Getting at Jesus

Getting at Jesus

A Comprehensive Critique of Neo-Atheist Nonsense
about the Jesus of History

PETER S. WILLIAMS

WIPF & STOCK · Eugene, Oregon

GETTING AT JESUS
A Comprehensive Critique of Neo-Atheist Nonsense about the Jesus of History

Copyright © 2019 Peter S. Williams. All rights reserved. Except for brief quotations in critical publications or reviews, no part of this book may be reproduced in any manner without prior written permission from the publisher. Write: Permissions, Wipf and Stock Publishers, 199 W. 8th Ave., Suite 3, Eugene, OR 97401.

Wipf & Stock
An Imprint of Wipf and Stock Publishers
199 W. 8th Ave., Suite 3
Eugene, OR 97401

www.wipfandstock.com

PAPERBACK ISBN: 978-1-5326-3424-6
HARDCOVER ISBN: 978-1-5326-3426-0
EBOOK ISBN: 978-1-5326-3425-3

Manufactured in the U.S.A. 01/28/19

Scripture quotations marked ISV are taken from the Holy Bible: International Standard Version®. Copyright © 1996-forever by The ISV Foundation. ALL RIGHTS RESERVED INTERNATIONALLY. Used by permission.

Scripture quotations marked RSV are from Revised Standard Version of the Bible, copyright © 1946, 1952, and 1971 National Council of the Churches of Christ in the United States of America. Used by permission. All rights reserved.

Scripture quotations marked ESV are from the ESV® Bible (The Holy Bible, English Standard Version®), copyright © 2001 by Crossway Bibles, a publishing ministry of Good News Publishers. Used by permission. All rights reserved.

Scripture marked The Voice are taken from The Voice™. Copyright © 2012 by Ecclesia Bible Society. Used by permission. All rights reserved.

Scripture quotations marked NLT are taken from the Holy Bible, New Living Translation, copyright © 1996, 2004, 2015 by Tyndale House Foundation. Used by permission of Tyndale House Publishers, Inc., Carol Stream, Illinois 60188. All rights reserved.

Scripture quotations marked MSG are taken from THE MESSAGE, copyright © 1993, 1994, 1995, 1996, 2000, 2001, 2002 by Eugene H. Peterson. Used by permission of NavPress. All rights reserved. Represented by Tyndale House Publishers, Inc.

Scripture quotations marked HCSB®, are taken from the Holman Christian Standard Bible®, Copyright © 1999, 2000, 2002, 2003, 2009 by Holman Bible Publishers. Used by permission. HCSB® is a federally registered trademark of Holman Bible Publishers."

Scripture quotations marked (NIV) are taken from the Holy Bible, New International Version®, NIV®. Copyright © 1973, 1978, 1984, 2011 by Biblica, Inc.™ Used by permission of Zondervan. All rights reserved worldwide. www.zondervan.com The "NIV" and "New International Version" are trademarks registered in the United States Patent and Trademark Office by Biblica, Inc.™

Dedicated to Dr. Sarah Campbell:
A dear friend in the real world,
and many virtual ones beside.

"I would only convert to a religion
if some evidence turned up to support it.
So far there is none . . ."
—Richard Dawkins, *Reddit* (2016)

"My encouragement to neo-atheists:
take a deep breath, open your eyes,
and allow the evidence to speak for itself."
—Paul M. Gould, "The Imperialistic, Elitist and Foolish Scientism of
Neo-Atheism"

Contents

Preface | ix

CHAPTER 1
Getting at Jesus | 1

CHAPTER 2
Getting at the Historical Jesus | 68

CHAPTER 3
Getting at the Gospels | 159

CHAPTER 4
Getting at Evidence for the Resurrection | 233

CHAPTER 5
Getting at the Best Explanation | 301

CONCLUSION
Getting at Jesus with Neo-Atheist Concessions to Historical Reality | 387

Selected Resources | 393
References | 397

Preface

"Is Truth Dead?" The question, posed in red letters on a black background, formed *Time Magazine*'s cover for April 2017. Inside, Washington Bureau Chief Michael Sherer mused that American President Donald Trump "has discovered something about epistemology in the twenty-first century. The truth may be real, but falsehood often works better."[1] The so-called New or Neo-Atheist movement has profited from the same phenomenon.[2]

The Oxford Dictionaries "Word of the Year" for 2016 was *post-truth,* an adjective defined as "relating to or denoting circumstances in which objective facts are less influential in shaping public opinion than appeals to emotion and personal belief."[3] Writing for the Oxford Dictionaries, Neil Midgley commented:

> in 2005 American comedian Stephen Colbert popularized an informal word relating to the same concept: *truthiness,* defined by Oxford Dictionaries as "the quality of seeming or being felt to be true, even if not necessarily true." *Post-truth* extends that notion from an isolated quality of particular assertions to a general characteristic of our age.

Neo-Atheism is a propaganda movement that thrives in the post-truth media environment. When a neo-atheist professor (Richard Dawkins, for example) makes confident assertions about the historical Jesus, their pronouncements carry an aura of truthiness, but are all too often the sort of "alternative facts" insisted upon by former White House Press Secretary Sean Spicer, who:

> used his first White House briefing to shout at journalists about what he incorrectly termed "deliberately false reporting" on Trump's inauguration, declaring: "We're going to hold the press accountable." "This was the largest audience ever to witness an inauguration, period," said Spicer, in one of several statements contradicted by photographs and transit data.[4]

---

1. Sherer, "Trump Truth."
2. See: "Post Truth & Fake News."
3. See: "Word of the Year 2016 is . . ."
4. Swaine, "Donald Trump's team defends 'alternative facts.'"

Preface

Journalist Jon Swaine commented: "While the topic of the inauguration attendance was trivial, that Trump's team was immediately willing to deny reality from the world's most powerful office alarmed figures across the political spectrum."[5] Many neo-atheist claims pertaining to the historical Jesus are similarly alarming to anyone with an informed understanding of the relevant subjects.

A second double-barreled epithet that hit the headlines in 2016 was "fake news," which journalist Fiona Macdonald describes as: "news from dubious sources, advertising content, or stories that are just totally made up—but which still go viral on Facebook and Twitter."[6] "Fake news" was named Collins Dictionary's official Word of the Year for 2017.[7] In our social-media-saturated environment, fake news claims about the historical Jesus garbed in the truthiness of neo-atheist academics get packaged into YouTube videos and Twitter memes that spread like the common cold among H.G. Well's ill-prepared Martian invaders.

A recent Stanford University study[8] of students in middle school, high school, and college: "found that most of them couldn't identify fake news on their own. Their susceptibility varied with age, but even a large number of the older students fell prey to bogus reports."[9] Researchers recommended that "students need to learn how to tell the difference between fake news and reality."[10] Learning the basics of critical thinking should be axiomatic to any education, but as Pulitzer Prize-winning journalist Bret Stephens warns:

> we in the United States are raising a younger generation who have never been taught either the how or the why of disagreement, and who seem to think that free speech is a one-way right: Namely, their right to disinvite, shout down or abuse anyone they dislike, lest they run the risk of listening to that person—or even allowing someone else to listen. The results are evident in the parlous state of our universities, and the frayed edges of our democracies.[11]

Professor Philip Seargeant says that although students are taught how to discern what academic information is trustworthy in higher education study-skills lessons, "these tools are rarely applied beyond their studies."[12]

This book applies standard canons of critical thinking to neo-atheist claims about the historical Jesus, putting before the public a comprehensive critique of neo-atheist nonsense about the Jesus of history. According to *The Concise Oxford*

---

5. Swaine, "Donald Trump's team defends 'alternative facts.'"
6. Macdonald, "Bad news."
7. Hunt, "'Fake news' named Collins Dictionary's official Word of the Year for 2017."
8. See: "Evaluating Information."
9. Fingas, "Study."
10. Vaughn, "University students 'need lessons in spotting fake news.'"
11. Stephens, "The Dying Art of Disagreement."
12. Quoted in Vaughn, "University students 'need lessons in spotting fake news.'"

Preface

Dictionary (Oxford, 1999), something is "comprehensive" if it includes or deals with "all or nearly all aspects of something," or is at least "of large content or scope," being "wide-ranging." In this sense of the term, this book is a "comprehensive" critique of neo-atheist views on the historical Jesus. The term can also be applied to winning a victory "by a large margin." Hence this book is also "comprehensive" in the sense that it demonstrates "by a wide margin" that the New Atheists' overall treatment of the historical Jesus is, to borrow a phrase from Jeremy Bentham, "nonsense on stilts."[13] Finally, an archaic meaning of "comprehensive" is "of or relating to understanding." I hope readers will not only understand and reject the insubstantial presuppositions and mistaken beliefs that lead the New Atheists to espouse such nonsense about Jesus, but that they will gain a new, evidence-based understanding of the sublime figure at the heart of our discussion.

Some notices: Biblical quotations are from the NIV translation unless otherwise indicated. Web addresses were functional when referenced. Although there's some overlap between parts of this book and the cumulative case for a Christian view of Jesus that I gave in *Understanding Jesus: Five Ways to Spiritual Enlightenment* (Paternoster, 2011), the relevant material has been fully revised. Part of Chapter One builds upon my article on the "New Atheism" in the peer-reviewed *Zondervan Dictionary of Christianity & Science* (Zondervan, 2017). Part of Chapter Two draws upon my peer-reviewed paper "The Epistle of James vs. Evolutionary Christology" in *Theofilos* (volume 9, number 1, 2016). I'm thankful to Dr. Stefan Lindholm (editor of *Theofilos*), Dr. K. Martin Heide (Professor of Semitic Languages at the Centre for Near and Middle-East Studies, Philipps-Universität in Marburg, Germany), and two anonymous reviewers for their comments on that paper.

I'd also like to record my thanks to: Dr. Luke Barnes, Dr. Sarah Campbell, Dr. William Lane Craig, the European Leadership Forum, Dr. Gary R. Habermas, Alice Harpole, Highfield Church Southampton (especially the members of my Bible study small group and participants in past "Reasonable Faith?" meetings), Peter Lambros, Peter Loose, Peter May MD, Nick and Carol Pollard, Philippa Roberts and Dr. Carl Stecher. Special thanks to Robin Parry et al at Wipf & Stock. Last but not least, thanks to my parents for their support and encouragement.

Peter S. Williams, Southampton, England, June 2018.

---

13. See: "Bentham, Jeremy."

CHAPTER 1

Getting at Jesus

> "Anyone should be able to see . . . whether a historical claim has merit or is pure fantasy driven by an ideological or theoretical desire for a certain set of answers to be right."
>
> —Bart Ehrman[1]

Victor J. Stenger (1935–2014) rose to public prominence as a member of the "New Atheism." In an interview published in 2014, Stenger (who was Adjunct Professor of Philosophy at the University of Colorado and Professor Emeritus of Physics and Astronomy at the University of Hawaii) summarized his critique of Christianity in the following terms:

> Physical and historical evidence might have been found for the miraculous events and the important narratives of the scriptures. For example, Roman records might have been found for an earthquake in Judea at the time of a certain crucifixion ordered by Pontius Pilate . . . In fact, there isn't a shred of independent evidence that Jesus Christ is a historical figure.[2]

There's so much wrong here that one hardly knows where to begin. Pointing out that objecting to believing anything in the absence of "independent evidence"[3] is to undermine *any* and *all* academic pursuits would be a good start. If "independent evidence" were essential for rational belief, it would never be rational to believe anything, because one's "independent evidence" would itself always stand in need of "independent evidence," and so on. Such a demand creates an insatiable, infinite regress.

---

1. Ehrman, *Did Jesus Exist,* 142.
2. Stenger, "Victor J. Stenger," 211.
3. Stenger, "Victor J. Stenger," 211.

Alternatively, we could question Stenger's assertion that "there isn't a shred of independent evidence that Jesus Christ is a historical figure,"[4] but we'll return to this subject in Chapter Two.

In the meantime, let's begin by focusing on a point of agreement. For although Stenger's critique is deeply flawed, it isn't entirely wrong-headed. Stenger clearly understands the *historical* nature of the Christian revelation claim.

The collection of first-century literature we call the "New Testament" (NT) contains a good deal of *purported historical reportage*: "since I myself have carefully investigated everything from the beginning," writes one of the authors, "I too decided to write an orderly account . . ." (Luke 1:3). The NT even contains some *purported eyewitness testimony*: "That . . . which we have heard, which we have seen with our eyes, which we have looked at and our hands have touched—this we proclaim" (1 John 1:1–2).

On the one hand: "You simply do not find this kind of empirical, verificationist language in the Bhagavad-Gita, the Granth, the Tripitaka, or the Qur'an."[5] On the other hand: "The writers of the New Testament were obsessed with this kind of language . . ."[6] As the neo-atheist author and neuroscientist Sam Harris recognizes: "One can speak about Buddhism shorn of its miracles . . . The same cannot be said of Christianity . . ."[7]

By making *an evidence-based critique* of Christianity, Stenger recognizes that there is an ineluctably *historical* dimension to the NT. As theoretical physicist turned theologian Sir John Polkinghorne comments:

> Christianity is a historically orientated religion. Its foundational stories . . . are not simply symbolic tales given us to stir our imaginations, but are . . . mediated through particular persons and events. Therefore there is an evidential aspect to what we are told in the Bible.[8]

Likewise, noted lawyer and Lutheran theologian Professor John Warwick Montgomery observes:

> Christianity . . . declares that the truth of its absolute claims rests squarely on certain historical facts open to ordinary investigation. These facts relate essentially to the man Jesus, his presentation of himself as God in human flesh, and his resurrection from the dead as proof of His deity.[9]

---

4. Stenger, "Victor J. Stenger," 211.
5. Hazen, "Ever Hearing but Never Understanding," 29.
6. Hazen, "Ever Hearing but Never Understanding," 29.
7. Harris, *Waking Up*, 23.
8. Polkinghorne, *Encountering Scripture*, x-xi.
9. Montgomery, *History, Law, and Christianity*, 48.

The evidential aspect of Christianity's historically-oriented foundational stories includes the miraculous claims listed by Montgomery, which are narrated by various NT documents as taking place *within history* rather than once upon a time in a mythical never-never land. As atheist John Gray writes: "If Jesus was not crucified and did not return from the dead the Christian religion is seriously compromised . . . Christianity is liable to falsification by historical fact."[10]

Of course, the fact that a claim is historically testable *in principle* doesn't guarantee it is historically testable *in practice*. The passage of time means that the contemporary reader of one of the first-century biographies of Jesus, later gathered into the NT and which we call "gospels" (from the Old English word *gōdspel* meaning "good news"), was obviously better able to check certain truth-claims made therein than is the modern-day reader. We in the fleeting present have only a very limited access to the past through the known chain of its effects.

It's worth pondering the fact that only 35 of 142 books written by the Roman historian Livy (c. 59/64 BC–c. AD 12/17) have survived (in 473 manuscripts, the oldest of which dates from the fourth century AD).[11] Likewise, only 4 1/2 of Tacitus's 14 books of Roman history have survived (in 36 manuscripts, the earliest of which dates from the ninth century).[12]

In light of the general paucity of our access to the past, a contemporary absence of evidence for a given historical claim is reasonably treated as evidence of historical absence *only* if one has a reasonable expectation that a) such evidence would exist in the first place, b) it would have survived into the present, and c) it would have been discovered by now. As Stenger observes: "Absence of evidence is evidence of absence *when the evidence should be there and is not*."[13] The history of biblical criticism is strewn with arguments from a purported lack of evidence ('arguments from silence') abandoned in the light of later discoveries.[14]

Stenger's selective argument from silence

Stenger's argument from silence against Christianity is suspiciously selective. Even if the lack of "Roman records . . . for an earthquake in Judea at the time of a certain crucifixion ordered by Pontius Pilate"[15] were evidence of absence (rather than a mere absence of evidence), why ignore the fact that we have "independent evidence" for the

---

10. Gray, *Seven Types of Atheism*, 14–15.
11. McDowell, *Evidence That Demands a Verdict*, 56.
12. McDowell, *Evidence That Demands a Verdict*, 56.
13. Stenger, *The New Atheism*, 58 (emphasis added).
14. See: Maier, "Biblical History."
15. Stenger, "Victor J. Stenger," 211.

existence of the Pontius Pilate who ordered "a certain crucifixion"[16]? According to one of the surviving *Annuls* of Tacitus (c. AD 116):

> to get rid of the report [that he caused the great fire of Rome], Nero fastened the guilt and inflicted the most exquisite tortures on a class hated for their abominations, called Christians by the populace. Christus, from whom the name had its origin, suffered the extreme penalty during the reign of Tiberius at the hands of one of our procurators, Pontius Pilatus, and a most mischievous superstition, thus checked for the moment, again broke out not only in Judaea, the first source of the evil, but even in Rome . . .[17]

Pilate is also mentioned by the first-century Jewish historian Flavius Josephus (see: *The Jewish War* 2.175–77 and *Jewish Antiquities* 18.60–62) and by the Jewish philosopher Philo of Alexandria (see: *Embassy* 299–305), writing c. AD 40.[18]

Moreover, archaeologists excavating the theatre at Caesarea Maritima in 1961 found a stone inscription that mentioned Pilate. The inscription is about a temple at Caesarea that Pilate built to honor the Roman emperor Tiberius (a "Tiberieum"). The Latin of the extant inscription reads:

S TIBERIEUM
IUS PILATUS
ECTUS IUDA

The original wording was probably:

S TIBERIUM
[PONT]IUS PILATUS
[PRAEF]ECTUS IDUA[EA]

Translated, this reads: "(this) Tiberium—Pontius Pilate, Prefect of Judea." Hence it appears that "Pilate had dedicated such a temple, and an inscription was made in the temple walls (or attached to the temple) to commemorate the event. Tiberius Caesar reigned from AD 14–37, so the inscription must have been created during that time. This fits the time-frame of the governorship of the Biblical Pilate."[19]

Whether or not an absence of independent evidence for an earthquake "at the time of a certain crucifixion ordered by Pontius Pilate" should count against the NT, the presence of independent evidence for the Pontius Pilatus who administered the "extreme penalty" to Jesus certainly counts in its favor! Stenger was either ignorant of the facts or he was offering a deliberately one-sided presentation of the evidence.

---

16. Stenger, "Victor J. Stenger," 211.
17. See: "Cornelius Tacitus."
18. See: Argubright, "Historical Evidence for Pontius Pilate;" Thatcher, "Philo on Pilate."
19. "Biblical Archaeology 40."

Fig. 1. The Pontius Pilate inscription
(B.R. Burton, Wikimedia Commons, 2012, http://bit.ly/20j3BLl).

Watch: "Pontius Pilate" Youtube playlist: www.youtube.com/playlist?list=PLQhh3qcwVEWjo6pSR-O1zeRUDyvT25B3b

Read: "The Quest for the Historical Pilate" by Paul Barnett: http://paulbarnett.info/2011/04/the-quest-for-the-historical-pontius-pilate/

'Was Pontius Pilate's Ring Discovered at Herodium?' by Robert Cargill: www.biblicalarchaeology.org/daily/biblical-artifacts/inscriptions/pontius-pilate-ring-herodium/

Again, one wonders why Stenger failed to mention the *geological* evidence[20] for an earthquake in Judea around the time of the crucifixion, which was published and widely discussed in 2012:

> geologist Jefferson Williams . . . and colleagues Markus Schwab and Achim Brauer of the German Research Center for Geosciences studied three cores from the beach of the Ein Gedi Spa adjacent to the Dead Sea. Varves, which are annual layers of deposition in the sediments, reveal that at least two major earthquakes affected the core: a widespread earthquake in 31 B.C. and an early first century seismic event that happened sometime between 26 A.D. and 36 A.D.[21]

---

20. See: Bargiel, "Phlegon of Tralles Scientifically Established as a Credible Source on Jesus."
21. Viegas, "Day of Jesus' Crucifixion Believed Determined."

Scholars agree that Jesus' crucifixion happened in AD 30 or 33 (I think it was the latter[22]) and both years are within the range of dates for the first-century seismic activity discovered by Williams et al.[23]

The literary genre of Matthew 27:51–54, which mentions an earthquake at the time of the crucifixion, is hotly debated.[24] Some scholars join Stenger in taking this passage to be making historical claims on par with Matthew's claims about Jesus' crucifixion. Some scholars think Matthew is using apocalyptic imagery to highlight the significance of Jesus' historical crucifixion. Perhaps the passage contains a combination of history and apocalyptic.

Williams is aware of this debate and notes that, whilst it is consistent with a historical reading of Matthew 27:51–54, the AD 26–36 date-range of the first-century quake in his team's research leaves open the possibility that the earthquake in Matthew 27 is an allegory, perhaps inspired by the first-century quake in their study.

Stenger's apparent ignorance of these matters puts him in the awkward position of complaining about a lack of independent evidence for something the author of Matthew may not have meant literally (although there is independent geological evidence consistent with a literal reading of Matthew), whilst ignoring the existence of independent evidence for something everyone agrees is meant historically: the existence of Pontius Pilate.

Prima facie evidence

As a matter of historical methodology, the fact that someone's testimony is open to empirical testing doesn't mean one must test it before rationally trusting it. I can empirically test your testimony that it's raining, but I needn't do so for my act of taking an umbrella from the stand as I head for the exit to be a rational act of trust. In the absence of sufficient reason for doubt (i.e. counter-evidence of equal or greater weight), testimony-based beliefs carry *prima facie* ("on the face of it") justification. This principle applies to what people write as well as what they say. Hence, as NT scholars David Wenham and Steve Walton observe: "The Gospels are prima facie evidence for what the historical Jesus said and did."[25] They are not alone in making this point:

- Montgomery affirms: "The benefit of the doubt is to be given to the document itself, and not arrogated by the critic to himself."[26]

---

22. See: Humphreys, *The Mystery of The Last Supper*.
23. Williams et al., "An early first-century earthquake in the Dead Sea."
24. See: Wilkins, *The Holman Apologetics Commentary on The Bible*, 182–83.
25. Wenham and Walton, *Exploring the New Testament*, 139. See also: Evans, *The Historical Christ*, 335.
26. Montgomery, *History and Christianity*, 29.

- Theologian Hugh Montefiore sets out "the criterion of historical presumption: a saying or story is likely to be authentic unless there are good reasons for thinking otherwise."[27]
- NT scholar Richard Bauckham argues that "testimony should not be treated as credible only to the extent that it can be independently verified . . . Trusting testimony is not an irrational act of faith that leaves critical rationality aside . . ."[28]
- NT scholar James H. Charlesworth concurs that we "should assume a tradition is authentic until evidence appears that undermines its authenticity."[29]

Note that this is *not* a matter of endorsing blind faith, but of forming a *falsifiable trust* in light of the *testimonial evidence*.

Of course, when it comes to assessing testimony concerning miracles, those who hold a worldview without room for miracles might take their worldview as reason for doubting such testimony. However, those who take this path should note that their objection to miracles isn't grounded in any supposed lack of publically-available evidence, but in a philosophical perspective that should be held no more immune to critical assessment than any other.

In sum, we should agree with Stenger that (at least in principle) biblical reports of miraculous events shouldn't be exempted from the empirically-testable, historical character of the Christian revelation claim. Stenger and his fellow neo-atheists are right to ask probing historical questions about Jesus. One just wishes that in the process of trying to answer those questions they paid closer attention to the actual evidence.

THE NEW ATHEISM

"Atheism deserves better than the new atheists . . ."

—Rabbi Jonathan Sacks[30]

The New Atheism (or neo-atheism) is a movement of anti-theistic *propaganda* in the modern, pejorative sense of the term that indicates "unfair, emotionally manipulative, and (in one way or another) misleading or dishonest efforts to influence opinion and sentiment."[31] Charitably-minded readers may suspect that this description is my own attempt at propaganda, but if their charity extends to an open-minded reading of this book, I hope they will conclude that it is merely a statement of publicly-demonstrable

---

27. Montefiore, *The Miracles of Jesus*, 20.
28. Bauckham, *Jesus and the Eyewitnesses*, 5.
29. Charlesworth, *The Historical Jesus*, 18.
30. Sacks quoted in *The Global Public Square* by Os Guinness, 31.
31. Blackford, "Philosophy in an age of propaganda," 27.

fact, a fact that explains why the movement has been stringently criticized by scholars of widely differing worldviews.

The New Atheist (or neo-atheist) movement came of age after Al-Qaeda terrorists flew passenger jets into the Twin Towers and the Pentagon on September 11 2001: "It is no coincidence that Sam Harris began writing *The End of Faith* the day after 9/11."[32] However, rather than condemning a particular interpretation of Islam,[33] Harris condemned religion in general. Sales of *The End of Faith* (W. W. Norton, 2004*)* revealed a public appetite for such broad-brush polemic,[34] heralding a slew of neo-atheist books aimed at the popular market, including:

- Richard Dawkins, *The God Delusion* (Bantam, 2006)[35]
- Daniel Dennett, *Breaking the Spell* (Allen Lane, 2006)[36]
- Sam Harris, *Letter to a Christian Nation* (Bantam, 2007)[37]
- Christopher Hitchens, *God is Not Great* (Atlantic, 2007)[38]
- A.C. Grayling, *Against All Gods* (Oberon, 2007)[39]
- Michel Onfray, *In Defence Of Atheism* (Serpant's Tail, 2007)[40]
- Victor J. Stenger, *The New Atheism* (Prometheus Books, 2009)
- Sam Harris, *The Moral Landscape* (Free Press, 2010)[41]
- Lawrence M. Krauss, *A Universe From Nothing* (Free Press, 2012)[42]
- A.C. Grayling, *The God Argument* (Bloomsbury, 2013)[43]

32. Bullivant, "The New Atheism And Sociology," 115.

33. See: Geisler and Saleeb, *Answering Islam*, 319–29; Harris and Nawaz, *Islam And The Future Of Tolerance*; Spencer, *A Religion of Peace?*

34. See: Shenvi, "A Long Response."

35. See: Williams, "Dissecting Dawkins' Defence of *The God Delusion*;" Beckwith, "The Irrationality of Richard Dawkins;" Brown, "Dawkins the Dogmatist;" Craig, "Richard Dawkins' Argument for Atheism;" Eagleton, "Lunging, Flailing, Mispunching;" Flew, "Professor Antony Flew Reviews *The God Delusion*;" Holt, "Beyond Belief;" Plantinga, "The Dawkins Confusion;" Swinburne, "Response to Richard Dawkins' comments;" Williams, "The Big Bad Wolf, Theism and the Foundations;" Williams, "Who's Afraid of the Big Bad Wolf?;" Zwartz, "*The God Delusion*."

36. See: Hart, "Daniel Dennett Hunts the Snark;" Kirsch, "If Men Are From Mars, What's God;" Stewart, *The Future of Atheism*; Wieseltier, "The God Genome;" Williams, *A Sceptic's Guide to Atheism*.

37. See: Holding, "Sam Harris' "Letter to a Christian Nation" Refuted."

38. See: Roberts, "*God is Not Great* by Christopher Hitchens."

39. See: Williams, "Contra Grayling."

40. See: Amarasingam, "A Review of Michel Onfray's *In Defense of Atheism;*" Plotinsky, "The Fanatical Philosopher."

41. See: Williams, *C.S. Lewis vs. the New Atheists*, 153–60.

42. See: Williams, "A Universe From Someone."

43. See: "A.C. Grayling vs. Peter S. Williams on *The God Argument;*" Ward, "*The God Argument* by A.C. Grayling."

- Jerry A. Coyne, *Faith vs. Fact* (Viking, 2015)[44]

As philosopher C. Stephen Evans generalizes: "The New Atheists do not want to write articles for philosophy periodicals; they want to write best sellers that will command cultural attention."[45] Scholars like Evans may try to do the latter, but they don't neglect the former foundation in scholarship.

What defines New Atheism? For a start, the movement embraces a historically naive conflict model of the relationship between science and monotheism.[46] Having swallowed the false myth of the "warfare between science and religion,"[47] neo-atheists see themselves as championing a scientific worldview based on evidence and opposed to religion, which they consider "the greatest threat to rationality and scientific progress"[48] because they mistakenly think that religion demands "irrationality . . . as a sacred duty."[49] They consequently believe that "religion is not only wrong; it's evil."[50]

Despite the fact that they generally reject moral objectivism and/or libertarian free will (rejections entailed by their materialistic worldview[51]), neo-atheists portray themselves as engaging in a heroic moral struggle to defend civilization against the evil irrationality of religion. This self-contradictory framework offers members of the neo-atheist community a sense of moral and intellectual superiority, together with a sense of meaning, purpose, and identity.[52]

French neo-atheist philosopher Michel Onfray admits that: "Never more than today has there been such evidence of vitality in . . . religious thinking, proof that God is not dead . . ."[53] As secular historian Michael Grant observes: "During the 1960s, it was widely forecast that we were entering upon a wholly secular period which would care nothing for religion. But this has proved a mistaken prophecy."[54] British scientist turned theologian Alister McGrath talks of the subsequent "crisis of confidence . . . gripping

---

44. See: Glass, "Jerry Coyne on the Incompatibility of Science and Religion;" Horgan, "Book by Biologist Jerry Coyne Goes Too Far in Denouncing Religion, Defending Science;" Hughes, "Faith, Fact, and False Dichotomies."

45. Evans, *Why Christianity Still Makes Sense*, 8.

46. See: Stenger, "What's New About The New Atheism?;" Williams, "Is Christianity Unscientific?;" Hannam, "How Christianity Led To The Rise Of Modern Science;" Koons, "Science and Theism;" Chapman, *Slaying The Dragons*; Chapman, *Stargazers*; Grant, *A History Of Natural Philosophy*; Hannam, *The Genesis of Science*; Hannam, *God's Philosophers*; Harrison, *The Bible, Protestantism, and the Rise of Natural Science*; Pearcey and Thaxton, *The Soul Of Science*.

47. Dennett, "Is Religion a Threat to Rationality and Science."

48. Dennett, "Is Religion a Threat to Rationality and Science."

49. Dennett, "Is Religion a Threat to Rationality and Science."

50. Wolf, "The Church of the Non-Believers."

51. See: Beckwith and Koukl, *Relativism*; Dawkins, "Afterword," 307; Dawkins, "Let's all stop beating Basil's car;" Goetz, "Is Sam Harris Right About Free Will?;" Harris, *Free Will*; Swinburne, *Mind, Brain, and Free Will*; Williams, *A Faithful Guide to Philosophy*.

52. See: Williams, "The Emperor's Incoherent New Clothes."

53. Onfray, *In Defence of Atheism*, 37.

54. Grant, *Jesus*, 193.

atheism"[55] in the twenty-first century. David Fergusson notes that "much modern atheism is . . . not merely dismissive of religion but angry and frustrated by its re-emergence as a powerful social force."[56] Atheist John Gray concurs with this analysis:

> Karl Marx and John Stuart Mill were adamant that religion would die out with the advance of science. That has not come about, and there is not the remotest prospect of it happening in the foreseeable future. Yet the idea that religion can be eradicated from human life remains an article of faith among humanists. As secular ideology is dumped throughout the world, they are left disorientated and gawping. It is this painful cognitive dissonance, I believe, that accounts for the particular rancour and intolerance of many secular thinkers. Unable to account for the irrepressible vitality of religion, they can react only with puritanical horror and stigmatize it as irrational.[57]

That *The End of Faith* is subtitled *Religion, Terror and the Future of Reason* encapsulates the neo-atheist reaction to the crisis of confidence described by McGrath: scapegoating Abrahamic religion for social evils,[58] among which the presumed irrationality of faith is seen as the primary culprit. Indeed, neo-atheism is characterized by "the blind faith that all faith is blind faith."[59] Hence zoologist Richard Dawkins worries that "Non-fundamentalist, 'sensible' religion . . . is making the world safe for fundamentalism by teaching . . . that unquestioned faith is a virtue."[60] This misrepresentation of faith as necessarily "unquestioned" is a corollary of the New Atheist's commitment to a self-contradictory and scientistic theory of rationality.

Watch: "Scientism" Youtube playlist: www.youtube.com/playlist?list=PLQhh3qcwVEWiIgrCwkM8Y-RoqU1TmYK8R

Listen: "Hebrews 11 & faith in the New Atheism" by Peter S. Williams: http://peterswilliams.podbean.com/mf/feed/dizgnf/Heb_11.mp3

"Knowledge, Faith & Knowing God" by Peter S. Williams: http://podcast.peterswilliams.com/e/knowledge-faith-knowing-god

---

Professor of philosophy Gary R. Habermas makes the disappointed observation that Christopher Hitchens's book *God is Not Great* contains "no serious discussion of any of the key issues that would occupy even an undergraduate discussion of metaphysics."[61] The same could be said of neo-atheism in general, which, for example,

---

55. McGrath, "The Spell of the Meme."
56. Fergusson, *Faith and Its Critics*, 7. See: McGrath, *The Twilight of Atheism*; Micklethwaite and Wooldridge, *God Is Back*; Siemon-Netto, "God Not So Dead."
57. Gray, "Sex, Atheism and Piano Legs," 46.
58. See: "Christianity Not A Source of Violence;" Ward, *Is Religion Dangerous*?
59. Lennox, *Gunning for God*, 56. See: Williams, "Hebrews 11 and faith in the new atheists."
60. Dawkins, *The God Delusion*, 286, 308.
61. Habermas, "The Plight of the New Atheism."

pays scant attention to the many serious problems with the materialism that the movement embraces. As atheist philosopher Mary Midgley muses:

> Even though the credo itself is already beginning to fray around the edges, people who think of themselves as scientifically orientated still often revere materialism in much the same way that their predecessors in Darwin's day revered Christianity. That is, they don't ask questions about it . . . They often assume that the only reasons for questioning it would be religious ones . . . But in truth the main difficulties here have nothing to do with religion.[62]

Watch: "Problems With Materialism/Metaphysical Naturalism" Youtube playlist: www.youtube.com/playlist?list=PLQhh3qcwVEWgolWsfZnhQvzNfRT_jHLJA

Read: "Naturalism and the First Person Perspective" by Lynne Rudder Baker: https://people.umass.edu/lrb/files/bak07natM.pdf

"Naturalism and Libertarian Agency" by Stewart Goetz: www.independent.org/issues/article.asp?id=1756

"The Incompatibility of Naturalism and Scientific Realism" by Robert C. Koons: http://robkoons.net/media/69b0dd04a9d2fc6dffff80b5ffffd524.pdf

"Epistemological Objections to Materialism" by Robert C. Koons: http://robkoons.net/media/3d211414d9a8a675ffff80b9ffaf2815.pdf

"Farewell to philosophical naturalism" by Paul K. Moser and David Yandell: www.researchgate.net/publication/292103014_Farewell_to_Philosophical_Naturalism

"Knowledge and Naturalism" by Dallas Willard: www.dwillard.org/articles/artview.asp?artid=64

The Soul Hypothesis: Investigations Into The Existence Of The Soul edited by Mark C. Baker and Stewart Goetz

The Devil's Delusion: Atheism and its Scientific Pretentions by David Berlinski

Naturalism: A Critical Analysis edited by William Lane Craig and J.P. Moreland

Science & Religion: Are They Compatible? by Daniel C. Dennett and Alvin Plantinga

Naturalism by Stewart Goetz and Charles Taliaferro

The Waining of Materialism edited by Robert C. Koons and George Bealer

Agents Under Fire: Materialism And The Rationality Of Science by Angus Menuge

Are You an Illusion? by Mary Midgley

The Recalcitrant Imagio Dei: Human Persons and the Failure of Naturalism by J.P. Moreland

Mind & Cosmos: Why The Materialist Neo-Darwinian Conception Of Nature Is Almost Certainly False by Thomas Nagel

C.S. Lewis' Dangerous Idea: In Defence of the Argument from Reason by Victor Reppert

Mind, Brain, & Free Will by Richard Swinburne

A Faithful Guide to Philosophy: A Christian Introduction to the Love of Wisdom by Peter S. Williams

---

62. Midgley, *Are You an Illusion?*, 14.

Similarly, philosopher James E. Taylor expresses surprise that "none of [the New Atheists] addresses either theistic or atheistic arguments to any great extent."[63] Indeed, they generally deal with arguments for God by either misrepresenting or outright ignoring them. Oxford mathematician and philosopher John C. Lennox rightly observes that: "The New Atheists are loud in their demand for evidence that a supernatural God exists; yet the genuineness of their demand is questionable since they seem reluctant to pay serious attention to evidence that is offered to them."[64] The same complaint applies to neo-atheist demands for evidence that God was incarnate in Jesus.

Alvin Plantinga (the leading philosopher of religion of the past half century) complains that neo-atheist philosopher of mind Daniel Dennett "doesn't know anything about contemporary analytic philosophy of religion, but that doesn't stop him from making public declarations on the subject."[65]

Watch: "Evidence for God's Existence" with William Lane Craig, Daniel Dennett and Alister McGrath: https://youtu.be/_WzolooG2MM

Listen: "On Daniel Dennett" by William Lane Craig: https://youtu.be/6UwvXBadRbw

Read: "Darwin, Mind and Meaning" by Alvin Plantinga: www.veritas-ucsb.org/library/plantinga/Dennett.html

"In Defence of Theistic Arguments" by William Lane Craig in *The Future of Atheism: Alister McGrath & Daniel Dennett in Dialogue* edited by Robert B. Stewart

Science & Religion: Are They Compatible? by Daniel C. Dennett and Alvin Plantinga

---

Dennett skirts over theistic arguments in *Breaking the Spell* and elsewhere declares himself content to punt the issue to Richard Dawkins. Dennett admits: "I give short shrift to the task of rebutting the standard arguments for the existence of God [in *Breaking the Spell*]" and welcomes what he calls "the . . . demolitions that Dawkins has assembled."[66] In his afterword to the tenth anniversary edition of *The God Delusion*, Dennett repeats this sentiment:

> (I devote a scant six pages of *Breaking the Spell* to the arguments for and against the existence of God, while Dawkins devotes roughly a hundred, laying out the standard arguments with admirable clarity and fairness, and answering them efficiently).[67]

Unfortunately, this is a case of the blind leading the blind. Dawkins's treatment of theistic arguments is anything but clear, fair, or efficient. As Taylor observes: "Dawkins . . . has been criticized for engaging in an overly cursory evaluation of

---

63. Taylor, "The New Atheists."
64. Lennox, *Against the Flow*, 134.
65. Plantinga, *Where the Conflict Really Lies*, 49.
66. Dennett, "Review of Richard Dawkins' *The God Delusion*."
67. Dennett, "Afterword," 422.

theistic arguments and for ignoring the philosophical literature in natural theology."[68] James Hannam accurately describes *The God Delusion* as "under-researched [and] under-argued" and observes that Dawkins's "treatment of the traditional proofs of God's existence is largely an attack on straw men . . . This refusal to engage with the serious literature is evident throughout . . ."[69]

Dennett praises Dawkins as "flattening all the serious arguments *for* the existence of God . . ."[70] *The God Delusion* does contain the most extensive neo-atheist examination of natural theology to date, but that's not saying much. Whereas Dawkins devotes *thirty-seven pages* (not the "roughly a hundred" pages claimed by Dennett) to the cursory rejection of *ten* theistic arguments, Plantinga once presented a paper outlining "a couple of dozen or so"[71] theistic arguments. That paper spawned an academic conference in 2014[72] and the book *Two Dozen (or so) Arguments for God: The Plantinga Project*, edited by philosophers Jerry L. Walls and Trent Dougherty (Oxford, 2018). Similarly, of the nine positive arguments for God in *The Blackwell Companion to Natural Theology* (Wiley-Blackwell, 2009), only five appear in *The God Delusion*. Thus, "Dawkins shows that he is totally unfamiliar with the wealth of literature on the subject . . ."[73] In other words, even if Dawkins offered the "demolitions" that Dennett imagines, *The God Delusion* wouldn't merit atheist P.Z. Myers's appraisal as "a thorough overview . . ."[74]

Moreover, Dawkins conspicuously fails in his attempt to rebut even those theistic arguments he does consider, mainly because he doesn't understand them.[75] As philosopher Barney Zwartz warns, Dawkins "is spectacularly inept when it comes to the traditional philosophical arguments for God . . ."[76] Likewise, the influential American philosopher William Lane Craig concludes that "the objections raised by Richard Dawkins to these arguments are not even injurious, much less deadly."[77]

In his afterword to the tenth anniversary edition of *The God Delusion*, Dennett concedes:

> There are indeed *recherché* versions of these traditional arguments [for God] that perhaps have not yet been exhaustively eviscerated by scholars . . .[78]

68. Taylor, "The New Atheists."
69. Hannam, "*The God Delusion* by Richard Dawkins."
70. Dennett, "Review of Richard Dawkins' *The God Delusion*."
71. Plantinga, "Two Dozen or so Theistic Arguments."
72. See: "Baylor ISR "Two Dozen (or so) Theistic Arguments" Alvin Plantinga Conference (2014)."
73. Edwards, "Dawkins' Delusional Arguments Against God."
74. Myers, "Bad Religion."
75. See: Williams, "Whose Afraid of the Big Bad Wolf?;" Williams, *C.S. Lewis vs. the New Atheists*; Williams, *A Sceptic's Guide to Atheism*.
76. Zwartz, "The God Delusion."
77. Craig, "Richard Dawkins on Argument for God," 30.
78. Dennett, "Afterword," 422.

But what becomes of Dawkins "flattening all the serious arguments *for* the existence of God . . ."[79] if there are theistic arguments—however rare, exotic, or obscure—that no one has as yet flattened or "exhaustively eviscerated"?

Dennett says Dawkins ignores these arguments because "his book is a consciousness raiser aimed at the general religious public, not an attempt to contribute to the academic micro-discipline of philosophical theology."[80] However, as H. Allan Orr comments:

> Dennett has apparently forgotten that the heart of Dawkins's book was his philosophical argument for the near impossibility of God . . . I can see why Dennett would like to forget about Dawkins's attempt at philosophy . . . but it's absurd to pretend now that *The God Delusion* had no philosophical ambitions . . . Dawkins explicitly stated that he was targeting *all* forms of the God Hypothesis . . . and insisted that all were victims of his arguments . . . It's one thing to think carefully about religion and conclude it's dubious. It's another to string together anecdotes and exercises in bad philosophy and conclude that one has resolved subtle problems. I wasn't disappointed in *The God Delusion* because I was shocked by Dawkins's atheism. I was disappointed because it wasn't very good.[81]

In a similar vein, the late Antony Flew complained about what he called Dawkins's "scandalous and apparently deliberate refusal to present the doctrine which he appears to think he has refuted in its *strongest* form."[82]

Contrary to neo-atheist bluster on the subject, I agree with John Pritchard that "There are very good intellectual reasons for believing in God, and it's worth having an honest look."[83] Readers interested in following this advice are referred to the following resources:

Watch: "Natural Theology" Youtube playlist: www.youtube.com/playlist?list=PLQhh3qcwVEWiDA8QN4h8wLrrbm49fLzPN

"Debating God" Youtube playlist: www.youtube.com/playlist?list=PLQhh3qcwVEWiY3UmTAiRdj2OW4SBG0y_W

"Baylor ISR "Two Dozen (or so) Theistic Arguments" Alvin Plantinga Conference (2014)" Youtube playlist: www.youtube.com/playlist?list=PLoJmtbsEea3gcN5eNq-0JXq2qTwDg7L_Q

"Deconstructing New Atheist Objections to the Arguments for God" by William Lane Craig: https://youtu.be/u14dtDuEf3E

"Deconstructing Dawkins' Defence: Responding to the New Edition of 'The God Delusion'" by Peter S. Williams: https://youtu.be/92v-mQjq9FY

---

79. Dennett, "Review of Richard Dawkins' *The God Delusion*."
80. Dennett, "Afterword," 422.
81. Orr, "*The God Delusion*."
82. Flew, "Book Review: *The God Delusion*," 473.
83. Pritchard, *Why go to Church?*, 2.

"Science, Scientism and the Knowledge of God" by Peter S. Williams: https://youtu.be/GkxCh45_VSc

Listen: "Dissecting Dawkins' Defence of The God Delusion" by Peter S. Williams: http://peterswilliams.podbean.com/mf/feed/rr7cd9/SUCU_Dawkins_Delusion_2016.mp3

"Scientism, Science & Half-a-Dozen or so Arguments for God" by Peter S. Williams: http://peterswilliams.podbean.com/mf/feed/isk6sb/Reading.mp3

"Defending C.S. Lewis' Argument from Desire" by Peter S. Williams: http://peterswilliams.podbean.com/mf/feed/i5z7d8/Oxford_Lewis_Society_Desire_2016.mp3

Read: "The New Atheism and Five Arguments for God" by William Lane Craig: www.reasonablefaith.org/the-new-atheism-and-five-arguments-for-god

"Richard Dawkins' Argument for Atheism in The God Delusion" by William Lane Craig: www.reasonablefaith.org/writings/question-answer/richard-dawkins-argument-for-atheism-in-the-god-delusion

"The General Argument from Intuition" by Robert C. Koons: http://robkoons.net/media/92f8093d1a9864c0ffff80ebffaf2815.pdf

"Two Dozen (or so) Theistic Arguments" by Alvin Plantinga: https://appearedtoblogly.files.wordpress.com/2011/05/plantinga-alvin-22two-dozen-or-so-theistic-arguments221.pdf

"Language, Being, God, and the Three Stages of Theistic Evidence" by Dallas Willard: www.dwillard.org/articles/individual/language-being-god-and-the-three-stages-of-theistic-evidence

"In Defence of Arguments from Desire" by Peter S. Williams: www.peterswilliams.com/2016/11/02/in-defence-of-arguments-from-desire/

The Rationality of Theism edited by Paul Copan and Paul K. Moser

On Guard For Students: A Thinker's Guide to the Christian Faith by William Lane Craig

Is Goodness without God Good Enough? A Debate on Faith, Secularism, And Ethics edited by Robert K. Garcia and Nathan L. King

Big Bang, Big God: A Universe Designed For Life? by Rodney Holder

God And Evil: The Case For God In A World Filled With Pain edited by Chad Meister and James K. Drew Jr.

Is Faith in God Reasonable? edited by Corey Miller and Paul Gould

Consciousness and the Existence of God: A Theistic Argument by J.P. Moreland

Scaling the Secular City: A Defence of Christianity by J.P. Moreland,

The Blackwell Companion to Natural Theology edited by J.P. Moreland and William Lane Craig

In Defence of Natural Theology: A Post-Humean Assessment by James F. Sennett and Douglas R. Groothuis

Atheism & Theism by J.J.C. Smart and J.J. Haldane

Two Dozen (or so) Arguments for God: The Plantinga Project by Jerry L. Walls and Trent Dougherty

A Faithful Guide to Philosophy: A Christian Introduction to the Love of Wisdom by Peter S. Williams

C.S. Lewis vs. the New Atheists by Peter S. Williams

Nonpartisan criticism

Plantinga castigates the New Atheists for "their close-mindedness, their reluctance to consider evidence, and their resort to ridicule, mockery, and misrepresentation in the place of serious argument..."[84] Evans complains that the New Atheists give "little in the way of detailed arguments" to back up their "grand claims," which, far from being new, are generally "stock claims made by atheists since at least the nineteenth century."[85] Philosopher Paul Copan decries the "sloppily argued attacks"[86] of New Atheists, describing them as "remarkably out of touch with [contemporary] sophisticated theistic arguments for God's existence."[87] Tom Gilson writes of the New Atheists that: "Their books, articles, and debates are riddled with fallacies, appeals to emotion, and mishandling of evidence."[88] Philosopher Charles Taylor condemns the New Atheists for "very intellectually shoddy" work and for advancing "the most incredibly bad arguments in a tone of indignation and anger."[89] Gary R. Habermas castigates them for using rhetorical methods "that are more bombastic than they are substantial."[90]

These trenchant criticisms of the New Atheism from Christian scholars cannot be dismissed with *ad hominem* accusations of bias, not least because similarly trenchant criticisms have been made by a host of atheist philosophers:

- Daniel Came: "there isn't much in the way of serious argumentation in the New Atheists' dialectical arsenal"[91]

- John Gray accuses Sam Harris of "cultivating a willed ignorance of the history of ideas..."[92]

- Thomas Nagel: "Dawkins dismisses, with contemptuous flippancy, the traditional ... arguments for the existence of God ... I found these attempts at philosophy ... particularly weak..."[93]

- Keith M. Parsons criticizes the New Atheists for "their logical lacunae and sophomoric mistakes..."[94]

---

84. Plantinga, endorsement quote for Lennox, *Gunning for God*.
85. Evans, *Why Christianity Still Makes Sense*, 5–6.
86. Copan, *Contending with Christianity's Critics*, vii.
87. Copan, "Interview with Paul Copan."
88. Gilson, "The Party of Reason?," 15.
89. Taylor, "The New Atheism and the Spiritual Landscape of the West."
90. Habermas, "The Plight of the New Atheism."
91. Came, "Richard Dawkins's refusal to debate is cynical and anti-intellectualist."
92. Gray, "Sex, Atheism and Piano Legs," 11.
93. Nagel, "Fear of Religion."
94. Parsons, "Old Atheism."

- Massimo Pigliucci describes *The God Delusion* as "historically badly informed polemic."[95]

- Michael Ruse says "Dawkins is brazen in his ignorance of philosophy and theology (not to mention the history of science)"[96] and adds: "It is not that the [new] atheists are having a field day because of the brilliance and novelty of their thinking. Frankly . . . the material being churned out is second rate. And that is a euphemism for 'downright awful.'"[97] Ruse complains that the New Atheists "are ignorant of anything outside their disciplines to an extent remarkable even among modern academics."[98]

- Erik Wielenberg argues that "the central atheistic argument of *The God Delusion* is unconvincing . . ."[99]

In short, there's a widespread, nonpartisan agreement that the neo-atheist oeuvre is laced with logical fallacies and peppered with factual errors.[100] These widely noted failings are summarized in Orthodox theologian David Bentley Hart's portrait of New Atheism as consisting of "vacuous arguments afloat on oceans of historical ignorance . . . a formidable collection of conceptual and historical errors."[101]

New Atheism gets a failing grade in history

Given our historical focus, it's worth noting that historian Borden W. Painter Jr. wrote *The New Atheist Denial of History* (Palgrave Macmillan, 2014) to call neo-atheists to account "for failing to take seriously the historical record to which they so freely appeal when attacking religion."[102] Borden comments:

> The New Atheists love to draw on history, but they show little evidence of having read much of it . . . New Atheist historiography . . . is dated and clumsy, manifesting little to no awareness of what mainstream historians of all stripes have to say on the subjects of interest to them. The New Atheists constantly claim the high ground of evidence based reasoning . . . yet they fail to heed readily available historical evidence that does not support their views . . . Ideology and a set of predetermined conclusions drive their way of doing history.[103]

---

95. Pigliucci, "New Atheism and the Scientistic Turn in the Atheism Movement."
96. Ruse, "*The God Delusion*."
97. Ruse, "*The God Delusion*."
98. Ruse, *Atheism*, 52.
99. Wielenberg, "Dawkins's Gambit, Hume's Aroma, and God's Simplicity."
100. See: Dickson, "The New Atheist's Questionable History: Part 1" and "Part 2;" Williams, "Dawkins and the Public Understanding of Scientism."
101. Hart, *Atheist Delusions*, 4, 19.
102. Painter, *The New Atheist Denial of History*, 1.
103. Painter, *The New Atheist Denial of History*, 3.

Borden proceeds to observe that "the New Atheists commonly use as evidence dated or second-rate sources while avoiding more recent and more credible work by major scholars."[104] He criticizes Dawkins, Hitchens, and Harris in particular for "a long list of false, misleading, and irresponsible historical pronouncements,"[105] complaining that they "ignore or manipulate history in ways that violate the basic canons of historical discourse. They do it in ways that undercut their constant calls for the rational consideration of evidence in constructing arguments and reaching conclusions."[106] Professor Borden gives Dawkins, Hitchens and Harris "a failing grade in history."[107]

Borden's focus is upon the New Atheist's use of European history since Constantine, but as one might expect, when we turn our attention to their treatment of the historical Jesus, we find a no less fecund and influential source of error. It is particularly perplexing to note with John Lennox that there is "no serious attempt by any of the New Atheists to engage with the evidence for the resurrection of Jesus Christ."[108] Contrary to their professed interest in evidence, the New Atheists largely ignore the historical evidence relating to Jesus' resurrection, often justifying their ignorance by appealing to some version of David Hume's philosophical case against miracles. Since the New Atheism follows Hume in this matter, it's hardly surprising to see that the failings philosopher Douglas R. Groothuis identifies in the latter are also to be found in the former. Both "end up either begging the question or not carefully considering the New Testament evidence."[109]

A comprehensive response to neo-atheist nonsense about the historical Jesus will therefore require us not only to set the record straight concerning the relevant *historical data*, but concerning certain *philosophical assumptions* that shape the New Atheist's reception and interpretation of that data.

Influential laymen

Despite the criticism of informed scholars on all sides of the God debate, the New Atheists have been and continue to be opinion shapers (at least in the Western world[110]). This is understandable. First, modern media thrives on conflict and gravitates towards anyone willing and able to clearly articulate controversial beliefs. The New Atheists fit the bill. Second, many New Atheists have a background in the hard sciences, and Western culture treats scientists as authority figures even when they

---

104. Painter, *The New Atheist Denial of History*, 18.
105. Painter, *The New Atheist Denial of History*, 10.
106. Painter, *The New Atheist Denial of History*, 11.
107. Painter, *The New Atheist Denial of History*, ix.
108. Lennox, *Gunning for God*, 188.
109. Groothuis quoted in Strobel, *The Case for Miracles*, 239.
110. See: Pew Research Center, "The Changing Global Religious Landscape."

speak on topics outside their academic training. On this point, it's worth bearing in mind Craig's word of caution:

> Academics are narrowly focused in their respective areas of specialization and remain largely ignorant on subjects—especially subjects in which they have little interest—outside their chosen fields. When it comes to topics outside their areas of expertise, the opinions of great scientists, philosophers, and other academics carry no more weight than the pronouncements of a layman—indeed, on these subjects they *are* laymen.[111]

When an articulate scientist like Dawkins makes a confident public pronouncement about the historical Jesus, one can understand why many laymen without the appropriate background knowledge to assess what they are hearing will find his pronouncement convincing.

There was a 0.8 percent increase in self-declared atheism amongst American adults between 2007 and 2012.[112] Likewise, the proportion of the combined English and Welsh populations who self-identify as having no religion (so-called "nones") rose from 46 percent in 2011 to 48.5 percent in 2014, thereby outnumbering those in the same population who self-identify as Christian (43.8 percent).[113] A Scottish social attitudes survey found that 52 percent of the population said they weren't religious in 2016, up from 40 percent at the turn of the century.[114] While the New Atheists are unlikely to be the sole cause of these changes, anecdotal evidence suggests they are a contributing cause. It's because of the high profile and influential nature of neo-atheist views, rather than their cogency, that they demand a public response.

Watch: "Concerning the New Atheism" Youtube playlist: www.youtube.com/playlist?list=PLQhh3qcwVEWifP3P_gIS8MMsRXLOGDiG_

Listen: "Dissecting Dawkins' Defence of *The God Delusion*" by Peter S. Williams: http://peterswilliams.podbean.com/mf/feed/rr7cd9/SUCU_Dawkins_Delusion_2016.mp3

"What Would C.S. Lewis say to Richard Dawkins?" by Peter S. Williams: http://peterswilliams.podbean.com/mf/feed/r46hka/ELF_2015_Lewis_Dawkins_Lecture.mp3

Read: "The New Atheism and Five Arguments for God" by William Lane Craig: www.reasonablefaith.org/the-new-atheism-and-five-arguments-for-god

"Richard Dawkins' Argument for Atheism in The God Delusion" by William Lane Craig: www.reasonablefaith.org/writings/question-answer/richard-dawkins-argument-for-atheism-in-the-god-delusion

"The Dawkins Confusion" by Alvin Plantinga: www.philvaz.com/apologetics/DawkinsGodDelusionPlantingaReview.pdf

"The God Argument by A.C. Grayling" by Keith Ward: www.bethinking.org/does-god-exist/book-review-ac-graylings-the-god-argument

---

111. Craig, "Atheists Gone Wild?"
112. See: Ambrosino, "From Nietzsche to Richard Dawkins."
113. Sherwood, "People of no religion outnumber Christians."
114. Sherwood, "People of no religion outnumber Christians."

"A Universe From Someone: Against Lawrence Krauss" by Peter S. Williams www.bethinking.org/is-there-a-creator/a-universe-from-someone-against-lawrence-krauss

Is God a Moral Monster? Making Sense Of The Old Testament God by Paul Copan

God Is Good, God Is Great: Why Believing in God Is Reasonable and Responsible edited by William Lane Craig and Chad Meister

A Reasonable God: Engaging the New Face of Atheism by Gregory E. Ganssle

True Reason: Confronting the Irrationality of the New Atheism edited by Tom Gilson and Carson Weitnauer

Atheism's New Clothes: Exploring And Exposing The Claims Of The New Atheists by David H. Glass

Atheist Delusions: The Christian Revolution and Its Fashionable Enemies by David Bentley Hart

The New Atheist Denial of History by Borden W. Painter Jr.

C.S. Lewis vs. the New Atheists by Peter S. Williams

A Sceptic's Guide to Atheism by Peter S. Williams

GETTING AT THE JESUS OF FAITH

Jesus of Nazareth intrigues and perplexes people from across the spectrum of beliefs about God. According to atheist author Phillip Pullman: "Jesus was a great storyteller. To invent the story about the Good Samaritan, you hear it once, you never forget it, you tell it to somebody else and it still has the same effect. The man was a genius of storytelling, if nothing else."[115] Author and agnostic Terry Pratchett once affirmed: "Jesus had a lot of good things to say."[116] New Testament scholar and self-described "agnostic with atheist leanings"[117] Bart D. Erhman describes Jesus as "a kind of religious genius . . ."[118] Peter Millican, an atheist philosopher at Oxford University, says that "for certain, Jesus has been extremely influential. I also think a lot of Jesus' moral teachings are actually quite enlightened."[119] In a similar vein, atheist philosopher of mind Colin McGinn writes: "I still admire many of the teachings of Jesus Christ, and find his life exemplary of some important moral truths, but I long ago rejected the supernatural baggage that accompanies Christian belief."[120]

Although "supernatural baggage" is a pejorative turn of phrase, one can see why an atheist (who believes that God doesn't exist[121]) wouldn't think about Jesus in Christian terms. Indeed, *if* atheism is true it follows that Jesus *cannot* be the person

---

115. Zaimov, "Atheist Author Phillip Pullman."
116. Prachett, "I create gods all the time."
117. Ehrman, *Did Jesus Exist?*, 5.
118. Ehrman, *Did Jesus Exist?*, 37.
119. Millican, the Craig-Millican debate.
120. McGinn, *The Making of a Philosopher*, 37.
121. See: Craig, "The Definition That Will Not Die."

Christianity says he is (conversely, if Jesus *is* the person Christianity says he is, then atheism is false). However, to rule out the *divinity* of Jesus isn't to rule out his *humanity*. Indeed, the above comments from Pullman, Pratchett, Erhman, Millican, and McGinn affirm not only the historical existence of Jesus, but the existence of sufficient evidence to justify various knowledge-claims about him.

Pullman thinks that "if nothing else" our evidence shows that Jesus was "a great storyteller" who invented "the story about the Good Samaritan."[122] Pratchett thought Jesus said some "good things."[123] Erhman thinks he can justifiably call Jesus a "religious genius" whose "teachings have impacted the world ever since."[124] Millican attributes the "quite enlightened"[125] moral teachings he praises to the historical Jesus. McGinn thinks the evidence gives us access not only to "many of the teachings of Jesus Christ" but to biographical details that are "exemplary of some important moral truths."[126]

The opinion of Jesus formed by many people today is a variation upon this theme: an interpretation of the relevant historical evidence (an interpretation that may or may not be grounded in an in-depth familiarity with either the historical data or the rules of historiography) that is molded by a pre-commitment to worldview beliefs that preclude a Christian understanding of Jesus. For example, according to NT scholar Helen K. Bond:

> modern *academic study* of the historical Jesus only really began in the wake of the eighteenth-century Enlightenment, with . . . its rejection of a God who intervenes in history in supernatural ways. The emergence of historical criticism in the nineteenth century allowed distinctions to be made between the 'Christ of faith' and the 'Jesus of history', distinctions that have underpinned the Quest [for the historical Jesus] ever since.[127]

We need to think carefully about this.

Light on the Enlightenment

For a start, the Enlightenment wasn't the monolithic movement portrayed by Bond. Historian Helena Rosenblatt explains:

> A widespread consensus used to exist that the very essence of the Enlightenment . . . was its attack on religion . . . We now know, however, that the relationship between Christianity and the Enlightenment was far more complex and interesting. We realize that these previous interpretations were overly

---

122. Zaimov, "Atheist Author Phillip Pullman."
123. Prachett, "I create gods all the time."
124. Ehrman, *Did Jesus Exist?*, 37.
125. Millican, the Craig-Millican debate.
126. McGinn, *The Making of a Philosopher*, 37.
127. Bond, *The Historical Jesus*, 7.

focused on France, and erroneously tended to posit a single Enlightenment . . . scholars have been 'pluralizing' the Enlightenment, the result being that we now see it not so much as a unified and Francophone phenomenon, but rather as a 'family of discourses' with many regional and national variations . . . It has become clear that earlier interpretations were based on an impoverished view of religious traditions and perhaps even an outright disdain for them.[128]

In other words, the association between the Enlightenment and Bond's "rejection of a God who intervenes in history" isn't a historical constant.

Atheist philosopher Julian Baggini comments that:

> Once upon a time . . . people believed in a wondrous time called the Enlightenment, a particularly triumphant period in the story of human progress from barbarism and superstition to civilized rationality. Nowadays, it is more fashionable to dismiss this narrative as a secular myth. Yet some still carry the torch for the old orthodoxy, none more energetically than AC Grayling, who has served as protector of the faith in several books.[129]

However, having done his PhD on the history and philosophy of science, Steve Fuller notes that "the scientific revolution . . . wasn't an anti-religious moment at all. In fact it coincides with the rise of Protestantism . . . and in particular the operative point . . . is the idea that human beings are made in the image and likeness of God."[130]

"The Enlightenment may have been troubled by the question of faith," writes Terry Eagleton, "but it was not especially anti-religious."[131] Eagleton elsewhere concludes that "The Enlightenment was deeply shaped by values which stemmed from the Christian tradition."[132] As historian Rodney Stark explains:

> The single most remarkable and ironic thing about the "Enlightenment" is that those who proclaimed it made little or no contribution to the accomplishments they hailed . . . Voltaire, Rousseau, Diderot, Hume, Gibbon, and the rest were literary men, while the primary revolution they hailed as the "Enlightenment" was scientific. Equally misleading is the fact that although the literary men who proclaimed the "Enlightenment" were irreligious, the central figures in the scientific achievements of the era were deeply religious. So much then for the idea that suddenly in the sixteenth century, enlightened secular forces burst the chains of Christian thought and set the foundation for modern times. What the proponents of "Enlightenment" actually initiated was the tradition of angry secular attacks on religion in the name of science . . . Presented as the latest word in sophistication, rationalism, and reason, these

---

128. See: Rosenblatt, "The Christian Enlightenment."
129. Baggini, "A flawed attempt to shed light on genius," 38.
130. Fuller, "Science & Religion."
131. Eagleton, *Culture and the Death of God*, 5.
132. Eagleton, *Reason, Faith, and Revolution*, 68.

assaults are remarkably naïve and simplistic—both then and now. In truth, the rise of science was inseparable from Christian theology, for the latter gave direction and confidence to the former . . .[133]

Many of the Enlightenment's leading philosophers were likewise Christian theists (e.g. George Berkley, Immanuel Kant, Gottfried Leibniz, John Locke, Thomas Reid, etc.). Hence, as historian of science Allan Chapman concludes, the Enlightenment: "transpires to be the creation of scholars with their own cultural and usually anti-Christian axes to grind."[134]

Finally, and most importantly, the Enlightenment did *not* draw a line of demarcation between critical scholars whose rejection of the supernatural left them free to engage in respectable academic study of the "Jesus of history," and un-critical folk whose religious beliefs excluded them from the scholarly guild and condemned them to blind adherence to the "Christ of faith." Indeed, the rejection of the supernatural expressed in the traditional anti-religious conception of "the Enlightenment" does not *allow* the distinction between the "Christ of faith" and the "Jesus of history" as Bond says; rather, it *requires* the distinction, and does so *regardless of the evidence!*

THE NEW ATHEISTS' JESUS OF FAITH

"Those who bang their heads against history's wall had better be equipped with some kind of a theoretical crash helmet."

—CHRISTOPHER HITCHENS[135]

According to philosopher Winfried Corduan: "To write history, it is always best to begin with the data supplied by one's sources and to build the theories around them, rather than beginning with certain theories and questioning the reliability of the written sources because they do not fit the theory."[136] In other words, *history should be an evidence led search for the truth*. Unfortunately, the "modern academic study of the historical Jesus" described by Bond is no more an evidence-led search for the truth than is the most critically ignorant Christian fideism. Rather, it's *the search for a Jesus consistent with the prior assumption of a standard conception of naturalism*. The Jesus happily acknowledged by many atheists and agnostics is, in this sense, *a Jesus of faith* (an understanding of Jesus shaped by trust in a naturalistic worldview) *rather than a Jesus of history* (an understanding of Jesus produced by following the evidence).

This is an irony that is intensified by the public statements of neo-atheists about the importance of empirical evidence in the process of rational belief-formation:

133. Stark, *The Triumph of Christianity*, 252.
134. Chapman, *Slaying The Dragons*, 67.
135. Hitchens, *Hitch-22*, 89.
136. Corduan, *In The Beginning God*, 313.

- Peter Atkins claims "that the scientific method is the only means of discovering the nature of reality . . . making observations and comparing notes, will forever survive as the only way of acquiring reliable knowledge."[137]
- Richard Dawkins criticizes religious faith as requiring "blind trust, in the absence of evidence, even in the teeth of evidence."[138] According to Dawkins: "the only good reason to believe that something exists is if there is real evidence that it does . . . it always comes back to our senses, one way or another."[139]
- A.C. Grayling condemns religious faith as "a stance or an attitude of belief independent of, and characteristically in the countervailing face of, evidence. It is non-rational at best, and is probably irrational given that it involves deliberate ignoring of evidence, or commitment despite lack of evidence."[140]
- Victor Stenger contrasts religious faith defined as "belief in the absence of supportive evidence"[141] with science defined as "belief in the presence of supportive evidence."[142]

In light of such repeated pronouncements about the importance of *a posteriori* evidence (pronouncements that evince a misunderstanding of faith, whilst promulgating a self-contradictory *scientistic* theory of knowledge), what are we to make of the New Atheists' ignorance of history, or their commitment to drawing a line of demarcation between the Jesus of faith and the Jesus of history *on a priori grounds*?

Sneer pressure

Richard Dawkins claims that "The nineteenth century is the last time when it was possible for an educated person to admit to believing in miracles . . . without embarrassment."[143] This un-evidenced psychological red herring is obviously false (being made in the teeth of overwhelming evidence to the contrary). Why make such a claim? Dawkins is borrowing a rhetorical method from Rudolf Bultmann, who notoriously proclaimed:

> it is impossible to use electric light and the wireless and to avail ourselves of modern medical and surgical discoveries, and at the same time to believe in the New Testament world of spirits and miracles.[144]

---

137. Atkins, *On Being*, xiii.
138. Dawkins, *The Selfish Gene*, 198.
139. Dawkins, *The Magic of Reality*, 16, 19.
140. Grayling, *Conversations on Religion*, 3.
141. Stenger, *The New Atheism*, 45
142. Stenger, *The New Atheism*, 15.
143. Dawkins, *The God Delusion*, 187.
144. Bultmann, *Kerygma and Myth*, 5.

What Bultmann meant was something along the lines of the assertion that "belief in the supernatural is an intellectually unsustainable position for well-educated adults in a scientific age." For the New Atheists, "intellectually sustainable" and "scientific" (defined to exclude any explanation incompatible with their naturalism) are synonymous. Hence the appeal to science is, for them, merely a roundabout way of asserting that theism is, as Antony O'Hear claims, "intellectually unsustainable."[145]

However, as atheist Nigel Warburton notes, "Confident assertion is no substitute for argument . . ."[146] Indeed, as C. Stephen Evans wryly observes, what we have here "is an unacknowledged, and perhaps unconscious, appeal to authority, the anonymous authority of the 'modern mind.'"[147] Of course, a great many modern minds manage this supposedly impossible feat! As theologian N.T. Wright notes: "I know plenty of scientists who firmly and avowedly believe in the resurrection, and some indeed who have given a solid and coherent account of why they do so."[148] Likewise, Plantinga observes:

> Very many well-educated people (including even some theologians) understand science and history in a way that is entirely compatible both with the possibility and with the actuality of miracles. Many physicists and engineers, for example, understand "electrical light and the wireless" vastly better than Bultmann or his contemporary followers, but nonetheless hold precisely those New Testament beliefs Bultmann thinks incompatible with using electric lights and radios . . . there are any number of . . . contemporary intellectuals very well acquainted with science who don't feel any problem at all in pursuing science and also believing in miracles . . .[149]

Neither intellect nor education is a barrier to holding supernatural beliefs. For example, 72 percent of Americans with postgraduate degrees believe in miracles.[150] A 2004 study reported that a majority of medical doctors surveyed thought that miracles have happened in history (74 percent) and that they could occur in the present (73 percent).[151]

Graham Veale is unfortunately correct when he warns that the New Atheism aims "to sell consumers a sense of intellectual superiority for a low intellectual price."[152] Dawkins's false psychological assertion about belief in miracles is deployed in an attempt to create peer pressure against belief. Veale comments: "We can dub this

---

145. O'Hear, *Beyond Evolution*, 201.
146. Warburton, *Thinking: From A to Z*, 19.
147. Evans, *The Historical Christ*, 200.
148. Wright, "Can a Scientist Believe," 42.
149. Plantinga, *Warranted Christian Belief*, 405.
150. Quarles, "Higher Criticism," 80.
151. Keener, *Miracles*, 721–22.
152. Veale, *New Atheism*, 11.

rhetorical strategy 'sneer pressure'. The aim is to gain converts by peer pressure, to make the faithful feel foolish and out of place in the modern academic environment."[153]

The rhetoric of sneer pressure is pervasive in Western culture. Theologian Randall Hardman remembers that in one of his undergraduate classes "the premise was put forward like this: 'We do history, not theology in here. Leave your faith at the door.'"[154] Hardman recalls hearing a number of similar statements, all of which reinforced the expectation "that being a critical historian implies rejecting any supernaturalism."[155] This biased expectation is commonplace, but it cannot survive critical scrutiny.

GETTING AT THE LINE OF DEMARCATION

> "While atheists may call themselves free thinkers,
> for many today atheism is a closed system of thought."
>
> —JOHN GRAY[156]

There are three basic approaches to drawing a line of demarcation between the "Jesus of history" and the "Christ of faith" (these approaches can be mixed):

1) *The metaphysical approach*—miracles *can't happen*

and/or:

2) *The espistemological approach*—miracles *can't be known*

and/or:

3) *The definitional approach*—miracles *can't be mentioned* within "history" as a subject.

The *metaphysical approach* denies the *possibility* of miracles by assuming an atheistic or deistic worldview. Critics who take this approach:

> assume that the Jesus of the Gospels is not the true Jesus of history. Since they reject the possibility of miracles, they cannot accept the miracle-working Jesus portrayed in the pages of the New Testament. Hence they are forced to try to discover a non-miraculous Jesus in history. This is a crucial point: they have not proven that the true Jesus of history is not the Jesus of the Gospels—they assume this to be the case before they begin their investigation.[157]

---

153. Veale, *New Atheism*, 17.
154. Hardman, "Historical Evidences For The Gospels," 227.
155. Hardman, "Historical Evidences For The Gospels," 227.
156. Gray, "Sex, Atheism and Piano Legs," 2.
157. Fernandes et al., *Hijacking The Historical Jesus*, 29.

For example, atheist historian Michael Grant stipulates that: "According . . . to the cold standard of humdrum fact . . . [Jesus'] nature-reversing miracles did *not* happen."[158] As C.S. Lewis complained: "The canon 'If miraculous, unhistorical' is one [these critics] bring to their study of the texts, not one they have learned from it."[159]

The *epistemological approach* denies the *knowability* of miracles by holding that it could never be more plausible to affirm than to deny the historicity of a miracle even if the miracle in question did in fact occur. Thus, Bart Ehrman states:

> even if miracles did happen in the past . . . there is no way to establish that they happened . . . that's not a result of atheist, anti-supernaturalist presuppositions. It is the result of historical method. Historians simply have no access to supernatural activities involving the actions of God . . . Theologians can certainly affirm that God has done miracles, but they are affirming this on theological grounds, not historical grounds.[160]

While this line of demarcation is epistemological rather than metaphysical, one may nevertheless suspect that Erhman's "anti-supernaturalist presuppositions" have some influence upon his understanding of "historical method"!

Unless it is combined with a metaphysical denial of miracles, embracing the epistemological line of demarcation means refusing to accept the occurrence of any miracle, regardless of the evidence, even though one acknowledges that a miracle may have actually occurred!

The *definitional approach* denies the *mentionability* of miracles *within history* by dint of *defining* history as *methodologically* naturalistic. Critics who take the definitional approach don't necessarily think miracles can't happen. Nor do they necessarily think of miracles as events that can't be known to have happened even if they do happen. Rather, they label miracles as events that can't feature within the academic discipline of history. As Craig observes: "It is frequently asserted that the professional scientist or historian is methodologically committed to seeking only natural causes as explanations of their respective data, which procedure rules out inference to God as the best explanation."[161] Put another way, the definitional approach seeks to limit academic freedom by enforcing a taboo against miracles.

For example, according to Albert Schweitzer: "the exclusion of miracle from our view of history has been universally recognized as a principle of criticism, so that miracle no longer concerns the historian either positively or negatively."[162] Likewise, scholars in the notorious Jesus Seminar affirm that a distinction between the historical

---

158. Grant, *Jesus*, 39.
159. Lewis, "Modern Theology and Biblical Criticism," 354.
160. Ehrman, "Bart D. Ehrman Interview."
161. Craig, "A Classical Apologist's Response," 124.
162. Schweitzer, *The Quest of the Historical Jesus*, 110–11.

Jesus and the Christ of faith is "the first pillar of scholarly wisdom"[163] and contend that by definition the historical Jesus must be a non-supernatural figure. The Jesus Seminar thereby guarantees by definition that miraculous explanations are non-historical irrespective of the evidence and irrespective of the facts of the matter.

William Lane Craig examines how methodological naturalism shapes the conclusions of seminar member Gerd Lüdemann:

> He states, "Historical criticism . . . does not reckon with an intervention of God in history." Thus, the resurrection *cannot* be historical; it goes out the window before you even sit down at the table to look at the evidence.[164]

Likewise, according to Jean-Pierre Isbouts:

> the Resurrection is beyond the grasp of science; it cannot be corroborated by historical or archaeological evidence.[165]

Isbouts's "cannot" appears to be a semantic rule about the use of the term "historical;" it's not an epistemological fact. As a matter of epistemology, it's obvious that the resurrection could be "corroborated" by historical and archaeological evidence. Indeed, we'll spend our final chapters examining how historical and archaeological evidence do just that.

Adopting a taboo against mentioning miracles in history means that history isn't an evidence-led search for the truth about the past. It means saying that even given that "Jesus was resurrected" is a true statement of fact warranted by historical evidence, it isn't a "historical" statement! In the absence of a metaphysical or epistemological justification, a mere taboo against miracles in history has no veto power over anyone with the strength of will to seek the truth about the past by following the evidence wherever it leads in an alternative academic pursuit we could call "What Happened Studies" (even if doing so means believing in a miracle). In sum, the definitional approach is just a sophisticated form of sneer pressure.

PHILOSOPHICAL QUESTIONS ABOUT MIRACLES

People who believe miracles are possible don't necessarily accept any miracle-claims. As Peter Kreeft and Ronald Tacelli observe: "If there is a God, miracles are *possible*. But perhaps God did not choose to actualize this possibility."[166] Then again, those who believe some miracle-claims don't necessarily believe all miracle-claims: "God is not compelled to act in a miraculous manner, and believers are not obligated to accept

---

163. Schweitzer, *The Quest of the Historical Jesus*, 2–3.
164. Craig, "Visions of Jesus."
165. Isbouts, *The Story of Jesus*, 96.
166. Kreeft and Tacelli, *Handbook of Christian Apologetics*, 109.

each and every purported case of a miraculous event as real . . ."[167] As C. Stephen Evans comments: "the believer in miracles does not deny that there is some presumption in favour of natural explanations. She merely denies that this presumption is so strong that it will always outweigh the evidence in favour of a miracle."[168] One might be agnostic about certain miracle-claims, believing some and disbelieving others. We certainly needn't be gullible when it comes to assessing miracle-claims. Rather, in response to each miracle claim we should ask whether there's sufficient evidence to convince us that a miracle has occurred.

The *a posteriori* question of whether any given miracle claim is true pre-supposes answers to a series of *a priori* philosophical questions, such as a) the *definitional* question of what is meant by "a miracle," b) the *metaphysical* question of whether a miracle can happen, c) the *epistemological* question of whether (and if so, how) a miracle can in principle be known to have happened, and d) the *definitional* question of whether methodological naturalism should be built into the definition of our search for the truth about the past.

For obvious reasons, one's intellectual openness to believing in miracles per se is deeply affected by one's beliefs about God. After all, it would be impossible for humans to show by investigation of the evidence that no miracles have happened. The skeptic can hardly examine every alleged miracle story in detail. Even if they did, there's always the possibility of miracles in prehistory. Hence people who reject miracles per se must do so by arguing either that:

1) Miracles cannot happen (the metaphysical approach)

or:

2) Even if miracles can happen, we cannot rationally believe in them (the epistemological approach).

HUME AGAINST MIRACLES

> "Hume's celebrated argument against miracles
> is now widely recognized as demonstrably fallacious."
>
> —William Lane Craig[169]

David Hume "is the most significant critic"[170] of miracles in the sense that, even today, his thoughts on the matter set the agenda for discussion. Hume made "a famous

---

167. Corduan, "Miracles," 169, 172–3.
168. Evans, *The Historical Christ*, 159.
169. Craig, "Creation and Divine Action," 326.
170. Mawson, *Belief In God*, 179.

and influential argument"[171] against belief in miracles, an argument that "has almost reached the level of canonical status amongst atheists and agnostics, who often cite it as the last word."[172] Indeed, according to Christopher Hitchens, Hume "wrote the last word on the subject"[173] of miracles. Such a statement exhibits a startling ignorance. That Richard Dawkins would call Hitchens "the leading intellect and scholar of our atheist secular movement, a formidable adversary to the pretentious, the woolly-minded or the intellectually dishonest"[174] consequently indicates that Dawkins must himself suffer from at least one of the conditions he lists.

In his *Enquiry Concerning Human Understanding* Hume wrote: "I flatter myself that I have discovered an argument . . . which, if just, will, with the wise and learned, be an everlasting check to all kinds of superstitious delusion, and consequently will be useful as long as the world endures."[175] This argument was that:

> A miracle is a violation of the laws of nature; and as a firm and unalterable experience has established these laws, the proof against a miracle, from the very nature of the fact, is as entire as any argument from experience can possibly be imagined.[176]

Some of Hume's interpreters have understood him as giving a *metaphysical* argument against miracles. Others have understood him to be giving an *epistemological* argument. We'll examine both interpretations, after passing some comments about the definition of "miracle" and the distinction between "natural" and "supernatural" explanations.

On the Nature of Miracles

"miracles do not, in fact, break the laws of nature."

—C.S. Lewis[177]

Hume notoriously defined a miracle as "a violation of the laws of nature"[178] and as a "transgression of a law of nature by a particular volition of the Deity . . ."[179] Dawkins follows Hume in defining a miracle as "a violation of the normal running of the natural

---

171. Wierenga, *The Philosophy of Religion*, 129.
172. Robertson, *Magnificent Obsession*, 41.
173. Hitchens, *God is Not Great*, 141.
174. Dawkins quoted in Taunton, *The Faith of Christopher Hitchens*, 175.
175. Hume, *An Enquiry Concerning Human Understanding*, 10.1.118.
176. Hume, *An Enquiry Concerning Human Understanding*, 10.1.118.
177. Lewis, *Miracles*, 99.
178. Hume, *An Enquiry Concerning Human Understanding*, 114:143.
179. Hume, *An Enquiry Concerning Human Understanding*, 115:154.

world"[180] that is "flatly contradictory not just to the facts of science but to the spirit of science."[181] Jerry A. Coyne likewise defines a miracle as "a divinely produced violation of nature's laws . . ."[182]

As Evans complains, the imagery of "violating" or "breaking" a "law" is prejudicial: "Since [natural] laws are not prescriptive but descriptive, it is misleading to describe God's action in deviating from them on occasion as a violation of a law . . . some people are no doubt misled by the connotations of the words *law* and *violation*."[183] Philosopher J.A. Cover comments:

> Miracles are not "violations" of the laws of nature at all. The laws of nature . . . describe what objects in nature are capable of producing in light of the powers that they have . . . Thus, miraculous events—those events not caused by the operation of natural powers in created objects—do nothing to threaten the truth of natural laws about natural causes . . . believing in events having supernatural causes needn't saddle one with believing that there are *false laws of nature*, laws having exceptions. Miracles are . . . occurrences having causes about which laws of nature are simply silent. The laws are true, but simply don't speak to events caused by divine intervention.[184]

On the nature of nature

C.S. Lewis explains that the distinction between natural and non-natural (or supernatural) things and explanations arose during the development of Greek thought:

> The pre-Socratic Greek philosophers had had the idea of taking all the things they knew or believed in—gods, men, animals, plants, minerals, what you will—and impounding them under a single name . . . the name they chose for it was *physis* . . . From *physis* this meaning passed to *natura* . . . Parmenides and Empedocles [who were materialists] had thought that they were giving, in principle, an account of everything. Later thinkers denied this; but in the sense that they believed in realities of a quite different order from any that their predecessors took account of. They expressed this not in the form "*physis* contains more than our ancestors supposed," but in the form (explicitly or implicitly), "there is something else besides *physis*." The moment you say this, *physis* is being used in what I call its demoted sense. For it had meant "everything" and you are now saying there is something in addition to it.[185]

180. Dawkins, *A Devil's Chaplain*, 150.
181. Dawkins, "Is Science a Religion?" 180.
182. Coyne, *Faith vs. Fact*, 124.
183. Evans, *Philosophy of Religion*, 108.
184. Cover, "Miracles and Christian Theism," 362.
185. Lewis, *Studies in Words*, 35–38.

Hence Lewis notes that "Aristotle criticised thinkers like Parmenides because 'they never conceived of anything other than the substance of things perceivable by the senses.'"[186] As Lewis observes:

> Christianity involves a God as transcendent as Aristotle's, but adds (this was what it inherited from Judaism and could also have inherited from Plato's *Timaes*) the conception that this God is the Creator of *physis*. *Nature (d.s.) demoted* is now both distinct from God [i.e. mono-theism isn't pantheism] and also related to him as artefact to artist, or as servant to master . . . [i.e. mono-theism isn't either polytheism or deism][187]

Today's "New Atheists" advocate a contemporary version of the materialism espoused by Parmenides and Empedocles, promoting a metaphysically naturalistic conception of "*physis*" that denies the existence of any realities of the "quite different" *supernatural* order embraced by the likes of Socrates, Plato and Aristotle.

Lewis traces the developing meaning of the term "nature":

> By far the commonest native meaning of *natura* is something like sort, kind, quality, or character. When you ask, in our modern idiom, what something "is like," you are asking for its *natura* . . . In nineteenth century English the word "description" itself ("I do not associate with persons of that description") is often an exact synonym for *natura*.[188]

In this native sense of the term, to give a natural or naturalistic explanation is to give an explanation in terms of "some idea of a thing's *natura* as its original or 'innate' character."[189] One could, in this sense, give a natural or naturalistic explanation of a supernatural reality (e.g. "God knows what I am praying because he is by nature omniscient"), no less than the behavior of an atom. Today, however, a naturalistic explanation has come to mean an explanation couched in terms of the sort of realities accepted by the Greek materialists (realities that are part of a non-intentional, closed, mechanistic system of things).

Lewis explains that:

> The nature of anything, its original, innate character, its spontaneous behaviour, can be contrasted with what it is made to be or do by some external agency. A yew tree is *natural* before the topiarist has carved it; water in a fountain is forced upwards against its *nature* . . .[190]

It isn't natural for a yew tree to form itself into the shape of an elephant; to do so outstrips its innate behavioral capacities as part of the natural world. Our observation

---

186. Lewis, *Studies in Words*, 38.
187. Lewis, *Studies in Words*, 39.
188. Lewis, *Studies in Words*, 24.
189. Lewis, *Studies in Words*, 25.
190. Lewis, *Studies in Words*, 45.

of such a tree excites an experience-based sense of wonder best resolved by explaining its elephantine shape as the product of design. We might consider attributing this design to any number of potential designer candidates. In this case the best explanation is the actions of a human being. However, in principle, there could be cases where the best explanation of an event that outstrips the innate behavioral capacities of the natural world would be the special action of *divine* agency.[191] We would call such an event "a miracle."

Given the obvious worldview ramifications of designating any event "a miracle," the naturalist may hope to find some principled way to permanently separate any and all nature-outstripping events from any and all explanations framed in terms of the special action of a *divine* agency. They might try to retain a standard form of naturalism despite acknowledging the occurrence of anomalous events that appear to outstrip the innate behavioral capacities of the natural world. Alternatively, they might consider adopting a non-standard version of naturalism that provides a naturalistically acceptable cause of any apparently miraculous event.

Miracles vs. undiscovered natural laws

Taking the first option, some argue that the only rational response to an apparently miraculous event is to revise our understanding of how nature works. Those who take this "undiscovered natural laws" approach conceded that it can be rational to conclude that a resurrection, for example, has occurred as an anomalous event; but they deny that it can be rational to conclude that a resurrection is "a miracle." However, as Moreland and Craig point out: "If an anomalous event occurs and we have reason to believe that this event would not occur again under similar circumstances [where we limit those circumstances to natural causes alone], then the law in question will not be abandoned."[192]

Indeed, it's one thing to *say* we should revise our understanding of nature to encompass an event we would otherwise describe as a miracle; it's quite another to actually formulate and scientifically validate such a revised understanding. Absent such work, this move is nothing but a question-begging, promissory naturalism of the gaps.

John Warwick Montgomery asks: "how likely is it that a new physical law might be discovered that would provide a satisfactory explanation of Jesus' resurrection from the dead after the systematic work of a Roman crucifixion team and three days in the grave?"[193] As Moreland and Craig argue:

> the evidence for the laws of nature . . . makes it probable that a resurrection from the dead is naturally impossible, which renders improbable the

---

191. See: Dembski, "The Incompleteness of Scientific Naturalism;" Monton, *Seeking God in Science*.
192. Moreland and Craig, *Philosophical Foundations for a Christian Worldview*, 568.
193. Montgomery, "Miracle Evidence," 199–200.

hypothesis that Jesus rose naturally from the grave. But such evidence is simply irrelevant to the probability of the hypothesis that God raised Jesus from the dead.[194]

Any skeptic who would insist we revise our scientific understanding of nature rather than accept that Jesus' admitted resurrection was a miracle would seem to be ignoring the *context* of the event in question, for "if a purported miracle occurs in a significant religio-historical context, then the chances of its being a genuine miracle are increased."[195] As philosopher William J. Wainwright explains:

> religiously significant events are those that "contribute significantly towards a holy divine purpose for the world." They can do this by bringing about good or by being a "contribution to or foretaste of the ultimate destiny of the world." Thus, an apparently inexplicable healing is religiously significant because its immediate effects are good and because it foreshadows the Kingdom of God . . .[196]

Hence, as Michael R. Licona concludes: "We may recognize that an event is a miracle when the event (a) is extremely unlikely to have occurred, given the circumstances and/or natural law and (b) it occurs is an environment or context charged with religious significance."[197]

The more reason we think there is to expect God to work miraculously to achieve certain goals *a priori*, the lighter the evidential load that falls upon *a posteriori* experience to convince us that a miracle has happened, and the more implausible the "undiscovered law of nature" response becomes with respect to the anomalous event in question. The same point applies to any case where we have some reason to believe that God has revealed his intention to work a specific miracle. As Kreeft and Tacelli argue:

> When we consider . . . the extraordinary deeds attributed to Jesus, and the special relationship he claimed to have with "the Father" (i.e., God), it is difficult to avoid one of three conclusions. Either Jesus was a sincere lunatic, or [a lying and blasphemous] fraud, or he really was the Son of God—and his extraordinary deeds were in the fullest sense miracles. This triple possibility arises not merely from the deeds considered by themselves; it arises primarily from the life, character and message of the one who performed them.[198]

Gary R. Habermas reports that:

---

194. Moreland and Craig, *Philosophical Foundations for a Christian Worldview*, 568.
195. Moreland and Craig, *Philosophical Foundations for a Christian Worldview*, 568.
196. Wainwright, *Philosophy of Religion*, 61–62.
197. Licona, "Historians and Miracle Claims," 106–29.
198. Kreeft and Tacelli, *Handbook of Christian Apologetics*, 114.

In recent decades, scholars have regularly taken a positive view of Jesus being aware of his impending death, and many are at least open to the resurrection predictions. This is probably due to several factors such as the embarrassment on the part of the disciples and especially Peter, who disbelieved and even resisted Jesus' comments, the multiple attestation found in [the sources drawn upon by the NT gospels] . . . and that these comments played no serious or extended function in a New Testament apologetic.[199]

Given the resurrection of Jesus, and given an attitude towards theism that falls short of a dogmatic atheism, it would surely be more reasonable to admit that his resurrection was a miracle than to insist: "Dead people naturally become resurrected people under certain, currently unknown physical conditions that have thus far only been met in the first-century case of a man who coincidentally just happened to be widely acclaimed as a miracle-worker and who predicted his resurrection as the crowning miraculous validation of his claim to be the Jewish Messiah."

The simulation hypothesis

Taking the second option, consider the fashionable hypothesis that our world is in fact a computer simulation (a virtual reality) created by naturalistically explicable beings in a physical reality that grounds and transcends our cosmos without thereby being supernatural in the traditional sense; for if the *natura* of our reality is simulated, any apparently miraculous event we notice would be best explained by reference to our naturalistic creators.

By postulating a transcendent but nonetheless naturalistic reality, the simulated reality (SR) hypothesis is able to uncouple the nature-outstripping effect from the supernatural cause that are united in the concept of a "miracle," thereby allowing the naturalist to admit the occurrence of events that outstrip the *natura* of our world (conceived of as a simulated reality) whilst assigning those events a naturalistic explanation. Thus, consideration of the SR hypothesis leads philosopher Richard Hanley to argue that "it would be dogmatic to insist" that all apparently "marvelous phenomenon" (i.e. miracles) must be "an illusion"; but this is only because he thinks the SR hypothesis demonstrates that the occurrence of nature-outstripping phenomena would be "a very long way from establishing that *it* is evidence for the divine."[200]

However, it seems to me that any hypothesis that tries to domesticate miracles by positing a naturalistically acceptable cause for nature-outstripping events will suffer from a number of drawbacks: First, any such hypothesis retains the metaphysical problems inherent within naturalism (including the many problems facing a naturalistic philosophy of mind). Second, any such hypothesis will be more complex than

---

199. Habermas, "Dale Allison's Resurrection Skepticism," 308.
200. Hanley, "Miracles and Wonders," 388.

standard naturalism. Third, any such hypothesis will be significantly *ad hoc*. For example, the SR hypothesis has to postulate the development of hardware that transcends "our current understanding of computing technology."[201] As mathematician Marcus Noack comments: "The more computing power I want, the bigger the computer must be . . . to accurately model the universe . . . I cannot overstate how far away that idea is from the reality of computation as we know it today."[202] Fourth, any such hypothesis will amount to an unfalsifiable conspiracy theory that disregards the religio-historical context of miracle claims. Fifth, any such hypothesis threatens to drown the scientific project in skepticism. On the SR hypothesis, what confidence can we have that our cosmos is as large or as old as it appears to us, that our memories are reliable, that everyone experiences the same world, or that other people aren't gaming avatars, etc?

I suggest we leave the SR hypothesis (and any hypothesis along the same lines) in the realm of science fiction, and that we join with the New Atheists in conceptualizing the naturalistic hypothesis in its standard form.

Watch: "The Simulation Hypothesis" YouTube playlist: www.youtube.com/playlist?list=PLQhh3qcwVEWhfgH84u_JzPzB4B8RPT5ca

Read: "Are You Living In A Computer Simulation?" by Nick Bostrom: www.simulation-argument.com/simulation.pdf

"Virtual Reality Poses the Same Riddles as the Cosmic Multiverse" by Joelle Daham: http://nautil.us/issue/46/balance/virtual-reality-poses-the-same-riddles-as-the-cosmic-multiverse

"Should we be Mormons in the Matrix?" by Sam Harris: www.samharris.org/blog/item/is-religion-true-in-the-matrix

"The Limits of Modern AI" by Erik J. Larson: https://thebestschools.org/magazine/limits-of-modern-ai/

"The Gödelian Argument: Turn Over the Page" by J.R. Lucas: http://users.ox.ac.uk/~jrlucas/Godel/turn.html

"Minds, Machines and Gödel" by J.R. Lucas: www.openstarts.units.it/bitstream/10077/5466/1/Lucas1_E&P_V_2003_1.pdf

"A paper read to the Turing Conference at Brighton on April 6th, 1990" by J.R. Lucas: http://users.ox.ac.uk/~jrlucas/Godel/brighton.html

"We Are Not Living In A Simulation. Probably." by Glenn McDonald: www.fastcompany.com/40537955/we-are-not-living-in-a-simulation-probably

"The Argument Against Quantum Computers" by Katia Moskvitch: www.quantamagazine.org/gil-kalais-argument-against-quantum-computers-20180207/

"Countering The Simulation Argument": https://philosophicalapologist.com/2016/06/08/countering-the-simulation-argument/

"Minds, brains, and programs" by John R. Searle: http://cogprints.org/7150/1/10.1.1.83.5248.pdf

---

201. McDonald, "We Are Not Living In A Simulation. Probably."
202. Noack quoted in McDonald, "We Are Not Living In A Simulation. Probably."

"A Critical Engagement of Bostrom's Computer Simulation Hypothesis" by Norman K. Swazo: http://philsci-archive.pitt.edu/11537/1/Computer_Simulation_paper_revised.pdf

Philosophy of Mind: A Short Introduction by Edward Feser

The Freedom of the Will by J.R. Lucas

The Recalitrant Imagio Dei: Human Persons and the Failure of Naturalism by J.P. Moreland

Science Fiction And Philosophy: From Time Travel To Superintelligence edited by Susan Schneider

Minds, Brains & Science by John Searle

The Rediscovery of the Mind by John Searle

A Faithful Guide to Philosophy: A Christian Introduction to the Love of Wisdom by Peter S. Williams

Supernatural miracles in a subordinate nature

The monotheistic tradition believes in a *physis* transcending, supernatural God who is the creator of a physical nature (nature in the demoted sense discussed by C.S. Lewis) able to achieve certain ends in virtue of its divinely given and sustained *natura*. Hence philosophers Michael Peterson, William Hasker, Bruce Reichenbach and David Basinger propose that:

> most events are acts of God in the broad, fundamental sense that God has created the universe, established the "laws" upon which causal interaction within this universe is based, and continues to sustain such interaction by divine power . . . however . . . there are some events . . . that would not have occurred in the exact manner in which they did . . . if God had not . . . manipulated the natural order.[203]

Experience shows that nature (d.s.) can attain ends beyond its *natura* with the help of an agent. That agent may be a finite agent, as when a human shapes a yew tree into topiary. However, if we admit that a divine agent might exist, we have to entertain the possibility that nature might attain ends beyond its *natura* with the help of a divine agent.

In either case this help might be supplied directly (as a basic action) or indirectly (through intermediaries), as when a gardener uses shears to cut a tree into the shape of an elephant. In the divine case, this help may include temporarily overriding, or perhaps adding to or subtracting from, the natural powers of certain substances; hence philosopher Peter van Inwagen suggests that "God always, or almost always,

---

203. Peterson et al., *Reason & Religious Belief*, 193.

supplies each particle with the same causal powers. But he may, *very rarely*, supply *just a few* particles . . . with different causal powers from the powers they normally have."[204]

As a divine agent is greater than a human agent, it follows that the ends reached by nature with assistance from a divine agent might be greater than the ends reached by nature with the assistance of human agency. Indeed, given that a divine agent could be omnipotent, the only ends nature couldn't attain with divine assistance would be ends that are logically impossible for the divine agency to bring about. That is, the only limiting factor where miracles are concerned isn't the *natura* of the created reality, but the *natura* of the Creator. As John Cottingham comments: "it seems plain that divine interventions . . . would necessarily be expressions of God's characteristics . . . [and hence, on a Judeo-Christian understanding of God,] they would be . . . manifestations of deep love and goodness."[205]

Any instance of nature transcending its *natura* due to the action of divine agency is a miracle. Hence Thomas Aquinas defined miracles as "works that surpass the ability of all nature"[206] and observed that such events are "*praeter naturam* (beyond physical nature) not *contra naturam* (violations of physical nature)."[207] As Ronald H. Nash reminds us: "the laws of nature do not and, indeed, cannot function as a kind of metaphysical straightjacket; they do not prescribe what can or cannot happen. And anyone who thinks this only reveals his need for a course in the philosophy of science."[208]

Hume inadvertently "gives away the store" on this very point when he poses the following rhetorical question:

> Why is it more than probable, that all men must die; that lead cannot, *of itself*, remain suspended in the air . . . unless it be, that these events are found agreeable to the laws of nature, and there is required a violation of these laws, or in other words, a miracle to prevent them?[209]

If God were to keep some lead suspended in the air, then the lead would clearly not remain suspended in the air "of itself" (i.e. by its created *natura*), but by the action of divine power (i.e. by God's *natura*). Hence, according to the definition given by Hume (and Dawkins et al), no *miracle*—that is, no "violation" of the natural law that "lead cannot, *of itself*, remain suspended in the air"—would have taken place! As David Glass argues:

> Science tells us how things *normally* work in the natural world, but science itself cannot tell us that nature is all there is and so cannot preclude the possibility of a supernatural event such as the resurrection. To use science to reject

---

204. Van Inwagen, "Of 'Of Miracles,'" 478.
205. Cottingham, *Why Believe?*, 94.
206. Aquinas, *Summa Contra Gentiles*, 1, 6, 1.
207. Feldmeier, *The God Conflict*, 95.
208. Nash, *Faith & Reason*, 227.
209. Hume, "Of Miracles," 34 (emphasis added).

the resurrection is a misuse of science and simply begs the question... A more scientific attitude would be to consider the actual evidence.[210]

Atheist William Stoeger objects that "an immaterial agent acting on or within a material context as a cause ... is not possible [since in that case] energy ... would be added to a system ... contravening the conservation of energy."[211] However, that's only to state the tautology that any miracle would involve a miracle, and the only way to turn this tautology into an objection to miracles is to beg the question against the possibility of miracles. As Robert A. Larmer points out, Stoeger confuses the *scientific* claim that energy remains constant in a physical system insofar as it is left to its own devices and the *metaphysical* claim that reality as a whole is a physical system that is necessarily left to its own devices. These claims are not synonymous, and the latter cannot be derived from the former:

> Theists ... reject not the scientific claim that energy is conserved in an isolated system but the speculative metaphysical claim that nature is an isolated system not open to causal influence by God ... attempts to move from the well-evidenced claim that, to the degree that a physical system is causally isolated, its energy will be conserved, to the speculative claim that energy can neither be created nor destroyed, cannot be justified on either conceptual or empirical grounds.[212]

Larmer concludes that "miracles do not violate the laws of nature. They threaten not our understanding of how nature works when not intervened upon by something other than itself, but rather the insistence that nature is never affected by supernatural agency."[213]

Michael R. Licona applies this line of argument to the resurrection of Jesus:

> A miracle is not a violation or suspension of the laws of nature. Rather, it is when the hand of God enters our world and alters the normal course of events. Everyone will agree that the laws of nature inform us that a corpse will not return to life when left to itself. But if Jesus's resurrection occurred, it was God, the author of life, who altered the normal course of events and raised Jesus. His corpse was not left to itself.[214]

From the theistic point of view "the laws of nature ... should be thought of as descriptions of the material universe when God is not treating what he has made in a special way."[215] As Evans muses:

210. Glass, "Four Poor Reasons for Rejecting the Resurrection."
211. Stoeger, "Describing God's Action in the World," 239–61.
212. Larmer, "Miracles and the Principle of the Conservation of Energy."
213. Larmer, *The Legitimacy of Miracle*, 86.
214. Licona, ""Michael Licona Interview."
215. Plantinga, *Where the Conflict Really Lies*, 119.

there are regular processes which bring about results in the natural order. These processes are certainly divine in origin, but they represent God's "constant" [secondary] activity. When God steps in in a special [primary] way, his activity is by definition exceptional in nature . . . Since God has acted specially, the effects will be somewhat special. No laws are violated in the sense that something irrational has occurred. Still, the events in question will be *different* from the normal course of nature.[216]

Watch: "Do Miracles Break the Laws of Nature, as David Hume Claimed?" by Tim McGrew: www.youtube.com/watch?v=-Hlo-PzoA-E

"Do Miracles Violate Natural Law?" by Alvin Plantinga et al.: http://youtu.be/uJk_TnDHhZo

---

Defining a miracle

A miracle can be defined as "an act God performs at a particular place and time, an act distinct from his 'normal' activity of sustaining the universe, including its natural processes."[217] In other words, a miracle is an event that transcends or surpasses the inherent causal capacities of the creation and is best explained as being primarily caused by God.

The NT writers use various Greek words to describe "miracles," including:

- *Dunamis*—an act of power ("*Dunamis*" is the root of English words such as "dynamic" and "dynamo")
- *Teras*—a wonder
- *Semeion*—a sign or omen

Michael Poole explains that "*Dunamis* focuses attention on the *cause* of a miracle in the power of God. *Teras* refers to its *effect*, and *Semeion* to its purpose."[218] Hence we may define a miracle as:

- A wondrous event wherein nature transcends its *natura*, best explained as having been caused (directly or indirectly) by an exceptional application of God's power and which consequently reflects something of God's character and purposes.[219]

216. Evans, *Philosophy of Religion*, 108–9.

217. Evans, *Philosophy of Religion*, 107.

218. Poole, *Miracles*, 32.

219. Two points about this definition of a miracle: First, the *natura* acted upon by God in a miracle may be natural or supernatural. Second, God's creation of the cosmos was not, by this definition, miraculous. As John Lennox observes: "Not all supernatural events are miracles in the strict sense. For instance, the origin of the universe and its laws, though a supernatural event, should probably not be subsumed under the rubric of miracle. Strictly speaking, miracles . . . *presuppose* the existence of the

Having investigated the definition of "miracle" and the distinction between natural and supernatural explanations, we can return to David Hume's argument against miracles.

The metaphysical interpretation of Hume's argument

On the *metaphysical* interpretation of Hume's argument against miracles (adopted by nineteenth-century theologian David Strauss), Hume is taken to be arguing along the following lines:

1) Miracles are by definition "violations of natural law."

2) Natural laws can't be violated because they have been established by uniform experience.

3) Therefore, miracles are impossible.

Hume does seem to use something like this argument when he writes: "There must... be a uniform experience against every miraculous event, otherwise the event would not merit that appellation."[220] Well, as C.S. Lewis commented:

> we must agree with Hume that if there is absolutely "uniform experience" against miracles, if in other words they have never happened, why then they never have. Unfortunately we know the experience against them to be uniform only if we know that all reports of them are false. And we can know all the reports to be false only if we know already that miracles have never occurred. In fact, we are arguing in a circle.[221]

Hume's attempt to establish the uniformity of natural laws by appealing to uniform human experience is contradicted by his own argument that because "it implies no contradiction that the course of nature may change, and that an object seemingly like those which we have experienced, may be attended with different or contrary effects,"[222] all reasoning about empirical matters proceeds "upon the supposition, that the future will be conformable to the past."[223] As Richard Purtill points out: "If we adopt a theistic view of natural laws, then we have a *reason* for thinking that such laws will hold in most cases. A Humean view, on the other hand, permits no such assurance."[224] Picking up on the same problem, Lewis comments:

---

normal course of things. It follows, then, that it does not really make sense to think of the creation of the normal course of things as a miracle."—*Gunning for God*, 167.

220. Hume, *An Enquiry Concerning Human Understanding*, 10.1.
221. Lewis, *Miracles*, 106.
222. Hume, *An Enquiry Concerning Human Understanding*, 4.2.18.
223. Hume, *An Enquiry Concerning Human Understanding*, 4.2.19.
224. Purtill, "Defining Miracles," 71.

> Theology says to you in effect, "Admit God and with Him the risk of a few miracles, and I in return will ratify your faith in uniformity as regards the overwhelming majority of events." The philosophy which forbids you to make uniformity absolute is also the philosophy which offers you solid grounds for believing it to be general . . . The alternative is really much worse. Try to make Nature absolute and you find that her uniformity is not even probable. You get the deadlock, as in Hume.[225]

In any case, recalling our discussion of how nature (d.s.) can attain ends beyond its *natura* with the help of an agent, it would be more accurate to say that the uniformity of natural law is the uniformity of laws with an implicit "all other things being equal" clause. If God causes a miraculous event, this obviously isn't a case of all other things being equal:

> The laws of nature are not properly defined as exceptionless regularities. Rather, they are our best attempt to say what nature will always do when left to itself . . . The question, then, is not, "How probable (or improbable) is it that we are wrong about the laws of nature?" Rather, it is, "How probable (or improbable) is it that, in this instance, God has reached into His creation to do something that nature alone could not?" A miracle, seen from this point of view, is not an exception to the exceptionless; it is, instead, an occasion when nature is not left to itself.[226]

As Michael L. Peterson et al. argue:

> *if* we assume that the water has been turned into wine as the result of direct divine activity, then those scientific laws leading us to believe that water does not turn into wine under any set of natural conditions have not been rendered inadequate. What has been rendered inadequate, rather, is the belief that all events can be explained adequately in terms of natural laws. And if this is so, then *unless* it can be demonstrated that supernatural causal activity is an impossibility, we can . . . have both the exception and the rule . . . However, few philosophers today believe that God's existence or ability to intervene directly can be shown to be impossible . . .[227]

Theists, agnostics, and even many atheists affirm the possibility of God's existence. But given the possibility of God's existence, the possibility of divine action, and thus the possibility of miracles, lies close at hand: "if there is a God who can act, there can be acts of God (miracles)."[228] While omnipotence doesn't extend to doing

---

225. Lewis, *Miracles*, 111.
226. McGrew, "Science, Doubt and Miracles."
227. Peterson et al., *Reason & Religious Belief*, 158–59.
228. Geisler and Turek, *I Don't Have Enough Faith To Be An Atheist*, 209.

the logically incoherent, there are logically coherent miracle-claims. Hence it seems that "if there is a God, miracles are possible."[229]

In sum, as Bart Ehrman acknowledges: "Miracles are not impossible."[230] Atheist Michael Ruse agrees: "Water could turn into wine and a dead man could come back to life. The question is whether they ever do..."[231] Even some neo-atheists concede this point. Lawrence Krauss states: "A god who can create the laws of nature can presumably also circumvent them at will."[232] Jerry Coyne warns: "It would be a closed minded scientist who would say that miracles are impossible in principle."[233]

The epistemological interpretation of Hume's argument

Contemporary philosophers generally take Hume to be arguing that even if miracles *can* happen, even if miracles *do* happen, we can never *reasonably believe* that they happen (at least, not on the basis of testimonial evidence). That is, Hume is taken as arguing "not for the impossibility of miracles but for the *incredibility* of accepting miracles."[234] On this understanding of Hume, he is thought to be arguing along the following *epistemological* lines:

1) As a violation of the laws of nature, a miracle is by definition a rare occurrence

2) A natural law is by definition a description of a regular occurrence

3) The evidence for the regular is always greater than the evidence for the rare

4) A wise man always bases his belief on the greater evidence

5) Therefore, a wise man should never believe a miracle has happened

Winfried Corduan objects that "this is really... nothing more than an expression of a predisposition against miracles..."[235]

The falsification falsification

Norman L. Geisler points out that Hume's "balance of probability" approach of weighing the infrequent evidence for rare events against frequent evidence for common events "would eliminate belief in any unusual or unique event from the past [e.g. the big bang]."[236] As Peter van Inwagen observes: "The first reports of someone's making a

---

229. Kreeft and Tacelli, *Handbook of Christian Apologetics*, 110.
230. Ehrman, "Opening Statement."
231. Ruse, *Atheism*, 161.
232. Krauss, *A Universe from Nothing*, 142.
233. Coyne, *Faith vs. Fact*, 124.
234. Geisler, "Miracles & the Modern Mind," 75.
235. Corduan, "Miracles," 172
236. Geisler, "Miracles & the Modern Mind," 79.

solo flight across the Atlantic or running a four-minute mile or reaching the summit of Mount Everest were contrary to the experience of those who heard them."[237] Yet people who believed a newspaper report of these events surely had a rationally warranted belief in them.

Then again, accepting Hume's principle about balancing probabilities would make it impossible to falsify scientific hypotheses concerning natural laws: "If we followed Hume's policy, we would in effect always reject an observation of an apparent counterinstance to a law of nature, on the grounds that its prior probability is too low . . ."[238] Thus the epistemological significance of falsification in science and everyday life falsifies Hume's understanding of how evidence should be weighed.

Moreover, philosopher Daniel Bonevac argues that since it's possible to falsify the hypothesis that a specific physical system is a closed system, it should be possible to falsify the hypothesis that the universe is a closed physical system:

> Within a physical system . . . it is possible to have evidence of various kinds that external forces are operating—that indicates, in other words, that the system is not closed. [This] is true of ecological systems . . . in which there can be empirical evidence for or against the operation of external forces on the system. There is nothing intrinsically mysterious about arguments that given systems are not closed. There appears to be nothing mysterious, therefore, about arguments that the order of nature itself is or is not closed.[239]

Since evidence for a miracle is evidence against the hypothesis that the universe is a closed system, to dismiss evidence for a miracle by appealing to the hypothesis that the universe is a closed system is a clear case of begging the question.

Problems with probability

"simply utilizing the frequency of an occurrence to determine its probability, as Hume does, simply won't do."

—CHAD MEISTER[240]

Francis J. Beckwith points out that:

> Just as our formulations of natural law are based on certain regularities, our standards of evaluating testimony and evidence are also based on certain regularities . . . Hume incorrectly assumed that because we *base* our knowledge of the past on regularities . . . the *object* of our knowledge must therefore be a

---

237. Van Inwagen, "Of 'Of Miracles,'" 483.
238. Evans, *The Historical Christ*, 156.
239. Bonevac, "The Argument from Miracles," 39.
240. Meister, *Philosophy of Religion*, 87.

regular event and not one that is either singular or highly improbable. Therefore, since we base both evidential and natural law judgements on regularities, it is certainly possible that we can have sufficient evidence to believe that an event highly improbable in terms of natural law has occurred . . . the question of the event's probability of having occurred must be answered in terms of the evidence for its occurrence on this single occasion, not exclusively on its antecedent improbability . . . an event's occurrence may be very improbable in terms of past experience and observation, but current observation and testimony may lead one to believe that the evidence for the event is good.[241]

Hume mistakenly thinks that the probability of an event is fixed by the frequency with which events of that type have been experienced hitherto. But as Evans says: "It is easy to see that this principle is unsound as a general way of estimating probability."[242] For example, we don't calculate the probability of Earth being struck by a meteor in the next year by simply observing how frequently Earth has been hit in the past:

When we estimate the probability of a meteor hitting the earth, we take into account all we know about meteors: how many of them there are, what orbits the ones we know follow, and so forth. Similarly, in estimating the probability of a miracle, we should not limit ourselves to considering how frequently miracles occur [in our limited experience]. Rather, we should take into account such facts as these: Is there a God? If there is a God, might God have reasons to perform a miracle?[243]

Hence, "Even if miracles do not happen every day, it might be highly probable that they occur at some times."[244]

Hume uses his prejudicial definition of miracles to create a false opposition between evidence for the laws of nature and evidence for miracles. Hume argues that testimonial evidence can never be sufficient for rational belief in a miracle even if a miracle has happened and the testimony is accurate. Even if Jesus did rise from the dead, Hume says that you oughtn't to believe any amount of testimony to this effect, because regular experience establishes that people do not naturally rise from the dead! But as theologian Craig S. Keener observes:

Claims about nature and miracles both rest on experience, so claimed experience of the former cannot cancel out claimed experiences of the latter. If experience is reliable in knowing that water is normally not turned to wine, why would it not be reliable in recognizing when water is turned to wine?[245]

241. Beckwith, *David Hume's Argument Against Miracles*, 37–38.
242. Evans, *Why Christian Faith Still Makes Sense*, 97.
243. Evans, *Why Christian Faith Still Makes Sense*, 98.
244. Evans, *Why Christian Faith Still Makes Sense*, 98–99.
245. Keener, *Miracles*, 144–45.

The same goes for a man who has been raised from the dead.

Indeed, when we correctly define a miracle (as an event wherein the primary activity of a divinity causes something to achieve an end beyond its *natura*) we can see that there's no either/or choice between evidence for regular laws of nature and evidence for irregular miraculous exceptions:

> Hume reaches his conclusion that evidence for a supposed miracle will always be overridden [by] the large body of (as Hume sees it) undeniably relevant evidence in favour of natural law, only by *assuming* that no god has acted miraculously . . . It is only by presupposing a conclusively justified *atheism*, or presupposing belief in a non-miracle-working god . . . that you are entitled to adduce with any cogency, say, evidence for Archimedes' Principle . . . as evidence against Christ's having walked on water . . .[246]

It follows that "balance of probability type arguments, depending as they do on a presumed conflict between the evidence for the laws of nature and the evidence for miracles, have no force . . ."[247] Thus Brian Hebblethwaite concludes that "Hume's main critique of belief in miracles has no force whatsoever . . . Accumulated evidence for what happens normally is totally irrelevant to the question of whether abnormal intervention by God, for good reasons, ever takes place."[248] Hence, as Larmer notes:

> The commonly accepted view that belief in events plausibly viewed as miracles can only be justified if there exists extraordinarily strong evidence in their favour is mistaken. Such a claim rests on the mistaken assumption that the evidence for such events must inevitably conflict with a body of conflicting evidence against their occurrence . . . Given there is no necessary conflict, it cannot be urged that belief in events best understood as miracles requires extraordinarily strong evidence before it is justified.[249]

In other words, because miracles surpass rather than violate natural laws, we don't need more evidence for a miracle than we have for the natural law or laws it surpasses. After all:

> unless there exists a conflict between two relevant bodies of evidence, it only takes a modest amount of evidence to justify that an event has occurred, even if the event is rare or unusual. We routinely accept claims with low pre-evidence probabilities on the basis of limited testimonial evidence.[250]

Looking carefully at a large snowflake under a microscope provides sufficient evidence that it exhibits a particular pattern, even though the pre-evidence chances

---

246. Huston, *Reported Miracles*, 134, 162.
247. Larmer, *The Legitimacy of Miracle*, 2.
248. Hebblethwaite, *In Defence of Christianity*, 105.
249. Larmer, *The Legitimacy of Miracle*, 132.
250. Larmer, *The Legitimacy of Miracle*, 125.

that any particular large snowflake would exhibit exactly that pattern (out of all the possible large snowflake patterns) is beyond astronomical.[251] Likewise, a scientist's testimony would normally be sufficient to convince us that the snowflake they examined had this or that particular pattern.[252]

Again, in order to believe a news report about winning lottery numbers, "Hume would require us to have enough evidence in favour of the morning news's reliability to counter-balance the improbability of the winning pick, which is absurd."[253] Probability theorists have pointed out that Hume overlooked the fact that "what also needs to be considered is the probability that if the reported event has *not* occurred, then the witness's testimony is just as it is."[254] The probability that the news would report the number they do if some other number was in fact the winning number is incredibly small, whilst the report made is much more probable given that the reported number was indeed the winning number. It is this comparative likelihood that "easily counter-balances the high prior improbability of the event reported."[255] In fact:

> Hume failed to distinguish . . . between the intrinsic probability of something like the resurrection, which may well be very low, and the probability of the resurrection in the light of the evidence we have for it, the improbability of having that evidence if the resurrection didn't happen and the low probability of naturalistic alternatives, which collectively could render the probability of the resurrection considerably higher than judgements of its intrinsic probability that fail to take such considerations into account.[256]

Moreover, when estimating the value of testimonial evidence, we can often go beyond assumptions about the reliability of witnesses in general. Not only can we have evidence about the general reliability (or otherwise) of a particular witness, we can have evidence relating to the reliability (or otherwise) of specific testimony from that witness. We might not be willing to accept the occurrence of a miracle on the testimony of just any witness, but testimony to a miracle can come from a witness who gives every general and/or specific evidence of testimonial reliability, honesty, sincerity, mental stability, etc. Hence, as Victor Reppert notes: "general considerations concerning the comparison between the reliability of testimony and the initial improbability of [miraculous] events may be overturned in the specific investigation of some particular case."[257]

---

251. See: Matthews, "It's True That No Two Snowflakes Are Alike, But Not For The Reason You Think;" Libbrecht, "Is it really true that no two snowflakes are alike?;" "Everyday Mysteries: Is it true that no two snow crystals are alike?"

252. Edward Wierenga uses a parallel example in *The Philosophy of Religion*, 127–28.

253. Craig, *Reasonable Faith*, 270.

254. Craig, *Reasonable Faith*, 270.

255. Craig, *Reasonable Faith*, 271.

256. Baggett, *Did the Resurrection Happen?* 140.

257. Reppert, "Miracles and the Case for Theism," 35–51.

Additionally, having multiple independent witnesses to a miracle adds to the evidence in its favor in an exponential manner. As Keener observes: "the probability of reliability is very high in multiple, independent testimony from persons normally deemed reliable . . . Detailed probability calculations show that even a very low *a priori* against miracles can be overcome by the sort of evidence available in multiple independent testimony."[258] Indeed, Moreland and Craig note that "the cumulative power of independent witnesses is such that individually they could be *un*reliable more than 50 percent of the time and yet their testimony combine to make an event of apparently enormous improbability quite probable in light of their testimony."[259]

Daniel Bonevac points out that "if there are several miracles supported by independent evidence, the probability of the disjunction of the miracle reports—that is the claim that at least one of the miracles occurred—may be high even if the probability of each miracle, considered in itself is very low."[260] In other words, "if we find reports of a series of miracles, there may be a significant probability that at least one happened."[261] Knowing that *a* miracle probably happened without knowing *which* miracle probably happened might be frustrating, but it's a start!

Bonevac also observes that "the miracles in the series set a context for each other."[262] Evidence for miracles earlier in a series of miracles raises the probability of miracles later in that series. Hence "the occurrence of miracles in series can have dramatic effects on the credibility of miracle reports."[263]

We should certainly insist that we should only conclude that a miracle has happened if this is the best explanation of all the relevant evidence available to us according to the standard rules for making inferences to the best explanation. The hypothesis of a miracle must out-compete alternative hypotheses (which will be variations on the twin themes of deception and delusion). Unfortunately, many self-styled skeptics are implicitly committed to an unsound but convenient argument that goes something like this:[264]

1) Extraordinary claims require extraordinary evidence.

2) The claim that God exists and/or worked a miracle is extraordinary.

3) Therefore, the claim that God exists and/or worked a miracle should be justified with extraordinary evidence.

4) I'm not sure what qualifies as "extraordinary evidence."

---

258. Keener, *Miracles*, 154.
259. Moreland and Craig, *Philosophical Foundations for a Christian Worldview*, 570.
260. Bonevac, "The Argument from Miracles."
261. Bonevac, "The Argument from Miracles."
262. Bonevac, "The Argument from Miracles."
263. Bonevac, "The Argument from Miracles."
264. See: McGrew, "Extraordinary claims require extraordinary evidence."

5) But I'm sure that whatever evidence you come up it isn't going to count.

6) Therefore, I win.

On the contrary, writes Larmer:

> Whether or not an unusual event, plausibly viewed as miraculous, occurred should be judged on the customary criteria by which we assess testimony, not on the basis of whether it fits a favoured worldview... extraordinary evidence is certainly welcome as a witness to the reality of miracles, but it is not necessary for belief in them to be rationally justified.[265]

We shouldn't proceed on the assumption that miracles are always intrinsically improbable to a degree that outweighs whatever specific evidence might be given for their occurrence. As J.C.A. Gaskin warns: "at some stage in his accumulation of respectable evidence the wise man would be in danger of becoming dogmatic and obscurantist if he did *not* believe the evidence."[266] To proceed on such a dogmatic and obscurantist assumption is to embrace an epistemology that rejects miracles regardless of evidence, and as J. Huston argues, absent a metaphysical proof against miracles:

> Only what one might call a fideistic atheism which refuses to consider its rational credentials will refuse to countenance the possibility that a theistic explanation may account *better* for the range of phenomena, including some putatively miraculous phenomena, than atheism.[267]

On the balance of evidence

Seemingly unaware of the contemporary philosophical discussion on the issue, Bart Ehrman rests his skepticism upon a Humean balance of probability-type argument against belief in miracles:

> We would call a miracle an event that violates the way nature always, or almost always, works so as to make the event virtually, if not actually, impossible. The chances of a miracle occurring are infinitesimal... Historians can establish only what probably happened in the past, but miracles, by their very nature, are always the least probable explanation for what happened... If historians can only establish what probably happened, and miracles by their definition are the least probable occurrences, then more or less by definition, historians cannot establish that miracles have ever probably happened.[268]

---

265. Larmer, *The Legitimacy of Miracle*, 130, 133.
266. Gaskin, *Hume's Philosophy of Religion*, 115.
267. Huston, *Reported Miracles*, 166.
268. Ehrman, *Jesus Interrupted*, 174–75.

Ehrman fails to distinguish between prior and posterior probabilities. Prior probability is the probability of X on our background information *before* we take into account the specific evidence for X. Posterior probability is the probability of X *after* we take into account the specific evidence for X. Something can be judged to be extremely improbable before the specific evidence is taken into account and yet extremely probable afterwards. As Craig points out:

> The probability of the resurrection on the background information and the evidence can be very high even though the probability of the resurrection on the background information alone is very low . . . thinking that because the probability of [the resurrection on the background information alone] is low therefore the probability of the resurrection is low . . . is a fallacious inference . . . there is no contradiction at all in saying that an intrinsically improbable event is the most probable event given the evidence.[269]

Francis J. Beckwith offers an illustration of why Humean balance of probability-type arguments are unsound:

> suppose a man, who had never [before] murdered anyone in his life, is accused of murder and brought to trial. Five responsible and upstanding citizens, with no reason to lie about what they had witnessed, testify on the witness stand that they had seen the accused commit an act of murder. However, the defense attorney . . . calls 925 people to the witness-stand to testify that they had known the accused for a good part of their lives and they had never seen him murder anybody . . . the defense attorney argues: "Let us weigh the 'evidence' of all the people who have seen my client not murdering against the evidence of the five people who say that they had seen my client commit murder at one single moment. Since the 'evidence' ('proof') of non-murdering is greater than the evidence of murdering, and the intelligent person always sides with what has greater evidence, my client is *not* guilty." If the jury in this case is any jury at all, it would see through the clever charade this defense attorney is trying to pull; for they know that what is most probable (i.e., that which occurs most often, like non-murdering), can never be weighed as irrefutable "evidence" against the evidence of a rare occurrence (like murdering).[270]

Beckwith helpfully points out that "since evidential criteria themselves are based on certain probabilities (that is, regularities), it is entirely possible that one can plausibly believe that a miracle has occurred if the converging of independent probabilities (that is, the pieces of evidence) 'outweighs' the antecedent improbability of the [miracle] occurring."[271] Thus he concludes that "if a number of independent probabilities converge upon an alleged miraculous event, and alternative naturalistic explanations

---

269. Craig, "The Work of Bart Ehrman."
270. Beckwith, *David Hume's Argument Against Miracles*, 33–34.
271. Beckwith, *David Hume's Argument Against Miracles*, 125.

are inadequate to explain the data . . . it becomes entirely reasonable to believe that this miraculous event has occurred."[272]

It seems to me that physicist Michael G. Strauss strikes the right epistemological stance here:

> I don't believe in fairies, unicorns, extrasensory perception, telekinesis, horoscopes . . . I don't believe in them, not because I require extraordinary evidence, but because I require just sufficient evidence. Rather than ask that some unattainable "extraordinary evidence" be presented as an excuse to dismiss any supernatural act, I instead want to carefully examine the evidence and to search for a conclusion that best explains all the evidence without, *a priori*, ruling out a conclusion based simply on my presuppositions.[273]

Watch: "Bart's Blunder and Egregious Errors" by William Lane Craig: https://youtu.be/IqZJvStSr-8

"Do Extraordinary events require extraordinary evidence?" by William Lane Craig: http://youtu.be/5M9pphsSLPs

"Don't Extraordinary Claims Require Extraordinary Evidence?" by William Lane Craig: https://youtu.be/5HgRWvqf-wM

"Extraordinary Claims Require Extraordinary Evidence" by Timothy McGrew: https://youtu.be/H7Gv8Fw_fFE

Read: "Extraordinary Claims ARE Extraordinary Evidence" by Robin Hanson: www.overcomingbias.com/2007/01/extraordinary_c.html

"When Do Extraordinary Claims Give Extraordinary Evidence?" by Robin Hanson: http://mason.gmu.edu/~rhanson/extraord.pdf

---

The verdict on Hume

Despite his continuing influence at the popular level, however his arguments are interpreted, "the fallaciousness of Hume's reasoning has been recognized by the majority of philosophers writing on the subject today."[274] For example:

- Hendrik van der Breggen: "Much critical examination of Hume's argument by philosophers has made it abundantly clear that Hume seriously overestimates the negative evidential weight the law-of-nature side of the scale bears on the credibility of miracle testimony."[275]

---

272. Beckwith, "Theism, Miracles, And the Modern Mind," 231.
273. Strauss, "Extraordinary Claims Require Extraordinary Evidence."
274. Craig, *Reasonable Faith*, third edition, 276.
275. Van der Breggen, "Hume's Scale," 443.

- William Lane Craig: "Hume's argument [against belief in miracles] is . . . demonstrably, irredeemably fallacious, based as it is upon an incomplete understanding of the probability calculus."[276]

- Stephen T. Davis: "it is generally recognised among philosophers that Hume overstates his case."[277] Davis says that Hume "is mistaken when he asserts that it can never be rational to believe that a miracle has occurred . . . Humean arguments against rational belief in miracles fail . . . miracles (so far as we know) *can* occur; the real question is whether any *have* occurred."[278]

- John Earman: "I find it astonishing how well posterity has treated 'Of Miracles,' given how completely the confection collapses under a little probing . . . I suspect that in more than a few cases it . . . involves the all too familiar phenomenon of endorsing an argument because the conclusion is liked."[279]

- Hugh G. Gauch Jr.: "David Hume wrote a powerful attack on miracles that has been enormously influential . . . But recently it has fallen on extremely hard times indeed . . ."[280]

- Norman L. Geisler: "Hume's argument confuses *quantity* of evidence with the *quality* of evidence . . . in the 'hard' form it begs the question by assuming that miracles are by definition impossible . . . in the 'soft' form the argument engages in special pleading, begs the question, proves too much . . . is inconsistent with Hume's own epistemology and makes scientific progress impossible . . . The wise do not *legislate* in advance that miracles cannot be believed to have happened; rather, they *look* at the evidence to see if God has indeed acted in history."[281]

- Douglas R. Groothuis: "Hume's critique, long (but not universally) hailed as definitively nailing the coffin shut on miracles, has been subjected to intense philosophical scrutiny in recent years and has lost much of its previous prestige."[282]

- David Johnson: "the view that there is in Hume's essay, or in what can be reconstructed from it, any argument or reply or objection that is even superficially good, much less, powerful or devastating, is simply a philosophical myth."[283]

- T.J. Mawson: "Hume has *not* shown that it is always irrational to believe miracles on the testimony of others. His A Priori Argument fails and his a posteriori

---

276. Craig, "Reply to Our Respondents," 160.
277. Davis, *Risen Indeed*, 4.
278. Davis, *Risen Indeed*, 5, 19.
279. Earman, *Hume's Abject Failure*, 71.
280. Gauch, "The Methodology of Ramified Natural Theology," 291.
281. Geisler, "Miracles & the Modern Mind," 79, 85.
282. Groothuis, *Christian Apologetics*, 534.
283. Johnson, *Hume*, 4.

concerns . . . could—unsurprisingly, their being a posteriori considerations—be met."[284]

- Brendan Sweetman: "it does seem wrong to rule out by definition, as Hume and others try to do, the possibility of [any] events providing evidence for miracles. Each person has to look at *specific* claims of the miraculous and make an informed judgement as to whether they are reasonable or not to believe."[285]

- Keith Ward: "any dispassionate thinker would have to conclude that David Hume's arguments against miracles are not at all convincing . . ."[286]

In sum, we may agree with Evans:

> Miracles seem possible, and it also seems possible for there to be compelling evidence for their occurrence . . . One's judgement here will be heavily shaped by his view of the likelihood of God's existence and his view of God's nature and purposes. It seems at least possible, however, that a reasonable person could be convinced that miracles have occurred even if he does not have a previously high estimate of the likelihood of God's existence, as long as he is not firmly convinced that God's existence is impossible.[287]

METAPHYSICS VERSES EVIDENCE

> "The scientists must sit down before fact as a little child, be prepared to give up every preconceived notion . . . or you shall learn nothing."
> —Thomas H. Huxley[288]

Epistemological skepticism about miracles ultimately requires metaphysical skepticism about miracles, since the only adequate justification for driving a wedge between history and evidence-led truth-seeking would come from having established, with a degree of confidence invincible to any practically conceivable *a posteriori* evidence, the truth of metaphysical naturalism (as a description of reality from which atheism can be deduced), atheism or deism (i.e. the existence of a deity who would never work a miracle, or who is *so unlikely* to work a miracle that no *a posteriori* evidence could ever justify the conclusion that a miracle had happened). If, and only if, such metaphysical skepticism was justified, would there be no danger that drawing a line of demarcation between the Jesus of history and the Christ of faith would drive a wedge between history and the evidence-led search for truth. For then, and only then, would

284. Mawson, *Belief In God*, 179.
285. Sweetman, *Religion*, 62.
286. Ward, *The Big Questions in Science and Religion*, 93.
287. Evans, *Why Christian Faith Still Makes Sense*, 117.
288. Huxley quoted in Hunter, *Science's Blind Spot*, 36.

the evidence-led search for truth be incapable of supporting a conclusion at odds with the *a priori* denial of miracles.

In the absence of such heavy-duty metaphysical justification, agnostic John Earman is surely right to argue that: "An epistemology that does not allow for the possibility that evidence, whether from eyewitness testimony or from other source, can establish the credibility of . . . a walking on water, or a resurrection is inadequate."[289]

William Lane Craig's analysis of the Jesus Seminar rightly highlights their blind faith in metaphysical naturalism:

> The number one presupposition of the Seminar is . . . *naturalism* . . . If you presuppose naturalism, then things like . . . Jesus' miracles . . . go out the window before you even sit down at the table to look at the evidence. As supernatural events, they *cannot* be historical. But if you are at least open to supernaturalism, then these events can't be ruled out in advance. You have to be open to looking honestly at the evidence . . . If you *begin* by presupposing naturalism, then of course what you wind up with is a purely natural Jesus! This reconstructed, naturalistic Jesus is not based on evidence, but on definition. What is amazing is that the Jesus Seminar makes no attempt to defend this naturalism; it is just presupposed.[290]

In response to this naturalistic presupposition, I register my agreement with philosopher Dallas Willard's opinion that:

> the governing assumption of the secularist approach to the Bible . . . that there is no God, or that if there is, he has nothing to do with the Bible or with the traditions or events cited in it—is an assumption totally without foundation in fact or in plausible theory. No one has proven it or rendered it plausible.[291]

At the very least, those with differing metaphysical assumptions should be equally open and honest in putting their cards on the table, and shouldn't obscure matters by hiding behind discredited methodological rules or question-begging claims to the mantle of enlightened, open-minded, empirical, scientific enquiry.

Biologist Denis Alexander reminds us that a properly scientific attitude towards miracles means being open-minded and following the evidence wherever it leads:

> The atheist who believes that the universe is essentially a closed system in which all matter "obeys" deterministic laws is unlikely to be very open to the possibility that the material world occasionally behaves in an unexpected way . . . Ironically it is therefore the stance of the atheist that is likely to lead to a closed mind when it comes to the question of evidence for claimed miraculous events . . . it is the stance of the theist that best exemplifies the general

---

289. Earman, *Hume's Abject Failure*, 4.
290. Craig, "Rediscovering the Historical Jesus."
291. Willard, *Knowing Christ*, 122–23.

attitude which one hopes characterizes the scientific community as a whole, namely, an openness to the way the world actually is . . . it is noticeable that the debate on miracles that Hume generated . . . has tended to get bogged down in circular arguments and question-begging prior commitments to philosophical positions that have excluded the possibility of miracles by means of prior definitions."²⁹²

DEMARCATION IS A RED HERRING

"When you have a concept of history which has decided before it investigates any empirical facts that dead men stay dead, then if this is what you mean by history (as many people do), historical investigation proves nothing."

—William Hordern²⁹³

In the opinion of NT scholar R.T. France, "the historical evidence [concerning Jesus] points to conclusions which lie outside the area which some modern scholars will allow to be 'historical.'"²⁹⁴ What's the historian to do if the evidence examined within their subject points to conclusions beyond the pale of how their discipline is currently defined? Do they refuse to follow the evidence in order to preserve a definition? Do they cede competence from their discipline by assigning a conclusion supported by historical evidence to a different discipline (e.g. theology)? Or might they re-think the definition of their subject to accommodate the truth?

It seems to me that even the potential for tension to arise between a methodologically naturalistic *definition* of history and the *evidence* of history is enough to undermine the "scholarly wisdom"²⁹⁵ of drawing a definitional line of demarcation between the Jesus of history and the Christ of faith.

Taken on its own, the definitional demarcation between the Jesus of history and the Christ of faith, enforced by methodological naturalism, is a red herring. What if the Jesus of "history" as an academic discipline must be rinsed clean of the supernatural? Without the backing of either (or both) of the other two approaches to demarcation, methodological naturalism acknowledges that even historians may truthfully affirm on adequate evidential grounds that the Jesus of historical reality is the man Christians believe him to be, just as long as they don't affirm this in their professional capacity historians. As atheist philosopher Thomas Nagel comments: "a purely semantic classification of a hypothesis or its denial as belonging or not to science [or

---

292. Alexander, *Rebuilding the Matrix*, 444, 450.
293. Hordern quoted in Montgomery, "Faith, History and the Resurrection," 88.
294. France, *The Evidence for Jesus*, 167.
295. Schweitzer, *The Quest of the Historical Jesus*, 2–3.

history] is of limited interest to someone who wants to know whether the hypothesis is true or false."[296]

Ditching methodological naturalism

"Dawkins knows practically nothing of the philosophy of science..."

—JOHN GRAY[297]

There's a growing recognition amongst philosophers of science that the attempt of nineteenth- and twentieth-century scholars to define science as methodologically naturalistic was a mistake.[298] As J.P. Moreland notes:

> Those who claim that one must do science, if it is being done at all, within a naturalistic methodological framework render as non-science 80 percent of the work done in the history of the disciplines. Such a radical reinterpretation is terribly wrong-headed. This commitment to methodological naturalism is not consistent with the history of science.[299]

To impose a methodological naturalism upon the practice of science is to render metaphysical naturalism immune to falsification by empirical evidence. Of course, if metaphysical naturalism is true, then methodological naturalism saves scientists from considering explanatory hypotheses that are false by definition (explanations that lie outside the strictures of a naturalistic worldview). However, if metaphysical naturalism is false, then methodological naturalism runs the risk of preventing scientists from ever discovering the truth about various matters. Hence atheist philosopher of science Bradley Monton argues that:

> rejection of the supernatural should not be a part of scientific methodology ... scientists should be free to pursue hypotheses as they see fit, without being constrained by a particular philosophical account of what science is ... If science really is permanently committed to methodological naturalism, it follows that the aim of science is not generating true theories. Instead, the aim of science would be something like: generating the best theories that can be formulated subject to the restriction that the theories are naturalistic ... science is better off without being shackled by methodological naturalism....[300]

---

296. Nagel, "Public Education and Intelligent Design," 195. See: Plantinga, "Whether ID Is Science Isn't Semantics."

297. Gray, "The Closed Mind of Richard Dawkins."

298. See: Bylica and Sagan, "God, Design, and naturalism;" Larmer, "Is Methodological Naturalism Question-Begging?"

299. Moreland, "Intelligent Design and the Nature of Science," 54.

300. Monton, "Is Intelligent Design Science?," 2, 9–10.

As William Lane Craig observes, "Methodology is supposed to aid us in the discovery of the truth about reality, not hinder it."[301]

According to sociologist of science Steve Fuller, the movement "to embrace a philosophy of science that extends beyond naturalism . . . probably represents the mainstream opinion of philosophers themselves."[302] Garry DeWeese and J.P. Moreland report that: "The inadequacy of methodological naturalism [is now] widely acknowledged by philosophers of science, even among those who are atheists . . ."[303] For example:

- Jonathan Bartlett: "methodological naturalism . . . as a total stricture on every type of scientific inquiry . . . is not philosophically sound."[304]

- Gregory Dawnes: "the naturalistic research tradition of the sciences . . . is poorly served by attempts to define science in such a way as to exclude the supernatural."[305]

- Philip Kitcher: "postulating an unobserved Creator need be no more unscientific than postulating unobservable particles."[306]

- Jeffrey Koperski: "If the best explanation for some new phenomenon is design, even supernatural design, it would still count as a scientific explanation. It borders on academic incompetence to pretend that science has strict boundaries and then gerrymander those boundaries to keep out the riffraff. Philosophers of science in particular should know better."[307]

- Robert A. Larmer: "Adopting methodological naturalism puts its practitioner in danger of violating a fundamental epistemic obligation to allow for some experience or set of experiences to serve as a defeater for the belief that natural causes are responsible for all that occurs in the physical universe . . . methodology should not be allowed to trump following the evidence where it leads."[308]

- Keith M. Parsons: "I can see no reason why, in principle, supernatural hypotheses might not be rigorously tested *vis-à-vis* natural ones . . ."[309]

---

301. Craig, "Naturalism and Intelligent Design," 67.
302. Fuller, *Science vs. Religion?*, 102–3.
303. DeWeese and Moreland, *Philosophy Made Slightly Less Difficult*, 146.
304. Bartlett, "Philosophical Shortcomings of Methodological Naturalism," 32.
305. Dawnes, *Theism and Explanation*, 146.
306. Kitcher, *Abusing Science*, 125.
307. Koperski, "Two Bad Ways to Attack Intelligent Design," 433–49.
308. Larmer, *The Legitimacy of Miracle*, 91, 95.
309. Parsons, "Review of Michael Ruse."

- Quine: "If I saw indirect explanatory benefit in positing sensibilia, possibilia, spirits, a Creator, I would joyfully accord them scientific status too, on a par with such avowedly scientific posits as quarks and black holes."[310]

Read: "God, design, and naturalism" by Piotr Bylica and Dariusz Sagan: https://docs7.chomikuj.pl/2540786018,PL,0,0,146.pdf

"Is Methodological Naturalism Question-Begging?" by Robert A. Larmer: http://epsociety.org/userfiles/art-Larmer%20(MethodologicalNaturalismQuestion-Begging).pdf

---

The overlapping magisteria of science and religion

Methodologically naturalistic history—whether our focus is human history or natural history—is committed to excluding the actions of any irreducible, transcendent, and/or supernatural agents from its description of past events, *regardless of the facts*. That is, the naturalist may permit historical explanations framed in terms of the actions of human agents (and they may even believe human agents have libertarian free will), but they will only permit this on the philosophical assumption that human agents must be ultimately explicable in terms of unintelligent and non-purposive natural causes. Of course, plenty of atheists and agnostics (as well as theists) think this naturalistic assumption—which remains a promissory note—is highly implausible.[311]

At the very least, many atheists and agnostics grant that naturalistic presuppositions ought to be subject to rigorous scrutiny in light of reason, experience, and evidence, rather than dogmatically defended by definition. As Phillip E. Johnson writes:

> the right question has been whether science and naturalism are really the same thing, or whether scientific evidence may be moving away from the materialist answers. If someone thinks this is a good question which deserves fair-minded investigation, he or she is travelling side-by-side with [proponents of an open philosophy of science] . . .[312]

The late Stephen Jay Gould held that science and religion treat distinct domains of reality using distinct methodologies:

> The net, or magisterium of science covers the empirical realm . . . The magisterium of religion extends over questions of ultimate meaning and moral value. These two magisteria do not overlap . . . To cite the old clichés, science gets the age of rocks, and religion the rock of ages; science studies how the heavens go, religion how to go to heaven.[313]

---

310. Quine, "Naturalism," 252.
311. See: Midgley, *Are You an Illusion?*; Nagel, *Mind and Cosmos*.
312. Johnson, *The Wedge of Truth*, 16–17.
313. Gould quoted in Dawkins, *The God Delusion*, 55.

Gould called this "independence" model of the relationship between science and religion "non-overlapping magisteria" or NOMA. However, as Michael Ruse argues:

> Gould's treatment of the problem is hardly adequate. Obviously, religious people do want to make factual claims. God exists and is creator. The universe has a purpose. We are special. We have distinctive abilities. Morality may be involved—it is involved—but Christianity goes beyond this. Simply labeling things different magisteria and leaving the discussion at that is not adequate.[314]

Rejecting NOMA means accepting that there is a relationship between science and theology, in that at least *one* truth-claim made by either discipline does, or at least could, come into contact with at least one truth-claim made by the other. Some scholars who reject NOMA think there's an inevitable conflict between science and religion. Others believe conflict isn't inevitable. Richard Dawkins, who belongs to the former camp, considers NOMA an act of "bending over backwards to positively supine lengths"[315] to avoid any possibility of conflict between science and theology.

The suggestion that science is about "how" while religion is about "why" contains a grain of truth (religion does deal with questions of meaning and value that science does not), but I agree with Dawkins that NOMA is far too simplistic. As Dawkins says, NOMA "sounds terrific—right up until you give it a moment's thought."[316] He dramatizes the point by imagining:

> that forensic archaeologists unearthed DNA evidence to show that Jesus really did lack a biological father. Can you imagine religious apologists shrugging their shoulders and saying anything remotely like the following? "Who cares? Scientific evidence is completely irrelevant to theological questions. Wrong magisterium! We're concerned only with ultimate questions and with moral values. Neither DNA nor any other scientific evidence could ever have any bearing on the matter, one way or the other." The very idea is a joke.[317]

Dawkins's general point is well-made, although his specific example is a bad one (by hypothesis, God presumably made up for Jesus' lack of a biological father in a miraculous manner with results that would be indistinguishable from organically conceived people, so DNA might be able to confirm that Joseph was not the biological father of Jesus, but not that Jesus had no biological father.) As Fuller comments:

> the people who do the greatest disservice to science and religion are the self-avowed "moderates" . . . who see science and religion as two non-overlapping spheres . . . In contrast, even though Richard Dawkins' theological competence is risible, he understands the one big point that these "moderates" miss

---

314. Ruse, *Atheism*, 112.
315. Dawkins, *The God Delusion*, 55.
316. Dawkins, *The God Delusion*, 55.
317. Dawkins, *The God Delusion*, 59.

completely—namely, that science and religion are both making truth and reality claims . . .[318]

Coyne sides with Dawkins in rejecting NOMA:

> We can, in principle allow a Divine Foot in the door . . . nothing in science prohibits us from considering supernatural explanations . . . If something is supposed to exist in a way that has tangible effects on the universe, it falls within the ambit of science. And supernatural beings and phenomena can have real-world effects.[319]

Christianity makes a number of real-world claims that intersect with fields of inquiry handled by science. For example, Jesus lived within and thus had effects upon the empirical world:

> it's inherent in the Christian faith to make claims about the real world. According to the Bible, God has revealed himself in time and space, and so Christianity—for good or ill—is going to intersect some of the factual claims of history and science. There's either going to be conflict or agreement. To make NOMA work, its advocates have to water down science or faith, or both. Certainly Gould did—he said religion was just a matter of ethical teaching, comfort, or metaphysical beliefs about meaning. But Christianity certainly claims to be more than that.[320]

This brings us back to our opening point of agreement with Victor J. Stenger. While his "absence of evidence" critique of Christianity is unsound, it does at least assume the falsehood of NOMA and so of any attempt to draw a line of demarcation between history and miracles, or between the Christ of faith and the Jesus of history.

Likewise, when Dawkins rejects NOMA he not only rejects methodological naturalism in the historical sciences, but he explicitly applies this rejection to the historical questions at the heart of Christianity:

> The presence or absence of a creative super-intelligence is unequivocally a scientific question, even if it is not in practice—or not yet—a decided one. So also is the truth or falsehood of every one of the miracle stories that religions rely upon to impress multitudes of the faithful. Did Jesus have a human father, or was his mother a virgin at the time of his birth? Whether or not there is enough surviving evidence to decide it, this is still a strictly scientific question with a definite answer in principle: yes or no. Did Jesus raise Lazarus from the dead? Did he himself come alive again, three days after being crucified?

---

318. "Interview with Steve Fuller."

319. Coyne, *Faith vs. Fact*, 93–94. I would say that "scientific expertise can help in investigating whether claims of the miraculous are valid or not. Even if science cannot definitively prove God exists or that something supernatural has occurred, it can provide empirical evidence that either supports or undermines miracle accounts."—Candy Gunther Brown quoted in Strobel, *The Case for Miracles*, 123.

320. Stephen C. Meyer quoted in Strobel, *The Case for a Creator*, 76.

There is an answer to every such question, whether or not we can discover it in practice, and it is a strictly scientific answer. The methods we should use to settle the matter, in the unlikely event that relevant evidence ever became available, would be purely and entirely scientific methods.[321]

The point is that methodological naturalism is just as much of a liability when applied to ancient history as it is when applied to natural history. As philosopher of science Jay Wesley Richards writes: "Methodological naturalism is very difficult to justify non-arbitrarily, and it contradicts the true spirit of science, which is to seek the truth about the natural world, no holds barred."[322] Indeed, methodological naturalism is in head-on collision with the fundamental intent of both science and history as disciplines that search for the truth. In either case, as Stephen C. Meyer points out, "Theoretically there are at least two possible types of causes: mechanistic and intelligent"[323]—and ruling out either type of cause by definition when arguing that the other type of cause is the best explanation of the evidence is an exercise in begging the question.

The admission that miracles *might* have occurred in history amounts to admitting miracles into the pool of live explanatory options, and the refusal to allow a miraculous explanation to be drawn out of that pool, regardless of evidence, drives a wedge between the discipline of history and the evidence-led search for truth. Hence Larmer concludes that: "Whether or not events best understood as miracles occur is not to be decided on the basis of armchair theorizing, but rather on the basis of meticulous examination of the evidence."[324] As Mark L. Strauss urges: "The historian's role is to find out what happened, not to assume what could or could not have happened."[325]

DOUBTING DEISM

Brian Hebblethwaite concludes that "Hume's main critique of belief in miracles has no force whatsoever"[326] and notes that "the possibility of miraculous intervention, given theism, is beyond doubt."[327] But what of the objection that even if God exists, he must be the non-interventionist God of *deism* rather than the God of *theism*?

Deism is "belief in a God who made the world but never interrupts it with supernatural events."[328] It's interesting to note that according to Richard Dawkins: "one

---

321. Dawkins, *The God Delusion*, 59.
322. Richards, "How Phil Johnson Changed My Mind," 58.
323. Meyer, "The Methodological Equivalence of Design and Descent," 97.
324. Larmer, *The Legitimacy of Miracle*, 187.
325. Strauss, *Introducing Jesus*, 124.
326. Hebblethwaite, *In Defence of Christianity*, 105.
327. Hebblethwaite, *In Defence of Christianity*, 105.
328. Geisler and Watkins, *Worlds Apart*, 147–48.

could make a reasonably respectable case"[329] for deism. However, as Geisler observes: "Deism is not presently a major worldview . . . The deistic movement arose during the seventeenth century and flourished in the eighteenth but largely died out by the nineteenth century."[330] Geisler argues that "Deism is defunct both historically and philosophically."[331]

Watch: "Deism" Youtube playlist: www.youtube.com/playlist?list=PLQhh3qcwVEWhXcclTKzr2wmV_xoO7xbgQ

Read: "Miracles as Inconsistent with the Perfection of God" by Robert A. Larmer: http://epsociety.org/library/articles.asp?pid=257

On the one hand, the standard philosophical motivation for preferring deism over theism is unsound. Historically speaking, deists were much taken with the design argument for God. Their focus was on the general lawful structure of the physical world as revealed, for example, by the natural philosophy of Newton's laws of motion. In an age when clockwork automata of various kinds were the technological cutting edge, deists likened the cosmos to a machine and God to an engineer:

> [Deists assumed that] . . . the most perfect mechanic could create the most perfect machine, which should need no subsequent "tune-ups." However, if God is personal, as even the deistic concept of God would admit, then there is no reason why a "perfect" universe for a personal God would not be one that involves personal attention.[332]

God may be an engineer, but perhaps God is also an artist. It takes engineering skill to design a musical instrument, but musical instruments are designed for playing. Then again, much of today's cutting-edge technology consists of devices designed for personal interaction (e.g. game consoles, touch-screen tablets, electronic personal assistants) and to facilitate personal interaction (e.g. mobile phones, e-mail). Since there's nothing second-rate about designing such a system and nothing inappropriate about the designer of such a system interacting with the system they designed, "Claims that belief in miracles is incompatible with affirming the perfection of God cannot be sustained. There is no inconsistency in believing that the God who creates and upholds the universe also on occasion acts in its history."[333]

Moreover, as philosopher Victor Reppert observes: "The mere belief that God is intelligent and has purposes"—a belief supported by design arguments[334]—"renders

---

329. Dawkins quoted in Lennox, "Has Science Buried God?"
330. Geisler, *Christian Apologetics*, 152.
331. Geisler, *Christian Apologetics*, 157.
332. Geisler, *Christian Apologetics*, 155.
333. Larmer, "Miracles as Inconsistent with the Perfection of God."
334. See: Williams, *A Faithful Guide to Philosophy*, chapters six and seven.

those [putative] miracles that serve some apparent divine purpose more likely to occur than [putative] miracles that seem to be just thrown into the universe for no reason. And other properties attributed to God, such as benevolence,"—which follows from the meta-ethical moral argument for theism[335]—"will provide some reason to think that certain miracles are more likely to occur than others."[336]

Furthermore, most people who believe in God (including deists) "maintain that God has endowed people with free will and consequently the capacity to influence history."[337] Indeed, if one believes humans have free will, God would appear to be the best explanation of this data.[338] Many people "also maintain that God has purposes that He wishes to see fulfilled."[339] Larmer points out that, given these beliefs, "the idea that God might at times intervene in the usual course of events, so as to bring about certain of His purposes which might otherwise be thwarted [by human free will] can scarcely be viewed as inconceivable."[340]

If God exists, humanity is surely among the closest known analogs to deity and thus an obvious source of clues as to God's general intentions. As personal beings, we seek and enter into a great variety of relationships. While God wouldn't *need* relationships with created beings, it would hardly be surprising if, having bothered to create us, our creator was to have an interest in relating in some way to at least some of us, under some conditions, at some time or other.

Sociologist Charles Taylor discusses the human desire for spiritual transcendence, a desire he describes as the "powerful intuition" that "in some activity, or condition, lies a fullness, a richness" a state wherein life is "more worthwhile, more admirable, more what it should be . . ."[341] Humanity is inveterately religious, and the majority of humans find a measure of satisfaction for their innate transcendent desires in various religious experiences. Most of these religious experiences have to do with God. Taylor explains that religious experiences "can help define a direction to our lives. But the sense of orientation also has its negative slope; where we experience above all a distance, an absence, an exile . . . the nostalgia for something transcendent."[342] That is, there seems to be an innate existential thirst in the human heart that only God could sate. Taylor notes the "need for meaning, a desire for eternity"[343] and concludes that

---

335. See: Williams, *A Faithful Guide to Philosophy*, chapter eight.
336. Reppert, "Miracles and the Case for Theism," 35–51.
337. Larmer, "Miracles as Inconsistent with the Perfection of God."
338. See: Moreland, *The Recalcitrant Imagio Dei*.
339. Larmer, "Miracles as Inconsistent with the Perfection of God."
340. Larmer, "Miracles as Inconsistent with the Perfection of God."
341. Taylor, *A Secular Age*, 5.
342. Taylor, *A Secular Age*, 6–7.
343. Taylor, *A Secular Age*, 723.

while, culturally speaking, "There are strong incentives to remain within the bounds of the human domain . . . yet the sense that there is something more presses in."[344]

While there are arguments for the existence of God from both the positive and negative slopes of religious experience,[345] this isn't my point here. Rather, my point is that both slopes offer some grounds for thinking that *if* God exists, *then* it isn't implausible to think he may have an interest in some sort of interaction with and/or on behalf of human beings.

Richard Swinburne suggests that if God exists he might choose to reveal various things to humans that it would be good for us to know, but which humans in general either could not or would not discover for themselves, such as:

- Evidence of God's existence that wouldn't be available without revelation
- Things about God's own nature
- Things about God's past actions
- Things about God's future plans for creation and/or humanity
- Information about our moral duties (especially any moral duties that wouldn't exist if God didn't enjoin them upon us)
- Encouragements to avoid doing what is bad and to choose what is good

Swinburne also argues that God, assuming he exists, would have reason to respond to human sin and suffering by becoming incarnate "and thereby providing atonement for our sins and identifying with our suffering."[346] Although an incarnation may not be the only way in which God might choose to do such things, it certainly is *a* way in which God might do them. Indeed, an incarnation along the lines suggested by Swinburne would be a way to elegantly accomplish several divine ends at once, including providing historically-situated evidence of God's existence that we'd otherwise lack. Hebblethwaite agues along similar lines:

> there are . . . good reasons for God to become incarnate: it would be appropriate for the Creator to identify himself with the creatures he has made in his image; it would teach the dignity of human nature; it would reveal the extent of God's love . . . it would show an exemplary human life; it would enable uniquely authoritative teaching; and it would manifest God's willingness to subject himself to the suffering and evil which creation entails.[347]

---

344. Taylor, *A Secular Age*, 727.

345. See: "Religious Experience;" "The Argument from Desire;" Williams, *The Case for God*; Williams, *A Faithful Guide to Philosophy*; Williams, *C.S. Lewis vs. the New Atheists*; Bassham, *C.S. Lewis' Apologetics*; Williams, "In Defence of Arguments from Desire."

346. Swinburne, *Revelation*, 81. See also: Swinburne, *The Resurrection of God Incarnate*, chapter two.

347. Hebblethwaite, *In Defence of Christianity*, 101–2.

That said, Swinburne cautions that "one would also expect [God], because he values our having creative powers, our making a difference to things, and our influencing each other and helping each other, not to intervene in the world too often."[348] Likewise, many philosophers argue that one shouldn't expect God to make his existence overwhelmingly obvious to humanity as a matter of course.[349] After all, if God is more interested in people freely choosing to know Him in a personal sense than in merely ensuring that everyone knows that he exists, Pascal was probably on the right track when he said that God provides "enough light for those who desire only to see and enough darkness for those of a contrary disposition."[350]

Gathering these points together, we can perhaps conclude that "given the nature of a personal God who made personal beings like himself, it is [not overwhelmingly unlikely] that such a God would want to communicate with those beings."[351] Given that God wanted to do this within human history—perhaps via an incarnation—he might well "confirm his messages as divine communication by miracles, thereby providing evidence of the message's divine origin . . ."[352]

In sum, there's nothing massively implausible about the thought that a personal God might create an interactive cosmos, one containing persons with whom he might interact and/or communicate in a non-coercive manner via the occasional miracle. At the very least, as Evans urges: "If strong reasons can be given for belief in a personal God, then it might be rash to give too low an estimate of the general probability of a miracle."[353]

CONCLUSION

"The viability of confirming a miracle cannot be ruled out prior to investigation."

—JOHN M. DEPOE[354]

Neo-atheist Jerry A. Coyne admits that when it comes to miracles:

> Hume took it too far. No amount of evidence, it seems, could ever override his conviction that miracles were really the result of fraud, ignorance, or

---

348. Swinburne quoted in Varghese, *Great Thinkers On Great Questions*, 212. See also: Meister and Drew, *God And Evil*.

349. See: "Divine Hiddenness;" Meister, "Evil and the Hiddenness of God;" Howard-Snyder, "The Argument from Divine Hiddenness."

350. Pascal, *Pensees*, 118.

351. Geisler, *Christian Apologetics*, 317.

352. Geisler, *Christian Apologetics*, 317.

353. Evans and Manis, *Philosophy of Religion*, 131.

354. DePoe, "How to Confirm a Miracle," 14.

misrepresentation. Yet perhaps there are some events . . . when a [miracle] is more likely than human error or deception.[355]

As Craig S. Keener observes:

> Our ability to quantify factors such as the probability of divine action might be extremely limited, but simply excluding it by presupposition is circular reasoning . . . Hume presupposes a standard of proof so high that any evidence is effectively ruled out in advance. That is, Hume so frames his position that he renders it unfalsifiable . . .[356]

Against the lazy, Humean skepticism of so much neo-atheism, C. Stephen Evans and R. Zachary Manis are right to argue that:

> Even in the absence of any firm knowledge about God and his purposes . . . it would still be rash to claim, with Hume, that the probability of miracles is vanishingly small . . . in which case, one should try to look at the evidence for miracles with a somewhat open, though cautiously sceptical, mind.[357]

In other words, to follow the example set by Victor J. Stenger's attempt to critically evaluate the historical aspects of the foundational Christian narratives, we need to reject "the false dichotomy between the historical Jesus and the Christ of faith . . ."[358], acknowledging with R. Douglas Geivett that: "We cannot foreclose on the question of God's willingness to disclose himself and his purposes in some concrete, particularized way without first looking into the evidence for the authenticity of an alleged revelation . . ."[359] Instead of sealing ourselves off from evidential considerations behind a wall of "sneer-pressure" and discredited Humean arguments, we should all welcome the intellectual freedom evinced by Wolfhart Pannenberg's declaration that "it is not clear why historiography should not in principle be able to speak about Jesus' resurrection as the explanation of the appearances and the discovery of the empty tomb."[360]

Watch: "Miracles" Youtube playlist: www.youtube.com/playlist?list=PLQhh3qcwVEWjIqwpnQZQfCxB-ZWLXNvh-

Read: "Of "Of Miracles"" by Peter van Inwagen: http://andrewmbailey.com/pvi/Of_Of_Miracles.pdf

David Hume's Argument Against Miracles: A Critical Analysis by Francis J. Beckwith

In Defence of Miracles: A Comprehensive Case for God's Action in History edited by R. Douglas Geivett and Gary R. Habermas

Hume's Abject Failure: The Argument Against Miracles by John Earman

355. Coyne, *Faith vs. Fact*, 124.
356. Keener, *Miracles*, 155.
357. Evans and Manis, *Philosophy of Religion*, 132.
358. Charlesworth, *The Historical Jesus*, 2.
359. Geivett, "Is Jesus The Only Way?," 194.
360. Pannenberg, *Jesus—God and Man*, 109.

The Historical Christ & The Jesus of Faith: The Incarnational Narrative as History by C. Stephen Evans

Reported Miracles by J. Huston

The Legitimacy of Miracle by Robert A. Larmer

Miracles C.S. Lewis

The Case For Miracles by Lee Strobel

The Philosophy of Religion by Edward Wierenga

CHAPTER 2

Getting at the Historical Jesus

"Blind faith without any historical knowledge is not the faith in Jesus
we find in the Evangelists and Paul."

—James H. Charlesworth[1]

For all their self-professed interest in evidence, the New Atheists' approach to Jesus is largely pre-determined by their philosophical commitment to naturalism. Not that they have a monopoly on this question-begging approach to New Testament (NT) historiography. As William Lane Craig explains:

> in explaining a body of data, we first assemble a pool of live options and then pick from the pool, on the basis of certain criteria, that explanation which, if true, would best explain the data. The problem at hand is that scientific naturalists will not permit supernatural explanations even to be in the pool of live options . . . [Gerd] Lüdemann is so sure that supernatural explanations are wrong that he thinks himself justified in no longer being open to them . . . But, of course, if only naturalistic explanations are permitted into the pool of live options, then [Lüdemann's] claim that the Hallucination Hypothesis is the best explanation [of the data for the purported resurrection of Jesus] is hollow. For . . . the question is not whether the Hallucination Hypothesis is the best naturalistic explanation, but whether it is true.[2]

An evidence-led approach to the Jesus of history is exemplified by the theory of knowledge adopted by atheist philosopher W.V. Quine (1908–2000), who affirmed: "If I saw indirect explanatory benefit in positing sensibilia, possibilia, spirits, a Creator, I would joyfully accord them scientific status too, on a par with such avowedly

1. Charlesworth, *The Historical Jesus*, 13.
2. Craig, "Visions of Jesus."

scientific posits as quarks and black holes."³ Atheists who adopt such an approach can, and sometimes do, critically assess the historical Jesus without a dogmatic pre-commitment to naturalism. For these atheists, naturalism is a working hypothesis, one they are willing to reconsider in the light of evidence.

If some people who take this non-dogmatic approach find that their consideration of Jesus overturns their worldview, while others don't, this may be due as much to differing evaluations of the relevant evidence as to differing degrees of commitment to naturalism. As Gary R. Habermas comments:

> everyone generally operates within his or her own concept of reality . . . having said this, however . . . We do need to be informed by the data we receive. And sometimes . . . the evidence on a subject convinces us against our indecisiveness or even contrary to our former position.[4]

In the words of N.T. Wright: "Sometimes, to make sense of the actual evidence before us, we have to pull our worldviews, our sense of what is after all possible, into a new shape."[5] Sam Harris puts the matter this way:

> Nothing is more sacred than the facts. No one, therefore, should win any points in our discourse for deluding himself. The litmus test for reasonableness should be obvious: anyone who wants to know how the world is, whether in physical or spiritual terms, will be open to new evidence.[6]

Likewise, Christopher Hitchens affirms that: "Objectivity means the search for truth no matter what."[7]

Neo-atheist hostility to evidence

Contrary to the spirit of open-minded enquiry endorsed by Harris and Hitchens, French neo-atheist Michel Onfray asserts that we should approach any purportedly holy book from "a [philosophical] standpoint hostile to [the possibility of] revelation."[8] Onfray assumes, dogmatically, that the answer to his rhetorical question "Who would have done the revealing?"[9] is "nobody." Anyone with this assumption had better not approach purportedly holy books wielding the demand that they provide adequate evidence to convince them of their revelatory status. Doing *that* would clearly involve a double standard.

3. Quine, "Naturalism," 252.
4. Habermas, "Did Jesus Perform Miracles?, 126.
5. Wright, *Simply Christian*, 98.
6. Harris, *The End of Faith*, 225.
7. Mann, *The Quotable Hitchens*, 207.
8. Onfray, *In Defence of Atheism*, 77.
9. Onfray, *In Defence of Atheism*, 77.

Daniel Dennett says of his naturalism: "It's defeasible. I could learn to abandon it if I encountered insuperable difficulties in carrying out the naturalist programme."[10] However, Dennett still rejects any evidence for miraculous acts of revelation on *a priori* grounds, stating: "historical arguments simply cannot be introduced into serious investigation [of God], since they are manifestly question begging."[11]

Far from begging the question of God's existence, historical arguments for miracles (such as the resurrection of Jesus) need only presuppose the possibility of God existing and acting in a revelatory manner. Then again, miracles might play a part in a cumulative case for theism or for a particular revelation claim wherein other arguments have already established a measure of plausibility for the proposition that God exists.

In point of fact, it's Dennett who begs the question against religious belief by invoking "the scientific method, with its assumption of no miracles"[12] as a bulwark against considering evidence for miraculous defeaters to his "naturalist programme." Dennett claims that: "Saying something is a miracle is basically just . . . a failure of imagination."[13] However, saying that the naturalist programme could be falsified by good evidence whilst failing to consider the case for miracles irrespective of the evidence is intellectually incoherent.

Jerry A. Coyne claims to reject all religions because "there is no good evidence supporting their truth claims."[14] Likewise, according to Richard Dawkins, "If you ask people why they are convinced of the truth of their religion, they don't appeal to evidence," and the reason they don't appeal to evidence is because "There isn't any."[15] These statements presupposes that Coyne and Dawkins are open to being convinced to accept a religion by an appeal to "good evidence."

Dawkins says: "I will respect your views if you can justify them. But if you justify your views only by saying you have faith in them, I shall not respect them."[16] In sum, Dawkins demands that if a religion wants him to respect it, that religion must have some evidential justification. He doesn't think any religion meets this demand, but the very act of issuing the demand implies that he is open to following the evidence wherever it leads.

Dawkins certainly *appears* to endorse an open-minded investigation when he asks: "Did Jesus . . . come alive again, three days after being crucified? There is an answer to every such question, whether or not we can discover it in practice, and it is

---

10. Dennett quoted in Spencer, "Mounting disbelief," 13.
11. Dennett, *Breaking the Spell*, 240.
12. Dennett, *Breaking the Spell*, 26.
13. Dennett, "The Q&A," 7.
14. Coyne, "What is a "true" religion?"
15. Dawkins, "Lecture at the Edinburgh International Science Festival."
16. Dawkins, "Lecture at the Edinburgh International Science Festival."

a strictly scientific answer."[17] However, to be genuine, such an investigation must include a commitment to following the evidence even if it entails a change of worldview. Unfortunately, Dawkins explicitly rejects such open-minded, evidence-led inquiry on *a priori* grounds:

> the water-into-wine story is pure fiction . . . We can say the same thing about all alleged miracles . . . Suppose something happens that we don't understand, and we can't see how it could be fraud or trickery or lies: would it ever be right to conclude that it must be supernatural? No! . . . that would put an end to all further discussion or investigation. It would be lazy, even dishonest, for it amounts to a claim that no natural explanation will ever be *possible*. If you claim that anything odd must be "supernatural" you are not just saying you don't currently understand it; you are giving up and saying that it can never be understood. There are things that not even the best scientists of today can explain. But that doesn't mean we should block off all investigation by resorting to phoney "explanations" invoking magic or the supernatural, which don't actually explain at all.[18]

Naturally, the conclusion that a given event was a miracle amounts to the claim that no *true* purely natural explanation of that event will ever be possible. But one might as well accuse *natural* explanations of blocking off "further discussion or investigation"! There's a sense in which *any* explanation brings a particular inquiry to an end. That's what explanations are for. However, in neither the miraculous nor the non-miraculous case is the exploration of consequent questions, or the re-consideration of one's original question, excluded.

Moreover, while I agree that an argument from ignorance is an inadequate basis for the conclusion that an event was a miracle, one simply needn't justify such a conclusion with this invalid form of argument. Because he has a dogmatic commitment to naturalistic explanations being the only possible kind of explanations, Dawkins refuses to countenance the idea that even a *true* supernatural explanation is an explanatory advance. Indeed, Dawkins tendentiously *defines* the claim that something is "supernatural" as the claim that "it can never be understood"! He thereby begs the question against all miracle claims, deducing their status as "pure fiction" from the procrustean presupposition that naturalism is true, without any regard for evidence. In light of Dawkins's statements about faith being belief in the absence of supportive evidence, science being belief in the presence of supportive evidence and the resurrection of Jesus being a strictly scientific question, this is what philosophers call "a double standard." All of which highlights the importance of Dawkins's own call for making

---

17. Dawkins, *The God Delusion*, 83.
18. Dawkins, *The Magic of Reality*, 262–63.

"disciplined precautions against personal bias, confirmation bias, prejudgement of issues before the facts are in."[19]

C. Stephen Evans calls all such "critics" out on their game of bait and switch:

> Critics . . . raise objections to historical religious knowledge that are apparently empirical in nature, and thus should presuppose [a] conception of religious knowledge that is open in principle to such historical knowledge. When we look more deeply, however, we find that these empirical objections are a smokescreen for covert [philosophical] presuppositions . . . Why should we assume that whatever religious knowledge takes as its object . . . can't manifest itself in the natural world at all? While it may be a genuinely empiricist claim to say that empirical religious knowledge is difficult to attain or can only be attained under certain conditions, empiricism provides no real support for the thesis that empirical religious knowledge is impossible.[20]

Being open to the evidence means being open to whatever theory is best supported by the evidence. A miraculous explanation should never be our first port of call (even people who believe in miracles think they are the rare exception rather than the frequent rule), but neither should our theory of knowledge preclude accepting a miracle regardless of the evidence. Hence, when it comes to claims about miracles, there's no avoiding the need to consider the evidence.

The agnostic will follow close behind both the theist and the Quinian atheist in approaching the historical Jesus with an openness to the possibility of his miracles and divinity. This open-mindedness need not and should not flout the appropriate critical demands of rational, rigorous, academic inquiry. Theists, agnostics and non-dogmatic atheists are all more open to following the evidence where it leads when it comes to investigating the historical Jesus than is the neo-atheist whose reasoning is blind to any evidence at odds with their faith in naturalism.

Unfortunately, the contemporary public debate about Jesus isn't conducted in a spirit of open-minded, evidence-led, critical enquiry. Instead, it's dominated by misinformation spread by neo-atheist ideologues whose historical ignorance is all too often justified by their overbearing pre-commitment to naturalism. Even Christopher Hitchens records his commitment to the *a priori* principle that "there has been no divine revelation. There could not be such a thing."[21] Such neo-atheist "skepticism" recapitulates the attitude of David Hume, who owned, according to Dr. Samuel Johnson: "that he had never read the New Testament with attention. Here then was a man who had been at no pains to inquire into the truth of religion, and had continually turned his mind the other way."[22]

---

19. Dawkins, *Science In The Soul*, 7.
20. Evans, *The Historical Christ*, 176–77.
21. Hitchens quoted in Taunton, *The Faith of Christopher Hitchens*, 89.
22. Johnson quoted in Taunton, *The Faith of Christopher Hitchens*, 167.

Getting at the Historical Jesus

THE MYTHICAL CHRIST MYTH

"The sure mark of an ideology, in science and philosophy as in politics
is the denying of obvious facts."

—COLIN MCGINN[23]

In 1916 an atheistic C.S. Lewis opined that: "after the death of a Hebrew philosopher Yeshua (whose name we have corrupted into Jesus) he became regarded as a god, a cult sprang up, which was afterwards connected with the ancient Hebrew Jahweh-worship . . . one mythology among many . . ."[24] By interpreting Jesus against the matrix of pagan mythology, Lewis was embracing the latest academic trend:

> The idea of a copycat religion really arose in Germany at the end of the nineteenth and the start of the twentieth century. It was put forward by the "History of Religions" school. It was popularised by Sir James Frazer in Britain when he published his readable, but unreliable, *The Golden Bough* . . . This seemed an attractive hypothesis for a while, but subsequent scholarship has examined this hypothesis and found it wanting . . . Nowadays it is regarded as a dead issue by almost all scholars.[25]

It's worth noting that among the presuppositions shaping the History of Religions School—that is, the *Religionsgeschichtliche Schule*—was an anti-Semitism that rejected the Jewishness of Jesus, if not his historical existence.[26] As Frazer wrote:

> My theory assumes the historical reality of Jesus of Nazareth as a great religious and moral teacher, who founded Christianity and was crucified at Jerusalem under the governorship of Pontius Pilate. The testimony of the gospels, confirmed by the hostile evidence of Tacitus (Ann, xv, 44) and the younger Pliny (Epist. X, 96), appears amply sufficient to establish these facts to the satisfaction of all unprejudiced enquirers . . . The doubts that have been cast upon the historical reality of Jesus are, in my judgement, unworthy of serious attention.[27]

Winfried Corduan laments that the central theory advanced in "Frazier's *Golden Bough*, despite its thoroughly fictional nature, continued to arouse fascination among readers a hundred years ago, and it still does so today."[28] Likewise, Michael Ruse warns:

---

23. McGinn, *The Making of a Philosopher*, 49.
24. Lewis, "Letter to Arthur Greeves," 52.
25. Green, *Lies, Lies, Lies!*, 59–60.
26. See: Hutchinson, *Searching For Jesus*, 50; Craig, "What About Pre-Christ Resurrection Myths?"
27. Frazer quoted in Short, *Why Believe?*, 28–29.
28. Corduan, *In The Beginning God*, 228.

Before you go off on flights of fantasy inspired by *The Golden Bough* (1890) by Sir James Frazer—about gods being sacrificed and eaten and resurrecting, and so the Jesus story is just a reflection of a common archetype—note that anthropologists these days are not that impressed by Frazer's conclusions and think he jumbled together a lot of very different stories and patterns.[29]

Atheist historian Michael Grant states that "modern critical methods fail to support the Christ-myth theory."[30] Consequently, as Gary R. Habermas notes, while "a reliance on legends was a popular thesis in times past [this approach] has been dismissed today by most researchers."[31]

So-called "mythicist" denials of Jesus' historical existence, which seek to employ the flawed arguments of the History of Religions School in support of an even less convincing conclusion, exist on the outer edge of the academic fringe (and beyond). Atheist NT scholar Maurice Casey reports that the History of Religions approach to Jesus is now "known a good century later to have been significantly mistaken."[32] As for mythicists who reject any historical core to historical testimony about Jesus, Casey chastises their "drastic reliance on work which is out of date, most of which was of questionable quality when it was written, mostly in the nineteenth and early twentieth centuries."[33] He concludes that "mythicist arguments are completely spurious from beginning to end."[34]

Likewise, James F. McGrath complains that modern mythicists are "not merely wrong in the ways that scholars are often wrong but rather grossly incompetent, shoddily argued and evidenced, utterly lacking in plausibility, and often seeming to willfully distort the evidence . . ."[35]

Unperturbed by scholarly criticism, New Atheism promotes "mythicist" theories according to which the NT accounts of Jesus are shaped by ideas borrowed from pagan mystery religions, being at best mythological re-interpretations of a mundane historical Jesus:

- According to Jerry A. Coyne: "arguments can be made that Jesus was a purely mythological figure, perhaps derived from earlier such figures . . ."[36] Coyne claims that there are "striking similarities of Jesus to other God-sons such as Mithra, Sandan, Attis, and Horus."[37]

29. Ruse, *Atheism*, 135.
30. Grant, *Jesus*, 200.
31. Habermas, *The Verdict of History*, 38.
32. Casey, *Jesus*, 1.
33. Casey, *Jesus*, 2.
34. Casey, *Jesus*, 245.
35. McGrath, "Maurice Casey, Jesus: Evidence and Argument or Mythicist Myths?"
36. Coyne, "It's Time to Ponder Whether Jesus Really Existed."
37. Coyne, "Once Again: Was There a Historical Jesus?"

- Richard Dawkins asserts that "all the essential features of the Jesus legend, including . . . the resurrection . . . are borrowed—every last one of them—from other religions already in existence in the Mediterranean and Near East region."[38]
- A.C. Grayling claims that "there is nothing particularly original about the core Christian stories. Think about the many other versions of what appears in the Christian story, versions long antedating it in Middle Eastern mythology or in Greek mythology . . ."[39]
- Lawrence Krauss once opined that Christian theology "is clearly derivative, based on earlier pagan theologies . . ."[40]

Parallelomania

Samuel Sandmel coined the term "parallelomania" to describe the mythicist tendency "which first overdoes the supposed similarity in passages, and then proceeds to describe source and derivation as if implying literary connection . . ."[41] As Craig notes, anyone advancing the copycat thesis: "has a burden of proof to bear . . . to show that the narratives are parallel and, moreover, that they are causally connected."[42] Failure to sustain this burden of proof led the academy to reject the History of Religions School of thought. Coyne et al. certainly don't supply this deficit.

Edwin M. Yamauchi (Professor Emeritus of History at Miami University) observes that: "by the mid-twentieth century, scholars had established that the sources used in [mythicist] writings were far from satisfactory and the parallels were much too superficial."[43] As J. Warner Wallace reports:

> Pre-Christian mythologies are far less similar to the story of Jesus Christ than critics claim. The gods of mythology were not born of a virgin as Jesus was born to Mary, they did not live a life that was similar to Jesus in detail, they did not hold the titles attributed to Jesus, and they were not resurrected in a manner that is remotely similar to the resurrection of Christ. Primitive mythologies simply fail to resemble the Biblical account of Jesus when they are examined closely.[44]

On the one hand, when mythicists make accurate claims about pagan mythology, those claims turn out to be irrelevant to a discussion about Jesus. For example, the conspiracy theory movie *Zeitgeist* (2007) claims that the Greek god Dionysus

---

38. Dawkins, *The God Delusion*, 119.
39. Grayling, *Conversations on Religion*, 5.
40. Krauss, "Krauss, Meyer, Lamoureux."
41. Sandmel, "Parallelomania," 1–13.
42. Craig, *A Reasonable Response*, 293.
43. Yamauchi quoted in Strobel, *The Case for the Real Jesus*, 165.
44. Wallace, "Why the pre-Jesus mythologies fail to prove Jesus was a myth."

resembles Jesus because he was born on December 25. However, the NT never dates the birth of Jesus (and the earliest source positing December 25 as Jesus' birthday is Hippolytus of Rome in the third century). Again, *Zeitgeist* claims that Christianity borrowed the idea of "three kings" for its nativity story from ancient religions, but the NT knows nothing of "three kings" (Matthew refers to an unspecified number of "magi"—i.e. astrologers—who give Jesus gifts of gold, frankincense, and myrrh).

On the other hand, when mythicists make relevant claims about pagan mythology, those claims turn out to be inaccurate. For example, while mythicists claim that various pagan gods were "virgin-born," none of the myths to which they point truly parallel the NT story. As Tertullian said in his second-century *Apology*, the virginal conception of Christ:

> was not from any incestuous mixture of brother and sister, not from any violation of a god with his own daughter, or another man's wife, in the disguise of a serpent, or a bull, or a shower of gold. These are the modes of generation with your Jove, and the offspring of deities you worship; but the Son of God we adore had a mother indeed, but a mother . . . without even that which the name of mother seems to imply, for she was a pure virgin.[45]

An oft-mentioned case in point: the Persian deity Mithra was supposedly born fully-grown from the rock of a mountain, thereby leaving behind a cave. He wasn't born as a baby from a virgin in a cave as some mythicists claim (an extrabiblical tradition, traceable to the middle of the second century, claims that Jesus was born in a cave; so perhaps the house in which Jesus was born incorporated a cave where animals were kept). In the Iranian version of the myth, Mithra's conception "was attributed, variously, to an incestuous relationship between Ahura-Mazda and his mother, or to the plain doings of an ordinary mortal woman, but there is *no* virgin conception/birth story to speak of."[46]

In general terms, alleged pagan parallels to the story of Jesus' conception "are exactly the opposite of the Gospel story of Mary's conceiving Jesus apart from any sexual relations. The Gospel stories of Jesus' virginal conception are, in fact, without parallel in the ancient Near East."[47]

Atheist Claire Rayner breezily dismisses the story of Jesus' resurrection as a myth: "the Christians, cleverly picking up on a very ancient human view of the springtime reappearance (i.e. resurrection) of dead plants and winter-vanished greenery, added on their version of a resurrection myth, telling the story of the magical return of a

---

45. Tertullian, *The Apology of Tertullian*, chapter 21.
46. Holding, "Pagan Christs, Persian Front: Mithra and Zoroaster," 207.
47. Craig, "Jesus and pagan mythology."

dead messiah."[48] A.C. Grayling likewise asserts that "Resurrection stories are commonplaces of religion and myth."[49] However, as Alister McGrath comments:

> The parallels between the pagan myths of dying and rising gods and the New Testament accounts of the resurrection of Jesus are now regarded as remote, to say the least . . . Furthermore, there are no known instances of the myth being applied to any *specific historical figure* in pagan literature . . . It is at this point that the wisdom of C.S. Lewis—who actually knew something about myths—must be acknowledged. Lewis intuitively realized that the New Testament accounts of the resurrection of Jesus bore no relation to "real" mythology . . . Perhaps most important, however, was the realization that the gnostic redeemer myths—which the New Testament writers allegedly took over and applied to Jesus—were to be dated later than the New Testament. The challenge posed to the historicity of the resurrection by these theories has thus passed into textbooks of the history of ideas.[50]

To quote Lewis himself:

> I have been reading poems, romances, vision-literature, legends, myths all my life. I know what they are like. I know that not one of them is like this . . . Either this is reportage—though it may no doubt contain errors—pretty close up to the facts . . . Or else, some unknown writer . . . without known predecessors or successors, suddenly anticipated the whole technique of modern, novelistic, realistic narrative. If it is untrue, it must be narrative of that kind. The reader who doesn't see this has simply not learned to read . . .[51]

Lewis further noted that "A *myth* is . . . not, save accidentally, connected with any given place or time."[52] Yet, as John Stonestreet observes: "Biblical faith is an historical faith. The accounts in the scripture do not take place in some mythical time-before-time like that of their pagan neighbors or the Bhagavad Gita in Hinduism."[53]

David H. Glass explains that: "In contrast to Christianity, which has a very definite link with history, the Mystery Religions were based on the annual cycle of birth and death in nature and not on specific historical claims."[54] As Michael R. Licona points out, unlike anything in the mystery religions, Jesus' resurrection "isn't repeated, isn't related to changes in the seasons, and was sincerely believed to be an actual historical event by those who lived in the same generation of the historical Jesus."[55] Indeed,

48. Rayner, "How to Have a Peaceful Pagan Christmas," 119.
49. Grayling, *The God Argument*, 227.
50. McGrath, "Resurrection and Incarnation," 30.
51. Lewis, *Christian Reflections*, 155, 157.
52. Lewis quoted in *C.S. Lewis & Philosophy as a Way of Life* by Adam Barkman, 117.
53. Stonestreet quoted in "Hello, Hezekiah!" by Eric Metaxas.
54. Glass, *Atheism's New Clothes*, 278.
55. Licona quoted in Strobel, *The Case for the Real Jesus*, 161.

while pagan mystery religions put a premium on secret knowledge (the clue is in the name), as Ronald H. Nash observes, *"early Christianity was an antimystery religion."*[56]

Bios not mythos

Scholars have reached a broad consensus that the literary genre of the NT gospels is *not* myth. Hence James D.G. Dunn begins his article on "Myth" in the *Dictionary of Jesus and the Gospels* by stating: "Myth is a term of at least doubtful relevance to the study of Jesus and the Gospels."[57]

E.M. Blaiklock (a respected classicist from the University of Auckland) writes of the synoptic gospels as a "record [that needs] to be approached as history . . ."[58] He explains that Mark's Gospel "concerns history . . ."[59] He concludes that "Matthew's gospel . . . appears to be an attempt to write history. Myth is not apparent."[60] He calls Luke's Gospel "the work of a first-rate historian."[61] Finally, Blaiklock affirms that "John was consciously writing history . . ."[62]

Far from being works of mythology, the consensus of contemporary scholarship affirms that the canonical gospels fall within the historical genre of ancient biography. In his influential study *What Are the Gospels? A Comparison with Graeco-Roman Biography*, Professor Richard A. Burridge concludes that "the gospels belong to the genre of Greco-Roman [*bios*]."[63] Burridge specifically rejects the relevance of "pure fiction" as a literary genre when reading the four gospels:

> the [*Bios*] genre of the gospels affects the "Quest for the historical Jesus," with particular respect to the use of sources by writers of [*Bioi*]. The selectivity allowed for an author to produce his portrait of the subject will form part of the redaction critical approach; however, because this is a Life of a historical person written within the lifetime of his contemporaries, there are limits on free composition.[64]

Today, most NT scholars hold that the gospels belong to the genre of ancient historical biography (*bios*):

---

56. Nash, *The Gospel and The Greeks*, 118.
57. Dunn, "Myth," 566.
58. Blaiklock, *Jesus Christ*, 46.
59. Blaiklock, *Jesus Christ*, 38.
60. Blaiklock, *Jesus Christ*, 43.
61. Blaiklock, *Jesus Christ*, 45.
62. Blaiklock, *Jesus Christ*, 68.
63. Burridge, *What Are the Gospels?*, 233.
64. Burridge, *What Are the Gospels?*, 249–50.

- Craig L. Blomberg: "Matthew, Mark, Luke, and John thought they were writing good history and biography by the standards of their day."[65]
- Darrell L. Bock: "a consensus has emerged that the Gospels are a form of ancient *bios*."[66]
- Helen K. Bond: "the Gospels present their material in biographical terms..."[67]
- Brant Pitre: "there are compelling historical reasons to conclude that the Gospels ... are ancient biographies written by the students of Jesus and their followers, written well within the lifetimes of the apostles and eyewitnesses to Jesus."[68]
- Graham Stanton (Lady Margaret's Professor of Divinity at the University of Cambridge): "the gospels are a type of Graeco-Roman biography."[69]
- N.T. Wright: "One of the great gains of New Testament scholarship in the last generation has been to re-establish that the canonical gospels certainly were intended, and certainly are to be read, within the framework of ancient biographical writing."[70]

Craig S. Keener states that: "Popular writers today who treat the Gospels as mythography act in a manner that is historically irresponsible."[71] He explains further:

> Myths and even legends normally involved characters placed centuries in the distant past. People wrote novels, but not novels claiming that a fictitious character actually lived a generation or two before they wrote. Ancient readers would most likely approach the Gospels as biographies, as a majority of scholars today suggest. Biographies of recent figures were not only about real figures, but they typically preserved much information... What was true of biographies in general could be even more true of biographies about sages. Members of sages' schools in this period typically preserved their masters' teachings, which became foundational for their communities.[72]

Introducing the multi-scholar volume *Biographies and Jesus: What Does It Mean for the Gospels to be Biographies?*, Keener writes:

> Genre does not answer all historical questions or eliminate the value of the more common historical-critical criteria. It does, however, rightly adjust our default expectations... With regard to biographies of recent characters [such

---

65. Blomberg, *Making Sense of the New Testament*, 31.
66. Bock and Wallace, "Precision and Accuracy," 368.
67. Bond, *The Historical Jesus*, 7.
68. Pitre, *The Case For Jesus*, 101.
69. Stanton, *A Gospel for a New People*, 64.
70. Wright, *Judas and the Gospel of Jesus*, 30.
71. Keener, "Introduction," 44.
72. Keener, "Jesus Existed."

as the canonical gospels], a default expectation that much of the information is accurate is usually likelier than are a priori skeptical assumptions.[73]

Michael R. Licona has reviewed the differences between the canonical gospels in light of an investigation of ancient compositional textbooks and biographical literature. He draws parallels between the gospels and Plutarch's *Parallel Lives*, which "provide modern historians with a rare opportunity to examine how one author narrates the same story differently in different contexts."[74] The *Lives* "belong to Greco-Roman biography, were written in . . . Greek, and were written within only a few decades of the Gospels."[75] In light of this material, Licona concludes:

> the extent of editing by the evangelists is minimal by ancient standards. As interesting as the differences in the Gospels may be, it is the refusal of their authors to paraphrase more freely that is striking to those readers familiar with both the Gospels and Plutarch's *Lives*.[76]

Professor Craig A. Evans comments that:

> compared to the compositional practice of Plutarch, the authors of the Gospels were far more conservative, especially when it comes to the editing and paraphrasing of the words of Jesus. Indeed, it has been observed that the authors of the New Testament Gospels are far more conservative in their paraphrasing of the words of Jesus than was Josephus in his paraphrasing of the words of Israel's ancient Scripture. What the evidence seems to show is that . . . the authors of the New Testament Gospels . . . had a very high regard for the stories of Jesus . . .[77]

The evangelists' use of the *bios* genre was undoubtedly shaped by the fact that they were working with contemporary oral history (and perhaps with written notes) about the teachings and deeds of Jesus:

> Many of the motifs that appear in the gospels can be paralleled in contemporary texts, especially in the anecdotal material which acted as a prime carrier of school traditions both in the rabbinic academies and in the Greek philosophical schools . . . what may be unique is the particular form this tradition takes when it is written down, a form whose external shape is strongly reminiscent of the Greek bios but whose narrative mode and theological framework (connectives, narrative structure, use of direct speech, intertextuality) owe much

---

73. Keener, "Introduction," 5.
74. Licona, *Why Are There Difference In The Gospels?*, 197.
75. Licona, *Why Are There Difference In The Gospels?*, 197.
76. Licona, *Why Are There Difference In The Gospels?*, 199.
77. Evans, "Foreword," x.

more to [Jewish scripture] . . . and shows no sign of being influenced by the philosophical ethos tradition which so dominated Greek biography . . .[78]

The historical, biographical character of the NT gospels clearly contradicts the idea that the Jesus we see therein is a purely or even mainly mythological figure: "while the Evangelists had an important theological agenda, the very fact that they chose to adapt Greco-Roman biographical conventions to tell the story of Jesus indicates that they were centrally concerned to communicate what they thought really happened."[79] As Douglas R. Groothuis comments:

> While some assert that Christianity stole the idea of resurrection from various mystery religions featuring a dying and rising figure, the Gospel accounts breath a far different air—the air of factual actuality, of dateable, verifiable history. The heroes or gods of the mystery religions are tied to vegetative patterns, a mythologizing of nature . . . They occur in a kind of dream world. The deities are, according to Bruce Metzger, "nebulous figures of an imaginary past." They were plainly not meant to be historical.[80]

Michael Green observes that:

> nobody had ever attributed divinity and a virgin birth, resurrection and ascension to a *historical person* whom lots of people knew. And certainly nobody claimed that the one and only God, the creator and judge of the whole earth, had embodied himself in Apollo, Hercules, Augustus, and the rest . . . Augustus had temples erected to him as *divus Augustus* in the East . . . but of course neither he nor anybody else imagined that by so doing he laid claim to embody the Godhead . . . Vesputin, dying in the seventies, quipped "Alas, I fear I am becoming a god!" It is very difficult to see the Christian conviction about Jesus springing from such roots. But no better ones have been put forward.[81]

By contrast with purveyors of mythology, the NT writers:

> were convinced the events in their accounts really happened. These were not sacred stories of netherworld gods and ethereal, supernatural heroes, but reports of actual historical events involving flesh and blood people . . . The Gospel writers intended to report history, not mythology. Their accounts include the vivid detail of an observer who had witnessed the events personally, or a chronicler who had obtained the information from people who were actually there . . . These facts on their own don't make the accounts true, of course. But

---

78. Alexander, "What is a Gospel?," 29.
79. Aune, "Greco-Roman Biography," 125.
80. Groothuis, *Christian Apologetics*, 527–28.
81. Green, "Jesus in the New Testament," 36–38.

they do seem to place these writings in a class of ancient literature that doesn't allow them to be dismissed for frivolous reasons.[82]

Indeed, various NT writers make a clear distinction between mythology on the one hand and what they have to say about Jesus on the other:

- 1 John 1:1–3: "That which... we have heard, which we have seen with our eyes, which we have looked at and our hands have touched—this we proclaim concerning the Word of life. The life appeared; we have seen it and testify to it, and we proclaim to you the eternal life, which was with the Father and has appeared to us. We proclaim to you what we have seen and heard, so that you also may have fellowship with us."
- 1 Timothy 1:3–4: "stay there in Ephesus so that you may command certain people not to teach false doctrines any longer or to devote themselves to myths and endless genealogies..."
- 1 Timothy 4:7: "Have nothing to do with godless myths..."
- 2 Timothy 4:3–4: "the time will come when people will... turn their ears away from the truth and turn aside to myths."
- Titus 1:13–14: "rebuke them sharply, so that they will be sound in the faith and will pay no attention to Jewish myths..."
- 2 Peter 1:16: "For we did not follow cleverly contrived myths when we made known to you the power and coming of our Lord Jesus Christ; instead, we were eyewitnesses of His majesty." (HCSB)

Jesus was Jewish

Today's quest for the historical Jesus is firmly grounded in the realization that "pagan mythology is simply the wrong interpretative context for understanding Jesus of Nazareth [because] Jesus and his disciples were first-century Palestinian Jews, and it is against that background that they must be understood."[83] As Gerald O'Collins comments, the myth thesis: "runs against the present tide of main-line scholarship, which—now drawing on extensive data from the Dead Sea Scrolls, recent archaeological discoveries, and other sources—insists that Jesus and the first Christians must be interpreted primarily against a Jewish and not a Hellenistic background."[84]

Michael Grant explains that "Judaism was a milieu to which doctrines of the deaths and rebirths of mythical gods seems so entirely foreign that the emergence of such a fabrication from its midst is very hard to credit."[85] A.C. Grayling may describe

82. Koukl, *Faith Is Not Wishing*, 22.
83. Craig, *Reasonable Faith*, 391.
84. O'Collins, "The Resurrection," 18.
85. Grant, *Jesus*, 199.

early Christianity as "a young and syncretistic religion drawing elements from many other faiths and superstitions that antedate it,"[86] but this claim is hard to square with J.P. Moreland's observation of the fact that "Jews were very much against allowing Gentile or Greek ideas to affect their worship."[87]

The Christian revelation claim stands or falls by the historicity of certain events said to have taken place in a socio-political context radically opposed to pagan mythology: "This is difficult," observed C.S. Lewis as an adult, "because [Jesus'] followers were all Jews; that is, they belonged to that Nation which of all others was most convinced that there was only one God—that there could not possibly be another."[88] As Green observes:

> The Jews had really learnt one lesson by the first century AD. That there is only one God, and no runners up. They believed this so strongly that they would allow no images of the divine to decorate their synagogue . . . So jealously did they stick to the Second Commandment that the Jews fought to the death rather than allow the Roman military standards, with their imperial medallions, to enter the Holy City. So seriously did Jews take their monotheism that they would not take the sacred name of God (Yahweh) upon their lips . . . In other words, if you had looked the whole world over for more stony and improbable soil in which to plan the idea of an incarnation you could not have done better than light upon Israel![89]

Phil Fernandes explains that:

> the mystery religions were syncretistic—they liked to blend beliefs from other religions with their own beliefs. Christianity, on the other hand, like the Judaism from which it came, was very exclusive. The early church, like first century Judaism, did not borrow from other religions. The early church believed that all non-Christian religions were false and that salvation comes only through Jesus. In short, the early church was not inclined to borrow from the pagan religions and their myths. In fact, many Christians were persecuted and martyred because they refused to blend Christianity with pagan beliefs.[90]

To suggest that the early Christians borrowed their central religious concepts from pagan culture evinces a fundamental misunderstanding of the Jewishness of Christianity. As Craig observes: "there is no causal connection between pagan myths and the disciples' belief in Jesus' resurrection. Jews were familiar with the seasonal deities (Ezek. 37:1–14) and found them abhorrent."[91]

86. Grayling, "A Happy Christmas," 197–98.
87. Moreland quoted in Strobel, *The Case for Christ*, 275.
88. Lewis, "What are we to make of Jesus Christ?", 82.
89. Green, "Jesus in the New Testament," 40.
90. Fernandes et al., *Hijacking the Historical Jesus*, 159.
91. Craig, *Reasonable Faith*, 391.

Chronos and historia

A nearly universal consensus of modern scholarship affirms that "there were *no* dying and rising gods that preceded Christianity. They all post-dated the first century."[92] As historian of religion Jonathan Z. Smith explains:

> The category of dying and rising gods, once a major topic of scholarly investigation, must be understood to have been largely a misnomer based on imaginative reconstructions and exceedingly late or highly ambiguous texts . . . There is no unambiguous instance in the history of religions of a dying and rising deity.[93]

Likewise, according to Gary R. Habermas:

> there is no case of a mythical deity in the mystery religions for which we have both clear and early evidence that a resurrection was taught prior to the late second century A.D. Thus, it is certainly a plausible theory that the mystery religions borrowed this aspect from Christianity, not the reverse.[94]

Bart Erhman acknowledges that "there is no unambiguous evidence that any pagans prior to Christianity believed in dying and rising gods . . ."[95] He concludes:

> there are serious doubts about whether there were in fact dying-rising gods in the pagan world, and if there were, whether they were anything like the dying-rising Jesus . . . There are, to be sure, scholars here or there who continue to think that there is some evidence of dying and rising gods. But even these scholars, who appear to be in the minority, do not think that the category is of any relevance for understanding the traditions about Jesus.[96]

Swedish scholar Tryggve N.D. Mettinger reports that "There is now what amounts to a scholarly consensus against the appropriateness of the concept [of dying and rising gods]. Those who still think differently are looked upon as residual members of an almost extinct species."[97]

That said, Mettinger takes what he admits is the "almost extinct" position that there are some (i.e. three to five) myths about dying and rising gods that predate Christianity. Mettinger nevertheless concludes that none of these myths serve as parallels to Jesus or as causal factors in the Christian understanding of Jesus.

In particular, Mettinger argues that there is "no *prima facie* evidence that the death and resurrection of Jesus is a mythological construct . . . The death and resurrection of

---

92. Licona quoted in Strobel, *The Case for Christ*, 160.
93. Smith, "Dying and Rising Gods," 227.
94. Habermas, *The Verdict of History*, 38–39.
95. Erhman, *Did Jesus Exist?*, 230.
96. Erhman, *Did Jesus Exist?*, 222–23.
97. Mettinger, *The Riddle of Resurrection*, 7, 40–41.

Jesus retains its unique character in the history of religions."[98] As Keener comments: "none of the alleged parallels involve a historical person (or anyone) resurrected in the strict sense. This is probably in part because resurrection in its strict (bodily and permanent) sense was an almost exclusively Jewish belief, and among Jewish people was reserved for the future."[99] Craig A. Evans concurs that "The idea of resurrection, whereby the dead are restored to life (and by this is meant a life superior to the previous life and almost always understood as everlasting life), appears to be distinctive of early Judaism and Christianity."[100] As Ehrman argues:

> Christian claims about Jesus's atoning sacrifice were not lifted from pagan claims about divine men. Dying to atone for sin was not part of the ancient pagan mythology . . . Even if—a very big if—there was an idea among some pre-Christian peoples of a god who died and rose, there is nothing like the Christian belief in Jesus's resurrection . . . The idea of Jesus' resurrection did not derive from pagan notions of a god simply being reanimated . . . Anyone who thinks that Jesus was modelled on such deities needs to cite some evidence—any evidence at all—that Jews in Palestine at the alleged time of Jesus's life were influenced by anyone who held such views. One reason that scholars do not think that Jesus was invented as one of these deities is precisely that we have no evidence that any of his followers knew of such deities in the time and place where Jesus was allegedly invented.[101]

In other words, the copycat theory simply can't avoid the need to engage with the historical evidence pertaining to Jesus' life, his death by crucifixion, his burial in a subsequently empty tomb, and so on. The resurrection of Jesus is reported as an observed historical reality, not a "myth." As Carl Braaten confirms: "Even the more skeptical historians agree that for primitive Christianity . . . the resurrection of Jesus from the dead was a real event in history, the very foundation of faith, and not a mythical idea arising out of the creative imagination of believers."[102] As atheist philosopher Kai Nielsen acknowledges concerning the resurrection: "it wasn't a myth that the Christian community tried to purvey, rather they were recording what they actually believed happened."[103]

Mythicism misses the mark

Lee Strobel summarizes the case against Jesus mythicism:

---

98. Mettinger, *The Riddle of Resurrection*, 221.
99. Keener, *The Historical Jesus of the Gospels*, 333.
100. Evans, "Resurrection," 566.
101. Erhman, *Did Jesus Exist?*, 215, 225–26, 230.
102. Braaten, *History and Hermeneutics*, 78.
103. Nielsen, "An Atheist's Rebuttal," 66.

First, "copycat" proponents often illogically assume that just because two things exist side by side, one of them must have caused the other. Second, many alleged similarities are exaggerated or fabricated . . . Third, the chronology is wrong. Writers cite beliefs and practices that postdate the first century in an attempt to argue that they influenced the first-century formation of Christianity. Just because a cult had a belief or practice in the third or fourth century AD doesn't mean it had the same belief or practice in the first century. Fourth, Paul would never have consciously borrowed from pagan religions; in fact, he warned against this very thing. Fifth, early Christianity was exclusivistic; any hint of syncretism in the New Testament would have caused immediate controversy. Sixth, unlike the mystery religions, Christianity is grounded in actual historical events. And seventh, what few parallels remain could reflect a Christian influence on pagan beliefs and practices.[104]

The New Atheists' collective failure to provide any documentary evidence that Christianity "borrowed" it's "essential features" from pagan religious culture reflects the fact that *there is no documentary evidence for this hypothesis.* Instead, the evidence is against the copycat theory. Accepting the copycat theory requires precisely the sort of blind faith in the teeth of overwhelming contrary evidence that New Atheism claims to reject. Little wonder that, as Ronald H. Nash reports: "The tide of scholarly opinion has turned dramatically against attempts to make early Christianity dependent on the so-called dying and rising gods of Hellenistic paganism."[105]

In a 2013 debate in Melbourne, Lawrence Krauss tried to use the copycat thesis as an objection to William Lane Craig's historical case for the resurrection; but under cross-examination Krauss conceded: "One may argue that these connections [between Jesus and pagan myths] are spurious, and I'm willing to accept that."[106] As Rice Broocks says: *"the real myth is that the story of Christ was borrowed from other ancient myths. Christ's story is unique and rooted in history, not mythology."*[107]

Watch: "Pagan Mythology and the Historical Jesus" Youtube playlist: www.youtube.com/playlist?list=PLQhh3qcwVEWgr9fxFD1VqQ33lTqFJYhmR

Read: "Jesus and Pagan Mythology" by William Lane Craig: www.reasonablefaith.org/jesus-and-pagan-mythology

What Are the Gospels? A Comparison with Graeco-Roman Biography by Richard A. Burridge

Reinventing Jesus: How Contemporary Skeptics Miss The Real Jesus And Mislead Popular Culture by J. Ed Komoszewski et al.

The Gospel And The Greeks: Did The New Testament Borrow from Pagan Thought? by Ronald H. Nash

---

104. Strobel, *The Case for the Real Jesus*, 186.
105. Nash, *The Gospel and the Greeks*, 162.
106. Krauss and Craig, "Life, The Universe, and Nothing."
107. Broocks, *God's Not Dead*, 150.

DID JESUS EXIST?

> "It is of no use to say that Christ as exhibited in the gospels is not historical..."
> —John Stewart Mill[108]

> "I am not a believer, but I must confess as a historian that this penniless preacher from Nazareth is irrevocably the very center of history."
> —H.G. Wells[109]

In January 2017, I was astonished to hear cultural critic Jonathan Meades declaring, in a BBC Four documentary on modernist Italian architecture, that Jesus was "probably fictional."[110] It's one thing to think (mistakenly) that the historical Jesus has been obscured from view by layers of mythology. It's quite another thing to think that there was no historical Jesus in the first place. As Helen Bond observes:

> ancient evidence for Jesus is remarkably early and widespread . . . Given that Jesus was a peasant from an insignificant part of the [Roman] Empire, we actually have surprisingly good evidence not only for his existence but for the course of his life and even the contents of his teaching. All of our sources need to be used with care, but there can be no doubt that he existed and that we can say something about him.[111]

It's a mark of the dogmatic, ideological nature of the New Atheism that some of its members promote a denial of the historical Jesus. As Randall Hardman comments:

> the number of times I have heard atheists say Jesus of Nazareth probably didn't exist bewilders me (and really any other scholar, liberal or not) simply on historical grounds, and suggests the term "dogmatic" may apply to certain militant atheists as well as it does to certain militant evangelicals . . .[112]

Dr. Andy Bannister chides neo-atheists for their historical ignorance:

> the New Atheists frequently castigate creationists, ripping into them like a *Tyrannosaurus rex* at an all-you-can-eat hog roast, in particular attacking them for their willful ignorance of the scientific literature. Yet, when it comes to *history*, you could thumb the bibliographies of the New Atheist literature until paper cuts have shredded your fingers to the bone, but you won't find them citing trained historians or their opinions on Jesus and the Gospels: they

---

108. Mill quoted in Kumar, *Christianity for Skeptics*, 85.
109. See: H.G. Wells, "H.G. Wells on the Historicity of Jesus."
110. Meades, "Ben Building."
111. Bond, *Jesus*, 3, 8.
112. Hardman, "Historical Evidences For the Gospels," 225.

are thus the historical equivalent of the Young Earth Creationists they love to criticize.[113]

Unfortunately, the New Atheists are better at promoting their views about Jesus than at researching them. A survey published by the Barna Group in 2015 reported that 22 percent of English people thought Jesus was a mythical figure, while 17 per cent are unsure whether he was real or not.[114] Moreover, 25 percent of 18–34-year-olds in the same survey thought Jesus was a mythical or fictional character.

Mark Allan Powell reports that: "A hundred and fifty years ago a fairly well respected scholar named Bruno Bauer maintained that the historical person Jesus never existed. Anyone who says that today—in the academic world at least—gets grouped with . . . the scientific holdouts who want to believe the world is flat."[115] Flat-earthers shouldn't make comfortable bedfellows for neo-atheists! Nevertheless, Daniel Dennett opines that Jesus is "probably a mythical character,"[116] adding: "I think the evidence that he was a historical personage is pretty thin . . ."[117] Christopher Hitchens, with only a pinch more caution, pondered what he called "the highly questionable existence of Jesus . . ."[118] but elsewhere stated that he didn't "really believe"[119] in Jesus' existence. In a 2011 article Lawrence Krauss was happy to note without caveat that "there are historians who doubt the historical existence of Jesus himself."[120]

According to Michel Onfray: "Jesus' existence has not been historically established."[121] Onfray insinuates a mythological status for Jesus when he states "the Messiah never hungers nor thirsts, he never sleeps . . ."[122] The significance of Onfray's observation is rather undermined by his remark that "Neither does Socrates,"[123] since Socrates is generally recognized as a historical figure. "Did Socrates really exist?," asks Avrum Stroll, "Some scholars, Winspear for example, have argued 'No.' Most historians of the period have rejected this view, and have argued that he did."[124] After all, contemporaneous eyewitnesses such as Aristophanes, Plato and Xenophon all mention Socrates (as does Aristotle).[125] Besides, Onfray has somehow missed the fact that according to the NT Jesus *does* hunger (see: Matthew 26:17–26; Mark 2:15, 3:20, and

---

113. Bannister, *The Atheist Who Didn't Exist*, 119–220.
114. See: www.talkingjesus.org/.
115. Powell, *The Jesus Debate*, 180.
116. Dennett, "Mounting disbelief," 16.
117. Dennett, "Mounting disbelief," 16.
118. Hitchens, *God is Not Great*, 114.
119. Hitchens, *Red Eye*.
120. Krauss, "Dealing with William Lane Craig."
121. Onfray, *Atheist Manifesto*, 115.
122. Onfray, *Atheist Manifesto*, 124.
123. Onfray, *Atheist Manifesto*, 124.
124. Stroll, "Did Jesus Really Exist?," 82–3.
125. See: Richard Kraut, "Socrates"; "Of Course Jesus Existed! Have a Bit of Sense!"

14:12–22; Luke 5:29, 7:33–36, 22:8–15, and 24:41; John 6:12 and 21:15; Acts 1:4), *does* thirst (see: John 19:28) and *does* sleep (see: Mark 4:38; Matthew 8:24). Onfray's conclusion that Jesus is merely "a concept" such that "he existed, but not as a historical figure..."[126] is built on a foundation of sand.

Jerry A. Coyne also references Socrates, stating: "I don't think most scholars would say that Socrates existed with the certainty that Christians (or even atheists like Bart Erhman) would say that Jesus existed."[127] Coyne appears to assume that Socrates' existence is in some doubt in a bid to highlight what he considers the even greater doubt surrounding the existence of Jesus, because he says that he is "surprised at how certain many biblical scholars are that Jesus existed (Bart Ehrman, to give a prominent example)"[128] and declares himself "a Jesus agnostic."[129] Coyne also ventures that "although I am the first to admit that I have no formal training in Jesusology, I think I've read enough to know that there is no credible extra-Biblical evidence for Jesus' existence..."[130] Coyne's too smart for school attitude is clear from his pejorative use of "Jesusology," and from the fact that his vaunted reading on the subject apparently extends to one magazine article by a journalist, an interview with Bart Ehrman, and a skim through a book by atheist Richard Carrier. Coyne seems to feel that his training in science absolves him of the need to conduct more than cursory research into matters outside his field of expertise upon which he wishes to pontificate: "As a scientist, I'll say that I don't regard the evidence that Jesus was a real person as particularly strong."[131]

Paul and Jesus

A further example of Coyne's hubris is his uncritical recycling of an absence of evidence argument much used by mythicists:

> The seven genuine letters of St. Paul [i.e. the undisputed letters of Romans, 1 & 2 Corinthians, 1 Thessalonians, Philippians, Philemon and Galatians] ... mention Jesus, by name or title, over 300 times, but none of them say anything about his life; nothing about his ministry, his trial, his miracles, his sufferings. Paul never uses an example from Jesus's sayings or deeds to illustrate a point or add gravitas to his advice...[132]

---

126. Onfray, *Atheist Manifesto*, 129.
127. Coyne, "It's time to ponder whether Jesus really existed."
128. Coyne, "It's time to ponder whether Jesus really existed."
129. Coyne, "It's time to ponder whether Jesus really existed."
130. Coyne, "It's time to ponder whether Jesus really existed."
131. Coyne, "It's time to ponder whether Jesus really existed."
132. Brian Bethune quoted in Coyne, "It's time to ponder whether Jesus really existed."

Of course, Paul wasn't writing a biography of Jesus, but pastoral letters addressing particular situations in communities with whom he shared an assumed background of knowledge (being part of a "high context" culture[133]):

> Paul's letters . . . are what scholars have called "occasional," responding to questions and problems that have arisen at a particular time in the place to which he is writing. So the fact that he recalls the Last Supper and the resurrection appearances but not other things from Jesus' life and ministry does not prove that he does not know anything else . . .[134]

Nevertheless, Paul's mention of the Last Supper and the resurrection appearances (in the undisputedly authentic 1 Corinthians) are enough to show how uninformed Coyne's agnosticism about Jesus really is. As Helen Bond reminds us:

> Although a native of Tarsis (in modern Turkey), Paul had spent time in Jerusalem and was in the city in the 30s. He knew many of Jesus' closest followers, such as Peter and other disciples, and Jesus' brother James . . . Clearly Paul was in an excellent position to hear reliable information about Jesus of Nazareth, and the date of his letters makes them first-rate testimony.[135]

Richard Dawkins complains that despite being the "earliest books of the New Testament . . . the epistles . . . say almost nothing about Jesus' life . . ."[136] However, A.N. Wilson admits that Paul "knew very well how Jesus died"[137] and adds: "He knew that Jesus was a good man, and, to judge from his letters, Paul also knew what some of the teaching of that good man was."[138]

In fact, Paul's letters reveal knowledge of Jesus' family background, as well as his ministry, teachings, passion and resurrection. Paul knew that Jesus was a Jew, born under the law (Galatians 4:4), a descendant of Abraham (Galatians 4:4) and a descendant of King David[139] (Romans 1:3). He knew Jesus had brothers (1 Corinthians 9:5),

---

133. See: "High-context and low-context cultures."
134. Wenham, *Did St Paul Get Jesus Right?*, 53.
135. Bond, *Jesus*, 6.
136. Dawkins, *Science In The Soul*, 280.
137. Wilson, *Paul*, 59.
138. Wilson, *Paul*, 59.
139. A decade or so ago scholars could truthfully claim that there was no evidence for a historical King David outside the Bible. Given how little survives from the tenth century BC, such a state of affairs wasn't surprising. Nevertheless, those with a bias against trusting the biblical evidence made much of this absence. However, several artefacts have now been discovered that confirm the historicity of King David: (1) The Tel Dan Stele—an inscribed monument erected by an Aramaic king in ancient Syria sometime before 800 BC that makes reference to "Jehoram son of Ahab, King of Israel" and "Ahaziahu son of Jehoram, king of the House of David." Both kings are biblically attested (2 Kings 9–10) and the language of the "House of David" parallels biblical language about the Davidic kingdom. (2) The Mesha Stele—a Moabite monument found in 1868 that, it was later noticed, probably mentions "the house [of Da]vid." (3) The Shoshenq Relief—a carving from the temple of Amun in Thebes that describes Pharaoh Shoshenq's raid into Palestine in 925 BC. In a list of places Shosenq

one of whom was James (Galatians 1:19). He knew Jesus was poor (2 Corinthians 8:9) and humble (Philippians 2:6–11); that he was loving and compassionate (Philippians 1:8) and lived an exemplary life (Romans 15:3 and 8:2; 2 Corinthians 5:21 and 8:9; Philippians 2:6–8). Paul knew that Jesus had a ministry among the Jews (Romans 15:8) and that he had twelve key disciples (1 Corinthians 15:5), including Cephas (i.e. Peter) and John (Galatians 1:19 and 2:9). Paul doesn't just mention, but goes into some detail about Jesus' last supper (1 Corinthians 11:23–25).

Paul carefully distinguishes between Jesus' teachings and his own teachings (1 Corinthians 11:1; 40:10–12; 1 Thessalonians 1:6); but how could Paul do this without any knowledge of what Jesus taught?[140] Indeed, Paul claims Christ as his authority when teaching Christians about divorce (1 Corinthians 7:11) and about supporting preachers (1 Corinthians 9:14). Paul may have been drawing upon the teachings of Jesus when he says taxes should be paid (Romans 13:7) and that the Law of Moses (with respect to human relations) boils down to loving one's neighbor (Galatians 5:14). Paul knew that Jesus taught about blessing those who persecute you (Romans 12:14), repaying no one evil for evil (Romans 12:14), and accepting all foods as clean (Romans 14:14). Paul seems to refer to Jesus' Sermon on the Mount several times in his letter to the Romans (12:14; 12:17; 14:13). Indeed: "repeated references to Jesus' extended discourses suggest that Paul knew more than individual teachings circulating in total isolation from each other. He was at the very least aware of clusters of teachings on similar topics, if not the entire messages themselves."[141] Thus, we should agree with Dale C. Allison that "the persistent conviction that Paul knew next to nothing of the teaching of Jesus must be rejected."[142]

Moreover, Paul knew that Jesus was betrayed at night (1 Corinthians 11:23), that he suffered death by crucifixion (1 Corinthians 2:2), and that having been buried (1 Corinthians 15:4), he was purportedly resurrected "on the third day" (1 Corinthians 15:5; Romans 4:24; Galatians 1:1), appearing to Cephas, to the twelve, to more than five hundred people, to James, and to all the apostles (1 Corinthians 15:5–7). Hence, purely on the basis of Paul's letters, we should agree with Stephen T. Davis that Jesus is "a person about whom we know a great deal."[143]

Watch: "Paul and Jesus" Youtube playlist: www.youtube.com/playlist?list=PLQhh3qcwVEWhQDIEFD5W1dsmnOawCvAIU

Read: *Paul: Missionary of Jesus* by Paul Barnett
   Did St Paul Get Jesus Right? by David Wenham

---

says he captured, a phrase appears that Egyptologist Kenneth Kitchen translates as "heights of David." See: Theophilogue, "Extrabiblical Evidence for King David."

140. See: Davis, *Rational Faith*, 58.
141. Blomberg, *Making Sense of the New Testament*, 76.
142. Allison quoted in Blomberg, *Making Sense of the New Testament*, 106.
143. Davis, "The Mad/Bad/God Trilemma."

Paul And Jesus: The True Story by David Wenham

Setting Stenger straight

Victor J. Stenger observes that "A number of scholars have made the case for the non-historicity of Jesus" before asserting that "their conclusions are convincing."[144] He conveniently fails to mention just how *small* "a number of scholars" have taken this point of view! In defense of this minority opinion Stenger makes the following points:

> There is not a single piece of independent historical evidence for the existence of Jesus or the veracity of the events described in the New Testament. Even the much-touted statement by the Jewish historian Flavius Josephus is now accepted by almost all scholars as a forgery. The paragraph in Antiquities that mentions Christ, his "wonderful works," death on the cross, and appearance three days later does not appear in earliest copies of that work and not until the fourth century.[145]

Stenger is wrong on each and every point.

Independent non Christian evidence

> "outside the gospels, there is almost no ancient source of information on a historical Jesus."
>
> —Clarke Rountree[146]

Readers may recall Stenger's preposterous assertion, to which I promised to return, that "there isn't a shred of independent evidence that Jesus Christ is a historical figure."[147] Onfray makes the only slightly less incautious claim that there are only "two or three vague references" to Jesus "in ancient texts."[148] Meanwhile, Dawkins inaccurately asserts: "There's a suspicious shortage of mentions of [Jesus] in any extrabiblical documents."[149] (Nevertheless, Onfray and Dawkins contradict Stenger's total denial about independent evidence.)

By "independent evidence" Stenger presumably means non-Christian evidence. Stenger's assertion is misguided on two counts. First, it's illegitimate to automatically

---

144. Stenger, *The New Atheism*, 58.
145. Stenger, *The New Atheism*, 58.
146. Rountree, "Faith, Not Reason, Underwrites the Belief in God," 142.
147. Stenger, "Victor J. Stenger," 211.
148. Onfray, *In Defence of Atheism*, 115.
149. Dawkins, *Science In The Soul*, 280.

discount evidence concerning the historical Jesus contained within first- and second-century Christian writings. Second, there's far more than a "shred" of non-Christian evidence for the historical Jesus.

Craig L. Blomberg (Distinguished Professor of New Testament at Denver Seminary) notes that by combining the evidence of first-to-third-century Greco-Roman writers:

> one can clearly accumulate enough evidence to refute the fanciful notion that Jesus never existed, without even appealing to the testimony of Jewish or Christian sources. [This evidence includes] references to his crucifixion, being worshipped as a god, working miracles, having an unusual birth, and being viewed as a sage, king and an instigator of a controversy . . .[150]

Gary R. Habermas summarizes the ancient non-Christian evidence:

> these sources include ancient historians such as Tacitus, Suetonius, and Thallus. Jewish sources such as Josephus and the Talmud add to our knowledge. Government officials such as Pliny the Younger and even Roman Caesars Trajan and Hadrian describe early Christian beliefs and practices. Greek historian and satirist Lucian and Syrian Mara Bar-Serapion provide other details . . . at least seventeen non-Christian writings record more than fifty details concerning the life, teachings, death, and resurrection of Jesus, plus details concerning the earliest church. Most frequently reported is Jesus' death, mentioned by twelve sources. Dated approximately 20 to 150 years after Jesus' death, these secular sources are quite early by the standards of ancient historiography.[151]

Taken together, these sources affirm that:

- Jesus lived during the time of Tiberius Caesar
- He was virtuous
- He worked wonders
- He had a brother named James
- Some people acclaimed him as the Messiah
- He was crucified under Pontius Pilate
- He was crucified on the eve of the Jewish Passover
- Darkness and an earthquake occurred when he died
- His disciples believed he rose from the dead
- His disciples were willing to die for their belief
- Christianity spread rapidly as far as Rome

---

150. Blomberg, *Making Sense of the New Testament*, 251.
151. Habermas, "Why I Believe the New Testament is Historically Reliable."

- Jesus' disciples worshiped him and denied the Roman gods[152]

Particularly well evidenced, being mentioned by twelve non-Christian sources as well as many independent first- and second-century Christian sources, is Jesus' crucifixion.

Independent Christian evidence

Consider the testimony of Ignatius, the bishop of Antioch who was hauled before the local governor for being a Christian: "when he refused to deny Christ he was sentenced to be transported to Rome to be thrown to the lions in the amphitheatre."[153] According to the early church historian Eusebius (c. AD 263–339), Ignatius was martyred in AD 108. The idea behind sending Ignatius to Rome was "to spread the fear of a similar fate to Christians all along the route of the martyr's last journey."[154] However, Ignatius actually became a source of encouragement to Christians, writing seven letters explaining why he was willing to be executed for his allegiance to Jesus: "We still possess these letters . . . and they are among the most important writings of the early church."[155] Bart Erhman comments:

> Ignatius . . . provides us with another independent witness to the life of Jesus. Again, it should not be objected that he is writing too late to be of any value in our quest. He cannot be shown to have been relying on the Gospels. And he was bishop in Antioch, the city where both Peter and Paul spent considerable time in the preceding generation, as Paul himself tells us in Galatians 2. His views [can] trace a lineage straight back to apostolic times.[156]

In his letter to the Ephesians, Ignatius writes about "our God, Jesus"[157] as a spiritual physician who is "fleshly and spiritual . . . God in man . . ."[158] He recounts how:

> God was displayed in human form to bring "newness of life" [see: Romans 6:4] with reference to the new man, Jesus Christ, which consists in faith towards him and love towards him, in his passion and resurrection . . . our antidote to ensure that we shall not die but live in Jesus Christ forever.[159]

Clearly, it was his confidence in a resurrected life through Jesus that lay behind Ignatius's willingness to suffer the death penalty.

---

152. See: Geisler and Turek, *I Don't Have Enough Faith to be an Atheist*, 223.
153. Churchill, *The Blood of Martyrs*, 60.
154. Churchill, *The Blood of Martyrs*, 60.
155. Churchill, *The Blood of Martyrs*, 60.
156. Erhman, *Did Jesus Exist?*, 103–4.
157. Bettenson, *The Early Christian Fathers*, 41.
158. Bettenson, *The Early Christian Fathers*, 41.
159. Bettenson, *The Early Christian Fathers*, 42.

Ignatius encouraged the Trallians about "Jesus Christ, who died for us that you might escape death through faith in his death,"[160] entreating them to ignore those who denied Jesus' humanity:

> Turn a deaf ear to any speaker who avoids mention of Jesus Christ,
> who was of David's line, born of Mary,
> who was truly born, ate and drank;
> was truly persecuted under Pontius Pilate,
> truly crucified and died . . .
> who also was truly raised from the dead,
> the Father having raised him,
> who in like manner will raise us who believe in him[161]

He likewise told the Smyrneans of his:

> full conviction with respect to our Lord that he is genuinely of David's line according to the flesh, son of God according to the divine will and power, really born of a virgin and baptized by John . . . really nailed up in the flesh for us in the time of Pontius Pilate and the tetrarchy of Herod . . . that he might "raise up a standard" for all ages through his resurrection . . . For he suffered all this on our account, that we might be saved. And he really suffered, as he really raised himself. Some unbelievers say he suffered in appearance only. Not so . . . when he came to Peter and his companions he said, "Take hold and feel me, and see that I am not a bodiless phantom." [see: Luke 23:36] And immediately they touched him and believed, when they had contact with his flesh and blood. Therefore also they despised death and proved superior to death.[162]

It's worth emphasizing that the pressing temptation for those attracted to a Jesus-centered spirituality in the first decade of the second century wasn't to deny Jesus' divinity, but to deny his humanity:

> The early church struggled hard to assert the full humanity of Christ against the "modern" and secular ethos that wanted to see him as a wholly divine figure, untouched by the world. The great heretics of the time, Arius, Apollinarius, Nestorius, and Eutyches, all proclaimed a divine Christ.[163]

It's also worth noting that in countering this temptation Ignatius appeals *to the historical testimony of the first Christians concerning the Jesus they knew in the flesh.*

The one personal letter written by Ignatius on his final journey was to Polycarp (c. AD 70–155),[164] a man who was to be a martyr himself and who had been a disciple

---

160. Bettenson, *The Early Christian Fathers*, 44.
161. Bettenson, *The Early Christian Fathers*, 44.
162. Bettenson, *The Early Christian Fathers*, 48–49.
163. Allison, "Modernity or Christianity?," 41.
164. See "Polycarp;" Churchill, *The Blood of Martyrs*, 77–82.

of one of Jesus' own disciples (John the apostle or the elder). Irenaeus (who was in turn Polycarp's disciple) reports that his teacher:

> was not only instructed by apostles, and conversed with many who had seen Christ, but was also by apostles in Asia appointed bishop . . . [He] always taught the things he had learned from the apostles . . .[165]

In his *Letter to Florinus* (preserved by Eusebius) Irenaeus wrote:

> I distinctly recall . . . the very place where the blessed Polycarp used to sit as he discoursed . . . how he would tell of his conversations with John and with the others who had seen the Lord, how he would relate their words from memory; and what the things were which he had heard from them concerning the Lord, his mighty works and his teaching, Polycarp, as having received them from the eyewitnesses of the life of the Logos, would declare . . .[166]

Polycarp was friends with Papias (c. AD 70–130), who had learnt about Jesus from "Ariston, the Elder John, and the [four] daughters of Phillip the evangelist."[167] In a surviving passage from his book *The Exposition of the Oracles of the Lord*, Papias explains:

> If, then, any one who had attended on the elders came, I asked minutely after their sayings—what Andrew or Peter said, or what was said by Philip, or by Thomas, or by James, or by John, or by Matthew, or by any other of the Lord's disciples: which things Aristion and the presbyter John, the disciples of the Lord, say. For I imagined that what was to be got from books was not so profitable to me as what came from the living and abiding voice.[168]

Ignatius was himself "the disciple of John the apostle"[169] (the Greek *apostolos* means "one sent forth as a messenger" and was a term used of Jesus' closest disciples). Moreover, both Eusebius[170] and Theodoret of Cyrrhus[171] (c. AD 393–457) testify that it was the apostle Peter who appointed Ignatius to the position of bishop.

Ignatius suffered a grisly and avoidable death because of his confidence in what Edwin M. Yamauchi calls "the historic underpinnings of Christianity . . ."[172] For Ignatius, those underpinnings weren't primarily provided by the testimony of what we now call the New Testament but by the living and abiding voice of testimony to the life, death, and resurrection of Jesus provided by people known to Ignatius who had

165. Irenaeus, *Against Heresies*, 3.3.4.
166. Irenaeus quoted in Bauckham, *Jesus and the Eyewitnesses*, 35.
167. Barnett, *Finding the Historical Christ*, 77–78.
168. See: Papias, "Fragments of Papias."
169. "The Martyrdom of Ignatius."
170. Eusebius, *Ecclesiastical History*, 3.36.1.
171. Theodoret of Cyrrhus, *Dial. Immutab.*, I.iv.33a.
172. Yamauchi quoted in Strobel, *The Case for Christ*, 89.

themselves known Jesus in the flesh (e.g. Peter and John) or who knew those who had done so (e.g. Polycarp and Papias). The multiple attestation of these witnesses clearly explains why Ignatius had the confidence to write as he did to the Christians in his final destination, Rome: "Let all come, fire and cross and conflicts with beasts, hacking, cutting, wrenching of bones, chopping of limbs, the crushing of my body . . . Only let me attain Jesus Christ . . . an imitator of the passion of my God . . ."[173]

1 Clement is a letter written from the church in Rome to the church in Corinth that tradition attributes to Clement of Rome. Clement was the fourth bishop of Rome from either AD 88 or 92 until he died c. AD 97—101. 1 Clement has been dated as early as the 60s (the letter doesn't mention the ecclesial status of its author). John A.T. Robinson argued for a date of AD 70. Bart Erhman thinks "the letter was written sometime during the 90s . . ."[174] The standard scholarly date for 1 Clement is c. AD 96. In short, 1 Clement is *a first-century source*; one that Erhman describes as "an independent witness not just to the life of Jesus as a historical figure but to some of his teachings and deeds."[175] Clement affirms: "that there shall be a future resurrection, of which [God] has rendered the Lord Jesus Christ the first-fruits by raising Him from the dead."[176]

Josephus and Jesus

"virtually no scholar today . . . doubts that . . .
Josephus did indeed make passing reference to Jesus."

—JOHN DICKSON[177]

Besides the many other non-Christian historical references to Jesus that have escaped his notice, Stenger appears to be ignorant of the fact that Josephus mentions Jesus in two separate passages in the *Antiquities*, as Paul L. Maier (the Russell H. Seibert Professor of Ancient History at Western Michigan University) explains:

> In *Antiquities* 18:63—in the middle of information on Pontius Pilate (A.D., 26–36)—Josephus provides the longest *secular* reference to Jesus in any first-century source [known as Testimonium Flavianum]. Later, when he reports events from the administration of the Roman governor Albinus (A.D. 62–64) in *Antiquities* 20:200, he again mentions Jesus in connection with the death of Jesus' half-brother, James the Just of Jerusalem.[178]

---

173. Bettenson, *The Early Christian Fathers*, 46.
174. Erhman, *Did Jesus Exist?*, 104.
175. Erhman, *Did Jesus Exist?*, 105.
176. Roberts, 1 Clement 24.
177. Dickson, "I'll Eat a Page From My Bible if Jesus Didn't Exist."
178. Maier, "Josephus and Jesus."

Atheist Paul Tobin argues that "Our confidence in the historicity of this account is bolstered by the fact that it was probably an eye witness account . . . at the time of James' execution, the twenty five year old Josephus was a priest in Jerusalem."[179] *Antiquities* 20:200 states that:

> Convening the judges of the Sanhedrin, [Ananus] brought before them the brother of Jesus who was called the Christ, whose name was James, and certain others. He accused them of having transgressed the law and delivered them up to be stoned. But those of the city residents who were deemed the most fair-minded and who were strict in observing the law were offended at this. Accordingly, they secretly contacted the king [Herod Agrippa II], urging him to order Ananus to desist from any more such actions, for he had not been justified in what he had already done.[180]

Maier comments:

> This, Josephus's second reference to Jesus, shows no tampering whatever with the text and it is present in all Josephus manuscripts. Had there been Christian interpolation here, more material on James and Jesus would doubtless have been presented . . . James would likely have been wreathed in laudatory language and styled, "the brother of the Lord," as the New Testament defines him, rather than "the brother of Jesus." Nor could the New Testament have served as Josephus's source since it provides no detail on James's death. For Josephus to further define Jesus as the one "who was called the *Christos*" was both credible and even necessary in view of the twenty other Jesuses he cites . . . Accordingly, the vast majority of contemporary scholars regard this passage as genuine in its entirety . . .[181]

Robert E. Van Voorst reports that "The overwhelming majority of scholars holds that the words 'the brother of Jesus called Christ' are authentic, as is the entire passage in which it is found."[182] The late Jewish NT scholar Geza Vermes (who was Professor Emeritus of Jewish Studies and Emeritus Fellow of Wolfson College, Oxford) affirms that Josephus's note about James "possesses all the appearances of authenticity"[183] and comments that "Josephus's identification of James as 'the brother of Jesus called Christ' would have made no sense unless there was an earlier mention of Jesus in Antiquities . . ."[184] Maier agrees that "the fact that the second reference to Jesus at

---

179. Tobin, "The Death of James."
180. Maier, "Josephus and Jesus."
181. Maier, "Josephus and Jesus."
182. Voorst, *Jesus Outside the New Testament*, 83.
183. Vermes, "Jesus in the Eyes of Josephus."
184 Vermes, "Jesus in the Eyes of Josephus."

Antiquities 20:200 which follows, merely calls him the *Christos* [Messiah] without further explanation suggests that a previous, fuller identification had already taken place."[185]

Turning to the earlier reference in *Antiquities* 18:63, known as the Flavian Testimony or *Testimonium Flavianum* (TF), we read:

> About this time lived Jesus, a wise man, if indeed one ought to call him a man. For he was the achiever of extraordinary deeds and was a teacher of those who accept the truth gladly. He won over many Jews and many of the Greeks. He was the Messiah. When he was indicted by the principal men among us and Pilate condemned him to be crucified, those who had come to love him originally did not cease to do so; for he appeared to them on the third day restored to life, as the prophets of the Deity had foretold these and countless other marvellous things about him, and the tribe of the Christians, so named after him, has not disappeared to this day.[186]

Stenger misleadingly states that this passage "does not appear in earliest copies of that work [i.e. the *Antiquities*] and not until the fourth century."[187] There *is* evidence for the TF in the early fourth century. However, this evidence doesn't feature in a copy of the *Antiquities*, as Stenger implies. Rather, it features as a quotation from the *Antiquities* found in several works by Eusebius. More importantly, Stenger's comments give the false impression (whether wittingly or unwittingly) that our earliest copies of the *Antiquities* not only pre-date the fourth century evidence for the TF, but that these earlier copies lack the TF. He thereby appears to insinuate that someone inserted the TF into the manuscript tradition of the *Antiquities* at some stage between our earliest copies and the fourth century. However, the quotations of the TF in Eusebius aren't just our earliest manuscript evidence for the TF, they are our earliest manuscript evidence for the *Antiquities*. There's no textual evidence against the TF, which is found in every extant manuscript of the *Antiquities*.[188]

Michael Green confirms that the TF "has as good attestation as anything in Josephus. It is included in all the manuscripts. The early church fathers knew it—the fourth century historian Eusebius quotes it . . ."[189] Vermes comments: "The textual evidence—the Greek manuscripts of Josephus, the quotation of the passage in Eusebius, and the Latin, Syriac and Arabic translations—contains no significant variants."[190]

In 1995 G.J. Goldberg used a digital database of ancient literature to identify a possible literary relationship between TF and the Gospel of Luke. He found several

---

185. Maier, "Josephus and Jesus."
186. Maier, "Josephus and Jesus."
187. Stenger, *The New Atheism*, 58.
188. See: Holding, "Secular references to Jesus: Jospehus."
189. Green, *Lies, Lies, Lies!*, 66.
190. Vermes, "Jesus in the Eyes of Josephus."

coincidences in word choice and word order between TF and the summary of Jesus' life in Luke 24:19–21, 26–27, called the "Emmaus narrative":

> And he said to them, "What things?" And they said to him, "Concerning Jesus of Nazareth, a man who was a prophet mighty in deed and word before God and all the people, and how our chief priests and rulers delivered him up to be condemned to death, and crucified him. But we had hoped that he was the one to redeem Israel. Yes, and besides all this, it is now the third day since these things happened" . . . Was it not necessary that the Christ should suffer these things and enter into his glory? And beginning with Moses and all the Prophets, he interpreted to them in all the Scriptures the things concerning himself.

By reading through the Greek of Luke 24:19 on, halting at each noun and verb of action and then looking to the TF for a corresponding phrase at the same location, Goldberg arrives at the following phrase-by-phrase outline of coincident points:

> [Jesus][wise-man/prophet man] [mighty/surprising] [deed(s)] [teacher/word] [truth/(word) before God] [many people] [he was indicted] [by leaders] [of us] [sentenced to cross] [those who had loved/hoped in him] [spending the third day] [he appeared/spoke to them] [prophets] [these things] [and numerous other things] [about him][191]

Goldberg explains: "Each of the nineteen brackets represents a location correspondence and contains the words or summarizes the meaning at each such point."[192] These coincidences led Goldberg to suggest that Josephus and Luke used a common first-century source.

Indeed, Goldberg observes that the Arabic version of the TF, quoted by the tenth-century historian Agapius: "is actually closer to Luke than it is to the Greek Testimonium. This tends to support the theory that Luke's narrative resembles the original version of the Testimonium, a resemblance that a later editor disrupted with interpolations."[193] The Arabic version of the TF reads:

> At this time there was a wise man called Jesus, and his conduct was good, and he was known to be virtuous. Many people among the Jews and the other nations became his disciples. Pilate condemned him to be crucified and to die. But those who had become his disciples did not abandon his discipleship. They reported that he had appeared to them three days after his crucifixion and that he was alive. Accordingly, he was perhaps the Messiah, concerning whom the prophets have reported wonders. And the tribe of the Christians, so named after him, has not disappeared to this day.[194]

---

191. Goldberg, "The Coincidences of the Emmaus Narrative," 6.
192. Goldberg, "The Coincidences of the Emmaus Narrative," 6.
193. Goldberg, "The Coincidences of the Emmaus Narrative," 14.
194. Maier, "Josephus and Jesus."

The original version of the TF was probably closer to this Arabic version than the Greek version quoted by Eusebius. Drawing upon the various manuscript traditions, and upon knowledge about Josephus's use of language, a variety of scholars have offered reconstructions of the original TF along the lines offered here by Vermes:

> About this time there lived Jesus, a wise man . . . For he was one who performed paradoxical deeds and was the teacher of such people as accept the truth gladly. He won over many Jews [and many Greeks?]. He was [called] the Christ. When Pilate, upon hearing him accused by men of the highest standing among us, had condemned him to be crucified, those who had in the first place come to love him did not give up their affection for him . . . And the tribe of the Christians, so called after him, has still to this day not disappeared.[195]

Whatever the precise wording of the original TF, Maier argues:

> Josephus must have mentioned Jesus in authentic core material at 18:63 since this passage is present in all Greek manuscripts of Josephus, and the Agapian version accords well with his grammar and vocabulary elsewhere. Moreover, Jesus is portrayed as a "wise man" [*sophos aner*], a phrase not used by Christians but employed by Josephus for such personalities as David and Solomon in the Hebrew Bible. Furthermore, his claim that Jesus won over "many of the Greeks" is not substantiated in the New Testament, and thus hardly a Christian interpolation but rather something that Josephus would have noted in his own day.[196]

Helen Bond notes that: "While an earlier generation of scholars assumed that the entire paragraph was a later Christian edition, it is more common nowadays to think that it has been altered by a Christian scribe . . ."[197] Bart Ehrman reports that: "The majority of scholars of early Judaism, and experts on Josephus, think that . . . one or more Christian scribes 'touched up' the passage a bit."[198] Maier confirms that the "the large majority position today"[199] among historians is that the *Testimonium Flavianum* "contains Christian interpolations in what was Josephus's original, authentic material about Jesus."[200] For example:

- F. Bermejo-Rubio: "I find most plausible the widespread view that an authentic core goes back to Josephus, although it has been partially interpolated."[201]

---

195. Vermes, "Jesus in the Eyes of Josephus." See: Slick, "Regarding the quotes from the historian Josephus about Jesus."
196. Maier, "Josephus and Jesus."
197. Bond, *Jesus,* 4–5.
198. Erhman, *Did Jesus Exist?*, 60.
199. Maier, "Josephus and Jesus."
200. Maier, "Josephus and Jesus."
201. Bermejo-Rubio, "Was the Hypothetical Vorlage of the Testimonium Flavianum," 326–65.

- Craig L. Blomberg: "most of the passage seems to be authentic."[202]

- R. Marcus: "The most probable view seems to be that our text represents substantially what Josephus wrote, but that some alterations have been made by a Christian interpolator."[203]

- Mark D. Smith: "While most scholars believe that this text contains scribal interpolations by later Christian copyists, the style of most of the text is consistent with Josephus."[204]

- Robert L. Webb: "many scholars conclude that the text probably did originally contain a description of Jesus, but that it was explicitly Christianized by early Christian scribes."[205] Webb affirms that "a non-Christianized version of the *Testimonium Flavianum* was originally present in Josephus' text . . ."[206]

- Edwin Yamauchi: "there's a remarkable consensus among both Jewish and Christian scholars that the passage as a whole is authentic."[207]

Indeed, contrary to the supposedly negative scholarly consensus about the *Testimonium Flavianum* invoked by Stenger, Peter Kirby reports:

> Louis H. Feldman surveyed the relevant literature from 1937 to 1980 in *Josephus and Modern Scholarship*. Feldman noted that 4 scholars regarded the *Testimonium Flavianum* as entirely genuine, 6 as mostly genuine, 20 accept it with some interpolations, 9 with several interpolations, and 13 regard it as being totally an interpolation. In my own reading of thirteen books since 1980 that touch upon the passage, ten out of thirteen argue the *Testimonium* to be partly genuine, while the other three maintain it to be entirely spurious. Coincidentally, the same three books also argue that Jesus did not exist.[208]

At this juncture, it's worth noting Vermes's comment that: "As an historian, Josephus is thought to be generally trustworthy except when he deals with matters in which he himself was involved."[209] It's also worth noting that Josephus (who also mentions the NT figures of James, John the Baptist and Pontius Pilate) wrote the *Antiquities* in the early nineties of the first century, i.e. about sixty years after the crucifixion. Hence, as Van Voorst comments: "If any [non-Christian] Jewish writer were ever in a position to know about the non-existence of Jesus, it would have been Josephus. His implicit

---

202. Blomberg, *The Historical Reliability of the Gospels*, 255.
203. Marcus quoted in Blaiklock, *Jesus Christ*, 29.
204. Smith, *The Final Days of Jesus*, 154.
205. Webb, "The Roman Examination and Crucifixion of Jesus," 685.
206. Webb, "The Roman Examination and Crucifixion of Jesus," 685.
207. Yamauchi quoted in Miller, *Did Jesus Really Rise From The Dead?*, 62.
208. Kirby, "Testimonium Flavianum: Josephus' Reference to Jesus."
209. Vermes, "Jesus in the Eyes of Josephus."

affirmation of the existence of Jesus has been, and still is, the most significant obstacle for those who argue that extrabiblical evidence is not probative on this point."[210]

Maier concludes:

> These passages [*Antiquities* 18:63 and *Antiquities* 20:200], along with other non-biblical, non-Christian references to Jesus in secular first [and second] century sources—among them Tacitus (*Annals* 15:44), Suetonius (*Claudius* 25), and Pliny the Younger (*Letter to Trajan*)—prove conclusively that any denial of Jesus' historicity is maundering sensationalism by the uninformed and/or the dishonest.[211]

Watch: "Josephus on Jesus" Youtube playlist: www.youtube.com/playlist?list=PLQhh3qcwVEWh-7X8CFtPpH8tPwEiVcnVW

Read: "The Coincidences of the Emmaus Narrative of Luke and the Testimonium of Josephus" by Gary J. Goldberg: www.josephus.org/GoldbergJosephusLuke1995.pdf

"The Testimonium Flavianum in Syriac and Arabic" by Alice Whealey: http://khazarzar.skeptik.net/books/whealey2.pdf

---

Inscriptional evidence for Jesus from archaeology

The "James Ossuary" is a mid-first-century limestone ossuary (or "bone box") discovered in the early 1970s but only recognized in 2002 as bearing the significant Aramaic inscription "Ya'akov bar Yosef akhui di Yeshua":

> Jacob, son of Joseph, brother of Jesus

In English, Jacob=James. NT scholar Ben Witherington III comments that: "If, as seems probable, the ossuary found in the vicinity of Jerusalem and dated to about AD 63 is indeed the burial box of James, the brother of Jesus, this inscription is the most important extrabiblical evidence of its kind."[212] The dating of the ossuary dovetails with the date of James's martyrdom (AD 62) reported by Josephus (*Antiquities* XX.9.1).[213]

---

210. Voorst, *Jesus Outside the New Testament*, 99.
211. Maier, "Josephus and Jesus."
212. Witherington quoted in Meister, *Building Belief*, 146.
213. See: Moo, *Tyndale New Testament Commentaries*, 21.

Fig. 2. The James Ossuary.[214]

Joseph M. Holden and Norman L. Geisler report:

> Experts have confirmed the presence of microbial patina on the ossuary and on both parts of the inscription: "James, the son of Joseph" and "brother of Jesus," demonstrating the unity and antiquity of the inscription . . . this patina is generally deemed ancient, without the possibility of it occurring naturally in less than 50 to 100 years, making a recent forgery impossible. The world's leading expert in bio-geology and the patination process, Wolfgang Krumbein of Oldenburg University in Germany, affirmed that the patina on the ossuary and inscription most likely reflects a development process of thousands of years . . . researchers from the Royal Ontario Museum in Toronto confirmed that the patina within the letter grooves is consistent with the patina on the surface of the ossuary; thus legitimizing the entire inscription's antiquity. According to expert paleographers Andre Lemaire and Ada Yardeni . . . the Aramaic is fully consistent with first-century style and practice.[215]

In 2014, a paper in the *Open Journal of Geology* validated the authenticity of the ossuary's inscription.[216] According to the paper's abstract:

---

214. Wikimedia Commons, "The James Ossuary," Paradiso (2005). http://commons.wikimedia.org/wiki/File:JamesOssuary-1-.jpg.

215. Holden and Geisler, *The Popular Handbook of Archaeology and the Bible*, 314.

216. See: Rosenfeld, "The Authenticity of the James Ossuary," 69–78.

An archaeometric analysis of the James Ossuary inscription "James Son of Joseph Brother of Jesus" strengthens the contention that the ossuary and its engravings are authentic.[217]

The patina on the ossuary contains various minerals that result from the activity of microorganisms over a long period of time, thereby demonstrating the antiquity of the ossuary. Moreover, the patina continues gradationally into the engraved inscription, striations on the ossuary crosscut the letters of the inscription, and dissolution pits are superimposed over several letters of the inscription. This evidence shows that the inscription is not a modern addition to an ancient ossuary. Finally: "wind-blown microfossils . . . and quartz within the patina of the ossuary, including the lettering zone, reinforces the authenticity of the inscription."[218] In sum, as Craig A. Evans writes: "Scientific study has determined that the inscription in its entirety is ancient and authentic."[219]

According to Professor Camil Fuchs, a statistician from Tel Aviv University: "with a confidence level of 95 percent, we can expect there to be 1.71 individuals in the relevant population named James with a father named Joseph and a brother Jesus."[220] Furthermore:

> Of those ossuaries bearing an inscription, almost all speak of the deceased occupant's father, and occasionally of the person's brother, sister, or other close relative if that person is well-known. The rare presence of the sibling's name (Jesus) would indicate that Jesus was a very prominent figure.[221]

Paul L. Maier concludes: "there is strong (though not absolutely conclusive) evidence that, yes, the ossuary and its inscription are not only authentic, but that the inscribed names are the New Testament personalities."[222] According to Hershel Shanks, former editor in chief of the *Biblical Archaeological Review*: "this box is [more] likely the ossuary of James, the brother of Jesus of Nazareth, than not. In my opinion . . . it is likely that this inscription *does* mention the James and Joseph and Jesus of the New Testament."[223] Hence the James ossuary plausibly provides inscriptional evidence for the existence of the biblical Jesus from a mere thirty years after the crucifixion.

Listen: "James Ossuary" by Ben Witherington III: http://restitutio.org/2015/10/26/james-ossuary/

---

217. Rosenfeld, "The Authenticity of the James Ossuary," 69.
218. Rosenfeld, "The Authenticity of the James Ossuary," 69.
219. Evans, *Jesus and the Remains of His Day*, 44.
220. Shanks, "The James Ossuary is Authentic."
221. Holden and Geisler, *The Popular Handbook of Archaeology and the Bible*, 314.
222. Maier, "The James Ossuary."
223. Shanks, *The Brother of Jesus*, 64.

Read: "The James Ossuary" by Gary Baxster: www.adefenceofthebible.com/2016/08/01/the-james-ossuary/

"Ossuary of James, son of Joseph and Brother of Jesus" by H. Wayne House: www.hwhouse.com/images/Ossuary_of_James.pdf

"The Aucenticity of the James Ossuary" by Amnon Rosenfeld et al.: http://file.scirp.org/pdf/OJG_2014031213484587.pdf

"'Brother of Jesus' Inscription is Authentic" by Hershel Shanks: http://members.bib-arch.org/publication.asp?PubID=BSBA&Volume=38&Issue=4&ArticleID=2

A historical consensus based on evidence

"for mainstream academics, the view that Jesus never existed belongs in the same category as those who claim that the moon landings were a hoax."

—JUSTIN BRIERLEY[224]

Responding to neo-atheist claims that Jesus didn't exist, atheist historian R. Joseph Hoffmann condemns "the provocative ignorance" of mythicists and states that: "Only in the age of instant misinformation . . . is this kind of idiocy possible . . . we know more about Jesus than we know about a great many figures that we think existed, from far fewer sources . . ."[225]

Atheist NT scholar Gerd Lüdemann states that "Jesus' death as a consequence of crucifixion is indisputable."[226] The Jesus Seminar co-founder John Dominic Crossan confirms: "That he was crucified is as sure as anything historical can ever be."[227] Jewish NT scholar Pinchas Lapide writes that "the death of Jesus of Nazareth on the cross . . . may be considered historically certain."[228] Likewise, Bart Erhman calls Jesus' crucifixion "One of the most certain facts of history."[229] Clearly, if Jesus' crucifixion is an indisputable fact of history, his existence can hardly be less certain!

Erhman observes that the denial of Jesus' existence "has no ancient precedents. It was made up in the eighteenth century. One might well call it a modern myth, the myth of the mythical Jesus."[230] He laments: "There are a lot of people who want to write sensational books and make a lot of money who say Jesus didn't exist, but I don't know any serious scholar who doubts the existence of Jesus . . ."[231] As Groothuis

---

224. Brierley, *Unbelievable?*, 105.
225. Hoffmann, "Mythic Pizza and Cold-Cocked Scholars."
226. Lüdemann, *The Resurrection of Christ*, 50.
227. Crossan, *Jesus: A Revolutionary Biography*, 145.
228. Lapide, *The Resurrection of Jesus*, 32.
229. Ehrman quoted in Licona, *The Resurrection of Jesus*, 600.
230. Erhman, *Did Jesus Exist?*, 96.
231. Erhman, "On the Existence of Jesus."

reports: "Biblical scholars and historians who have investigated this issue in detail are virtually unanimous today in rejecting this view, regardless of their theological or ideological perspectives."[232] For example:

- E.M. Blaiklock: "no responsible historian can dismiss the historical reality of Jesus."[233]

- Marcus Borg: "Jesus really existed, and he really was crucified, just as Julius Caesar really existed and was assassinated . . . We can in fact know as much about Jesus as we can about any figure in the ancient world."[234]

- Maurice Casey: "the whole idea that Jesus of Nazareth did not exist as a historical figure is verifiably false."[235]

- James H. Charlesworth: "The references to Jesus by a Roman historian [Tacitus] and a Jewish historian [Josephus] disprove the absurd contention that Jesus never lived . . ."[236]

- John Dickson: "the basic Gospel narrative that Jesus was a celebrated Galilean teacher and healer who heralded the 'kingdom of God' and died by crucifixion in Jerusalem under Pontius Pilate . . . is the bedrock of historical discussion about Jesus today."[237] Dickson concludes that the New Atheists "are either ignoring" or "deliberately misrepresenting"[238] this historical bedrock.

- Simon Edwards says the view that Jesus didn't exist is "entirely against the weight of modern scholarly opinion."[239]

- Craig A. Evans: "Apart from a few eccentrics, no historian doubts that such a person [as Jesus] actually lived in the first century and that in one sense or another was the founder of a movement that in time became known as Christianity."[240]

- Michael Grant: "if we apply to the New Testament, as we should, the same sort of criteria as we should apply to other ancient writings containing historical material, we can no more reject Jesus' existence than we can reject the existence of a mass of pagan personages whose reality as historical figures is never questioned."[241]

---

232. Groothuis, *Christian Apologetics*, 439.
233. Blaiklock, *Jesus Christ*, 11.
234. Borg, "The Meaning of Jesus: Two Visions."
235. Casey, *Jesus*, 243.
236. Charlesworth, *The Historical Jesus*, 35.
237. Dickson, "The Nouveau Atheists on the Historical Jesus."
238. Dickson, "The Nouveau Atheists on the Historical Jesus."
239. Edwards quoted in Lodge, "New book claiming Jesus did not exist dismissed by historians."
240. Evans, "The Christ of Faith is the Jesus of History," 459.
241. Grant, *Jesus*, 199–200.

- James Hannam: "the idea that [Jesus] never existed is untenable."[242]

- E.A. Judge (Emeritus Professor of History at Macquarie University): "An ancient historian has no problem seeing the phenomenon of Jesus as an historical one. His many surprising aspects only help anchor him in history. Myth or legend would have created a more predictable figure."[243]

- Paul L. Maier: "there is more evidence that Jesus of Nazareth certainly lived than for most famous figures of the ancient past."[244]

- Eric Meyers (Emeritus Professor in Judaic Studies at Duke University): "The details have been debated for centuries, but no one who is serious doubts that [Jesus is] a historical figure."[245]

- Simon Seabag Montefiore writes that the existence of Jesus "is confirmed not only by the Gospels but in Tacitus and Josephus . . ."[246]

- Lydia McGrew: "That Jesus was a real person who died by crucifixion some time in the early first century AD is hardly a matter in historical doubt."[247]

- John Romer: "Jesus lived, of that there can be little doubt."[248]

- Graham Stanton: "Today nearly all historians, whether Christians or not, accept that Jesus existed and that the gospels contain plenty of valuable evidence which has to be weighed and assessed critically."[249]

- Avrum Stroll: "the number of modern, or even relatively modern, scholars who explicitly deny the existence of Jesus is few indeed." Of the hypothesis that Jesus did not exist he states: "I do not think that this conjecture is a likely one."[250]

- Christopher Tuckett (Professor of New Testament Studies and Fellow of Pembroke College Oxford): "The fact that Jesus existed, that he was crucified under Pontius Pilate (for whatever reason) and that he had a band of followers who continued to support his cause, seems to be part of the bedrock of historical tradition. If nothing else, the non-Christian evidence can provide us with certainty on that score."[251]

---

242. Hannam, "A Historical Introduction to the Myth that Jesus Never Existed," xiii.
243. Judge, "Foreword," v.
244. Maier, "Did Jesus Really Exist?," 143.
245. Meyers quoted in Romey, "The Real Jesus," 42.
246. Montefiore, *Jerusalem*, 119.
247. McGrew, "Probabilistic Issues Concerning Jesus of Nazareth," 311.
248. Romer, *Testament*, 166.
249. Stanton, *The Gospels and Jesus*, 145.
250. Stroll, "Did Jesus Really Exist?," 85.
251. Tuckett quoted in Lennox, *Gunning For God*, 189.

- Geza Vermes: "Jesus was a real historical person. In my opinion, the difficulties arising from the denial of his existence, still vociferously maintained in small circles of rationalist 'dogmatists', far exceed those deriving from its acceptance."[252]

This consensus is grounded in the relevant historical evidence. For example, consider how the criterion of *explanatory economy* (i.e. Occam's razor) applies to the existence of Jesus. This takes us back to Philip Pullman's point that our evidence justifies the contention that Jesus was "a great storyteller" who invented "the story about the Good Samaritan."[253] Dr. Peter J. Williams, an affiliated lecturer in the Faculty of Divinity at Cambridge University, points out that there's no evidence for the widespread use of parables prior to Jesus. There are two examples in the Old Testament book of 2 Samuel (see: 2 Samuel 12:1–10; 14:5–20), but there are no parables in the Jewish Apocrypha or the Dead Sea Scrolls, and few if any examples from other Jewish rabbis or from the early church fathers. In other words, the widespread use of parables is a distinctive feature of Jesus' pedagogical style. Parables attributed to Jesus are spread throughout the synoptic gospels.[254] Some parables appear in two or three sources, but others appear uniquely in one source or another. If there was no historical Jesus, then instead of believing in one genius teller of parables, the evidence would lead us to believe in several genius storytellers who just happened to live around the same time and place, all of whom put their parables into the mouth of the same fictional character. This more complex hypothesis strains credulity.

Broadening the point somewhat, C.H. Dodd argues that:

> the first three gospels offer a body of sayings on the whole so consistent, so coherent, and withal so distinctive in manner, style and content, that no reasonable critic should doubt, whatever reservations he may have about individual sayings, that we find reflected here the thought of a single, unique teacher.[255]

Consider the criteria of having *multiple early witnesses*. Geisler points out that while "Most events from the ancient world are known on the basis of one or two writers from the time period or some time after it" the first-century evidence for Jesus collected in the NT comes from (or through) nine different writers: "(Matthew, Mark, Luke, John, Paul, James, Jude, and the writer of Hebrews)."[256] Then there's the extrabiblical Jewish, Roman and Christian evidence from the first and second centuries.

Graham Stanton applies the criterion of *enemy attestation* to the non-Christian data when he notes that "the early Christian's opponents *all* accepted that Jesus existed, taught, had disciples, worked miracles, and was put to death on a Roman cross.

---

252. Vermes, *The Resurrection*, 1.
253. Zaimov, "Atheist Author Phillip Pullman."
254. See: McGuire, A. "List of the Parables of Jesus."
255. Dodd, *The Founder of Christianity*, 33.
256. Geisler, *A Popular Survey Of The New Testament*, 20.

As in our day, debate and disagreement centred largely not on the story but on the significance of Jesus."[257]

Much more could be said; but enough has been said to indicate why, as Keener comments:

> Contrary to some circles on the Internet, very few scholars doubt that Jesus existed, preached and led a movement. Scholars' confidence has nothing to do with theology but much to do with historiographic common sense. What movement would make up a recent leader, executed by a Roman governor for treason, and then declare, "We're his followers"? If they wanted to commit suicide, there were simpler ways to do it.[258]

Grudging admissions of a historical Jesus

"I don't think you can take the easy way out by denying that Jesus ever existed..."

—MICHAEL RUSE[259]

Having been content to draw attention to the existence of "historians who doubt the historical existence of Jesus"[260] in 2011, Lawrence Krauss conceded in 2013 that Jesus "was a real, historical person."[261] Krauss said:

> If you asked me, is the weight of historical evidence such that Jesus was a real historical figure, I would say, the weight of historical evidence is that Jesus was a historical figure... I do not dispute that the weight of historical evidence suggests that he was a real person.[262]

In *The God Delusion* Richard Dawkins acknowledges that "Jesus probably existed..."[263] Nevertheless, the admission is begrudging. It seems calculated to plant doubt in the uninformed reader's mind. Dawkins writes that "it is even possible to mount a serious, though not widely supported, historical case that Jesus never lived at all, as has been done by, among others, Professor G.A. Wells of the University of London..."[264] Dawkins fails to inform readers that Wells is Professor Emeritus *of German Language* at Birkbeck College, London.

---

257. Stanton, *The Gospels and Jesus*, 145.
258. Keener, "Jesus Existed."
259. Ruse, *Atheism*, 134.
260. Krauss, "Dealing with William Lane Craig."
261. Krauss and Craig, "Life, The Universe, and Nothing."
262. Krauss and Craig, "Life, The Universe, and Nothing."
263. Dawkins, *The God Delusion*, 122.
264. Dawkins, *The God Delusion*, 122.

In response to Dawkins's use of Wells, John Dickson wryly asks us to: "Imagine the response from the new atheists if someone were to argue that a serious scientific case can be made that evolution by natural selection has never occurred and then offered as the sole authority a language professor."[265]

Dawkins also fails to inform readers that since the late 1990s Wells has actually accepted that the gospels of Matthew and Luke "may contain a core of reminiscences of an itinerant Cynic-type Galilean preacher . . ."[266] Indeed, James Hannam reports:

> When I met him briefly in 2003, [Wells] accepted that Paul knew that Jesus had been crucified by the Romans in Jerusalem. He also believed that the teaching of Jesus that we find in the Gospels had come from a real Galilean preacher. He just didn't accept that they were one and the same person. I suppose that Wells had gone from believing that there was no historical Jesus to concluding that there were two of them. This is an improvement of sorts.[267]

In the course of a 2008 public discussion with John Lennox at the Oxford Museum of Natural History (which I attended), Dawkins said: "maybe I alluded to the possibility that Jesus never existed. I take that back. Jesus existed."[268] Sam Harris likewise accepts the existence of Jesus, writing of "Jesus, the Buddha, Lao Tzu, and the other saints and sages of history . . ."[269]

Watch: "The Existence of Jesus" Youtube playlist: www.youtube.com/playlist?list=PLQhh3qcwVEWiCALtjBWyxo78Dxxib4g8E

Read: "Did Jesus Exist?" by Gary R. Habermas: www.bethinking.org/jesus/did-jesus-exist

"A Historical Introduction to the Christ Myth" by James Hannam: http://jameshannam.com/christmyth.htm

---

WAS THE IDEA OF JESUS' DIVINITY A LATE DEVELOPMENT?

> "even the most elevated Christological notions are very old indeed."
> —STEPHEN T. DAVIS[270]

Anyone who wants to deny that Jesus saw himself as divine is forced to introduce a sufficient period of time in between the historical Jesus and belief in his divinity (a so-called "high Christology"). This period of time must be long enough for the

---

265. Dickson, "The Nouveau Atheists on the Historical Jesus."
266. Wells, "Earliest Christianity." See: Hannam, "An Evening With G.A. Wells."
267. Hannam, "A Historical Introduction to the Myth that Jesus Never Existed," xvi.
268. Dawkins, "Richard Dawkins Admits Jesus Existed."
269. Harris, *Waking Up*, 5.
270. Davis, *Rational Faith*, 56.

evolution of a high Christology to plausibly take place in the absence of the sort of factors Christians believe shaped the Christology of the first Christians. To posit such an evolution is to embrace an evolutionary Christology. The time period postulated needs to move belief in the divinity of Jesus away from the Jewish roots of Christianity, because it is highly implausible to think that monotheistic Jews like Peter, John, Paul, or James would divinize Jesus without being given sufficient reason to do so. As Green reminds us: "if you had looked the whole world over for more stony and improbable soil in which to plan the idea of an incarnation you could not have done better than light upon Israel!"[271]

Dan Brown's best-selling novel *The Da Vinci Code* popularized an extreme version of the idea that belief in the divinity of Jesus was a late arrival on the theological scene, suggesting the concept was foisted upon Christ by a narrow vote at the Council of Nicea in AD 325.

In *The Da Vinci Code* Professor Teabing and Sophie Neveu discuss the matter as follows:

> "Constantine needed to strengthen the new Christian tradition, and held a famous ecumenical gathering known as the Council of Nicaea. At this gathering," Teabing said, "many aspects of Christianity were debated and voted upon—the date of Easter, the role of bishops, the administration of sacraments, and, of course, the *divinity* of Jesus."
>
> "I don't follow. His divinity?"
>
> "My dear," Teabing declared, "until *that* moment in history, Jesus was viewed by His followers as a mortal prophet . . . a great and powerful man, but a man nevertheless . . ."
>
> "Not the Son of God?"
>
> "Right," Teabing said. "Jesus' establishment as the Son of God was officially proposed and voted on by the Council of Nicaea."
>
> "Hold on. You're saying Jesus' divinity was the result of a *vote*?"
>
> "A relatively close vote at that," Teabing added. "By officially endorsing Jesus as the Son of God, Constantine turned Jesus into a deity who existed beyond the scope of the human world, an entity whose power was unchallengeable."[272]

---

271. Green, "Jesus in the New Testament," 40.
272. Brown, *The Da Vinci Code*, 232–33.

However: "the best historical scholarship shows that simply is not the case."[273] Bart Ehrman explains which aspects of Brown's novel account are fictional:

> this was not a council that met to decide whether or not Jesus was divine . . . everyone at the Council—and in fact, just about every Christian everywhere—already agreed that Jesus was divine, the Son of God. The question being debated was how to *understand* Jesus' divinity in light of the circumstance that he was also human . . . And there certainly was no vote to determine Jesus' divinity: this was already a matter of common knowledge among Christians, and had been from the early years of the religion . . . Christians before Nicea already did accept Jesus as divine; the Gospels of the New Testament portray him as human as much as they portray him as divine; the Gospels that did *not* get included in the New Testament portray him as divine as much, or more so, than they portray him as human.[274]

Ancient historian Paul Barnett responds to the idea that the divinity of Jesus is a late theological development:

> This is simply untrue historically! In the immediate years after Jesus, the New Testament authors refer to him as God [Romans 9:5; Hebrews 1:8; John 1:1]. Paul's letters contain evidence 270 years *before* Nicea that Christians worshipped Jesus as God. Pliny's letter to his emperor, written 215 years *before* Nicea, reports that Christians expressed worship to Jesus, 'as if to a god'.[275]

Writing to the Emperor Trajan, Pliny the Younger (who was governor of Bithynia in Asia Minor) recounts:

> An anonymous information was laid before me containing a charge against several persons, who upon examination denied they were Christians, or had ever been so. They repeated after me an invocation to the gods, and offered religious rites with wine and incense before your statue . . . and even reviled the name of Christ: whereas there is no forcing, it is said, those who are really Christians into any of these compliances: I thought it proper, therefore, to discharge them. Some among those who were accused by a witness in person . . . owned indeed that they had been of that number formerly, but had now (some above three, others more, and a few above twenty years ago) renounced that error . . . They affirmed the whole of their guilt, or their error, was, that they met on a stated day before it was light, and addressed a form of prayer to Christ, as to a divinity, binding themselves by a solemn oath, not for the purposes of any wicked design, but never to commit any fraud, theft, or adultery, never to falsify their word, nor deny a trust when they should be called

---

273. Mittleberg, *The Questions Christians Hope No One Will Ask*, 102.
274. Ehrman, "What was the Council of Nicea?"
275. Barnett, *Messiah*, 120.

upon to deliver it up; after which it was their custom to separate, and then reassemble, to eat in common...²⁷⁶

Note that although Pliny writes this report c. AD 112, the intelligence he passes on about Christians praying "to Christ, as to a divinity" comes from multiple eyewitness sources who claim to have renounced their faith "above twenty years ago," that is, c. AD 92, which is *59 years after* the crucifixion.

The anti-Christian Greek philosopher Celsus (writing c. AD 177–80) stated that Jesus "gave himself the title of God."²⁷⁷ Likewise, writing c. AD 165–75, the Greek satirist Lucian of Samosata wrote of Christians as those who "worship the crucified sage."²⁷⁸

Watch: "The Truth About the Council of Nicea": http://youtu.be/WSKBGdvo7nQ

"The Real Da Vinci Code with Tony Robinson": https://youtu.be/UAtoP5nFhh4

Read: "What was the council of Nicea?" by Bart D. Ehrman: www.beliefnet.com/Faiths/Christianity/2005/06/What-Was-The-Council-Of-Nicea.aspx

Breaking the Da Vinci Code by Darrell L. Bock

Exploring "The Da Vinci Code": Investigating the Issues Raised by the Book and Movie by Lee Strobel and Gary Poole

The Gospel Code: Novel Claims about Jesus, Mary Magdalene and Da Vinci by Ben Witherington III

Archaeological evidence of belief in the divinity of Jesus

The archaeological record provides a material case sufficient in and of itself to debunk the claim that, prior to the council of Nicea, Jesus was viewed by his followers merely as a prophet.

Dura-Europos wall paintings

The early third-century church at Dura-Europos (in modern-day Syria) contains a baptistery with several significant wall paintings dated to around AD 240, including:

> Christ Healing the Paralytic . . . one of Jesus' earliest healings from Mark 2. Then there is a picture of the Good Shepherd, a popular image amongst the earliest Christian art. Also shown is the story from Matthew 14 of Jesus and Peter walking on the water . . . although Jesus' face appears not to have

---

276. See: "Pliny, Letters 10.96-97": http://faculty.georgetown.edu/jod/texts/pliny.html
277. Celsus in Origen's *Contra Celsus*, 1.38.
278. Habermas, *The Historical Jesus*, 206.

survived. Lastly there is what appears to be part of a picture of the two/three women at Jesus' empty tomb.[279]

There is also a painting of a woman drawing water out of a well. This is probably a depiction of the Samaritan woman at Jacob's well to whom Jesus talks in John's Gospel. The crux of their conversation is Jesus' claim to be the Messiah and the source of eternal life (John 4:5–41). These paintings contain the earliest known depictions of Jesus, and bear testimony to belief in both the divinity and resurrection of Jesus.

The painting of Christ healing a paralytic (Fig. 3) depicts a clean-shaven Jesus in a toga with an outstretched right arm, standing over and pointing at a figure lying upon a rather substantial bed. To their left, a male figure carries his bed upon his back. This is a "before" and "after" picture. Everett Ferguson writes:

> The healing miracle might be either from John 5:2–9 (where the reference to the pool suggested a baptismal interpretation) or the synoptics (Matthew 9:2–8; Mark 2:1–12, where the healing of the paralytic is associated with Jesus' power to forgive sins).[280]

It seems to me that the baptismal context actually favors the synoptic interpretation, where the narrative is focused upon the apparently blasphemous authority of Jesus as "the Son of Man" to pronounce the forgiveness of sin on his own authority, rather than John 5's relatively incidental mention of water. This being so, one of the earliest extant paintings of Jesus may well depict an incident the central point of which is Jesus making an indirect claim to divinity (Fig. 3). Atheist historian Michael Grant acknowledges that "Jesus . . . claimed that he *himself* could forgive sins."[281]

---

279. Dyke, "Earliest Known Picture of Jesus Goes on Display."
280. Ferguson, *Baptism in the Early Church*, 442.
281. Grant, *Jesus*, 50.

Fig. 3.

Jesus' reported self-designation as "the good shepherd" (John 10:11)—represented in the painting directly above the baptistery (Fig. 4)—can be seen as a claim to both Messiahship (see: Micah 5:2) and divinity (see: Ezekiel 34:11–12 and Psalm 23) as Jesus is represented as applying to himself a title that the Old Testament Scriptures apply to God.

Fig. 4.

The picture of Jesus walking on the water (Fig. 5, see: Matthew 14:25–33), when read against the Old Testament background (see: Job 9:8), can likewise be seen as depicting an enacted claim to divinity.

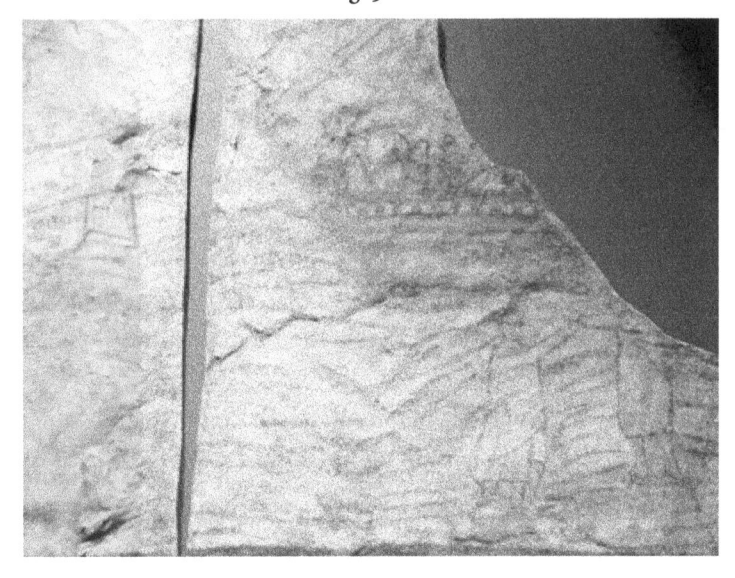

Fig. 5.[282]

Then there's a painting that shows some women approaching the (empty) tomb of Jesus (Fig. 6). They are holding lighted candles, indicating that they are walking in

---

282. Picture credit Simon Jenkins, used with permission. See: Williams, *Digging For Evidence*.

the gloom of the early dawn (see: Matthew 28:1, Mark 16:2, Luke 24:1 and John 20:1). The women are also carrying bowls, probably indicating spices being brought for the purpose of anointing the body of Jesus (see: Mark 16:1 and Luke 24:1). The artist has depicted the inside of the tomb as being decorated with vine patterns painted onto the walls.[283] An example of just such a decoration can be seen in a tomb excavated for the Jordanian Department of Antiquities in 1959 by Hassan Awad Qutshan, known as tomb Q-4.[284] In the gospels, the significant point of the event herein depicted is of course that the women discover that Jesus' tomb was empty, bearing indirect witness to his resurrection from the dead and thereby also to his divinity.

Fig. 6 (Part of the scene of women visiting Jesus' tomb).[285]

These paintings indicate that around a century before the Council of Nicea some people *believed* that Jesus did and said things that indirectly laid claim to divinity, and that they *believed* Jesus wrought miracles in confirmation of the truth of his claims. Against the background of his crucifixion for blasphemy, Jesus' resurrection—referenced by the fourth painting—is obviously the premier miraculous confirmation thereof.

Finally, the fact that these paintings adorn a baptistery is significant:

> The early church adopted a form of baptism from their Jewish upbringing, called proselyte baptism. When Gentiles wanted to take upon themselves the laws of Moses, the Jews would baptize those Gentiles in the authority of the God of Israel. But in the New Testament, people were baptized in the name of

283. See: "Removal of fill from inside of the Christian House Church at Dura Europos."
284. See: "Abila—Tomb Q-4."
285. Picture credit Simon Jenkins, used with permission. See: Williams, *Digging For Evidence*.

God the Father, God the Son, and God the Holy Spirit [see: Matthew 28:19[286] as well as Acts 2:38, 10:48 and 1 Corinthians 1:13]—which meant they had elevated Jesus to the full status of God.[287]

Christian Church near Megiddo

Archaeologist Yotam Tepper and epigraphist Leah Di Segni have dated a church discovered in 2005 near Megiddo to c. AD 230.[288] Writing in *National Geographic News*, Mati Milstei comments that: "Dating to roughly the third century, it is popularly accepted as the oldest church ever discovered."[289] Vassilios Tzaferis (who thinks that the church dates to the second half of the third century) writes:

> Tepper... exposed... probably the earliest church ever discovered in the Holy Land (the excavators date it to the first half of the third century, around 230 A.D.) and one of the very few churches from this early period anywhere in the world—from a time before Christianity became the religion of the Roman empire in the early fourth century during the reign of Constantine the Great.[290]

The remains primarily consist of a series of mosaics grouped around a stone plinth that once held a table used for the celebration of communion. One large mosaic displays at its center a picture of several fish. The fish was an early Christian symbol due to the acrostic formed from the letters of the Greek word for fish (*Ichthys*): Iēsous Christos Theou Yios Sōtēr. That is: "Jesus Christ, God's Son, Savior." For example, discussing an early fifth-century mosaic discovered at Stobi, Ruth E. Kolarik observes: "The large Greek letters... inscribed into the geometric pattern, form the common acrostic for the name of Christ followed by a cross."[291] Hence the fish mosaic at Megiddo plausibly testifies to belief in Jesus as "God's Son."

Even more impressive is a Greek inscription (Fig. 7) about the donation of the table placed in the center of the hall (the plinth of which is still extant) for the celebration of communion. This reads:

> The God-loving Akeptous has offered the table to God Jesus Christ as a memorial.

---

286. The baptism formula from Matthew 28:19 is also found in *Didache* 7:1. See: Shamoun, "A Series of Answers to Common Questions."

287. Moreland quoted in Strobel, *The Case for Christ*, 275.

288. See: "Prison Makes Way for the Holy Land's Oldest Church;" Tepper, *A Christian Prayer Hall of the Third Century CE at Kefar 'othnay (legio)*.

289. Milstei, ""Oldest Church"" Discovery "Ridiculous," Critics Say."

290. Tzaferis, "Inscribed to 'God Jesus Christ.'"

291. Kolarik, "Mosaics of the Early Church at Stobi," 295–306.

Fig. 7.[292]

Charlie Campbell comments: "This discovery at Megiddo demonstrates that a belief in Jesus' deity was already in place long before the fourth century."[293]

Watch: "Megiddo Church": https://youtu.be/a2lcDvAMzQ8
Read: "Oldest church found? Inscribed "to God Jesus Christ'" by Vassilios Tzaferis: www.bib-arch.org/online-exclusives/oldest-church-02.asp

---

The Alexamenos graffito

This stark piece of graffiti, discovered on a wall near the Palatine Hill in Rome in 1857, dates to "c. AD 200."[294] It depicts a man named Alexamenos, who stands with an up-stretched arm facing a donkey-headed figure on a cross. In rough-hewn scratches the picture is accompanied by a Greek inscription that means "Alexamenos worships/worshipping god." The only known crucifixion victim that Alexamenos might have worshiped is Jesus. Indeed, the late second-century Christian writer Tertullian tells of an arena worker in Carthage who had a picture ridiculing the Christian God by showing him with the head of a donkey.[295]

It's worth pondering the fact that, in the ancient Roman context of this graffiti, one simply wouldn't worship a crucified man, not unless one thought that something *extraordinary* happened that somehow set aside the shame of his crucifixion.

292. Image from Williams, *Digging for Evidence*.
293. Campbell, *Archaeological Evidence for The Bible*, 119.
294. Bauckham, *Jesus: A Very Short Introduction*, 96.
295. See: Roberts et al., *The Ante-Nicene Fathers Vol. III*, 31.

Getting at the Historical Jesus

Fig. 8. Alexamenos Graffito

Read: "Alexamenos Execution Graffito" by H. Wayne House: www.hwhouse.com/images/8.ALEXAMENOS_CRUCIFIXION_GRAFFITI.pdf

---

Nuovo catalogo epigrafico 156.

As reported in a September 2011 article on Livescience.com:

> Researchers have identified what is believed to be the world's earliest surviving Christian inscription . . . Officially called NCE 156, the inscription is written in Greek and is *dated to the latter half of the second century*. . . NCE 156. . . alludes to Christian beliefs . . . Gregory Snyder, of Davidson College in North Carolina . . . who detailed the finding in the most recent issue of the *Journal of Early Christian Studies*, believes it to be a funeral epigram, incorporating both Christian and pagan elements . . .[296]

These mixed elements suggest that the inscription is of a gnostic provenance. As translated by Snyder, the inscription reads:

296. Jarus, "World's Earliest Christian Engraving Shows Surprising Pagan Elements."

Getting at Jesus

> To my bath, the brothers of the bridal chamber carry the torches,
>
> [here] in our halls, they hunger for the [true] banquets,
>
> even while praising the Father and glorifying the Son.
>
> There [with the Father and the Son] is the only spring and source of truth.[297]

Despite the possible influence of second-century gnostic beliefs, here we find "the Son" being glorified in the same breath as praise is offered to "the Father" (i.e. God). We also find "the Father" and "the Son" being treated *together* as "the only spring and source of truth." As Dean L. Overman observes: "the gnostic gospels, as the vast majority of New Testament scholars agree, proclaim a gnosticism that emphasizes that Jesus was too divine to be human, not that he was only a human and not divine."[298]

Digging down to a high Christology

In sum, archaeological evidence demonstrates that belief in the deity of Jesus pre-dates the Council of Nicea by *well over a century* (Fig. 9). Moreover, since belief in the deity of Jesus was spread over a wide geographical area (the relevant archaeological evidence comes from places as far-flung from Jerusalem as Dura-Europos and Rome) the origins of this belief must predate the archaeological evidence by a time period sufficient to account for its geographical spread and appearance in the material culture.

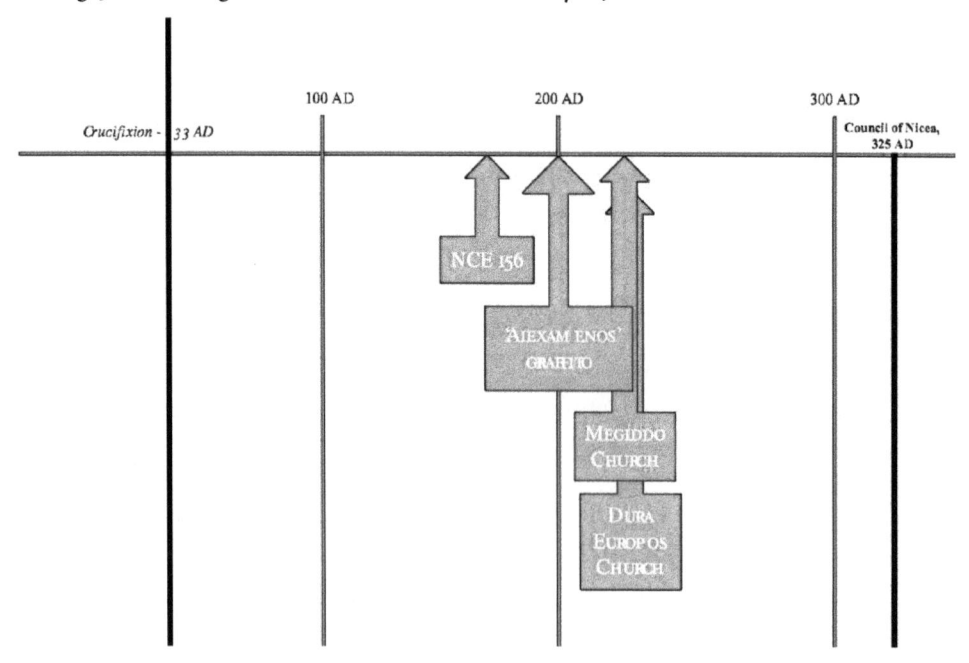

Fig. 9. Archaeological evidence of belief in the divinity of Jesus before the Council of Nicea

---

297. Jarus, "World's Earliest Christian Engraving Shows Surprising Pagan Elements."
298. Overman, *A Case for the Divinity of Jesus*, 5.

High Christology in the epistolary literature

Whilst avoiding the extremes of *The Da Vinci Code*, novelist Matthew Kneale asserts that "Jesus had never considered himself a god"[299] and that "in the first decades after his death, Jesus still appears to have been regarded by his followers—including Paul—as thoroughly human and not a god,"[300] but that "By the early second century. . . Jesus had become fully supernatural."[301] The Jesus Seminar co-founder Robert W. Funk suggests a four-stage development within which Jesus went from being seen as a mere human who became "a son of God by virtue of his resurrection" to being thought of as "pre-existent from the beginning" by the time of the Gospel of John towards the end of the first century.[302] Atheist John W. Loftus appeals to Funk's thesis to support his own claim that Christians gradually "developed a higher, more glorified view of Jesus"[303] in a process of deification "that took at least seventy years . . ."[304] We can call the end of this supposed seventy-year process "the Loftus line" (c. AD 103).

Luke Timothy Johnson observes that "Paul's letters (and probably other epistolary literature such as James and Hebrews) provide first-hand evidence for the Christian movement in its first three decades."[305] Reading the NT letters (see Fig. 10 for a chart showing the dates of these letters), it's hard to see how the first-century followers of Jesus could have been any clearer in affirming their belief in his divinity. For example, the writer of Hebrews (c. AD 65) addresses Jesus as Christ by declaring: "Thy throne, O God, is for ever and ever" (Heb 1:8).[306]

J.P. Moreland notes that "we possess from seven to thirteen letters from the hand of Paul. Most of these letters are dated from 49 to 65."[307] Alister McGrath confirms that Paul's letters "date mainly from the period AD 49–69, and provide confirmation of the importance and interpretations of Jesus in this formative period."[308] As Geisler reports: "Even critical scholars agree that 1 Corinthians was written by c. AD 55 to 56, and 2 Corinthians, Romans, and Galatians were written shortly thereafter. Yet these books provide the same basic information about the life, teaching, death, and resurrection of Christ found in the Gospels."[309] Paul Barnett comments:

---

299. Kneale, *An Atheist's History of Belief*, 125.
300. Kneale, *An Atheist's History of Belief*, 106.
301. Kneale, *An Atheist's History of Belief*, 125.
302. Funk, *Honest to Jesus*, 279–96.
303. Loftus, *Why I Became An Atheist*, 329.
304. Loftus, *Why I Became An Atheist*, 330.
305. Johnson, *The Real Jesus*, 87.
306. See: Bruce, *The Epistle to the Hebrews*, 59–60; Fudge, *Hebrews: Ancient Encouragement For Believers Today*, 52–53; Montefiore, *A Commentary on the Epistle to the Hebrews*, 47.
307. Moreland, *Scaling the Secular City*, 148.
308. McGrath, *Jesus: Who He Is and Why He Matters*, 69.
309. Geisler, *A Popular Survey Of The New Testament*, 23.

there are early copies (of copies?) of Paul's original letters that have survived and are safely housed in museums around the world. Furthermore, as well as their earliness, the number and wide geographic distribution of editions of the whole NT mean that textual critics are able to reconstitute versions of Paul's original texts that are for practical purposes what Paul actually wrote. Disputed readings of Paul's texts are minimal and are usually limited to isolated words. As well, the next wave of Christian writers (in the early second century) quotes extensively from Paul and provides a further check alongside his manuscripts.[310]

The so-called "undisputed" letters of Paul—Galatians, 1 Thessalonians, Romans, 1–2 Corinthians, Philippians, and Philemon—were all written by the early sixties AD. These letters "confirm at least thirty-one facts recorded in the Gospels"[311] and demonstrate that "a concept of a divine Jesus was already present, at the latest, within sixteen to twenty years after the crucifixion."[312]

For example, in his letter to Titus (c. AD 64), Paul calls Jesus "our great God and Savior" (2:13). Likewise, in 1 Thessalonians 3:11–13 (c. AD 50) Paul *prays to* "our God and Father himself and our Lord Jesus."[313]

Moreover, as I. Howard Marshall observes:

> One of the most important insights of modern Pauline study is its realisation that at point after point Paul was not the great innovator who recreated Christianity in his own image; his indebtedness to his Christian predecessors was deep and far-reaching, and there was no essential point at which he was far out on a limb compared with his predecessors.[314]

---

310. Barnett, *Paul: Missionary of Jesus*, 3.
311. Geisler, *A Popular Survey Of The New Testament*, 26.
312. Moreland, *Scaling the Secular City*, 148.
313. See: Schmit, "The Contribution of 1 Thessalonians 3:11–13 to a Pauline Christology."
314. Marshall, *I Believe in the Historical Jesus*, 69.

Fig. 10. Approximate dates of the New Testament letters.[315]

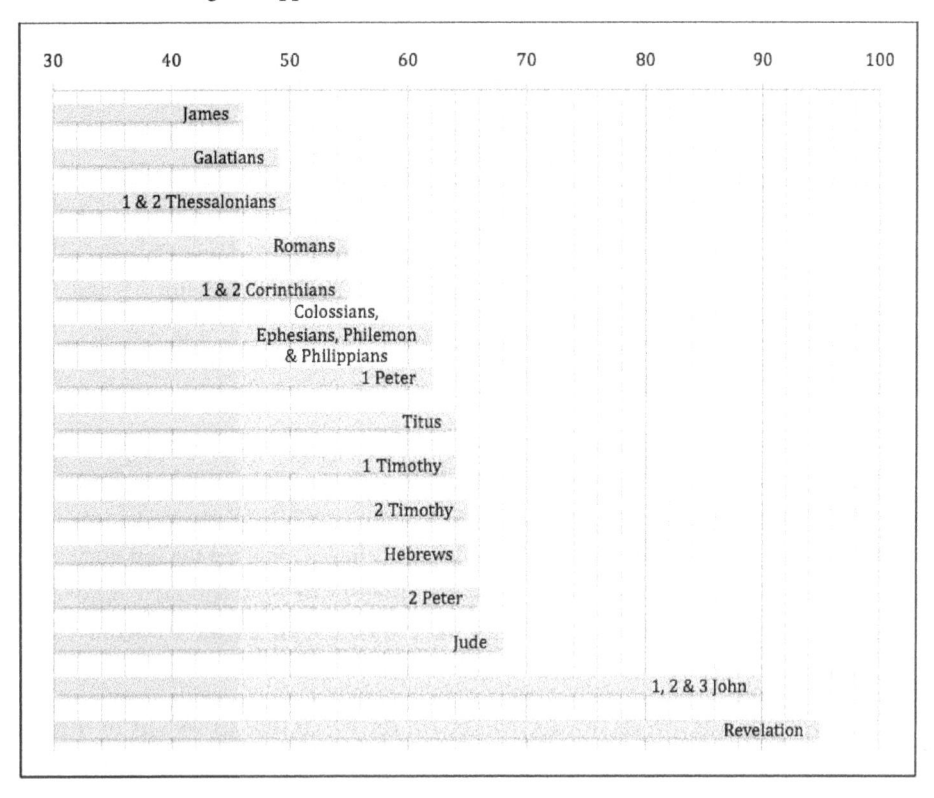

Letter	Approximate Date Range
James	~35–48
Galatians	~40–55
1 & 2 Thessalonians	~45–55
Romans	~50–60
1 & 2 Corinthians	~48–58
Colossians, Ephesians, Philemon & Philippians	~55–65
1 Peter	~55–65
Titus	~60–70
1 Timothy	~55–70
2 Timothy	~60–70
Hebrews	~60–70
2 Peter	~60–70
Jude	~60–70
1, 2 & 3 John	~85–95
Revelation	~90–100

High Christology in the epistle of James

The first-century epistle of James offers a particularly interesting case study in high Christology, since the letter "reflects the issues and theology of early Jewish Christians."[316] James not only refers in exulted terms to "the Lord Jesus Christ" (James 1:1), describing his readers as "believers in our glorious Lord Jesus Christ" (James 2:1), but talks to them about "the ones who are *blaspheming* the noble name of him to whom you belong" (James 2:7, emphasis mine).[317] Although the Greek for "blaspheming" can refer to speech that "speaks evil of" or "reviles" non-divine persons, the context clearly favors taking the term as a reference to blaspheming *in the strongest sense*[318] and this is how most English translations understand the reference.[319]

---

315. Chart draws upon various sources, including: *NIV Thompson Student Bible*; *The Apologetics Study Bible*; Geisler, *A Popular Survey of the New Testament*.

316. Serrao, *James: A Commentary in the Wesleyan Tradition*, 23.

317. See: Bible Hub Commentaries, "James 2:7."

318. See: *Thayer's Greek-English Lexicon of the New Testament*, 102; Bible Hub Commentaries, "blasphémó."

319. See: Bible Hub Commentaries, "James 2:7;" "James 2:7." 'Parallel English translations' can be found at https://biblehub.com/james/2-7.htm & 'Commentaries on James 2:7' can be found at https://biblehub.com/commentaries/james/2-7.htm.

Getting at Jesus

Calling Jesus "Lord"

In light of the Jewish *Shema*—"Hear, O Israel: The Lord our God, the Lord is one" (Deuteronomy 6:4)—Paul Barnett argues that by calling Jesus *Lord*, early Christians like Paul and James were:

> identifying the risen and ascended Jesus with the Lord of the Old Testament. This is clear from Paul's words, which echo but radically adapt the Jewish creed ... "There is *one* God, the Father ... and one Lord, Jesus Christ" (1 Corinthians 8:6). The *one* Lord of his Jewish faith Paul now redefined as the *one* Father and the *one* Lord.[320]

As Dean L. Overran explains:

> By the time of Jesus' birth, devout Jews avoided speaking the Hebrew name for God because the word was considered too sacred to be pronounced out loud. God's name was composed of four Hebrew letters: YHWH (*Yahweh*), known as the Hebrew tetragrammaton. When Jewish believers referred to God, they used the Hebrew word *adonai* in speaking about or to God. Among Greek-speaking Jews, the Greek word *kyrios* was read out loud for the tetragrammaton (*Yahweh*).[321]

Linguistically, the Greek word *kyrios* could refer to *a* lord as well as to *the* Lord (i.e. *adonai* or *Yahweh*). However, Josephus reports that first-century Jews refused to address the Roman emperor as *kyrios* because they believed this term should only be applied to *Yahweh*.[322] Since the first disciples were Jewish, Overman argues that:

> When the early church proclaimed that "Jesus is Lord," it was using *kyrios* in its most exalted sense. For example, the author of the first letter of Peter, writing in the early 60's, ascribes to Jesus an Old Testament passage in which the term "Lord" refers to the Hebrew *Yahweh*. In First Peter 3:15, the author writes: "... but in your hearts sanctify Christ as Lord (*kyrios*)." (Careful study shows that "Christ" in the New Testament always refers to Jesus.) This passage refers to Isaiah 8:13: "*Yahweh Saboath*, him you shall sanctify."[323]

Moreover, James describes Jesus as not only "Lord," but as "the Lord of glory" (James 2:1). According to Douglas J. Moo: "This translation, which takes *doxēs* as a descriptive genitive dependent on 'Lord', is probably correct. Paul describes Jesus similarly in 1 Corinthians 2:8 and James is fond of this type of genitive construction."[324] To refer to Jesus in this way "suggests particularly the heavenly sphere to which he has

---

320. Barnett, *Messiah*, 40.
321. Overman, *A Case for the Divinity of Jesus*, 21–22.
322. See: Overman, *A Case for the Divinity of Jesus*, 22.
323. Overman, *A Case for the Divinity of Jesus*, 23.
324. Moo, *Tyndale New Testament Commentaries: James*, 92.

been exulted and from which he will come at the end of history to save and to judge (See Jas 5:9)."³²⁵

The application of "Lord" to Jesus in the Epistle of James evinces an early, high Christology amongst Jewish Christians.

"Blaspheming the noble name"

The Greek word *Christianos* comes from *Christos*, meaning "anointed one," plus an adjectival ending borrowed from Latin to denote adhering or belonging to (as in slave ownership). The Septuagint translation of the Old Testament used *Christos* to translate the Hebrew word *Mašiaḥ* (Messiah), meaning "[one who is] anointed." So, Christians are those who are called upon by the name of, belong to, and/or are slaves of Jesus "the Christ," where "Christ" is "the noble name of him," i.e. Jesus, to whom Christians adhere or belong. The NLT translation of James 2:7 makes this explicit:

> Aren't they the ones who slander Jesus Christ, whose noble name you bear?

Several translations of the Bible contextually link James's description of the Christian belonging to the noble name with the Christian practice of being baptized into the name of Christ:

- "Don't they blaspheme the noble name that was pronounced over you at your baptism?" (HCSB)
- "Is it not they who blaspheme the noble name that was invoked over you?" (NABRE)
- "Is it not they who blaspheme the excellent name that was invoked over you?" (NRSV)
- "Aren't they the ones who scorn the new name—'Christian'—used in your baptisms?" (MSG)

Christians originally described themselves as "followers of 'the way'" (see: John 14:6, Acts 19:9, 19:23, 22:4, 24:14, 24:22, and perhaps Romans 3:17 and 9:31). The use of "Christian" began as "outsider language":

- Tacitus informs us in his *Annals* (15:44) that the Emperor Nero blamed the AD 64 Great Fire of Rome upon those "whom the crowd called Christians."
- The letter known as 1 Peter, written in Rome, shows (see: 1 Peter 4:16) that the crowd's terminology had been appropriated by at least some in the Jesus-following community by c. AD 62.³²⁶

---

325. Moo, *Tyndale New Testament Commentaries: James*, 92–93.

326. On the dating of 1 Peter, see: Clowney, *The Message of 1 Peter*; Grudem, *Tyndale New Testament Commentaries: 1 Peter*; Marshall et al., *Exploring the New Testament*, 285–88; Powers, *New Beacon Commentary: 1 & 2 Peter, Jude*.

- Luke reports Herod Agrippa II teasing Paul the Apostle c. AD 61 by saying: "In a short time would you persuade me to be a Christian?" (Acts 26:28, ESV).
- Indeed, Luke notes that "the disciples were called Christians first in Antioch." (Acts 11:26.) The context here suggests that the term "Christian" was already in use by critics of "the way" c. AD 46.

James's talk of "the noble name of him to whom you belong" is clearly a reference to the term "Christian" (i.e. "One who is a slave of Christ") being used as a term of abuse, and it follows that James's reference to "the ones who are blaspheming the noble name of him to whom you belong" (James 2:7) is a reference to people blaspheming Jesus Christ.

James 2:7 echoes several Old Testament passages that speak of humans being "called upon" *by God's name* (Deuteronomy 28:10; 2 Chronicles 7:14; Isaiah 4:1, and Amos 9:12). As Heinrich Meyer observes: "The expression . . . is borrowed from the O.T., where it often occurs, and in the sense that one becomes the property of him whose name is called upon him; particularly it is said of Israel that the name of God was called upon them."[327]

Interestingly, in Luke's report of the Council at Jerusalem (c. AD 49), James quotes the Septuagint translation of the prophet Amos, to the effect that "the rest of mankind may seek the Lord, even all the Gentiles who bear my name, says the Lord, who does these things" (Acts 15:17).[328] Thus James 2:7 puts Jesus Christ into the position of God in the Old Testament.

This conclusion is re-enforced by James's elliptical style, for as *The Expositor's Greek New Testament* explains:

> the omission of all mention of the name, which would have come in very naturally, betrays Jewish usage; as Taylor truly remarks. . . "A feeling of reverence leads the Jews to avoid, as far as possible, all mention of the Names of God. This feeling is manifested . . . in their post-canonical literature, even with regard to less sacred, and not incommunicable Divine names. In the Talmud and Midrash, and . . . in the Rabbinic writings generally, it is the custom to abstain from using the Biblical names of God, excepting in citations from the Bible; and even when Elohim is necessarily brought in, it is often intentionally misspelt . . ."

Indeed, the International Standard Version translation of James 2:7 footnotes "the noble Name" with the comment "i.e. God," while The Voice translation makes the connection explicit within the text: "Aren't they the ones mocking the noble name of our God, the One calling us?"[329]

---

327. See: "James 2:7 Commentary."

328. See: Hicks, "James Interprets Amos 9:11-12;" Braun, "James' Use of Amos at the Jerusalem Council."

329. See: Bible Hub Commentaries, "James 2:7 Commentaries;" "Blasphemy."

The Authorship of James

A consideration of the authorship of the Epistle of James isn't a precondition for the fruitful discussion of either the publication date of the letter or the significance of its high Christology, but it is helpful. So-called "liberal" scholars often attribute the epistle to an admirer of James writing under a pseudonym between AD 80 and 100. In favor of this view, scholars from Erasmus to Joseph F. Kelly[330] have argued that the Greek of the letter is too good to be plausibly attributed to a Galilean Jew. The same supposition leads other scholars to suggest that James's original material was later reworked by an unknown editor (a more complex compositional theory that lacks manuscript evidence).[331] It has also been suggested that the mention of elders in James 5:14 reflects a church leadership more advanced than existed prior to the fall of Jerusalem. Catholic theologian Scott Hann responds to these arguments:

> scholarship continues to produce evidence that Galilee was thoroughly bilingual during the NT period (Aramaic and Greek), so the ability of a Palestinian Jew, especially one who was intellectually gifted, to write in excellent Greek is far from impossible (e.g., the Jewish historian Flavius Josephus was educated in first-century Jerusalem and acquired an impressive command of Hellenistic Greek, as well as classical Greek literature). Second, unless one disregards the Book of Acts as a witness to history, it is clear that a hierarchical system of leadership (with 'elders' or 'presbyters') had emerged well before the end of the first century (Acts 14:23; 20:17; cf. 1 Peter 5:1–2).[332]

Sophie Law confirms that "it is no longer possible to assert with complete confidence that James of Jerusalem could not have written the good Greek of the epistle, since the wide currency of language in Palestine is increasingly appreciated."[333] Craig S. Keener points to "excavations showing that most of Galilee was not as backward as was once thought" and to "the widespread use of amanuenses (scribes) who might, like Josephus's editorial scribes, help a writer's Greek. This last point would be especially appropriate for the leader of the mother church, in the one overwhelmingly Jewish city that also provided advanced education in Greek works (cf. the Greeks in Acts 15:23–29)."[334] Besides, as Alec Motyer points out: "Artistic skills and exceptional abilities owe nobody an explanation. Time and again they arise where least expected."[335]

As for church leadership, Michael J. Townsend observes that according to James:

---

330. See: Kelly, *An Introduction to the New Testament for Catholics*, 222.

331. See: Wallace, "James: Introduction, Outline, and Argument."

332. Hann and Mitch, *Ignatius Catholic Study Bible, The Letter of St. James, the First and Second Letters of St. Peter and the Letter of St. Jude*, 13.

333. Laws quoted in Motyer, *The Message of James*, 19. See: Richardson, *The New American Commentary: James*, 23–24.

334. Keener, *The IVP Bible Background Commentary: New Testament*, 668.

335. Motyer, *The Message of James*, 17.

Those who hold authority within the Christian community are simply teachers (3.1) or elders (5.14) from which it seems as if the various orders of Christian ministry have not by this stage managed to develop into anything like the formal positions we find in say, 1 Cor. 12:28, let alone the Pastoral Epistles. It also fits well with the kind of leadership Luke describes in the Jerusalem church at this period (Acts 11.30; 15.2; 16.4; 21.18).[336]

In sum: "the arguments proposed for later dates [and thus non-traditional authorship] lack impressiveness."[337] Moreover, even if it were correct, the liberal dating of the epistle nevertheless permits it to stand in contradiction to the Council of Nicea thesis advanced by Dan Brown. The lower end of the liberal date-range is likewise incompatible with the theory of an evolving Christology that took at least seventy years to attribute divinity to Jesus.

James of Jerusalem, son of Joseph and brother of Jesus

There's a strong cumulative case for attributing the epistle to James the brother of Jesus:

Unanimous testimony

On the one hand, early church fathers such as Athanasias, Cyril of Jerusalem, Eusebius, and Origen unanimously attributed the Epistle of James to James the (half) brother of Jesus. No alternative author was ever suggested in ancient times.[338]

Argument by elimination

On the other hand, the other men by the name of James known from the NT are generally thought not to have been prominent enough to write an authoritative general epistle:

> Two men of this name were among the apostles of Jesus: James son of Zebedee (Mk 1:19; 3:17) and James son of Alphaeus (Lk 6:15; Acts 1:13) . . . but most scholars think it improbable that either one wrote the Letter of James—the former was martyred in AD 44, probably too early to have been the author (Acts 12:2) and very little is known about the latter . . . Instead, scholars through the centuries have given preference to a third figure of the apostolic age: James of Jerusalem, also known as "the Lord's brother" (Gal 1:19).[339]

---

336. Townsend, *The Epistle of James*, xxxi.
337. Motyer, *The Message of James*, 18.
338. See: "The Authorship of James" in Holding, *Trusting the New Testament*, 221.
339. Scott and Mitch, *Ignatius Catholic Study Bible, The Letter of St. James, the First and Second Letters of St. Peter and the Letter of St. Jude*, 13. See: Moo, *Tyndale New Testament Commentaries:*

Getting at the Historical Jesus

Local Knowledge

James of Jerusalem obviously fits the geographical situation of the epistle:

> James lived in Jerusalem . . . and his readers are probably to be found in the regions just outside of Palestine along the coastline to the north, In Syria and perhaps southern Asia Minor. Several allusions in the letter, most notably the reference to the "earlier and latter rains" (5:7), seem to confirm this location; for only along the eastern coast of the Mediterranean Sea do the rains come in this sequence.[340]

Jewishness

The highly Jewish nature of the epistle, including its reverence for the Jewish Law and the book of Proverbs, is consistent with the background of someone like James.

Linguistic links

There are linguistic similarities (Fig. 11) between the epistle and both the speech of James at the Council of Jerusalem reported by Luke in Acts 15 and the letter sent under the authority of James as recorded in Acts 15:23–29.

Fig. 11.

Epistle of James	James in Acts 15
Listen, my beloved brothers	Brothers, listen
the noble name of him to whom you belong	the Gentiles who bear my name
my beloved brethren	our beloved Barnabas and Paul

Authorial prominence

The lack of any qualifying designation specifying which James is writing the letter indicates that no further explanation was needed: "the opening self-description of James as a 'servant of the Lord Jesus' (Jas 1:1) . . . presupposes that he is already known to his readers and feels no need to assert his authority or credentials."[341] The brother of Jesus would certainly fit the requirement for a James who needs no introduction:

James, 13.
  340. Moo, *Tyndale New Testament Commentaries: James*, 36.
  341. Moo, *Tyndale New Testament Commentaries: James*, 36.

A pseudonymous author, hoping to borrow the reputation of James for himself, would more likely have described him in exulted rather than humble terms. Or, at least, he would have given a sufficiently explicit description of James to help readers identify which of the ancient Jameses he was claiming to be.[342]

Peter H. Davids agrees that "there was but one James in the early church who was well enough recognized to be able to use such a simple greeting and that was James the son of Joseph . . ."[343]

The epistle of James, from James

In sum, "All the characteristics of the letter support the traditional attribution of it to James the brother of the Lord."[344] Thus Alister McGrath concludes: "The letter of James was probably [written by] James the brother of Jesus . . ."[345] Many other NT scholars reach the same conclusion:[346]

- James B. Adamson affirmed the "probability that the Epistle is by James, the Lord's brother."[347]

- Kent Dobson: "The author . . . was probably the brother of the Lord and the leader of the Jerusalem council . . . martyred c. AD 62, an event recorded by the Jewish historian Josephus (*Antiquities*, 20.9.1)."[348]

- Walter A. Elwell and Robert W. Yarbrough write that the author of James "is most likely James the (half-) brother of Jesus . . ."[349]

- Donald Guthrie concludes: "the authorship of James, the Lord's brother, must still be considered more probable than any rival."[350]

- Luke Timothy Johnson: "there are strong reasons for arguing that the extant letter was composed by James of Jerusalem, whom Paul designates as 'brother of the Lord.' . . . the preponderance of evidence makes that position one that can be held with a high degree of confidence."[351]

---

342. Moo, *Tyndale New Testament Commentaries: James*, 36.
343. Davids, "James," 1354.
344. Doulas and Tenny, *Zondervan Illustrated Bible Dictionary*, 691.
345. McGrath, *NIV Bible Handbook*, 477.
346. See: Holding, "The Authorship of James," 221–24; Cook, "Introduction to the Letter of James;" Howe, "The Letter of James."
347. Adamson, *The Epistle of James*, 22.
348. Dobson, "James: Introduction," 1579.
349. Elwell and Yarbrough, *Encountering the New Testament*, 345.
350. Guthrie, *New Testament Introduction*, 746.
351. Johnson, *Brother of Jesus*, 3.

- Craig S. Keener rejects pseudonomy (whilst allowing for the involvement of an editor) and states: "the material in the letter should be viewed as genuinely from James."[352]
- I. Howard Marshall, Stephen Travis and Ian Paul agree: "There is . . . no strong reason to question the tradition of authorship by James of Jerusalem."[353]
- Douglas J. Moo argues for "James, the Lord's brother, as the most likely author of the epistle."[354]
- Daniel B. Wallace affirms: "The traditional view, that James the Just, the brother of our Lord, is the author, stands as most probable over against any other James and over against any claim of pseudonymity."[355]

Dating the epistle of James according to its author

Hegesippus (c. AD 165–175, as preserved by Eusebius) tells us that James was stoned to death for refusing to renounce his faith in Jesus.[356] James's martyrdom is independently confirmed by Josephus (*Antiquities* XX.9.1) in a manner that enables us to date the event to AD 62.[357] Corroboration of this date comes from the James Ossuary.

If James the brother of Jesus is indeed the author of James's letter, then it must have been written before his death. Moreover, because James writes to "the twelve tribes scattered among the nations" (James 1:1) the letter must date from long enough after Jesus' crucifixion for the Christian belief in his resurrection and divinity to have spread a fair way: "The Epistle must have been written, therefore, sometime between the late A.D. 30s and the early A.D. 60s."[358]

Dating the epistle of James apart from its author

There are good reasons for dating the Epistle of James prior to the Jewish War (which began in AD 66) quite apart from consideration of the letter's authorship. Hann observes that "Evidence within the letter is generally supportive of an early date."[359] John

---

352. Keener, *The IVP Bible Background Commentary*, 668.
353. Marshall et al., *Exploring the New Testament*, 266.
354. Moo, *Tyndale New Testament Commentaries: James*, 20.
355. Wallace, "James."
356. See: "Hegesippus."
357. See: Moo, *Tyndale New Testament Commentaries: James*, 21.
358. Elwell and Yarbrough, *Encountering the New Testament*, 345.
359. Hann and Mitch, *Ignatius Catholic Study Bible, The Letter of St. James, the First and Second Letters of St. Peter and the Letter of St. Jude*, 13.

Drane concurs that "a number of facts suggest very strongly that it belongs to an early period of the church's life rather than a later one."[360] For example:

- There are signs of James in *The Shepherd of Hermas* (c. AD 85–140)[361] and in the first letter of Clement (often dated to AD 96 but possibly as early as AD sixties).[362]

- "In favour of the early date are the striking simplicity of church organization and discipline, the fact that Christians still met in the synagogue (Jas. 2:2), and the general Judaic tone."[363] Hann concludes that the epistle of James comes from "a time . . . before Christianity and Judaism had irrevocably distinguished themselves from one another . . ."[364]

- Drane notes that "much of the imagery of James is clearly Palestinian. The mention of 'autumn and spring rains' (5:7) would have meant nothing at all in other parts of the Roman empire, while the agricultural practices mentioned in the preceding verses are of a type that disappeared for good in Palestine after AD 70, but which were widespread in the days of Jesus."[365]

- Keener states: "The situation depicted in the letter best fits a period before A.D. 66 (the Jewish war with Rome) . . ."[366]

Given just this data, we might agree with Peter H. Davids in dating the Epistle of James to the mid-sixties.[367] Alister McGrath suggests that the epistle was written "at some point in the late 50's or early 60's."[368] Townsend suggests that "a date somewhere between 55 and 66 is the most likely."[369] I. Howard Marshall, Stephen Travis and Ian Paul likewise suggest the letter was written "most likely between AD 50 and 66."[370] However, there's more evidence to take into consideration.

For example, Douglas J. Moo points to "the absence of any reference to the controversy between Jew and Gentiles, particularly with respect to the 'ritual law.'"[371] In

---

360. Drane, *Introducing The New Testament*, 415.

361. For a defense of the earlier dating of *The Shepherd of Hermas*, see: Robinson, *Redating the New Testament*.

362. See: Holding, "The Authorship of James," 221.

363. Douglas and Tenny, *Zondervan Illustrated Bible Dictionary*, 692.

364. Hann and Mitch, *Ignatius Catholic Study Bible, The Letter of St. James, the First and Second Letters of St. Peter and the Letter of St. Jude*, 13. See: Moo, *Tyndale New Testament Commentaries: James*, 13.

365. Drane, *Introducing The New Testament*, 415.

366. Keener, *The IVP Bible Background Commentary: New Testament*, 668.

367. See: Davids, "James."

368. McGrath, *NIV Bible Handbook*, 477.

369. Townsend, *The Epistle of James*, xxxv.

370. Marshall et al., *Exploring the New Testament*, 267.

371. Moo, *Tyndale New Testament Commentaries: James*, 35.

particular, James shows no awareness of the Acts 15 council (c. AD 49), "which would have been relevant to his theme had it already occurred."[372]

Noting similarities between parts of James's letter and teachings of Jesus reported in Matthew's Gospel, John Drane argues that:

> the writer of James knew these sayings of Jesus in a slightly different form than they now have in the New Testament gospels . . . and the fact that some of this teaching has a more primitive form in James than it does in Matthew might imply that James has access to it at an earlier stage than the writers of the gospels.[373]

According to Davids:

> No other letter of the NT has as many references to the teaching of Jesus per page as this one does. It is not that James quotes Jesus directly, although he sometimes does (see in 5:12), but he normally simply uses phrases and ideas which come from Jesus. His readers would have memorized much of the Lord's teaching, so they would recognize the source. Most of these phrases come from the teaching of Jesus now in Matthew's Sermon on the Mount (Mt. 5–7) or Luke's Sermon on the Plain (Lk. 6).[374]

Johnson likewise notes "the way James's speech is shaped by the sayings of Jesus. And when we realize that the form of some of the more certain allusions is simpler than the redacted form of the sayings found in the Synoptics, then we appreciate that James may be very close indeed to the formative stage of the Jesus traditions."[375] That is: "the use of an early form of the Jesus tradition suggests that the letter of James was written either before the composition of the Synoptic Gospels, or at the very least before their version of Jesus' teachings became standard."[376]

I won't go into the dating of the synoptic gospels at this juncture (this is a topic we will examine later). However, I believe there are good arguments for dating the publication of Luke and Matthew some time around the early sixties, arguments that therefore add to the case for dating James to within two-to-three decades of the crucifixion. Indeed, the parallel between James 1:6 and Mark 11:22–24 suggests that James was written prior to the publication of Mark's Gospel, which I would place in c. AD 49. Even on a more standard dating of Mark (c. AD 65–75[377]), this point alone would still place James early in the second half of the first century.

---

372. Geisler, *A Popular Survey of the New Testament*, 243.
373. Drane, *Introducing The New Testament*, 414.
374. Davids, "James," 1354.
375. Johnson, *Brother Of Jesus Friend Of God*, 38.
376. Johnson, *Brother Of Jesus Friend Of God*, 154.
377. See: Cline, "Dating and Origins of Mark's Gospel."

Moo observes that "The general social conditions in the Near East in the middle of the first century also correspond with the situation presupposed in James."[378] For example, the merchants who ranged far and wide in search of profits (4:13–17) and the wealthy, often "absentee" landlords who exploited an increasingly large and impoverished labour force (5:1–6) were familiar figures."[379] Another familiar feature of the times were the Zealots, who sought to win freedom for Israel by violent means: "Some scholars, in fact, think that James 4:2—'you desire and do not have; so you kill'—may refer to zealot partisans who had brought their violent ideology into the church."[380]

Furthermore, Professor Barry D. Smith argues that a relationship exists between the letter of James and the letters of Paul, especially Romans and Galatians:

> Paul must contend with Jewish believers who determined that gentiles should submit to the Law as a condition of final salvation; because of James' authority . . . his opponents use portions of the Letter of James in support of their position. This forces Paul to correct their erroneous extrapolations . . . and, in so doing, sometimes to appear to be in direct opposition to James . . . (It is probable that the Letter of James quickly reached Antioch, where Paul resided, from Jerusalem.) . . . On the assumption that Paul had read the Letter of James before he wrote his Letter to the Galatians . . . the *terminus a quo* [for the publication of James] is some time before 48, when Paul probably wrote the Letter to the Galatians . . .[381]

Finally, Smith argues:

> If James wrote his letter before 48 A.D, then the persecution that he mentions in the present tense as still occurring (see Jas 1:2–12) could be the result of the persecution of the church instigated by Herod Agrippa I . . . In addition, it is possible that the references to helping the poor who are hungry and naked (see Jas 2:1–17) could be inspired by the fact that there were Jewish believers who were suffering deprivation during the famine that occurred c. 45–46.[382]

As Johnson observes: "Everything in the letter and everything lacking from the letter help confirm the impression that this social world was one shared by a leader of the Jerusalem church and Jewish messianists of the diaspora during the first decades of the Christian movement."[383] Hann likewise argues that James comes from "the earliest decades of the Church, i.e. at a time when the mission field of the gospel was still

---

378. Moo, *Tyndale New Testament Commentaries: James*, 36.

379. Moo, *Tyndale New Testament Commentaries: James*, 36.

380. Moo, *Tyndale New Testament Commentaries: James*, 36–37. See: Reiher, "Violent Language—a clue to the Historical Occasion of James."

381. Smith, "James."

382. Smith, "James."

383. Johnson, *Brother Of Jesus Friend Of God*, 122.

concentrated in Israel and its environs . . ."³⁸⁴ Other scholars venture more precise estimates for the date of James's letter:

- James H. Charlesworth: "Some experts . . . think that the Epistle of James, which contains the most allusions to Jesus' thoughts in the New Testament corpus (except for the Gospels), derives from Jesus' brother [and] probably took shape between 30 and 60 C.E."³⁸⁵

- Kent Dobson: "Some date the letter in the early 60s. There are indications, however, that it was written before AD 50."³⁸⁶

- Donald Guthrie wrote of James that "a date before AD 50 . . . has much to be said for it and is probably to be preferred."³⁸⁷

- Mark Allan Powell: "a date in the late 40s to mid-50s might make the most sense . . ."³⁸⁸

- R. Gregg Watson: "James was probably written between A.D. 48 and 52 . . ."³⁸⁹

- Craig L. Blomberg: "The Epistle of James may in fact be the earliest of all the New Testament documents, written in the late 40s."³⁹⁰

- According to Paige Patterson: "many scholars are convinced that James is the first book of the New Testament to be written, some dating it as early as A.D. 48."³⁹¹

- John A.T. Robinson thought James was written c. 47–48 AD.³⁹²

- Henry Thiessen dated James from 45 to 48 AD.³⁹³

- Kendell H. Easley: "the epistle is likely to be dated between 44 and 49, with the year 45 being a reasonable estimate . . ."³⁹⁴

- Daniel B. Wallace writes: "It is our tentative conclusion that James was written . . . c. 44–45 [AD], making it the earliest writing in the New Testament canon."³⁹⁵

---

384. Hann and Mitch, *Ignatius Catholic Study Bible, The Letter of St. James, the First and Second Letters of St. Peter and the Letter of St. Jude*, 13. See: Moo, *Tyndale New Testament Commentaries: James*, 13.
385. Charlesworth, *The Historical Jesus*, 41.
386. Dobson "James: Introduction," 1579.
387. Guthrie, *New Testament Introduction*, 753.
388. Powell, *Introducing the New Testament*, 451.
389. Watson, "James," 1347.
390. Blomberg, *Making Sense of the New Testament*, 60.
391. Patterson, "James the Letter."
392. Fernandes and Larson, *Hijacking The Historical Jesus*, 144.
393. Fernandes and Larson, *Hijacking The Historical Jesus*, 144.
394. Easley, *Holman Quick Source Guide To Understanding The Bible*.
395. Wallace, "James."

In sum, the author and audience of the Epistle of James were early-mid first-century Jewish monotheists who considered Jesus Christ to be their divine Lord. The evidence favors the traditional attribution of authorship to James of Jerusalem, the (half) brother of Jesus. This attribution both makes the high Christology of the letter all the more startling and suggests a publication date before AD 62 (when James was martyred).

Even apart from the evidence for James of Jerusalem being the author, there's every reason to date the epistle and its Christology to before the Jewish War that began in AD 66 (i.e. within 33 years of the crucifixion). Indeed, there's strong evidence for Alister McGrath's conclusion that James was written no later than "the late 50's or early 60's."[396] There's some reason to think that Daniel B. Wallace (Professor of New Testament Studies at Dallas Theological Seminary) is correct when he concludes "that James was written . . . c. 44–45, making it the earliest writing in the New Testament canon."[397] As Phil Fernandes and Kyle Larson conclude: "A date of 45 AD for James's epistle is not extreme."[398]

Of course, the author of James arrived at his belief in Jesus' divinity *before* writing his epistle. Likewise, the recipients of the epistle obviously arrived at their belief in Jesus' divinity, and were suffering the abuse of being called "Christians," at some time *before* the epistle was written to them. Since the intended audience were "scattered among the nations" (James 1:1), sufficient time must have passed for the gospel message—including the belief that Jesus was divine—to have gone out from Jerusalem where Christianity originated to the then-current geographical spread of this Jewish-Christian diaspora. These factors plausibly push the high Christology reflected in James's letter back by several years.

Since the balance of evidence suggests that the epistle was published c. AD 45, and since belief in the divinity of Jesus pre-dates its publication, we may conclude that the Epistle of James offers us glimpses of the high Christology embraced by Jewish Christians *within a decade of the crucifixion*. At the very least, the Epistle of James demonstrates the high Christology of Jewish Christians *before the Jewish War*. Either scenario excludes the sort of evolutionary Christology proposed by the likes of Loftus, Kneale, Funk and Brown.

---

396. McGrath, *NIV Bible Handbook*, 477.
397. Wallace, "James."
398. Fernandes and Larson, *Hijacking The Historical Jesus*, 144.

Fig. 12. The plausible range of dates for the Epistle of James, c. 12–27 years after the crucifixion and thus c. 43–58 years before the "Loftus line" for the evolution of a high Christology.

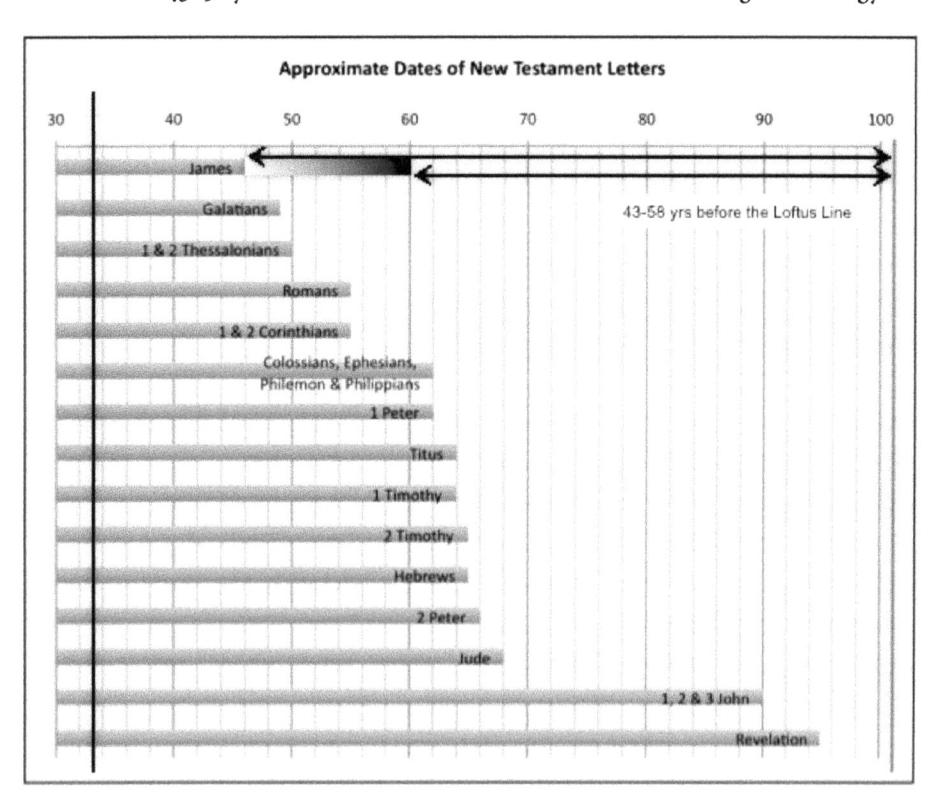

Early creeds and hymns

J.P. Moreland draws attention to the fact that:

> Paul's letters contain a number of creeds and hymns [e.g. Rom 1:3–4; 1 Cor. 11:23 ff.; 15:3–8; Phil. 2:6–11] . . . they use language which is not characteristically Pauline, they often translate easily back into Aramaic, and they show features of Hebrew poetry and thought-forms. This means that they came into existence while the church was heavily Jewish and that they became standard, recognized creeds and hymns well before their incorporation into Paul's letters.[399]

These and other early NT creeds and hymns testify to "the death, resurrection, and deity of Christ. They consistently present a portrait of a miraculous and divine Jesus who rose from the dead . . . In sum, the idea of a fully divine, miracle-working Jesus who rose from the dead was present during the first decade of Christianity."[400]

---

399. Moreland, *Scaling the Secular City*, 148–49.
400. Moreland, *Scaling the Secular City*, 149.

Getting at Jesus

The crucified Lord of glory

Paul quotes a hymn in his letter to the Philippians c. AD 60–62. This speaks of Christ Jesus "being in the form of God [*en morphe theos*]" prior to his incarnation, wherein he took up "the form of a servant, being born in the likeness of men" (see: Philippians 2:6–7, ESV).

Although the NIV translates *en morphe theos* as "being in very nature God," the majority of instances where *morphe* and its cognates occur mean simply "outward appearance."[401] However, by describing Jesus as "being in outward appearance God" the hymn presents a metaphorical "picture of the pre-existent Christ clothed in the garments of divine majesty and splendour,"[402] garments "by which His divine nature may be known."[403] The hymn assumes that Christ rightfully deserves the public status indicated by these poetic divine garments, but goes on to explain that despite "being in outward appearance Divine, Christ didn't count it something to be held onto [i.e. 'grasped for personal advantage'], to be like God ('*isa*[404] *Theō*')" (Philippians 2:6, my translation). That is, Jesus didn't stand on his rights and exploit his status for personal gain. More specifically, he didn't count receiving public recognition as someone who could rightfully be wrapped up within the divinity of God in the Jewish sense of the term as more important than becoming our "servant" on a publically shaming cross:

> being found in human form, he humbled himself by becoming obedient to the point of death, even death on a cross. (Philippians 2:8, ESV)

Paradoxically, this inglorious crucifixion of Jesus simultaneously hides and reveals his true glory. Philippians 2:9–11 proceeds to quote God's words about himself in Isaiah 45:23 and to apply them *to Jesus*:

> Therefore God exalted him to the highest place and gave him the name that is above every name, that at the name of Jesus "every knee should bow," in heaven and on earth and under the earth, and "every tongue confess" that Jesus Christ is Lord, to the glory of God the Father.

Charles A. Wanamaker explains that these verses "are a remarkable statement because they predicate to Christ Lordship which Isa 45:23 reserves for God alone . . ."[405] As Michael Green comments: "In the face of this, to argue that the full deity of Christ was only gradually asserted after decades had rolled by is not only inaccurate, it is very bad scholarship. Jesus was accorded this status by his followers from the earliest days of the Christian church."[406]

---

401. Fabricatore, *Form of God, Form of a Servant*.
402. O'Brien, *Philippians*.
403. Behm, *TDNT*, 4:752.
404. See: Bible Hub Commentaries, "isos."
405. Wanamaker, "Philippians," 1398.
406. Green, "Jesus in the New Testament," 24.

High Christology in the first decades of Christianity

Having made an in-depth study of the earliest Christians' devotion to Jesus (including Philippians 2:5–11) theologian Larry W. Hurtado concludes that:

> well within the first couple of decades of the Christian movement . . . Jesus was treated as a recipient of religious devotion and was associated with God in striking ways . . . devotion to Jesus was not a late development . . . it was an immediate feature of the circles of those who identified themselves with reference to him . . . this intense devotion to Jesus, *which includes reverencing him as divine*, was offered and articulated characteristically within a firm stance of exclusivist monotheism . . .[407]

Elsewhere, Hurtado observes that:

> our earliest Christian writings . . . presuppose cultic devotion to Jesus as a familiar and defining feature of Christian circles wherever they are found . . . So, instead of an evolutionary/incremental model, we have to think in terms of something more adequate . . . a religious development that was more like a volcanic eruption.[408]

James D.G. Dunn comments on "the striking fact that within a few years the first Christians were speaking about Jesus in divine terms" and notes that the earliest testimony to this belief "comes from Jews . . . the most fiercely monotheistic race of that age."[409] As Muslim-turned-Christian Nabeel Qureshi came to admit:

> The very earliest Christian records are unanimous: Jesus is God. All four gospels teach that Jesus is divine, and even before they were written, Christians had firmly established God's incarnation as the core of their faith. This was not a teaching that evolved over time but one that was present at the inception of the church and had its roots in Jesus' proclamation.[410]

Richard Bauckham observes that the first Christians:

> include Jesus in the unique divine identity as Jewish monotheism understood it. The writers do this deliberately and comprehensively by using precisely those characteristics of the divine identity on which Jewish monotheism focused in characterizing God as unique. They included Jesus in the unique divine sovereignty over all things, they included him in the unique divine creation of all things, they identified him by the divine name which names the

---

407. Hurtado, *Lord Jesus Christ*, 2–3 (emphasis added).
408. Hurtado, *How on Earth Did Jesus Become a God?*, 25.
409. Dunn, *The Evidence for Jesus*, 61.
410. Qureshi, *No God But One*, 233.

unique divine identity, and they portray him as accorded the worship which, for Jewish monotheists, is recognition of the divine identity.[411]

As Overman explains:

> the earliest literary sources in our possession that we know for certain were written within decades of Jesus' death . . . contain devotional creeds, hymns, and liturgical formulae that pre-existed these literary sources and were then incorporated into them. They present compelling evidence of a pattern of worship of Jesus of Nazareth as a resurrected, divine being . . . This means that we have solid, historical evidence that persons who were alive and presumably eyewitnesses to Jesus' life worshipped him as divine within an astonishingly short time frame of the crucifixion.[412]

Indeed:

> The devotional practices of the primitive church, for which there is substantial evidence, clearly demonstrate that Jesus was worshipped as divine right from the beginning of the Christian movement. This is nothing short of astounding, considering that this worship practice erupted in the context of an exclusivist monotheistic Judaism and that the early disciples did not see this worship as inconsistent with Judaism, but as the fulfilment of Jewish prophecy.[413]

Theologians Robert M. Bowman and J. Ed Komoszewski point out that the NT literature describes Jesus as sharing in the *honors* due to God, the *attributes* of God, the *names* of God, the *deeds* of God, and the *seat* of God's metaphoric throne.[414]

All of this goes to show, as Michael Bird says, that "the first few decades of the church saw the rise of a form of devotion and types of Christological confession that clearly placed Jesus within the orbit of the divine identity."[415] Barnett confirms: "We are on firm ground historically in asserting that the early Christians worshipped Jesus as Lord."[416]

While the theological and philosophical articulation of this basic Christian belief continues to undergo development to the present day,[417] Louis Markos correctly states that "belief in Jesus' divinity is not a later development."[418] Komoszowski, Sawyer and

---

411. Bauckham, *God Crucified*, 26.
412. Overman, *A Case for the Divinity of Jesus*, 3–4.
413. Overman, *A Case for the Divinity of Jesus*, 20.
414. See: Bowman Jr. and Komoszewski, *Putting Jesus in His Place*.
415. Bird, "The Story of Jesus and the Story of God," 13.
416. Barnett, *Messiah*, 119.
417. See: Moreland and Craig, *Philosophical Foundations for a Christian Worldview*; Morris, *Our Idea of God*; Owen, *Christian Theism*; Senor, "The Incarnation and the Trinity;" Swinburne, *Was Jesus God?*; Swinburne, *The Christian God*; Werther, "Freedom, Temptation, and Incarnation; Williams, "Understanding the Trinity.'"
418. Markos, *Apologetics for the 21st Century*, 186.

Wallace agree that "this much is certain: Jesus' earliest followers viewed him as divine. Even scholars who do not personally embrace the divinity of Jesus readily recognize that the New Testament authors did."[419] Having previously been skeptical about Jesus being presented as divine in the synoptic gospels, in 2014 Bart Ehrman conceded that: "Jesus is portrayed as a divine being, a God-man, in all the Gospels."[420]

As Ronald H. Nash concludes: "The early church clearly believed that Jesus Christ is God."[421] Indeed, that *the very first generation of Christians believed in Jesus' deity* is a historical fact attested by multiple, early independent historical sources in multiple literary forms.

JESUS' SELF-UNDERSTANDING

Richard Dawkins's assertion that "there is no good historical evidence that [Jesus] ever thought he was divine"[422] rests not only upon his nineteenth-century hyper-skepticism concerning the NT, but also upon his failure to grapple with the indirect evidence of early Christian beliefs.

Contemplating Philippians 2:5–11 as a hymn "dating perhaps to less than twenty years after the death of Jesus,"[423] A.N. Wilson finds himself "compelled to wonder and awe at the fact that out of this strict and monotheistic religion, there was born such an all-but-idolatrous worship of a prophet."[424] He adds that "common sense . . . is bound to ask, "What can it have been about this man that inspired such thoughts?'"[425]

The radical theological shift embraced by the first Christians demands an adequate explanation. As Paul Copan observes: "Orthodox Jews considered worshipping a mere human blasphemous and detestable (Acts 10:25–26; 14:11–15), so the church's without-controversy acceptance of Christ-worship is stunning."[426] The most plausible explanation is that Jesus deliberately encouraged people to relate to him in such terms, and did so in a manner sufficiently compelling to convince them that this theological innovation was warranted. As agnostic philosopher Anthony O'Hear writes:

> We should remember that [Jesus'] first followers were pious Jews, to whom the claims being made would have seemed blasphemous had they not been given strong reason to believe them—and where better than from Jesus himself?[427]

419. Komoszewski et al., *Reinventing Jesus*, 169.

420. Ehrman, "Jesus as God in the Synoptics." Ehrman thinks Jesus is presented as being divine in different ways in different gospels, but this is a secondary issue.

421. Nash, *The Gospel and the Greeks*, 158.

422. Dawkins, *The God Delusion*, 117.

423. Wilson, *Paul*, 114.

424. Wilson, *Paul*, 114.

425. Wilson, *Paul*, 115.

426. Copan, *True For You But Not For Me*, 167.

427. O'Hear, *Jesus for Beginners*, 84.

Indeed, as James E. Taylor argues:

> critics need to avoid committing themselves to the extremely implausible view that the followers of Jesus did not believe he was the Messiah and the Son of God and deliberately fabricated the grounds for attributing divine status to him. It is unlikely that they would have subjected themselves (as they did) to ridicule, persecution, ostracism, imprisonment, and, in some cases, death for the sake of a claim they did not really believe to be true. But if we assume . . . that the early Christians *believed* Jesus was Lord and God, we must look for the best explanation of this fact. In particular, could so many have come to believe this—including many eyewitnesses to the life of Jesus—within so few years of Jesus' death if Jesus himself had never explicitly claimed or implied that he was divine? . . . It is implausible to hold that merely subjective factors, such as self-deception and wishful thinking—especially among hardcore monotheistic Jews—could account for the worship of Jesus as God.[428]

Contra Dawkins, the best explanation of the historical data is that "The New Testament deification of Jesus Christ . . . has its roots in the words and activities of the historical Jesus."[429]

During a Jewish-Christian dialogue, Jewish Professor of Religious Studies Peter Zaas commented:

> Did Jesus claim to be divine? I don't think that's quite as closed a question as you think it is. But perhaps he did. Did his followers claim that he was not only divine, but the only way that people could achieve some kind of notion of salvation? They certainly did.[430]

However, the conundrum produced by admitting that Jesus' original disciples claimed that he was divine whilst denying that Jesus claimed the same thing, is both obvious and very great. How could the Jewish disciples of a Jewish rabbi so radically misunderstand their teacher's self-image in so blasphemous a manner? As Craig A. Evans writes:

> To assert that Jesus did not regard himself as in some sense God's son makes the historian wonder why others did. From the earliest time Jesus was regarded by Christians as the son of God. Why not regard him as the great Prophet, if that is all that he had claimed or accepted? Why not regard him as the great Teacher, if that had been all that he had ever pretended to be? Earliest Christianity regarded Jesus as Messiah and as son of God, I think, because that is how his disciples understood him and how Jesus permitted them to understand him.[431]

---

428. Taylor, *Introducing Apologetics*, 180–81.
429. Evans, "The Historical Jesus and the Deified Christ," 67.
430. Zaas in Copan and Evans, *Who Was Jesus?*, 40.
431. Evans "The Jesus of History and the Christ of Faith," 66.

If Jesus didn't claim to be divine, then, when his disciples claimed that he was, were they promulgating a deliberate lie about their teacher? That seems highly unlikely:

> if the story in the Gospels is a myth, if the historical Jesus never claimed divinity . . . then this myth was invented by Jesus' apostles themselves, not by later generations or the early Christian community. But why would the apostles lie? What would motivate such a massive conspiracy of deceit? . . . If they lied, what was their motive, what did they get out of it? What they got out of it was misunderstanding, rejection, persecution, torture, and martyrdom. Hardly a list of perks! And if they lied, why did not one of the liars ever confess this, even under torture? Martyrdom does not prove truth, but it certainly proves sincerity.[432]

Even Michel Onfray concedes that "Mark, Matthew, Luke, and John did not knowingly deceive. Neither did Paul . . . they said that what they believed was true and believe that what they said was true . . . Clearly they believed what they wrote."[433]

But if not a lie, then the disciple's claim must have been a sincere delusion, a case of mistaken identity qualifying as the most radical and blasphemous of misunderstandings regarding the identity of a fellow human being available to any Jew. Hence Onfray accuses the disciples of suffering from "Intellectual self-intoxication, ontological blindness."[434] However, the hypothesis of such a misunderstanding, by such people and despite the lack of sufficient prompting in this direction from Jesus himself, seems highly unlikely.

By the elimination of alternatives, then, it appears most plausible to think that the disciple's declaration of Jesus' divinity was at the very least *a sincere belief rooted in Jesus' own teaching*; that is, it was a belief rooted in Jesus' communication of his own self-image. Thus, we have a strong indirect case for J.P. Moreland's conclusion that "a high Christology goes back to Jesus himself."[435]

"The Son of Man" on trial

> "famous terms for Jesus such as 'son of man' and 'son of God' really were being used by or of Jesus when he was alive . . ."
>
> —JAMES G. CROSSLEY[436]

Much could be said about the direct evidence for Jesus' self-consciousness that we don't have room to explore in any depth here. For example, as Scott McKnight

---

432. Kreeft, "Why I Believe Jesus is the Son of God," 250.
433. Onfray, *In Defence of Atheism*, 125.
434. Onfray, *In Defence of Atheism*, 126.
435. Moreland, *The God Question*, 111.
436. Bird and Crossley, *How Did Christianity Begin?*, 1.

observes, "there is a consistent strain in the records about Jesus that he, in some way, claimed to be uniquely the Son of God."[437] There are, for example, numerous examples of Jesus referring to himself as God's "Son" in a manner that lays claim to a "unique filial relation to God and his special role in ushering in the kingdom [of God]."[438] Craig explains:

> Jesus' parable of the wicked tenants of the vineyard (Mk 12.1–9) tells us that Jesus thought of himself as God's only son, distinct from all the prophets, God's final messenger, and even the heir of Israel itself. Notice that one cannot delete the figure of the son from the parable as an inauthentic, later addition, for then the parable lacks any climax and point. Moreover, the uniqueness of the son is not only explicitly stated but inherently implied by the tenants' stratagem of murdering the heir in order to claim possession of the vineyard. So this parable discloses to us that the historical Jesus believed and taught that he was the *only* Son of God.[439]

However, Jesus' preferred self-designation in the gospels is "Son of Man" (the title features in multiple early sources) "and this title is central for spelling out Jesus' relation to the coming kingdom."[440] David Wenham and Steve Walton caution: "A common mistake that is made is to think that 'son of man' refers to Jesus' humanity and 'son of God' to his divinity, whereas . . . both phrases seem to have both elements at least to some degree."[441] Indeed, if anything, it's the "Son of Man" title that carries the more explicit claim to divinity. Oscar Cullmann concludes that "by means of this very term Jesus spoke of his divine heavenly character . . ."[442] Licona explains:

> Many sceptical scholars believe that Jesus referred to Himself as the Son of Man, because it is unlikely to have been an invention of the early Church. For example, in the Gospels, 'Son of Man' is Jesus' favourite self-designation. Yet in the epistles, it is never used of Jesus. In fact, the term appears in the New Testament only 4 times outside of the Gospels and never in extra-biblical Christian writings during the first 120 years following Jesus. The point is: How likely is it that the Church originated the title Son of Man as Jesus' favourite self-description, when the Church itself did not refer to him in this manner?[443]

---

437. McKnight, "Who Is Jesus? An Introduction to Jesus Studies," 67.
438. Bird and Crossley, *How Did Christianity Begin?*, 29.
439. Craig, "Jesus the Son of God."
440. Bird and Crossley, *How Did Christianity Begin?*, 26.
441. Wenham and Walton, *Exploring the New Testament*, 184.
442. Cullmann quoted in Miethe and Habermas, *Why Believe?*, 278, 280.
443. Licona, "Jesus—the Son of Man?"

Robert H. Stein affirms the authenticity of Jesus' self-designation as *the* (not merely "a") "Son of Man," stating that: "The only clear instance of this title in contemporary Judaism in the sense in which Jesus used it is found in [Daniel] 7:13."[444] Daniel wrote:

> In my vision at night I looked, and there before me was one like a son of man, coming with the clouds of heaven. He approached the Ancient of Days and was led into his presence. He was given authority, glory and sovereign power; all nations and peoples of every language worshiped him. His dominion is an everlasting dominion that will not pass away, and his kingdom is one that will never be destroyed. (Daniel 7: 13–14)

Here, God the Father ("the Ancient of Days") receives into his divine presence "one like a son of man" who "was given authority, glory and sovereign power," who is described as the appropriate recipient of worship, who has an "everlasting dominion" and a "kingdom" (i.e. *the kingdom of God*) that "will never be destroyed."

In the light of this background, consider the report of Jesus' trial included within Mark's Gospel:

> They took Jesus to the high priest, and all the chief priests, the elders and the teachers of the law came together. Peter followed him at a distance, right into the courtyard of the high priest. There he sat with the guards and warmed himself at the fire. The chief priests and the whole Sanhedrin were looking for evidence against Jesus so that they could put him to death, but they did not find any. Many testified falsely against him, but their statements did not agree. Then some stood up and gave this false testimony against him: 'We heard him say, "I will destroy this temple made with human hands and in three days will build another, not made with hands."' Yet even then their testimony did not agree. Then the high priest stood up before them and asked Jesus, 'Are you not going to answer? What is this testimony that these men are bringing against you?' But Jesus remained silent and gave no answer. (Mark 14:53–61)

As Craig explains: "In Jewish thinking God is the one who built the temple . . . and who threatens the destruction of the temple . . . The charges brought against Jesus, that he threatened the destruction of the temple and promised to rebuild it, show that he was being charged with arrogating to himself divine roles."[445]

However, with the witnesses' testimony failing to cohere, the trial seems to be going well for Jesus. So the high priest gambles upon a more direct approach:

> Again the high priest asked him, 'Are you the Messiah, the Son of the Blessed One?' 'I am,' said Jesus. 'And you will see the Son of Man sitting at the right hand of the Mighty One and coming on the clouds of heaven.' (Mark 14:61–62)

---

444. Stein, "Criteria for the Gospel's Authenticity," 95.
445. Craig, *Reasonable Faith*, 307.

Jesus' response is made in terms of theologically-charged symbolic images:

- Jesus identifies himself as the "Son of Man" from Daniel 7.

- Furthermore: "it was one thing to enter God's presence and yet another to sit in it. But to sit *at God's right side* was another matter altogether. In the religious and cultural milieu of Jesus' day, to claim to sit at God's right hand was tantamount to claiming equality with God [see: Psalm 110:1] . . ."[446]

- "In other Old Testament writings, the image of riding on clouds was used exclusively of divinity [Exodus 14:20; 34:5; Numbers 10:34; Psalm 104:3; Isaiah 19:1]. Daniel employed this image, and Jesus embraced it as his own."[447]

- Jesus "claimed to exercise the authority of God, implying that he would sit in judgment over the Jewish council—not the other way around."[448]

As Craig L. Evans explains:

> Jesus had claimed that the day will come when Caiaphas and company will see Jesus, the "Son of Man," seated at God's right hand, on God's chariot throne, thundering through heaven and coming in judgement. That a man would dare claim such a thing was indeed blasphemous.[449]

Jesus' self-designation here coheres with "Documents like 4 *Ezra* and parts of 1 *Enoch*, probably written in the same century in which Jesus lived, [which] clearly make the Son of Man a messianic figure."[450]

In short, Jesus deliberately incriminated himself in the council's eyes:

> The high priest tore his clothes. 'Why do we need any more witnesses?' he asked. 'You have heard the blasphemy. What do you think?' They all condemned him as worthy of death. (Mark 14:63–64)

Overman explains that "In Jewish tradition the high priest was to tear his garments if he ever heard blasphemy."[451] In other words, with his reply to the high priest:

> Jesus affirms that he is the Messiah, the Son of God, and the coming Son of Man. He compounds his crime by adding that he is to be seated at God's right hand, a claim that is truly blasphemous in Jewish ears. The trial scene beautifully illustrates how in Jesus' self-understanding all the diverse claims blend together, thereby taking on connotations that outstrip any single term taken out of context.[452]

---

446. Bowman and Komoszewski, *Putting Jesus In His Place*, 244.
447. Komoszewski et al., *Reinventing Jesus*, 179.
448. Komoszewski et al., *Reinventing Jesus*, 179.
449. Evans, "The Jesus of History and the Christ of Faith," 66.
450. Bird and Crossley, *How Did Christianity Begin?*, 27.
451. Overman, *A Case for the Divinity of Jesus*, 59.
452. Craig, *Reasonable Faith*, 317.

People sometimes wonder what the source could have been for this conversation between Jesus and the high priest. Several relevant sources were available to the gospel writers. Since the trial was "probably carried out at Herod's palace,"[453] Luke's mention that one of the women who supported Jesus financially was Joanna, the wife of Herod's steward (see: Luke 8:3 and 24:10), has an obvious relevance. Moreover, "The texts say that the 'whole' council was gathered. This would have included Joseph of Arimathea and Nicodemus. They could easily have given eyewitness testimony to what happened."[454] Then again, "Some court records were public, and therefore available to those willing to do some research (see: Luke 1:1–4)."[455] Finally, it should be remembered that Peter (a major source behind Mark's Gospel) was present at the trial, having been taken along by a disciple of Jesus who was known personally to the high priest (see John 18:15).

It is because of the direct and indirect evidence for Jesus' self-consciousness that, as Craig reports: "most New Testament critics acknowledge that the historical Jesus acted and spoke with a self-consciousness of divine authority . . ."[456] For example:

- Richard Bauckham: "The only Jesus we can plausibly find in the sources is a Jesus who . . . speaks and acts for God in a way that far surpassed the authority of a prophet in the Jewish tradition. His opponents recognized this."[457]

- Michael F. Bird: "Jesus identified himself as a divine agent with a unique authority and a unique relationship with God. In addition, he spoke as one who spoke for God in an immediate sense and believed himself to be embodying the very person of God in his mission to renew and restore Israel."[458]

- Stephen T. Davis: "a convincing case can be made that much of the material in the Gospels that implies a high Christology can be traced back to Jesus . . . He was, in some robust sense, conscious of himself as divine . . ."[459]

- Simon J. Gathercole: "Several stories and sayings in the Synoptic Gospels point toward Jesus's unique role as a divine *agent* with an unprecedented *authority* and who undertakes divine *action*."[460]

- Michael R. Licona: "the Gospels present Jesus making divine claims in so many ways and in such varied contexts that attributing all of them to the creativity of the Evangelists or their sources stretches credulity."[461]

---

453. *Archaeological Study Bible*, 1714.
454. McDowell and Wilson, *He Walked Among Us*, 334.
455. Carson, *The Gospel According to John*, 587.
456. Craig, *Reasonable Faith*, 323.
457. Bauckham, *Jesus*, 93–94.
458. Bird, "Did Jesus Think He Was God?," 46.
459. Davis, *Christian Philosophical Theology*, 92.
460. Gathercole, "Did Jesus Think He Was God?," 57.
461. Licona, *The Resurrection of Jesus*, 606.

- Horst Georg Pohlmann: "there is virtually a consensus . . . that Jesus came on the scene with an *unheard of authority*, namely with the authority of God, with the *claim of the authority to stand in God's place . . .*"[462]
- Carsten Peter Thiede: "Jesus claimed to be the Messiah, the Son of God and God himself."[463]
- N.T. Wright: "Jesus was aware of a call, a vocation, to do and be what, according to the scriptures, only Israel's God gets to do and be."[464]

Christopher Hitchens admitted that Jesus "reportedly believed himself, at least some of the time, to be god or the son of god."[465] Lawrence Krauss states that Jesus "had delusions of being God."[466] Whilst rejecting the truth of Jesus' claim to divinity, Hitchens and Krauss both admit the existence and sincerity of that claim. Such an admission leads one facing what C.S. Lewis called "the old *aut deus aut malus homo*"[467] (i.e. "either god or a bad man") argument for the divinity of Jesus.

Watch: "Christology" Youtube playlist: www.youtube.com/playlist?list=PLQhh3qcwVE WgjXlj2cVn_ZjOE8Wd9dVbv

Listen: "Who was Jesus of Nazareth?" by William Lane Craig: www.bethinking.org/jesus/who-was-jesus-of-nazareth

"Defending an Early High Christology from Archaeology and the New Testament Letters (with special reference to the Epistle of James)" by Peter S. Williams: http://podcast.peterswilliams.com/e/european-leadership-forum-2018-defending-an-early-high-christology-from-archaeology-and-new-testament-letters/

Read: *How God Became Jesus: The Real Origins of Belief in Jesus' Divine Nature—A Response to Bart D. Ehrman* by Michael F. Bird et al.

Putting Jesus In His Place: The Case for the Deity of Christ by Robert M. Bowman and J. Ed Komoszewski

Lord Jesus Christ—Devotion to Jesus in Earliest Christianity by Larry W. Hurtado

Reinventing Jesus: How Contemporary Skeptics Miss The Real Jesus And Mislead Popular Culture by J. Ed Komoszewski et al.

A Case for the Divinity of Jesus: Examining the Earliest Evidence by Dean L. Overman

No God But One: Allah or Jesus? by Nabeel Qureshi

The Case For Christ by Lee Strobel

Understanding Jesus: Five Ways to Spiritual Enlightenment by Peter S. Williams

---

462. Pohlmann quoted in Craig, *Reasonable Faith*, 327.
463. Thiede, *Jesus, Man or Myth?*, 136.
464. Wright, *Simply Christian*, 101.
465. Hitchens, *God is Not Great*, 118 (emphasis added).
466. Krauss and Craig, "Life, The Universe, and Nothing."
467. Lewis, "Letter to Owen Barfield," 306.

Getting at the Historical Jesus

AUT DEUS AUT MALUS HOMO

"Someone who claims to be God is either evil or crazy or exactly who he said he was."

—Francis S. Collins[468]

G.K. Chesterton asks us to "imagine what would happen to a man who did really read the story of Christ as a story . . . of a man of whom he had never heard before."[469] According to Chesterton: "a really impartial reading of that kind would lead, if not immediately to belief, at least to a bewilderment of which there is really no solution except in belief."[470] The bewilderment to which Chesterton refers results from the paradox of Jesus' claims and character as depicted by the NT sources. For here we have a man who, by saying and doing things by which he lays hold of a divine status, leaves himself open to charges of insanity (if he is sincere) or blasphemy (if he is insincere), but whose general character appears to be the very definition of sanity and sincerity. This paradox lies at the heart of an ancient argument summarized in Latin by the phrase: "*aut deus aut malus homo*," which means "either God or a bad man":

> The first premise is that Christ must be either God, as he claims to be, or a bad man, if he wasn't who he claims to be. The second premise is that he isn't a bad man. The conclusion is that he is God . . . You see, he either believes his claim to be God, or he doesn't. If he does [and the claim is false], then he is intellectually bad—very bad, in fact, because that's a pretty large confusion! And if he does not believe his claim [and it is false], then he is morally bad: a deceiver and a terrible blasphemer.[471]

In contemporary English, this argument is often referred to as the "Mad, Bad or God" argument, or (with alliteration) as the "Lunatic, Liar, Lord" argument. The thing is, as Stephen T. Davis comments:

> there is precious little in the Gospels to suggest that Jesus was either a lunatic or a liar, and much to suggest strongly that he was neither. Virtually everyone who reads the Gospels . . . comes away with the conviction that Jesus was a wise and good man . . . Jesus shows none of the character traits usually associated with those who have delusions of grandeur or "divinity complexes." Such people are easily recognizable by their egotism, narcissism, inflexibility, predictable behaviour, and inability to relate understandingly and lovingly to others . . . We live in an age when scholars confidently make all sorts of bizarre claims about the historical Jesus. But few scripture scholars of any theological

---

468. Collins, *The Language of God*, 97.
469. Chesterton, *The Everlasting Man*, 215.
470. Chesterton, *The Everlasting Man*, 215.
471. Kreeft, *Between Heaven & Hell*, 38–39.

stripe seriously entertain the possibility that Jesus was either a lunatic or a liar.[472]

Scottish minister John Duncan (1796–1870) seems to have first applied the term "trilemma" to this argument when he observed: "Christ either deceived mankind by conscious fraud, or He was Himself deluded and self-deceived, or He was Divine. There is no getting out of this trilemma. It is inexorable."[473] As Chesterton mused:

> Stark staring incredulity is a far more loyal tribute to that truth than a modernist metaphysic that would make it merely a matter of degree. It were better to rend our robes with a great cry against blasphemy . . . or to lay hold of the man as a maniac possessed of devils . . . rather than to stand stupidly debating . . . in the presence of so catastrophic a claim. There is more of the wisdom that is one with surprise in any simple person, full of the sensitiveness of simplicity, who should expect the grass to wither and the birds to drop dead out of the air, when a strolling carpenter's apprentice said calmly and almost carelessly, like one looking over his shoulder: "Before Abraham was, I am." [John 8:58, see also Mark 14:62.][474]

C.S. Lewis famously re-phrased Chesterton's argument:

> Among these Jews there suddenly turns up a man who goes about talking as if He was God. He claims to forgive sins . . . He says He is coming to judge the world at the end of time . . . I am trying here to prevent anyone saying the really foolish thing that people often say about Him: "I'm ready to accept Jesus as a great moral teacher, but I don't accept his claim to be God." That is the one thing we must not say. A man who was merely a man and said the sort of thing Jesus said would be either a lunatic—on a level with the man who says he is a poached egg—or else he would be the Devil of Hell. You must make your choice. Either this man was, and is, the Son of God: or else a madman or something worse. You can shut him up for a fool, you can spit at him and kill him as a demon or you can fall at his feet and call him Lord and God, but let us not come with any patronising nonsense about his being a great human teacher. He has not left that open to us . . . Now it seems to me obvious that He was neither a lunatic nor a fiend: and consequently, however strange or terrifying or unlikely it may seem, I have to accept the view that He was and is God.[475]

Lewis's somewhat hyperbolic phrasing brings us back to the many contemporary atheists (including neo-atheists) who admit sufficient historical knowledge of Jesus to laud him as "a great human teacher" whilst rejecting "the supernatural baggage that

---

472. Davis, *Christian Philosophical Theology*, 154.
473. Duncan quoted in Brazier, *C.S. Lewis*, 110.
474. Chesterton, *The Everlasting Man*, 229–30.
475. Lewis, *Mere Christianity*, 42–43.

accompanies Christian belief," even when that "supernatural baggage" is warranted by stronger evidence than the moral "teachings" they readily acknowledge. What we have in such cases is an interpretation of the available historical evidence that's moulded by a pre-commitment to naturalistic worldview beliefs that preclude the Christian understanding of Jesus. If one pays consistent attention to the relevant historical data, to call Jesus merely a good moral teacher is to warp the evidence in the name of one's philosophical preference. As Sir Thomas More put the matter in 1534: "surely, if the Christ were not God, he would be no good man either, since he plainly said he was God."[476]

Hitched to Lewis's logic

Writing for the *New York Times* in 2010, Christopher Hitchens contrasted two views of Jesus. On the one hand, he quoted deist Thomas Jefferson, who thought that Jesus was merely human despite promulgating "the most sublime and benevolent code of morals which has ever been offered to man."[477] Likewise, Ernest Renan "repudiated the idea that Jesus was the Son of God while affirming the beauty of his teachings."[478] On the other hand, Hitchens referenced "In rather striking contrast, C.S. Lewis"[479] who "maintained in his classic statement *Mere Christianity*"[480] that "A man who was merely a man and said the sort of things Jesus said would not be a great moral teacher . . . Either this man was, and is, the Son of God; or else a madman or something worse."[481]

Hitchens finds himself in agreement with Lewis: "As an admirer of Jefferson and Renan and a strong non-admirer of Lewis, I am bound to say that Lewis is more honest here."[482] As Hitchens said in a 2009 interview:

> so many times you come up against the Jefferson line, that Jesus may not have been divine, but that his morality was divine. No. It's a wicked doctrine if it isn't fed by the force of revelation . . . the stuff is, as Lewis quite rightly said, wicked gibberish.[483]

In *God Is Not Great*, Hitchens likewise hailed Lewis's argument as a "stinging riposte"[484] to "those who argue that Jesus may have been a great moral teacher without

---

476. More, *Dialogue of Comfort Against Tribulation*, 3.14.179.
477. Jefferson quoted in Hitchens, "In the Name of the father, the Sons . . ."
478. Hitchens, "In the Name of the father, the Sons . . ."
479. Hitchens, "In the Name of the father, the Sons . . ."
480. Hitchens, "In the Name of the father, the Sons . . ."
481. Lewis, *Mere Christianity*, 54–56.
482. Hitchens, "In the Name of the father, the Sons . . ."
483. Hitchens, "Q&A: Christopher Hitchens."
484. Hitchens, *God is Not Great*, 119.

being divine,"[485] and wrote that "Lewis . . . deserves some credit for accepting the logic and morality of what he has just stated."[486]

Despite recognizing the logic of Lewis's argument, Hitchens briefly attempts to evade the trilemma, asserting that Lewis "takes his two false alternatives as exclusive antitheses, and then uses them to fashion a crude non-sequitur . . ."[487] However, Hitchens conspicuously fails to elaborate a fourth option that would allow him to escape the trilemma. Instead, he vacillates between endorsing the non-Christian options presented by the argument.

Hitchens asserts: "There were many *deranged* prophets roaming Palestine at the time, but this one reportedly believed himself, at least some of the time, to be god or the son of god. And that has made all the difference."[488] Hitchens apparently acknowledges that Jesus may have thought of himself as divine, whilst seeking to portray Jesus as a madman. However, Hitchens doesn't offer any independent *evidence* that Jesus was "deranged," a designation that doesn't square with the lucidity of Jesus' teaching: "in view of the eminent soundness of Jesus' teachings" writes Montgomery, "few have been able to give credence to the idea of mental aberration."[489]

Elsewhere Hitchens seems to prefer the highly implausible *ad hoc* suggestion that Jesus was a huckster, describing him as "an exorcist *on the make*."[490] But as Montgomery comments:

> The idea of Jesus as a charlatan — as an intentional deceiver who claimed to be something he knew he was not—has never had much appeal, even among fanatical anti-religionists. Jesus' high ethical teachings and noble personal character have made such an interpretation extremely improbable.[491]

Besides, if Jesus was "on the make," he failed to make much of his opportunities: "Foxes have dens and birds have nests, but the Son of Man has no place to lay his head" (Luke 9:58/Matthew 8:20); at least, not until the authorities were so provoked by him that they secured him lodgings in a local tomb.

Hitchens's acknowledgement of "the logic and morality" of the trilemma, his failure to justify picking either non-Christian horn thereof, or to produce a mooted fourth option, all combine to highlight the strength of the argument.

---

485. Hitchens, *God is Not Great*, 119.
486. Hitchens, *God is Not Great*, 119.
487. Hitchens, *God is Not Great*, 120.
488. Hitchens, *God is Not Great*, 118 (emphasis added).
489. Montgomery, *History And Christianity*, 65.
490. Hitchens quoted in Mann, *The Quotable Hitchens*, 187 (emphasis added).
491. Montgomery, *History And Christianity*, 62.

Dawkins' quadrilemma

Unlike Hitchens, Richard Dawkins recognizes the problems with calling Jesus mad or bad. On the one hand, Dawkins admits: "There's no evidence Jesus himself was barking mad."[492] On the other hand, Dawkins admits the implausiblity of categorizing Jesus as a morally bad man. Indeed, Dawkins thinks that Jesus "was a great moral teacher."[493] He describes Jesus as "a charismatic young preacher who advocated generous forgiveness" and praises "his genuinely original and radical ethics."[494] Dawkins acknowledges "the moral superiority of Jesus"[495] and states:

> Jesus . . . was surely one of the great ethical innovators of history. The Sermon on the Mount is way ahead of its time. His 'turn the other cheek' anticipated Gandhi and Martin Luther King by two thousand years. It was not for nothing that I wrote an article called 'Atheists for Jesus' (and was later delighted to be presented with a T-shirt bearing the legend).[496]

Sam Harris goes even further than Dawkins here, not only grouping Jesus together with "the other saints and sages of history [e.g. the Buddha, Lao Tzu],"[497] but repudiating any dismissal of Jesus or those "other saints and sages" as "epileptics, schizophrenics, or frauds."[498]

Like Hitchens, Dawkins suggests that the "*aut deus aut malus homo*" argument poses a false dilemma. Unlike Hitchens, Dawkins actually specifies a fourth option to which he appeals in an attempt to sustain his objection. In an interview on Canadian TV, Dawkins responded to a question about C.S. Lewis:

> Fanny Kiefer: When you read some of C.S. Lewis' work . . . a Christian communicator with a fertile mind and a great intellect, why do you think someone who is a scholar . . . is grabbed by faith?
>
> Richard Dawkins: Well, you could pick a much better target than C.S. Lewis . . . when you read some of his arguments, they are just pathetic. Things like: Well, Jesus claimed to be the Son of God, so either Jesus was mad, or bad, or He really was the Son of God. It did not seem to occur to him that Jesus could simply be mistaken, sincerely and honestly mistaken. I mean, what a pathetic argument.[499]

---

492. Dawkins, *Playboy* interview.
493. Dawkins, "Atheists for Jesus."
494. Dawkins, "Atheists for Jesus."
495. Dawkins, *The God Delusion*, 284.
496. Dawkins, *The God Delusion*, 283–84.
497. Harris, *Waking Up*, 5.
498. Harris, *Waking Up*, 5.
499. See: "Richard Dawkins on Studio 4 in Vancouver—Part 3 of 5."

As Dawkins concludes in *The God Delusion*: "A fourth possibility, almost too obvious to need mentioning, is that Jesus was honestly mistaken. Plenty of people are."[500]

People can be honestly mistaken about plenty of things, but as Stephen T. Davis observes: "it is not easy to see how any sane religious first-century Jew could sincerely but mistakenly hold the belief, *I am divine*."[501] Mike King's response to Dawkins hits the nail on the head:

> anyone "honestly mistaken" in such a way would inevitably be considered insane. But why should Dawkins *et al.* not be content to simply dismiss Jesus as mad or bad? Quite clearly, it is because even a rudimentary flick through Jesus' life demonstrates both of these possibilities to be untenable.[502]

As Nicky Gumbel comments: "The irony of *The God Delusion* is that Dawkins... says that all Christians are deluded because they believe there is a God, but Jesus was not deluded even though he thought he was God."[503]

Dawkins's attempt to disarm Lewis' trilemma by inventing the even more implausible *ad hoc* escape-hatch of calling Jesus "honestly mistaken" ends up being a backhanded compliment to the argument's strength. As philosopher Richard Purtill affirms: "the old [argument] still holds: if Christ claimed to be God, he was speaking the truth, or was lying, or was insane. If common sense and available evidence rule out the last two hypotheses, the first must be true."[504]

In the end, Dawkins resorts to rejecting the starting-point of the "*aut deus aut malus homo*" argument, asserting: "the evidence that Jesus claimed any sort of divine status is minimal."[505] He doesn't explain or engage with whatever evidence it is that he has in mind (acting as if "minimal" and "false" were synonyms). He takes no account of scholars who take a different view, or the arguments they offer. He doesn't even seem to have checked with his fellow neo-atheists, since Christopher Hitchens admitted that Jesus "reportedly believed himself, at least some of the time, to be god or the son of god"[506] and Lawrence Krauss affirms that Jesus "had delusions of being God."[507] Of course, that brings us back to the problems (acknowledged by Dawkins and Harris) with saying that Jesus was a deluded "*malus homo*."

Watch: "The "Lunatic, Liar or lord" Argument" Youtube playlist: www.youtube.com/playlist?list=PLQhh3qcwVEWiCA7mwy67RLgGt_2n4jzra

---

500. Dawkins, *The God Delusion*, 117.
501. Davis, "The Mad/Bad/God Trilemma."
502. King, *The God Delusion Revisited*, 63.
503. Gumbel, *Is God a Delusion?*, 80.
504. Purtill, *Reason to Believe*, 138.
505. Dawkins, *The God Delusion*, 117.
506. Hitchens, *God is Not Great*, 118 (emphasis added).
507. Krauss and Craig, "Life, The Universe, and Nothing."

Read: "The Mad/Bad/God Trilemma: A Reply to Daniel Howard Snyder" by Stephen T. Davis: www.lastseminary.com/trilemma

"Jesus: Considering the Options" by Peter Kreeft: www.bethinking.org/jesus/jesus-considering-the-options

"Was Jesus Mad, Bad or God?" by Stephen T. Davis in *Christian Philosophical Theology*

"Aut Deus Aut Malas Homo: A Defense of C.S. Lewis' "Shocking Alternative"" by David A. Horner in *C.S. Lewis as Philosopher: Truth, Goodness and Beauty* edited by David Baggett, Gary R. Habermas and Jerry L. Walls

Between Heaven & Hell: A Dialog Somewhere Beyond Death with John F. Kennedy, C.S. Lewis & Aldous Huxley by Peter Kreeft

"What are we to make of Jesus Christ?" by C.S. Lewis in *God in the Dock*

Mad or God? Jesus: The Healthiest Mind Of All by Pablo Martinez & Andrew Sims

"The Validity of Lewis's Trilemma" by Donald T. Williams in *Reflections from Plato's Cave: Essays in Evangelical Philosophy*

CONCLUSION

"To try to make Jesus into a humanistic ideal instead of a divine Savior is to run counter to all the historical facts about Him."

—John Warwick Montgomery[508]

When it comes to critically assessing the Christian revelation claim, C.S. Lewis argued that "The question is, I suppose, whether any hypothesis covers the facts so well as the Christian hypothesis . . . The alternative . . . is either lunacy or lies. Unless one can take the . . . alternative (and I can't) one turns to the Christian theory."[509] Stephen T. Davis lays out his version of the "Mad, Bad or God" argument like so:[510]

1) Jesus claimed, either explicitly or implicitly, to be divine.

2) Jesus was either right or wrong in claiming to be divine.

3) If Jesus was wrong in claiming to be divine, Jesus was either mad or bad.

4) Jesus was not bad.

5) Jesus was not mad.

6) Therefore, Jesus was not wrong in claiming to be divine.

7) Therefore, Jesus was right in claiming to be divine.

8) Therefore, Jesus was divine.

---

508. Montgomery, *How Do We Know There is a God?*, 17.
509. Lewis, "What are we to make of Jesus Christ?" 41.
510. Davis, *Christian Philosophical Theology*, 152.

The inadequate and conflicting responses of New Atheists don't show that "*aut deus aut malus homo*" is a knock-down argument for Christianity; but they do suggest it is a serious argument that carries some weight.

CHAPTER 3

Getting at the Gospels

"You are not educated if you don't know the Bible."
—Christopher Hitchens[1]

Richard Dawkins' breezy separation of a high Christology from the historical Jesus illustrates the intellectual laziness that characterizes neo-atheist "skepticism." Dawkins is wedded to what Robert J. Hutchinson calls "a largely discredited and obsolete" understanding of the New Testament (NT) gospels rooted in a "nineteenth-century rationalism [whose faulty] assumptions, methods, and conclusions are still widely seen today."[2] Reputable scholarship has long abandoned the so-called "no quest" phase of historical Jesus research—a period associated with figures from the early twentieth century such as Albert Schweitzer and Rudolf Bultmann (both of whom, it should be noted, believed in the existence of Jesus)—but Dawkins is content to uncritically regurgitate outdated positions as if scholarship has been idle for a century, and as if the gospels are the only evidence relevant to Christology. Hence, in a frankly astonishing litany of (mainly recycled) inaccurate accusations, Dawkins opines:

> since the nineteenth century, scholarly theologians have made an overwhelming case that the gospels are not reliable accounts of what happened in the history of the real world. All were written long after the death of Jesus, and also after the epistles of Paul, which mention almost none of the alleged facts of Jesus' life. All were then copied and recopied, through many different "Chinese Whisper generations" . . . The four gospels that made it into the official canon were chosen, more or less arbitrarily, out of a larger sample of at least a

1. Hitchens quoted in Belz, "The World According to Hitch."
2. Hutchinson, *Searching For Jesus*, 49.

dozen . . . Nobody knows who the four evangelists were, but they almost certainly never met Jesus personally. Much of what they wrote was in no sense an honest attempt at history . . . reputable Bible scholars do not in general regard the New Testament . . . as reliable records of what actually happened in history . . . The only difference between *The Da Vinci Code* and the gospels is that the gospels are ancient fiction while *The Da Vinci Code* is modern fiction.[3]

Now, as Professor Borden W. Painter Jr. observes: "It is reasonable to hold the New Atheists to the standards they constantly set in criticizing others."[4] So, what evidence does Dawkins provide for his assertions? Hardly any. On the issue of which gospels found their way into the NT (a topic to which we will return), a footnote refers readers to a couple of works by textual critic Bart Erhman. And that's it. Indeed, as far as one can tell from Dawkins's bibliography, his familiarity with anything like relevant NT scholarship extends to three books by Ehrman, one by Elaine Pagels (a Professor of Religion at Princeton University)[5] and one by episcopal bishop John Shelby Spong.[6] As Thomas A. Miller observes, Dawkins's attack upon the NT gospels is out of touch with contemporary scholarship:

> Dawkins derives many of these conclusions from a few selected sources that are clearly on the fringe and at odds with . . . the preponderance of contemporary New Testament scholarship, which offers an entirely different analysis of the Gospels. Not only does this scholarship challenge much of what is presented as the "final" word in Dawkins' book, but it also provides overwhelming evidence that the Gospels are very reliable historical sources [and] were written much earlier than originally thought . . .[7]

Broadening the point, Borden observes that neo-atheists:

> present no evidence in their texts or notes that they have bothered to read much of what historians have written on the subjects they purport to cover . . . In the endnotes and bibliographies of the New Atheists, the first notable problem is the missing sources. Given the great amount of space they devote to historical arguments to assault religion, it is remarkable what a small, often dated, list of sources they use. They cite very few historians with sound reputations, and they manage to misread, misrepresent, or neglect some of the better ones they do use.[8]

Anyone acquainted with contemporary scholarly discussions of the resurrection will recognize that in this context, Dawkins's assault upon the gospels is of limited

---

3. Dawkins, *The God Delusion*, 118, 121, 122–23.
4. Painter, *The New Atheist Denial of History*, 5.
5. See: Licona, "Michael Licona vs Elaine Pagels: The Gospel of Thomas."
6. See: Moore, *Can A Bishop Be Wrong?*
7. Miller, *Did Jesus Really Rise From The Dead?*, 23.
8. Painter, *The New Atheist Denial of History*, 32, 132.

relevance. First, much of the discussion centers upon the letters of Paul. Second, discussion of relevant data from the gospels revolves around their use of sources *predating* their composition. Third, NT scholars use "criteria of authenticity" (looking for independent testimony, etc.) that sidestep questions about the *general* reliability or unreliability of the gospels and/or their sources. These points also apply when the subject of discussion is Christology, since relevant evidence comes from a wide variety of sources outside of and often pre-dating the gospels (recall our discussion of the hymn to Christ in Philippians).

Dawkins's disdain for the NT gospels is out of touch with contemporary historical scholarship; but then, as atheist John Gray complains: "Today's atheists cultivate a broad ignorance of the history of the ideas they fervently preach."[9] Randall Hardman pulls no punches when he states that "One of the most unfortunate features of the New Atheist movement is its poor understanding of the interplay between the New Testament and history."[10] As illustrated by the following quotations, that interplay is regarded more positively today than at any time since the beginning of modern NT studies:

- Craig L. Blomberg: "the so-called Third Quest for the historical Jesus over the past quarter-century has for the most part been proving more and more optimistic about how much we can know about the founder of Christianity."[11]

- Darrell L. Bock: "those who participate in the third quest have tended to see far more historicity in the Gospels than either of the previous quests, showing a renewed respect for the general historical character of the Gospels."[12]

- Phil Fernandes: "The skepticism of Rudolph Bultmann concerning the historical Jesus has been replaced by a confidence that, through serious historical research, we can uncover much about the true Jesus of history."[13]

- David H. Glass: "scholarship on the historical Jesus has become much less sceptical in recent decades . . . While few scholars of the historical Jesus treat the Gospels as faultless historical records, nearly all would be horrified at the claims of the New Atheists . . . With the advent of what has become known as the "third quest" for the historical Jesus, since about 1980, the consensus about what can be known on the basis of the evidence has shifted considerably."[14]

- A.E. Harvey: "the information about Jesus which we can derive from the Gospels enjoys a high degree of historical reliability. The Gospels can be subjected to investigation with all the tools and methods of modern historical study, and

9. Gray, "The ghost at the atheist feast," 42.
10. Hardman, "Historical Evidences For The Gospels," 225.
11. Blomberg, *Making Sense of the New Testament*, 19.
12. Bock, *Studying the Historical Jesus*, 147.
13. Fernandes, *Hijacking The Historical Jesus*, 23.
14. Glass, *Atheism's New Clothes*, 266.

come remarkably well out of the process. So far as their historical reporting is concerned, they bear comparison with the work of any ancient historian, and at many points the information they offer is not merely credible but impressive."[15]

- T.W. Manson: "I am increasingly convinced that in the Gospels we have the materials—reliable materials—for an outline account of the ministry [of Jesus] as a whole."[16]

- Carl E. Olson: "the fog of skepticism that settled upon Scripture scholarship in the nineteenth and twentieth centuries has not only lifted in recent decades, it has increasingly been pierced by the clear light of a new and rigorous body of scholarship. There is a renewed recognition that the four Gospels have to be taken seriously as historical texts, especially mindful of the first-century Jewish context, as works meant to be not just theological in nature but also biographical and historical . . ."[17]

As Bart Erhman states: "To dismiss the Gospels from the historical record is neither fair nor scholarly."[18]

GOSPEL FICTION?

"we have good reason to believe that the evangelists were seeking to tell a reliable story of what happened, expressed within the historical conventions of their time."

—JOHN POLKINGHORNE[19]

Sam Harris likens the biblical story of Jesus to "a gratuitous, and rather gruesome, fairy tale."[20] Christopher Hitchens once complained about being made to "sit through lessons in the sinister fairy tales of Christianity"[21] at school, opining that "Holy writ is probably fiction, of a grand sort, to begin with."[22] He asserts that "the Gospels are most certainly not literal truth."[23] Dawkins writes that the four gospels are "pure fiction"[24]

---

15. Harvey, "Christology and the Evidence of the New Testament," 46.
16. Manson, *Studies in the Gospels and Epistles*, 11.
17. Olson, *Did Jesus Really Rise From The Dead?*, 47–48.
18. Erhman, *Did Jesus Exist?*, 73.
19. Polkinghorne, *Encountering Scripture*, 57.
20. Harris, *The End of Faith*, 204.
21. Hitchens quoted in Taunton, *The Faith of Christopher Hitchens*, 31.
22. Hitchens quoted in Mann, *The Quotable Hitchens*, 134.
23. Hitchens, *God Is Not Great*, 120.
24. Dawkins, *The Magic of Reality*, 262.

and that the gospel writers "blithely made stuff up."[25] Likewise, Alex Rosenberg thinks that "the Bible [is] fictional."[26]

While the Bible certainly contains a variety of literary genres, including fiction (e.g. Jesus' parable of the good Samaritan), the sweeping use of the category, especially with respect to the gospels, is inaccurate. The gospel writers "were writing fact, not fiction. They were trying to give an honest account of Jesus . . ."[27] As James D.G. Dunn affirms: "There can be little question that the New Testament is history at least in the sense that the New Testament writers were concerned with the historical reality of the events on which Christianity's distinctive claims were based."[28]

It is true that since the gospel writers wanted people to put their trust in Jesus, "Their books are not neutral or unbiased. But of course that fact by itself does not entail that what they say about Jesus is false."[29] One might as well say that accounts of the Holocaust written by Holocaust survivors must be unreliable because the authors are biased! Concerning the NT gospels, Jewish archaeologist Dr. Megan Broshi (Dead Sea Scrolls scholar and former curator of the Shrine of the Book) emphatically states (in slightly broken English): "There is absolutely no fiction there, they are not historical novellas, they are as far as accurate as they could have gone."[30]

Ancient historian Paul Barnett complains that:

> Dawkins . . . makes the ludicrous claim that the Gospels are as much works of fiction as Dan Brown's *The Da Vinci Code*. One of the results of painstaking research into ancient biographies and the Gospels has been to reveal that the Gospels belong to the genre of biography, not fiction. All credit to Dawkins for his accomplishment in his chosen area of scholarship, but his basic errors about the Gospels diminish his credibility to pass historical judgements on them.[31]

Those "basic errors" include confusing the apocryphal *Gospel of Thomas* with the apocryphal *Infancy Gospel of Thomas* and misattributing the story of the wise men to Luke rather than Matthew.

The Greek term *euangelion*—which means "good news" and is translated by the English term "gospel"—wasn't used to describe written accounts of Jesus' ministry until the middle of the second century. Originally the gospels "were called narratives and memoirs. A narrative tells a story; a memoir is a narrative composed from personal

---

25. Dawkins, *Science In The Soul*, 280.
26. Rosenberg, *The Atheist's Guide to Reality*, 208.
27. Green, *The Books The Church Suppressed*, 37.
28. Dunn, "The New Testament As History," 47.
29. Davis, *Rational Faith*, 52.
30. Broshi quoted in "Archaeology and the New Testament."
31. Barnett, *Gospel Truth*, 22–23.

experience... The four Gospels are biographical memoirs."[32] Richard Bauckham agrees that "the best way of categorizing the Gospels as literature is to see them as biographies, more precisely biographies of a contemporary person, based (as such biographies were expected to be) on eyewitness testimony."[33] Indeed, as Craig A. Evans observes: "There is credible, early testimony to the effect that the material in the four New Testament Gospels reaches back to the original followers of Jesus and that this material circulated and took shape during the lifetime of eyewitnesses."[34] This gives the lie to Christopher Hitchens's claim that "many of the 'sayings' and teachings of Jesus are hearsay upon hearsay..."[35]

I Hear the Gospels are Hearsay...

Lawrence Krauss agrees that the gospels are "hearsay."[36] Hitchens seeks to bolster this claim with a cherry-picking reference to one of a very small number of gospel passages widely thought to be a late addition to the text, namely John 8:3–11. According to Mark D. Roberts: "It's likely that this story is true, but that it was added to John well after the evangelist finished his task."[37] Blomberg concurs that the story "stands a fairly good chance of being historically accurate."[38] It was concerning this very incident from the Gospel of John that C.S. Lewis argued:

> Of this text there are only two possible views. Either this is reportage—though it may no doubt contain errors—pretty close up to the facts... Or else, some unknown writer... without known predecessors or successors, suddenly anticipated the whole technique of modern, novelistic, realistic narrative. If it is untrue, it must be narrative of that kind. The reader who doesn't see this has simply not learned to read.[39]

In any case, even if we concede for the sake of argument that John 8:3–11 is unreliable, to draw the conclusion that the four NT gospels are therefore *in general* "fiction" and "not literal truth" would be like pointing to a single instance of scientific fraud to discredit the entire scientific enterprise. On the one hand, one needn't accept the *general* historicity of the NT for the evidence to warrant *particular* conclusions about the historical Jesus. On the other hand, contrary to the outdated skepticism of the New Atheists, there's a strong case for the *general* historicity of the NT gospels.

32. Comfort and Driesbach, *The Many Gospels of Jesus*, 2.
33. Bauckham, *Jesus*, 15.
34. Evans, "Textual Criticism And Textual Confidence," 171.
35. Hitchens, *God Is Not Great*, 120.
36. Krauss and Craig, "Life, The Universe, and Nothing."
37. Roberts, *Can We Trust the Gospels?*, 35.
38. Blomberg, *Making Sense of the New Testament*, 23.
39. Lewis, "Fern-seed and Elephants," 108.

Hitchens admits that "Either the Gospels are in some sense literal truth, or the whole thing is essentially a fraud and perhaps an immoral one at that."[40] In other words, either the NT writer's core claims about Jesus are true or they are false; if false then either sincere or insincere; if sincerely false then massively deluded; if insincere then brazenly fraudulent. Hence to the extent one thinks the evidence is against delusion or fraud, so to that extent the truth of the gospel's basic portrait of Jesus becomes more plausible. In this context, it's worth recalling Michel Onfray's concession that "Mark, Matthew, Luke and John did not knowingly deceive. Neither did Paul . . . they said what they believed was true and believed that what they said was true . . . Clearly they believed what they wrote."[41]

Devastating differences?

"The past is a foreign country, they do things differently there."
—L.P. Hartley[42]

The New Atheists repeatedly point to differences between the NT gospels in an attempt to cast doubt on their *general* reliability. Hitchens asserts that "The gospels do not agree on the life of the man Jesus . . ."[43] and complains about the lack of "consistent witnesses"[44] for the resurrection. Likewise, Jerry A. Coyne complains that "the details of the Resurrection and empty tomb . . . show serious discrepancies."[45] Lawrence Krauss states that the gospels are "contradictory."[46]

The "discrepancies" charge is a red herring when the issue is the critical search for data about the historical Jesus that can be established on the basis of standard historical principles. As atheist Michael Grant comments: "we do not deny that an event ever took place just because pagan historians such as, for example, Livy and Polybius, happen to have described it in differing terms."[47]

Ancient historians are used to seeing past discrepant data (whether apparent or actual). For example, although the ancient "historians who narrate the Great Fire of Rome in AD 64 disagree about Nero's whereabouts during the fire and whether he 'fiddled' (played the lyre) or sang while the city burned . . . no one doubts that Nero failed to show leadership while the city was being destroyed."[48] Analogous to the

---

40. Hitchens, *God is Not Great*, 120.
41. Onfray, *In Defence of Atheism*, 125.
42. Hartley, *The Go-Between*.
43. Hitchens quoted in Mann, *The Quotable Hitchens*, 29.
44. Hitchens, *God Is Not Great*, 143.
45. Coyne, *Faith vs. Fact*, 121.
46. Krauss and Craig, "Life, the Universe, and Nothing."
47. Grant, *Jesus*, 200.
48. Barnett, *The Truth about Jesus*, 136.

agreement that Rome burnt, the biblical sources consistently agree upon the fundamental facts of Jesus' teachings, death, burial, empty tomb, and resurrection.

Apparent discrepancies certainly exist between the gospels concerning matters of circumstantial detail, but "the presence of discrepancies in circumstantial detail is no proof that the central fact is unhistorical."[49] As atheist John W. Loftus comments: "all the New Testament writers agree . . . that God raised Jesus from the dead. Should this unanimous agreement alone be enough of a reason to believe Jesus was resurrected from the dead? It is a reason, no doubt."[50]

Of course, critics often rush to judgement without adequate cause. As Louis Markos observes, when the apparent discrepancies between the gospels are listed:

> they turn out to be few in number, and most can be resolved either by some help from history or archaeology or by a more careful reading of the text . . . [while some] can be shown to be the result either of minor textual errors in transmission or of the fact that much of the Bible, especially the Gospels, is based on eyewitness accounts that complement rather than contradict each other.[51]

J. Warner Wallace helpfully address the issue of discrepancies in eye-witness testimony from his professional experience as a police detective:

> when witnesses are allowed to sit together (prior to being interviewed) and compare notes and observations, I'm likely to get one harmonized version of the event . . . While this may be tidier, it will come at the sacrifice of some important detail that a witness is willing to forfeit in order to align his or her story with the other witnesses. I'm not willing to pay that price. I would far rather have three messy, apparently contradictory versions of the event than one harmonized version that has eliminated some important detail. I know in the end I'll be able to determine the truth . . . The apparent contradictions are usually easy to explain once I learn something about the witnesses and their perspectives (both visually and personally) at the time of the crime.[52]

Mark L. Strauss, University Professor of New Testament at Bethel Seminary, argues that:

> most claims of contradictions result from demanding more historical precision than the authors intended to provide. The Gospels were never meant to be videotapes of events or word-for-word transcripts. It is the normal method of history writing—both ancient and modern—to summarize accounts, paraphrase speeches, omit extraneous details, and report events from a particular

---

49. Harris, *Raised Immortal*, 68.
50. Loftus, *Why I Became An Atheist*, 363.
51. Markos, *Apologetics*, 150.
52. Wallace, *Cold-Case Christianity*, 74–75.

vantage point. Most supposed contradictions in the Gospels can be readily explained from common practices in history writing.[53]

For example, Strauss notes:

> scholars have long recognized that in most cases we have not the exact words (*ipsissima verba*) of Jesus, but rather his authentic voice (*ippssima vox*). The essential meaning is communicated using different words. In one sense this is obvious, since Jesus normally spoke Aramaic but the Gospels are in Greek. Many differences in wording or idiom may be attributed to differences in translation and style.[54]

Moreover, it's fruitless to criticize ancient texts without paying attention to the cultural, literary, and linguistic conventions that formed them. As theologian Trent Horn observes: "The authors of the Gospels . . . were concerned with recording history, but their style of historical writing was not the same as the histories we are familiar with today."[55] Hence Richard Burridge warns that: "Trying to decode the Gospels through the genre of modern biography, when the author encoded his message in the genre of ancient [biography], will lead to . . . blaming the text for not containing modern predilections which it was never meant to contain."[56] As Darrell L. Bock comments: "the way ancients . . . related events with variation tells us that we should be slow to make the assumption of a contrary stance behind differences in detail . . ."[57]

For example, different gospel reports put Jesus' resurrection on "the third day," "after three days," and after "three days and three nights." To many modern readers these statements appear contradictory. If they were contradictory, that wouldn't disprove the fact that Jesus' body was only entombed for a short period of time. However, in accordance with ancient Jewish idiom, these different temporal statements actually all mean the same thing: "in Jewish reckoning any part of a day could count as a day (cf. Gen. 42:17–18; 1 Sam. 30:1, 12–13; 1 Kings 20:29; 2 Chron. 10:5, 12; Esther 4:16–5:1)" such that "we may say that Jesus was in the grave three (parts of) days."[58] Jesus' corpse was in the tomb a part of Friday (a "day"), all of Saturday (a second "day"), and a part of Sunday (a third "day"):

> In the first century, any part of a day could be computed for the whole day and the night following it . . . The *Jerusalem Talmud* quotes rabbi Eleazar ben Azariah, who lived around A.D. 100, as saying: "A day and night are an Onah [a portion of time] and the portion of an Onah is as the whole of it." . . . a person in ancient times could legitimately speak of something occurring "on

---

53. Strauss, *Introducing Jesus*, 95.
54. Strauss, *Introducing Jesus*, 95–96.
55. Horn, *Hard Sayings*, 125.
56. Burridge, *What Are the Gospels?*, 249.
57. Bock and Wallace, "Precision and Accuracy," 280, 368.
58. Pate, *40 Questions About the Historical Jesus*, 344, 346.

the third day," "after three days," or after "three days and three nights," yet still be referring to the same exact day.[59]

To consider one further example, American atheist Carl Stecher insists that the resurrection appearances in Luke's Gospel are presented as having all happened on Easter day in Jerusalem, a reading that's contradicted by the other gospels (which either indicate or narrate resurrection appearances in Galilee).[60]

However, Luke stitches together his gospel's resurrection narratives using the Greek particle "*de*," which connects events as happening one after the other without necessarily implying that they happened in immediate conjunction ("*de*" can be translated as "moreover, on-top of this, then or next").[61] Hence it's possible that while the events of Luke 24:1–43 happened on Easter day, those of Luke 24:44 and following ("Then he said to them . . . ") happened some time later.

The process of Jesus teaching the disciples' about himself through the Old Testament Scriptures (Luke 24:45–49) presumably took some days, while Jesus' subsequent instruction to "stay in the city [Jerusalem] until clothed with power from on high" was given shortly before he led them to the location of his ascension on the slope of the Mount of Olives (about a thousand yards outside Jerusalem, see: Luke 24:49–50 and Acts 1:9–12).

In sum, Luke's Gospel leaves grammatical space between the events of Easter day and the ascension for heeding the instructions about Jesus meeting with his disciples in Galilee (see: Mark 16:7, Matthew 28:7 and 10), instructions that were probably addressed to a wider group than just the remaining members of "the twelve" upon whom Matthew focuses (see: Matthew 28:16, Luke 8:3, 10:1, 24:33–35, Acts 1:21–26, and 1 Corinthians 15:6).

To insist upon reading Luke's Gospel as restricting the resurrection appearances to Easter day in Jerusalem not only uncharitably creates an unnecessary contradiction with the other canonical gospels, but between Luke's Gospel and his own follow-up book of Acts, where he says that Jesus "presented himself alive to them after his suffering by many proofs, *appearing to them during forty days . . .*" (Acts 1:3, ESV, emphasis added); and where he explains that Jesus' command about staying in Jerusalem came "*not many days*" before their "baptism with the Holy Spirit" (Acts 1:5, ESV, emphasis added) clothed them "with power from on high" at Pentecost. Luke's accounts of the resurrection *complement* both each other and the other gospels.

Watch: "Gospel Contradictions?" Youtube playlist: www.youtube.com/playlist?list=PLQh h3qcwVEWjt9SKTdFKEqLkUpwJYxCit

Read: "Passion Problems" by Craig L. Blomberg: www.4truth.net/fourtruthpbjesus. aspx?pageid=8589952881

59. Lyons, "Did Jesus Rise "On" or "After" the Third Day?"
60. See: Blomberg and Stecher, *Resurrection: Faith or Fact?*
61. See: Bible Hub Commentaries, "de."

"Are There Contradictions in the Bible?" by Douglas S. Huffman: www.goodshepherdarp.org/images/uploads/Are-There-Contradictions-in-the-Bible.pdf

"How Many Times Did the Rooster Crow?" by Eric Lyons: www.apologeticspress.org/apcontent.aspx?category=6&article=759

"Sabbath Day's Journey" by H. Porter: www.biblestudytools.com/encyclopedias/isbe/sabbath-days-journey.html

"Differences in the Gospels: A Closer Look" by Robert H. Stein: www.christianitytoday.com/edstetzer/2012/march/differences-in-gospels-closer-look.html

"Bible Contradictions Explained: 4 Reasons the Gospels 'Disagree'" by Mark Strauss: https://zondervanacademic.com/blog/bible-contradictions-explained/

The Historical Reliability of the Gospels by Craig L. Blomberg

The Historical Reliability of John's Gospel: Issues & Commentary by Craig L. Blomberg

"Precision and Accuracy: Making Distinctions in the Cultural Context" by Darrell L. Bock in *Do Historical Matters Matter To Faith? A Critical Appraisal of Modern and Postmodern Approaches to Scripture* edited by James K. Hoffmeier and Denis R. Magary

The Holman Apologetics Commentary On The Bible: The Gospels and Acts edited by Jeremy Royal Howard

The Final Days Of Jesus by Andreas J. Kostenberger and Justin Taylor

"Viewing the Gospels as Ancient Biographies Resolves Many Perceived Contradictions" by Michael R. Licona in *Biographies of Jesus: What Does It Mean for the Gospels to be Biographies?* edited by Craig S. Keener and Edward T. Wright

---

TESTING THE TESTIMONY OF THE FOUR GOSPELS

> "There is much to be said for Jesus at a historical level as one studies the Gospels as ancient literary texts."
>
> —Darrell L. Bock[62]

Our investigation thus far bears out the verdict delivered by David H. Glass:

> Ironically, given their emphasis on the importance of evidence, the New Atheists have uncritically adopted some of the most extreme views on the Gospels instead of taking the best evidence and scholarship into account . . . No matter how much the New Atheists might like to think otherwise, there is no disputing the fact that the Gospels provide us with historical information about Jesus.[63]

The NT gospels aren't works of mythology or fiction, but first-century biographies about a recent historical figure. As David Robertson observes: "The Gospel accounts are not written as mythical accounts—'In a hole in the ground there lived a

---

62. Bock, *Studying the Historical Jesus*, 215.
63. Glass, *Atheism's New Clothes*, 270, 278.

hobbit.' They are written as historical accounts which were dependent on witnesses and must be judged as such."[64]

But how should we go about judging the gospels as historical accounts? Discussing the supposed paucity of evidence for Jesus, Dawkins patronizingly opines: "The fact that something is written down is persuasive to people not used to asking questions like: 'Who wrote it, and when?'"[65] However, the pursuit of answers to obvious questions like "Who wrote it, and when?" has actually led to a far greater receptivity towards the NT gospels as generally "reliable accounts of what happened" on the part of modern scholars in the so-called "third quest" for the historical Jesus. As Blomberg explains: "if we limit ourselves to the approaches taken by classical historians who study other people, events, and institutions from the ancient Jewish, Greek, and Roman worlds, a cumulative case emerges which suggests that the gospels and Acts are very historically reliable."[66] Writing as a classical historian of Rome, Professor Mark D. Smith comments: "The Gospels are, relative to the material regularly utilized by ancient historians, very early, and the fact that there are four is a form of riches rare in our profession."[67]

Testimonial knowledge

According to philosopher Ernest Sosa:

> Testimonial knowledge is a collaborative accomplishment involving . . . the gathering, retaining, transmitting, and receiving of information . . . Think of the documents consulted by a historian, of those responsible for their production, for their preservation and transmission unaltered, and so on.[68]

When assessing written testimony, we want to know the strength of the various "links" in the "chain of testimony" stretching from the events about which a source of testimony purports to inform us, through that source and the written use of their testimony, to the contemporary reception thereof. There are thus four basic stages or links in the *chain of testimony* behind the NT gospels:

Link 1) Between the reported events and the reporting source or sources

Link 2) Between the reporting source or sources and the written use of their testimony in one or more of the gospels

Link 3) Between the original written/published gospel reports (the "autographs") and the surviving copies thereof

---

64. Robertson, *Magnificent Obsession*, 102.
65. Dawkins, *The God Delusion*, 118.
66. Blomberg, *Making Sense of the New Testament*, 21.
67. Smith, *The Final Days of Jesus*, 17–18.
68. Sosa, "Knowledge," 116.

Link 4) Between the autographs and the text we can reconstruct today from surviving copies thereof

In each case, the stronger the link, the better (although the failure of any link in the chain leads to the failure of that chain of testimony). The first two links in the chain of testimony concern the *origins* of the gospel testimony, whereas the last two links concern the *transmission* of the gospel testimony.

Looking in greater detail at the origins of the gospel testimony, Mark L. Strauss discerns "four main stages in the development of the Gospels"[69]:

Stage 1: The historical Jesus

Stage 2: The period of oral history, when the teaching of and stories about Jesus were preserved primarily in the oral memory of the eyewitnesses and of the wider Christian community

Stage 3: The period of written sources, when collections of sayings and other material were collected

Stage 4: The writing of the gospels

The earlier stages should probably be pictured as overlapping with the later stages of this process. The prologue of Luke's Gospel helpfully touches upon all four stages:

> Many have undertaken to draw up an account [stages 3 & 4] of the things that have been fulfilled among us [stage 1], just as they were handed down to us by those who from the first were eyewitnesses and servants of the word [stages 2 & 3]. With this in mind, since I myself have carefully investigated everything from the beginning [stages 2–4], I too decided to write an orderly account for you, most excellent Theophilus [stage 4]. (Luke 1:1)

The origins of testimony: Link 1

Most relevantly-qualified scholars think Mark was the first published gospel, and hence "the gospel with the highest claims [in terms of historical proximity] to be accepted as a reliable historical source."[70] Moreover, as Bart Erhman explains:

> It is often thought Mark used a passion narrative that had been written years earlier in which the episodes of Jesus' arrest, trials, death, and resurrection were already put into written form. The most recent and most authoritative two-volume commentary on Mark, by Joel Marcus, contends that Mark used a source, or a number of sources, for his account of Jesus' words and deeds prior to the passion narrative.[71]

---

69. Strauss, *Four Portraits, One Jesus*, 44.
70. Stanton, *The Gospels and Jesus*, 35. See: Hengel, *Studies in the Gospel of Mark*, 7.
71. Erhman, *Did Jesus Exist?*, 81–82.

Getting at Jesus

On the basis of early and unanimous tradition, it is generally acknowledged that, in addition to this passion narrative, Mark's main source of testimony was the apostle Peter.

The gospel according to Mark is generally taken to have been followed by the gospels of Matthew and Luke, which given the significant overlap in the traditions reported therein are collectively known as "the Synoptic Gospels," from the Greek words *optic* (meaning "see") and *syn* (meaning "together").

Christopher Hitchens mistakes "synoptic" for a term that distinguishes between the canonical and non-canonical ("apocryphal") gospels, writing of "early church councils that decided which Gospels were 'synoptic' and which were 'apocryphal.'"[72]

Of course, no apocryphal gospels competed with the four canonical gospels until the second century when such texts began to be written. By the time any church council discussed which gospels were to be considered as Scripture, it was merely a matter of officially ratifying a pre-established convention against obvious late-comers and forgeries.

Michael Ruse notes that "the Synoptic Gospels (Matthew, Mark and Luke) . . . are clearly (at least some of them) using earlier writings . . . and also oral traditions of people who certainly had the chance to see and hear Jesus."[73] Strauss explains:

> scholars today hold the view that Matthew and Luke both used (1) The Gospel of Mark [and if they didn't use Mark, they must have had access to a source or sources very similar to Mark], (2) a source or sources which Matthew and Luke had in common, conveniently referred to as Q [an abbreviation of the German *Quelle*, "source"], and (3) unique material which each had in hand, conveniently designated as M (Matthew's unique material) and L (Luke's unique material).[74]

The Synoptic Gospels were followed by the Gospel of John, which offers a complementary picture of Jesus that is independent of the former gospels, at least in the sense that it doesn't depend upon them in literary terms. Indeed, 92 percent of the Gospel of John presents us with material not found in the synoptic traditions.

John Dickson reports that "many scholars . . . detect an earlier source within the Gospel of John. They call it the Signs Source or SQ for short . . . SQ appears to have been a collection of seven miracle stories or signs highlighting Jesus' status as Messiah."[75] The Jesus Seminar postulates a signs source behind John's Gospel that dates between AD 50 and 70. Erhman reports that "scholars have long suspected that John had at his disposal an earlier written account of Jesus' miracles (the so-called Signs Source), at least two accounts of Jesus' long speeches (the Discourse Sources),

---

72. Hitchens, *God Is Not Great*, 117.
73. Ruse, *Atheism*, 134.
74. Strauss, *Four Portraits, One Jesus*, 53.
75. Dickson, *Investigating Jesus*, 118.

Getting at the Gospels

and possibly another passion source as well."[76] According to Norman L. Geisler: "John uses independent sources of his own that can be traced on linguistic grounds to between A.D. 30 and 66 . . ."[77]

However, there's more caution amongst scholars concerning sources used by John than sources used by the synoptic gospels. For example, Blomberg writes that:

> While it is quite plausible to believe that the Fourth Gospel utilized written source material, as did the Synoptics (and most other ancient historians for that matter), it is quite another matter for us to declare with any confidence that we can determine what they are.[78]

What can be said with some confidence is that the four gospels provide us with access to between five and eight different sources of information about Jesus, all of which take us back to the pre-gospel period of written sources and/or oral history. Both types of source plausibly include the apostolic witnesses behind the gospels, for although the culture of the time was as much as 95 percent illiterate, many of Jesus' disciples were fishermen, and as Ben Witherington III notes: "Fisherman were not peasants . . . fisherman were businessmen, and they had to either have a scribe or be able to read and write a bit to deal with tax collectors, toll collectors, and other business persons."[79]

Paul Barnett notes that ""Q" texts are cited or echoed in letters of Paul written in the mid-fifties."[80] Likewise, D.C. Allison concludes that "Paul knew material from Mark, material common to Luke and Matthew ("Q"), material unique to Luke "L," and perhaps material unique to Matthew ("M")."[81] Thus it appears that at least elements of Q, L, and M existed within twenty years of the historical Jesus.

Indeed, the NT letter of James contains many allusions to the teachings of Jesus, especially teaching found in the Q tradition's "beatitudes" material that found its way into the gospels of Matthew and Luke.[82] Given that the Epistle of James was written c. AD 45–48 (as argued previously), these elements of Q can thus be traced back to within 12–15 years of the historical Jesus.

Bart Erhman hammers home a key point here:

> We cannot think of the early Christian Gospels as going back to a single solitary source that "invented" the idea that there was a man Jesus. The view that Jesus existed is found in multiple independent sources that must have been

---

76. Erhman, *Did Jesus Exist?*, 82.
77. Geisler, *Christian Apologetics*, 313.
78. Blomberg, *The Historical Reliability of John's Gospel*, 47.
79. Witherington quoted in Kostenberger et al., *Truth Matters*, 60.
80. Barnett, *The Birth of Christianity*, 147.
81. Barnett, *The Birth of Christianity*, 125.
82. See: Meadors, "The 'Poor' in the Beatitudes of Matthew and Luke;" Lyons, "Jesus' Sermon on . . . the Mount or the Plain?"

circulating throughout various regions of the Roman Empire in the decades before the Gospels that survive were produced . . . In addition to Mark, we have Q, M (which is possibly made of multiple sources), L (also possibly multiple sources), two or more passion narratives, a signs source, two discourse sources . . . and possibly others.[83]

The gospel sources were either written sources, which may or may not have been dependent upon oral sources, or were themselves oral sources. As Blomberg reminds us: "It would have been quite normal and expected for Jesus' disciples, revering their teacher, to commit to memory significant portions of his teaching and even brief narratives of his great works, and to have remembered those accounts accurately for a considerable span of time."[84] As the *Mishna* says, a good pupil is like a "plastered cistern that loses not a drop."[85] Moreover, "rabbis and their followers often took private notes of important material, which they consulted from time to time to refresh their memories. It would be unusual if Jesus' followers had not done the same."[86] Thus Erhman states that the "traditions [about Jesus] can be dated back to Aramaic sources of Palestine, almost certainly from the 30s of the Common Era (i.e. of the first century AD)."[87]

Furthermore, as Dunn comments, the oral history preserved in the NT isn't "casual recall across several decades or something once heard and little thought about since" but "a deliberate attempt to implant firmly and rootedly matters of importance in the memory of individuals motivated to listen, to absorb and to live accordingly."[88] For example, some 80 percent of Jesus' sayings in the gospels when translated back into Aramaic (the language Jesus normally spoke): "show signs of poetic and mnemonic structure. They are brief, vivid, and show signs of alliteration, assonance, parallelism, symmetry, repetition, rhythm, and rhyme."[89]

Discussing research into oral cultures, theologians Gregory A. Boyd and Paul Rhodes Eddy argue:

> the case for accepting the early church tradition regarding the authorship and relatively early dating of the four Gospels is stronger than many suppose. But . . . not too much hangs on this . . . even if we grant that the Gospels were written between AD 70 and 100 . . . and even if we grant that we don't know who wrote these books, this still doesn't warrant the conclusion that these authors were not in a position to pass on reliable history.[90]

---

83. Erhman, *Did Jesus Exist?*, 82–83.
84. Blomberg, *Jesus and the Gospels*.
85. Montgomery, *History And Christianity*, 37–38.
86. Blomberg, *Jesus and the Gospels*, second edition, 94.
87. Erhman, *Did Jesus Exist?*, 97.
88. Dunn, "Social Memory and the Oral Jesus Tradition," 186.
89. Hardman, "Historical Evidences For The Gospels," 241.
90. Boyd and Eddy, *Lord or Legend?*, 92.

This is because oral cultures:

> are invested in accurately preserving the memory of events that shape their communal identity . . . while tradents entrusted with the task of retelling a community's oral traditions are allowed creative flexibility in how they express traditional material, the community as a whole typically assumes responsibility to ensure that the tradent's creative performance doesn't alter the substance of the tradition he or she is passing on. So it is, as many orality specialists now argue, that orally dominant communities typically evidence the ability to reliably transmit historical material for long periods of time—in some cases, for centuries.[91]

A recent study found that "Aboriginal stories of lost islands match up with underwater finds in Australia."[92] *Scientific American* reported that: "Without using written languages, Australian tribes passed memories of life before, and during, postglacial shoreline inundations through hundreds of generations as high-fidelity oral [traditions]."[93] This research demonstrates that historically accurate oral traditions can be reliably preserved within an oral culture over a period of 10,000 years. As the researchers concluded: "Indigenous languages can be repositories for factual knowledge across time depths far greater than previously imagined . . ."[94]

Oral traditions exhibit a characteristic balance between form and freedom. The tradent "is granted a certain amount of creativity and flexibility in how he or she presents the traditional material, but there are also strong constraints when it comes to altering the core content of traditional material . . . if the narrator alters the material too much, the community objects and corrects him or her in the midst of the performance."[95] As Groothuis explains, in studies of oral traditions:

> 60–90 percent of the information remained unvarying, including all elements deemed necessary for the lessons of the stories to remain intact. Tradents who left out or garbled any of these elements were to be interrupted and corrected by those in the audience who recognized the mistakes . . . This kind of tradition does not produce verbatim reproduction of every minor word but it is true to the details that make a story or a teaching what its author intended it to be.[96]

Examining the gospels, we notice the same balance between form and freedom:

---

91. Boyd and Eddy, *Lord or Legend?*, 92.
92. John Upton, "Ancient Sea Rise Tale Told Accurately for 10,000 Years."
93. John Upton, "Ancient Sea Rise Tale Told Accurately for 10,000 Years."
94. John Upton, "Ancient Sea Rise Tale Told Accurately for 10,000 Years."
95. Boyd and Eddy, *Lord or Legend?*, 69–70.
96. Groothuis, *Christian Apologetics*, 451–52.

The order of events and wording of Jesus' sayings, for example, often varies from Gospel to Gospel, though the basic content and broad narrative framework is similar. In light of the new discoveries in orality studies, this suggests that we should view the Gospels as written versions—or "textualizations"—of the oral performances that would have been so common among the early Christian communities . . . this suggests that the oral traditions about Jesus that lie behind the Gospels—including their overall narrative framework of his life—are solidly rooted in history.[97]

J.P. Moreland writes that "a strong case could be made for the fact that much of the New Testament, including the Gospels and the sources behind them, was written by eyewitnesses."[98] Likewise, Richard Bauckham argues that:

> Gospel traditions did not, for the most part, circulate anonymously but in the name of the eyewitnesses to whom they were due . . . in imagining how the traditions reached the Gospel writers, not oral tradition but eyewitness testimony should be our principle model.[99]

In other words, the gospels aren't based upon oral traditions (a designation that technically applies to the oral transmission of information over at least a generation) but upon the testimony of contemporary, eyewitness, oral history.

Bauckham argues that the presence of various named characters in the synoptic gospels is best explained by the hypothesis that these characters were the eyewitness tradents of the tradition to which their names are attached: "many of these named characters were eyewitnesses who not only originated the traditions to which their names are attached but also continued to tell these stories as authoritative guarantors of their traditions."[100] As Boyd and Eddy explain:

> Orality specialists now realize that, while the community plays a significant role in preserving the accuracy of an oral tradition . . . oral communities typically designate individual tradents . . . to be the primary and official transmitters of the tradition. When an individual was an eyewitness to events that have to become part of a community's oral historical traditions, he or she is often recognized as a crucial link in the communal preservation of that tradition . . . this discovery of the crucial role of individual tradents suggests that we can no longer conceive of the traditional material about Jesus being transmitted in the early church *apart from the strong influence of original eyewitnesses*. This renders it virtually impossible to conceive of the oral traditions in the early church veering too far from the historical events observed by eyewitnesses.[101]

97. Boyd and Eddy, *Lord or Legend?*, 70.
98. Moreland, *The God Question*, 137.
99. Bauckham, *Jesus*, 8.
100. Bauckham, *Jesus*, 39.
101. Boyd and Eddy, *Lord or Legend?*, 73.

Taking all of these points into consideration:

> it should be clear that, whoever they were and whenever they wrote, we have good reasons to accept that the Gospel authors were in a position to transmit reliable reports about Jesus. Unless we arbitrarily assume that the early Christian communities were remarkably atypical for orally dominant communities, the sheer fact that the Gospel authors wrote as tradents of an early church tradition should incline us to accept this much.[102]

After all, "historians frequently trust authors who wrote about events that preceded them by greater spans of time than forty to sixty years and who were not directly connected to the events they wrote about via a community's orally transmitted history."[103] Moreover, "A broad range of studies—from ancient Greece to nineteenth-century Serbo-Croatia to contemporary Africa—have all confirmed that orally orientated historical traditions (both oral and written in medium) . . . within roughly 80 to 150 years of the event recorded—tend to be quite reliable."[104] It is clear that "The picture of Jesus in the New Testament was established well within that length of time."[105]

So, as Paul Copan argues:

> Given (1) the importance of memorization and oral tradition in first-century Palestine, (2) the practice of (occasionally) writing down and preserving the teachings of rabbis by their disciples, (3) the fact that the vast majority of Jesus' teaching was in poetic (and easily memorable) form, (4) the importance and revered status of religious traditions in Palestine, and (5) the presence of apostolic authority in Jerusalem to ensure the accurate transmission of tradition . . . we have good reason to believe that the material in the Gospels was carefully and correctly set down.[106]

Finally, it's worth noting with Stephen T. Davis that there are powerful arguments against the idea that the gospel writers felt free to simply invent content:

> First, had the early Christians engaged in such a practice, it is highly probable that sayings would have been placed in the mouth of Jesus that were relevant to the central concerns and controversies of the church in the second half of the first century. But notice that there are no sayings of Jesus in the canonical gospels that are directly relevant to such burning issues in the late-first-century church as the proper use of spiritual gifts, whether male Gentile converts were obliged to be circumcised, whether Christians should divorce their non-Christian spouses, the proper practice of the Lord's supper, how churches ought to be governed, etc. Second, notice that the church preserved

---

102. Boyd and Eddy, *Lord or Legend?*, 92–93.
103. Boyd and Eddy, *Lord or Legend?*, 93.
104. Eddy and Boyd, *The Jesus Legend*, 395.
105. Moreland, *Scaling the Secular City*, 156.
106. Copan, *"True For You, But Not For Me,"* 103.

and passed on 'difficult' sayings of Jesus . . . for example, sayings about the human failings of some of the church's greatest leaders (e.g. Peter, in Mark 14:66–72) . . . these arguments show . . . the respect that the church had for the actual teachings of Jesus—I believe they were reliably preserved and passed on rather than amended or even made up.[107]

Watch: "Oral History and the Gospels" Youtube playlist: www.youtube.com/playlist?list=PLQhh3qcwVEWgzSQQrmuWAifmpNURBFlaL

Confirmation from local knowledge

The gospel writers display a detailed local knowledge unlikely to be available to ancient writers much removed in time and/or space from their subject matter; when a source of testimony proves accurate in matters we can check, our confidence concerning their accuracy in matters we cannot check is thereby increased. As Lydia McGrew observes: "If you sample a loaf of bread on both ends and at several points in the middle and find it good, it would be caviling to say that perhaps just the parts you haven't tasted happen to be the moldy ones."[108]

CONFIRMATION FROM ARCHAEOLOGY

As Craig L. Blomberg observes:

> A particularly significant subcategory of corroborating external evidence outside of the Gospels and Acts, or any other explicitly Christian sources, is that which archaeology unearths . . . there are books filled with items that confirm the kinds of details in the New Testament that lend themselves to archaeological proof or disproof. In no instance has any detail been disproved; countless items have been corroborated.[109]

For example, writing about Luke's account of rioting in Ephesus (Acts 19:23–40), Professor James R. Edwards comments:

> Some 18 historical references or terms occur in Acts 19:23–40. Apart from the personal identities of Demetrius and Alexander, all these references and terms are repeated and reported in the archaeological or inscriptional remains of Ephesus, affording a remarkably complete "material commentary" on the riveting drama . . . Luke knew what he was talking about in recording the riot in the theatre. His claim at the outset of the two-part work (Luke and Acts) to have "investigated everything accurately and reported them orderly"

---

107. Davis, *Disputed Issues*, 12.
108. McGrew, *Hidden In Plain View*, 225.
109. Blomberg, *Making Sense of the New Testament*, 53.

(Luke 1:3) is substantiated in Acts 19 . . . The archaeological and inscriptional remains of Ephesus allow modern readers to appreciate the credibility with which Luke's account would have been read by first-century citizens of Ephesus and Roman Asia.[110]

Watch: "New Evidences the Gospels were Based on Eyewitness Accounts" by Peter J. Williams: https://youtu.be/r5Ylt1pBMm8

Listen: "Archaeological Evidence and Jesus" by Peter S. Williams: http://podcast.peterswilliams.com/e/archaeological-evidence-and-jesus/

Read: "Digging For Evidence" by Peter S. Williams: http://christianevidence.org/docs/booklets/digging_for_evidence.pdf

Jesus And His World: The archaeological evidence by Craig A. Evans

---

Confirmation from geography

Archaeologist Steven Collins points out that the NT:

> often refers to the features of the land in which the gospel events occurred. Many of the mountains, valleys, rivers, and lakes of Palestine are mentioned by name . . . Even the lay of the land is precisely indicated by statements like "going *up* to Jerusalem" from Jericho and other locations. Indeed you always go *up* to Jerusalem from the east or west because it sits on the pinnacle of Israel's hill country.[111]

Read: *In The Steps of Saint Paul: An Illustrated Guide To Paul's Journeys* by Peter Walker

---

Confirmation from names

As Andy Bannister observes:

> if I asked you to start naming minor villages a hundred miles from Paris, you'd probably struggle unless you'd actually visited the region. Yet that's precisely the level of detail the Gospels get right, managing to know not just major cities such as Jerusalem but minor villages like Cana and Chorazin, one-goat towns in their day. The Gospels also get a wealth of other local information right, from politics to agriculture, economics to weather patterns; they even get people's names right.[112]

---

110. Edwards, "Archaeology Gives New Reality To Paul's Ephesus Riot."
111. Collins, *The Defendable Faith*, 188.
112. Bannister, *The Atheist Who Didn't Exist*, 221.

Indeed, a recent in-depth study of personal names in Israel at the time of Jesus shows that the gospel writers had the kind of intimate and detailed knowledge of life in that time and place one could only expect of authors from that time and place. In 2002 an Israeli scholar called Tal Ilan:

> sorted through documents, engravings, scraps of papyrus, ossuaries and the like from the time period surrounding Jesus and the apostles in order to make a list of over 3,000 personal names — along with whatever bits of information she could find about those names. It was as if she were compiling a phone book from ancient trash heaps. Because of her work, it became possible for the first time to find out what personal names were the most popular during the time of Jesus and how those names were used.[113]

If the gospel writers lacked reliable contact with the culture depicted in their stories then they would be very unlikely to get that culture's use of names right: "It would be as if a person who had never set foot out of California were attempting to write a story about people living in Portugal 60 years ago and the writer perfectly captured all the details of the personal names of the day without traveling, without the Internet, without encyclopedias or libraries."[114] But as Craig Hazen explains: "the Gospel writers were 'spot on' in regard to the popularity, frequency, proportion and usage of personal names in the text of Scripture, indicating very deep familiarity with life in the exact area and timeframe of Jesus and his earliest followers."[115]

Richard Bauckham has built upon Ilan's work by correlating NT names with names compiled from the extrabiblical sources to show that the gospels accurately captured the frequency of names among Palestinian Jews of the time. For instance, Ilan's list of the ten most popular names matched rank for rank the list of the most frequent names in the gospels and Acts. This is an extraordinary confirmatory correlation:

> the *relative* frequency of names in the Gospels and Acts corresponds to that in the other sources . . . it is hard to see how such a close correspondence could have occurred if the names in the Gospels were invented. . . since the relative popularity reveals itself only when we put occurrences in all four Gospels and Acts together. Even supposing that a Gospel writer would try to make the range of his names realistic . . . he was only responsible for one Gospel. Nobody planned the onomastic data that we get from putting all four Gospels together (along with Palestinian Jewish names in Acts) . . . while contemporaries would realize that some names were common and others rare, they are unlikely to have known . . . the relative proportions of name usage . . . In any society, such things are only known by gathering and analyzing. There was

---

113. Hazen, "What's in a Name?"
114. Hazen, "What's in a Name?"
115. Hazen, "What's in a Name?"

no *Jerusalem Times* that at the end of the year listed the most popular names given to babies that year (as the London Times now does).[116]

By contrast:

> if you examine the most popular Jewish names in a different region (such as Egypt) at the time, the list is dramatically different ... Also by contrast, if you examine the names that appear in the Apocryphal Gospels (such as the Gospels of Thomas, Mary, Judas), you discover that the frequency and proportion of names in these writings do not match what we know to be true of names from the land and time of Jesus. Hence the Apocryphal Gospels do not have the ring of authenticity with regard to personal names and are rightly called into question.[117]

Watch: "New Evidences the Gospels were Based on Eyewitness Accounts" Peter J. Williams: https://youtu.be/r5Ylt1pBMm8

Read: *Jesus and the Eyewitnesses: The Gospels as Eyewitness Testimony* by Richard Bauckham

Can We Trust the Gospels? by Peter J. Williams

Confirmation from undesigned coincidences

An "undesigned coincidence" exists where one source of testimony mentions in passing information that answers a question arising from a different source of testimony, thereby bearing witness to the common information that lies beneath them. There are many instances where one NT source fills an informational gap in another, including where one gospel "completely in passing and therefore almost certainly inadvertently explains a question that other Gospels raise but leave unanswered by gaps in their narratives."[118] For example:

> in Matthew 26:67–68, the chief priest and members of the council struck Jesus and asked Him to prophesy who hit Him. It wouldn't seem to have been a difficult thing to do, unless one had read Luke 22:63–64, which included the added detail that Jesus had been blindfolded. In the feeding of the five thousand, Jesus asked Philip where they should buy food (John 6:5) ... Why did Jesus ask him rather than one of the other disciples? It turns out that Philip was from Bethsaida (John 12:21), the location of the feeding of the five thousand. However, John's gospel does not tell us where the feeding occurred. Although the account of the feeding is in all four gospels, we only get the location from

---

116. Bauckham, *Jesus and the Eyewitnesses*, 543.
117. See: Hazen, "What's in a Name?"
118. Craig in endorsement for McGrew, *Hidden In Plain View*.

Luke's gospel (Luke 9:10). But Luke did not indicate whom Jesus asked and did not state where Philip had lived. So, we can only figure out why Jesus asked Philip where to get food by reading parallel [but independent] accounts from Luke and John.[119]

Now, as Timothy McGrew observes: "One undesigned coincidence might be an accident—like having two unrelated pieces of a jigsaw puzzle fit together, just by chance. But if we discover numerous undesigned coincidences crisscrossing the documents, it becomes ridiculous to insist that they are all just accidental."[120] Hence, as Lydia McGrew argues: "The occurrence of multiple undesigned coincidences between and among these documents supports the conclusion that the Gospels and Acts are historically reliable and that they come from people close to the facts who were attempting to tell truthfully what they knew."[121]

Lydia McGrew notes that even the two gospels that most resemble each other (i.e. Mark and Matthew): "have undesigned coincidences that couldn't have arisen from copying between them; this is a reason to believe that they are reliable and to an important degree *independent*."[122]

Watch: "Undesigned Coincidences" YouTube playlist: www.youtube.com/playlist?list=PLQhh3qcwVEWgZ_2TLqaPchdovuItTyZll

Listen: "The Ring of Truth" by Timothy McGrew: http://firstkenner.org/audio/jan2011/010911A%20.mp3

Read: "Tim McGrew replies to Ed Babinski's Critique of his Discussion of Undesigned Coincidences": http://dangerousidea.blogspot.com/2011/01/tim-mcgrew-replies-to-ed-babinskis.html

"Undesigned Scriptural Coincidences: The Ring of Truth" by Jonathan McLatchie: http://christianapologeticsalliance.com/2012/08/22/undesigned-scriptural-coincidences-the-ring-of-truth/

"Forgotten Arguments for Christianity: Undesigned Coincidences—The argument stated" by J.W. Wartick: https://jwwartick.com/2012/11/26/undesigned-coinc-1/

Hidden In Plain View: Undesigned Coincidences in the Gospels and Acts by Lydia McGrew

---

In light of all the evidence reviewed above, we can agree with philosopher William P. Alston that "the Gospels embody items from the tradition that stretches to them from Jesus himself during his life on earth," and that they do so in a manner that is "sufficiently free from distortion" to count as "an accurate account."[123]

---

119. Deem, "Book Review: *Cold-Case Christianity*."
120. McGrew, "Internal Evidence for the Truth of the Gospels and Acts."
121. McGrew, *Hidden In Plain View*, 14.
122. McGrew, *Hidden In Plain View*, 28.
123. Alston, "Historical Criticism of the Synoptic Gospels," 167.

Getting at the Gospels

The origins of testimony: Link 2

Who wrote the gospels?

> "it is well known to scholars that the Gospels were not actually written by their traditional authors..."
>
> —Russell Blackford and Udo Schuklenk[124]

Of the "tales about Jesus in the New Testament," Jerry A. Coyne asserts that our sources "are not only second hand but produced by unknown writers."[125] Concerning NT sources about Jesus' resurrection in particular, he opines that "none are by eyewitnesses..."[126] Coyne doesn't explain how he knows the NT sources are second-hand and not by eyewitnesses if we don't know who wrote them. Similarly, Richard Dawkins asserts: "Nobody knows who the four evangelists were, but they almost certainly never met Jesus."[127] Despite not knowing who wrote the gospels, Dawkins is nonetheless sure that "not one of them" was "an eyewitness."[128] Likewise, Michel Onfray opines that "none of the four evangelists ever know Christ in the flesh."[129]

Missing a Key Point

As seen in our review of the role played by testimonial sources in the formation of the gospels, these expressions of skepticism are somewhat beside the point. As John Polkinghorne reminds us: "the essential question is not the identity of the particular person who wrote a particular text, but the historical reliability of what was written."[130] The gospels clearly weave together a number of pre-existing sources (Luke does so explicitly). The reliability of those sources and the faithfulness of their transmission by the gospel writers, whoever they were, is validated by multiple lines of evidence. That evidence includes our general knowledge of oral history, numerous lines of corroborative evidence (including extrabiblical writers such as Josephus), as well as evidence from archaeology, geography, the undesigned coincidences between the gospels, and their statistically accurate use of names.

---

124. Blackford and Schuklenk, *50 Great Myths About Atheism*, 173.
125. Coyne, *Faith vs. Fact*, 121.
126. Coyne, *Faith vs. Fact*, 121.
127. Dawkins, *The God Delusion*, 122.
128. Dawkins, *The Magic of Reality*, 262.
129. Onfray, *In Defence of Atheism*, 155.
130. Polkinghorne, *Encountering Scripture*, 54.

Getting at Jesus
Defending the Tradition

The idea that the NT gospels weren't written by the traditional authors within a generation of Jesus, but by anonymous authors towards the end of the first century (or even the beginning of the second century), "was formulated in the early twentieth century by scholars known as 'form critics,' who believed that the Gospels were not biography but folklore."[131] However, this European folklore model "has been discredited..."[132] The form critic's comparison has been replaced by the realization that the NT Gospels were ancient biographies composed against the backdrop of Jewish oral culture. Hence "a good case can still be made for Matthew, Mark, Luke, and John as the authors of the Gospels that have traditionally been attributed to them."[133] For example, Lydia McGrew argues that "the hypothesis that these Gospels were written by their traditionally ascribed authors is a good explanation for the data found in them, including the undesigned coincidences."[134]

The gospels were originally written on scrolls, which would have had name tags (called "syllabus") on the outside that identified the author. When the codex (the early form of the book) was first used to make a copy of a scroll, the author's name would naturally have been written in at the beginning of the codex. That name would have been copied from the scroll's tag, or else it would have been written in from memory if the tag was missing. Works without named or known authors would likely be given the name of a pseudepigraphical author; but such works would probably be attributed to several different authors as names were given to them in different communities:

> Since even critics admit that the NT documents were intended for a wide audience... they must explain why these practical factors would be irrelevant and allow a NT document to remain "anonymous" and then later not be attributed to multiple authors. Critics would have a better case if they could find a copy of Matthew that is instead attributed to, say, Andrew; or to no one at all, followed by confusion over authorship from external sources; or a copy of what is obviously Mark that is attributed to Barnabas. But the internal evidence of attribution from the NT documents is unanimous and unequivocal.[135]

As Bauckham observes: "if the Gospels had originally circulated without titles, a variety of different titles would have been generated as various Christian communities invented titles for their own use. But we have no evidence that there were ever titles other than the ones we know."[136] Thus Lydia McGrew concludes that "all of our

---

131. Pitre, *The Case For Jesus*, 13.
132. Bauckham, *Jesus and the Eyewitnesses*, 300.
133. Blomberg, *Jesus and the Gospels*, 365.
134. McGrew, *Hidden In Plain View*, 30.
135. Holding, *Trusting the New Testament*, 140.
136. Bauckham, *Jesus and the Eyewitnesses*, 536.

Getting at the Gospels

manuscript evidence . . . is fully compatible with the hypothesis that the gospels *never* circulated without their present titles."[137]

Brant Pitre reports that "When it comes to the titles of the Gospels, not only the earliest and best manuscripts, but *all of the ancient manuscripts—without exception, in every language—attribute the four Gospels to Matthew, Mark, Luke, and John.*"[138] Pitre notes that "In the first three centuries after Christ, even those identified as heretics and enemies of the Church seem to have accepted that the four Gospels were actually written by Matthew, Mark, Luke and John."[139] Indeed, as far as we know, "no one in antiquity ever attributed the Gospels to anyone other than the four traditionally accepted authors."[140]

Christians probably wouldn't attribute gospels to such peripheral characters as Mark, Luke, and even the apostle Matthew, if they didn't at least have a major input to their content: "Mark and Luke, after all, were not among Jesus' twelve apostles . . . Though an apostle, Matthew is best known for . . . his unscrupulous past as a [tax-collector]."[141] By contrast with the canonical gospels, "the later second-through fifth-century apocryphal Gospels and Acts are [generally speaking] (falsely) ascribed to highly reputable, influential early Christians to try to make them appear as authoritative and credible as possible."[142] Hence Timothy Paul Jones argues that there is:

> no compelling reason to reject the ancient oral traditions that connected the New Testament Gospels to Matthew, Mark, Luke and John. Given the evidence that's available, no one can be certain who wrote these books . . . still, the best evidence that we possess suggests that the sources for the four Gospels were a tax collector named Matthew, Simon Peter's translator Mark, the physician Luke and a fisherman named John.[143]

Mark D. Roberts reports that:

> in recent years many have come to believe that the first and fourth Gospels reflect the memory and the perspective of Jesus' own disciples, both Matthew and John . . . Matthew and John may not have been the ones who finally put pen to papyrus, but they, their memory, and their authority stand behind the Gospels that bear their names.[144]

Michael Licona comments that while "A number of scholars hold to the traditional authorship of John," nevertheless "today's majority contends that a minor

137. McGrew, "Bart Ehrman and the Authorship of the Gospels."
138. Pitre, *The Case For Jesus*, 17.
139. Pitre, *The Case For Jesus*, 52.
140. Wallace, *Cold-Case Christianity*, 172.
141. Blomberg, "Where Do We Start Studying Jesus?," 28.
142. Blomberg, "Where Do We Start Studying Jesus?," 24.
143. Jones, *Misquoting Truth*, 119.
144. Roberts, *Can We Trust the Gospels?*, 49.

disciple who was not one of the Twelve but who had travelled with Jesus and was an eyewitness to his ministry is the source behind John's Gospel."[145] In either case, John's Gospel provides "eyewitness testimony from one of Jesus' disciples who had travelled with him."[146]

J.P. Holding reports that among NT scholars: "Mark and Luke-Acts are usually granted their assigned authorship..."[147] R.T. France comments:

> Luke, the doctor who was a companion of Paul (Colossians 4:14; 2 Timothy 4:11; Philemon 24) is the most widely accepted, as the author of both the third gospel and its sequel, the Acts of the Apostles. Mark, similarly a colleague of Paul (Acts 12:25; 15:37-41; Colossians 4:10; 2 Timothy 4:11; Philemon 24), but also, if the same Mark is intended, a companion of Peter (1 Peter 5:13), is accepted by many as at least a possible author of the second gospel... There are in fact weighty defenders today of the traditional authorship of all four gospels... I find all four traditional ascriptions at least plausible.[148]

The New Atheist's blanket claims about the gospel writers being unknown authors who didn't know Jesus in the flesh are both unjustified and wide of the mark.

Watch: "Who Wrote the NT Gospels?" Youtube playlist: www.youtube.com/playlist?list=PLQhh3qcwVEWg2vHjaH7hwE3BdtZao15CS

When were the gospels written?

"the gospels were written down and circulated during the first generation after the event."

—William Lane Craig[149]

"the Gospels originated within a few decades of the death of Jesus."

—Michael Green[150]

Richard Dawkins writes that: "All four of the gospels... were written long after the events that they purport to describe..."[151] Again, he states: "The gospels were written

---

145. Licona, "Fish Tales," 141.
146. Licona, "Fish Tales," 141.
147. Holding, *Trusting the New Testament*, 137.
148. France, *The Evidence for Jesus*, 122, 124.
149. Craig, *On Guard*, 191.
150. Green, *The Books The Church Suppressed*, 34.
151. Dawkins, *The Magic of Reality*, 262.

decades after Jesus' purported death."[152] As our discussion of gospel sources shows, such an emphasis upon the publication dates of the gospels is naive. Moreover, how long after the events is "long after"? How many "decades" are we talking about?

A.N. Wilson once opined that "the Jesus of the Gospels is an artificial creation, a collective work of art who evolved through the combined consciousness of two generations of Christian worship."[153] Likewise, Matthew Kneale asserts that "The gospels ... were written two and more generations after Jesus' death."[154] If we take a generation to be thirty-forty years, this suggests the NT gospels were written some sixty-eighty years after Jesus' death, around the turn of the second century.

According to Jerry A. Coyne, although the events of Jesus' life "were not written down within Jesus' lifetime, they were described only a few decades later."[155] This suggests the NT gospels were written within thirty to forty years of Jesus' death, and within the first century. Roy Williams reports that the "rough consensus" of scholarship puts the authorship of the NT gospels "some time between AD 60 and AD 90, though both earlier and later dates have been proposed."[156] As Stanley E. Porter writes: "The estimated dates for the composition of the Gospels vary considerably, but all [scholars of the NT] agree that they were written in the first century."[157] N.T. Wright reports the scholarly consensus that "The 27 books of the New Testament were written ... by the end of the first century at the latest. Most scholars would put most of them earlier than that..."[158] For example, W.F. Albright argued that "every book of the New Testament was written ... between the forties and the eighties of the first century A.D. (very probably sometime between about A.D. 50 and 75)."[159]

Indeed, as John J. Bombaro observes: "scholars almost universally are dating the New Testament documents earlier."[160] Geisler confirms: "There is a growing acceptance of earlier New Testament dates..."[161] In particular, as Josh McDowell and Bill Wilson report: "scholars are increasingly opting for earlier dates of composition for the gospel accounts."[162] J.P. Moreland concurs that: "in recent years, there has been a trend in New Testament studies towards dating the Gospels earlier."[163]

---

152. Dawkins, *Science in The Soul*, 280.
153. Wilson, *Paul*, 144.
154. Kneale, *An Atheist's History of Belief*, 78.
155. Coyne, *Faith vs. Fact*, 121.
156. Williams, *God, Actually*, 161–62.
157. Porter, *How We Got the New Testament*, 85.
158. Wright, *Why Read the Bible?*, 4.
159. Albright quoted in Montgomery, *History, Law and Christianity*, 17–18.
160. Bombaro, "Introduction," 5.
161. Geisler, *Baker Encyclopedia of Christian Apologetics*, 529.
162. McDowell and Wilson, *He Walked Among Us*, 128.
163. Moreland, *Scaling the Secular City*, 151.

For example, atheist James G. Crossley (of the Department of Biblical Studies at the University of Sheffield and co-chair of the Jesus Seminar for the British New Testament Conference) argues that Mark was written between the mid-30s and mid-40s. Atheist NT scholar Maurice Casey likewise dates Mark to the 40s. As Carsten Peter Thiede states: "those who argue for early dates of authentic Gospels as sources of information about an historical Jesus . . . are no longer the conservative or fundamentalist outsiders."[164]

Biblical historian and Fellow of the British Academy F.F. Bruce comments that, even with the later range of dates considered by mainstream NT scholarship: "the situation is encouraging from the historian's point of view, for the first three Gospels were written at a time when many were alive all who could remember the things that Jesus said and did, and some at least would still be alive when the fourth Gospel was written."[165]

Genesis of the four-fold gospel

It's impossible to say with certainty when in the first century AD the four gospels were written: "The Gospels do not say when they were written and there is no unambiguous external evidence."[166] Nevertheless, scholars offer historical reconstructions for the historical genesis of the gospels, and the following reconstructions strike me as the most plausible.

Paul Barnett argues that in the early church, four overlapping mission groups emerged by the forties AD "led by Peter, James, John, and Paul,"[167] and that each mission group is associated with "one gospel and one or more letters"[168] that were gathered into the NT during the second century (having been recognized and passed on as authentic by the first-century Christian community).

Fig. 13.

Mission Group Leader:	Mission Group Literature:
Peter	1 & 2 Peter, Gospel of Mark
Paul	Paul's Letters, Gospel of Luke, Acts
James	Epistle of James, Gospel of Matthew
John	Gospel of John, 1 John, Revelation

---

164. Thiede, *Jesus*, 9.
165. Bruce, *The New Testament Documents*, 17.
166. Barnett, *The Truth About Jesus*, 50.
167. Barnett, *Finding the Historical Christ*, 14.
168. Barnett, *Finding the Historical Christ*, 16.

This hypothesis "explains the dissemination of Christian belief as well as the origin and purpose of the greater part of the NT."[169]

Let's consider the origins of each of the four gospels in what I take to be their likely historical order.

The gospel according to Mark: c. AD 49

Matthew Kneal asserts that "Mark's gospel was written almost two generations after Jesus' death..."[170] If we take a generation to be about 40 years, that would date Mark's Gospel to around the first decade of the second century. Jerry A. Coyne writes of "the four or five decades spanning the reported date of Jesus' death and the first written scriptural account of his deeds (the Gospel of Mark),"[171] thereby placing Mark's Gospel around AD 70–80 (and overlooking the NT letters). According to Russell Blackford and Udo Schuklenk: "The first of the Gospels, traditionally attributed to Mark, was probably written about 70 CE..."[172] Michel Onfray agrees that "Mark wrote his text around the year 70."[173] Note that this is within living memory, being about 40 years after Jesus' death.

On the one hand, scholars who advocate composition dates "around," or more precisely after, AD 70 for the NT gospels often rely upon the question-begging assumption that miracles of prophecy are impossible: "all the Gospels record Jesus prophesying the destruction of Jerusalem. Now, scholars who don't believe anything supernatural can occur, argue that this shows that the Gospels must be written after the fall of Jerusalem [in AD 70] (a main reason they date the Gospels late)."[174]

It's interesting to note that Josephus records the prophecy of one Jesus son of Ananias, who predicted the destruction of Jerusalem and its temple at the Feast of Tabernacles in AD 60. Still, the fact that Jesus' prediction was purportedly made further before the event and also has a high degree of specificity to it is a stumbling-block to those with dogmatic miracle-excluding presuppositions.

On the other hand, plenty of eminent scholars would date Mark earlier than AD 70. For example, Rowan Williams records that he thinks "of Mark being written some time in the 60s—that is, before the fall of Jerusalem" whilst also noting that "the issue of the date of Mark is very far from being closed, less so than seemed to be the case half a century ago."[175]

---

169. Barnett, *Finding the Historical Christ*, 16.
170. Kneale, *An Atheist's History of Belief*, 111.
171. Coyne, "It's Time to Ponder Whether Jesus Really Existed."
172. Blackford and Schuklenk, *50 Great Myths About Atheism*, 173.
173. Onfray, *In Defence of Atheism*, 121.
174. Boyd, *Letters From a Skeptic*, 95.
175. Williams, *Meeting God in Mark*, 19.

The early church historian Eusebius (AD 340) "fixes a date for Mark during the reign of the Emperor Claudius between A.D. 41 and 54,"[176] and I think there's a plausible case for dating Mark's Gospel to c. AD 49, sixteen years after the crucifixion of Jesus.

Concerning the gospel traditionally attributed to Mark, Blomberg notes that "the oldest and most important testimony, from very early in the second century and recorded by Eusebius in the early 300s, is that of Papias."[177] Papias cites the apostle John as having taught that:

> Mark became Peter's interpreter and wrote accurately all that he remembered, not indeed, in order, of the things said or done by the Lord. For he had heard not the Lord, nor had he followed him, but later on, as I said, followed Peter, who used to give teaching as necessity demanded but not making, as it were, an arrangement of the Lord's oracles, so that Mark did nothing wrong in writing down single points as he remembered them. For to one thing he gave attention, to leave out nothing of what he had heard and to make no false statement in them.[178]

Peter's reported influence upon the first gospel fits the observation that "the general outline of Mark's Gospel is similar to Peter's presentation of the gospel in Acts 10:36–43."[179] Martin Hengel notes that while the disciples are mentioned 43 times in Mark, Peter is clearly singled out, being mentioned 25 times. He also notes the number of times Peter is mentioned per the number of words in the three Synoptic Gospels, a ratio that is higher in Mark (at 1:443) than in Matthew (1:772) or Luke (1:648).[180] Again, Peter is the first and last disciple mentioned in the Gospel of Mark. Bauckham argues that "the pattern of reference to Peter in Mark is an authorial indication that Peter is the main eyewitness behind this Gospel . . ."[181]

John Mark is a minor character in the NT, mentioned in only a smattering of passages:

- Mark 14:51–52: The young man who fled naked from Gethsemane, having left his linen garment behind with his would-be captors, is generally thought to have been John Mark.

- Acts 12:12–13: Mark is the son of Mary, a wealthy woman in whose house the early church meets to pray for Peter while he is in prison c. AD 42.

- Colossians 4:10: Mark is the cousin of Barnabas.

---

176. *Ignatius Catholic Study Bible New Testament*, 61.
177. Blomberg, *Jesus and the Gospel*, 123.
178. Papias quoted in Blomberg, *Jesus and the Gospels*, 123.
179. *Ignatius Catholic Study Bible New Testament*, 61.
180. See: Holding, *Defending the Resurrection*, 324.
181. Bauckham, *Jesus and the Eyewitnesses*, 511.

- Acts 12:25: Mark returned to Antioch from Jerusalem with Barnabas and Paul c. AD 47.

- Acts 13:5: Mark accompanied Barnabas and Paul on a missionary journey c. AD 47–48, but left part way through.

- Acts 15:37–39: Mark was consequently the cause of a dispute between Barnabas and Paul c. AD 49.

- Philemon 24 and 2 Timothy 4:11: Mark is described as being "a fellow worker" with Paul.

- 1 Peter 5:13: Peter refers to "my son Mark," in a spiritual rather than biological sense.

Blomberg comments: "Given that Mark was not one of the Twelve [apostles] but a relatively obscure character with a mixed record of ministry during his lifetime, it is unlikely that anyone unfamiliar with the true author of this Gospel but desiring to credit it to an authoritative witness would have selected Mark as his man."[182] Indeed, why not attribute the gospel to Peter?

Hengel concludes that Mark's Gospel "was written by a Jewish Graeco-Palestinian, John Mark, who was a missionary companion of Peter for some time."[183] David Wenham and Steve Walton report:

> This remains a widely held view in scholarship [as it] offers a plausible explanation for many incidental details in the Gospel. It also fits well with Mark's reports of occasions when only Peter and a few others were present (e.g. 1:16–20, 29–31; 9:2–8; 14:27–31), and the frequent mentions of Peter's failures and mistakes (e.g. 8:32f.; 9:5f.; 10:28–31; 14:29–31, 66–72).[184]

Early church fathers such as Irenaeus, Clement, Justin Martyr, Tatian, Tertulian, Origen, Jerome, and Eusebius all accept Mark as the author. Oscar Cullmann observes that "there is no serious reason to doubt"[185] this tradition. Michel Onfray accepts that Mark was "probably the companion of Paul of Tarsus on his missionary wanderings."[186] Given that Mark died in AD 62, as reported by both Jerome and Eusebius, he must have written his gospel beforehand.

David Winter suggests that the failure to name "the young man who fled, leaving behind his tunic, on the occasion of the arrest of Jesus [an incident mentioned only by Mark]"[187] may indicate the gospel's antiquity, inasmuch as naming him could still have led to trouble with the authorities. Again, Simon of Cyrene (who bore the cross-beam

---

182. Blomberg, *Jesus and the Gospel*, 125.
183. Hengel, *Studies in the Gospel of Mark*, 29.
184. Wenham and Walton, *Exploring the New Testament*, 205.
185. Cullmann, *The New Testament*, 37.
186. Onfray, *In Defence of Atheism*, 121.
187. Winter, *The Search for the Real Jesus*, 29.

for Jesus) is only identified indirectly by Mark, via the names of his sons Alexander and Rufus. As Hengel observes, this probably indicates that they were "still known to the audience of the Gospel."[188]

R. Alan Cole likewise points out that:

> No identification is made in Mark either of the wounded servant of the high priest or of the disciple who struck the blow which wounded him (14:7) and presumably for exactly the same reason; it was not safe at the time. Not until John's gospel, probably written long afterwards . . . will it be safe to identify both servant and disciple (John 18:10).[189]

As Simon Greenleaf observed:

> Peter's agency in the narrative of Mark is asserted by all ancient writers, and is confirmed by the fact that his humility is conspicuous in every part of it, where anything is or might be related to him; his weaknesses and fall being fully exposed, while things which might redound to his honor, are either omitted or but slightly mentioned; that scarcely any transaction of Jesus is related, at which Peter was not present, and that all are related with that circumstantial minuteness which belongs to the testimony of an eye-witness.[190]

Another indication of an early date is that the Gospel of Mark contains "more Aramaic formulae than any other original Greek literary text."[191] Atheist NT scholar Maurice Casey has argued that much of Mark is easily retrojected back into Aramaic. This supports "the suggestion of Bauckham that Mark translated Peter's Aramaic recollections into his Gospel. Peter spoke in Aramaic and perhaps some wooden Greek, remembering various things Jesus did and said, and Mark wrote it down in better Greek."[192] Casey consequently concludes that Mark was written c. AD 40.[193]

Mark also contains more Latinisms than other Greek texts, which is interesting in light of Carsten Peter Thiede's observation that early Christian writers Papias, Eusebius, and Jerome "supply valuable information from first-generation eyewitness accounts (Papias) and from massive archival material . . . that Peter first visited Rome in the second year of the Emperor Claudius who ruled from AD 41–54."[194]

Peter's escape from the prison of Herod Agrippa I[195] and his fleeting visit thereafter to the home of Mark's mother in Jerusalem (see: Acts 12) must have happened c. AD 42: "then Luke simply says, 'And he left for another place.' If Papias, Eusebius, and

---

188. Hengel, *Studies in the Gospel of Mark*, 9.
189. Cole, *Tyndale New Testament Commentaries: Mark*, 24.
190. Greenleaf, *The Testimony of the Evangelists*, 23.
191. Hengel, *Studies in the Gospel of Mark*, 9.
192. Witherington, "Christianity in the Making," 223.
193. See: Casey, *Jesus of Nazareth*.
194. Thiede, *Jesus*, 44.
195. See: Williams, *The Case for Angels*, 127–29.

Jerome are correct, then the final destination of this journey must have been Rome."[196] This fits the fact that the phrase "to another place" is found in the Septuagint Greek version of the Old Testament, where it refers to Babylon, the mantle of which had figuratively fallen on Rome by NT times (see: Revelation 17:5. This association was also made by Roman writers such as Plautus). Indeed, this identification is made explicit at the end of Peter's first letter written in Rome: "She who is in Babylon, chosen together with you, sends you her greetings and so does my son Mark." Luke is thus obliquely referring to Peter's destination. This fits with Paul's statement in Romans 15:20–24 (written c. AD 57) that he intended only to pay a passing visit to Rome "lest I build on another man's foundation" (see: Galatians 2:7–9). The other man was presumably Peter, whom tradition unanimously cites as the founder of the Roman church:

> So Rome it was for Peter. And Mark probably went with him straightaway. That he was with Peter in Rome at some stage at least is clearly stated in 1 Peter 5:13 . . . But all other early sources also confirm that he was present when Peter preached the gospel to the Romans. And Peter could have spent at least two, perhaps three, years in the city during his first stay. When Herod Agrippa died in AD 44, the man who had put him into prison back in Jerusalem could no longer endanger his safety . . . Therefore, in AD 44 at the earliest, Peter could have left Rome to return to Jerusalem . . . One way or another, he was back in Jerusalem in time for the apostolic council mentioned in Acts 15:1–29 . . . And this council can be dated to about AD 48.[197]

Thiede hypothesizes that "Soon . . . after the 'exodus' of Peter from Rome—a term used by the second-century author Irenaeus in his brief report about the four Gospels, and all too often mistranslated as 'death' instead of 'departure'—the Christians would have asked Mark to write down . . . what Peter had taught him about the life and sayings of Jesus."[198] This would seem to be a natural reaction to the departure of the community's primary trident of the oral history about Jesus. John Wenham argues that: "Peter's departure from Rome seems to provide the ideal *Sitz im Leben* for the writing of Mark's Gospel . . . it is reasonable to suppose that Peter left Mark behind and that he then wrote his Gospel."[199]

Another possible spur to Mark to begin writing down things about Jesus was his participation c. AD 47–48 in Paul's first missionary journey (see: Acts 13:5). In any case, as Robert J. Hutchinson observes: "It is possible, even likely, that the author of Mark spent many years collecting sayings and anecdotes about Jesus' life, both written and oral, perhaps in the AD 30s and 40s."[200] There's certainly no need to hypoth-

---

196. Thiede, *Jesus*, 44.
197. Thiede, *Jesus*, 46.
198. Thiede, *Jesus*, 46.
199. Wenham, "Did Peter Go To Rome In AD 42?," 94–102.
200. Hutchinson, *Searching For Jesus*, 34.

esize that Mark's material came *only* from the apostle Peter. Mark clearly wasn't an eyewitness to Jesus' ministry in the way that the apostles were, but as a resident of Jerusalem he had the opportunity to have been an eyewitness to some of the events in his gospel (as suggested by the cameo of the young man who flees in an embarrassing state of undress from the garden of Gethsemane). It's possible that his mother, Mary, was an eyewitness to something of Jesus' career (at least within the environs of Jerusalem). In addition, he would probably have known other residents of Jerusalem who may have witnessed Jesus.

In any case, I propose that Mark's writings by AD 48 formed *a first draft of* what was to become his gospel. Thiede addresses a paradox arising from the writings of Clement of Alexandria (c. AD 150–214) who:

> wrote twice about the reception given to Mark's Gospel. Both statements are quoted by the historian Eusebius of Caeserea, and they appear to contradict each other. In one report, having told how the Roman Christians asked Mark to write down Peter's preaching after his departure, he says 'When the matter came to Peter's knowledge, he neither expressly hindered it nor actively encouraged it.' But in another report, Clement states . . . that Peter was pleased at the zeal of the Roman Christians and ratified the Gospel for study in the churches.[201]

Thiede's reconstruction resolves this paradox: "Clement, quoted by Eusebius in different contexts, describes a development. The first stage describes the collection of the material, the composition of a first version of the Gospel. The second stage is the refined version, the finished product, proofread perhaps by Peter himself."[202] Hence, on the basis of the testimony available to him from the 30s and 40s (including, perhaps, his own): "Mark . . . could have started to write his Gospel . . . in AD 44 . . ."[203] John A.T. Robinson concludes that "the first draft of Mark's gospel could be as early as 45 AD."[204] By assuming that Mark had completed a first draft of his gospel by c. AD 48, we can perhaps illuminate the incident recorded by Luke in Acts 13:13, where Mark suddenly leaves his cousin Barnabas and Paul in the lurch and returns to Jerusalem. When Barnabas later suggested taking Mark on a second journey, Paul refuses "because he had deserted them in Pamphylia and had not continued with them in their work" (Acts 15:37–38). Even though Barnabas defends Mark, "They had such a sharp disagreement that they parted company. Barnabas took Mark and sailed for Cyprus" (Acts 15:39). So why did Mark leave Paul and Barnabas in the lurch on their first journey, and why was Barnabas happy to go it alone with Mark on that second occasion? Maybe Mark:

201. Thiede, *Jesus*, 48–49.
202. Thiede, *Jesus*, 49.
203. Thiede, *Jesus*, 49.
204. Robinson, *Can We Trust The New Testament?*, 73.

left them and returned to Jerusalem because he had heard that Peter had returned there. For Mark . . . this would have been the long-awaited chance to show his work to the man on whose preaching it was based. And here, at this meeting or soon after, the second stage of the completion of the Gospel may have begun—the drafting of the one which was to meet with Peter's approval, the one ratified by him for copying and distribution . . .[205]

According to this reconstruction, Mark, who was already in touch with information about Jesus, began writing his gospel based primarily upon Peter's teaching stories after Peter's departure from Rome c. AD 44 and/or whilst on mission with Paul and Barnabas c. AD 47. Mark left Paul and Barnabas to show his "work in progress" to Peter in Jerusalem c. AD 48. Revisions and/or additions may have been made at this stage, given Mark's renewed access both to Peter and to various Jerusalem sources. Perhaps it was at this stage that Mark married his record of Jesus' teaching and deeds to our earliest narrative account of Jesus' passion:

> The story of Jesus' suffering and death, commonly called the passion story, was probably not originally written by Mark. Rather Mark used a source for this narrative. Mark is the earliest gospel, and his source must be even earlier still. In fact, Rudolf Pesh, a German expert on Mark, says the passion source must go back to at least AD 37.[206]

Once Mark had Peter's blessing on his completed *bios* of Jesus, it was arranged to have copies written and circulated. Plausibly, this publication process took place fairly soon after Peter and Mark returned to Rome following the Jerusalem Council in the winter of AD 48/49 (hence this hypothesis agrees with the testimony of Clement of Alexandrea to the effect that Mark's Gospel was issued while Peter was still alive in Rome).[207]

A reconstruction along these lines is comfortably within the mainstream of contemporary scholarly thought on the dating of Mark's Gospel. Andreas J. Kostenberger and Justin Taylor date Mark's Gospel to "the mid-to late 50s".[208] Walter Elwell and Robert W. Yarborough report: "W.C. Allen dated Mark to about 50 AD . . . John Wenham . . . favors 45, but says any date between 44 and the early 50s is possible."[209] James G. Crossley argues that Mark was written between AD 35 and 45. Maurice Casey concludes that "Mark's Gospel was written c. 40 CE."[210] Clearly, as J. Warner Wallace

---

205. Thiede, *Jesus*, 51.
206. Craig, *On Guard*, 191.
207. On the chronology of Paul's life and the dating of the Jerusalem Council, see: McCallum, "A Chronological Study of Paul's Ministry;" "Timeline of the Apostle Paul."
208. Kostenberger and Taylor, *The Final Days of Jesus*, 15.
209. Elwell and Yarborough, *Encountering the New Testament*.
210. Casey, *Jesus*, 90.

concludes: "Mark's gospel . . . can be sensibly placed in either the late 40's or very early 50's."[211]

The Roman historian Suetonius reports (c. AD 120) that the Emperor Claudius expelled the Jews from Rome in AD 49: "As the Jews were making constant disturbances because of the instigator Chrestus . . ."[212] This comports with Luke's contemporaneous observation in Acts 18:2 "that Claudius had commanded all Jews to depart from Rome." Suetonius's "Chrestus" rests on a confusion of "Christ/Christus" with the slave-name Chrestus:

> It is just conceivable that the riots mentioned by Suetonius were caused by the activity of an otherwise unknown Chrestus, but in that case he would probably have said "at the instigation of a certain Chrestus" (impulsore Chresto quodam). It is more natural to suppose that he intended his readers to understand that Chrestus who, as a matter of general knowledge, was the founder of Christianity. To be sure, Christ was not in Rome in the time of Claudius; but Suetonius, writing seventy years later, may have thought that he was. If his sources indicated that the riots which provoked Claudius's edict of expulsion were due to the introduction and propagation of Christianity in the capital, he could well have drawn the mistaken inference that it had been introduced there by Christ in person.[213]

In which case, might the disturbances in Rome have been sparked *by the publication of Mark's Gospel*? Having researched this question, Peter May argues for what he calls "these distinct and fascinating possibilities":[214]

- That Peter laid the foundations of the church in Rome between AD 44–49
- That Peter's preaching caused uproar among the Jews in Rome, as it had done in Jerusalem (see: Acts 4:2–4)
- That John Mark wrote it down
- That publishing it, in whole or in part, precipitated the riots in Rome

---

Watch: "Mark's Gospel" Youtube playlist: www.youtube.com/playlist?list=PLQhh3qcwVEWj9-pNNYrUA4RWZPzcr_IGJ

Read: "Did Peter Go To Rome In AD 42?" by John Wenham: https://legacy.tyndalehouse.com/tynbul/Library/TynBull_1972_23_04_Wenham_PeterInRome.pdf

Zondervan Illustrated Bible Background Commentary: Volume 1—Matthew, Mark, Luke edited by Clinton E. Arnold

---

211. Wallace, *Cold-Case Christianity*, 170.

212. See: Greg Magee, "The origins of the church at Rome;" Bruce, "Christianity Under Claudius," 309–26; Voorst, *Jesus Outside the New Testament*, 30–39.

213. Wallace, *Cold-Case Christianity*, 170.

214. See: May, *The Search for God and the Path to Persuasion*.

The Holman Apologetics Commentary On The Bible: The Gospels and Acts edited by Jeremy Royal Howard

Baker Exegetical Commentary on the New Testament: Mark by Robert H. Stein,

The Gospel of Mark: Socio-rhetorical Commentary by Ben Witherington III

Quibbles about specific dates aside, the main take-home point here is that "virtually whatever sensible date is accepted for the Gospel of Mark, it was written at a time when the events it records were within the living memory of at least some individuals."[215] As Bauckham affirms: "Mark is a contemporary biography, one written within living memory of its subject."[216]

The Gospel according to Luke: c. AD 59–60.

When it comes to internal evidence for the authorship of Luke-Acts:

> There are no questions to be had: all copies of Luke and Acts say that Luke is the author. Additionally, Luke is the best candidate among Paul's listed companions to be selected from the travelling group designated by "we" in Acts.[217]

Irenaeus, Clement of Alexandria, Origen, Tertullian, Eusebius, and Jerome all attest to Luke's authorship.

Michael R. Licona reports that "the majority of modern scholars hold to the traditional authorship of Luke and Acts."[218] Montefiore acknowledges that Luke's authorship "seems probable".[219] Geisler reports that "Sir William Ramsay supported Luke's authorship . . . Even a liberal scholar like Adolph Harnack agreed that Luke wrote it. Finally, a noted Roman historian, Colin Hemer, agrees with the Lucan authorship."[220] Maurice Casey writes:

> Early church tradition is unanimous in supposing that this Gospel was written by Luke, a companion of Paul, who was not present during the historical ministry of Jesus. This part of church tradition should be accepted, because it is soundly based in the primary source material.[221]

Luke's Gospel combined much of Mark's volume with the sources known as "Q" and other material collected by Luke (known to scholars as "L"). Barnett notes that Luke "had extensive associations with Paul [the leader of our third missionary

---

215. Davis, *Christian Philosophical Theology*, 90.
216. Bauckham, *Jesus and the Eyewitnesses*, 511.
217. Holding, *Trusting the New Testament*, 163.
218. Licona, "Bart D. Ehrman, *Forged: Writing in the Name of God*."
219. Montefiore, *The Womb And The Tomb*, 137.
220. Geisler, *A Popular Survey Of The New Testament*, 77.
221. Casey, *Jesus*, 96.

group], considerable contact with Mark, and opportunity to meet Peter (in Rome—2 Tim 4:11; 1 Peter 5:13)."[222] It therefore seems likely that "L" consists of multiple oral sources. Hence it's not the publication or even writing dates of Luke that's of primary importance but the fact that, as detailed in the gospel's prologue, Luke "received the 'narratives' of the 'eyewitnesses' *while they were still alive* and their memory of the historical Christ was current."[223]

Moreover, since Luke is explicitly writing his gospel to confirm Christian beliefs already received from other witnesses by his patron, Theophilus (Luke 1:3), the information contained in this gospel must at least be consistent with those prior sources. That "Theophilus" means "lover of God" doesn't suggest he was a made-up figure. Indeed, "symbolic dedicatees were virtually unknown"[224] in the ancient world, so it's likely Theophilus was a real person "of status . . . whose name in the dedication might be thought useful to circulating the work."[225] The title "most excellent," given to Theophilus in Luke 1:3, suggests he was "a high official in the service of Rome."[226] This position would have given him sufficient wealth to act as Luke's literary patron, paying for the publication of his two-scroll biography/history of Jesus and the early church (Luke-Acts). As C.H. Dodd writes, Luke-Acts is "an historical composition in the full sense . . . a history of the Beginnings of Christianity, in two parts or volumes."[227]

Luke (the only Gentile contributor to the NT) opens his gospel by recording that since he has "carefully investigated everything from the beginning," in the style of a proper classical historian, he "decided to write an orderly account for you, most excellent Theophilus, so that you may know the certainty [*asphaleia*—literally 'not-totter', meaning 'firmness that equates to security'[228]] of the things you have been taught." (Luke 1:3–4.) Luke doesn't speak in terms of "proof" in the logical or mathematical sense, but he does write that Jesus gave "convincing evidences that he was alive" (Acts 1:3).[229] This proof was pragmatically beyond a reasonable doubt to the eyewitnesses.

Thus, it appears Theophilus was an official of Rome who had heard about Jesus but who wanted more evidence (and wanted to make that evidence available to a wider audience). Luke's two-volume response to Theophilus demonstrates that far from requiring "commitment despite lack of evidence,"[230] Christian faith can be a commitment because of the evidence. Luke doesn't encourage Theophilus to ignore evidence:

---

222. Barnett, *Finding the Historical Christ*, 114.
223. Barnett, *Finding the Historical Christ*, 112.
224. Keener, *The IVP Bible Background Commentary: New Testament*, 319.
225. Keener, *The IVP Bible Background Commentary: New Testament*, 319.
226. Bruce, *Zondervan Bible Commentary*, 1243.
227. Dodd, *The Founder of Christianity*, 29.
228. See: Bible Hub Commentaries, "asphaleia."
229. See: Polhill, *The New American Commentary: Acts*, 81.
230. Grayling, "A.C. Grayling," 3.

far from it! Luke provides Theophilus with evidence "handed down to us by those who from the first were eyewitnesses . . ." (Luke 1:2)

Given that Luke was the author of the gospel "according to Luke," it must have been written before he died. Tradition says Luke died in Thebes aged 84, whilst differing as to whether he died c. AD 70–74[231] or c. AD 150. However, the latter date doesn't fit with the very plausible identification of Luke the evangelist with Luke the traveling companion of Paul, making the earlier date the more likely and pegging AD 74 as the latest possible date for Acts.

In 2001 a paper on the contents of the coffin traditionally held to be that of Luke the evangelist was published in the *Proceedings of the National Academy of Sciences*. The *New York Times* reported:

> A new DNA analysis gives tentative support to the belief that the remains in an ancient lead coffin are those of St. Luke, traditionally considered the author of the third Gospel and the Acts of the Apostles. Dr. Guido Barbujani, a population geneticist at the University of Ferrara, Italy, has extracted DNA from a tooth in the coffin. He concluded that the DNA was characteristic of people living near the region of Antioch, on the eastern Mediterranean, where Luke is said to have been born. Radiocarbon dating of the tooth indicates that it belonged to someone who died between 72 A.D. and 416 A.D.[232]

Thiede described this discovery as "extremely exciting" and stated: "We can never prove definitely that this is St Luke . . . but the evidence is very encouraging."[233]

Simply taking into account the time required for Luke to write Acts before his death plausibly pushes the publication of Luke's Gospel back into the early 70s. Furthermore, Luke's explanation of Jesus' presentation at the temple 32 days after circumcision (Luke 2:22–24) would have been anachronistic unless the temple was still standing when he wrote (and the temple was destroyed in AD 70).

Scholars debate whether or not Luke's work displays any subtle sign of knowing about the destruction of Jerusalem in its report of Jesus' prophecy thereof, but since one might reasonably expect rather obvious references to such a historically and theologically important event, we might well count the absence of any such references as favoring a pre-70 date for Luke-Acts. As David Wenham and Steve Walton comment:

> Some argue that Luke's version of Jesus' prophecy of the fall of the city (Luke 21) is written up in the light of the knowledge of actual events. For example, Luke omits Matthew and Mark's verses inviting the disciples to pray that the siege of the city will not be in winter (Matt. 24:20; Mark 13:18)—and the siege happened during April to September AD 70. However, Luke 21:21 reports the same saying as Mark 13:14, that the disciples should flee to the mountains, and

---

231. See: Tidmarsh, "Saint Luke;" Zalonski, "Saint Luke the Evangelist."
232. Wade, "Body of St. Luke Gains Credibility."
233. Thiede quoted in Craig, "DNA Test Pinpoints St Luke the Apostle's Remains to Padua."

> while we know that the early Christians did flee Jerusalem at this stage, they went to Pella, which is several hundred feet lower than Jerusalem—hardly "the mountains" at all! Further, much of the imagery of Luke 21 reflects the OT accounts of earlier sieges of the city, which could have been done at any time prior to AD 70 . . .[234]

The earliest date at which Luke's Gospel could have been written is of course just after the composition of Mark's Gospel, much of which is incorporated within Luke. We have dated the completed Mark to c. AD 49. So, we can narrow down the timeframe for the publication of Luke to between c. 50 and 70.

On the basis of the first of the famous "we" passages in Acts (where Luke goes from third person to first person description of events), we can infer that Luke joined Paul and his companions in Troas (a major seaport on the west coast of Asia Minor) and went on with them to Philippi in Macedonia c. AD 51. Luke either stayed put in Philippi or he traveled elsewhere without Paul before returning. Either way, from the second "we" passage in Acts it appears that c. AD 58 Luke reconnected with Paul in Philippi when the apostle was on his way to Jerusalem with a relief fund for the church there: "After Paul's arrest in that city and during his extended detention in nearby Caesarea, Luke may have spent considerable time in Palestine working with the apostle as the occasion allowed and gathering materials for his future two-volume literary work, the Gospel and the Acts."[235]

In October-November of AD 60 (see: Luke 27:9),[236] Paul was sent to Rome. Acts describes the voyage, including a shipwreck on Malta,[237] in another of Luke's "we" passages. The narrative of Acts ends with Paul "enjoying considerable personal liberty and opportunities to preach the gospel (Acts 28:30–31) even though a prisoner"[238] in Rome. Paul was released after two years (Acts 28:30), but was re-imprisoned and subsequently martyred during the Neronian persecution c. AD 65. However, Luke only mentions Paul's first imprisonment, leading Wenham and Walton to argue:

> If Luke writes shortly after the events described in Acts 28 (which takes place about AD 62), then Acts appears prior to the execution of Paul (most probably in AD 65), and Luke's Gospel is likely to be at least a little earlier . . . The positive elements in the portrait of Roman authorities would fit well with a date prior to Nero's persecution of Christians in AD 65.[239]

---

234. Wenham and Walton, *Exploring the New Testament*, 297.
235. "Saint Luke."
236. See: Nelson, "Paul Survives a Shipwreck."
237. See: Gatt, "The mystery of St. Paul's shipwreck."
238. "Luke, Gospel of."
239. Wenham and Walton, *Exploring the New Testament*, 297.

Following the same line of argument, Roman historian Mark D. Smith concludes: "it is very probable that Acts was composed before 64 . . ."[240]

Likewise, that nothing is said about the martyrdom of James the brother of Jesus in Jerusalem c. AD 62 indicates that Acts was published before news of this event reached Rome, which in turn suggests that Luke's Gospel was completed no later than AD 63.

Indeed, Paul appears to have been aware of Luke's Gospel c. AD 64, when he wrote his first letter to Timothy:[241]

> The elders who direct the affairs of the church well are worthy of double honor, especially those whose work is preaching and teaching. For Scripture says, 'Do not muzzle an ox while it is treading out the grain,' and 'The worker deserves his wages.' (1 Timothy 5:17–18)

The first quotation is from the Old Testament (Deuteronomy 25:4), but the second quotation is Luke 10:7. Paul isn't merely quoting the same tradition as Luke, since he explicitly notes he is quoting what "Scripture says." Moreover, theologian Michael J. Kruger argues that "Although Paul might be citing some unknown apocryphal gospel (that just happens to have the exact same wording of Luke 10:7), why should we prefer an unknown hypothetical source over a known source?"[242] (2 Peter 3:15–16 likewise refers to the letters of Paul as Scripture in c. AD 65.[243])

Furthermore, it seems to me that John Wenham makes a good point when he observes:

> Luke's Gospel . . . is better dated before the [late 60 AD] shipwreck (in which all manuscripts would have been destroyed) than after. Luke was nearby during Paul's two-year stay at or near Caeserea about 57–59, and this would make a very suitable period for the final preparation of his material for publishing.[244]

Our argument to this point dovetails nicely with the fact that "the early external sources [suggest] that Luke and Acts were written early, while Paul was still alive. See, for example, sections 2:22, 3:4, and 6:25 in Eusebius' *Church History* and section 7 in Jerome's *Lives of Illustrious Men*."[245]

Origen interpreted Paul's comment in 2 Corinthians 8:18 about the brother "whose praise [is] in the gospel throughout all the congregations"[246] as a reference to Luke's written gospel, which would date it to the mid-fifties AD. However, the refer-

---

240. Smith, *The Final Days of Jesus*, 21.
241. See *NIV Thompson Student Bible*, 1627.
242. Kruger, "Some NT Writers Quote Other NT Writers as Scripture."
243. See: Kruger, "Some NT Writers Quote Other NT Writers as Scripture."
244. Wenham, "Did Peter Go to Rome in AD 42?," 95.
245. Engwer, "Early External Evidence for an Early Date for Luke-Acts."
246. See: Bible Hub Commentaries, "2 Corinthians 8:18."

ence isn't explicitly about either Luke or a written gospel. The verse may be taken as referring to "the brother who is praised throughout the churches for his gospel ministry" (HSCB), and Paul could easily have in mind Mark, Silas, or Barnabas, etc. This hook can't bear the weight of dating Luke's Gospel.

J. Warner Wallace points out similarities between Luke's report of the Last Supper (Luke 22:19-20) and Paul's description of the same event in 1 Corinthians 1:23-25. *If* Paul is quoting Luke, *then* Luke's Gospel must predate 1 Corinthians, placing his gospel before c. AD 55. However, the similarities between these two accounts is less striking than the quotation from Luke 10:7 in 1 Timothy, so it seems more plausible in this case to think that Paul and Luke are being jointly influenced by the same tradition.

John Warwick Montgomery urges that "Luke-Acts should probably be dated prior to 64 . . ."[247] Leon Morris reckons that for Luke's Gospel "there seems most to be said for a date in the early 60s."[248] The *Holman Bible Dictionary* suggests we "date the writing of Luke somewhere between A.D. 61, 63."[249] Brant Pitre argues that "the Gospel of Luke was written while Paul was still alive . . . sometime before AD 62."[250] Mark Strauss argues that Luke's Gospel dates to "the late 50's or early 60's," and suggests a date around about "A.D. 60-63."[251] Elwell and Yarborough conclude that Luke "must have been completed somewhere in the late 50s or early 60s . . . there is no reason to date Luke any later than the early 60s."[252] John Wenham, drawing upon work by F.F. Bruce, argues Luke was published around A.D 59.[253] William Lane Craig concludes that "Luke was written probably around A.D 57 or so."[254] I suggest that a publication date for Luke's Gospel c. AD 59-60 is most plausible given the available evidence. This places Luke's Gospel within 26-27 years of Jesus' crucifixion.

Whatever its precise date of composition/publication, it's important to note that leading NT scholar James D.G. Dunn praises Luke as "one of the most reliable historians of his age, whose account can be credited with a high degree of trustworthiness."[255] Likewise, John Stott reports that "Luke has been vindicated in recent years as an accurate and painstaking historian . . ."[256] As Craig explains:

> The book of Acts overlaps significantly with secular history of the ancient world, and the historical accuracy of Acts is indisputable. This has recently been demonstrated anew by Colin Hemer, a classical scholar who turned to

247. Montgomery, *History And Christianity*, 35.
248. Morris, *Tyndale New Testament Commentaries: Luke*, 33.
249. "Luke, Gospel of."
250. Pitre, *The Case For Jesus*, 100–1.
251. Strauss quoted in Arnold, *Zondervan Illustrated Bible Backgrounds Commentary*, 322.
252. Elwell and Yarborough, *Encountering the New Testament*, chapter 6—Kindle version.
253. Wenham, "Did Peter Go To Rome In AD 42?," 94–102.
254. "William Lane Craig at the Bible and Beer Consortium in Dallas, Texas (2015)."
255. Dunn, "The New Testament As History," 51.
256. Stott, *Basic Introduction to the New Testament*, 26.

New Testament studies, in his book *The Book of Acts in the Setting of Hellenistic History*. Hemer goes through the book of Acts with a fine-toothed comb, pulling out a wealth of historical knowledge, ranging from what would have been common knowledge down to details which only a local person would know. Again and again Luke's accuracy is demonstrated: from the sailings of the Alexandrian corn fleet to the coastal terrain of the Mediterranean islands to the peculiar titles of local officials, Luke gets it right . . . Given Luke's care and demonstrated reliability as well as his contact with eyewitnesses within the first generation after the events, this author is trustworthy.[257]

Archaeologist William M. Ramsay said that "Luke's history is unsurpassed in respect of its trustworthiness."[258] Lydia McGrew calls Luke "a careful, conscientious historian."[259]

Watch: "Luke's Gospel" Youtube playlist: www.youtube.com/playlist?list=PLQhh3qcwVEWgrfQ_3f22WAVZZ4F1Y7KIM

Read: *Zondervan Illustrated Bible Background Commentary: Volume 1—Matthew, Mark, Luke* edited by Clinton E. Arnold

The Holman Apologetics Commentary On The Bible: The Gospels and Acts edited by Jeremy Royal Howard

The Book of Acts in the Setting of Hellenistic History by Colin Hemer

---

The Gospel according to Matthew: c. AD 61–65.

Following Peter's escape from prison and his departure for Rome, "the leadership of the Jerusalem church passed to James, the Lord's brother."[260] This brings us to the missionary group that adopted the Jewish-flavored gospel according to Matthew, which is named as such by every intact manuscript except for a third-century manuscript P1, which doesn't offer any inscription. In other words: "No traces of a rival tradition have survived from Christian antiquity."[261]

Irenaeus says Matthew was written "While Peter and Paul were preaching the gospel and founding the church in Rome,"[262] which would require a date for Matthew prior to the mid 60s.

Michael Green notes the claim that "We have fragments of Matthew chapter 26 in Oxford which look on palaeographical grounds to have been written before 70

---

257. Craig, "The Evidence for Jesus."
258. Ramsay quoted in Montgomery, *History, Law and Christianity*, 15.
259. McGrew, *Hidden In Plain View*, 226.
260. Barnett, *Is The New Testament Reliable?*, 75.
261. *Ignatius Catholic Study Bible New Testament*, 3.
262. Irenaeus quoted in Blomberg, *Matthew*, 42.

AD, though this is disputed."[263] We are on firmer ground with Norman L. Geisler and Peter Bocchino's observation that "various passages in Matthew refer to details of temple worship, which would be unnecessary anachronisms after AD 70, and one passage (17:24–27) would be positively misleading since it approves the payment of the temple tax, which after AD 70 was diverted to the upkeep of the temple of Jupiter in Rome!"[264] Dale C. Allison Jr. begrudgingly acknowledges that "there has recently been a slight tendency to date Matthew before 70."[265] Elwell and Yarborough agree that "Matthew was written before the fall of Jerusalem in AD 70."[266]

J.P. Holding reports that "there is significant external evidence attributing to Matthew a Gospel, and connecting it to a version originally composed in a Semitic language."[267] As quoted by Eusebius, Papias reports that Matthew collected the "oracles" of Jesus and that everyone "translated" or "interpreted" them as best they could. Blomberg notes that the Greek word for "oracles" (*logia*) "most naturally means 'sayings,' not a full-fledged narrative Gospel, so perhaps Matthew himself was the author of something like 'Q' before he (or a translator?) turned it into Greek."[268]

The "Matthew wrote Q" hypothesis comports with the explanation offered by James D.G. Dunn for the twin facts of Q's "marked Galilean character" and "lack of a passion narrative;" namely, that *"the Q material first emerged in Galilee and was given its lasting shape there prior to Jesus' death in Jerusalem."*[269] Dunn agrees that "Matthew, the tax collector, is the most obvious candidate for the role of a literary disciple (one who could read and write), who, conceivably, could have taken notes during Jesus' preaching and teaching sessions."[270] Indeed, "Papias—a man who seems to have been in direct contact with the apostle John—mentions that Matthew was a designated note-taker among the earliest disciples."[271]

Timothy Paul Jones explains that "Tax collectors carried *pinakes*, hinged wooden tablets with beeswax coating on each panel. Tax collectors etched notes in the wax using styluses; these notes could be translated later and rewritten on papyrus."[272] Hence, as Casey observes: "It is entirely natural that one of the Twelve, who was a tax collector, selected himself to write down material about Jesus during the historic ministry."[273] Green comments:

263. Green, *The Books The Church Suppressed*, 39
264. Geisler and Bocchino, *Unshakeable Foundations*, 121.
265. Allison, "Matthew," 27.
266. Elwell and Yarborough, *Encountering the New Testament*,
267. Holding, *Trusting the New Testament*, 147.
268. Blomberg, *Jesus and the Gospels*, 102.
269. Dunn, "Remembering Jesus," 205.
270. Dunn, "Remembering Jesus," 209.
271. Boyd and Eddy, *Lord or Legend?*, 68–69.
272. Jones, *Why Trust the Bible?*, 72.
273. Casey, *Jesus*, 91.

> Probably the name Matthew became associated with this Gospel because it embodies a lot of special material that the apostle Matthew gathered . . . Scholars call this the "Q" material, and it is clearly very ancient. Probably Matthew the apostle assembled "Q," the teachings of his master, Jesus, and quite possibly during his ministry. He certainly had ample opportunity to do this, as he followed Jesus for those three years. And as a tax-gatherer he must have had the writing skills and probably shorthand as well, which was well known in the ancient world.[274]

Hardman concludes: "it is a strong possibility that Matthew wrote Q."[275] Thiede muses:

> Matthew, the shorthand-writing tax and customs official, was the ideal man to safeguard the beginnings of a literary tradition; but Mark, following the oral message of Peter, was the first to write a complete, fully developed Gospel.[276]

Grappling with comments from Irenaeus and Papias about Matthew writing in Hebrew, Barnett hypothesizes:

> One possible solution is that Matthew originally wrote Q . . . In this case, Matthew, or some other writer unknown to us, subsequently translated these "Hebrew oracles" into Greek and combined them with Mark and [M], thus completing the Gospel in its present form . . .[277]

Mark Strauss likewise leaves open the possibility that Matthew wrote the whole of the gospel to which his name was attached:

> Perhaps Matthew wrote an original Gospel (or a collection of Jesus' sayings: Q?) in Aramaic or Hebrew. He could have later published a Greek edition of this Gospel (not a translation but a new edition). As a tax collector, Matthew no doubt would have been proficient in both Aramaic and Greek.[278]

As Casey observes, in addition to the material designated as "Q," material in Matthew's Gospel designated as "M"—the material unique to Matthew's Gospel—may also have been "written down accurately in Aramaic on a wax tablet by Matthew, the apostle and tax collector."[279] Moreover, Casey points out that since Matthias or Matthew were common Jewish names, there'd be nothing "improbable or peculiar in the author of one of the synoptic Gospels having more or less the same name as one of the Twelve."[280] In other words, Matthew's Gospel may have been compiled and ed-

---

274. Green, *The Books The Church Suppressed*, 32.
275. Hardman, "Historical Evidences for the Gospels," 252.
276. Thiede, *Jesus*, 56.
277. Barnett, *Is The New Testament Reliable?*, 92.
278. Strauss, *Four Portraits, One Jesus*, 252.
279. Casey, *Jesus*, 96.
280. Casey, *Jesus*, 92.

ited by someone called "Matthew" who drew heavily upon the writings of the apostle Matthew. The one may even have been a disciple of the other. Ben Witherington III likewise suggests:

> Matthew [could have been] responsible for both the M (or special Matthew) material in the Gospel as well as the Q (non-Markan sayings source) material. That is, he contributed a large proportion of the material in this Gospel . . . The finished document then was attributed to its apostolic contributor—Matthew.[281]

Blomberg argues that "Perhaps the apostle Matthew wrote a first draft of Jesus' teachings, possibly also including certain narratives, which either he or someone else later revised in light of Mark,"[282] before concluding: "Matthew remains the most plausible choice for author."[283] Indeed, this conclusion is favored both by tradition and Occam's razor.

It's interesting to note that, in keeping with the interests of a tax collector, Matthew's Gospel features a good many unique references to "currency, debts, business transactions, and other financial matters (17:24-27; 18:23-35; 20:1-16; 25:14-30; 26:25; 27:3-10)."[284] R.T. France comments:

> We may safely say that the unanimous tradition of the early church . . . offers us a candidate who on other grounds is likely to have been the sort of person indicated by the character of the Gospel. But no doubt there were other such people among the disciples. And even if the patristic association of Matthew's name with the Gospel is given full weight, this does not rule out the possibility of more than one stage in its composition. The later the Gospel is dated, the more likely it becomes that Matthew's contribution was at an earlier stage than the final "edition." So in the end we simply do not know the extent of the role of the apostle Matthew in the composition of ["Matthew"], but the tradition of the early church encourages us to believe that it was a major one.[285]

Returning to the question of dating the publication of Matthew, Blomberg suggests the evidence "favors a date from ca. 58-69."[286] Michael J. Wilkins reckons Matthew was published c. AD 60-61.[287] Casey argues that "the Gospel of Matthew . . .

---

281. Witherington, *Invitation to the New Testament*, 87.
282. Blomberg, *Jesus and the Gospels*, 40.
283. Blomberg, *Jesus and the Gospels*, 44.
284. *Ignatius Catholic Study Bible New Testament*, 3.
285. France, *Matthew*, 37.
286. Blomberg, *Matthew*, 42.
287. Wilkins quoted in Arnold, *Zondervan Illustrated Bible Backgrounds Commentary: Volume 1*, 7.

should be dated c. 50–60 CE . . ."[288] Andreas J. Kostenberger and Justin Taylor concur that Matthew wrote "in the 50s or 60s."[289]

Given that Luke's Gospel incorporates material from Q but not from Matthew's Gospel per se,[290] we might hazard that Matthew was published *after* Luke published his gospel, which was plausibly before Luke left Jerusalem for Rome with Paul in October-November of AD 60 (see: Luke 27:9).[291] *Perhaps* it was the publication of Luke's Gospel that spurred Matthew to expand his Q material to produce his own biography of Jesus. Thus, I would suggest a publication date for Matthew's Gospel of c. AD 61–65, around thirty years after Jesus' crucifixion.

Watch: "Matthew's Gospel" Youtube playlist: www.youtube.com/playlist?list=PLQhh3qcwVEWieyXg1yfsvMkdgZM1H-OpF

Zondervan Illustrated Bible Background Commentary: Volume 1—Matthew, Mark, Luke edited by Clinton E. Arnold

The New American Commentary: Matthew by Craig L. Blomberg

The Holman Apologetics Commentary On The Bible: The Gospels and Acts edited by Jeremy Royal Howard

---

The Gospel According to John: c. AD 60–90.

The fourth gospel mentions "the disciple whom Jesus loved . . . who had leaned back against Jesus at the supper" (John 21:20, see also 11:3, 11:36, 13:23, 19:26, 20:2, 21:7 and 21:20) and identifies this disciple as the "the disciple who testifies to these things and who wrote them down" (John 21:24).

The early church fathers unanimously attribute the fourth gospel to the apostle John, one of the sons of Zebedee (see: Mark 3:17 & 10:35, Luke 5:10 and John 21:2). Writing c. AD 180, Irenaeus (a protégé of John's disciple Polycarp, c. 70–155) says that: "John, the disciple of the Lord, who leaned back on his breast, published the Gospel while he was resident at Ephesus in Asia."[292]

In the fourth century, Eusebius quotes Papias via Irenaeus:

> If, then, any one came, who had been a follower of the elders, I questioned him in regard to the words of the elders . . . what was said by Philip, or by Thomas or by James, or by John, or by Matthew or by any other of the disciples of the Lord, and what things Aristion and the presbyter [or "elder"] John, the

---

288. Casey, *Jesus*, 90.
289. Kostenberger and Taylor, *The Final Days Of Jesus*, 15.
290. See: Friedrichsen, "Critical Observations on a Team Effort;" Goodacre, "Beyond the Q Impasse or Down a Blind Alley?;" Head and Williams, "Q Review."
291. See: Nelson, "Paul Survives a Shipwreck."
292. Irenaeus quoted in Wilkins, *The Holman Apologetics Commentary On The Bible*, 500.

disciples of the Lord, say. For I did not think that what was to be gotten from the books would profit me as much as what came from the living and abiding voice."[293]

Some scholars think that Papias (writing c. 95–110[294]) distinguished between John the apostle and John the presbyter/elder, while others think these phrases have the same referent. Several scholars who distinguish between Johns attribute the fourth gospel to the elder rather than the apostle.

However, that the apostle John is in some sense the author of the fourth gospel would explain why it never mentions him by name although the Synoptic Gospels all present him as one of Jesus' inner circle. Dr. Bruce Milne draws attention to how "the notably close association in this gospel of the 'disciple whom Jesus loved' with Peter [echoes] the close association of John and Peter in Acts."[295] Moreover, while the Synoptic Gospels are careful to distinguish between John "the Baptist" and John "the Apostle," the fourth gospel simply refers to the Baptist as "John." As A. Rendle Short observes: "If there are two boys at school, J. Smith and T. Smith, other boys in writing will distinguish them by their initial, but when J. is writing, he will speak of the other simply as Smith."[296] Besides, as Blomberg comments: "No orthodox writer ever proposes any other alternative for the author of the Fourth Gospel . . . The external evidence must be deemed to opt overwhelmingly in favour of John, the son of Zebedee, as author of this document."[297]

That said, John 21:20–24 appears to distinguish between the "beloved disciple" as the eyewitness author of the bulk of the gospel (see: John 13:23, 18:16, 19:26, 20:2–8, 21:7 and 21:20), and the commenting voice of the gospel's editor/s:

> Peter turned and saw that the disciple whom Jesus loved was following them. (This was the one who had leaned back against Jesus at the supper and had said, "Lord, who is going to betray you?") When Peter saw him, he asked, "Lord, what about him?" Jesus answered, "If I want him to remain alive until I return, what is that to you? You must follow me." Because of this, the rumor spread among the believers that this disciple would not die. But Jesus did not say that he would not die; he only said, "If I want him to remain alive until I return, what is that to you?" *This is the disciple who testifies to these things and who wrote them down. We know that his testimony is true.*

On the basis of this passage, John Drane observes:

> It seems at least possible that the gospel was first written in Palestine, to demonstrate that "Jesus is the Christ" (20:31), perhaps over against the views of

---

293. Eusebius, *Ecclesiastical History* 3.39.1–7.
294. See: Yarborough, "The Date of Papias: A Reassessment."
295. Milne, *The Message of John*, 17.
296. Short, *Why Believe?*, 37.
297. Blomberg, *The Historical Reliability of John's Gospel*, 25–26.

sectarian Jews influenced by ideas like those of the Qumran community, and then when the same teaching was seen to be relevant to people elsewhere in the Roman empire, it was revised, with Jewish customs and expressions being explained, and the prologue and epilogue added. The advice to church leaders in chapter 21 suggests that the final form of the gospel might have been directed to a Christian congregation comprised of both Jews and Gentiles somewhere in the Hellenistic world, perhaps at Ephesus.[298]

Blomberg suggests that "the peculiar ending of chapter 21 is to be explained at least by John's advancing age if not his actual, recent death"[299] and comments: "There may have been something of a gap between the draft of the Gospel . . . (which itself could have circulated locally in and around Ephesus) and its final redaction . . . especially if that editing took place posthumously."[300] On this theory, whether before or after his death, one or more of the apostle John's disciples published a second edition of his gospel (the first edition may not have been circulated if John didn't consider it to have been finished).

Alternatively, if we assume that Polycarp and/or Irenaeus made a mistake in identifying "the disciple whom Jesus loved" with "John," then "John" (whether the apostle and/or the elder) was probably the lead compiler/editor of this gospel, which incorporates material written by "the disciple whom Jesus loved." A confusion between John the apostle and "the disciple whom Jesus loved" would be understandable if both men were disciples who played a role in authoring the fourth gospel.

Professor Ben Witherington III (among others) argues for identifying the disciple "whom Jesus loved" as Lazarus (whom Jesus is said to have miraculously brought back to life—see: John 11:1–45):

> There are a number of odd features in the Gospel itself that cry out for explanation and suggest that a distinction must be made between the Beloved Disciple and the final editor of the document . . . the internal evidence of this Gospel itself tells us that the Beloved Disciple is not someone named John but rather one named Lazarus [see: John 11:1–44, especially verses 3 and 36] . . . The "we" [of John 21:24] is presumably the Johannine community who knows the full story of Lazarus and knows he is now dead. Some other member of that community has then assembled this Gospel after the death of the Beloved Disciple. Here perhaps is where John the elder or presbyter comes in . . .[301]

Witherington allows that "it is not *impossible* that John son of Zebedee had something to do with this Gospel."[302]

---

298. Drane, *Introducing the New Testament*, 217.
299. Blomberg, *The Historical Reliability of John's Gospel*, 44.
300. Blomberg, *The Historical Reliability of John's Gospel*, 44.
301. Witherington, *Invitation to the New Testament*, 135–40.
302. Witherington, *Invitation to the New Testament*, 138.

It's fair to observe that naturalists will have an obvious philosophical issue with attributing the bulk of the fourth gospel to Lazarus, and will tend to prefer one of the other theories of authorship on offer. Besides John the apostle and/or elder, a few scholars propose other alternative candidates, such as "Doubting" Thomas, but as Milne writes: "Sufficient to say, the traditional view, that John the son of Zebedee was the author, certainly continues to be defensible."[303]

Whoever "the disciple whom Jesus loved" was, the hypothesis of a two-stage process behind the composition of the fourth gospel as we have it today neatly explains the distinction apparently drawn in John 21:24, as well as the otherwise anachronistic present tense of John 5:2: "By the Sheep Gate in Jerusalem there *is* a pool, called Bethesda in Hebrew, which has five colonnades." This architectural reference (which archaeological investigation has validated) displays a detailed local knowledge of Jerusalem before AD 70. Indeed, "The author characterizes himself as an eyewitness to Jesus' ministry (19:35), and the style and content of the book substantiate that claim by detailing weights and measurements, distances, personal names, and features of the typography of Jerusalem before its destruction by the Romans . . ."[304] As Angus Moyes observes:

> An eyewitness should get details right, even background information like names and places and geography. And that's exactly what we find in John—the names and locations of towns, the distances between them and the best route to take from one to the other are all correct . . . several places mentioned in the Gospel were long thought to be fictional, but recent archaeology has proved John accurate. The Pool of Bethesda where Jesus healed a man born blind (John 5), the Stone Pavement where Pilate sentenced Jesus to death, and Golgotha—"the place of the skull"—where He was crucified, all show John's Gospel to be right, and previous assumptions wrong (both John 19). So not only is the Gospel early enough to be have been written within living memory of the events, it had to have been written by someone with intimate knowledge of where these events took place.[305]

Israeli archaeologist Ravi Arav and John Rousseau, a research associate at the University of California, Berkley and a fellow of the Jesus Seminar, both concur that "the primary author of the Gospel of John was probably an eyewitness to several events in the life of Jesus," being "well acquainted with Jerusalem and its surroundings."[306]

Ancient historian Paul Barnett writes that he sees "no reason for John being written later than the 60's, especially since his references to buildings and topography for Jerusalem fit the period before the Roman invasion of AD 66–70 after which much of

---

303. Milne, *The Message of John*, 19.
304. Tappy, "The Gospels and Acts: John," 586.
305. Moyes, "The Reliability of John's Gospel."
306. Arav and Rousseau, *Jesus and His World*, 157.

pre-war Palestine was unrecognizable."[307] Thus "a date in the 60s [is] a viable option"[308] for the composition of John's Gospel, or at least for the bulk of the material (written by "the disciple whom Jesus loved"). Adele Reinhartz reckons that "an early version of the Gospel may have originated in Judea," although "a late first century date for the Gospel's final version is likely."[309]

In line with the testimony of the early church fathers, John (or the finalized form thereof) is usually held to be "the last of the Gospels to be written, in the 80s or early 90s . . ."[310] For example, in his commentary on John's Gospel, Barnabas Lindars states: "the most probable date of composition is about A.D. 85–95."[311]

As Blomberg explains: "Older views that placed John well into the second century have been discarded . . . with the discovery of the John Ryland's fragment—already at least one stage of copying removed from John's original and yet dating from c. 125–140."[312] According to Phil Fernandes and Kyle Larson: "Thiede has persuasively argued that this fragment of a copy of John's Gospel should probably be dated earlier—as early as 100 AD . . ."[313] Be that as it may, "Since [the Rylands fragment] was found in Egypt, the original of John's Gospel would have had to be written considerably earlier [than the Ryland's fragment]; for, the Gospel did not immediately spread to Egypt from Israel."[314] Consequently, "few scholars today would . . . want to date John much later than about AD 100."[315]

Montefiore says that John's Gospel: "could hardly have been written after AD 100, and its generally agreed date has been around AD 90–100."[316] Cullmann states: "it is no longer possible to admit any period after the years 90 to 95 for the composition of the Fourth Gospel."[317] Stanley E. Porter writes that: "Virtually all scholars agree that John's Gospel was the last written and that this would have occurred, at the latest, around AD 90. It may have been written earlier."[318] Blomberg dates John "either to the late 80s or to the 90s."[319] Kostenberger and Taylor place John's Gospel in the "late 80s or early 90s'.[320] Geisler dates John to "during the reign of Domitian (81–96)."[321]

307. Barnett, "Is The New Testament Historically Reliable?," 229.
308. *Ignatius Catholic Study Bible New Testament*, 157.
309. Reinhartz, "John," 265.
310. Green, *The Books The Church Suppressed*, 33.
311. Lindars, *The New Century Bible Commentary: The Gospel of John*, 42.
312. Blomberg, *Jesus And The Gospel*, 170.
313. Fernandes et al., *Hijacking The Historical Jesus*, 129.
314. Fernandes et al., *Hijacking The Historical Jesus*, 129.
315. Blomberg, *The Historical Reliability of John's Gospel*, 42.
316. Montefiore, *The Womb And The Tomb*, 109.
317. Cullmann, *The New Testament*, 48.
318. Porter, *How We Got The New Testament*, 86.
319. Blomberg, *The Historical Reliability of John's Gospel*, 44.
320. Kostenberger and Taylor, *The Final Days Of Jesus*, 16.
321. Geisler, *A Popular Survey Of The New Testament*, 95.

Regardless of continuing debates about the compositional process involved, the significant point to bear in mind is the probability that at least the bulk of the fourth gospel presents us with *first century eyewitness testimony*.[322] Moreover, as F.F. Bruce comments, the historical tradition preserved by the fourth gospel "is independent of those traditions represented in the Synoptic Gospels, but no less authentic."[323] In sum:

> most scholars affirm that the Gospel of John was produced in a community founded by one of Jesus' original disciples, and that it was written, preserved, and edited by leaders who had close ties with the apostolic tradition . . . It retains elements of very early eyewitness tradition not recorded elsewhere . . . John is usually said to have been produced in the 90s, since that is when the final redaction is likely to have taken place, but the scholars who say this generally recognize that much of the material in John comes from an earlier time.[324]

Watch: "John's Gospel" Youtube playlist: www.youtube.com/playlist?list=PLQhh3qcwVE WjZ96UEngK_Iojs-_hX-H9O

Read: "59 Confirmed or Historically Probable Facts in the Gospel of John": http://truth-bomb.blogspot.com/2012/02/59-confirmed-or-historically-probable.html

"'The Disciple Jesus Loved": Witness, Author, Apostle—A Response to Richard Bauckham's Jesus and the Eyewitnesses" by Andreas J. Köstenberger and Stephen O. Stout; www.ibr-bbr.org/files/bbr/bbr18b02_kostenberger.pdf

"Did Lazarus of Bethany Write John's Gospel?": http://christiancadre.blogspot.com/2007/01/did-lazarus-of-bethany-write-gospel-of.html

"Is the raising of Lazarus fictional?" by J. Warner Wallace: http://coldcasechristianity.com/2017/is-the-raising-of-lazarus-fictional/

"Was Lazarus the Beloved Disciple?" by Ben Witherington III: www.beliefnet.com/columnists/bibleandculture/2007/01/was-lazarus-the-beloved-disciple.html

The Historical Reliability of John's Gospel: Issues & Commentary by Craig L. Blomberg

The Holman Apologetics Commentary On The Bible: The Gospels and Acts edited by Jeremy Royal Howard

---

Back to the early sources

As has already been noted, it's impossible to be certain about the publication dates of the four gospels. Most scholars accept a spread of dates ranging from the 60s to 90s (c. 30 to 60 years after the crucifixion). However, it seems to me that the synoptic gospels were probably all published *within c. 30 years of the crucifixion*—in

---

322. Indeed, if the fourth gospel was completed by John the apostle using material written by Lazarus, then it presents us with material from *two* eyewitnesses!

323. Bruce, *The Gospel of John*, 5.

324. Powell, *Introducing the New Testament*, 176.

the order of Mark (c. AD 49), followed by Luke (c. AD 59–60) and Matthew (c. AD 61–65) (all drawing upon earlier sources), with John arriving on the scene *within c. 60 years of the crucifixion* (c. AD 90), though based on a first draft written before the fall of Jerusalem.

Dawkins' decades-long doubt

In light of this evidence, it won't do for Dawkins to object, as he did in the course of an interview with Catholic law professor Hugh Hewitt, that the gospels "were written decades after the alleged events were supposed to happen. No historian would take that seriously."[325] Hewitt didn't let Dawkins get away with such an obvious falsehood:

> HH: Well . . . teachers routinely rely on things like Tacitus and Pliny, and histories that were written centuries after the events in which they are recording occur.

> RD: There's massive archaeological evidence, there's massive evidence of all kinds. It's just not comparable. No . . . if you talk to any ancient historian of the period, they will agree that it is not good historical evidence.[326]

Note that Dawkins implicitly concedes Hewitt's point by shifting his objection away from the time-gap between event and report. Not that Dawkins's new objection is any better:

> HH: Oh, that's simply not true. Dr. Mark Roberts, double PhD . . . has written a very persuasive book upon this . . . Are you unfamiliar with him? [Hewitt is referring to Mark D. Robert's *Can We Trust The Gospels?* (Crossway, 2007)]

> RD: All right, then there may be some, but a very large number of ancient historians would say . . .[327]

Dawkins concedes Hewitt's point before automatically shifting his ground to the next most damning accusation in line:

> HH: Well, you just said there were none. So there are some that you are choosing not to confront.

> RD: You sound like a lawyer.

> HH: I am a lawyer.

---

325. Dawkins, "Hugh interviews atheist Richard Dawkins."
326. See: Dawkins, "Hugh interviews atheist Richard Dawkins."
327. Dawkins, "Hugh interviews atheist Richard Dawkins."

RD: ... I didn't know that. All right. I will accept that there are some ancient historians who take the Gospels seriously. But they were written decades after the events that happened ...[328]

The most intriguing aspect of this exchange is how Dawkins returns to the time-gap objection only moments after he has implicitly conceded the point! Yet, even when we set aside the discussion about earlier sources and first drafts, the NT gospels compare very favorably with other ancient works in terms of the interval between their date of composition and the events they report.[329]

Figs. 14 and 15 compare the NT gospels to a range of ancient historical literature in terms of the lapses involved between the relevant historical events and the published reports of those events.

Fig. 14.

Author/Work:	Reported Events:	Report Published:	Lapse between events & report:	Average lapse:
Mark	c. AD 30–33	c. AD 49	c. 16–19 yrs	c. 17.5 yrs
Luke	c. 6 BC–AD 33	c. AD 60	c. 27–66 yrs	c. 46.5 yrs
Matthew	c. 6 BC–AD 33	c. AD 65	c. 32–71 yrs	c. 51.5 yrs
John	c. AD 30–33	c. AD 90	c. 57–60 yrs	c. 58.5 yrs
Pliny, Letters	AD 97–112	AD 100—112	0–3 yrs	1.5 yrs
Thucydides, History	431–411 BC	410—400 BC	0–30 yrs	15 yrs
Xenophon, Anabasis	401–399 BC	385—375 BC	15–25 yrs	20 yrs
Polybius, History	200–120 BC	150 BC	20–70 yrs	45 yrs
Tacitus, Annuls	AD 14–68	c. AD 100—110	c. 32–100 yrs	c. 66 yrs
Heroditus, History	546–478 BC	430—425 BC	50–125 yrs	87.5 yrs
Suetonius, Lives	50 BC–AD 95	c. AD 120	c. 25–170 yrs	c. 97.5 yrs
Josephus, War	200 BC–AD 70	c. AD 80	c. 10–280 yrs	c. 145 yrs
Josephus, Antiquities	200 BC–AD 65	c. AD 95	c. 30–295 yrs	c. 162.5 yrs
Plutarch, Lives	500 BC–AD 70	c. AD 100	c. 30–600 yrs	c. 315 yrs

328. Dawkins, http://radioblogger.townhall.com/talkradio/transcripts/transcript.aspx?ContentGuid=77fe9a0d-d15d-4f33-af90-d4685976f8e0.

329. Data for the following figures was sourced from Montgomery, *Evidence for Faith*.

Getting at the Gospels

Fig. 15.
Average gap between events and written report

Source	Gap
Plutarch	~315
Josephus, Antiq	~160
Josephus, War	~145
Suetonius	~95
Heroditus	~85
Tacitus	~65
John	~60
Matthew	~50
Luke	~45
Polybius	~45
Xenophon	~20
Mark	~18
Thucydides	~15
Pliny	~1

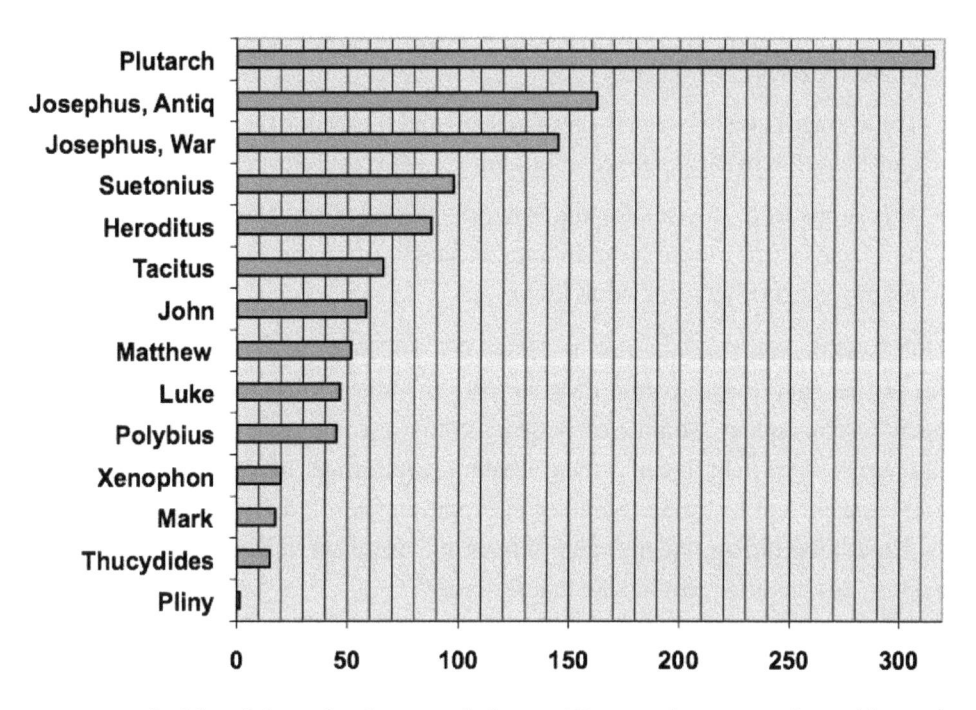

Even the liberal dates for the gospels (i.e. c. AD 60–95) compare favorably on this score, with the average gaps falling into the range indicated in figure 16.

Fig. 16.
Average 'liberal' gap between events and written report

(Same data as Fig. 15, with a shaded band highlighting the range approximately 65–95.)

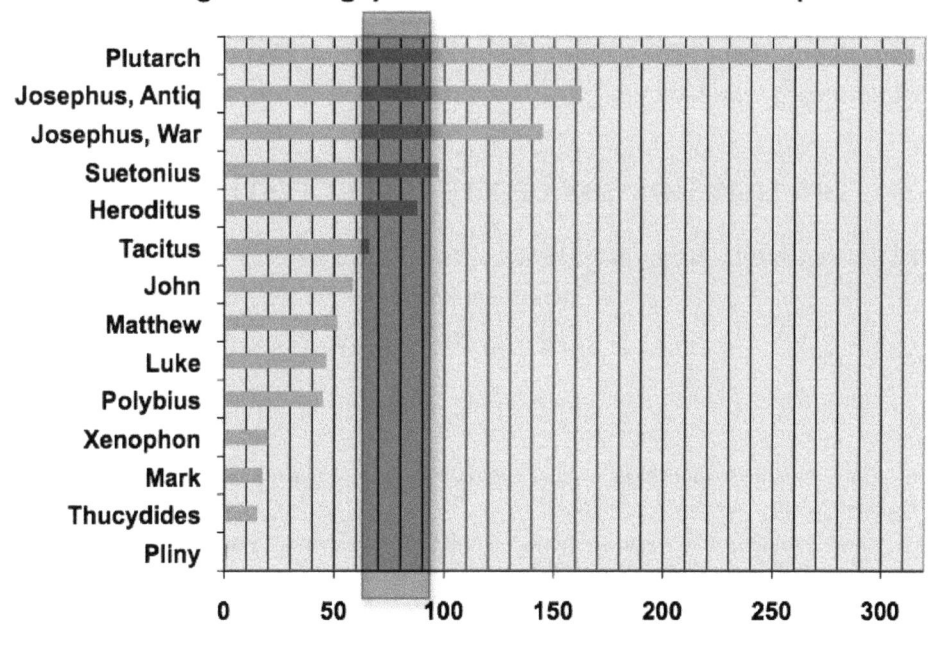

- The average gap between event and written report for the ten non-biblical sources listed above is c. 94 years.
- Even if we exclude Plutarch's *Lives*, the average time-lapse for the remaining non-biblical texts is c. 71 years.
- The average lapse between the four gospels and the events they report (excluding consideration of earlier gospel drafts and/or sources) is just over 43 years.
- This drops to c. 38 years for the Synoptic Gospels (less if we exclude Matthew and Luke's stories about Jesus' infancy and focus upon the Synoptic Gospels' testimony concerning Jesus' adult life).

If Dawkins wants to question the historical reliability of the NT gospels on the grounds that they "were written decades after the alleged events were supposed to happen,"[330] consistency would clearly demand that on the same grounds he should doubt most of ancient history! A consistent application of Dawkins's objection would leave ancient historians bereft of information from Plutarch, Josephus, Suetonius, Heroditus, Tacitus, Polybus and Xenophon. However, to borrow a phrase from Dawkins: "No historian would take that seriously."[331]

Whatever dates are assigned to the NT gospels, it should be remembered that all four gospels incorporate material predating their composition. It would appear that, at the very least, elements of Q, L, and M existed *within twenty years of the crucifixion*. Indeed, there's reason to suspect that Q was written *during the lifetime of Jesus*.

Lawrence Krauss can't be allowed to get away with his (unsubstantiated) complaint that "everything [about] this word of God that we're told about was written by people well after the fact . . ."[332] By the standards of ancient history (where the average gap between an event and a written report is about a century), the NT gospel sources, along with the NT letters and the various creeds and hymns therein, all count as extraordinarily *early* sources.

THE TRANSMISSION OF THE GOSPEL TESTIMONIES

"The New Testament is far and away the best-attested work of Greek or Latin literature from the ancient world."

—Darrel L. Bock and Daniel B. Wallace[333]

---

330. Dawkins, http://radioblogger.townhall.com/talkradio/transcripts/transcript.aspx?ContentGuid=77fe9a0d-d15d-4f33-af90-d4685976f8e0.

331. Dawkins, http://radioblogger.townhall.com/talkradio/transcripts/transcript.aspx?ContentGuid=77fe9a0d-d15d-4f33-af90-d4685976f8e0.

332. Krauss, "Krauss, Meyer, Lamoureux."

333. Bock and Wallace, *Dethroning Jesus*, 48.

Getting at the Gospels

Having covered the link between the original events of Jesus' life and the written reports of those events in the four gospels, we now turn to the transmission of those reports over time to the present day.

Link 3

"The NT is simply the best textually supported book from the ancient world."
—NORMAN L. GEISLER[334]

Richard Dawkins misrepresents the NT manuscript tradition as a matter of being "copied and recopied, through many different 'Chinese Whisper generations.'"[335] However, the game of one-time-only *serial* "Chinese whispers" (Americans call it "The Telephone Game") is a poor analogy for the *parallel* processes of repeatedly disseminating written (or oral) information in the ancient world. As textual critic Daniel B. Wallace points out:

> In the telephone game . . . [there is] only one line of transmission, it is oral rather than written, and the oral critic (the person who is trying to figure out what the original utterance was) only has the last person in line to interrogate. When it comes to the text of the NT, there are multiple lines of transmission . . . Further, the textual critic doesn't rely on just the last person in the transmissional line, but can interrogate many scribes . . . way back to the second century. And even when the early manuscript testimony is sparse, we have the early church fathers' testimony as to what the original text said. Finally, the process is not intended to be a parlor game but is intended to duplicate the original text faithfully—and this process doesn't rely on people hearing a whole utterance whispered only once, but seeing the text and copying it. The telephone game is a far cry from the process of copying manuscripts of the NT.[336]

Watch: "Is the oral tradition comparable to the telephone game?" by William Lane Craig: https://youtu.be/VKudgsPT6No

"Jesus, the Gospels and the Telephone Game": https://youtu.be/-PZEYfLxtsM

Sam Harris worries about the modern text of the NT being "evidenced by discrepant and fragmentary copies of copies of copies of ancient Greek manuscripts."[337] However, according to N.T. Wright: "It needs to be stressed that our evidence for

---

334. Geisler, "Has the Bible Been Accurately Copied Down Through the Centuries?," 45.
335. Dawkins, *The God Delusion*, 118.
336. Wallace, "Symposia Christi."
337. Harris, *The Moral Landscape*, 168.

the text of the New Testament is in a completely different league to our evidence for every single other book from the ancient world."[338] As Winfried Corduan reports: "No other ancient document equals the New Testament when it comes to the preservation of manuscripts, both in terms of number and closeness in time to the original autographs."[339] Bart Ehrman acknowledges that the NT is "the best-attested book from antiquity"[340] and notes that "we have more manuscripts of the New Testament than for any other book from Greek and Roman antiquity—far, far more..."[341]

Consider the link between the original "autographs" and the earliest surviving complete manuscript copies in the following representative cases from ancient literature[342]:

- Between Homer's *Illiad* (an epic poem composed in the eighth century BC) and our earliest complete copy ("Venetus A") lies c. 1,800 years.
- Between the Roman poet Gaius Valerius Catullus and our earliest copy or copies lie c. 1,500 years.
- Between the Greek playwright Sophocles and our earliest copy lies c. 1,500 years.
- Between the philosopher Aristotle and our earliest copy of one of his manuscripts lies c. 1,400 years.
- Between the historian Herodotus and our earliest copy lies c. 1,350 years.
- Between Plato's writings and our earliest copy lies c. 1,300 years.
- Between the historian Thucydides's *History of the Peloponnesian War* and our earliest copies lies c. 1,300 years.
- Between the playwright Aristophanes and our earliest copy lies c. 1,200 years.
- Between Josephus' *Jewish War* and our earliest copies lies c. 900 years.
- Between the poet Horace and our earliest copies lie c. 900 years.
- Between the historian Suetonius and our earliest copy lies c. 800 years.
- Between the historian Tacitus and our earliest copy (of the first six books of the *Annals*) lies c. 800 years.
- Between the writings of Pliny the Younger and our earliest copy lies c. 750 years.

---

338. Wright, *Why read the Bible?*, 5.
339. Corduan, *No Doubt About It*, 193.
340. Ehrman, "The Significance of an Astounding New Discovery."
341. Ehrman, "The Significance of an Astounding New Discovery."
342. Data taken from various sources including: Collins, *The Defendable Faith*, 98, Geisler, "Updating the Manuscript Evidence for the New Testament;" Kostenberger et al., *Truth Matters*, 115; McDowell and McDowell, *Evidence That Demands A Verdict*; Moreland, *Scaling the Secular City*, 135; Morrow, *Questioning the Bible*, 96.

- Between Pliny the Elder's *Historia Naturalis* and our earliest copies lie c. 400 years.

- Between Gaius's second-century *Institutes of Roman Law* and our only complete copy lies c. 300 years.

Norman L. Geisler notes that "The average time span between the original and earliest [complete] copy of the other ancient texts [those outside the New Testament] is over 1,000 years."[343] Complete manuscripts of NT gospels appear some 235–400 years after the autographs, with the whole NT likewise appearing within about 400 years of the autographs. The closest ancient comparisons are the works of Pliny the Elder, where our earliest complete manuscripts appear c. 400 years after he wrote, and Gaius's *Institutes*, where our earliest complete manuscript appears c. 300 years after he wrote.

The following graph compares the gap between autograph and the earliest extant complete manuscript copies for both the NT Gospels and a dozen representative ancient literary examples from the above list:

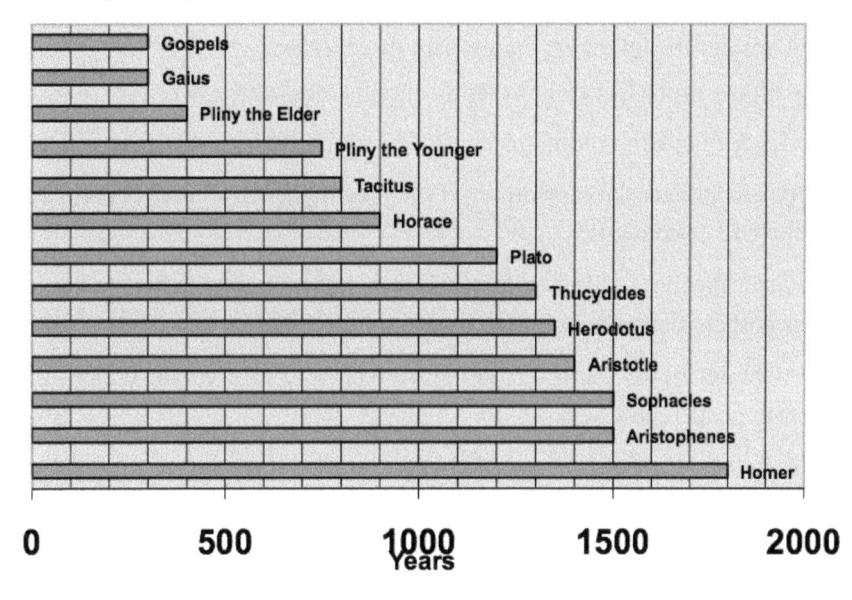

Fig. 17. Gap between autographs and complete manuscript copies.[344]

Work	Years
Gospels	~250
Gaius	~300
Pliny the Elder	~400
Pliny the Younger	~700
Tacitus	~900
Horace	~1000
Plato	~1300
Thucydides	~1400
Herodotus	~1450
Aristotle	~1500
Sophocles	~1600
Aristophenes	~1600
Homer	~1800

Moreover, in the case of the NT we have early papyrus fragments from within fifty years of the autographs. Although these fragments only provide direct evidence of the text they bear, they bear indirect witness to the surrounding text from which they come and into which they fit.

---

343. Geisler and Bocchino, *Unshakeable Foundations*, 257.

344. See: Geisler, "Updating the Manuscript Evidence for the New Testament;" Morrow, *Questioning the Bible*, 96.

The earliest known fragment from the NT is currently the Rylands Papyrus (P52),[345] containing John 18:31–33 and 37–38. P52 is generally dated to the first half of the second century, which likely takes us within c. 50 years of the autograph.

In 2018 the Egypt Exploration Society published a Greek papyrus (P137) that's likely the earliest known fragment of the Gospel of Mark, dating from c. AD 150–250 and bearing a few letters on each side from verses 7–9 and 16–18 of Mark 1.[346] Other recent NT papyrus publications include a third-century papyrus of Luke 13:13–17 and 13:25–30 (P138) and a fourth-century papyrus of Philemon 6–8 and 18–20 (P139).[347] Speaking in 2012, Professor Daniel B. Wallace observed: "we have as many as eighteen New Testament manuscripts (all fragmentary, more or less) from the second century... Altogether, about 33% of all New Testament verses are found in these manuscripts."[348]

The closest comparison from ancient literature on this score are the plays of Sophocles, with fragments from within c. 100–200 years of the originals. In the same ballpark, we have several fragments of Plato's works within c. 200 years, and 49 fragments of Herodotus' work within c. 225 years.

In sum, NT fragments appear within c. 50–200 years of the autographs, whole pages within c. 150 years, and whole gospels within c. 235–350 years of the autographs. Consider the following manuscript discoveries:

- The fifth-century Codex Ephraemi contains most of the NT.
- Codex Alexandrinus contains almost the entire Bible, c. AD 400.
- Codex Sinaiticus, dating from c. AD 350, contains the whole NT (and about half of the Old Testament).
- Codex Vaticanus, dating from c. AD 325–350, contains complete copies of the four gospels along with most of the rest of the Bible.
- The Chester Beatty Papyri,[349] dating from c. AD 250, contains major portions of all four gospels and Acts.
- The Bodmer Papyri,[350] from c. AD 200, contains several pages of Luke and most of John.

Craig A. Evans draws attention to the fact that:

> a recent study of libraries, collections and archives from late antiquity... found that manuscripts were in use anywhere from 150 to 500 years before being discarded... The fourth-century Codex Vaticanus was re-inked in the

---

345. See: "Papyrus 52."
346. See: Hixson, "Despite Disappointing Some, New Mark Manuscript Is Earliest Yet."
347. See: Hixson, "Despite Disappointing Some, New Mark Manuscript Is Earliest Yet."
348. Wallace, "Earliest Manuscript of the New Testament Discovered?"
349. See: "Chester Beatty Papyri."
350. See: "Bodmer Papyri."

tenth century . . . many other biblical codices show signs of re-inking, correcting and annotations hundreds of years after they were produced . . . If the first-century originals . . . of the Gospels continued in use for 150 years or more, they would still have been in circulation when the oldest copies of the Gospels that we possess today were copied."[351]

The upshot of this study is that our earliest NT manuscripts (including the Bodmer and Chester Beatty Papyri) were likely contemporaneous with the autographs: "The evidence of [MS] longevity suggests that the autographs and first copies remained in circulation until the time of our earliest, extant papyri . . . and that these papyri remained in circulation until the production of the first great codices in the fourth century." Hence, "there is no significant gap in the history of the transmission of the text of the Greek NT."[352]

Finally, Christian writers of the first-to-fourth centuries quote over 20,000 times from the Gospels and Acts, over 14,000 times from the NT letters, and over 600 times from Revelation in various extrabiblical texts. These quotations add up to about 46 percent of the NT.[353]

Link 4

"We possess a text of the Greek New Testament that is accurate enough to be more than adequate for religious and theological purposes."

—STEPHEN T. DAVIS[354]

Concerning the biblical text, atheist songwriter Robie Fulks asks: "how many generations of translation stood between me and whoever [wrote the original text]? The Christians around me were as in the dark as I was."[355] If Fulks would simply read the preface to a modern Bible (such as the *English Standard Version* or the *New International Version*), he would find himself in a position to inform his ignorant Christian neighbors that the translation is based on the modern critical text of the original Greek, as established by textual critics, and are not the product of a chain of translations at all! As Antony Flew acknowledged: "the earliness and the number of manuscripts for most of the Christian documents, is unusually great . . . that's . . . very good authority for the accuracy of the text that is provided in translation in the New Testament."[356]

---

351. Evans, *Jesus And His World*, 75–76.

352. See: Tweet by @ApologeticsCA: https://twitter.com/ApologeticsCA/status/442441771608317952/photo/1.

353. See: "Modern Myth."

354. Davis, *Rational Faith*, 53–54.

355. Fulks, "God isn't Real," 266.

356. Flew quoted in *Did Jesus Rise From the Dead?*, 66.

Fig. 18 compares the *Greek* manuscript evidence for the NT with the *total* manuscript evidence for a representative selection of other works by ancient authors. Homer's *Illiad* provides the closest ancient comparison to the NT on this score, with recent discoveries pushing the number of manuscripts from the oft-quoted 643 up to some 1,900 (a number that includes about 188 medieval and renaissance manuscripts).[357] However, the text of the NT currently comes to us through about 23,980 manuscripts, including around 975 Coptic manuscripts, 10,000 Latin manuscripts, 350 Syriac manuscripts, and 5,680 Greek manuscripts.[358]

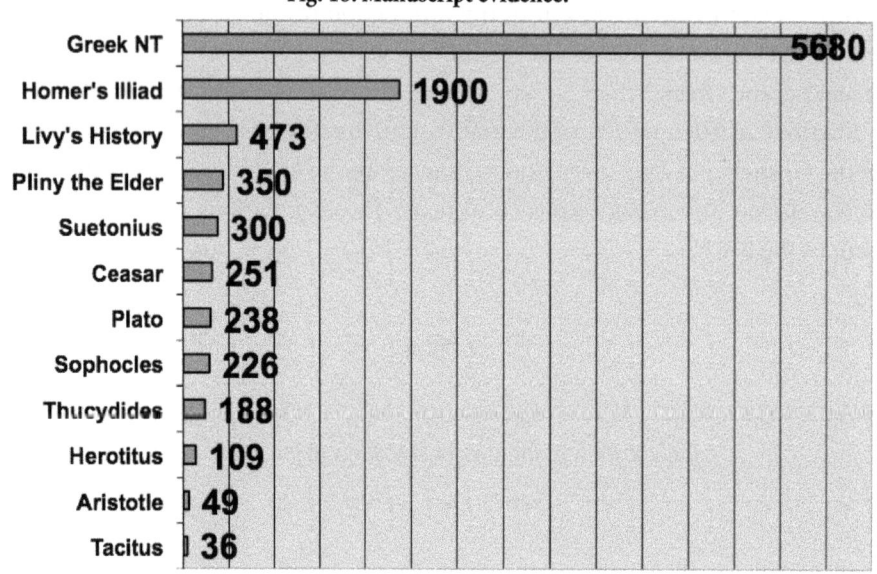

Fig. 18. Manuscript evidence.[359]

Greek NT	5680
Homer's Illiad	1900
Livy's History	473
Pliny the Elder	350
Suetonius	300
Ceasar	251
Plato	238
Sophocles	226
Thucydides	188
Herotitus	109
Aristotle	49
Tacitus	36

Discussing the detail of the Greek NT manuscript tradition, Wallace explains:

> The official count . . . is somewhere over 5800. Now [this count assigns] what's called the Gregory-Aland number, that's the official cataloging number that New Testament scholars know these manuscripts by . . . Well, maybe in the past, they did it in haste . . . or they didn't have photographs of these manuscripts, and what they didn't realize is that the manuscript discovered in Ireland is actually a part of the manuscript that was discovered in North Carolina. They're a part of the same manuscript. They may have actually different catalog numbers given to them, and so when we discovered later that

---

357. See: Geisler, "Updating the Manuscript Evidence for the New Testament;" McDowell and McDowell, *Evidence That Demands A Verdict*, 56.

358. See: "Jesus of Testimony;" Wallace, "Daniel B. Wallace Interview Transcript;" Fernandes et al., *Hijacking The Historical Jesus*, 73; Geisler, "Updating the Manuscript Evidence for the New Testament;" McDowell and McDowell, *Evidence That Demands A Verdict*, 46–68.

359. See: Geisler, "Updating the Manuscript Evidence for the New Testament;" Morrow, *Questioning the Bible*, 96.

they're part of the same manuscript, we don't change the catalog numbers. Otherwise, you have gaps in the catalog. We simply say for this particular manuscript, codex 2112, see also codex 1793, and that's when you realize it's part of the same. When you get all that kind of data, what we have is just over 5600 manuscripts, but still an awful lot of manuscripts.[360]

Theologians Kostenberger, Bock, and Chatraw point out that: "In almost every case even the most widely accepted works from ancient philosophers and historians are considered verifiable with only a small handful of available sources to vouch for them."[361] As Geisler and Turek note, many ancient works survive "on fewer than a dozen manuscripts [and the average is about twenty manuscripts], yet few historians question the historicity of the events those works describe."[362] Geisler summarizes the situation, writing: "The New Testament has more manuscripts, earlier manuscripts, and more accurately copied manuscripts than any other book from the ancient world."[363] Hence, as John Warwick Montgomery observes: "the documentary attestation for these [NT] records is so strong that a denial of their reliability carries with it total scepticism toward the history and literature of the classical world."[364]

According to Doug Powell, "scholars can recover 97 to 99 percent of the original content of the New Testament with certainty."[365] As Timothy Paul Jones explains:

> the 5,700 or so [Greek] New Testament manuscripts that are available to us may differ from one another in as many as 400,000 places—and there are only 138,000 or so words in the Greek New Testament in the first place . . . [However] Most of these 400,000 variations stem from differences in spelling, word order, or the relationships between nouns and definite articles—variants that are easily recognizable and, in most cases, virtually unnoticeable in translations . . . In the end, more than 99 percent of the 400,000 differences fall into this category of virtually unnoticeable variants! Of the remaining 1 percent or so of variants, only a few have any significance for interpreting the biblical text. Most important, *none* of the differences affects any central element of the Christian faith.[366]

Bart Ehrman acknowledges that:

---

360. See: Wallace, "Daniel B. Wallace Interview Transcript."

361. Kostenberger et al., *Truth Matters*, 112.

362. Geisler and Turek, *I Don't Have Enough Faith to be an Atheist*, 225. See also Komoszewski et al., *Reinventing Jesus*, 71.

363. Geisler, *A Popular Survey Of The New Testament*, 20.

364. Montgomery, *History And Christianity*, 43.

365. Powell, *Holman Quick Source Guide to Christian Apologetics*, 161.

366. Jones, *Why Trust the Bible?*, 42–44. See: "Apologia: A Sermon Series in Defense of the Faith—Part IIb: "Can We Trust the Bible?""

most of the changes found in early Christian manuscripts have nothing to do with theology or ideology. Far and away the most changes are the result of mistakes pure and simple—slips of the pen, accidental omissions, inadvertent additions, misspelled words, blunders of one sort of another.[367]

He also recognizes that the vast majority of textual differences:

> are immaterial, insignificant, and trivial . . . Probably the majority matter only in showing that Christian scribes centuries ago could spell no better than my students can today . . . [N]one of the variants that we have ultimately would make any Christian in the history of the universe come to think something opposite of what they already think about whatever doctrines are usually considered "major."[368]

Ehrman consequently concludes: "scholars are convinced that we can reconstruct the original words of the New Testament with reasonable (although probably not 100 percent) accuracy."[369]

Wallace summarizes the case for the reliability of the transmission of the NT gospels:

> When you start looking at classical Greek or Latin literature and compare it to the New Testament, the first thing you will recognize is that the New Testament . . . has more manuscripts, more translations, more comments on its text than any other ancient writer in the Greco-Roman world . . . We have manuscripts that are written within decades of the original New Testament. For the average classical Greek or Latin author, we are waiting half a millennium, 500 years, before we get any copies at all . . . We have approximately one thousand times more manuscripts for the New Testament than we do for the average classical Greek or Latin author. So if you're gonna be skeptical about what the original New Testament says because we don't have the original manuscripts, then we might as well just shove ourselves right into the Dark Ages again, because we don't know what any of the ancients ever said about anything.[370]

The bottom line here is that we can be more certain that the critical text of the Greek NT reflects the original than we can be that the text of any other ancient work reflects the original. As Mark D. Roberts observes:

> the abundance of manuscripts and the antiquity of manuscripts, when run through the mill of text-critical methodology, allows us to know with a very high level of probability what the evangelists and other New Testament authors wrote . . . We can have confidence that the critical Greek texts of Matthew,

---

367. Ehrman, *Misquoting Jesus*, 55.
368. Ehrman, "Who Cares?"
369. Erhman, *The New Testament*, 481.
370. Wallace, "Daniel B. Wallace Interview Transcript."

Mark, Luke, and John represent, with a very high degree of probability, what the autographs of the Gospels actually contained.[371]

N.T. Wright is clearly on solid ground when he affirms: "There is better evidence for the New Testament than for any other ancient book . . . The New Testament we have printed in our Bibles does indeed go back to what the very early Christians wrote."[372] Dawkins's concern over what he calls "the huge uncertainty befogging the New Testament texts"[373] is misinformed and misplaced.

Watch: "The Biblical Text" Youtube playlist: www.youtube.com/playlist?list=PLQhh3qcwVEWhx61s1CiNf9_CATxat5bn8

Read: *The Text Of The New Testament: From Manuscript to Modern Edition* by J. Harold Greenlee

Reinventing Jesus: How Contemporary Skeptics Miss The Real Jesus And Mislead Popular Culture by J. Ed Komoszewski et al.

How We Got The New Testament: Text, Transmission, Translation by Stanley E. Porter

---

CANON UNDER FIRE

"The four Gospels in our Bible had all been written by the end of the first century. Apparently no other gospels were written by this time."

—GRAHAM H. TWELFTREE[374]

The NT gospels give every indication of being faithfully transmitted, early sources of generally reliable testimony to the historical Jesus; but must these sources compete with other, equally authoritative but less orthodox accounts of Jesus found in extrabiblical "gospels"? David Robertson asks and answers a related rhetorical question: "Is it not the case that at the Council of Nicea, in A.D. 325, the church decided to keep some books and got rid of a whole lot of others which were considered to be inconvenient? No—that is another myth in the Dan Brown mould."[375]

Dawkins claims that "The four gospels that made it into the official canon were chosen, more or less arbitrarily, out of a larger sample of at least a dozen . . . additional

---

371. Roberts, *Can We Trust the Gospels?*, 37.

372. Wright, "Foreword," x.

373. Dawkins, *The God Delusion*, 120.

374. Twelftree, "What About 'Gospels' Not In Our New Testament?," 57.

375. Robertson, *Magnificent Obsession*, 142.

gospels,'[376] but this is misleading, because "our earliest and in fact our only first century gospels are those by Matthew, Mark, Luke, and John."[377]

Christopher Hitchens mentions the existence of various "gospels" discovered near an ancient Coptic Christian site at Nag Hammadi in Egypt, and asserts: "These scrolls were of the same period and provenance as many of the subsequently canonical and 'authorized' Gospels, and have long gone under the collective name of 'Gnostic.'"[378] Unfortunately, Hitchens fails to take into account the fact that several Nag Hammadi writings (for example, the third-century Gospel of Philip) actually use material from the canonical NT, which they therefore post-date. The reason the non-canonical Gnostic gospels "were omitted by those ecclesiastics"[379] was quite simply because the "early Christians knew that these documents came too late to represent eyewitness testimony about Jesus."[380]

Michael Green points out that the *earliest* of the non-canonical "gospels" is probably the Gospel of Thomas, "but this shows evidence of knowing all four canonical Gospels and is therefore later than them."[381] Indeed, Thomas contains a distinctive Syriac form of the canonical gospel material:

> the Syrians did not have the Gospels in their own language until Tatian produced his *Diatessaron* [a harmony of the four canonical gospels], around AD 160 . . . In this blend of the Gospel material Tatian created some new forms of expression, and it is these which appear in Thomas. What is more, Thomas is called Judas Thomas in this gospel, and that name is found only among Syrian Christians. Syriac scholars have also noticed that although the 114 sayings in *Thomas* seem to have no rhyme or reason about their sequence in Coptic or the underlying Greek, as soon as you translate them into Syriac you discover many catch-words which link almost all the 114 sayings in order to aid memorization. All of this adds up to the strong probability that *Thomas* was written towards the end of the second century.[382]

As Philip W. Comfort and Jason Driesbach report:

> it is almost universally recognized that the four Gospels were penned in the first century and that all others came in the second century or thereafter . . . The four Gospels (1) were written on the basis of eyewitness authority; (2) were written in the first century; (3) have substantial second-century manuscript support; (4) were written as memoirs of the apostles in the form of

---

376. Dawkins, *The God Delusion*, 121.
377. Barnett, *Finding the Historical Christ*, 12.
378. Hitchens, *God Is Not Great*, 112.
379. Dawkins, *The God Delusion*, 121
380. Jones, *Misquoting Truth*, 134.
381. Green, *Lies, Lies, Lies!*, 44.
382. Green, *Lies, Lies, Lies!*, 37–38.

narratives; and (5) ring true and accord with what the apostles taught about Jesus [in their 1st century letters]. On the other hand, the non-canonical Gospels were not eyewitnesses' accounts [but] were written in the second century or thereafter; they usually have no manuscript support earlier than the third century or no Greek manuscript support at all. They were written in the form of dialogues or sayings, thereby revealing the author's lack of credibility as eyewitnesses; and they lacked that ring of truth, failing to accord with what the apostles taught about Jesus.[383]

Contrary to the claims of Dawkins and Hitchens: "these extracanonical Gospels do not offer early, reliable tradition, independent of what we possess in the New Testament Gospels. The extracanonical Gospels are late and almost always reflect a context far removed in time and place from first-century Palestine."[384]

Michel Onfray asserts that "The testamental canon arose from later political decisions, particularly those reached when Eucebius of Caeserea, mandated by the emperor Constantine, assembled a corpus stitched together from twenty-seven versions of the New Testament in the first half of the fourth century."[385] However, as Wallace confirms: "There is absolutely nothing to suggest in any of the historical literature that Constantine ever influenced what books belonged in the New Testament."[386] As James Bishop complains:

> It is common for skeptics to claim that the New Testament Canon was formed during 4th Century Church Councils (such as the Council of Nicea or Laodicea), however, that is not the truth as the earliest believers had already preserved the canonical gospels and letters centuries prior to the time of these Church Councils. For instance, the early church leaders prior to the first council at Nicea (known as the Ante-Nicene Church Fathers) began to collect and affirm the canon of Scripture in three separate geographical areas.[387]

Halvor Moxnes, Professor Emeritus of New Testament Studies at the University of Oslo, explains that:

> The process towards establishing a canon, especially a canon of gospels, started much earlier than Constantine, and was not a unified effort directed by a central authority. The geographically disparate and culturally diverse context of early Christianity, lacking as it was in centralised powers, made the process towards canonisation in the first three centuries a local and unstructured affair.[388]

---

383. Comfort and Driesbach, *The Many Gospels of Jesus*, xii, xvi.
384. Evans, *Fabricating Jesus*, 99.
385. Onfray, *In Defence of Atheism*, 78.
386. Wallace, "Predictable Christmas fare."
387. Bishop, "30 Common New Testament Challenges by Skeptics Answered."
388. Moxnes, *A Short History Of The New Testament*, 85.

Eusebius (in Palestine) affirmed 26 of the NT books around AD 324. Origen (in Egypt) affirmed as many as 27 NT books around AD 225. Hippolytus (in Italy) affirmed 24 of the NT books around AD 220. Irenaeus (in France) affirmed 24 of the NT books around AD 185.[389] As Professor C.E. Hill writes:

> In the last two or three decades of the second century Irenaeus in Gaul, Clement in Alexander, Theophilus and Serapion in Antioch, and the author of the Muratorian Fragment in or near Rome, at points far distant from each another on the map, are all saying or implying that the church has the same four acknowledged Gospels... The testimony of these authors is that the four Gospels were not recently foisted on them... but has been passed down to them from their forebears in their local Christian communities.[390]

It's noteworthy that "the [Muratorian] Canon—most likely the earliest list of authoritative Christian books (around 180 AD)—affirms the four New Testament Gospels as being the only ones recognized as Scripture."[391] Professor Michael J. Kruger argues that "by the second century most of the New Testament books were already seen as fully authoritative."[392]

Paul D. Wagner, Terry L. Wilder and Darrell L. Bock explain that when it came to the formation of the NT canon:

> the only significant question the early church had was whether or not a book carried the apostolic imprimature. Such authority was recognized in books that were seen to be authored or endorsed by an apostle, were consistent with apostolic doctrine, and were widely accepted in the apostolic churches. The twenty-seven books of the NT passed these tests... the Gnostic Gospels, did not.[393]

Kruger comments:

> The Council of Nicea had nothing to do with the formation of the New Testament canon (nor did Constantine)... When people discover that Nicea did not decide the canon, the follow up question is usually, "Which council did decide the canon?"... The fact of the matter is that when we look into early church history there is no such council. Sure, there are regional church councils that made declarations about the canon (Laodicea, Hippo, Carthage). But these regional councils did not just "pick" books they happened to like, but affirmed the books they believed *had functioned as foundational documents for the Christian faith*. In other words, these councils... did not create, authorize, or determine the canon. They simply were part of the process of *recognizing*

---

389. See: Bishop, "30 Common New Testament Challenges by Skeptics Answered."
390. Hill, *Who Chose the Gospels?*, 99–101.
391. Kostenberger et al., *Truth Matters*, 49.
392. Kruger, *The Question of Canon*, 206.
393. Wagner et al., "Do We Have the Right Canon?," 428.

a canon that was already there . . . Here we can agree with Bart Ehrman, 'The canon of the New Testament was ratified by widespread consensus rather than by official proclamation.'[394]

According to John Dickson:

> The four New Testament Gospels were a fixed, authoritative collection by at least the middle of the second century, before most of the Gnostics had even begun to put pen to papyrus . . . When the great church councils got together in the third and fourth centuries to discuss which books were part of the canon . . . there was no argument about the Gospels. Their inclusion, along with the letters of the apostle Paul, had long been established.[395]

Charlotte Allen comments:

> Within a century of Jesus' death, all four Gospels were in wide circulation, often as a unit . . . Today's Christian "canon" . . . was not the product of church councils, although the rulings of bishops and the opinions of theologians undoubtedly played a role in its formation. By and large, it was created by consensus . . . While the New Testament canon was not officially codified until sometime during the fourth century, as early as 200 [AD] it was more or less in place . . .[396]

Green notes that "As early as the Chester Beatty papyrus P45, written in about 200 AD, we actually possess the fourfold Gospels bound together in a codex (book) form."[397] He reckons that: "by 100, if not a little earlier—that is to say within the lifetime of some who had known Jesus—the New Testament was not only written but was on the way to being collected."[398] Wright confirms that: "The four canonical gospels . . . The Acts of the Apostles, and the 13 letters ascribed to Paul were regarded by the early Christians as authentic and authoritative from very early on, by the early to mid second century at least."[399] Comfort and Driesbach concur, writing that: "the Gospels and the major epistles of Paul were 'canonized' in the minds of many Christians as early as A.D. 90–100 . . ."[400]

Watch: "The New Testament Canon" Youtube playlist: www.youtube.com/playlist?list=PLQhh3qcwVEWgB1baV-0QrZ3f0JRkj74hM

Read: "The Canon of the New Testament" by F.F. Bruce: www.bible-researcher.com/bruce1.html

394. Kruger, "The NT Canon was Not Decided at Nicea."
395. Dickson, *Investigating Jesus*, 46.
396. Allen, *The Human Christ*, 80–81.
397. Green, *The Books The Church Suppressed*, 58.
398. Green, *Lies, Lies, Lies!*, 79.
399. Wright, *Why Read the Bible?*, 4–5.
400. Comfort and Driesbach, *The Many Gospels of Jesus*, 11.

"What About the Gospel of Thomas?" by Glenn M. Miller: http://christianthinktank.com/gthomas.html

"The Foreign God and the Sudden Christ: Theology and Christology in Marcion's Gospel Redaction" by Peter M. Head: https://legacy.tyndalehouse.com/tynbul/Library/TynBull_1993_44_2_06_Head_ForeignGodSuddenChrist.pdf

The Books The Church Suppressed: What The Da Vinci Code Doesn't Tell You by Michael Green

Reinventing Jesus: How Contemporary Skeptics Miss The Real Jesus And Mislead Popular Culture by J. Ed Komoszewski et al.

The Question Of Canon: Challenging the status quo in the New Testament debate by Michael J. Kruger

---

GETTING AT THE KEY QUESTION

"the four Gospels in our New Testaments are substantially reliable sources for knowing quite a lot about Jesus."

—RICHARD BAUCKHAM[401]

Gary R. Habermas neatly summarizes many of our conclusions thus far:

> The charge that Jesus did not (or probably did not) exist is certainly a minority view . . . open to several especially strong negative critiques. It cannot stand in light of the early and eyewitness testimony presented by Paul and others, the early date, historicity and trustworthiness of the Gospels (as well as the New Testament as a whole) and the failure of legendary and mythical theories, such as the mystery religions, to explain Christian origins.[402]

Robert Martin's assessment of neo-atheist engagement with the canonical gospels is spot on:

> The New Atheists . . . fail to support their, often wild, assertions with rigorous well-reasoned evidence. They misunderstand ancient historiography and the nature of historical reporting . . . Their conclusions fail to adequately account for the evidence. It is ironic that a group so intent on rationality and evidence can overlook and ignore so much. The New Atheist case against the reliability of the canonical Gospels is hardly proven.[403]

Indeed, in light of the evidence one can see why Blomberg concludes that "on sheer historical grounds alone there is substantial reason to believe in the *general*

---

401. Bauckham, *Jesus*, 6.
402. Habermas, *The Verdict of History*, 54.
403. Martin, "The New Atheists and the New Testament," 67–68.

trustworthiness of the Gospel tradition."[404] Contrary to the woefully uninformed hyper-skepticism of the New Atheists, it should be clear that we have good reason to agree with Green that: "the four Gospels . . . emerge from every test with their integrity unimpeached. [That] is a very good reason for taking with the utmost seriousness the accuracy of the picture of Jesus that they paint."[405]

The key question about the picture of Jesus we get from critically investigating the canonical gospels and the rest of the NT, as well as the ancient non-Christian evidence, is obviously *this*:

- What is the truth status of the "high Christology" we've traced to Jesus and his original, first-century followers?

Jesus' earliest followers arrived at and defended their belief in a high Christology via a handful of arguments. As Green says of Jesus:

> his influence, his teachings, his claims, his miracles, his fulfilment of prophecy, his death and his resurrection all combine to convince the first disciples that their Master is no mere man but Lord and God.[406]

We've already examined the "trilemma" argument based upon the combination of Jesus' claims and character (see chapter Two). However, the crowning argument here (which was clearly the clinching piece of evidence for the first Christians) is undoubtedly the argument that will occupy our attention in our final chapters, namely, the argument from Jesus' resurrection.

It's worth noting that an atheist like Michael Ruse can "agree on the fairly uncontroversial claim that if the miracles of the Gospels did occur, then we have some pretty strong evidence for the truth of Christianity."[407] In particular, Ruse affirms that "If Jesus was really dead on Friday and really alive on Sunday, then I for one will be satisfied."[408] Anyone who is serious about following the evidence where it leads should obviously echo this commitment.

Read: "Recent Perspectives on the Reliability of the Gospels" by Gary R. Habermas: www.garyhabermas.com/articles/crj_recentperspectives/crj_recentperspectives.htm

"Why I Believe the New Testament is Historically Reliable" by Gary R. Habermas: www.monergism.com/thethreshold/sdg/Why%20I%20Believe%20the%20New%20Testament%20is%20Historically%20Reliable(1).pdf

"Bart Ehrman's Forged: Writing in the Name of God—a review" by Michael Licona: www.bethinking.org/is-the-bible-reliable/forged-writing-in-the-name-of-god

---

404. Blomberg, *The Historical Reliability of the Gospels*, 381.
405. Green, *The Books The Church Suppressed*, 34.
406. Green, *The Books The Church Suppressed*, 27.
407. Ruse, *Atheism*, 161.
408. Ruse, *Atheism*, 161.

"The Historicity of the New Testament" by J.P. Moreland: www.bethinking.org/is-the-bible-reliable/the-historicity-of-the-new-testament

"Bart Ehrman's Misquoting Jesus—an analysis" by Peter J. Williams: www.bethinking.org/is-the-bible-reliable/bart-ehrmans-misquoting-jesus-an-analysis

"Digging For Evidence" by Peter S. Williams: http://christianevidence.org/docs/booklets/digging_for_evidence.pdf

Jesus and the Eyewitnesses: The Gospels as Eyewitness Testimony by Richard Bauckham

Is The New Testament Reliable? by Paul Barnett

The Historical Reliability of the Gospels by Craig L. Blomberg

The Jesus Legend: A Case For The Reliability of the Synoptic Jesus Tradition by Paul Rhodes Eddy and Gregory A. Boyd

Fabricating Jesus: How Modern Scholars Distort the Gospels by Craig A. Evans

Jesus And His World: The Archaeological Evidence by Craig A. Evans

The Books The Church Suppressed: What The Da Vinci Code Doesn't Tell You by Michael Green

The Early Text of the New Testament by Charles E. Hill and Michael J. Kruger

The Holman Apologetics Commentary On The Bible: The Gospels and Acts edited by Jeremy Royal Howard

Searching For Jesus: New Discoveries In The Quest For Jesus Of Nazareth—And How They Confirm The Gospel Accounts by Robert J. Hutchinson

Misquoting Truth: A Guide to the Fallacies of Bart Ehrman's Misquoting Jesus by Timothy Paul Jones

The Real Jesus: The Misguided Quest For The Historical Jesus And The Truth Of The Traditional Gospels by Luke Timothy Johnson

Biographies and Jesus: What Does It Mean for the Gospels to be Biographies? edited by Craig S. Keener and Edward T. Wright

Reinventing Jesus: How Contemporary Skeptics Miss The Real Jesus And Mislead Popular Culture by J. Ed Komoszewski et al.

Hidden In Plain View: Undesigned Coincidences in the Gospels and Acts by Lydia McGrew

The Case For Jesus: The Biblical And Historical Evidence For Christ by Brant Pitre

How We Got The New Testament: Text, Transmission, Translation by Stanley E. Porter

Midrash Criticism: Introduction and Appraisal by Charles L. Quarles

Can We Trust the Gospels? by Mark D. Roberts

Introducing Jesus: A short guide to the gospels' history and message by Mark L. Strauss

Memories of Jesus: A Critical Appraisal of James D.G. Dunn's Jesus Remembered edited by Robert B. Stewart and Gary R. Habermas

Can We Trust the Gospels? by Peter J. Williams

CHAPTER 4

Getting at Evidence for the Resurrection

> "In the end, there is no 'true' religion in the factual sense,
> for there is no good evidence supporting their truth claims."
> —Daniel Dennett[1]

> "The evidence for the resurrection is better than for claimed miracles in any other religion. It's outstandingly different in quality and quantity."
> —Anthony Flew[2]

CHRISTOPHER HITCHENS ONCE ASKED his opponent in a debate on the existence of God: "Do you believe Jesus Christ was . . . resurrected from the dead?" His opponent (philosopher Jay W. Richards) obligingly affirmed his belief in the resurrection. Hitchens acted as if this were a telling admission:

> I rest my case. This is an honest guy, who has just made it very clear science has nothing to do with his worldview.

Well, as philosopher Timothy McGrew says: "Hitchens rarely let slip an opportunity for good theatre. But good theatre is not always good reasoning."[3]

Hitchens' theatrics assumed that "science" was on his side and that nothing trumps "science." However, it wasn't *science* that Hitchens had on his side, but *a dogmatic philosophy of science*. As documented in chapter one, we should be skeptical

---

1. Dennett, "What is a "true" religion?"
2. Flew, "My Pilgrimage from Atheism to Theism."
3. McGrew, "Do Miracles Really Violate the Laws of Science?"

about attempts to demarcate science from philosophy and about *a priori* arguments against the miraculous. Instead, we should favor an open philosophy of science that allows supernatural theories into the pool of live explanatory hypotheses and recognizes the importance of following the evidence wherever it leads.[4] Indeed, several New Atheist writers endorse an open philosophy of science:

- Jerry Coyne: "nothing in science prohibits us from considering supernatural explanations . . . If something is supposed to exist in a way that has tangible effects on the universe, it falls within the ambit of science. And supernatural beings and phenomena can have real-world effects."[5]

- Richard Dawkins: "Did Jesus . . . come alive again, three days after being crucified? There is an answer to every such question, whether or not we can discover it in practice, and it is a strictly scientific answer."[6]

- Sam Harris: "Nothing is more sacred than the facts . . . anyone who wants to know how the world is, whether in physical or spiritual terms, will be open to new evidence."[7]

- Victor J. Stenger: "Physical and historical evidence might have been found for the miraculous events . . . of the scriptures."[8]

Christianity is founded upon the historical occurrence of the miraculous. As Ben Witherington III observes: "Acts indicates, as the Pauline Epistles also suggest, that the basic confession of the early church was the acknowledgement that Jesus is the (risen) Lord."[9] N.T. Wright elaborates the point:

> The question of Jesus' resurrection lies at the heart of the Christian faith. There is no form of Christianity known to us—though there are some that have been invented by ingenious scholars—that did not affirm at its heart that after Jesus' shameful death God raised him to life again. Already by the time of Paul . . . the resurrection of Jesus is not just a single, detached article of faith. It is woven into the very structure of Christian life and thought, informing (among other things) baptism, justification, ethics, and the future hope both for humans and for the cosmos.[10]

---

4. See: Bylica and Sagan, "God, design, and naturalism;" Larmer, "Is Methodological Naturalism Question-Begging?;" Monton, "Is Intelligent Design Science?;" Bartlett, "Philosophical Shortcomings of Methodological Naturalism and the Path Forward."

5. Coyne, *Faith vs. Fact*, 93–94.

6. Dawkins, *The God Delusion*, 59.

7. Harris, *The End of Faith*, 225.

8. Stenger, "Victor J. Stenger," 211.

9. Witherington, *The Acts Of The Apostles*, 149.

10. Wright, *The Challenge of Jesus*, 94.

For example, Paul connects the death and resurrection of Christ to Christian beliefs about "baptism, justification, ethics and the future hope" in his letter to Christians in Rome c. AD 55:

> Or don't you know that all of us who were baptized into Christ Jesus were baptized into his death? We were therefore buried with him through baptism into death in order that, just as Christ was raised from the dead through the glory of the Father, we too may live a new life. For if we have been united with him in a death like his, we will certainly also be united with him in a resurrection like his. For we know that our old self was crucified with him so that the body ruled by sin might be done away with, that we should no longer be slaves to sin - because anyone who has died has been set free from sin. Now if we died with Christ, we believe that we will also live with him. For we know that since Christ was raised from the dead, he cannot die again; death no longer has mastery over him. The death he died, he died to sin once for all; but the life he lives, he lives to God. In the same way, count yourselves dead to sin but alive to God in Christ Jesus. (Romans 6:3–11)

Jesus' resurrection was *not* a Christian metaphor for a post-crucifixion revival of faith on the part of the disciples (as some nineteenth-century theologians suggested), but a description of something that was thought to have happened to the corpse of Christ:

> the Christian claim was from the beginning that Jesus' resurrection was a question not of the internal mental and spiritual states of his followers a few days after his crucifixion but of something that had happened in the real, public world, leaving among its physical mementoes not only an empty tomb but a broken loaf at Emmaus and footprints in the sand by the lake. This left his followers with a lot of explaining to do but with a transformed worldview that is only explicable on the assumption that something really did happen, even though it stretched their existing worldviews to breaking point.[11]

Christopher Hitchens confuses resurrection in its strongest theological sense with resurrection in the lesser sense of a miraculous resuscitation or revivification when he asserts that "Just in the life of Jesus of Nazareth there's the raising of Lazarus and of the daughter of Jairus . . . making it seem that resurrection is a relative commonplace."[12] However, these incidents involve miraculous *resuscitations* to earthly life, and as Marcus J. Borg concedes: "whatever happened at Easter was not a resuscitation."[13] Stephen T. Davis explains that, in the strongest sense of the term:

> resurrection is not *resuscitation* . . . The difference is this: in resuscitations, the revived persons are restored to their old lives and will certainly die again at

---

11. Wright, "Can a Scientist Believe," 43. See: Dodd, *The Founder of Christianity*, 172.
12. Hitchens, "Zombies?"
13. Borg and Wright, *The Meaning of Jesus*, 131.

some later point . . . A resurrected person is raised to a new and exulted state of life and will never die again.[14]

Bart Ehrman agrees that "the early teachings about Jesus were . . . not simply that his corpse was restored to the living. It is that he experienced a resurrection. That's not the same thing."[15] He notes: "The resurrection claims are claims that not only [did] Jesus' body came back alive; it came back alive never to die again."[16] As Davis observes: "The New Testament's witness holds that Jesus was not merely restored to his previous life, but rather was transformed to a new and glorious life fit for the kingdom of God."[17] This isn't the case with Lazarus or the daughter of Jairus.[18]

Paul discourses upon the nature of the resurrection body intended for the kingdom life of the new heavens and earth[19] in his first letter to Christians in Corinth (c. AD 54), saying:

> The body that is sown is perishable, it is raised imperishable; it is sown in dishonor, it is raised in glory; it is sown in weakness, it is raised in power; it is sown a natural body, it is raised a spiritual body. (1 Corinthians 15:42; see Philippians 3:21)

Atheist John W. Loftus concedes that "What little Jesus himself said about the resurrection leads us to think both he and Paul shared the same view."[20] Indeed, Carl E. Olson points out that "the early Christian testimony to the bodily nature of the Resurrection and on the resurrection to come is constant and unanimous."[21]

This understanding of resurrection wasn't unique to Christianity, but was adopted from Judaism. As James H. Charlesworth observes: "the concept of a general resurrection was developed by Jews long before Jesus . . . the Christian belief in Jesus' resurrection is founded on Jewish concepts and beliefs . . ."[22] For example, in the book of 2 Maccabees a Jewish martyr states that "the king of the universe will raise us up to an everlasting renewal of life . . ." while another contrasts being put to death "at the

---

14. Davis, *Rational Faith*, 69.
15. Erhman, *Did Jesus Exist?*, 225.
16. Ehrman, "Is There Historical Evidence for the Resurrection of Jesus?"
17. Davis, *Christian Philosophical Theology*, 134.
18. See: Blomberg, *The Historical Reliability of John's Gospel*, 164–72 and Wright, *The Resurrection of the Son of God*, 443–49.
19. According to *Meyer's NT Commentary* on 1 Corinthians 15:42: "Paul, in his whole discussion regarding the nature of the future bodies, has in view only . . . future sharers in the resurrection of the righteous (comp. on Php 3:11), whose resurrection-hope was being assailed." Likewise, Matthew Poole's commentary on 1 Corinthians 15:42 notes: "that is, so shall it be, as to the bodies of the saints, in the resurrection."
20. Loftus, *Why I Became An Atheist*, 363.
21. Olson, *Did Jesus Really Rise From The Dead?*, 39.
22. Charlesworth, *The Historical Jesus*, 56.

hands of mortals" with "being raised again" by God in the "resurrection to life!"[23] On this shared Judeo-Christian view, the dead body laid in the tomb is raised from the tomb in a *physical but metaphysically-renovated form*. As Wright explains:

> from the start within early Christianity it was built in as part of the belief in resurrection that the new body, though it would certainly *be* a body in the sense of a physical object occupying space and time, will be a *transformed* body, a body whose material, created from the old material, will have new properties.[24]

Atheist James Crossley confirms that Paul "refers to bodily resurrection in the strongest sense . . . of the sort that would have left behind an empty tomb."[25] Matthew Kneale reveals his confusion on this point by asserting that "Paul reports that they saw Jesus not in a *bodily* but in a *spiritual* form."[26] However, Paul's qualifications of "body" with the terms "natural" (*psychikon*, which literally means "soulish") and "spiritual" (*pneumatikon*) in 1 Corinthians 15:42 do *not* contrast physicality with non-physicality.[27] Both qualifications apply *to one and the same body*:

> Virtually every modern commentator agrees on this point: Paul is not talking about a rarefied body made out of spirit or ether; he means a body under the lordship and direction of God's Spirit . . . The contrast is not between physical body / non-physical body, but between naturally oriented body / spiritually oriented body.[28]

For Paul, the *psychikon* ("soulish" or "natural") man is a person with an antithetical attitude to spiritual things springing from a worldly, egotistical dedication to a sensuous, animalistic lifestyle. Hence Paul writes *of those still living* that:

> the *psychikon* man does not readily welcome the things of the Spirit of God, for they are foolishness to him; nor can he know them by acquaintance, because they are spiritually discerned. But he who is spiritual judges all things, yet he himself is rightly judged by no one. (1 Corinthians 2:14–15, my translation.)

Paul's contrast between the "natural" and the "spiritual" person isn't a contrast between material and immaterial *substances* but between opposite spiritual *orientations*. Paul's thinking about the resurrection follows on from this distinction, such that a "spiritual body" is a *physical* human body *transformed by God so that it fitted to eternal life in a re-created cosmos without sin*—the "new heavens and earth" (see: 2 Peter

---

23. 2 Maccabees 7:9, 14.
24. Wright, *Surprised by Hope*, 55.
25. Bird and Crossley, *How Did Christianity Begin?*, 52.
26. Kneale, *An Atheist's History of Belief*, 103.
27. See: Licona, "Paul and the Nature of the Resurrection Body;" Davis, "Was Jesus Raised Bodily?;" Davis, "James D.G. Dunn on the resurrection of Jesus;" Wright, *Surprised by Hope*.
28. Craig, "The Bodily Resurrection of Jesus."

3:13; Revelation 21:1)—a "new creation" (or re-creation) *of which Jesus' resurrection is an advanced sample*: "Christ has indeed been raised from the dead, the first-fruits of those who have fallen asleep" (1 Corinthians 15:20). Hence, while Paul believes that the immaterial spirits of the Christian dead are currently "with Christ" (Philippians 1:22–24),[29] he looks forward to the end of earthly history wherein:

> We will not all sleep [i.e. die physically], but we will all be changed—in a flash, in the twinkling of an eye . . . the dead will be raised imperishable, and we [i.e. Christians then living] will be changed. For the perishable [human body] must clothe itself with the imperishable, and the mortal [human body] with immortality. When the perishable has been clothed with the imperishable, and the mortal with immortality, then the saying that is written will come true: "Death has been swallowed up in victory" [Isaiah 25:8]. (1 Corinthians 15:51–54.)

Just as the first Christians believed that the resurrected Jesus was a miraculously transformed pre-resurrection Jesus, so they believed that the "new creation" would be the old (i.e. current) creation miraculously transformed by the Spirit of God: "Paul conceived of the resurrection body as a powerful, glorious, imperishable, Spirit-directed *body*, created through a transformation of the earthly body or the remains thereof, and made to inhabit the new universe in the eschaton [i.e. in the goal of the present world]."[30] As Davis explains:

> We should not be misled by Paul's use of the term "spiritual body." He is not using the term to signify a body "formed out of spirit" . . . whatever that might mean, but rather a body that has been glorified or transformed by God and is now fully dominated by the power of the Holy Spirit.[31]

Watch: "The Resurrection Body" Youtube playlist: www.youtube.com/playlist?list=PLQh h3qcwVEWjzzSCvGeMMTrijW81-JDvf

"Heaven & Hell" Youtube playlist: www.youtube.com/playlist?list=PLQhh3qcwVEWiI mwioEwFZIiNXYAVEQpvN

Read: "Sentiments of Reason and Aspirations of the Soul" by John Haldane: https://muse.jhu.edu/article/170324/pdf

"The Possibility of Life After Death" by Richard Swinburne: http://people.ds.cam.ac.uk/dhm11/Swinburne.html

Heaven: The Heart's Deepest Longing by Peter Kreeft

The God of Hope and the End of the World by John Polkinghorne

Surprised by Hope by N.T. Wright

29. See: Craig, "The Soul Provides Continuity Between the Physical and Resurrection Body;" Cooper, *Body, Soul & Life Everlasting*.

30. Craig, "The Bodily Resurrection of Jesus."

31. Davis, *Risen Indeed*, 56. It thus appears that the resurrected bodies of non-believers at the last judgment will not be spiritual bodies (see: John 5:28-29; Revelation 20:12-15).

Heaven: The Logic of Eternal Joy by Jerry L. Walls
Christian Eschatology And The Physical Universe by David Wilkinson

---

Jesus' resurrection underpins Christian hope in a future resurrected life of flourishing relationships purged of evil, a *pneumatikon* cosmos. If Jesus was *not* resurrected, Christianity is false. *Theism* could be true without *Christianity* being true, but *Christianity* can't be true without the belief that Jesus rose from the dead being true. As Paul put it:

> if Christ has not been raised, our preaching is useless [fallacious] and so is your faith. More than that, we are then found to be false witnesses about God, for we have testified about God that he raised Christ from the dead . . . (1 Corinthians 15:14–15.)

On the other hand, if Jesus *has* been resurrected, that clearly confirms Jesus' teaching (including his teaching about himself). As John Warwick Montgomery argues:

> Once the facticity of Christ's resurrection has been granted, all explanations for it reduce to two: Christ's own (He rose because He was God) and any and every interpretation of the event in contradiction to this explanation. Surely it is not difficult to make a choice here, for Jesus (unlike anyone else offering an explanation of the Resurrection) actually rose from the dead! His explanation has prima facie value as opposed to those in contradiction to it, presented as they are by persons who have not managed resurrections themselves.[32]

STANDING UP TO THE NEW ATHEISTS ON THE RESURRECTION

> "Jesus was neither divine nor resurrected..."
>
> —Jerry A. Coyne[33]

Paul W. Barnett contends that "So comprehensive and pervasive is the resurrection of Jesus" within our historical sources "that, historically speaking, the onus is on the skeptic to overturn it."[34] Although Jerry A. Coyne devotes a couple of pages to the subject in his book *Faith vs. Fact*—a challenge we will meet in our final chapter—John Lennox is right to complain that there's "no serious attempt by any of the New Atheists to engage with the evidence for the resurrection of Jesus Christ."[35] As Habermas

---

32. Montgomery, *Faith Founded On Fact*, 62.
33. Coyne, *Faith vs. Fact*, 259.
34. Barnett, "Is The New Testament Historically Reliable?," 250.
35. Lennox, *Gunning for God*, 188.

wryly observes: "sometimes critics . . . have done the least thinking about this."[36] For example, Barnett's evidence-led challenge contrasts starkly with Lawrence Krauss's assertion that "the point about the resurrection is that there's no evidence of it!"[37]

Dawkins's dismissal of Jesus' resurrection is wholly unencumbered by interaction with contemporary scholarship on the subject. He simply opines that "the evidence that [Jesus] worked miracles [or] rose from the dead . . . is zero."[38] He just asserts that "Accounts of Jesus' resurrection . . . are about as well documented as Jack [and] the Beanstalk."[39] Thomas A. Miller complains:

> Dawkins conveniently bypasses any serious discussion of evidence for [Jesus'] resurrection by insisting that modern scholarship has clearly shown that the New Testament Gospels (which are the primary sources describing the resurrection) are not reliable historical accounts about Jesus, since they were written long after his alleged death by individuals who clearly did not know him, making the possibility of myth and legend very likely.[40]

As documented in chapter three, modern scholarship has shown no such thing; but even if it had, Dawkins's skepticism would be unjustified. In the first place, given the multiple lines of evidence that support the general historical reliability of the NT gospels (see: chapter three), one is in fact faced with a wealth of evidence for the resurrection of Jesus. As James H. Charlesworth observes: "with the Passion Narrative we have the most reliable historical traditions because they were written first, portray events when Jesus' followers were present, and were verifiable public occurrences."[41] In the second place, one can argue for the resurrection without relying on arguments for the general historical reliability of the NT, by focusing on specific data established by historical "criteria of authenticity." This approach was pioneered by theologian Wolfhart Pannenberg, who:

> opined that the Gospel accounts of Jesus's resurrection are so legendary that they have scarcely a historical kernel in them; yet . . . stunned German theology by arguing for the historicity of Jesus' post-mortem appearances and empty tomb and, hence, for his resurrection sheerly on historical grounds.[42]

Pannenberg's approach to the resurrection is perfectly compatible with the false belief, which he shared with Dawkins, that the NT is generally unreliable.

---

36. See: Habermas, "Filling the Naturalistic Void."
37. Krauss and Craig, "Life, The Universe, and Nothing."
38. Dawkins, "Hugh interviews atheist Richard Dawkins."
39. Dawkins quoted in Lennox, *Gunning for God*, 187.
40. Miller, *Did Jesus Really Rise From The Dead?* 23.
41. Charlesworth, *The Historical Jesus*, 63.
42. Craig, "Qualms about the resurrection of Jesus."

AUTHENTICATED DATA

> "I am an atheist because I reject all stories that are not rooted in and supported by empirical data..."
>
> —EMERY EMERY[43]

Gary R. Habermas argues that any conclusion about the historicity of the resurrection must accommodate historical data that exhibits two characteristics: "they are well evidenced, usually for multiple reasons, and they are generally admitted by critical scholars who research this particular area."[44] The second characteristic should not be dismissed as merely an appeal to the authority and common consent of "biased" conservative Christian scholars. On the one hand, accusations of bias cut both ways, and one must demonstrate rather than simply assume that a scholar's bias renders their arguments and/or conclusions unsound. On the other hand, this appeal (despite being hard to objectively quantify in absolute terms) is designed to include the opinions of liberal, Jewish, agnostic, and atheist scholars precisely as a check against bias. As Halvor Moxnes explains: "Since the end of the twentieth century, studies of the historical Jesus and of the New Testament in general have been an ecumenical enterprise including Christian, Jewish and non-religious scholars."[45] In his review of *Jewish Scholarship on the Resurrection of Jesus* (Pickwick, 2017), David Mishkin observes that:

> Many non-Jewish scholars already have a faith commitment to Jesus. This does not mean that their scholarship should summarily be discarded as biased. It should be evaluated on its own merit. Nevertheless, the reality is that presuppositions are influential. Jewish scholars begin with a different set of presuppositions. But, what is interesting to note is that the main historical events that make up this discussion are virtually the same for both groups: crucifixion, burial, disciples' belief, empty tomb, and Paul's dramatic turnaround.[46]

Moreover, Habermas proposes that well supported data beyond those admitted by scholars regardless of their religious beliefs can be taken into account as part of a supplementary argument, or as a tiebreaker between otherwise evenly-matched hypotheses. So, while trans-worldview consent is *desirable*, good evidence is *essential*.

Watch: "The Minimal Facts Approach to the Resurrection" Youtube playlist: www.youtube.com/playlist?list=PLQhh3qcwVEWibeo-6SuXmjOkmFE_4C8Vx

---

43. Emery, "A Child Was Born on Christmas Day," 18.
44. Habermas, "Evidential Apologetics," 100.
45. Moxnes, *A Short History Of The New Testament*, 181.
46. Mishkin, *Jewish Scholarship on the Resurrection of Jesus*, 210.

Criteria of authenticity

> "The criteria for determining what Caesar did at Gaul, or how the Goths sacked Rome, or what happened at Waterloo, are the criteria by which we determine what happened on this first Easter Sunday."
>
> —Wilbur M. Smith[47]

As we've seen, an accumulation of both archaeological and literary-historical factors "suggests a presumption in favor of the quality of the tradition as it appears in the New Testament."[48] Nevertheless, it will be useful in what follows to bear in mind that the field of "Tradition Criticism"[49] utilizes "criteria of authenticity" to establish historical facts without reference to our background knowledge about the historical reliability of the NT testimony.

The criteria of authenticity "contribute to a cumulative argument about particular texts,"[50] such that even if one thought the NT contained generally unreliable testimony about the historical Jesus, those elements of the NT that are supported by these criteria should nevertheless be regarded as historically reliable:

> the chief point here is that, as applied to ancient history, the textual "criteria of authenticity" provide some of the very best insights that particular Gospel passages have probably narrated actual historical incidents. This is especially the case when more than one criterion affirms the same event or saying.[51]

These criteria include:

1) Eyewitness sources

All other things being equal, first-hand evidence is preferable to second-hand evidence. Some atheists point to studies on problematical aspects of eyewitness evidence in order to dismiss historical data that passes this criterion. However, as Timothy McGrew observes:

> The critical literature on eyewitness testimony is largely focused on cases where various confounding estimator variables are in play; for example, the people are strangers to one another, witnesses are intoxicated, cross-racial identification is involved, the initial situation involves short exposure (typically 12–45 seconds), and high levels of stress or a weapon are involved. Not one of these factors are plausibly in play in the case of the witnesses to the resurrected Jesus. Far from undermining the value of the evidence we do have,

---

47. Smith, *Therefore Stand*, 361.
48. Bock, *Studying the Historical Jesus*, 199.
49. Bock, *Studying the Historical Jesus*, 199.
50. Wenham and Walton, *New Testament: Volume One*, 139.
51. Habermas, *The Investigator*, 19.

the study of the vagaries of eyewitness testimony heightens the puzzle of how Jesus's intimate acquaintances could have been so profoundly mistaken as to have believed that he had appeared to them alive after his crucifixion again and again over a period of many weeks.[52]

Psychologist Susan A. Clancy adds that "The most recent research indicates that although some details of traumatic events may be forgotten or confused, the core of the memory—what actually happened—generally remains intact."[53]

2) Early sources

All things being equal, we should privilege earlier sources over later sources: "The less time there is between an event and its written description, the less the margin for error—for forgetting or adding."[54] As classical historian Mark D. Smith avers: "In particular, there is a significant watershed between first-generation sources, written during the lifetime of at least some who knew the person or experienced the event in question, and sources from subsequent generations."[55]

Jerry Coyne demands "accounts that are contemporaneous with the event."[56] Interpreted strictly, this rule would make ancient history all but impossible; but if we take this to mean that historians should prefer accounts written within living memory of an event, this is simply a restatement of the criteria of early sources. Hence it is significant to note with I. Howard Marshall that: "It is generally accepted among scholars that the passion story existed in a form of a continuous narrative from an early date."[57]

3, 4 & 5) Multiple and/or *Independent attestation of Sources and/or Forms*

According to John P. Meier: "The criterion of multiple attestation focuses on those saying or deeds of Jesus that are attested in more than one independent literary source and/or in more than one literary form or genre. The force of this criterion is increased if a given motif or theme is found in both literary sources and different literary forms."[58]

Attestation from multiple testimonial sources that agree although they can be shown to have been unaware of each other's testimony is a historical ideal devoutly to be desired. For obvious reasons, though, it's very often impossible to establish more than a presumption of such informational independence among historical sources. Indeed, scholars generally treat the different NT sources (Q, L, M, Peter, Paul, etc.) as independent witnesses on account of their literary independence. Although literary independence doesn't guarantee testimonial independence, it is indicative thereof.

---

52. McGrew, "There Are Serious Reasons for Belief," 106.
53. Clancy, *Abducted*, 13.
54. Dickson, *Investigating Jesus*, 124.
55. Smith, *Therefore Stand*, 29.
56. Coyne, *Faith vs. Fact*, 121.
57. Marshall, *I Believe in the Historical Jesus*, 166.
58. Meier, *A Marginal Jew*, 175.

On the other hand, literary dependence doesn't necessarily negate the value of multiple source attestation.[59] That author B makes the same claim as author A, of whose testimony on the matter at hand they are aware (and even if they do so using similar language or even wholesale quotation), doesn't mean that B didn't independently check the veracity of A's information. For example, although Luke is often dependent upon Mark in literary terms, he clearly states in his prologue that he has carefully checked the truth of his account with many different sources. As David Wenham and Steve Walton comment:

> if [something] is attested by several NT writings, then this is in its favour . . . if, for example, we argue that the feeding of the 5,000 has a high claim to being historical, being attested in the four canonical Gospels, the immediate objection could be that the other evangelists were using Mark as a source, so what appears to be four witnesses is really only one. This objection is not a total knockout blow to the proposed criterion: even if it is correct that the other evangelists used Mark, it is also clear that they had their own non-Markan sources . . .[60]

Likewise, Robert H. Stein argues:

> Does not the fact that two Gospel writers chose to incorporate the account of another Gospel writer into their works witness to a three-fold testimony to that tradition? Unless we assume that the later Evangelists were totally unfamiliar with the traditions found in Mark (or Matthew), then we must grant additional credence to the testimony of an account found in the triple tradition, for in their acceptance of the traditions in their source they give corroborative testimony to the primitiveness of those traditions.[61]

We can follow Blomberg in distinguishing between different types of multiple attestation. First, "if a story or saying is found in more than one of the Gospel sources which scholars postulate, then this is possibly more significant."[62] Second, "another form of multiple attestation that has been proposed looks for ideas or themes that are found in different types of Gospel teaching: thus the 'kingdom of God' is a theme that permeates all sorts of Jesus' teaching (parables, miracle stories, etc.) and is seen therefore as having huge historical probability."[63] These forms of multiple attestation occur "when a saying appears either in multiple sources (M, L, Q, Mark) or in multiple forms (i.e. in a miracle account, a parable, and/or apocalyptic sayings)."[64] As Blomberg writes: "That which appears in . . . more than one Gospel source, or more than one

---

59. See: Evans, *The Historical Christ*, 331.
60. Wenham and Walton, *New Testament: Volume One*, 135.
61. Stein, "The "Criteria" for Authenticity," 88–103.
62. Wenham and Walton, *New Testament: Volume One*, 136.
63. Wenham and Walton, *New Testament: Volume One*, 136–37.
64. Bock, *Studying the Historical Jesus*, 92.

form stands a better chance of being authentic than that which is singly attested."[65] Thomas R. Yoder Neufeld agrees that "if one can find the same saying or deed attributed to Jesus in several different sources, especially different kinds of sources and different layers of tradition, confidence in its authenticity is greatly strengthened."[66]

In short, as Smith explains: "Strong corroborations are agreements between different types of evidence, such as nuministics and literary evidence, or two independent strands of literary evidence, while weaker corroborations exist among sources that have some sort of connection."[67]

Coming back to the concept of "independent" attestation, note that my testimony about events in my life surely counts as independent testimony even though I am aware of friends and family members who would testify to the same events. In sum, testimony from sources that know of other sources making the same claim, can sometimes be shown to be "independent" in the still robust sense that they don't believe the claim they are asserting because of that other testimony. For example, many of those who bear witnesses to the resurrection of Jesus clearly disbelieved prior testimony on the matter and only came to believe on the basis of their personal experience.

6) *Embarrassing sources*

The criterion of embarrassment "refers to sayings or deeds that are not easily explained as inauthentic creations of the early church, simply because there are aspects about them that would have been potentially embarrassing."[68] As Graham Stanton notes: "traditions which would have been an embarrassment to followers of Jesus in the post-Easter period are unlikely to have been invented."[69]

7) *Divergent/Enemy sources*

Mark L. Strauss explains: "The *criterion of divergent traditions* says that when an author preserves traditions which do not serve his purposes, they are more than likely to be authentic."[70] Wenham and Walton comment that "if a Gospel contains a saying or story of Jesus which is contrary to the evangelist's own particular interests or tendencies, then this is likely to be a tradition that is being passed on, not something coming from the evangelist himself."[71]

Information from sources opposed to the gospel writers' viewpoint, but which nevertheless agrees with some element of that viewpoint, is often called "enemy attestation."

8) *Criterion of public falsifiability*

65. Blomberg, *Jesus and the Gospels*, 186.
66. Neufeld, *Recovering Jesus*, 44.
67. Smith, *Therefore Stand*, 30.
68. Evans, *Fabricating Jesus*, 140.
69. Stanton, *The Gospels and Jesus*, 175.
70. Strauss, *Four Portraits, One Jesus*, 361
71. Wenham and Walton, *New Testament: Volume One*, 138.

As Mark D. Smith explains:

> Any claims about [a] public event by a first-generation source are subject to the immediate review of those who were there. Any author making claims contrary to the public memory of those who experienced the event in question would be committing reputational suicide. Falsifiable evidence, while quite rare in the ancient world, provides an extremely high level of probability. When Josephus, for example, writes of the Aqueduct riot, that evidence is falsifiable.[72]

Public falsifiability comes in degrees of strength, depending upon the degree to which a given event was public.

9) *Criterion of historical verisimilitude (e.g. Palestinian Coloring and Semitisms)*

James A. Beverley and Craig A. Evans explain that "One of the most important indications of an ancient document's veracity is something historians call verisimilitude. That is, do the contents of the document match with what we know of the place, people and period described in the document?"[73] Verisimilitude includes "linguistic and cultural features that fit what we know of first-century Palestine."[74]

For example, "There are particular words in the Gospels, such as '*Abba*', '*talitha cum*', '*eloi, eloi, lama sabachthani*', which are Aramaic, the common language of Palestine in Jesus' day (Mark 5:41; 14:36; 15:34). Their appearance in the Greek Gospels is most simply explained in terms of Jesus' own usage."[75] Other examples are *ephphatha* in Mark 7:34; *Golgotha* in Mark 15:22, Matthew 27:33, and John 19:17; *rabi* in Mark 9:5; *rabonni* in Mark 10:5; and *Siloam* in John 9:7. Moreover, "Sometimes translating the text from Greek back into Aramaic will reveal Semitic meter, word plays, or other evidence that points to a Semitic context."[76]

In addition to linguistic verisimilitude, the NT gospels exhibit "geographic and topological verisimilitude, cultural and archaeological verisimilitude, and religious, economic and social verisimilitude."[77]

10) *Criterion of memorability*

John Dickson explains: "The criterion of memorability suggests that teachings of Jesus which are inherently memorable are more likely to have been remembered accurately in oral tradition and therefore recorded correctly in the later Gospels."[78] Much of Jesus' teaching seems to have been designed for memorization using mnemonic devices

---

72. Smith, *Therefore Stand*, 30.
73. Beverley and Evans, *Getting Jesus Right*, 22.
74. Neufeld, *Recovering Jesus*, 44.
75. Wenham and Walton, *New Testament: Volume One*, 138.
76. Bock, *Studying the Historical Jesus*, 202.
77. Beverley and Evans, *Getting Jesus Right*, 23.
78. Dickson, *Investigating Jesus*, 143.

"such as rhyme, rhythm, alliteration and parallelism which aid the disciple to recall and pass on the teaching."[79]

This criterion would also apply to the various creeds and hymns quoted within the NT letters, and to the core elements of inherently memorable, dramatic and/or life-changing events reported within the pages of the NT. As J. Warner Wallace says: "When witnesses experience something that's unique, unrepeated, and personally important or powerful, they're much more likely to remember it."[80]

11) *Criterion of unintentional signs of history*

This criterion "argues that particularly vivid details of an eyewitness can demonstrate accurate knowledge of the environment and the event. This contributes to the credibility of a text."[81]

12) *Criterion of historical coherence*

Wenham and Walton note that this criterion is "ancillary to the other criteria. If any of the other criteria enable us to identify some sayings or stories of Jesus that are probably historical, then we may build on that, and include other sayings and stories, which may not 'pass the test' in their own right, but which fit in with the emerging picture."[82] As Bock observes: "This criterion is dependent upon the previous . . . It argues that whatever coheres or 'jives' with the application of the other criteria should be accepted as authentic."[83]

Watch: "Historical Criteria of Authenticity" Youtube playlist: www.youtube.com/playlist?list=PLQhh3qcwVEWg6gh7wSlE4EWoDtTHaq--5

Read: "Criteria for the Gospel's Authenticity" by Robert H. Stein in *Contending with Christianity's Critics* edited by Paul Copan and William Lane Craig

---

Using the criteria

While the criteria of authenticity cannot guarantee the historicity of data to which they apply, they do provide reasons to take such data with greater seriousness than would otherwise be the case. All things being equal, the more criteria of authenticity a saying or event passes, the more seriously we must take it. Of course, we must bear in mind that some criteria are more telling than others (for example, passing the criterion of multiple attestation is more impressive than passing the criterion of coherence). The criteria work best when combined in a cumulative case.

---

79. Dickson, *Investigating Jesus*, 144.
80. Wallace quoted in Strobel, *The Case for Miracles*, 197.
81. Bock, *Studying the Historical Jesus*, 201.
82. Wenham and Walton, *New Testament: Volume One*, 139.
83. Bock and Wallace, "The Words of Jesus in the Gospels," 93.

While the criteria of authenticity are useful tools of historiography, recent academic discussion has tended to highlight the fact that they "manifest several important limitations" including "the narrow types and amounts of data that they generate."[84] Craig cautions:

> it is somewhat misleading to call these "criteria," for they aim at stating sufficient, not necessary, conditions of historicity . . . what the criteria really amount to are statements about the effect of certain types of evidence upon the probability of various sayings or events . . . all else being equal . . . the probability of some event or saying is greater given, for example, its multiple attestation than it would have been without it . . . these "criteria" . . . focus on a particular saying or event and give evidence for thinking that specific element of Jesus' life to be historical, regardless of the general reliability of the document in which the particular saying or event is reported.[85]

Thus, as Darrell L. Bock observes: "One should remember that failure to meet the criteria does not establish a text's inauthenticity, because the criteria cover only a limited amount of assessment factors . . ."[86], such that "these criteria serve better as a supplemental argument for authenticity . . ."[87] Bock also notes that "some of these criteria can only test the conceptual level of Jesus' teaching—i.e., did Jesus teach this theme with this emphasis? These criteria cannot prove that he used a specific wording to make his point. Such tests are almost impossible to create for any ancient document."[88]

The repeated applicability of the criteria of authenticity to the NT in specific instances constitutes additional cumulative grounds for a more general trust in the NT. After all:

> Historians working with the writings of people like Julius Caesar and Josephus are much more open to their historical sources than skeptical Gospel critics—they do not insist on weighing individual sayings and stories . . . The Gospels are prima facie evidence for what the historical Jesus said and did . . . they describe the same real Palestinian world as does Josephus, and they deserve to be taken at least as seriously.[89]

---

84. Porter, "How Do We Know What We Think We Know?," 99.
85. Craig, *Reasonable Faith*, 298.
86. Bock, *Studying the Historical Jesus*, 202–3.
87. Bock, *Studying the Historical Jesus*, 202–3.
88. Bock, *Studying the Historical Jesus*, 90.
89. Wenham and Walton, *New Testament: Volume One*, 139.

Historical ground zero

> "The great majority of scholars believe that the passion narratives assumed a fairly fixed form early on rather than coming together at the tail end of the process..."
>
> —MARK ALLAN POWELL[90]

The shocking, life-changing and therefore inherently memorable story of Jesus' death, burial, empty tomb, and resurrection clearly isn't a legendary accretion that grew over the historical ground zero of Jesus' life as it receded into the mists of time. In contrast to the divinization of Buddha in the Mahayana tradition, for example, the divinity-proclaiming resurrection of Jesus is part of our historical ground zero: "Historical research can confirm that belief in Jesus' resurrection goes back to the earliest days of the Christian community."[91] Lawrence Krauss's assertion that the earliest reports of Jesus' resurrection come from "decades or hundreds of years after the fact"[92] is wrong.

Atheists Russell Blackford and Udo Schuklenk concede "that some kind of resurrection story was in place before the Gospels were written."[93] German scholar Rudolph Pesch thinks that Mark's passion source goes back to *at least* AD 37. That's within *four years* of the crucifixion. N.T. Wright argues that the lack of OT allusion, the lack of explicit connection to Christian eschatology, and the inclusion of culturally embarrassing *female* witnesses (side-lined by the early creedal material quoted by Paul in 1 Corinthians 15—about which, more later) all point to the gospel resurrection narratives being "essentially very early, pre-Pauline . . . The stories, though lightly edited and written down later, are basically very, very early."[94] Wright adds:

> The very strong historical probability is that, when Matthew, Luke, and John describe the risen Jesus, they are writing down very early oral tradition, representing three different ways in which the original astonished participants told the stories. These traditions have received only minimal development, and most of that probably at the final editorial stage, for the very good reason that stories as earth-shattering as this, stories as community-forming as this, once told, are not easily modified. Too much depends upon them.[95]

Quite apart from the gospels, Jesus' resurrection "is explicitly mentioned in every New Testament [letter] apart from the short letters of Philemon, James, 2 Peter, 2 John, 3 John, and Jude."[96] For example, c. AD 49 (a mere sixteen years after the cruci-

---

90. Powell, *The Jesus Debate*, 106.
91. Watson, "The Quest for the Real Jesus," 159.
92. Krauss and Craig, "Life, the Universe, and Nothing."
93. Blackford and Schuklenk, *50 Great Myths About Atheism*, 174–75.
94. Wright, *Surprised by Hope*, 68.
95. Wright, *The Resurrection of the Son of God*, 611.
96. Chaffey, *In Defence of Easter*, 39.

fixion) the letter to the Galatians opens with a reference to "Jesus Christ and God the Father who raised him from the dead." In other words, the resurrection of Jesus easily passes the historical criteria of attestation from multiple early sources and literary forms: "The claim that 'Jesus is risen' occurs in practically all the New Testament texts, in a wide variety of forms (narrative, creed, argument etc.)."[97]

The 1 Corinthians 15 creed

"the first resurrection stories began to be told very early."
—MICHAEL GRANT[98]

Written c. AD 54, Paul's first letter to the Corinthian church refers to early testimony that he had "received" as a formal oral tradition before he had personally "handed over" or "delivered" said tradition to the Corinthians c. AD 51:

> For I delivered to you as of first importance what I also received, that:
> *Christ died for our sins*
> *in accordance with the scriptures*
> *and that he was buried*
> *and that he was raised on the third day*
> *in accordance with the scriptures*
> *and that he appeared to Cephas*
> *then to the Twelve* [some manuscripts have "the eleven"]
> then he appeared to more than five hundred brethren at one time
> (most of whom are still alive, though some have fallen asleep)
> then he appeared to James
> then to all the apostles.
>
> Last of all, as to one untimely born, he appeared also to me.
> (1 Corinthians 15:3–8 [RSV] my italics, brackets, and pagination)

NT scholars universally recognize the italicized words as belonging to an early Christian creed. Some would also include the phrases "then he appeared to more than five hundred brethren at one time," "then he appeared to James" and "then to all the apostles" within this creed. Everyone agrees that the lines about some of the five hundred still being alive and about Paul's own experience are comments additional to the creed.

It's worth noting that there's excellent manuscript evidence for Paul's first letter to the Corinthians (most significant is P46, dating from around AD 200). Consequently,

---

97. Barclay, "The Resurrection In Contemporary New Testament Scholarship," 15.
98. Grant, *Jesus*, 177.

the modern critical Greek text of 1 Corinthians has an estimated word-for-word accuracy of 97.9 percent.[99] Moreover, "there are . . . quotations and clear allusions to 1 Corinthians 15:3–11 in the Apostolic fathers . . ."[100]

Theologian Robert L. Reymond explains why scholars are agreed that at least verses 3–5 of 1 Corinthians 15 contains an early creed:

> This assertion is based upon (1) Paul's references to his "delivering" to the Corinthians what he had first "received," terms suggesting that we are dealing with a piece of "tradition," (2) the stylized parallelism of the "delivered" material itself (see the four *hoti* [that] clauses and the repeated *kata tas graphas* [according to the scriptures] phrases in the first and third of them), (3) the Aramaic "Cephas" for Peter, suggesting an earlier Palestinian milieu, not a later Greco-Roman milieu, for this tradition, (4) the traditional description of the disciples as "the Twelve," and (5) the omission of the appearances to the women from the list.[101]

Stephen T. Davis concurs that 1 Corinthians 15:3 "Is a technical first-century reference to the handing on of tradition,"[102] and comments that "It doubtless refers to what he had been taught about Jesus and the resurrection by the Christians who received him in Damascus soon after his conversion (or perhaps to what Jerusalem believers told him when he visited there in AD 36 [Galatians 1:18])."[103] As a creed, this early material obviously passes the criterion of memorability. The use of Peter's Aramaic name means the creed also passes the criterion of Semitisms.

Atheist James Crossley concludes that in the 1 Corinthians creed we have "reliable reports"[104] from "eyewitnesses"[105] that "must be taken very seriously"[106] and which provide "good evidence that the first Christians did not invent the resurrection from scratch."[107] Habermas notes that "the original resurrection proclamation was exceptionally early and linked to the initial eyewitnesses themselves,"[108] and he emphasizes that "scholars are persuaded almost unanimously that the appearance reports [in the 1 Corinthians 15 creed] came from the eyewitness themselves, based on their own original experiences . . ."[109] For example:

---

99. See: "Bible Query—Early Manuscripts of 1 Corinthians."
100. Davis, *Disputed Issues*, 58.
101. Reymond, *Faith's Reasons for Believing*, 149.
102. Davis, *Rational Faith*, 75.
103. Davis, *Rational Faith*, 75.
104. Crossley, *The Date of Mark's Gospel*, 140.
105. Crossley, "Against the Historical Plausibility of the Empty Tomb Story," 171–86.
106. Crossley, "Against the Historical Plausibility of the Empty Tomb Story," 171–86.
107. Crossley, *The Date of Mark's Gospel*, 140.
108. Habermas, "Tracing Jesus' Resurrection to Its Earliest Eyewitness Accounts," 202.
109. Habermas, "Tracing Jesus' Resurrection to Its Earliest Eyewitness Accounts," 214.

- Robert L. Reymond argues that the 1 Corinthians 15 creed "reflects what those who were the earliest eye-witnesses to the events that had taken place in Jerusalem were teaching on *Palestinian* soil within days after the crucifixion . . . the material in 1 Corinthians 15:3b-5 is based on *early, Palestinian* eyewitness testimony . . ."[110]

- Richard Bauckham: "There can be no doubt that . . . Paul is citing the *eyewitness testimony* of those who were recipients of the resurrection appearances."[111]

- Jewish NT scholar Pinch's Lapide writes of 1 Corinthians 15:3–8 that: "this unified piece of tradition which soon was solidified into a formula of faith may be considered as *a statement of eyewitnesses* for whom the experience of the resurrection became the turning point of their lives."[112]

Habermas summarizes the generally-accepted scholarly reconstruction of how Paul received this creed:

> Critical scholars take very seriously Paul's statement in Galatians 1:18–19 that he went up to Jerusalem just three years after his conversion [according to the Jewish idiom, Paul's "after three years" probably means "two years later"], to meet with Peter and James the brother of Jesus . . . Paul tells us that he went back to Jerusalem fourteen years later, specifically to discuss the nature of the gospel [2:2] The other apostles, Peter, James and John, agreed with his message and added nothing to it [2:6 & 9]. As Paul said several years later, he and the other apostles were preaching the same message with regards to Jesus' resurrection [1 Corinthians 15:11] . . . Paul probably received the creedal material when he visited Jerusalem the first time [c. AD 35–36]. At the very least, from an exceptionally early date, these four major disciples discussed the nature of the gospel message and agreed on the details . . . But note carefully, this is when Paul received and confirmed the message. The other apostles who passed it on to him had it before he did . . . So we are essentially back to the exact time when it all happened, as critical scholars have noted.[113]

For example:

- John G.M. Barclay writes that the 1 Corinthians 15 creed "may date from as early as the 30s."[114]

- Paul W. Barnett says the creed received by Paul "had been formulated in Jerusalem beforehand, very soon after Jesus' death in 33."[115]

---

110. Reymond, *Faith's Reasons for Believing*, 149.

111. Bauckham quoted by Habermas, "Tracing Jesus' Resurrection to Its Earliest Eyewitness Accounts," 215.

112. Lapide, *The Resurrection of Jesus*, 99 (emphasis added).

113. Habermas quoted in Baggett, *Did the Resurrection Happen?*, 56.

114. Barclay, "The Resurrection in Contemporary New Testament Scholarship," 16.

115. Barnett, "Is The New Testament Historically Reliable?," 251."

- C.H. Dodd argued that 1 Corinthians 15:3–5 was "the earliest known recital of the facts" which takes us back "a long way behind the gospels" and provides "a solid body of evidence from a date very close to the events."[116]

- James D.G. Dunn: "This tradition, we can be entirely confident, was formulated as tradition within months of Jesus' death."[117]

- Michael Goulder writes that this testimony "goes back at least to what Paul was taught when he was converted, a couple of years after the crucifixion."[118]

- Timothy Paul Jones: "Most likely, Paul learned this tradition around A.D. 35 when he visited the city of Jerusalem."[119]

- Barnabas Lindars: "we have here an official formulary which can be traced back to the earliest period of the primitive Church . . ."[120]

- Gerd Lüdemann: "the elements in the tradition are to be dated . . . not later than three years after the death of Jesus . . ."[121]

- Hugh Montefiore: "We have thus taken the testimony to the Resurrection back to within three years of the time when it is said to have taken place. By that time, according to the evidence of Paul, the testimony had already taken a semi-creedal form."[122]

- Ulrich Wilkens affirms that this material "indubitably goes back to the oldest phase of all in the history of primitive Christianity."[123]

This creed bears witness to Jesus' death and burial. Inasmuch as it states that Jesus was "raised on the third day," it presupposes an empty burial site of some kind and bears witness to the disciple's belief in Jesus' resurrection. As Crossley notes: "1 Corinthians 15:4 ('that he was buried, and that he was raised') refers to bodily resurrection in the strongest sense: Jesus was literally and bodily *raised up* from the dead."[124] However, the focus of the creed is the provision of a list of witnesses who testify to having met the resurrected Jesus.

Jake O'Connell observes that "the pre-Pauline material of 1 Corinthians 15:3–8, which surely dates to within years of the resurrection, and is nearly universally regarded as summarising extremely early material, ensures that the appearances enumerated

---

116. Dodd, *The Founder of Christianity*, 173–74.
117. Dunn, *Jesus Remembered*, 825.
118. Goulder quoted in Habermas, *The Risen Jesus*, 79.
119. Jones, *Misquoting Truth*, 92.
120. Lindars, "The Resurrection and the Empty Tomb," 124.
121. Lüdemann quoted in Habermas, "Tracing Jesus' Resurrection to Its Earliest Eyewitness Accounts," 212.
122. Montefiore, *The Womb And The Tomb*, 139.
123. Wilkins quoted in Habermas, *The Risen Jesus*, 79.
124. Bird and Crossley, *How Did Christianity Begin?*, 52.

there cannot be legendary."[125] Craig concurs that: "given its early date, as well as Paul's personal acquaintance with the people involved, the list of eyewitnesses to Jesus' resurrection appearances, quoted by Paul in 1 Cor. 15.5–8, guarantees that such appearances [that is, as genuinely reported subjective experiences] occurred."[126]

James G.D. Dunn points out that: "the apostles" of verse 8 "were a wider group than 'the twelve'. Of the former, Andronicus and Junia may well have been appointed by the risen Christ within forty days, since Paul says that they 'were in Christ' before him (Romans 16:7)."[127]

That many of the eyewitnesses listed in 1 Corinthians 15 went on to die for their belief in the resurrection confirms their certainty that it happened. If they were unsure, they would have admitted their doubts and been spared execution:

> Consider James the brother of Jesus. Josephus . . . tells us that he died a martyr's death for his faith in his brother. Yet the Gospels tell us that during Jesus' life, he was an unbeliever and opposed to Jesus. Why did he change? What could cause a Jew to believe that his own brother was the very Son of God and to be willing to die for such a belief? . . . the appearance of Jesus to James (1 Cor. 15:7) can explain his transformation. As with James, so it is with the other disciples. One who denies the resurrection owes us an explanation of this transformation which does justice to the historical facts.[128]

At this point it is worth highlighting N.T. Wright's argument that, given the low status of women in the first century, had the tradition started in the form that is only explicit about male witnesses found in 1 Corinthians 15, "it would never have developed—and in such different ways—into the female-first stories we find in the gospels."[129] Hence: "The gospels must embody the earliest storytelling, and 1 Corinthians 15 a later revision."[130] Thus it would seem that the passion account in Mark, at the very least, puts us in touch with testimony that predates the already extremely early 1 Corinthians 15 creed!

Although it seems that the gospel resurrection accounts all reflect oral history that predates the formulation of the 1 Corinthian creed, those oral histories reach us through later publications that probably involved an editorial process, however minimal. What Paul quotes in 1 Corinthians 15 is an example of early oral history itself.

Watch: "Resurrection Evidence: That Amazing Creed in 1 Corinthians 15": http://youtu.be/DL1bDzq5zg4

125. O'Connell, "Jesus' Resurrection and Collective Hallucinations," 75.
126. Craig and Sinnott-Armstrong, *God?*, 23.
127. Dunn, *Why Believe in Jesus' Resurrection?*, 22.
128. Moreland, *Scaling the Secular City*, 179.
129. Wright, "Can a Scientist Believe in the Resurrection?," 54.
130. Wright, "Can a Scientist Believe in the Resurrection?," 54.

"Paul's Corinthian Quotation of an Early Creed" by Gary R. Habermas: http://youtu.be/7QDCnYwJv6M

Read: "The Resurrection of Jesus and the Witness of Paul" by Peter May: www.bethinking.org/did-jesus-rise-from-the-dead/the-resurrection-of-jesus-and-the-witness-of-paul

---

Primal reports

Fig. 19 shows the common content of the primal reports pertaining to Jesus' death, burial, and resurrection (a concept which implies the empty tomb) that can be established from the *early* testimonies contained within the *multiple forms* of 1) the (*memorable, Aramaic-containing, eyewitness*) creed quoted by Paul in 1 Corinthians 15:3–5; 2) the pre-Marcan passion *narrative* of Mark 15:37–16:7; 3) Peter's Pentecost *sermon* recorded in Acts 2:23–32 (an *eyewitness* source, albeit second hand) and 4) Paul's *sermon* (another—second hand—*eyewitness* source) recorded in Acts 13:28–31.

Concerning speeches in Acts, Dunn explains that "Luke has sought out much earlier material and has incorporated it into the brief formalized expositions which he attributes to Peter, Stephen, Paul, etc."[131] Montefiore comments:

> These speeches have been examined in considerable detail, and there are indications that the author did use sources for them . . . there is the presence of Semitisms in the speeches . . . It is held by many that these speeches represent the primitive *kerygma* (preaching of the Gospel in the early Church).[132]

John Drane affirms: "there can be no doubt that in the first few chapters of Acts its author has preserved material from very early sources."[133] Bart Erhman concurs: "the speeches in Acts are particularly notable because they are, in many instances, based . . . on oral traditions . . . these speeches incorporate materials from the traditions about Jesus that existed long before Luke put pen to papyrus."[134] Another example is Luke's outline of eyewitness Peter's speech to some Gentile God-fearers in Caesarea (Acts 10:34–43), in which he recounts: "They killed [Jesus] by hanging him on a cross, but God raised him from the dead on the third day and caused him to be seen . . . by us who ate and drank with him after he rose from the dead." (Acts 10: 39–41)

---

131. Dunn, *Why Believe in Jesus' Resurrection?*, 22.
132. Montefiore, *The Womb And The Tomb*, 134.
133. Drane quoted in Strobel, *The Case for Christ*, 256.
134. Erhman, *Did Jesus Exist?*, 109, 111.

Fig. 19. Four Early Sources on Easter

Acts 2:23-32 Peter's Pentecost sermon, AD 33.	1 Corinthians 15:3-5 Early Creed, c. AD 33-34.	Mark 15:37—16:7 Pre-Marcan passion narrative, c. AD 33-37.	Acts 13:28-31 Paul's Pisidian Antioch sermon, c. AD 45.
you . . . put him to death by nailing him to the cross.	Christ died . . .	Jesus breathed his last.	they asked Pilate to have him executed.
David died and was buried, and his tomb is here to this day [Peter thereby implies Jesus' empty tomb].	he was buried . . .	Joseph bought some linen cloth, took down the body, wrapped it in the linen, and placed it in a tomb . . .	they took him down from the tree and laid him in a tomb.
God has raised this Jesus to life. . . [which likewise implies an empty tomb]	he was raised . . . [which implies an empty grave or tomb]	He has risen! [The empty tomb is thereby implied]	But God raised him from the dead . . . [which implies the empty tomb]
we are all witnesses of the fact.	he appeared . . .	He is going ahead of you into Galilee. There you will see him . . .	for many days he was seen by those who had travelled with him from Galilee to Jerusalem.

The canonical gospels alone provide four sources relating to Jesus' death, burial, empty tomb, and resurrection appearances. Adding information from speeches by Peter in Acts, from Paul in Acts and in Paul's own letters, and from the creed quoted by Paul in 1 Corinthians 15, gives us seven sources of *early* testimony about Easter. This testimony is presented in *multiple forms* and includes *multiple eyewitness sources*.

Fig. 20. Seven First Century Sources on Easter

	Peter in Acts	1 Corinthians	Mark's Passion Source	Paul in Acts & Letters	Luke	Matt.	John
Death	2:23 & 10:39	15:3	15:37	13:28-29	23:46	27:24	19:30
Burial		15:4	15:46	13:29; Rm 6:4; Col 2:13	23:53	27:64	19:42
Empty Tomb	Implied by 2:29-32		16:6		24:2, 10, 12, 23	28:6 & 12-13	20:2, 6
Appearances	2:32 &10:41	15:5-8	16:7	13:31, 22:6-9 & 26: 13-14; 1 Cor 9:1 & 15:8; Gl 1:13-17	24:12, 15 & 36	28:9-10 & 16-17	21:14

Let's examine the relevant historical data in greater detail, bearing in mind the criteria of authenticity reviewed above:

Fact 1: Jesus' death by crucifixion

Michael Onfray claims that Jesus' crucifixion is an "improbability" because history "bears witness: at that time Jews were not crucified but stoned to death."[135]

History bears witness to Jewish use of crucifixion as well as stoning. Geza Vermes reports that "the Hasmonaean priest-king Alexander Jannaeus (103–76 BCE) crucified 800 of his political opponents" and that "in the late Second Temple period, during the Maccabaean-Hasmonaean rule (c. 160–60 BCE), death penalty by crucifixion was part of Jewish penal legislation."[136] However, after the Roman Republic conquered the Jews, "the right to impose the death penalty had been taken away from the Jewish courts by the Roman authorities"[137]—hence the rigmarole of getting Jesus tried before Pilate (see: John 18:31).[138] The traditional Roman method of execution was crucifixion. Contrary to Onfray's assertion, the history of "that time" proves that Jews certainly *were* crucified. Vermes reports:

> We learn from Josephus that the violent repression of the rebellion which followed the death of Herod the Great (4 BCE) involved mass crucifixions . . . ordered by the general of the Roman forces . . . During the final stages of the siege of Jerusalem in 69–70 CE, when crowds of rebels sought to escape from the city, no fewer than 500 captured Jews were crucified every day so that, to quote Josephus, "there was not enough room for the crosses and not enough crosses for the bodies." Whether the remains of a crucified man whose bones were discovered in Jerusalem in 1968 in an ossuary inscribed with the name of Yohanan son of Ezekiel were one of these we cannot say, but the nail piercing his anklebone, to which bits of olive wood are still attached, and his broken shinbones clearly indicate how Yohanan died.[139]

According to Hugh Montefiore: "There is . . . quite sufficient evidence from the gospels for us to conclude that Jesus did indeed die upon the cross. His death is corroborated by St Paul in his Epistles . . . and also by Peter's speeches in Acts shortly after Pentecost."[140] Robert L. Webb observes that "the ancient sources with reference to the death of Jesus are numerous and varied—not only that he was executed, but that the

---

135. Onfray, *Atheist Manifesto*, 128.
136. Vermes, "Was Crucifixion a Jewish Penalty?"
137. Jacobs, "The Death Penalty in Jewish Tradition."
138. See: Stewart, "Judicial Procedure in New Testament Times."
139. Vermes, "Was Crucifixion a Jewish Penalty?" See: Biblical Archaeological Society Staff, "A Tomb in Jerusalem."
140. Montefiore, *The Womb And The Tomb*, 104.

means of execution was crucifixion."[141] For example, c. AD 108 Ignatius encouraged the Trallians about "Jesus Christ, who died for us,"[142] going on to report that Jesus "was truly persecuted under Pontius Pilate, truly crucified and died."[143] The second-century Greek satirist Lucian of Samosata wrote of Christians as those who "worship the crucified sage."[144] Ancient historians such as Josephus and Tacitus also mention Jesus' crucifixion. In a letter written at some time between AD 74 and 165, the Syrian Stoic philosopher Mara bar-Serapion refers to the death of Jesus when he asks: "What advantage did the Jews gain from executing their wise King?"[145] Habermas points out that:

> Of all the events in Jesus' life, more ancient sources specifically mention his death than any other single occurrence ... twenty-two [ancient sources] relate this fact, often with details. Eleven of these sources are non-Christian, which exhibits an incredible amount of interest in this event.[146]

Jesus' publically falsifiable death by crucifixion is thus confirmed by multiple, early sources, including enemy sources:

> within approximately the first 100 years after Jesus' death there are six witnesses that are certainly independent and another five that are probably independent. And of these witnesses, three of them are non-Christian, and of these three, two of them are explicitly anti-Christian. There are witnesses to the specific fact of Jesus' execution by crucifixion. If one were to broaden the scope to include references to Jesus' death more generally, the number of independent witnesses, both Christian and non-Christian would increase. Thus, of all the events and/or sayings of Jesus, there is probably no other that has such an extensive collection of witnesses that meets the criterion of multiple attestation.[147]

Again, in the second-century Jewish Babylonian Talmud, in a tradition the core of which David Instone Brewer argues goes back to "the actual court records from the time of Jesus,"[148] it is stated: "On the eve of Passover they hung Yeshu [i.e. Jesus] for sorcery and enticing Israel [to idolatry]." One version of the text actually says that they hung "Yeshu the Notzarine" (i.e. Jesus the Nazarene). The term "hung/hanged" (*kremannumi*) can be applied to crucifixion, as shown by the NT's own usage in Luke 23:39, Acts 5:30 and 10:39, and Galatians 3:13.

141. Webb, "The Roman Examination and Crucifixion of Jesus," 671.
142. Webb, "The Roman Examination and Crucifixion of Jesus," 44.
143. Webb, "The Roman Examination and Crucifixion of Jesus," 44.
144. Lucian quoted in Habermas, *The Historical Jesus*, 206.
145. See: Mara bar Serapion's "Testimony on Jesus."
146. Habermas, *The Verdict of History*, 178.
147. Webb, "The Roman Examination and Crucifixion of Jesus," 689–90.
148. Brewer, "Jesus of Nazareth's Trial in Sanhedrin 43a," 20.

Read: "Jesus of Nazareth's Trial in Sanhedrin 43a" by David Instone Brewer: www.tyndale.cam.ac.uk/Tyndale/staff/Instone-Brewer/prepub/Sanhedrin%2043a%20censored.pdf

---

Writing to the Corinthian church c. AD 54, Paul describes Jesus' institution of the Last Supper in wording that closely parallels the Synoptic Gospel reports of the same event (see: 1 Corinthians 11:23–26, Luke 22:14–20, Matthew 26:26–29, and Mark 14:22–25). Paul is once again quoting a piece of oral tradition that he had "received" and had in turn already "passed on" to the Corinthians c. AD 51:

> For I received from the Lord what I also passed on to you: The Lord Jesus, on the night he was betrayed, took bread, and when he had given thanks, he broke it and said, "This is my body, which is for you; do this in remembrance of me." In the same way, after supper he took the cup, saying, "This cup is the new covenant in my blood; do this, whenever you drink it, in remembrance of me." For whenever you eat this bread and drink this cup, you proclaim the Lord's death until he comes. (1 Corinthians 11:23–26)

This discussion of the Last Supper contains very early testimony to the death of Jesus.

Note that the Last Supper, celebrated by Christians as the communion, instituted *a repeated memorial of Jesus' death*. It's worth pondering the paradox of why, on the one hand, the first Christians would memorialize Jesus' death by crucifixion if he *hadn't* died, and why, on the other hand, they would *memorialize* Jesus at all given that he died by crucifixion. This paradox is resolved by their belief in Jesus' resurrection.

Then again, Paul's letter to the Galatians talks about believers' sinful natures being metaphorically "crucified with Christ" (Galatians 2:20; see also: Galatians 5:24) c. AD 49. These references to Jesus' death are theological reflections in pastoral letters that complement the biographical reportage of the gospels and so pass the criterion of *multiple forms*.

Jesus says the Aramaic phrase recorded in Mark 15:34—"*eloi, eloi, lama sabachthani*"—the opening line of Psalm 22:1, *from the cross*. Then again, multiple sources of testimony, including eyewitness testimony, specify the Aramaic name of the place where Jesus was crucified as *Golgotha* (Matthew 27:33, Mark 15:22, and John 19:17). Hence Jesus' crucifixion gains a two-fold warrant from the *criterion of Semitisms*.

That Jesus was crucified is probably the most widely accepted historical fact about him:

- Reza Aslan: "Jesus was most definitely crucified."[149]
- S.G.F. Brandon: "[Jesus] was crucified by the Romans . . ."[150]

---

[149] "Reza Aslan vs Lauren Green."
[150] Brandon, *Jesus and the Zealots*, 13.

- James H. Charlesworth: "Roman soldiers, following the command of the prefect, Pontius Pilate, crucified Jesus."[151]
- John Crossan: "There is not the slightest doubt about the *fact* of Jesus' crucifixion under Pontius Pilate."[152]
- Stephen T. Davis: "It cannot sensibly be denied that there existed a man Jesus who was crucified."[153]
- C.H. Dodd: "Jesus was led to the place of execution [and] crucified, after the brutal Roman practice."[154]
- Bart Erhman: "Jesus . . . was crucified (a Roman form of execution) in Jerusalem during the reign of the Roman emperor Tiberius, when Pontius Pilate was governor of Judea."[155] According to Erhman: "it is highly improbable that the earliest Palestinian Jewish followers of Jesus would have made up the claim that the messiah was crucified . . . And it is a claim found multiply attested throughout our tradition (Mark, M, L, John, Paul, Josephus, Tacitus) . . . this is a highly probable tradition.[156]
- Craig A. Evans states the proposition that Jesus "was condemned to death and crucified" is "disputed by almost no one."[157]
- Jean-Pierre Isbouts: "Jesus . . . was crucified."[158]
- Matthew Kneale: "Jesus endured the slow horror of crucifixion . . ."[159]
- Amy-Jill Levine: "Jesus . . . was crucified by Roman Soldiers during the governorship of Pontius Pilate."[160]
- I. Howard Marshall says Jesus "was arrested, tried . . . and crucified."[161]
- Simon Seabag Montefiore: "Jesus, like most crucifixion victims, was scourged with a leather whip tipped with either bone or metal, a torment so savage that it often killed the victim."[162]

---

151. Charlesworth, *The Historical Jesus*, 118.
152. Crossan, *The Historical Jesus*, 375.
153. Davis, *Christian Philosophical Theology*, 92.
154. Dodd, *The Founder of Christianity*, 167.
155. Ehrman, *Did Jesus Exist?* 12.
156. Ehrman, *Did Jesus Exist?* 188.
157. Evans, "The Christ of Faith is the Jesus of History," 464.
158. Isbouts, *Jesus and the Origins of Christianity*, 23.
159. Kneale, *An Atheist's History of Belief*, 78–79.
160. Levine quoted in Kessler, *Jesus*, 22.
161. Marshall, *I Believe in the Historical Jesus*, 216.
162. Montefiore, *Jerusalem*, 127.

- John Romer: "Jesus [was] crucified by the Roman authorities."[163]
- Michael Ruse: "Jesus . . . got himself crucified by the Romans . . ."[164]
- Christopher Tuckett: "The fact that Jesus existed, that he was crucified under Pontius Pilate . . . seems to be part of the bedrock of historical tradition. If nothing else, the non-Christian evidence can provide us with certainty on that score."[165]
- N.T. Wright: "The crucifixion of Jesus of Nazareth is one of the best attested facts in ancient history."[166]

Although evidence of Jesus' crucifixion isn't synonymous with evidence of his death by crucifixion, the former is nevertheless a strong indication of the latter!

Jesus' *death* by crucifixion passes the *criterion of historical verisimilitude*, for as Nabeel Qureshi points out: "never in recorded history has anyone survived a full Roman crucifixion."[167] Roman law placed a death penalty "on any soldier who let a capital prisoner escape in any way, including bungling a crucifixion."[168] Roman executioners were thus highly motivated and knew what they were doing.

Not that their job was particularly complicated. Crucifixion was, in general terms, a cruel death by asphyxiation:

> Since the muscles used for inhaling are stronger than the muscles used for exhaling, carbon dioxide would build up and the victim would die an uncomfortable death. Experiments on live volunteers, suspended with the inability to touch the ground, revealed that one could not remain conscious longer than twelve minutes in this position, as long as their arms were at a 45-degree angle or less. Breaking the legs of a crucified victim would prevent them from pushing up against the nail in their feet, an excruciating move, in order to make it easier to breath, albeit temporarily. It is the opinion of my two ER physician friends that, due to the trauma already experienced by a crucified victim, once He had died on a cross from a lack of oxygen, and had remained dead in that position for five minutes, there would be no chance of resuscitating Him.[169]

The fact that the soldiers didn't bother to break Jesus' legs (the practice of breaking legs in order to expedite death by crucifixion is related by ancient sources including Cicero's *Orations*) shows that they were sure he was already dead. Archaeologist Shimon Gibson notes that the earlier scourging suffered by Jesus "would undoubtedly

---

163. Romer, *Testament*, 171.
164. Ruse, *Atheism*, 135.
165. Tuckett, "Sources and Methods," 124.
166. Wright quoted in Brierley, *Unbelievable?*, 114.
167. Qureshi, *No God But One*, 167.
168. Kreeft and Tacelli, *Handbook of Christian Apologetics*, 183.
169. Licona, "Can We Be Certain that Jesus Died on a Cross?"

have led to a massive loss of blood... Hence, it is not surprising that Jesus did not last very long on the cross, perhaps 3 to 6 hours at the most."[170]

Nevertheless, to eliminate all doubt one of the soldiers stabbed Jesus' corpse with a spear, a *coup de grace* mentioned by the first-century Roman author Quintilian. John provides an *eyewitness* (phenomenological) report of "blood and water" coming out of the spear-wound (John 19:34). Truman Davis, MD argues that this is "conclusive post-mortem evidence" that Jesus actually died "of heart failure..."[171] As Alexander Metherall, MD explains:

> hypovolemic shock would have caused a sustained rapid heart rate that would have contributed to heart failure, resulting in the collection of fluid in the membrane around the heart, called a pericardial effusion, as well as around the lungs, which is called a pleural effusion [sometimes referred to as "water on the lungs"]... The spear apparently went through the right lung and into the heart, so when the spear was pulled out, some fluid—the pericardial effusion and the pleural effusion—came out. This would have had the appearance of a clear fluid, like water, followed by a large volume of blood, as the eyewitness John described...[172]

The ancient writer of this eyewitness testimony in John's Gospel wouldn't have known these medical details, and so had no reason for his report of it besides fidelity to the facts (hence his *eyewitness* report passes the *Criterion of Unintentional Signs of History*). As an article in the *Journal of the American Medical Association* concluded:

> Clearly, the weight of historical and medical evidence indicates that Jesus was dead before the wound to his side was inflicted and supports the traditional view that the spear, thrust between his right rib, probably perforated not only the right lung but also the pericardium and heart and thereby ensured his death. Accordingly, interpretations based on the assumption that Jesus did not die on the cross appear to be at odds with modern medical knowledge.

Since it bears the hallmark of an unintentional sign of historicity, the observation of blood and water emerging from Jesus' spear-wound counts as a demonstrably independent witness to the fact of Jesus' death by crucifixion, meaning that Jesus' death by crucifixion passes the criteria of independent testimony in its most stringent form.

It's worth noting at this juncture that "Tannaitic sources repeatedly emphasize that it is forbidden to treat a person as dead until it is clearly ascertained that he has expired (Semahoth I)."[173] Simon Seabag Montefiore observes: "Jewish dead were not buried in the earth during the first century but laid in a shroud in a rock tomb, which [was] always checked, partly to ensure that the deceased were indeed dead and not

---

170. Gibson, *The Final Days of Jesus*, 123.
171. Davis, "The Crucifixion of Jesus."
172. Metherell quoted in Strobel, *The Case For Christ*, 215–16.
173. Safrai, *The Jewish People in the First Century*, 773.

merely comatose..."[174] Thus, as A. Rendle Short comments: "The Roman soldiers, the priests and His friends who buried Him would all look carefully to make certain that He was dead."[175] Homicide detective J. Warner Wallace comments:

> Three conditions become apparent in the bodies of dead people: temperature loss, rigidity, and lividity . . . dead bodies look, feel, and respond differently from living, breathing humans . . . Is it reasonable to believe that those who removed Jesus from the cross, took possession of His body, carried him to the grave, and spent time treating and wrapping His body for burial would not have noticed any of these conditions common to dead bodies?[176]

Apparently, the people who a) crucified Jesus or saw him crucified,[177] b) took Jesus down from the cross, c) prepared him for burial, and d) entombed him all thought he was dead.

Likewise, the Jewish authorities at whose behest Jesus had been executed conceded that Jesus had died when they accused the disciples of stealing his corpse away from his tomb, a conspiracy theory discussed in Matthew 28:12-14 and reflected in Jewish tradition (as gathered into the fifth-century *Toledoth Jesu*).

The synoptic gospel accounts of Jesus' death mention people that the audience would have been able to check facts with. For example, they all mention Simon of Cyrene, who is compelled to carry Jesus' crossbeam after Jesus (suffering from blood loss, dehydration, and shock consequent to his scourging) stumbles under the load (see: Mark 15:21; Matthew 27:32; Luke 23:26). Simon's sons Alexander and Rufus were known within the early church and are mentioned by the pre-Marcan passion account, as if to say "if you don't believe this, go and check with them" (see: Mark 15:21 and Romans 16:13).

The existence of Simon and Alexander has been corroborated by archaeology. In 1941, Israeli archaeologist Eleazar Sukenik discovered a tomb in the Kidron valley in eastern Jerusalem. Pottery dated it to the first century. The tomb contained eleven ossuaries bearing twelve names in fifteen inscriptions. Some of the names were particularly common in Cyrenaica. An inscription on one of these ossuaries says: "Alexandros (son of) Simon." The lid of this ossuary bears an inscription with the name Alexandros in Greek, followed by the Hebrew QRNYT. The meaning of this isn't clear, but one possibility is that the person making the inscription meant to write QRNYH—the Hebrew for "Cyrenian." Writing in *Biblical Archaeological Review*, Tom Powers comments:

---

174. Montefiore, *Jerusalem*, 130.
175. Short, *Why Believe?*, 48-9.
176. Wallace, *Cold-Case Christianity*, 42.
177. Those who saw him crucified include: John, Jesus' mother, Mary Magdalene, Mary the mother of James and Joses, Mary the wife of Clopas, and Salome the mother of the sons of Zebedee (see: Matthew 27:56, Mark 15:40-41, Luke 23:49; John 20:1-18.).

When we consider how uncommon the name Alexander was, and note that the ossuary inscription lists him in the same relationship to Simon as the New Testament does and recall that the burial cave contains the remains of people from Cyrenaica, the chance that the Simon on the ossuary refers to the Simon of Cyrene mentioned in the Gospels seems very likely.[178]

Finally, Jesus' death by crucifixion would have been so *embarrassing* to Jesus' followers (who expected him to destroy the Romans and who mostly ran away when he didn't) that they wouldn't have made it up. As Craig A. Evans asks:

> Had Jesus not been executed, had Jesus not been crucified, why make up such a preposterous story? No, the death of Jesus is no fiction. It is a grim historical reality. It was known to non-Christians, and it was demoralizing even for Jesus' followers—at least initially—and an ongoing embarrassment as the church proclaimed Jesus as Savior and Son of God throughout the Roman Empire. There can be no doubt that Jesus was executed.[179]

Likewise, archaeologist John Romer comments:

> the act of Jesus' crucifixion convinces because of its extremely degrading nature. In the Roman Empire crucifixion was a most shameful death, even in the minds of the early Christian congregations, as Paul's letters make clear . . . Crucifixion was considered to be one of the most severe Roman punishments, worse than decapitation, burning, or exposure to wild beasts . . .[180]

As Graham Veale writes: "Crucifixion was such a way to die that it is absurd to suppose that any group would *pretend* that their leader had been crucified!"[181] Michael Grant agrees that "no one would have invented such a degraded end, a fatal objection to Jesus' Messiahship in Jewish eyes."[182]

Indeed, it is the scandalous nature of crucifixion (recall the "Alaxamenos worships his god" graffiti!) that leads Muslims to deny Jesus suffered such a fate. As Lee Strobel notes: "The idea that Jesus never really died on the cross can be found in the Koran, which was written in the seventh century."[183] However, the Quran can't compete on historical grounds with the unanimous voice of the early sources that record Jesus' death by crucifixion. According to former Muslim Nabeel Qureshi:

> as a historical source about Jesus's life there is very little reason to trust the Quran because it was composed six hundred years after Jesus and more than six hundred miles away from where he lived. Although there are accounts in

---

178. Powers, "Treasures in the Storeroom: Family Tomb of Simon of Cyrene."
179. Evans, *Jesus and the Remains of His Day*, 148.
180. Romer, *Testament*, 178–79.
181. Veale, *New Atheism*, 80.
182. Grant, *Jesus*, 166.
183. Strobel, *The Case for Christ*, 192.

the Quran that come from an earlier period, those are from late, fictitious gospels that are historically unreliable.[184]

Charles Foster reports that such historically late denials of Jesus' crucifixion "have been laughed out of court by serious scholars . . . The overwhelming conclusion of the mainstream literature, even that written by virulent opponents of Christianity, is that Jesus did indeed die on the cross."[185] Habermas confirms that "Almost no scholar today questions Jesus' death by crucifixion"[186] since it is "is one of the best attested facts in ancient history."[187] Likewise, Francis J. Beckwith reports that "nearly all scholars agree that Jesus died by crucifixion . . ."[188] For example:

- Reza Aslan: "Jesus was executed by the Roman state for the crime of sedition."[189]
- Raymond Brown: "Except for the romantic few who think that Jesus did not die on the cross but woke up in the tomb and ran off to India with Mary Magdalene, most scholars accept the uniform testimony of the Gospels that Jesus died . . ."[190]
- James H. Charlesworth: "Jesus died by Roman execution . . ."[191]
- John Dominic Crossan: "Jesus' death by crucifixion under Pontius Pilate is as sure as anything historical can ever be."[192]
- Bart Erhman: "Was Jesus killed? Yes. By the Romans? Yes. By crucifixion? Yes."[193]
- Adam S. Francisco: "The evidence from history is quite clear about certain facts pertaining to Jesus. He was crucified and died on a Roman cross."[194]
- Paula Fredriksen: "The single most solid fact about Jesus' life is his death; he was executed by the Roman prefect Pilate, on or around Passover, in the manner Rome reserved particularly for political insurrectionists, namely, crucifixion."[195]
- Michael Grant: "Jesus . . . was arrested by the high-priest and Sanhedrin and handed over to the Roman governor, Pontius Pilate, who found him guilty of seditious designs and had him executed by crucifixion."[196]

---

184. Qureshi, *No God But One*, 183.
185. Foster, *The Jesus Inquest*, 72, 220.
186. Habermas quoted in Baggett, *Did the Resurrection Happen?*, 26.
187. Habermas, *The Verdict of History*, 178.
188. Beckwith, *David Hume's Argument Against Miracles*, 65.
189. Aslan, *Zealot*, 156.
190. Brown, *The Death of the Messiah*, 1373.
191. Charlesworth, *The Historical Jesus*, 111.
192. Crossan, *Jesus*, 145.
193. Erhman, "Bart D. Ehrman Interview."
194. Francisco, "Can a Historian explain the Empty Tomb with the Resurrection of Jesus?," 56.
195. Fredriksen, *Jesus of Nazareth*, 8.
196. Grant, *Jesus*, 10.

- Luke Timothy Johnson: "Even the most critical historian can confidently assert that a Jew named Jesus . . . was executed by crucifixion under the prefect Pontius Pilate and continued to have followers after his death."[197]

- Craig Keener: "To claim that Jesus died by crucifixion is also not controversial . . ."[198]

- Pinchas Lapide: "the death of Jesus of Nazareth on the cross . . . may be considered historically certain."[199]

- Gerd Lüdemann: "Jesus' death as a consequence of crucifixion is indisputable."[200]

- Alexander Metherell: "There was absolutely no doubt that Jesus was dead."[201]

- John Warwick Montgomery: "Jesus surely died on the cross . . ."[202]

- Hugh Montefiore: "Jesus did indeed die upon the cross."[203]

- Simon Seabag Montefiore: "It may have actually been the spear that had killed him."[204]

- Nabeel Qureshi: "Jesus died by crucifixion."[205]

- Mark D. Smith: "The trial of Jesus may have been private, but his execution was ruthlessly public. Naked, humiliated, and riven with agony, Jesus was lifted up to public scrutiny and public ridicule. Some of the sources mention the presence of some of his friends and family members, as well as mockers, including the chief priests' . . . Jesus seems to have died quickly and in great agony."[206]

- Geza Vermes: "The passion of Jesus is part of history."[207]

- Robert L. Webb: "on the basis of the diverse multiple attestation to this event and the actual evidence that this event was a source of embarrassment for the early Christian movement, it is reasonable to conclude that Jesus' execution by crucifixion is one of the more probable events that can be established in ancient history . . ."[208]

---

197. Johnson, *The Real Jesus*, 123.
198. Keener, *The Historical Jesus of the Gospels*, 323.
199. Lapide, *The Resurrection of Jesus*, 32.
200. Lüdemann *The Resurrection of Christ*, 50.
201. Metherell, op cit, 216.
202. Montgomery, *History, Law and Christianity*, 42.
203. Montefiore, *The Womb And The Tomb*, 104.
204. Montefiore, *Jerusalem*, 129.
205. Qureshi, *No God But One*, 162.
206. Smith, *Therefore Stand*, 195–96.
207. Vermes, *The Passion*, 9.
208. Webb, "The Roman Examination and Crucifixion of Jesus," 693.

- A.N. Wilson: "The Cross, and the Crucifixion, are at the very centre of this religious vision, not as an airy concept or a metaphor, but as a bloody death actually recollected."[209]

In sum:

> the historical evidence is very strong that Jesus died by crucifixion. It is attested to by a number of ancient sources, some of which are non-Christian ... the chances of surviving crucifixion were very bleak; the unanimous professional medical opinion is that Jesus certainly died due to the rigors of crucifixion, and even if Jesus somehow managed to survive crucifixion, it would not have resulted in the disciples' belief that he had been resurrected.[210]

Even Jerry Coyne affirms that: "Jesus was crucified, ending everyone's hope of glory."[211]

The conclusion that Jesus died due to crucifixion is warranted by at least twelve criteria of authenticity:

- Eyewitness sources
- Early sources
- Independent sources
- Multiple sources
- Multiple forms
- Enemy sources
- Embarrassing sources
- Public falsifiability
- Unintentional signs of history
- Historical verisimilitude
- Memorability
- Historical coherence

Watch: "Jesus died on the cross" Youtube playlist: www.youtube.com/playlist?list=PLQhh3qcwVEWjXGlCNqo8jcoNAXYnyDNoa

Read: "A Tomb in Jerusalem Reveals the History of Crucifixion and Roman Crucifixion Methods": www.biblicalarchaeology.org/daily/biblical-topics/crucifixion/a-tomb-in-jerusalem-reveals-the-history-of-crucifixion-and-roman-crucifixion-methods/
  "The Medical Evidence: Was Jesus' Death a Sham?" by Lee Strobel and Alexander Metherell: www.willowcreek.com/caseforeaster/Chapter%20One.pdf

---

209. Wilson, *Paul*, 117.
210. Licona, "Can We Be Certain that Jesus Died on a Cross?," 167.
211. Coyne, *Faith vs. Fact*, 123.

"The Science of the Crucifixion" by Cahleen Shrier and Tally Flint: www.apu.edu/articles/15657/

"An Examination of the Medical Evidence for the Physical Death of Christ" by Bert Thompson and Brad Harrub: http://apologeticspress.org/apcontent.aspx?category=13&article=145

Fact 2: Jesus' burial in a tomb (by Joseph of Arimathea)

Michael Onfray asserts that, as a victim of crucifixion, Jesus "would have been left hanging there, at the mercy of wild beasts. There was no question of bodies being laid to rest in tombs."[212] There are indeed historical records of crucifixion victims being left "hanging on a cross to feed the crows."[213] However, Onfray's blanket claim is demonstrably wrong.

For one thing, it is contradicted by archaeology. The *entombed* remains of Yohanan (mentioned above) came complete with the nail that had been driven through the heel bone of his left foot during crucifixion.[214]

Moreover, archaeologists have recently reassessed the skeletal materials and nails from the ossuary in Abba Cave in Jerusalem, concluding that the deceased—identified by an inscription in the cave as "Mattathias son of Judah"—was the man known in Greek as Aristobulus II, the last Hasmonean ruler, whom Marcus Antonius had crucified. Three nails, still bearing traces of human calcium, were recovered from his ossuary.

Furthermore, Craig A. Evans points out that "138 iron nails have been recovered from [Jewish] tombs and many of them have imbedded in the rust human bone and calcium. So there we've got . . . evidence probably of dozens of crucifixion victims who were properly buried."[215]

In first century Israel:

> The commands of Scripture, taken with traditions regarding piety (as especially exemplified in Tobit), corpse impurity, and the avoidance of the defilement of the land, strongly suggest that under normal circumstances (i.e., peacetime) no corpse would remain unburied—neither Jew nor Gentile, neither innocent nor guilty. All were to be buried.[216]

---

212. Onfray, *Atheist Manifesto*, 128.

213. Horace, *Epistles*, 1.16.48.

214. See: Biblical Archaeological Society Staff, "A Tomb in Jerusalem Reveals the History of Crucifixion and Roman Crucifixion Methods."

215. Evans, "The Burial and Empty Tomb Traditions."

216. Evans, "Jewish Burial Traditions and the Resurrection of Jesus."

Indeed, Josephus commented: "Jews are so careful about funeral rights that even malefactors who have been sentenced to crucifixion are taken down and buried before sunset."[217]

Historian of Rome Mark D. Smith observes that:

> According to Roman law, criminals condemned to death must be buried. Only in the case of the highest form of treason . . . was denial of burial permitted (but not required). Roman cultural values combined with Roman law to demand that even the destitute and abandoned, even executed criminals, most of whom, then as now, were from the lower classes, would not rot in the streets or the places reserved for executions, but would receive at least the minimal burial or cremation . . . these factors, combined with the traditional Roman respect for the autonomy of the cultural practices of provincials, suggest that standard Roman procedure would be to allow Jews to handle their dead as they wished, including those who were executed.[218]

Hence, contrary to Onfray, reports of Jesus' burial pass the *criterion of historical verisimilitude*: "Jews buried all dead, including the executed, and the Romans complied with Jewish customs—at least during peacetime."[219] Jewish archaeologist Jodi Magness, an expert on burial traditions in Jerusalem in the late Second Temple period, states that "The Gospel accounts describing Jesus' removal from the cross and burial are consistant with archaeological evidence and with Jewish law."[220]

The 1 Corinthians 15 creed and the passion source used by the Gospel of Mark provide exceptionally early sources of testimony to Jesus' burial. Early testimony to Jesus' burial is also provided by the special sources used by Luke and John in their gospels. The sermons recorded in Acts 2:29–31 and 13:36–37 likewise provide early testimony to Jesus' burial. Finally, Paul alludes to Jesus' burial when he speaks of believers being metaphorically "buried with" Jesus in Romans 6:4 and as "having been buried with him in baptism" in Colossians 2:13. We can therefore note that the burial passes the criterion of *multiple forms*.

Although a few critics have suggested that the specific burial place of Jesus may have been unknown, Pannenberg observes that "this is a pure invention of modern scholarship without the slightest evidence."[221] The gospels contain multiple early reports of multiple individuals (both friend and foe) who knew the specific burial place of Jesus (e.g. Mary the mother of Jesus, the female disciples including Mary Magdalene, the Jewish authorities, the guards, the cemetery groundskeeper, Nicodemus, and Joseph of Arimathea).

---

217. Josephus quoted in Evans, "Jewish Burial Traditions and the Resurrection of Jesus."
218. Smith, *Therefore Stand,* 204, 206.
219. Evans, "The Christ of Faith is the Jesus of History," 464.
220. Magness quoted in Strobel, *The Case for Miracles,* 205.
221. Pannenberg, "History and the Reality of the Resurrection," 69.

As Craig observes:

> Even the most skeptical scholars acknowledge that Joseph was probably the genuine, historical individual who buried Jesus, since it is unlikely that early Christian believers would invent an individual, give him a name and nearby town of origin, and place that fictional character on the historical council of the Sanhedrin, whose members were well known.[222]

J.P. Holding notes that "Arimathea" can be identified with ancient Ramah, which was later named as Ramathaian or Aramathaim (see: Josephus *Antiquities* 13.4.9). Joseph's coming from Aramathaim would have very naturally led to a pun on the Greek phrase "best disciple" (*aristos mathetes*). "Metheia" means "disciple" and "ari" is a common Greek prefix denoting superiority:

> Far from suggesting that Joseph was a fiction, the punning implies that Joseph's role as a "best disciple" was an early and well-known figure, recognized by the Greek-speakers of the church who, in line with the Jewish tendency to make puns, came up with this clever joke which became implanted in the diverse Gospel tradition.[223]

C. Marvin Pate reports that: "Even the most skeptical biblical scholars agree that Joseph of Arimathea was a historical person, actually a member of the Jewish Sanhedrin . . . it is highly unlikely that [Christians] would invent such an individual who would do the right thing regarding the burial of Jesus."[224] Indeed, as Michael Grant observes, the absence of Jesus' circle of male disciples from his burial is "too unfortunate, indeed disgraceful, to have been voluntarily invented by the evangelists at a later date."[225]

Finally, Jesus' somewhat *publically falsifiable* burial is implicitly conceded by the *enemy attestation* of the Jewish polemic concerning the empty tomb that lies behind Matthew 27:62–66 and 28:11–15. There would have been no need to explain the emptiness of the tomb had it not been occupied in the first place: "The fact that the enemies of Christianity felt obliged to explain away the empty tomb by the theft hypothesis shows . . . that the tomb was known (confirmation of the burial story) . . ."[226]

Robert J. Hutchinson reports that:

> many scholars, and not merely Christian ones, insist that Jesus' body was almost certainly taken down from the cross and buried, in deference to the Jewish holiday of Passover . . . contemporary historians and archaeologists—such as Shimon Gibson, Jodi Magness, James Dunn, N.T. Wright, Raymond Brown,

---

222. Craig, *The Son Rises*, 53.
223. Holding, "Was Joseph of Arimathea a Myth?," 286.
224. Pate, *40 Questions About The Historical Jesus*, 258.
225. Grant, *Jesus*, 175.
226. Craig, "The Empty Tomb of Jesus," 193.

Getting at Evidence for the Resurrection

E.P. Sanders, James Tabor, Michael Grant and Craig Evans—believe that Jesus was indeed given a proper burial.[227]

Again:

- Rudolph Bultmann called the burial story: "an historical account which creates no impression of being a legend..."[228]
- Raymond Brown: "That Jesus was buried is historically certain."[229]
- C.H. Dodd: "Jesus... was given decent, though hasty, burial through the good offices of a well-to-do sympathizer."[230]
- Gerd Lüdemann: "Jesus was obviously buried... There is the tradition of the burial in Paul; it's a very old tradition, and it's likely to be historical."[231]
- Simon Seabag Montefiore: "It is likely that the present Church of the Holy Sepulchre, which encloses both the place of crucifixion and the tomb, is the genuine site since its tradition was kept alive by local Christians for the next three centuries."[232]
- John A.T. Robinson states that the burial of Jesus is: "one of the earliest and best attested facts about Jesus."[233]
- Mark D. Smith: "Our evidence consistently supports the conclusion that Jesus was buried in the new family tomb of Joseph of Arimathea."[234]
- Geza Vermes: "The Bible orders that a person condemned to death by a court should be buried on the day of his execution before sunset [Deuteronomy 21:22–23], as happened to Jesus, too."[235]

The conclusion that Jesus was buried is warranted by at least ten criteria of authenticity:

- Early sources
- Independent sources
- Multiple sources
- Multiple forms
- Enemy sources

---

227. Hutchinson, *Searching for Jesus*, 232–33.
228. Bultmann, *The History of the Synoptic Tradition*, 274.
229. Brown, *The Death of the Messiah*, 1240.
230. Dodd, *The Founder of Christianity*.
231. Lüdemann quoted in *Jesus' Resurrection*, 52.
232. Montefiore, *Jerusalem*, 130.
233. Robinson, *The Human Face of God*, 131.
234. Smith, *Therefore Stand*, 207.
235. Vermes, *The Resurrection*, 22.

- Embarrassing sources
- Public falsifiability
- Historical Verisimilitude
- Memorability
- Historical coherence

Watch: "Jesus was buried in a tomb" Youtube playlist: www.youtube.com/playlist?list=PLQhh3qcwVEWjOA69as_NWrHsBRBLY_a3Y

Listen: "A Tomb in Jerusalem Reveals the History of Crucifixion and Roman Crucifixion Methods": www.biblicalarchaeology.org/daily/biblical-topics/crucifixion/a-tomb-in-jerusalem-reveals-the-history-of-crucifixion-and-roman-crucifixion-methods/

"The burial and empty tomb traditions" by Craig A. Evans: www.youtube.com/watch?v=ZKvy9e5UMKE

Read: "The Historicity of the Empty Tomb of Jesus" by William Lane Craig: www.reasonablefaith.org/the-historicity-of-the-empty-tomb-of-jesus

"Getting the Burial Traditions and Evidences Right" by Craig A. Evans in *How God Became Jesus: The Real Origins Of Belief In Jesus' Divine Nature* edited by Michael F. Bird

The Final Days of Jesus: The Thrill of Defeat, The Agony of Victory—A Classical Historian Explores Jesus's Arrest, Trial, and Execution by Mark D. Smith

---

Fact 3: Jesus' empty tomb

German NT critic Klaus Berger states that "The reports about the empty tomb are related by all four Gospels (and other writings of early Christianity) in a form independent of one another."[236] Moreover, as William Lane Craig points out: "Behind the fourth gospel stands the Beloved Disciple, whose reminiscences fill out the traditions employed. The visit of the disciples to the empty tomb [see: John 20:1–10] is therefore attested not only in tradition but by this disciple."[237] That is, the *publically falsifiable* claim that Jesus' tomb was empty enjoys *eyewitness attestation*. Moreover, John's observation of the positioning of the grave clothes in the tomb (John 20:7) is plausibly an *unintentional sign of historicity*.

J.P. Moreland notes that within the pages of the NT the main debate between the disciples and the Jewish establishment "was over why [the tomb] was empty, not whether it was empty."[238] The reality of the empty tomb (and hence the burial) is thereby implicitly conceded by the *enemy source* of the Jewish establishment, who focus upon trying to explain why the tomb was empty.

---

236. Berger quoted in Copan and Tacelli, *Jesus' Resurrection*, 35.
237. Craig, "The Empty Tomb of Jesus," 192.
238. Moreland, *Scaling the Secular City*, 163.

Moreland also notes that:

> the resurrection was preached in Jerusalem just a few weeks after the crucifixion. If the tomb had not been empty, such preaching could not have occurred. The body of Jesus could have been produced, and since it is likely that the location of Joseph of Arimathea's tomb was well known (he was a respected member of the Sanhedrin), it would not have been difficult to find where Jesus was buried.[239]

As Holding writes: "That such an important personage buried Jesus in his personal tomb is taken to be a failsafe for the historicity of the burial, for it is assumed to be impossible that the New Testament could make such an important person or his role up and get away with it."[240]

Positing that Jesus' corpse would have been unrecognizable by the time the disciples publically proclaimed the resurrection doesn't work. Stephen T. Davis comments:

> I do not agree that Jesus' corpse would have been unrecognizable after seven weeks . . . I myself also checked with an eminent pathologist on this point, who told me that when a body is in fact buried, and the climate is dry and fairly cool, a corpse can be readily identified for much longer than that. Moreover, we must note that any body that was found in Jesus' tomb and put on display, even an unrecognizable one, would have spelled disaster for the Christian movement.[241]

The gospel reports all pass the criteria of *embarrassment* because it was Jesus' *female* disciples who discovered the empty tomb. In first-century Jewish culture, women were considered so unreliable that their testimony was automatically suspect.[242] Rabbi Ben Herman explains that:

> The Talmud, in Shevuot 30a and Gittin 46a, states that a woman cannot be a witness because her place is at home and not in court. As a result, women were only used as witnesses in matters related to them (things involving their families or their bodies), for identification of people or for events regarding places frequented only by women.[243]

The *Mishnah* states that women are "unsuitable to bear witness."[244] Josephus writes of not allowing women to be witnesses "on account of the levity and boldness of their

---

239. Moreland, *Scaling the Secular City*, 161.
240. Holding, "Was Joseph of Arimathea a Myth?," 285.
241. Davis, *Disputed Issues*, 67.
242. See: Lapide, *The Resurrection of Jesus*, 95–96.
243. Herman, "Jewish Witnesses: Who Qualifies?"
244. *Mishnah Shabout* 4.1 quoted in Dickson, *Investigating Jesus*, 130.

sex."²⁴⁵ That early *Christian* culture quickly became more egalitarian is beside the point, for as Vermes comments:

> The evidence furnished by female witnesses had no standing in a male-dominated Jewish society . . . If the empty tomb story had been manufactured by the primitive Church to demonstrate the reality of the resurrection of Jesus, one would have expected a uniform and fool proof account attributed to patently reliable witnesses.²⁴⁶

That is, males. It is, then, highly significant that the gospel writers relate that women first discovered the empty tomb. As Gerald O'Collins observes:

> Surprisingly, women enjoy a witness function in both the passion and resurrection narratives . . . they could testify both to the fact of his burial and the location of his grave. Subsequently they discover that grave to be empty. If the discovery story were simply a legend created by the early Christians, it remains difficult to explain why women find a place in the story. In Jewish society they did not count as valid witnesses . . . The role of the women in the story provides a sound argument for its historical reliability.²⁴⁷

Furthermore, although it coheres with prevailing patriarchal attitudes, the male disciples' failure to believe the women's report of the empty tomb is, at least in terms of Christian tradition, likewise rather embarrassing: "they would not believe it," ruminates Mark (16:8), while Luke narrates that the women's report to the male disciples "seemed to them an idle tale, and they did not believe them" (Luke 24:11). Hence: "the fact that it is women, rather than men, who are the chief witnesses to the empty tomb is best explained by the historical facticity of the narrative in this regard."²⁴⁸ As Craig A. Evans comments:

> The story of the women who witness Jesus' burial and then return early Sunday to anoint his body smacks of historicity. It is hard to see why relatively unknown women would feature so prominently in such an important story, if what we have here is fiction. But if the women's intention is to mourn privately, as Jewish law and custom allowed, and, even more importantly, to note the precise location of Jesus' tomb, so that the later gathering of his remains for burial in his family tomb is possible, then we have a story that fits Jewish customs, on the one hand, and stands in tension with resurrection expectations and supporting apologetics, on the other.²⁴⁹

---

245. Josephus, *Jewish Antiquities*, 4.8.15.
246. Vermes, *The Resurrection*, 142.
247. O'Collins, *The Resurrection of Jesus Christ*, 42–43.
248. Craig and Sinnott-Armstrong, *God?*, 23
249. Evans, "Jewish Burial Customs and the Resurrection of Jesus."

An objection often raised against the women being witnesses to the empty tomb is that the different gospels report slightly different lists of women on the scene. However, all fours gospels agree on the primary (and culturally embarrassing) point that it was *some women* who discovered the empty tomb. Besides, the overlapping lists of names are in fact compatible with one another; it's just that none of the lists is exhaustive. If this lack of unanimity has any significance, it actually lies in indicating the *independence* of these reports, which adds to their historical value!

Jerry A. Coyne complains that "despite ardent searching," archaeologists have not "found such a tomb."[250] In point of fact, archaeologists have found over a thousand "such" rock-cut tombs in Jerusalem:

> What is clear is that the kind of tomb suggested by the Gospel accounts *is* consistent with what is now known of contemporary practice in the Jerusalem area: i.e. a rock-cut tomb, a low entrance closed by a moveable stone, and a raised burial couch within.[251]

Moreover, according to archaeologist John McRay, "the archaeological and early literary evidence argues strongly for those who associate [Jesus' tomb] with the Church of the Holy Sepulchre."[252] James D.G. Dunn allows that "the site has about as much plausibility as could be hoped for. Other sites for the original tomb of Jesus have been suggested, but hardly with the same credibility."[253] Simon Seabag Montefiore affirms: "It is likely that the present Church of the Holy Sepulchre, which encloses both the place of crucifixion and the tomb, is the genuine site since its tradition was kept alive by Christians for the next three centuries."[254] Dan Bahat, former city archaeologist of Jerusalem, concludes: "We may not be absolutely certain that the site of the Holy Sepulchre Church is the site of Jesus' burial, but we certainly have no other site that can lay a claim nearly as weighty, and we really have no reason to reject the authenticity of the site."[255]

In 2016 a conservation team from the National Technical University of Athens set to work on restoring the shrine within the Holy Sepulchre Church and "the marble covering protecting the original limestone slab upon which Jesus was believed to have been laid [was] temporarily removed for restoration and cleaning, thereby exposing to view the original slab, [not] seen since 1555."[256] According to National Geographic's archaeologist-in-residence, Fredrik Hiebert, this "appears to be visible proof that the location of the tomb has not shifted through time, something that scientists and his-

---

250. Coyne, *Faith vs. Fact*, 121.
251. Biddle, *The Tomb of Christ*, 55.
252. McRay, *Archaeology & the New Testament*, 216.
253. Dunn, *Why Believe in Jesus' Resurrection?*, 32.
254. Montefiore, *Jerusalem*, 130.
255. Bahat, "Does the Holy Sepulchre Church Mark the Burial of Jesus?," 26–45.
256. Craig, "Excavating the Tomb of Jesus."

torians have wondered for decades."²⁵⁷ Mortar recovered during the renovation was dated (by optically stimulated luminescence) to as early as AD 345, supporting the traditional dating of the first Church of the Holy Sepulchre to the reign of Emperor Constantine. Archaeologist Jodi Magness observes:

> All of this is perfectly consistent with what we know about how wealthy Jews disposed of their dead in the time of Jesus. This does not, of course, prove that the event was historical. But what it does suggest is that whatever the sources were for the gospel accounts, they were familiar with this tradition and these burial customs.²⁵⁸

At the very least, then, archaeology demonstrates that the NT reports of Jesus' burial and empty tomb pass the criterion of *historical verisimilitude*. However, one might well argue that *we have the tomb of Jesus, and it is empty*.

We may also note that discovering the tomb of one's recently interned rabbi to be unexpectedly empty is certainly the sort of thing that would prove *memorable*.

William Lane Craig recounts that "the consensus of scholarship affirms the historicity of the empty tomb of Jesus."²⁵⁹ For example:

- Klaus Berger: "Without a doubt the grave of Jesus was found to be empty . . ."²⁶⁰
- D.H. Van Dallen: "It is extremely difficult to object to the empty tomb on historical grounds; those who deny it do so on the basis of theological or philosophical assumptions."²⁶¹
- John Dickson: "Most experts accept that Jesus' tomb was empty within days of his burial."²⁶²
- C.H. Dodd: "I should be disposed to conclude that . . . tradition . . . preserved also a genuine memory that on that Sunday morning [Jesus'] tomb was found broken open and to all appearance empty."²⁶³
- James D.G. Dunn: "it is hard to escape the conclusion: that on the Sunday following Jesus' crucifixion, the tomb in which his dead body had been laid was found to be empty."²⁶⁴

---

257. Hiebert quoted in Romey, "Unsealing of Christ's Reputed Tomb."
258. Magness quoted in Romey, "Unsealing of Christ's Reputed Tomb."
259. Craig, "Who Was Jesus?," 25.
260. Berger quoted in Craig, *A Reasonable Response*, 300.
261. Dallen quoted in Craig, "Who Was Jesus?," 25.
262. Dickson and Clarke, *Life of Jesus*, 117.
263. Dodd, *The Founder of Christianity*, 173.
264. Dunn, *Why Believe in Jesus' Resurrection?*, 34.

- Michael Grant: "The historian cannot justifiably deny the empty tomb . . . the evidence necessitates the conclusion the tomb was found empty."[265]

- Michael Green: "There can be no doubt that the tomb of Jesus was, in fact, empty on the first Easter day."[266]

- Jacob Kremer: "By far most exegetes hold firmly to the reliability of the biblical statements concerning the empty tomb."[267]

- Alister McGrath: "the empty tomb . . . is such a major element in each of the four gospels . . . that it must be considered to have a basis in historical fact."[268]

- Jeffrey L. Morrow: "The empty tomb is almost certainly pre-Markan and historical."[269]

- Jake H. O'Connell concludes it is "certainly more probable than not [that] Jesus' *tomb* was discovered empty."[270]

- Mark D. Smith: "some women among the disciples visited the tomb of Jesus to provide for a fuller preparation of the body . . . When they arrived, they found the tomb empty."[271]

- Geza Vermes: "the women belonging to the entourage of Jesus discovered an empty tomb and were definite that it was the tomb [in which Jesus had been placed]."[272]

Facts 1–3 are *mutually supportive* in that the significant thing about Jesus' empty tomb was that it previously housed his body, and if the tomb housed Jesus' body this was most likely because Jesus was dead. Likewise, the empty tomb coheres with the disciple's belief that Jesus had been resurrected, as an occupied tomb would have precluded this belief. This mutual support means that Jesus' empty tomb passes the *criterion of historical coherence*.

The conclusion that after his burial Jesus' tomb was found empty is warranted by at least eleven criteria of authenticity:

- Eyewitness testimony
- Early sources
- Independent sources

---

265. Grant, *Jesus*, 176.
266. Green quoted in McDowell, *The New Evidence That Demands a Verdict*, 245.
267. Craig, "Who Was Jesus?," 25.
268. McGrath, *Jesus*, 89.
269. Morrow, *Jesus' Resurrection*, 59.
270. O'Connell, *Jesus' Resurrection and Apparitions*, 150.
271. Smith, *Therefore Stand*, 210.
272. Vermes, *Jesus the Jew*, 40.

- Multiple sources
- Enemy sources
- Embarrassing sources
- Public falsifiability
- Unintentional Signs of History
- Historical Verisimilitude
- Memorability
- Historical coherence

Watch: "Jesus' tomb was empty" Youtube playlist: www.youtube.com/playlist?list=PLQhh3qcwVEWhqraAeJ8gVcSlbXhZR2R6p

Read: "The Historicity of the Empty Tomb of Jesus" by William Lane Craig: www.reasonablefaith.org/writings/scholarly-writings/historical-jesus/the-historicity-of-the-empty-tomb-of-jesus/

"The Disciples' Inspection of the Empty Tomb" by William Lane Craig: www.reasonablefaith.org/writings/scholarly-writings/historical-jesus/the-disciples-inspection-of-the-empty-tomb/

"Reply to Evan Fales: On the Empty Tomb of Jesus" by William Lane Craig: www.reasonablefaith.org/writings/scholarly-writings/historical-jesus/reply-to-evan-fales-on-the-empty-tomb-of-jesus/

"The Empty Tomb of Jesus" by Gary R. Habermas: www.4truth.net/fourtruthpbjesus.aspx?pageid=8589952861

"Unsealing of Christ's Reputed Tomb Turns Up New Revelations" by Kristen Romey: http://news.nationalgeographic.com/2016/10/jesus-christ-tomb-burial-church-holy-sepulchre/

As Eric Metaxas writes: "it's clear that Jesus really lived and was crucified and lain in a tomb and that on the third day, that tomb was found to be empty. On those points there is almost zero doubt."[273] It's what happened next that caused, and continues to cause, controversy.

Fact 4: Jesus' apparent postmortem appearances

Lawrence Krauss begs the question against any testimony supporting Jesus' resurrection by asserting that a resurrection "has never been observationally verified."[274] How very Humean of him. However, early testimony to "observationally verified" encounters with the resurrected Jesus is laced throughout the NT letters, the NT gospels, and Acts in multiple and often independent forms, and includes eyewitness testimony. As

---

273. Metaxas, *Miracles*, 100.
274. Krauss and Craig, "Life, the Universe, and Nothing."

Getting at Evidence for the Resurrection

John M.G. Barclay observes, these appearance stories are "of early provenance and multiple attestation (Paul and the Gospels)."[275] Michael Grant acknowledges:

> those who believed that Jesus had appeared to them on the earth after his death have their alleged experiences recorded in a number of passages of the New Testament. Their testimony cannot prove them to have been right in supposing that Jesus had risen from the dead. However, these accounts do prove that certain people were utterly convinced that that's what he had done.[276]

Bart Ehrman adds that the author of Acts had:

> access to traditions that are not based on his Gospel account so that we have yet another independent witness. For the writer of Acts, Jesus is very much a man who really lived and died in Judea, as can be seen in the accounts of Jesus' resurrection in chapter 1 and in the speeches that occur abundantly throughout the narrative. Chapter 1 portrays the disciples meeting with Jesus after the resurrection.[277]

Not only did the early Christians clearly *believe* that Jesus had been resurrected, they believed that many of their number had personally met (i.e. seen, heard, talked with, and even touched) the resurrected Jesus, both individually and in groups, over an extended period of time; *this early, multiple, and often independent verification was why they believed Jesus had been resurrected.*

The fact that Jesus reportedly appeared mainly to people who had been his disciples before his death is an apparent weakness in the evidence for the resurrection that actually indicates the reliability of the NT reports, for if the appearance reports were either lies or legends, it is likely that hostile witnesses would feature more prominently. Indeed, this is just what we see in later, extrabiblical literature such as the Gospel of Peter and the Gospel to the Hebrews, which both add "neutral and even hostile witnesses to the resurrection."[278]

Fig. 21 lists post-resurrection appearances of Jesus referenced by the NT (in their apparent historical order).[279] References to Mark 16:9 and following are in brackets as this section of text doesn't appear in the earliest manuscripts; but note that Mark 16:7 (which *is* in the earliest manuscripts) implies at least one group resurrection appearance in Galilee.

---

275. Barclay, "The Resurrection in Contemporary New Testament Scholarship," 16.
276. Grant, *Jesus*, 176.
277. Erhman, *Did Jesus Exist?*, 107.
278. O'Collins, *Jesus' Resurrection and Apparitions*, 66–67.
279. Based on the chart given by Miller, *Did Jesus Really Rise From The Dead?*, 106, and Wilkins' list of resurrection appearances in *The Holman Apologetics Commentary on the Bible: The Gospel and Acts*, 190–91.

Fig. 21.

Resurrection Witnesses:	Location:	Senses Involved:	Sources:
Mary Magdalene	Empty Tomb	Saw and talked with Jesus (perhaps touching him)	John 20:11–18 (see: Mark 16:9)
At least four other women, including Joanna and Mary the mother of James	Jerusalem	Saw, heard, and touched Jesus	Matthew 28:1–10
Cleopas and Mary	Emmaus Road	Saw and talked with Jesus	Luke 24:13–32 (see: Mark 16:12)
Peter	Unspecified	Saw Jesus	1 Corinthians 15:5; Mark 16:7; Luke 24:34
Ten disciples (and others)	Unspecified room	Saw and talked with Jesus	John 20:19–23; Luke 24:36–49 (see: 1 Corinthians 15 and Mark 16:14)
Eleven disciples including Thomas	Unspecified room	Saw, talked with, and touched Jesus	John 20:24–30; Luke 24:33–43; (see: 1 Corinthians 15)
Seven disciples	Along the Sea of Galilee (Tiberius)	Saw and talked with Jesus	John 21:1–25 (see: Mark 16:7)
500 individuals at once	Unspecified	Saw Jesus	1 Corinthians 15:6 (see: Mark 16:7)
Eleven disciples	Galilee/Unspecified	Saw and heard Jesus	Matthew 28:16 [18]-20 (see: Acts 1:3–8 and Mark 16:7)
Eleven disciples	Mount of Olives	Saw and heard Jesus	Luke 24:44–53; Acts 1:4–12 (see: Mark 16:19–20)
Saul	Road to Damascus	Saw and talked with Jesus	1 Corinthians 15:8 and Acts 9:1–19

From this data, it would appear that we should take notice of eleven distinct appearance incidents.[280] These appearance reports all qualify as *early* reports that pass the criteria of *memorability*. In addition:

- Six of these reported encounters with the resurrected Jesus (the encounters witnessed by Mary Magdalene, the group of women, the two disciples on the road to Emmaus, the ten disciples, Thomas, and Saul) come from testimonial sources that are *independent* in the sense that they all accepted Jesus' resurrection because of their personal appearance experiences and not because of any testimony they had heard.

---

280. Michael R. Licona has suggested that Matthew relocates the first appearance to the male disciples from Jerusalem to Galilee, but see: McGrew, "Licona gospel examples IV: More over-reading."

- We have *multiple early sources* for at least two individual and three group appearances: "The appearance to Peter is independently attested by Paul and Luke (1 Cor 15:5; Lk 24:34) [as well as by Mark 16:7], the appearance to the [disciples *as a group*] by Paul, Luke and John (1 Cor 15:5; Lk 24:36–43; Jn 20:19–20) . . . and appearances to the disciples in Galilee by Mark . . . and John (Mk 16:7 . . . Jn 21)."[281]

- The appearance to Peter passes the criteria of *historical verisimilitude* (see: 1 Corinthians 15:5's use of *Cephus*) and is *multiply attested in different forms.*

- The appearance to Mary Magdalene passes the criteria of *embarrassment* and the criteria of *historical verisimilitude* (note the popularity of the name *Mary* and the Aramaic *Rabboni* in John 20:16).

- The *group* appearance to the other women likewise passes the criteria of *embarrassment* and *historical verisimilitude* (the most common female name at the time was Mary).

- The appearance to the two disciples on the road to Emmaus passes the criterion of *historical verisimilitude.*[282]

- The appearance to the *group* of ten male disciples[283] (plus others) is attested by literarily *independent* sources and is reported by an *eyewitness* (see: John 20:19–23).

- The *group* appearance to the eleven including Thomas is attested by literarily *independent* sources, passes the criteria of *embarrassment* and is reported by an *eyewitness* (see: John 20:24–30).

- The *group* appearance to seven disciples by the Sea of Galilee is reported by an *eyewitness* (See John 21:1–25).

- The appearance to Saul is *multiply attested*, including an *eyewitness* report (from the formerly-hostile Saul himself).

As for the content of these eleven reports:

- Jesus was *seen* on every occasion.[284]

- At least eight reports concern appearances to *groups* of two, four, seven, ten, eleven and even five hundred people.

---

281. Craig quoted in Copan and Tacelli, *Jesus' Resurrection*, 182.

282. Note the hospitality culture and the meal etiquette of prayer and bread breaking. See also: Bivin, "Farewell to the Emmaus Road;" Thiede, *The Emmaus Mystery*; Walker, *In The Steps of Jesus*.

283. Luke employs a figurative synecdoche when he writes that "the eleven" were assembled with those with them: "because Judas was now gone from them, and dead; and this being their whole number, it is used, though every one might not be present, as particularly Thomas was not; see: John 20:19."—Gill's Exposition of the Entire Bible. See also: Jackson, "Does the Expression "the Eleven" (Luke 24:33) Constitute an Error?"

284. See: Davis, *Christian Philosophical Theology*, 136–37.

- While Jesus appeared to Saul rather than his traveling companions, they nevertheless saw and heard something (so we should class this as a *group* appearance).

- On nine occasions, it is additionally reported that people heard and/or talked with Jesus.

- On three occasions, *independent* sources (including *eyewitnesses* John) state or imply that people *touched* Jesus.

From Saul to Paul

On several occasions, the apostle Paul claims that *he is himself an eyewitness to the resurrected Jesus* (see: 1 Corinthians 9:1 and 15:8; Galatians 1:13–17). Paul's claim is corroborated by Acts (written by Paul's traveling companion Luke) and given the stamp of sincerity by Paul's martyrdom. As Antony Flew observed:

> the evidence of Paul is certainly important and strong precisely because he was a convert. He was not a prior believer, and the evidence that he hadn't been previously a believer is about as clear as it could have been because he had been an active opponent. I think this has to be accepted as one of the most powerful bits of evidence that there is [for the resurrection of Jesus] . . .[285]

William Lane Craig notes that "when Paul speaks of his 'visions and revelations of the Lord' (II Cor 12.1–7) he does *not* include Jesus' appearance to him. Paul and the early Christian community as a whole were familiar with religious visions and sharply differentiated between these and an appearance of the risen Lord."[286]

Atheists Russell Blackford and Udo Schuklenk incorrectly assert that "the only New Testament narrative of the actual road to Damascus conversion is in the Acts of the Apostles (chapter 9), traditionally attributed to Luke."[287] In fact, Paul's conversion (c. AD 34) is also narrated in Luke's summary of two speeches *made by Paul* in Acts 22 and 26. Blackford and Schuklenk claim that Luke's report "is consistent with a visionary experience . . ."[288] However, both Luke and Paul (as related by Luke) make it clear that Paul's experience wasn't a subjective visionary experience.

Paul's traveling companions all saw the same bright light and heard a voice (*phóné*).[289] Moreover, according to Acts 26:13–14, it wasn't just Saul who fell to the ground on the road to Damascus, but his traveling companions as well: "I saw a light from heaven, brighter than the sun, blazing around me and my companions. We all

---

285. Flew quoted in Baggett, *Did the Resurrection Happen?*, 57.
286. Craig, "The Bodily Resurrection of Jesus."
287. Blackford and Schuklenk, *50 Great Myths About Atheism*, 175.
288. Blackford and Schuklenk, *50 Great Myths About Atheism*, 175.
289. See: Bible Hub Commentaries, "phóné."

fell to the ground . . ." As Bock comments: "this shows that it was a real, external event, not merely an internal vision of Jesus."[290]

According to some translations of Acts 22:9, Paul says that "those who were with me saw the light, but they did not hear the voice of the One who was speaking to me" (HSBC). So, did Luke fail to notice a glaring contradiction between the reports he recorded in Acts? That seems unlikely.

On the one hand, one might accept that the supposed "contradictions" between the various accounts in Luke of Paul's conversion are real whilst yet concluding that they fall within the acceptable limits of variation in matters of secondary detail accorded by the genre rules of first-century historiography. On the other hand, one can argue that the supposed "contradictions" are merely apparent. For example, one might conclude from Acts 9:7 that having fallen to the ground Saul's companions stood up before he did: "The men who were traveling with him stood speechless, hearing the voice but seeing no one" (ESV). Likewise:

> it is over-interpretation to suggest that Acts 9:7 says that they did not see the light . . . All that is said here is that they did not see anyone. For those with Saul, there was neither an appearance nor a revelation. The point is that the others knew something happened and that Saul did not have a merely inner, psychological experience. Those with Paul, however, did not know exactly what took place.[291]

Jesus once spoke of those who: "Though seeing, they do not see; though hearing, they do not hear or understand" (Matthew 13:13). As in English, the Greek for "hearing/hear" is ambiguous. It can refer to "hearing" plain and simple, or it can refer to "hearing with understanding." By the principle of interpretive charity, we may conclude that Paul's companions *heard* the voice but didn't *understand* it: "This distinction would neatly parallel the distinction the two texts make with regard to what Paul's companions saw: they saw the light (22:9) but did not see the person whom Paul saw in the light (9:7)."[292]

Interestingly, in Acts 26:14 Paul specifically notes that Jesus spoke to him "in the Aramaic dialect." Hence the lack of comprehension on the part of Paul's companions may have been due to their being unfamiliar with Aramaic (perhaps they only spoke Greek and Syriac). Alternatively, it may simply be that they heard the sound of Jesus' voice without being able to make out what he said (perhaps because they were further away than was Saul). In any case, Paul's companions "did not understand the voice of him who was speaking . . ." (Acts 22:9).

---

290. Bock, *Acts*, 716.
291. Bock, *Acts*, 660.
292. Bowman, "Did they hear what Paul heard?"

Putting these accounts together, it becomes apparent that Paul's Damascus road experience cannot be dismissed as merely some subjective, visionary event in Paul's psyche. As theologian R. Albert Mohler comments:

> These texts are perfectly complementary . . . both affirm that Paul, and Paul alone, saw Christ and both heard and understood his voice. Paul's associates heard the voice without understanding and saw the light without seeing the appearance of Christ . . . Paul's associates witnessed the supernatural character of the event, seeing the light and hearing a voice, but they neither saw Christ nor understood his words.[293]

Paul and his compatriots all saw a light and heard a voice (note the parallel with the incident reported in John 12:28–29). Only Paul saw a figure in the light or understood the voice. Only Paul suffered from temporary blindness as a result of the encounter. Perhaps this was because only Paul looked *into* the light.

In any case, unless we countenance a group hallucination, the *similarities* between the unanticipated experiences of Paul and of his companions tell us that *something objective happened*. Luke's point "is that the others knew something happened and that Saul did not have a merely inner, psychological experience. Those with Paul, however, did not know exactly what took place."[294] The *differences* between the experiences of Paul and his companions fit with Paul's claim that the resurrected Jesus' specific intent was to reveal himself to Paul in order to appoint him as an apostle (see: Acts 26:16). There's no contradiction between Paul's Damascus road experience and that of his traveling companions, and Paul's eyewitness testimony (corroborated by Luke) must be taken seriously.

Paul's conversion experience doesn't begin and end on the Damascus road. Luke recounts how Paul's encounter left him temporarily blinded, and how Paul was healed of his blindness when a Damascene Christian called Ananias came to Paul in fear and trembling after both men were given a vision of the other from God:

> Placing his hands on Saul, he said, "Brother Saul, the Lord—Jesus, who appeared to you on the road as you were coming here—has sent me so that you may see again and be filled with the Holy Spirit." Immediately, something like scales fell from Saul's eyes, and he could see again. (Acts 9:17–18)

The specified complexity of these accurate visions (God reportedly even told Ananias that Paul was staying in "the house of Judas on Straight Street") and the healing of Paul's blindness both confirmed to Paul, and to the early church, that Jesus had indeed appeared to Paul on the road to Damascus. Luke recounts:

> When [Paul] came to Jerusalem, he tried to join the disciples, but they were all afraid of him, not believing that he really was a disciple. But Barnabas took

---

293. Mohler, "When The Bible Speaks, God Speaks," 53.
294. Bock, "Precision and Accuracy," 370.

him and brought him to the apostles. He told them how Saul on his journey had seen the Lord and that the Lord had spoken to him, and how in Damascus he had preached fearlessly in the name of Jesus. (Acts 9:26–27)

Jesus, or a meteor?

William Hartmann, co-founder of the Planetary Science Institute in Tucson, Arizona, advances an alternative theory of what happened to Paul. Hartmann claims that the biblical descriptions of Paul's conversion closely match accounts of the fireball meteor seen above Chelyabinsk, Russia, in 2013. The Chelyabinsk meteor provides what Hartmann calls "observational data that match what we see in this first-century account."[295] *New Scientist* laid out the claimed parallels:

> The most obvious similarity is the bright light ... That's in line with video from Chelyabinsk showing a light ... around three times as bright as the sun ... After witnessing the light, Paul and his companions fell to the ground. Hartmann says they may have been knocked over when the meteor exploded ... At Chelyabinsk, the shock wave ... knocked people off their feet. Paul then heard the voice of Jesus ... Chelyabinsk produced a thunderous, explosive sound. Paul was also blinded ... A few days later, "something like scales fell from his eye and he regained his sight' ... Hartmann ... suggests that Paul was suffering from photo keratitis ... "It's basically a bit of sunburn on the cornea of the eye. Once that begins to heal, it flakes off," ... The UV radiation at Chelyabinsk was strong enough to cause ... temporary blindness.[296]

Dr. Guy Consolmagno, Director of the Vatican Observatory, comments that Hartmann's thesis "was first presented at the Meteoritical Society meeting in Edmonton and rather thoroughly refuted in the discussion there; I am surprised that the author has decided to submit it for publication ..."[297] Consolmagno points out the fallacy at the heart of Hartmann's paper:

> impact events like that of Chelyabinsk ... are accompanied by large, blinding flashes of light and loud noises. [Hartmann] notes that the event of Paul's conversion was also accompanied by a large flash of light and a loud noise. He then concludes that the one event was the same as the other. This is equivalent to saying that "the sun is yellow; bananas are yellow; therefore the sun is a banana."[298]

---

295. Hartmann quoted in Aron, "Falling meteor may have changed the course of Christianity."
296. Aron, "Falling meteor may have changed the course of Christianity."
297. Consolmagno, "Was St. Paul converted by a meteor fall?"
298. Consolmagno, "Was St. Paul converted by a meteor fall?"

The match between Paul's experience and a falling meteor isn't specific enough to warrant a reductive explanation of the former in terms of the latter. For example, Hartmann suggests that Paul and his companions were knocked to the ground by a shockwave. However, Paul doesn't say they were *knocked* to the ground, but that upon seeing the "light from heaven" he and his companions "all fell to the ground . . ." (Acts 26:13–14). The Greek verb translated here as "fell" means "I fall down, fall prostrate."[299] I. Howard Marshall explains the import of this phrase as being that, "Overwhelmed by the experience they all fell *to the ground* . . ."[300] In other words, they weren't knocked to the ground by a shockwave, but chose to prostrate themselves on the ground. Hartmann forces the biblical report to fit his theory by rewriting history. Indeed, Hartmann buys explanatory scope and power for his theory by simply rejecting Paul's testimony of having seen and heard the resurrected Jesus!

Hartmann's thesis is disconfirmed by a triple lack of expected evidence:

> In Chelyabinsk . . . We have the widespread accounts of more than a million people who saw the bolide in the sky; we have the craters and other physical damage made by the falling stones; and we have many examples of the stones themselves. These three lines of evidence are specifically lacking in the proposed Damascus event . . .[301]

It's implausible to imagine that such a large event would go unnoticed:

> at no point in the journey would St. Paul have been more than 110 km away from [either Jerusalem or Damascus]. In fact the distance between Nazareth and Damascus (which is on a likely route between Jerusalem and Damascus) is only about 130 km so at no point in the journey would St. Paul have been more than 65 km from either city. By contrast, the strewn field alone of the Chelyabinsk pieces extends for roughly 50 km. The Chelyabinsk fireball . . . was observed from places as far apart as of more than one thousand kilometres . . .[302]

Hence the meteor hypothesis is caught in a catch-22 situation:

> a meteorite might not be found, or a crater not formed, if the event [was] large enough to result in an airburst. . . But that makes the problem even worse . . . the Tunguska event resulted in . . . a visible night light glow seen across Europe and Asia for several nights. Effects from the blast were felt as far away as London. The bigger the event, the more likely it is that it would have been seen and recorded . . . if one argues that the meteorite fall was small enough to

---

299. See: Bible Hub Commentaries, "katapiptó."
300. Marshall, *Acts*, 414.
301. Consolmagno, "Was St. Paul converted by a meteor fall?"
302. Consolmagno, "Was St. Paul converted by a meteor fall?"

go unnoticed except nearby, then one no longer has a fall of sufficient energy to produce the blinding flash . . .[303]

Raj Das-Bhaumik, a consultant surgeon at Moorfields Eye Hospital in London, observes that the symptoms of photokeratitis[304] are not as Hartmann claims: "You wouldn't expect bits of the eye to fall off; I've not come across that at all."[305] It's hard to be sure whether Luke's description that "there fell from his eyes as it were [or 'something like'] scales" (Luke 9:18, YLT) is meant literally or metaphorically, but even assuming Paul's blindness had both a natural cause and a natural cure, it's still miraculous that Ananias and Paul should have mutual visions that arranged their meeting in Damascus. It's worth noting the *historical verisimilitude* of the instruction for Ananias to find Paul's lodging on "Straight Street" (see: Acts 9:11), the main east-west route through Damascus, part of the colonnaded first-century incarnation of which has been uncovered by archaeologists.[306]

In sum, Hartmann's thesis lacks the explanatory scope and power needed to explain away Paul's conversion. It is *ad hoc*, disconfirmed by a lack of expected evidence and by knowledge about photo keratitis, and it relies upon simply *ignoring* the details of Luke's early reports about Paul's conversion (not only on the road to Damascus, but in Damascus) and Paul's own testimony to having met the risen Jesus. With Consolmagno: "I find the proposal of this work to be highly unlikely and of dubious merit, either scientifically or historically."[307]

Watch: "From Saul to Paul" Youtube playlist: www.youtube.com/playlist?list=PLQhh3qcwVEWgxr-o_wjk56gosqehDX-x7

Read: "Heard but Not Understood? Acts 9:7 and 22:9 and Differing Views of Biblical Inerrancy" by Rob Bowman: www.academia.edu/19770469/Heard_but_Not_Understood_Acts_9_7_and_22_9_and_Differing_Views_of_Biblical_Inerrancy

"Acts vs. Epistles" by J.P. Holding: www.tektonics.org/ntdocdef/actspaul.php

---

Krauss concedes to appearances

"there were people who believed that they saw the risen Jesus."

—James Crossley[308]

---

303. Consolmagno, "Was St. Paul converted by a meteor fall?"
304. See: Porter, "What is Photokeratitis — Including Snow Blindness?"
305. Das-Bhaumik quoted in Aron, "Falling meteor may have changed the course of Christianity."
306. See: Arnold, *Zondervan Illustrated Bible Backgrounds Commentary: Acts*, 77.
307. Consolmagno, "Was St. Paul converted by a meteor fall?"
308. Crossley, "The Resurrection Probably Did Not Happen," 492.

Lawrence Krauss concedes that people had apparent experiences of a resurrected Jesus: "In fact, the fact that people may have seen Jesus walking [after his death], if they did, if they report that, I'm willing to accept their belief that they did."[309] Indeed, as William Lane Craig reports: "Most New Testament critics are prepared to admit that [subjectively speaking] the disciples did see appearances of Jesus . . ."[310] For example:

- Dale Allison: "I am sure that the disciples saw Jesus after his death."[311]
- Maurice Casey: "I conclude that the evidence for early appearances, from the women to St Paul, is unimpeachable . . ."[312]
- James G. Crossley: "certain people believed they saw Jesus . . ."[313]
- C.H. Dodd writes that the disciples "were *dead sure* that they had met with Jesus' after his death."[314]
- Bart D. Ehrman: "some of the disciples believed they saw Jesus later, and on that basis they came to believe he had been raised and exalted to heaven."[315]
- David Flusser: "The Lord's brother, James, came to believe as a result of a resurrection appearance."[316]
- Reginald Fuller confirms that the disciples' subjective experience of seeing Jesus after his death "is a fact upon which both believer and unbeliever may agree."[317]
- Paula Fredriksen: "I know in their own terms what they saw was the raised Jesus. That's what they say, and then all the historic evidence we have afterwards attests to their conviction that that's what they saw. I'm not saying that they really did see the raised Jesus. I wasn't there. I don't know what they saw. But I do know as a historian that they must have seen something."[318]
- Traugott Holtz says the disciples' "experiences of resurrection . . . is in fact an undeniable historical event."[319]
- Ed Kessler: "his followers continue to experience Jesus after his death. According to Luke, he first appeared to Mary . . ."[320]

---

309. Krauss and Craig, "Life, the Universe, and Nothing."
310. Craig, *The Son Rises*, 108.
311. Allison, *Resurrecting Jesus*, 283.
312. Casey quoted in Veale, *New Atheism*, 81.
313. Bird and Crossley, *How Did Christianity Begin?*, 52.
314. Dodd, *The Founder of Christianity*, 176.
315. Ehrman, "Bart D. Ehrman Interview."
316. Flusser, *The Sage from Galilee*, 16.
317. Fuller, *The Foundations of New Testament Christology*, 142.
318. Fredriksen quoted in *The Search for Jesus* with Peter Jennings (2000).
319. Holtz quoted in Habermas, "The Case for Christ's Resurrection," 191.
320. Kessler, *Jesus*, 37.

- Helmut Koester: "with respect to the appearances of the risen Jesus . . . That Jesus also appeared to others (Peter, Mary Magdalene, James) cannot very well be questioned."[321]

- Gerd Lüdemann: "It may be taken as historically certain that Peter and the disciples had experiences after Jesus's death in which Jesus appeared to them as the risen Christ."[322]

- Hugh Montefiore: "The disciples were clearly convinced of the reality of the risen Jesus whom they saw and with whom they conversed."[323]

- Lindija Novakovic: "There is little doubt that the followers of Jesus were convinced that they saw Jesus alive. Moreover, they were convinced that what they saw was some form of embodied life and that the one who appeared to them was the same person who had been crucified a short time ago."[324]

- Norman Perrin: "The more we study the tradition with regard to the appearances, the firmer the rock begins to appear upon which they are based."[325]

- E.P. Sanders: "That Jesus' followers (and later Paul) had resurrection experiences is, in my judgment a fact. What the reality was that gave rise to the experiences I do not know."[326]

- Geza Vermes: "No doubt the New Testament characters believed in the reality of their visions of Jesus."[327]

- David Mishkin: "There may be a variety of suggestions about why the disciples believed they encountered [a resurrected] Jesus, for example, but whether or not they themselves believed this is virtually beyond dispute."[328]

- A.J.M. Wedderburn: "It is an indisputable historical datum that sometime, somehow the disciples came to believe that they had seen the risen Jesus."[329]

As Jonathan Kendall writes:

> That numerous individuals, including Jesus' closest disciples, had experiences subsequent to the crucifixion that led them to conclude that Jesus had been resurrected from the dead is a fact accepted by essentially all New Testament

---

321. Koester quoted in Godfrey, "What do Biblical scholars make of the Resurrection?"
322. Lüdemann, *What Really Happened?*, 80.
323. Montefiore, *The Womb And The Tomb*, 126.
324. Novakovic, "Jesus' Resurrection and Historiography," 923.
325. Perrin quoted in Godfrey, "What do Biblical scholars make of the Resurrection?"
326. Sanders, *The Historical Figure of Jesus*, 280.
327. Vermes, *Jesus the Jew*, 149.
328. Mishkin, *Jewish Scholarship on the Resurrection of Jesus*, 203.
329. Wedderburn, *Beyond Resurrection*, 13.

scholars, even those that are most skeptical of Christianity and of the resurrection itself.[330]

Note that, alongside the *general* fact that there were multiple apparent resurrection appearances of Jesus (involving a variety of people in a variety of individual and group settings), adherence to the criteria of historicity should lead us to acknowledge certain *specific* appearance experiences, including group appearances (see Figures 20 and 21).

The conclusion acknowledging apparent postmortem experiences of Jesus is warranted by at least ten criteria of authenticity:

- Eyewitness sources
- Early sources
- Independent sources
- Multiple sources
- Multiple forms
- Embarrassing sources
- Enemy sources
- Historical Verisimilitude
- Memorability
- Historical coherence

Watch: "The Resurrection Appearances of Jesus" Youtube playlist: www.youtube.com/playlist?list=PLQhh3qcwVEWgUZZO-MUpLJhm7ZmscmAk6

Read: "The Resurrection Appearances of Jesus" by Gary R. Habermas: www.4truth.net/fourtruthpbjesus.aspx?pageid=8589952867

Fig. 22. Five historical criteria that eight resurrection appearance reports pass in addition to being early and historically-coherent reports of memorable events

Witnesses	Reported	Eyewitness testimony	Multiple Literarily Independent sources	Multiple forms	Embarrassment	Verisimilitude
Mary Magdalene	John 20:11-18 (see Mark 16:9)				X	X

---

330. Kendall, "Hallucinations and the Risen Jesus," 307.

Witness	Reference						
At least four other women, (Joanna, Salome & Mary the mother of James)	Matthew 28:1-10; Luke 24:8-11					X	X
Cleopas and Mary	Luke 24:13-32 (see Mark 16:12)					X	X
Peter	1 Corinthians 15:5; Luke 24:34		X	X			X
Ten disciples (and others)	John 20:19-23; Luke 24:36-49 (see Mark 16:14)	X	X				
Eleven disciples including Thomas	John 20:24-30; see 1 Corinthians 15:5	X			X		
Seven disciples	John 21:1-25: see Mark 16:7	X					
Saul (& others)	1 Corinthians 15:8 & Acts 9:1-19	X	X	X			

Fact 5: The first Christian's ground-breaking belief in the resurrected Jesus

The first Christians were Jews who sincerely believed that the crucified Jesus had been resurrected from the dead. Each and every first century individual who claims to share this belief gives *independent* testimony to the existence of this belief. There is therefore a large amount of independent evidence for our fifth fact, spread across multiple early sources and presented in multiple literary forms (see: Mark 16:4; Acts 2:32, 4:2, and 4:33; Romans 1:4; 1 Corinthians 15:4; 1 Corinthians 15:21; Philippians 3:10).

C.H. Dodd observes that belief in Jesus' resurrection "is not a belief that grew up within the church; it is the belief around which the church itself grew up, and the 'given' upon which its faith was based. So much the historian may affirm."[331] As Stephen T. Davis comments:

> the earliest Christians unanimously and passionately believed that Jesus was alive. This belief sustained the Jesus movement and allowed it to survive and thrive (unlike, say, that of John the Baptist or even Bar-Kochba a century

---

331. Dodd, *The Founder of Christianity*, 169.

later). The conviction allowed Christians to overcome both the discouragement of their leader's death and their later persecution.[332]

Robert J. Hutchinson reports that "many secular, agnostic, and atheist scholars now accept that something extraordinary happened to Jesus' earliest followers—something that led them to believe Jesus had come back to life after death."[333] After all, we have *multiple early* examples of *independent first-hand* testimony, as well as *enemy attestation* (e.g. Celsus, c. AD 178), to the *publically falsifiable* existence of this *culturally embarrassing* and highly *memorable* (counter-cultural) belief, which is presented in *multiple literary forms*:

- Reza Aslan: "the followers of Jesus believed in his resurrection . . . belief in the resurrection seems to have been part of the earliest liturgical formula of the nascent Christian community."[334]
- Rudolph Bultmann: "historical criticism can establish . . . the fact that the first disciples came to believe in the resurrection."[335]
- James H. Charlesworth: "the historian knows that belief in Jesus' resurrection by God appeared around 30 C.E. in both Galilee and Jerusalem."[336]
- Stephen T. Davis: "the earliest Christians truly *believed* that God had raised Jesus."[337]
- James D.G. Dunn: "The first Christians, of course, were convinced that Jesus had been raised from the dead."[338]
- Bart Ehrman: "It is a historical fact that some of Jesus' followers came to believe that he had been raised from the dead soon after his execution."[339]
- Robert Funk: "The conviction that Jesus had risen from the dead had already taken root by the time Paul was converted . . ."[340]
- Jean-Pierre Isbouts: "The Apostles certainly believed that Jesus had risen, and they chose martyrdom rather than recant that belief."[341]
- Matthew Kneale: "Jesus' resurrection became central to Christianity so quickly that it makes little sense as a mere invention. Why lie?"[342]

---

332. Davis, *Christian Philosophical Theology*, 94.
333. Hutchinson, *Searching for Jesus*, 250.
334. Aslan, *Zealot*, 175.
335. Bultmann, *Kerygma and Myth*, 42.
336. Charlesworth, *The Historical Jesus*, 113.
337. Davis, *Rational Faith*, 63.
338. Dunn, *Why Believe in Jesus' Resurrection?*, 30.
339. Ehrman, *The New Testament*, 276.
340. Funk quoted in Hoover and the Jesus Seminar, *The Acts of Jesus*, 466.
341. Isbouts, *National Geographic: The Story of Jesus*, 96.
342. Kneale, *An Atheist's History of Belief*, 103.

The conclusion acknowledging early belief in the resurrection of Jesus is warranted by at least ten criteria of authenticity:

- Eyewitness sources
- Early sources
- Independent sources
- Multiple sources
- Multiple forms
- Enemy sources
- Public falsifiability
- Embarrassing sources
- Memorability
- Historical coherence

Against the grain

The evidence shows that belief in the death and the resurrection of Jesus went against the grain of the disciples' expectations. According to Hutchinson: "belief in a suffering and even dying messiah . . . was part and parcel of the tapestry of messianic expectations that existed in the time of Jesus . . . *some* Jews in Jesus' time did very much expect a suffering messiah, perhaps even one who would die."[343] However, Jesus' disciples didn't share such expectations (see: Mark 8:31–33 and 9:31–32; John 20:9). Instead, they held to the *general* expectation of the day, centered upon a messianic king who would triumph over the occupying Romans (see: John 12:12–16; John 18:10; Acts 1:6). As Hutchinson concedes: "perhaps most [Jews] thought the messiah would be a military hero who would rescue the Jewish people from their oppressors."[344]

Some Jews (i.e. the Sadducees who ran the temple) didn't believe in resurrection at all. The majority who did accept the concept of resurrection thought in terms of a mass resurrection at the final judgement. According to Timothy Keller:

> The idea of an individual being resurrected, in the middle of history, while the rest of the world continued on burdened by sickness, decay and death, was inconceivable. If someone had said to any first-century Jew, "So-and-so has been resurrected from the dead!" the response would be, "Are you crazy? How could that be? Has disease and death ended? Is true justice established in the world? Has the wolf lain down with the lamb? Ridiculous!" The very idea of

---

343. Hutchinson, *Searching For Jesus*, 119–20.
344. Hutchinson, *Searching For Jesus*, 268.

an individual resurrection would have been as impossible to imagine to a Jew as to a Greek.³⁴⁵

The disciples' culture militated *against* any thought that Jesus might rise from the dead before the end of the age:

- Darrell L. Bock: "The Jews believed in a general bodily resurrection at the end of time . . . before the judgment (Isa. 66; Dan 12:1–2; 2 Macc. 7) but did not have an expectation of an earlier, immediate, special resurrection for anyone."³⁴⁶
- Joachim Jeremias: "Ancient Judaism did not know of an anticipated resurrection as an event of history."³⁴⁷
- Gerald O'Collins: "Within the context of late Jewish apocalyptic thought, to claim the resurrection of a single individual before the end of the world was to introduce a quite new element."³⁴⁸
- Rowan Williams: "The Easter event . . . comes to his followers as a surprise . . ."³⁴⁹
- Ulrich Wilkins: "nowhere do the Jewish texts speak of the resurrection of an individual which already occurs before the resurrection of the righteous dead at the end of time and is differentiated and separate from it . . ."³⁵⁰

The disciples' expectations were clearly congruent with their cultural background. As William Lane Craig writes: "The disciples had no idea of the resurrection of an isolated individual, especially of the Messiah."³⁵¹ Stephen T. Davis concludes that "the resurrection accounts in the New Testament make it quite clear that Jesus' disciples were not expecting him to be raised."³⁵²

Jesus, John and the cloak of Elijah

Some critics assert that Herod's reaction to Jesus' miracles (reported by the synoptic gospels) is at odds with the claim that the concept of an isolated resurrection (in the strongest sense of the term) was unknown in ancient Judaism:

> Jesus' name had become known. Some said, "John the baptizer has been raised from the dead; that is why these powers are at work in him." But others said, "It is Elijah." And others said, "It is a prophet, like one of the prophets of old."

---

345. Keller, *The Reason for God*, 205.
346. Bock, *Acts*, 125.
347. Jeremias, "Die alteste Schicht der Osterberlieferung," 194.
348. O'Collins, *Jesus' Resurrection and Apparitions*, 31.
349. Williams, *Meeting God in Mark*, 67.
350. Wilkins, "Auferstehung," 131.
351. Craig, *Reasonable Faith*, 393.
352. Davis, *Christian Philosophical Theology*, 116.

> But when Herod heard of it he said, "John, whom I beheaded, has been raised."
> (Mark 6:14–16)

However, Herod's comment is no more a counterexample to the claim that the concept of an isolated resurrection was unknown in ancient Judaism than is the story about Jesus reviving Lazarus. That said, Craig argues:

> Herod and the people were not talking about either John's revivification or resurrection. This is blindingly obvious from the fact that Jesus and John were *contemporaries*... Before John was arrested and beheaded, Jesus was alive and active. So people couldn't possibly have thought that Jesus was literally the beheaded corpse of John the Baptist brought back to life. Rather what's going on here, as the comment "that is why these powers are at work in him" reveals, is that people see that the mantle of John the Baptist has now fallen on Jesus. The same power that inspired John rests on Jesus, and Jesus continues what John began... In a Jewish context, one would say, as Herod did, that Jesus is John risen from the dead—not literally but figuratively.[353]

In the Old Testament story of the prophet Elijah (note that the historicity of this story is immaterial with respect to the argument here), before he "went up to heaven in a whirlwind" (2 Kings 2:11), he asks Elisha what he can do for him and Elisha replies: "Let me inherit a double portion of your spirit" (2 Kings 2:9). When he has gone, Elisha picks up Elijah's discarded cloak and figuratively inherits the prophet's capacity to work miracles (see: 2 Kings 2:14). When he causes the river Jordan to stop flowing,[354] a chorus of bystanding prophets declare: "The spirit of Elijah is resting on Elisha." (2 Kings 2:15) Michael Grant comments:

> More than eight hundred years later, John the Baptist believed himself to be the heir of these two prophets. Indeed, one reason why he chose the area of the Jordan as the scene of his ministry and used the waters of that river for his baptisms was because this was said to be the place where Elijah had ascended to heaven, and this was the stream in which Elisha had commanded the leper Naaman to wash and be miraculously cured... [Jesus] also seemed to his followers, like John the Baptist before him, to be the heir of the ancient Israelite prophets, especially Elijah and Elisha.[355]

---

353. Craig, "What was Herod thinking?" Luke's account of this incident includes the suggestion that "one of the prophets of old has risen [or 'arisen' - anestē]" (Luke 9:8, ESV), but the parallel with Mark 6:15 ("He is a prophet, like one of the prophets of long ago") suggests the thought is figurative. Alternatively, the phrase may envisage an apparition/objective vision of a dead prophet, or a miraculous revivification.

354. See: Humphreys, *The Miracles of Exodus,* chapter two.

355. Grant, *Jesus,* 79, 171.

Against this cultural background, Herod's comment about Jesus being "John, whom I beheaded . . . raised [i.e. ēgerthē—meaning 'to lift up or raise up'[356]]," is clearly consonant with the story of Elijah and Elisha, with the way in which it was prophesied that John would go before Jesus "in the spirit and power of Elijah" (Luke 1:17, see: Luke 7:27) and with Jesus' own description of John as "the Elijah who was to come" (Matthew 11:7–14, see: Malachi 3:1 and 4:5).

Read: "What was Herod Thinking?" by William Lane Craig: www.reasonablefaith.org/question-answer/P40/what-was-herod-thinking

"Was John the Baptist Really Elijah?" by Matt Slick: www.carm.org/bible-difficulties/matthew-mark/was-john-baptist-really-elijah

"A Hypernatural Miracle: Elijah and the Fire From Heaven" by Daniel J. Dyke and Dr. Hugh Henry: www.reasons.org/articles/a-hypernatural-miracle-elijah-and-the-fire-from-heaven

"The Cave of Prophet Elijah Under Threat?" by Henry Curtis Pelgrift: www.biblicalarchaeology.org/daily/biblical-sites-places/biblical-archaeology-places/the-cave-of-elijah-the-prophet-under-threat/

"Have Archaeologists Found Elisha's House?" by Chris Mitchell and Julie Stahl: www.cbn.com/cbnnews/insideisrael/2013/july/have-archaeologists-found-prophet-elishas-house/?mobile=false

"Did Herod think Jesus was John the Baptist" by B.J.E. Van Noort: www.contradicting-biblecontradictions.com/?p=1602#.XDg4hOD4P7s

---

Messianic expectations

The obscure "Gabriel's Revelation" tablet has been thought by some to evince Jewish belief in a dying and rising messiah dating from either the second half of the first century BC or the very early first century AD. In particular, line 80 of the text appears to read something like "In three days, live, I Gabriel command you" or "On the third day: the sign! I am Gabriel, the king of kings," or some combination thereof. Unfortunately, the inked text is faint and the word that could be the Hebrew *hayeh* ("live") is smudged and could easily be a very similar Hebrew word meaning "sign." Hutchinson reports that "Israel Knohl, a leading Israeli Bible scholar at Hebrew University in Jerusalem who originally translated the text as 'live,' recently changed his mind and now says the word reads 'sign.'"[357] The idea of a sign of God coming on the "third day" has precedence in the Jewish Scriptures (see: Exodus 19; 2 Kings 20:8; Ezra 6:15; Ezekiel 31:1; Hosea 6:2) and does not in itself suggest a resurrection. Hence the Gabriel inscription is a thin thread upon which to hang any theory about Jewish messianic expectation in the thirties of the first century.

---

356. See: Bible Hub Commentaries, "egeiró."
357. Hutchinson, *Searching For Jesus*, 118.

That the Gabriel tablet is messianic "seems fairly clear, but what it is saying about the Messiah is garbled and very unclear. For this reason, any conclusion about its meaning—never mind its significance—should be correspondingly quite tentative."[358] As Ben Witherington III comments: "the text is hard to read at crucial junctures, and it is not absolutely clear it is talking about a risen messiah."[359] Even if it is talking about a risen messiah, it's not clear that it predates Christianity. Tom Gilson assesses the significance of the "Gabriel Revelation":

> Does it undermine what we know of Christianity? Hardly. The followers of Christ—even those closest to him—are depicted as being completely caught off guard, first by Jesus' predictions of his death, and then by the actual event. Their expectations were hardly molded by this stone or any related beliefs.[360]

Josephus reports half a dozen rebels against Rome with messianic aspirations. No one suggested that any of *them* were resurrected after their deaths. Rather, the death of the messiah figure in question was taken as disproof of their messianic pretensions. As Graham Veale comments:

> We know of "messianic" types who tried to found movements in this period. Theudas claimed that he would part the waters of the Jordan; an Egyptian who said that he would cause the walls of Jerusalem to come tumbling down. Would-be kings like the shepherd Athronges or John of Gischala. In each case Rome executed the leader; in each case the movement died. So the question arises: "what was different about Jesus' movement?" The simplest answer is the answer provided by Paul (in 1 Corinthians) and the Gospel writers. Jesus' followers, on the basis of eyewitness reports, believed that their leader had returned from the dead.[361]

If Jesus' contemporaries made anything of his predictions about the Son of Man (i.e. himself) "rising" (and note that while Jesus uses cognates of *ēgerthē* in Mark 14:28 and Matthew 26:32, his predictions in Mark 8:31, 9:9 and 10:34, as well as Luke 18:33, 24:7, and 24:46, use words such as *anastēsetai* and *anastēnai* that literally mean to "stand up again"—the semantic range of both terms co-inside with that of the English term "resurrection"[362]), they wouldn't have understood his comments in a Christian manner. Instead, they'd have thought in terms of a) the resurrection of the righteous dead *at the last judgement* (see: Mark 12:25 and John 11:24[363]), b) resurrection in the sense of *resuscitation* to earthly life (as with Jesus resuscitating Lazarus (see: John 11:23)—though they probably assumed a dead man couldn't resuscitate *himself*), or c)

358. Oakes, "What is the significance of the Gabriel Stone?"
359. Witherington, "The Death and Resurrection of Messiah—written in stone."
360. Gilson, "Gabriel Revelation (Stone Tablet)."
361. Veale, *New Atheism*, 80.
362. See: Bible Hub Commentaries, "Mark 12:25" and "John 11:24."
363. See: Bible Hub Commentaries, "Mark 12:25" and "John 11:24."

the story of Elijah "rising up" and being "assumed" into the heavenly presence of God (see: 2 Kings 2:1–12).

The dominance of these cultural assumptions is seen in the Jewish Sanhedrin's reason for having Jesus' tomb guarded, namely: "lest his disciples go and steal him away and tell the people, 'He has risen from the dead'" (Matthew 27:64, ESV). The Greek translated as "risen from the dead" here isn't *anastēsetai* (resurrected) but *ēgerthē* (the same term Herod uses when he says Jesus is "John, whom I beheaded . . . raised [*ēgerthē*]"). Interestingly, the Jewish polemic *Toledot Yeshu* inaccurately claims that: "On the first day of the week [Jesus'] bold followers came to Queen Helene with the report that he who was slain was truly the Messiah and that he was not in his grave; *he had ascended to heaven as he prophesied*."[364] Hence, as J.P. Holding surmises, the Sanhedrin's concern was most likely "that the disciples would steal the body and claim it had ascended to heaven."[365]

It was against this Jewish background, in the very city just outside of which he'd recently been publically executed and entombed, that Jesus' dispirited Jewish disciples suddenly risked their lives to proclaim *Jesus' resurrection within history* as the fulcrum at the heart of God's relationship with humanity!

Jesus may have predicted that he would die and be resurrected soon thereafter, but his disciples were too enthralled by their cultural expectations to understand him. And yet, despite Jesus' ignominious public execution, and despite the persecution that would obviously ensue, the disciples (along with James and Saul) swiftly embraced belief in Jesus' *resurrection* and reoriented their religious identity accordingly.

CONCLUSION

"there are a number of essential events in the Gospels that historians across the spectrums of faith and personal philosophy accept as real events, based on the criteria used in studying ancient texts."

—Carl E. Olson[366]

Lawrence Krauss asserts that "there's no evidence"[367] for the resurrection. He is mistaken. In point of fact, there's plenty of evidence. After Jesus was dead and buried, his tomb was found empty. Soon thereafter we find sincere testimony concerning multiple, unexpected appearances (to individuals and groups of people, including women and skeptics) of a living (albeit transformed) Jesus. Quite apart from the appearance

---

364. Emphasis added. See: Wallace, "Is there any evidence for Jesus outside the Bible?"
365. Holding, "Hallucinations and Expectations," 369.
366. Olson, *Did Jesus Really Rise From The Dead?*, 29.
367. Krauss and Craig, "Life, the Universe, and Nothing."

reports, it's clear that soon after Jesus' shameful death, numerous people (including some skeptics) were sincerely convinced, against their expectations, not merely that Jesus was *alive* again, but that he'd been *resurrected*.

What explains the New Atheist's ironic failure to recognize or engage with this evidence? Many neo-atheists exhibit "the tendency . . . to work with the *assumption* that miracles cannot occur, with little or no discussion of individual cases."[368] As Lennox says: "the New Atheists are not always as scientific as they profess to be, particularly when it comes to following evidence where it leads—especially when that evidence threatens their materialistic or naturalistic presuppositions."[369]

Many neo-atheists hold that miracles cannot happen, or at least cannot be believed to have happened, often due to a blind faith that Hume said the last word on miracles. David H. Glass summarizes the proper reaction to this appeal to authority:

> There are no quick and easy ways to reject the resurrection of Jesus. The sceptic needs to step up from his armchair to investigate the evidence and not simply presuppose that atheism is true.[370]

Some neo-atheists seem to believe their own narrative about religious faith necessarily being a matter of blind trust, and from this false premise they appear to invalidly *deduce* the false conclusion that "there's no evidence"[371] for the resurrection. Finally, some neo-atheists mistakenly think that if they argue against the *general* historical reliability of the NT they can avoid dealing with *specific* historical claims about Jesus, such as those summarized in Fig. 23.

Fig. 23. Five historical facts supported by multiple historical criteria.

	Jesus' Death by Crucifixion	Jesus' Burial	Jesus' Empty Tomb	Putative Resurrection Appearances	Disciples' Resurrection Belief
Eyewitness sources	X		X	X	X
Early sources	X	X	X	X	X
Independent sources	X	X	X	X	X
Multiple sources	X	X	X	X	X
Multiple forms	X	X		X	X

368. Sweetman, *Religion*, 62.
369. Lennox, *Gunning for God*, 30.
370. Glass, "Four Poor Reasons to Reject the Resurrection."
371. Krauss and Craig, "Life, the Universe, and Nothing."

Enemy sources	X	X	X	X	X
Embarrassing sources	X	X	X	X	X
Public falsifiability	X	X	X		X
Historical verisimilitude	X	X	X	X	
Unintentional signs of history	X		X		
Memorability	X	X	X	X	X
Historical coherence	X	X	X	X	X

CHAPTER 5

Getting at the Best Explanation

"In the preceding phase contextual information was considered to evaluate the data's evidentiary value, but in this second phase the primary function is to explore alternative hypotheses."

—Robert L. Webb[1]

A CONNECTED SERIES OF miracle claims constitutes a cumulative case for divine intervention. First, "if there are several miracles supported by independent evidence, the probability of the disjunction of the miracle reports—that is the claim that at least one of the miracles occurred—may be high even if the probability of each miracle, considered in itself is very low."[2] In other words, "if we find reports of a series of miracles, there may be a significant probability that at least one happened."[3] Second, "the miracles in the series set a context for each other."[4] Evidence for miracles earlier in a connected series of miracle claims raises the probability of miracles later in that series. Hence "the occurrence of miracles in series can have dramatic effects on the credibility of miracle reports."[5]

Jesus' resurrection is the crowning miracle claim in a series of connected miracle claims stretching back through Jesus' ministry and into Jewish history. Hence, in the course of assessing the evidence for the resurrection, one might profitably examine the miracle claims made within what Christians call the Old Testament,[6] including

---

1. Webb, "The Historical Enterprise and Historical Jesus Research," 35.
2. Bonevac, "The Argument from Miracles," 33.
3. Bonevac, "The Argument from Miracles," 33.
4. Bonevac, "The Argument from Miracles," 33.
5. Bonevac, "The Argument from Miracles," 34.
6. See: "The Exodus;" Williams, "Old Testament Archaeology;" Williams, "Old Testament Miracles;" Dyke and Henry, "A Hypernatural Miracle: Elijah and the Fire from Heaven;" "Parting the waters;" Ehrenkranz and Sampson, "Origin of the Old Testament Plagues;" Hoffmier, *Ancient Israel in*

the intricate web of Old Testament prophecies and their historical fulfilments, most especially prophecies about the Messiah, which have been fulfilled by Jesus.

Watch: "Biblical Prophecy" Youtube playlist: www.youtube.com/playlist?list=PLQhh3qcwVEWgq_Hba52LXvmcUHR4T010a

Listen: "Arguments For and From Fulfilled Biblical Prophecy" by Peter S. Williams: http://podcast.peterswilliams.com/e/arguments-for-and-from-fulfilled-biblical-prophecy-1467022784/

"Archaeological Evidence for Biblical History and Fulfilled Prophecy" by Peter S. Williams: http://peterswilliams.podbean.com/mf/feed/vfaihr/history_archaeology_prophecy.mp3

Read: "Is Fulfilled Prophecy of Value for Scholarly Apologetics?" by John A. Bloom: www.bethinking.org/is-christianity-true/is-fulfilled-prophecy-of-value-for-scholarly-apologetics

"Ezekiel 26:1–14: A Proof Text For Inerrancy or Fallibility of The Old Testament?" by Paul Ferguson: www.biblearchaeology.org/post/2009/12/07/Ezekiel-261-14-A-Proof-Text-For-Inerrancy-or-Fallibility-of-The-Old-Testament.aspx

"Miraculous Bible Prophecy Fulfilments" Norman L. Geisler: https://philosophical11.wordpress.com/2012/09/12/miraculous-bible-prophecy-fulfillments/#more-151

Answering Jewish Objections to Jesus, Volume Three: Messianic Prophecy Objections by Michael L. Brown

Against the Flow: The Inspiration of Daniel in an Age of Relativism by John C. Lennox

"Fulfilled Prophecy as Miracle" by Robert C. Newman in *In Defence of Miracles* edited by Douglas R. Geivett and Gary R. Habermas

The Evidence of Prophecy: Fulfilled Prediction as a Testimony to the Truth of Christianity edited by Robert C. Newman

Understanding Jesus: Five Ways to Spiritual Enlightenment by Peter S. Williams

There's good evidence for a series of miracles performed by Jesus, and "if Jesus really performed the miracles the Gospels say he did, then both the existence and the character of these miracles add substantial confirmation to Jesus' claim to be the Messiah and one with the Creator and Redeemer God."[7]

As Bruce Chilton and Craig A. Evans insist: "Any fair reading of the Gospels and other ancient sources (including Josephus) inexorably leads to the conclusion that Jesus was well known in his time as a healer and exorcist."[8] Indeed: "The miracle stories are now treated seriously and are widely accepted by Jesus scholars as deriving from Jesus' ministry. Several specialized studies have appeared in recent years, which conclude that Jesus did things that were viewed as 'miracles.'"[9]

Sinai; Hoffmier, *Israel in Egypt*; Hoffmier et al., *"Did I Not Israel Out Bring of Egypt?;"* Humphreys, *The Miracles of Exodus*; Kitchen, *On the Reliability of the Old Testament*; Provan et al., *A Biblical History of Israel*.

7. Taylor, *Introducing Apologetics*, 194–96.
8. Chilton and Evans, *Authenticating the Activities of Jesus*, 11–12.
9. Chilton and Evans, *Authenticating the Activities of Jesus*, 11–12.

Atheist NT scholar Maurice Casey concludes: "Jesus was by far the most successful exorcist and healer of his time. That judgement is based on a massive amount of evidence in our oldest primary sources, critically assessed within the criterion of historical plausibility."[10] Marcus Borg of the Jesus Seminar affirms that "on historical grounds it is virtually indisputable that Jesus was a healer and exorcist."[11] Mark L. Strauss argues that:

> If miracles are not ruled out in advance, the accounts of Jesus' miracles fare well under critical scrutiny. They are widely attested to in a range of Gospel sources and forms, and they cohere well with the almost certainly authentic preaching of Jesus about the kingdom.[12]

Likewise, historian Paul Barnett observes that:

> the *sheer number and variety* of Jesus' miracles are extraordinary. Mark reports no fewer than *eighteen* miracles, the majority of which are reproduced in Matthew and Luke. Found only in the source common to Matthew and Luke (Q) are *two* miracles, Matthew's special source (M) has *three*, Luke's special source (L) has *seven* and John has *six*. In other words, five independent sources report about forty miracles of Jesus.[13]

In terms of different *categories* of miracle, "there are many examples of multiple attestations to exorcisms, nature miracles, healings and the raising of the dead spread across the primary Gospel sources Mark, John [QS], Q, L and M . . ."[14] This plethora of testimony—which includes multiple eyewitnesses reports and reports based upon eyewitness evidence—follows extremely close upon the events reported. As Paula Fredriksen writes:

> Jesus as exorcist, healer (even to the point of raising the dead), and miracle worker is one of the strongest, most ubiquitous, and most variously attested depictions in the Gospels. All strata of this material—Mark, John, M-traditions, L-traditions, and Q—make this claim.[15]

Figure 24 lists eighteen specific miracles of Jesus that are reported by more than one canonical gospel (note that the first four miracles here all pass the criteria of multiple early, literarily independent sources, including at least one eyewitness):

---

10. Casey, *Jesus*, 68.
11. Borg, *Jesus*.
12. Strauss, *Introducing Jesus*, 128.
13. Barnett, *Messiah*, 86–87.
14. Barnett, *Messiah*, 90.
15. Fredriksen, *Jesus of Nazareth*, 114.

Fig. 24.

Miracle:	Type:	Mark:	Matt:	Luke:	John:
In all four gospels					
1. Feeding 5,000 people	Nature	6:35f	14:15f	9:12f	6:5f
In three gospels including John					
2. Walking on water	Nature	6:48f	14:25f		6:19f
3. Peter's mother-in-law	Healing	1:30f	8:14f		4:38f
4. Roman centurion's servant	Healing (at a distance)		8:5f	7:1f	4:47f
In all three Synoptic Gospels					
5. Man with leprosy	Healing	1:40f	8:24f	5:12f	
6. Paralyzed man	Healing	2:3f	9:2f	5:18f	
7. Man with shriveled hand	Healing	3:1f	12:10f	6:6f	
8. Calming the storm	Nature	4:37f	8:23f	8:22f	
9. Gadarene demoniac(s)	Exorcism	5:1f	8:28f	8:27f	
10. Jairus's daughter	Resuscitation	5:22f	9:18f	8:41f	
11. Hemorrhaging woman	Healing	5:25f	9:20f	8:43f	
12. Demon-possessed boy	Exorcism	9:17f	17:14f	9:38f	
13. Two blind men	Healing	10:46f	20:29f	18:35f	
In two gospels (Mark and Matthew)					
14. Canaanite woman's daughter	Exorcism (at a distance)	7:24f	15:21f		
15. Feeding of 4,000	Nature	8:1f	15:32f		
16. Fig tree withered	Nature	11:12f	21:18f		
In two gospels (Mark and Luke)					
17. Possessed man in synagogue	Exorcism	1:23f		4:33f	
18. Blind, mute and possessed man	Exorcism		12:22	11:14	

Some of these reports pass the criteria of *embarrassment* in that they portray the disciples in an unflattering light (see: Mark 4:37–40, 6:49–50, and 9:17–27). The miracle reports of Mark 5:41 and 7:31–35 both pass the criterion of *Aramaic language*.

Outside the gospels, the apostle Peter appeals to a *publically falsifiable common knowledge* of Jesus' miracles in one of the speeches reported in Acts, speaking at the first Pentecost of "Jesus the Nazarene, a man attested to you by God with miracles and wonders and signs which God performed through Him in your midst, just as you yourselves know" (Acts 2:22).

The Athenian church leader Quadratus, writing c. AD 125, provides further *independent testimony* about Jesus' miraculous power:

> But the works of our Saviour were always present, for they were true, those who were cured, those who rose from the dead, who not merely appeared as cured and risen, but were constantly present, not only while the Saviour

was living, but even for some time after he had gone, so that some of them survived even to our own time.[16]

The claim that Jesus worked miracles passes the criterion of *enemy attestation*. As Alan Richardson observes: "It cannot be disputed upon historical grounds that all the people who came into contact with Jesus during his ministry in Galilee believed that He worked miracles, for even his enemies believed it."[17] James H. Charlesworth confirms that:

> the literary form of these accounts, along with the criteria of multiple attestation and polemical ambience, indicates that none of Jesus' contemporaries seems to have doubted that he was able to do and did perform healing miracles. His opponents did not deny that Jesus performed miracles; they judged that he did so because he was in league with Satan . . .[18]

Both "Mark and Q include the accusation of Jesus' opponents that he was able to exorcise demons *because he was in league with the devil* (Mark 3:20–30; Matthew 12:22–32). Not only is this doubly attested, but it is an unlikely fabrication."[19] As N.T. Wright argues: "the Church did not invent the charge that Jesus was in league with Beelzebub, but charges like that are not advanced unless they are needed as an explanation for some quite remarkable phenomenon."[20]

Several other hostile witnesses independently concede Jesus' miraculous powers. Using a phrase that he applied to the miracles of Elisha in the Old Testament, Josephus concedes in the first century that Jesus was "*a doer of startling deeds . . .*"[21] Writing c. AD 180 the pagan philosopher Celsus opined that Jesus learned magic in Egypt (an idea based on Jesus' time as a child refugee, see: Matthew 2:13–15) and that: "It was by magic that [Jesus] was able to do *the miracles which he appears to have done*."[22] Moreover, Celsus states that it was "on account of those powers" that Jesus "gave himself the title of God."[23] According to the Babylonian Talmud:

> On the eve of Passover they hanged Yeshu [i.e. Jesus]. And an announcer went out, in front of him, for forty days (saying): "He is going to be stoned [i.e. suffer capital punishment], because *he practiced sorcery* and enticed and led Israel astray. Anyone who knows anything in his favor, let him come and plead in

---

16. Quadratus quoted in Woolmer, *Healing and Deliverance*, 159.
17. Richardson, *Christian Apologetics*, 170.
18. Charlesworth, *The Historical Jesus*, 84.
19. Price, "The Miracles of Jesus: A Historical Inquiry."
20. Wright, *Jesus and the Victory of God*, 188.
21. Josephus, *Antiquities*, Book 18.
22. Celsus quoted in Origen, *Contra Celsum*, 1.6 (emphasis added).
23. Celsus quoted in Origen, *Contra Celsum*, 1.38.

his behalf." But, not having found anything in his favor, they hanged him on the eve of Passover.[24]

In the context of Jesus' teaching about the kingdom of God and his own role therein, evidence that he worked miracles is evidence that confirms the truth of his teaching. Indeed, as Michael Symonds Roberts observes, many of Jesus' miracles "were acts that first-century Jews expected only God to perform."[25]

Watch: "Did Jesus Perform Miracles?" Youtube playlist: www.youtube.com/playlist?list=PLQhh3qcwVEWi1yi_tcY-Ptl9nNJzRCeiN

Read: "Did Jesus Use Magic And Sorcery?" by Etian Bar: https://www.oneforisrael.org/bible-based-teaching-from-israel/did-jesus-use-magic-and-sorcery/

"Thinking About Magic: (1) Was Jesus a Magician?" by Kirtsy Birkett: https://au.thegospelcoalition.org/article/thinking-about-magic-1/

Jesus the Miracle Worker: A Historical and Theological Study by Graham Twelftree

Jesus The Healer: Paradigm Or Unique Phenomenon by Keith Warrington

---

Taking into account both the evidence for the occurrence of various specific miracles and the evidential relevance of having a connected series of miracle claims, we must surely agree with Steven B. Cowan that "the evidence for the veracity of at least some of the biblical miracles is quite strong."[26] In my estimation, this evidence—which the New Atheists overlook—justifies a receptive attitude towards the resurrection of Jesus as the evidential *pièce de résistance* of the Christian revelation claim.

INFERRING THE BEST EXPLANATION FROM MULTIPLE COMPETING HYPOTHESES

Each of the five historical facts established in the previous chapter is supported by a cumulative case that uses multiple standard criteria of historical authenticity. In a sense, we have a surfeit of evidence, inasmuch as to show that Jesus was miraculously alive again after his death it would be enough to establish that he died and that he was alive at some time thereafter. "Here's how I look at the evidence for the resurrection," says Gary R. Habermas: "First, did Jesus die on the cross? And second, did he appear later to people? If you can establish these two things, you've made your case, because dead people don't normally do that."[27] Of course, Habermas is here using "resurrection" as a synonym for miraculous resuscitation. Still, *a miraculous resuscitation can't be ignored*. Indeed, it may be a stepping-stone to the conclusion that we have a full-blown *resurrection* on our hands.

24. Babylonian Talmud, *Sanhedrin* 43a (emphasis added).
25. Roberts, *The Miracles of Jesus*, 97.
26. Cowan, "Discerning the Voice of God," 11.
27. Habermas quoted in Strobel, *The Case for Christ*, 248.

Getting at the Best Explanation

There are basically five competing categories of hypotheses proposed to explain our five historical facts (although there can be overlap between some of these categories):

1) The first hypothesis (the "myth theory") is that the reports of the resurrection are myths that weren't intended to be understood historically.

2) The second hypothesis holds that "Jesus didn't die on the cross" (perhaps because he wasn't put on the cross in the first place). A major variant on this hypothesis (known as "swoon theory") holds that the disciples were deceived into thinking Jesus had been resurrected when he appeared to them having survived crucifixion.

3) The third hypothesis is that the evidence for Jesus' resurrection is best explained by a conspiracy to deceive (e.g. the disciples stole the body and invented the story of his resurrection to deceive people, or Jesus had a secret twin brother who deceived the disciples into thinking Jesus had been raised, etc.).

4) The fourth hypothesis holds that the witnesses to Jesus' resurrection were sincerely deluded (e.g. they hallucinated the resurrection, or they misinterpreted objective supernatural visions of Jesus).

5) The final hypothesis (given by those closest to the events) is that Jesus was miraculously resurrected.

As Kreeft and Tacelli write: "All five possibilities are logically possible, and therefore must be fairly investigated."[28]

Our investigation of these explanatory possibilities and their various sub-theories will proceed according to the method of "multiple competing hypotheses" or "inference to the best explanation," wherein one "infers that hypothesis among a competing group which would, if true, provide the best explanation of some set of relevant data."[29]

The warrant of a historical explanation depends on several factors, including its *simplicity*, *explanatory scope* (whether it encompasses the relevant facts), *explanatory power* (whether it raises the probability of the facts to be explained), *explanatory plausibility* (how far our background knowledge implies the hypothesis), degree of *explanatory ad hoc-ness* (the fewer contrived, un-evidenced hypotheses, the better) and degree of *explanatory disconfirmation* (i.e. conflict with our background knowledge).[30]

The resurrection hypothesis offers a relatively simple[31] explanation of the relevant historical evidence that combines excellent explanatory scope (i.e. *if* the resurrection

---

28. Kreeft and Tacelli, *Handbook of Christian Apologetics*, 182.
29. Meyer, "The Return of the God Hypothesis."
30. See: Craig, "The Doctrine of Christ (Part 18);" Meyer, "The Return of the God Hypothesis;" McCullagh, *Justifying Historical Descriptions*, 19.
31. See: Richards, "Divine Simplicity."

happened, it would explain "why the tomb was found empty, why the disciples saw post-mortem appearances of Jesus, and why the Christian faith came into being"[32]) and excellent explanatory power (i.e. *if* God chose to resurrect Jesus from the dead, *then* the empty tomb, postmortem appearances of Jesus and the origin of belief in Jesus' resurrection all become highly probable) with a fair degree of plausibility (especially in light of Jesus' purported miracles, etc.) and low degrees of ad hoc-ness and evidential disconfirmation (especially if one already accepts theism).

Indeed, the failure of arguments against the possibility of miracles (including the failure of arguments against theism) means that the resurrection hypothesis isn't contradicted by any of our background knowledge. As Craig comments: "I can't think of any accepted beliefs that disconfirm the resurrection hypothesis—unless one thinks of, say, 'Dead men do not rise' as disconfirmatory. But this generalization based on what naturally happens when people die does nothing to disconfirm the hypothesis that *God* raised Jesus from the dead."[33]

Although the resurrection hypothesis posits an explanation that's miraculous—and therefore unlikely *a priori* (being inherently unusual)—I've already indicated why I think the hypothesis gains plausibility from our background knowledge of the case for theism, Jesus' claims in the context of his character, his reported miracles and his fulfillment of prophecy. As Craig observes: "The plausibility of Jesus' resurrection grows exponentially once we consider it in its historical context, namely, Jesus' unparalleled life and radical personal claims, and in its philosophical context, namely, the evidence for God's existence."[34]

Clearly, the degree to which one finds the resurrection hypothesis *ad hoc* and/or *disconfirmed* by what one counts as background knowledge ultimately depends upon the worldview expectations one brings to considering the arguments for the resurrection (and its implications as one understands them), most especially the degree to which one thinks our background knowledge supports a) belief in a deity who b) might choose to raise Jesus from the dead, so that "given the historical context of Jesus' own unparalleled life and claims, the resurrection serves as divine confirmation of those radical claims."[35]

The question isn't whether the resurrection hypothesis *can* explain the relevant evidences, but whether any other hypothesis does *a better job*. The New Atheists don't tout all of the explanations that seek to outperform the resurrection hypothesis. This is to their credit, because some of the alternative explanations are pretty "far out"! Nevertheless, for the sake of a comprehensive investigation, we will consider the full range of explanations sketched out above.

32. Craig, "The Resurrection of Jesus."
33. Craig, *On Guard*, 261.
34. Craig, *On Guard*, 259.
35. Craig, "The Resurrection of Jesus."

Alternative 1: Myth

The thesis promoted by several neo-atheists, that Christianity is the mythological outcome of a Jewish messianic movement submerged by pagan religious ideas, is flatly contradicted by the historical testimony of those first-century Jews who came to believe that Jesus was resurrected within days of his crucifixion. Contrary to the myth hypothesis, the evidence shows that those who first changed their minds about Jesus being just another dead and buried pretender to the title of "messiah" (see: Luke 24:21) did so with shocking rapidity *within a thoroughly Jewish milieu*. Hence, as Carl Braaten reports:

> Even the more sceptical historians agree that for primitive Christianity . . . the resurrection of Jesus from the dead was a real event in history, the very foundation of faith, and not a mythical idea arising out of the creative imagination of believers.[36]

By their own testimony, the first Christians didn't come to believe that Jesus had been resurrected after a process of reflection upon pagan religious thought. Nor was the disciples' belief in the resurrection of Jesus analogous to Greek belief in the myth of, say, Persephone in the underworld. According to 2 Peter 1:16: "we did not follow cleverly devised stories when we told you about the coming of our Lord Jesus Christ in power, but we were eyewitnesses of his majesty." Regardless of debates about authorship, this canonical text is representative of the repeated NT emphasis upon the *historical* nature of the Christian revelation claim (see: Luke 1:1–4). Paul criticizes those who "turn their ears away from the truth and turn aside to myths" (2 Timothy 4:4). John testifies that it was that "which we have heard, which we have seen with our eyes, which we have looked at and our hands have touched" that the disciples proclaimed concerning Jesus (1 John 1:1).

Quite apart from the fact that it would have been uncharacteristic for Jews to permit their beliefs to be reshaped by pagan mythology, even if they had gone down that road it would have steered them *away* from belief in the bodily resurrection of Jesus (or anyone else):

> Gentile culture wasn't happy with the idea of bodily resurrection. Greek philosophy tended to think that the body was an impediment to spiritual development. Jews, however, believed that the body was good because it belonged to God, and they looked forward to the resurrection of their bodies on judgement day. But the legendary development hypothesis asks us to believe that Jewish Christians first believed that Jesus only spiritually survived the cross; then Greek and Gentile Christians hijacked this idea to promote a physical resurrection. This is wildly implausible.[37]

---

36. Braaten, *History and Hermeneutics*, 78.
37. Veale, *New Atheism*, 81–82.

To dismiss the resurrection of Jesus as a myth is to ride roughshod over the evidence demonstrating belief on the part of the first Christians that, despite Jesus' ignominious crucifixion, he had been resurrected from the dead; and that's not even to mention the evidence that Jesus' corpse went missing from his tomb just before multiple eyewitnesses (including enemies) sincerely believed they actually met with a resurrected Jesus in person.

The earliest Christians were Jews who believed Jesus had been resurrected in space-time history, not "once upon a time" in some mythological never-never land.

Alternative 2: Jesus didn't die

2i) Substitution Theory—Jesus wasn't crucified (that was someone else)

According to the Qur'an (4:157–158):

> That they said (in boast), "We killed Christ Jesus the son of Mary, the Messenger of Allah"—But they killed him not, nor crucified him, but so it was made to appear to them, and those who differ therein are full of doubts, with no (certain) knowledge, but only conjecture to follow, for of a surety they killed him not—Nay, Allah raised him up unto Himself . . .[38]

At least, this is what the standardized Qur'anic text we have today says. As Keith E. Small explains:

> what has been preserved and transmitted for the Qur'an is a text-form that was chosen from amidst a group of others, which was then edited and canonized at the expense of these others, and has been improved upon in order to make it conform to a desired ideal . . . what cannot be determined are the Autographic text-forms of what the earliest Muslims considered to be the full corpus of revelations given through Muhammad and left at his death or the Authoritative text-forms of his Companions. Instead, a strongly edited version of one corpus has been preserved and transmitted, made between twenty and one hundred years after Muhammad's death.[39]

Still, as David Marshall comments:

> According to mainstream Muslim interpretation the Qur'an states that Jesus did not die on the Cross . . . in context this is not a piece of anti-Christian polemic, even if it has subsequently been used as such; the Qur'an is here primarily concerned to reject the claim of the unbelieving Jews that they had been able to triumph over God's messenger.[40]

---

38. Quoted in Licona, *Paul Meets Muhammad*, 41.
39. Small, *Textual Criticism and the Qur'an Manuscripts*, 184–85.
40. Marshall, "The Resurrection of Jesus in the Qur'an," 171.

Of course, one can argue that Jesus' (prophesied) passion is of a piece with the suffering and persecution of prophets recorded throughout the Old Testament (see: 1 Kings 19:10; 2 Chronicles 24:21–22; Matthew 23:37; Luke 6:23, 11:47, 13:33; Acts 7:52) and even with the sufferings undergone by Muhammed himself.[41]

Discussing Sura 4, noted Qur'anic translator and commentator Abdullah Yusuf Ali states: "The Qur'anic teaching is that Christ was not crucified nor killed by the Jews . . ."[42] The central problem with this hypothesis is of course that *it involves setting aside our first historical fact* (that Jesus died on the cross).

Some Muslims mistakenly believe evidence supporting the rejection of our first historical fact is provided by the pseudepigraphical Gospel of Barnabas, in which Judas Iscariot is crucified in Jesus' stead (having been transformed by God "in speech and in face to be like Jesus"[43]) and some of the disciples steal his entombed corpse under the mistaken impression that it is the corpse of Jesus (who, meanwhile, has been miraculously removed from the world without dying).

Quite apart from the intrinsic implausibility of this conspiracy theory, the plain fact of the matter is that the Gospel of Barnabas "is a medieval forgery"[44] that dates "to the thirteenth or fourteenth century"[45] (and is known to us through two later manuscripts). As John Oaks observes, this fake gospel is in fact "a compilation of the four canonical gospels, with the principle difference being interpolations rather obviously placed there in an attempt to reverse engineer the gospel to make room for statements about Jesus in the Qu'ran."[46] James A. Beverley and Craig A. Evans report that "Scholars readily recognize the lateness of the Gospel of Barnabas and its unreliability because of its many historical errors and anachronisms."[47]

At best, the medieval author of the Gospel of Barnabas may have drawn on some earlier apocryphal sources (e.g. gnostic sources) and upon the *Diatessaron* (a second-century harmony of the canonical gospels), albeit "edited to conform to Islam."[48] Indeed, the rejection of Jesus' death by crucifixion in both the *Gospel of Barnabas* and the Qur'an may ultimately derive from the second-century gnostic Gospel of Basilides. Ignatius reports Basilides' teaching that:

> Christ did not himself suffer death, but Simon, a certain man of Cyrene, being compelled, bore the cross in his stead; so that this latter being transfigured by him, that he might be thought to be Jesus, was crucified, through ignorance

---

41. See: Saaduev, "What Is The Meaning of Prophet Muhammad's (PBUH) Suffering?"
42. Ali, *The Meaning of the Holy Qur'an*, 236.
43. Gospel of Barnabas, chapters 216–17.
44. Beverley and Evans, *Getting Jesus Right*, 174. See: Geisler and Saleeb, *Answering Islam*, Appendix 3.
45. Beverley and Evans, *Getting Jesus Right*, 174.
46. Oakes, "A Response to Recent False Claims by Muslims About the Gospel of Barnabas."
47. Beverley and Evans, *Getting Jesus Right*, 174.
48. Hashim, "The Gospel of Barnabas."

and error, while Jesus himself received the form of Simon, and, standing by, laughed at them.[49]

Neither the medieval Gospel of Barnabas, nor the seventh-century Qur'an, nor even the second-century Gospel of Basilides can plausibly claim to provide more reliable historical information about the fate of Jesus than the first-century testimony gathered into the New Testament (not to mention the multiple first- and second-century extrabiblical sources that report Jesus' execution). Basilides's gnostic gospel is no more a rival source of historical information about Jesus than is the apocryphal Gospel of Barnabas. Rather, it's a late work of fiction concerned with propogating a polytheistic worldview. In other words, on this point of dispute (as on several others[50]) it is the Qur'anic Jesus that is a demonstrably mythical Jesus.

The *ad hoc* suggestion that the man who died on the cross wasn't Jesus entails that the corpse subsequently laid in the tomb was also not Jesus' corpse; but what then of that tomb being discovered empty on Sunday morning? A second *ad hoc* hypothesis (such as the one offered by the Gospel of Barnabas) is then required to account for the empty tomb without the resurrection of Jesus.

Moreover, the hypothesis that Jesus wasn't crucified doesn't do anything to account for the resurrection appearances or the origin of the disciples' belief in Jesus' resurrection. Once again, further *ad hoc* hypotheses would have to be advanced to explain away these facts.

Most importantly, the evidence shows that Jesus was killed on a cross. Notwithstanding later assertions on the matter in unreliable sources with anti-Christian agendas, there's simply no credible historical evidence to the contrary.

At this juncture, the final recourse for the Muslim apologist would be to demonstrate that there's a better case for the proposition that the Qur'an is a genuine revelation than there is against this proposition, thereby providing sufficient indirect reason to trust the Qur'anic account of what happened to Jesus over and above the account supported by the historical evidence. This is, of course, a matter on which the Christian and New Atheist can make common cause. In the words of Sam Harris:

> The burden is upon them to prove their beliefs about God and Muhammad are valid. They have not done this.[51]

This point of agreement aside, when Harris tells Christians that "every devout Muslim has the same reasons for being a Muslim that you have for being a Christian,"[52] he is simply displaying his ignorance. The confusion may stem from the neo-atheist dogma that all religious faith is a matter of blind faith, from which mistaken assumption it follows that no religion has better warrant than any other.

49. See: Qureshi, *No God But One*, 179.
50. See: Qureshi, *No God But One*.
51. Harris, *Letter to a Christian Nation*, 6.
52. Harris, *Letter to a Christian Nation*, 6.

For example, whilst Christianity hinges upon miracles, in many places the Qur'an stresses that Muhammad had no truck with miracles (see: Q 6:35; 6:37; 17:93; 28:48; 29:50), besides his alleged inspiration in writing the Qur'an (see: Q Al-Qasas 29:48–51). Ayman S. Ibrahim comments:

> Of course many Muslims, past and present, still assume, claim, insist, or at least wish that Muhammad did actually perform miracles, especially when they debate other faiths. In so doing, they rely on later sayings attributed to Muhammad or works written about him centuries after his death. Not only the reliability of these sources is questionable, but also their emphasis on supernatural miracles goes against the clear Quranic witness.[53]

On the one hand: "the Quran gives us clear evidence that Muhammad did not have any personal miracles."[54] On the other hand, later attributions of miracles to Muhammad (such as the story of Muhammad splitting the moon, or of the "night journey") are legends, often based upon misreadings of the Qur'an.[55] The earliest biographical source for the life of Muhammad (known to us via quotations in later writings) dates from over a hundred years after his reported death, and cannot compete with the Qur'an on this score.[56] Nor can the *hadiths*, which were "written at least two hundred years after the time of Muhammad."[57]

In sum, Muslims can't uphold their burden of proof in the face of the historical evidence for Jesus' death by crucifixion, etc. To press the point further would take us beyond our current remit, so readers who wish to pursue this issue are referred to the recommended resources.

Watch: "Islam" Youtube playlist: www.youtube.com/playlist?list=PLQhh3qcwVEWjhD84EB0jEG5PswCOcDsmJ

"Gospel of Barnabas According to Islam": https://youtu.be/b9m1YKgqvmM

"Muslim Scholar Reza Aslan Admits That the Quran Is Wrong about Jesus": https://youtu.be/q0-7D75ftmk

"What Does the Quran Say About the Crucifixion of Jesus?" by William Lane Craig: https://youtu.be/xQbKXfi5EXQ

"Did Jesus Die by Crucifixion?" Michael Licona vs. Yusuf Ismail: https://youtu.be/V6P2uVyVOTc

Websites: *Answering Islam:* www.answering-islam.org/index.html

Bethinking: Islam www.bethinking.org/islam

Pfander Centre for Apologetics: www.pfander.uk

---

53. Ibrahim, "Did Muhammad Perform Miracles?"
54. See: "Did Prophet Muhammad Split the Moon?" and "Muhammad and Miracles."
55. Geisler and Saleeb, *Answering Islam*, 163–66.
56. Townsend, *Questioning Islam*, 43.
57. Townsend, *Questioning Islam*, 176.

Listen: "Historical Jesus vs. Historical Muhammad" by Andy Bannister and Jay Smith: www.bethinking.org/islam/historical-jesus-vs-historical-muhammed

"The Qur'an vs. the Bible": www.bethinking.org/islam/the-quran-vs-the-bible

"The Textual Histories of the Qur'an and NT" by Keith Small: www.bethinking.org/islam/textual-histories-of-quran-and-nt

Read: "Who Is the Real Jesus: the Jesus of the Bible or the Jesus of the Qur'an?" by William Lane Craig: www.reasonablefaith.org/who-is-the-real-jesus-the-jesus-of-the-bible-or-the-jesus-of-the-quran

"The Concept of God in Islam and Christianity" by William Lane Craig: www.reasonablefaith.org/concept-of-god-in-islam-and-christianity

"Is There a 'Gospel of Barnabas'?" by Norman L. Geisler: www.jashow.org/wiki/index.php/Is_There_a_"Gospel_of_Barnabas"%3F

"Did Muhammad Perform Miracles?" by Ayman S. Ibrahim: www.firstthings.com/web-exclusives/2015/09/did-muhammad-perform-miracles

"The Date and Provenance of the Gospel of Barnabas" by Jan Joosten: www.academia.edu/1151977/_The_Date_and_Provenance_of_the_Gospel_of_Barnabas_

Getting Jesus Right: How Muslims Get Jesus And Islam Wrong by James A. Beverley and Craig A. Evans

Answering Islam: The Crescent in Light of the Cross by Norman L. Geisler and Abdul Saleeb

Paul Meets Muhammad: A Christian-Muslim Debate On The Resurrection by Michael Licona

Textual Criticism And The Qur'an Manuscripts by Keith E. Small

Did Muhammad Exist? An Inquiry Into Islam's Obscure Origins by Robert Spencer

Questioning Islam: Tough Questions & Honest Answers About the Muslim Religion by Peter Townsend

No God But One: A Former Muslim Investigates The Evidence For Islam & Christianity by Nabeel Qureshi

---

2ii) Swoon theories—Jesus survived crucifixion

According to Cambridge scholar Murray Harris: "the 'swoon theory' or the 'apparent death theory,' enjoyed considerable popularity among eighteenth and nineteenth-century German rationalists . . . but the theory is now totally discredited."[58] As John Foster reports, claims that Jesus didn't die on the cross "have been laughed out of court by serious scholars."[59] Nevertheless, as Eric Metaxas comments: "Although this is generally now—because of medical science and other evidence—thought risible, we should compose ourselves to consider it, because it still makes its appearance in books every few years."[60]

---

58. Harris, *From Grave to Glory*, 114.
59. Foster, *The Jesus Inquest*, 72.
60. Metaxas, *Miracles*, 106.

For example, some Muslims accept a strained interpretation of the Qu'ran's fourth chapter (4:157–58), according to which Jesus *was crucified* but was *not killed* in the process, divine aid guaranteeing he only swooned on the cross before being entombed and thereafter miraculously assumed into heaven (thereby explaining the empty tomb). This Muslim swoon theory (which has also been called the rescue theory) avoids the problems faced by an injured and shroud-wrapped Jesus in exiting his (guarded) tomb, but it does so at the price of positing miracles that lack the scope or power to explain either the resurrection appearances or the origin of the disciples' belief therein. In short:

> rescue theory . . . accounts for the empty tomb but has to strain to explain the evidence for the death of Jesus and his post-resurrection appearances . . . The rescue theory likewise leads to the suggestion that the prophet Jesus was mistaken in his belief that he would soon die . . .[61]

Atheist philosopher Theodore M. Drange suggests that an alternative explanation of the relevant facts that would be both naturalistic and "far more reasonable" than belief in a resurrection "is that Jesus didn't really die, but regained consciousness, escaped the tomb, and left town, perhaps with the aid of someone else who subsequently kept quiet on the matter."[62]

A more fulsome secular swoon theory might go like this: Jesus either fell unconscious or somehow faked his death on the cross. Despite having been flogged, crucified, and speared through his side, Jesus resuscitated "in the cool of the tomb" (for some reason "the cool of the tomb" always seems to help in these scenarios, rather than being the final straw that does Jesus in). He removed his own shroud (despite having hands that wouldn't function because nails had been driven through his wrists). Although rolling a tombstone back up its groove would normally require several men pushing it from the side, Jesus got the tombstone out of the way by pushing on its inside face (despite his injuries). Having opened his tomb, and having evaded or subdued the guards, Jesus tracked down his disciples (as well as James and Saul) so that he could deceive them into thinking (against their expectations and against every social inducement to the contrary) that he'd been gloriously *resurrected*, before leaving his friends and family to risk their lives spreading this delusion in his name whilst he hobbled off, eventually dying elsewhere without leaving any further historical trace.

While the secular swoon theory attempts to provide resources with which to explain away the empty tomb and resurrection appearances—by having a post-swoon Jesus appear to his disciples—this (rather meager) explanatory gain comes at the high cost of the implausibility attached to getting Jesus to survive crucifixion and exit the tomb without divine aid, as well as the implausibility of the injured Jesus accounting for the resurrection appearances and the beliefs adopted by the disciples thereafter. As

---

61. Licona, *Paul Meets Muhammad*, 152–53.
62. Drange, "Some Philosophical Aspects of the Craig-Rosenberg Debate," 91.

many scholars observe, a Jesus who swooned on the cross lacks the explanatory causal power to account for the resurrection appearances or the origin of the disciples' belief in the resurrection:

- J.N.D. Anderson is skeptical that "instead of proving the inevitable end to His flickering life, that he would have been able to loose Himself from yards of graveclothes weighted with pounds of spices, roll away a stone that three women felt incapable of tackling, and walk miles on wounded feet."[63]

- Christopher Bryan: "Anyone who imagines that the survivor of a crucifixion would be in a state to convince anyone that he was the victorious conqueror of death clearly has very little idea what a crucifixion was like."[64]

- Gary R. Habermas: "A crucified but still-living Jesus would have been in horrible physical shape: bloodied, bruised, pale, limping, unwashed, and in obvious need of medical assistance. Such a condition would have hopelessly contradicted the disciples' belief that Jesus had appeared to them in a resurrected body."[65]

- J.P. Holding asks us to consider "the fact that the temperature in the tomb was probably about 56–58 degrees Fahrenheit, which would cause death by exposure on its own after 36 hours (note that linen is not much of a protector in this context) . . . lain out shivering and losing energy in a tomb . . . after hanging for hours on a cross (how do those dislocated shoulders and/or strained muscles feel about pushing anything?)."[66]

- Karl Theodor Keim: "Then there is the most impossible thing of all; the poor, weak, sick Jesus, with difficulty holding himself erect, in hiding, disguised, and finally dying—this Jesus an object of faith, of exalted emotion, of the triumph of his adherents, a risen conqueror, the Son of God! Here, in fact, the theory begins to grow paltry, absurd, worthy only of rejection."[67]

- John Stott: "are we to believe that after the rigours and pains of . . . flogging and crucifixion He could survive thirty-six hours in a stone sepulchre . . . then rally sufficiently to perform the superhuman feat of shifting the boulder which secured the mouth of the tomb."[68]

- David Strauss: "It is impossible that a being who had stolen half-dead out of the sepulchre, who crept about weak and ill, wanting medical treatment, who required bandaging, strengthening and indulgence, and who was still at last yielding to his sufferings, could have given the disciples the impression that he was a

---

63. Anderson, "The Resurrection of Christ," 7.
64. Bryan, *The Resurrection of the Messiah*, 163.
65. Habermas, *The Risen Jesus*, 16.
66. Holding, *Defending the Resurrection*, 382.
67. Keim, *Jesus of Nazareth*, 327–28.
68. Stott, *Basic Christianity*, 48–49.

Conqueror over death and the grave, the Prince of life, an impression which lay at the bottom of their future ministry."[69]

Swoon theory entails the hypothesis that, after somehow duping the disciples into thinking he was resurrected (and somehow duping them into thinking that he'd ascended to God the Father), Jesus "abandoned all those who loved and trusted him, leaving them to their own fate, and crept away out of Palestine with his tail between his legs . . ."[70] Such a theory is *ad hoc, implausible,* and strongly *disconfirmed* by our evidence about Jesus' character.

Finally, any suggestion that Jesus had help—whether divine (according to some Muslims) or secular (according to Drange)—turns the swoon theory into a conspiracy theory. Indeed, to explain away the reports of Jesus' resurrection appearances, the swoon theory requires (and is thus a worse explanation than) either a conspiracy theory or some sort of delusion theory, since "the disciples testified that Jesus did not swoon, but really died and really rose."[71] It is to such theories that we turn next.

Watch: "Can the "swoon" hypothesis explain the resurrection?" Youtube playlist: www.youtube.com/playlist?list=PLQhh3qcwVEWgpajHFMToSTLx1QEKaoTAo

"What Does the Quran Say About the Crucifixion of Jesus?" by William Lane Craig: https://youtu.be/xQbKXfi5EXQ

"Islam and Christianity? Did Jesus Physically Rise From the Dead?" William Lane Craig vs. Shabir Ally: https://youtu.be/ofyy4q8z4us

"Did Jesus Die by Crucifixion?" Michael Licona vs. Yusuf Ismail: https://youtu.be/V6P2uVyVOTc

Read: "The Guard on the Tomb" by William Lane Craig: www.reasonablefaith.org/writings/scholarly-writings/historical-jesus/the-guard-at-the-tomb/

No God But One: A Former Muslim Investigates The Evidence For Islam & Christianity by Nabeel Qureshi

---

Alternative 3: Conspiracy theories

Robert J. Hutchinson poses the question: "What caused the followers of Jesus to adopt their new, bold, and courageous faith if Jesus died like every other man—and stayed dead? Did the disciples gather together in the upper room at Pentecost and simply decide to go out and pretend Jesus had risen? *How likely is that?*"[72] Not very. For one thing, Jesus' disciples clearly had no expectation that the messiah they sought would be killed, let alone that he'd be resurrected within human history.

---

69. Strauss, *A New Life of Jesus*, 412.
70. Foster, *The Jesus Inquest*, 72.
71. Kreeft and Tacelli, *Handbook of Christian Apologetics*, 184.
72. Hutchinson, *Searching For Jesus*, 223.

As N.T. Wright observes, conspiracy hypotheses tend "to be disconfirmed by our general knowledge of conspiracies, their instability and tendency to unravel."[73] J. Warner Wallace explains that:

> For a conspiracy to succeed, you need the smallest number of conspirators; holding the lie for the shortest period of time; with excellent communication between them so they can make sure their stories line up; with close familial relationships, if possible; and with little or no pressure applied to those who are telling the lie. Those criteria don't fit the resurrection witnesses.[74]

Any conspiracy theory must take into account the fact that "the testimony on behalf of Christ's Resurrection held firm under the most extraordinary affliction."[75] If nothing else, martyrdom assures both sincerity and psychological certitude:

> no one, weak or strong... Christian or heretic, ever confessed, freely or under pressure, bribe or even torture, that the whole story of the resurrection was a fake, a lie, a deliberate deception. Even when people broke under torture, denied Christ and worshiped Caesar, they never let that cat out of the bag, never revealed that the resurrection was their conspiracy. For that cat was never in that bag.[76]

Reza Aslan points out that, in the case of the disciples, such steadfastness is indicative of truth as well as sincerity:

> Many zealous Jews died horribly for refusing to deny their beliefs. But these first followers of Jesus were not being asked to reject matters of faith based on events that took place centuries, if not millennia, before. They were being asked to deny something they themselves personally, directly encountered. The disciples... were beaten, whipped, stoned, and crucified, yet they would not cease proclaiming the risen Jesus.[77]

As William Paley famously asked:

> Would men in such circumstances pretend to have seen what they never saw; assert facts which they had not knowledge of, go about lying to teach virtue; and, though not only convinced of Christ's being an imposter, but having seen the success of his imposture in his crucifixion, yet persist in carrying on; and so persist, as to bring upon themselves, for nothing, and with full knowledge of the consequences, enmity and hatred, danger and death?[78]

---

73. Wright, *Surprised by Hope*, 251.
74. Wallace quoted in Strobel, *The Case for Miracles*, 206.
75. Sullivan and Menssen, "Revelation and Miracles," 215.
76. Kreeft and Tacelli, *Handbook of Christian Apologetics*, 184–85.
77. Aslan, *Zealot*, 174–75.
78. Paley, *A View of the Evidences of Christianity*, 327–28.

The original conspiracy theory, discussed in Matthew's Gospel and reflected in Jewish tradition (see: Justin Martyr's second-century *Dialogue with Trypho*, the fifth-century AD *Toledoth Jesu*, and the medieval Gospel of Barnabas), suggested that Jesus' disciples stole the corpse from the tomb and invented Jesus' resurrection (see: Matthew 28:12–14).

Against this, Matthew points out that the Jewish authorities had put a guard on the tomb.[79] Grant R. Osborne argues that "there is a great deal of non-Matthean language that likely points to tradition rather than Matthean creation behind the material"[80] about the guard. William Lane Craig concurs that the story of the guard "is peppered with non-Matthean vocabulary, indicative of a prior tradition."[81] The Jewish authorities responded in turn with the claim that their guards had all fallen asleep on the job! Not only is this claim intrinsically unlikely, but how could the guards identify the disciples as those responsible for emptying the tomb if they'd been asleep when the emptying happened?

Atheist Richard Carrier notes that there was a window of time between the burial and the posting of the guard (see: Matthew 27:62). However, any thieves would need good timing to exploit this opportunity. Moreover, it's plausible to think that the guard who "made the tomb secure and sealed the stone" (Matthew 27:66) would have checked its contents. As Tim Chaffey observes: "Carrier's hypothesis depends upon an incredibly inept group of soldiers."[82]

If the body (whether of Jesus of someone else mistakenly thought to be Jesus) had already been taken by the time the guard arrived, we must face the question asked by Frank Morrison in the title of his classic book *Who Moved the Stone*? All four gospels report that the stone rolled in place[83] by Joseph and Nicodemus was found some way away from the tomb on Sunday morning (this is how the women disciples were able to see inside when they arrived on the scene). If this happened *before* the soldiers arrived at the tomb, they could hardly have failed to notice that something was wrong! However, if the stone was moved *after* the soldiers arrived at the tomb, then it would seem that the body must have left the tomb *whilst the guard was onsite*, and we're back to official claims of mass sleepiness.

Perhaps the disciples rolled the stone away, removed the body (having spent the time to divest it of the expensive grave-clothes in order to leave them behind), rolled the stone back, waited for the guards to arrive and fall asleep (without checking the tomb), and *then* quietly moved the stone a second time without waking the slumbering soldiers. . . the more one thinks through this conspiracy theory the more *ad hoc* and implausible it becomes. Perhaps the inclusion of the "Jesus' disciples stole the

79. See: Craig, "The Guard on the Tomb."
80. Osborne, "Jesus' Empty Tomb and His Appearances in Jerusalem," 788.
81. Craig, "Dale Allison on Jesus's Empty Tomb," 296.
82. Chaffey, *In Defence of Easter*, 102.
83. See: "Was the stone sealing Jesus's tomb square-shaped?"

body" theory in Matthew's Gospel is a double bluff on behalf of a conspiracy by the disciples.

If the disciples *invented* the resurrection, isn't it rather odd that none of the NT literature ever narrates the event itself? Such narration appears in the apocryphal literature (see: the Gospel of Peter), but not in the NT. As Paul Avis notes:

> There were, as far as we know, no witnesses present to observe the act of Resurrection itself. Belief in the Resurrection was an inference drawn immediately by the disciples from their experiences of the Risen Christ, and subsequently, and to a lesser extent, from the empty tomb.[84]

Any resurrection conspiracy would probably have produced multiple accounts of the resurrection itself as observed by reliable, upstanding males (perhaps placing Joseph and Nicodemus at the tomb to greet the resurrected Christ, together with Peter and John). Instead, the NT not only fails to narrate the resurrection, but makes the first witnesses to both the empty tomb and the resurrected Jesus *female* (considered unreliable by the chauvinistic culture of the day): "if the disciples stole Jesus' corpse, then it would be utterly pointless to fabricate a story about *women* finding the tomb to be empty [and being the first witnesses to the resurrected Jesus]. Such a story would not be the sort of tale Jewish men would invent."[85] As Kostenberger et al. comment:

> The claim is the disciples fabricated a culturally unpopular idea (resurrection), using people who do not count as witnesses for it (women), presented to a host of unbelieving followers (doubting disciples) as the way to persuade a doubting audience. Not one of these elements passes the smell test for the fabrication theory.[86]

Moreover, calculated deception would have produced unanimity among our sources. Instead, we have stories from different viewpoints. Differences over the presentation of minor details combined with similarity in the presentation of major details of the kind that we find in the passion narratives are generally seen as indicating historical reliability. If Christianity was a conspiracy, it was a spectacularly inept one. Or is this too a double bluff? Such a hypothesis is *ad hoc*.

After the crucifixion (indeed, mainly before the crucifixion) the NT says that the disciples (prudently, albeit embarrassingly in light of the story they would subsequently tell) ran away:

> In the everyday religious politics of the time, if the Messiah you followed died it was proof positive that you had backed the wrong man. The movement surrounding a failed Messiah was either wiped out or broke up as quickly as possible. Nobody wanted to voice support for Judas the Galilean when he

---

84. Avis, "The Resurrection of Jesus," 3.
85. Craig, *On Guard*, 245.
86. Kostenberger et al., *Truth Matters*, 169.

and his rebel army ended up on crosses, and we have no reason to think that Peter, James and John had any other hope after the death of Jesus than to distance themselves from him and disappear unnoticed. A hint of this attempt is preserved in the story of Peter's [embarrassing] denial, which all four Gospels relate . . .[87]

These are not moves made by a group of men with "a cunning plan." Nor is it the self-portrait of a group of conspirators expecting to overpower a group of soldiers or dupe the world at the risk of their lives.

Any disciple-centric conspiracy theory for the origin of Christianity is morally and psychologically implausible given what we know about the disciples, and especially so given what we know about Jesus' antagonistic brother James and the Christian-persecuting Saul, who were each converted by their personal experiences of Jesus after his death. As Flew admits: "virtually all the major people are people who are above suspicion of deliberate distortion . . . I believe they had some sort of experience."[88] In short, the principle witnesses to the resurrection are, to borrow a phrase from Hume: "of such undoubted integrity, as to place them beyond all suspicion of any design to deceive others . . ."[89] Thus, having considered the hypothesis that the disciples stole Jesus body, Gezer Vermes concludes: "Its value for the interpretation of the resurrection is next to nil."[90] Likewise, E.P. Sanders concluded: "I do not regard deliberate fraud as a worthwhile explanation."[91]

Alternatively, if it isn't the disciples, but Joseph and/or Nicodemus and/or the person in charge of the cemetery ("the gardener" of John 20:15) who supposedly moved the body *against Jewish custom*,[92] then surely, as Vermes argues: "the fact that the organizer(s) of the burial was/were well known and could have easily been asked for and supplied an explanation, strongly mitigates against this theory."[93] Richard Purtill likewise eliminates the obvious candidates:

> Early Christians claimed that the tomb of Christ was empty and that Christ had risen from the dead. The Roman and Jewish authorities did not refute this claim by producing the body, as they certainly would have done had *they* removed it from the tomb. The Apostles suffered persecution, hardship, and martyrdom to proclaim the message of Christ risen from the dead, which they surely would not have done if *they* had removed and hidden Christ's body.[94]

---

87. Tilby, *Son of God*, 161.
88. Habermas, Flew and Miethe, *Did Jesus Rise from the Dead?*, 79.
89. Hume, "Of Miracles," 36.
90. Vermes, *Jesus the Jew*, 145.
91. Sanders, *The Historical Figure of Jesus*, 279.
92. See: Miller, "Was the Burial of Jesus a Temporary One."
93. Vermes, *Jesus the Jew*, 144.
94. Purtill, "Miracles: What If They Happen?," 196.

As for the suggestion that unknown grave-robbers are to blame for the empty tomb, quite apart from problems involving the guards, robbers "would not have gone through the time-consuming effort of carefully removing and folding the linen cloths ... only to carry away a naked corpse. What is more, grave robbers would not have left the most valuable material, the cloths and spices."[95]

Some have suggested that, notwithstanding the guards, necromancers might have conspired to steal Jesus' corpse with some kind of magical purpose. However, the necromancer hypothesis is *ad hoc*, for as Craig Keener points out: "our evidence for the theft of corpses appears in Gentile regions, never around Jerusalem."[96] Worse than being *ad hoc*, the necromancer hypothesis is actually *disconfirmed* by accepted facts. In the 30s, Jerusalem was mainly inhabited by devout Jews who regarded graveyards as ritually unclean and considered necromancy to be sacrilegious (see: Leviticus 20:27 and Deuteronomy 18:10), a highly implausible environment for necromancy. Furthermore, as Holding explains:

> all the evidence suggests that when necromancers had need of a body for their arts, they did not steal the whole body from the tomb. Instead, they would either conduct their rituals in the tomb itself, leaving the body where it was when they were finished; or, they would slice off whatever they needed, mutilating the body and taking the selected parts with them, leaving the rest behind. It does not help critics to argue that Jesus' nose and ears may have been missing, while the rest of the body was still in the tomb![97]

The hypothesis that the soldiers at the crucifixion were bribed to allow Jesus' burial before returning to remove the evidence of their corruption (as Carl Stecher suggests) neglects the fact that no guards would need to be bribed, because the burial was according to custom. Indeed, the hypothesis disregards the evidence that the authorities knew about Jesus' burial (see: Mark 15:43; Matthew 27:57–66 and 28:11; John 19:38–42), and fails to explain why the grave-clothes and spices were left behind in the tomb.

Finally, these attempts to explain away the empty tomb by invoking conspiracy all suffer from *a lack of explanatory scope*, since they fail to explain (or else implicitly deny) either the reported resurrection appearances or the origin of the disciples' belief in Jesus' resurrection.

3a) Conspiracy theories involving an identical twin

An alternative form of the conspiracy theory depends upon the *ad hoc* suggestion that Jesus had a long-lost identical twin brother! This hypothetical twin either died

---

95. Kostenberger and Taylor, *The Final Days of Jesus*, 184.
96. Keener, *The Historical Jesus of the Gospels*, 341.
97. Holding, *Defending the Resurrection*, 391.

in Jesus' place so Jesus could deceive his disciples into believing that he'd been resurrected (the twin substitution theory), or waited until Jesus was dead to make his appearance, thereby deceiving people into believing he was Jesus resurrected from the dead (the twin replacement theory).

Of course, there's no evidence Jesus had a twin, despite the fact that two gospels provide independent accounts of Jesus' birth[98] and that the NT tells us about his younger half-brothers who were prominent members of the early church (e.g. James and Jude). Roping various NT writers and/or Jesus' family (i.e. Matthew, Luke, and/or Mary, James, Jude, etc.) into a conspiracy of silence about Jesus' identical sibling makes the twin theory even less plausible.

The twin substitution theory (which denies Jesus' death) assumes: that Jesus' hypothetical twin was willing to be crucified in his place for the sake of a hoax; that nobody at the crucifixion and/or burial—including the Roman and Jewish authorities, Mary Magdalene, Salome, Joseph of Arimathea, Nicodemus, John the apostle, and Jesus' mother—realized the wrong man was executed and laid to rest; and that Jesus both could and would foist the blasphemous and culturally implausible lie that he'd been resurrected from the dead upon friends and family alike. As Doug Powell observes:

> Jesus' twin would have had to follow Jesus around without being recognized and be willing to swap places with him just before being arrested so he could willingly die in Jesus' place in order that Jesus could create the hoax of being resurrected from the dead. Who would willingly die for a hoax their brother wanted to play? Also, this deception goes against everything we know about Jesus' character and teaching.[99]

The twin replacement theory (which accepts Jesus' death) asks us to suppose Jesus' hypothetical twin thought it a good idea to impersonate a man who had just been executed. It also asks us to suppose that Jesus' friends and/or family wouldn't notice that the "resurrected Jesus" was an imposter. Remember, the resurrection appearances included several extended conversations, some of a highly personal nature (e.g. John 21:15–19) with people who knew Jesus intimately.

Detective J. Warner Wallace comments:

> Con artists are successful if, and only if, they know more about the focus of their lie, than the people to whom they are lying. If you're trying to con someone out of money in a phony investment scheme, you better know more about investment businesses than your victims. You'll need to sound like you know

---

98. See: "The Nativity;" Williams, "The Nativity;" Ernie Rea et al., "Virgin Birth;" Brindle, "The Census and Quirinius;" McLatchie, "The Nativity Defended;" Scott, "Matthew's Intention to Write History;" Barnett, *Messiah*; Crowe, *Was Jesus Really Born Of A Virgin?*; Edwards, *The Virgin Birth In History And Faith*; Foster, *The Christmas Mystery*; Machen, *The Virgin Birth of Christ*; Nicholl, *The Great Christ Comet*; Quarles, *Midrash Criticism*; Redford, *Born Of A Virgin*.

99. Powell, *Resurrection iWitness*, 27.

what you're doing if you want to convince someone to give you their money, and they better not be able to detect your deception. So if someone wanted to con those closest to Jesus into believing that Jesus had actually risen from the dead, he would need to know Jesus (his mannerisms, figures of speech and behaviors) better than the disciples themselves.[100]

So, how could anyone so dupe Peter that he would later die for his faith in the resurrected Jesus? How could anyone so thoroughly convince James and Jude to believe that their brother was resurrected that they likewise died as martyrs for this proclamation? As Frank Morison mused: "The terrors and the persecutions which these men ultimately had to face and did face unflinchingly, do not admit of a half-hearted adhesion secretly honeycombed with doubt."[101] Roping the likes of Peter, James and Jude into the hypothetical conspiracy means increasing its *ad hoc* implausibility.

The twin replacement theory is also disconfirmed by the secondary, but still multiply attested data concerning the unexpected characteristics of the resurrection appearances [see: Luke 24:13–43 and 51; John 20:19–26, 21:6, and 21:12; Acts 1:3 and 1:9]. As Wallace observes:

> The behavior of Jesus following the Resurrection was simply too remarkable to have been achieved by an imposter. Remember that Jesus spent forty days with the disciples, providing many "convincing proofs" to demonstrate that he was truly raised from the dead (see: Acts 1:2–3). His behavior following the Resurrection included miraculous, supernatural deeds.[102]

At the very least, our imposter would have needed to convince Jesus' friends and family that he did a variety of miraculous actions, including somehow appearing to vanish from the Mount of Olives (see: Luke 24:50–51; Acts 1:9–11).

Although a post-crucifixion appearance of either an un-crucified Jesus or a Jesus-impersonating identical twin (in either case lacking the crucifixion scars referenced by Luke 24:39–40 and John 20:24–29) would occasion surprise, such an appearance (even in conjunction with an empty tomb) *lacks the explanatory power* to account for the disciples' belief in Jesus' *resurrection*. As N.T. Wright argues: "If the disciples had simply seen, or thought they had seen, someone they took to be Jesus, that would not by itself have generated the stories we have."[103] The twin theory doesn't help explain the empty tomb (if a corpse—whether of Jesus or his hypothetical twin—remained in the tomb, the disciples couldn't have believed in or got away with proclaiming a resurrected Jesus). Nor can the twin theory easily account for the appearance to Saul on the road to Damascus.

---

100. Wallace, "The Post Resurrection Behavior of Jesus."
101. Morison, *Who Moved the Stone?*, 114.
102. Wallace, "The Post Resurrection Behavior of Jesus."
103. Wright, *Surprised by Hope*, 69.

Watch: "Was the Resurrection a Conspiracy?" Youtube playlist: www.youtube.com/playlist?list=PLQhh3qcwVEWjQhRvN7_VM8D4oLHVEa6AD

Read: "The Guard on the Tomb" by William Lane Craig: www.reasonablefaith.org/writings/scholarly-writings/historical-jesus/the-guard-at-the-tomb/

"Was Jesus' Body Reburied?" by Robert Martin: https://atheistforum.wordpress.com/2016/03/20/was-jesus-body-reburied/

"Was the burial of Jesus a temporary one because of time constraints?" by Glenn Miller: http://christianthinktank.com/shellgame.html

3b) Alien conspiracy

"Extraterrestrials are like deities for atheists."

—MICHAEL SHERMER[104]

Many agree with Richard Dawkins that "there probably is intelligent life elsewhere in the Universe,"[105] a thesis that underpins the conspiracy theory (which Dawkins does not advocate) "that Jesus was really [an alien] who came in a flying saucer."[106] Alternatively, and accommodating the existence of two independent birth accounts for Jesus,[107] perhaps aliens "implanted" Jesus into Mary's womb or used artificial insemination.[108] Perhaps they were merely Jesus' co-conspirators, unless, unlikely as it may seem, he was their patsy. In any case, aliens might have used hypothetical technology to fake Jesus' resurrection, etc.

For example, might a "matter transporter" *a la* Star Trek have been used to remove Jesus from the tomb so he could be brought back to life somehow (using "science") before being beamed into Jerusalem to surprise the disciples? Given the scientific problems attendant upon such technology, that seems unlikely. For one thing, as Lawrence Krauss explains:

> building a transporter would require us to heat up matter to a temperature a million times the temperature at the centre of the Sun, expend more energy in

---

104. Shermer quoted in Bromwich, "Bright Lights, Strange Shapes and Talk of U.F.O.'s."
105. Dawkins quoted in Stannard, *Science and Wonders*, 73.
106. Kreeft and Tacelli, *Handbook of Christian Apologetics*, 182.
107. See: "The Nativity;" Williams, "The Nativity;" Ernie Rea et al., "Virgin Birth;" Brindle, "The Census And Quirinius;" McLatchie, "The Nativity Defended;" Scott, "Matthew's Intention to Write History;" Barnett, *Messiah*; Crowe, *Was Jesus Really Born Of A Virgin?*; Edwards, *The Virgin Birth In History And Faith*; Foster, *The Christmas Mystery*; Machen, *The Virgin Birth of Christ*; Nicholl, *The Great Christ Comet*; Quarles, *Midrash Criticism*; Redford, *Born Of A Virgin*.
108. See: "Was Jesus an Alien?;" Millar, "Question: Was Jesus of Alien Parentage?"

a single machine than all of humanity presently uses, build telescopes larger than the size of the Earth . . . and avoid the laws of quantum mechanics.[109]

Then again, perhaps aliens brainwashed all the witnesses to *think* they saw an empty tomb and/or met Jesus alive after his death. Perhaps aliens are making you *think* you are reading this book and living on Earth, when in reality you aren't! The mere *possibility* of such skeptical scenarios doesn't undermine the testimony of our senses.[110] The existence of alien life is currently an open question, let alone the existence of intelligent alien life with the means, motive, and opportunity to participate in such a bizarre religious conspiracy.

Barring intelligent intervention of some kind, the origin and subsequent macroevolution of life (whether on Earth or elsewhere in the cosmos) is a "non-trivial" contingency that cannot be taken for granted.[111] Atheist philosopher Thomas Nagel takes Richard Dawkins to task over the origin of life:

> Dawkins . . . says that there are . . . a billion billion planets in the universe with life-friendly physical and chemical environments like ours. So all we have to suppose [to account for the origin of life on Earth] is that the probability of something like DNA forming . . . is not much less than one in a billion billion . . . [However] no one has a theory that would support anything remotely near such a high probability . . . at this point the origin of life remains, in light of what is known about the huge size, the extreme specificity, and the exquisite functional precision of the genetic material, a mystery . . .[112]

Neo–atheist and chemist Peter Atkins concedes that "One problem with evolution is how it began,"[113] admitting that on this issue "science is a bit stuck"[114] and that the origin of life "is still a real puzzle."[115] Indeed, synthetic chemist James Tour writes that:

> In contrast to the ubiquity of life on earth, the lifelessness of other planets makes far better chemical sense . . . The appearance of life on earth is a mystery.

---

109. Krauss, *The Physics of Star Trek*, 83.
110. See: Van der Breggen, "Reasonable Skepticism about Radical Skepticism."
111. See: "The Origin of Life;" "Intelligent Design;" Meyer, "DNA and the Origin of Life;" Tour, "An Open Letter to My Colleagues;" Abel, *Primordial Prescription*; Abel, *The First Gene*; Axe, *Undeniable*; Behe, *The Edge of Evolution*; Behe, *Darwin's Black Box*; Campbell and Meyer, *Darwinism, Design, and Public Education*; Dembski, *Uncommon Dissent*; Dembski, *No Free Lunch*; Dembski and Wells, *The Design of Life*; Gordon and Dembski, *The Nature of Nature*; Johnson, *Programming of Life*; Johnson, *Darwin on Trial*; Klinghoffer, *Debating Darwin's Doubt*; Klinghoffer, *Signature Of Controversy*; Lennox, *God's Undertaker*; Menuge, *Agents Under Fire*; Marks et al., *Introduction To Evolutionary Informatics*; Meyer, *Darwin's Doubt*; Meyer, *Signature in the Cell*; Pullen, *Intelligent Design or Evolution?*; Swift, *Evolution Under the Microscope*.
112. Nagel, "Dawkins and Atheism," 24–25.
113. Atkins, *On Being*, 38.
114. Atkins, *On Being*, 38.
115. Atkins, *On Being*, 60.

> We are nowhere near solving this problem. The proposals offered thus far to explain life's origin make no scientific sense . . .[116]

The pre-conditions for eukaryotic plant and animal life are nowhere near as simple as the "star plus rock plus water" formula popularized by media reports about the discovery of extrasolar planets: "complex animal life . . . may only be possible around Sun-like stars, on very Earth-like planets with plate tectonics, oceans of water, continental land, a thick oxygen-rich atmosphere and large moon."[117] Currently, no such planet is known besides our own.

Science writer Geoff Watts observes that: "Of the search for *intelligent* life in particular, many scientists are skeptical."[118] Unlike the reports of Jesus' resurrection appearances, purported alien space-craft and visitations (whether ancient or modern) are susceptible to mundane explanations.[119]

According to psychologist Susan A. Clancy: "alien-abduction memories are best understood as resulting from a blend of fantasy-proneness, memory distortion, culturally available scripts, sleep hallucinations, and scientific illiteracy, aided and abetted by the suggestions and reinforcement of hypnotherapy."[120]

Upon investigation, most Unidentified Flying Objects (UFOs) become Identified Flying Objects (IFOs) of a non-alien nature. That some remain *unidentified* is, like the existence of unsolved crimes, hardly supportive of the hypothesis that technologically advanced aliens exist. As physicist Stephen Webb notes, "the percentage of 'inexplicable' UFOs does not vary much within the overall number of sightings . . . whether it is a busy year or a quiet year for UFO sightings, the IFO/UFO ratio is about the same"[121] and "This is not at all what one would expect if the 'inexplicable' UFO sightings represent alien craft."[122] On the basis of this data, Robert Sheaffer concludes that "the apparently unexplainable residue is due to the essentially random nature of gross misperception and misreporting."[123]

---

116. Tour, "An Open Letter to My Colleagues." See also: Tour, "The Origin of Life."

117. Dartnell, *Life in the Universe*, 171. See also: Berger, *How Unique Are We?*; Peter D. Ward and Donald Brownlee, *Rare Earth* (New York: Copernicus, 2000); David Waltham, *Lucky Planet* (London: Icon, 2014).

118. Watts, "Is There Life on Other Planets?," 203.

119. See: "Aliens & UFOs;" Akpan and Barajas, "7 times that science explained aliens;" Blackmore, "Abduction by Aliens or Sleep Paralysis?;" Blackmore and Cox, "Alien Abductions, Sleep Paralysis and the Temporal Lobe;" Clancy, *Abducted*; Colavito, *The Cult of Alien Gods*; Feder, "Help! I'm Being Followed by Ancient Aliens!;" French, "Close Encounters of the Psychological Kind;" French et al., "Psychological Aspects of the Alien Contact Experience;" Goode, "What About Alien Abductions?;" Nickell, "Abductions and Hoaxes;" Omohundro, "Von Däniken's Chariots;" Perina, "Alien Abductions;" Webb, *Where Is Everybody?*, 29–34; White, *The Past Is Human*.

120. Clancy, *Abducted*, 138.

121. Webb, *Where Is Everybody?*, 31.

122. Webb, *Where Is Everybody?*, 31.

123. Sheaffer, "An Examination of the Claims that Extraterrestrial Visitors to Earth are Being Observed."

Over half a century of the "search for extra-terrestrial intelligence" (SETI)—"mainly in the radio, but occasionally in the infrared and increasingly in the visible"[124]—has thus far produced a null result.[125] Historian of science George Basalla notes that "Many SETI supporters expected extraterrestrial contact well before the coming of the millennium."[126] Hence, as Webb observes: "the continuing silence, despite intensive searches, is beginning to worry even some of the most enthusiastic proponents of SETI."[127] William Borucki, the principal investigator of NASA's planet-hunting Kepler mission (and recipient of the prestigious Shaw Prize in Astronomy) comments: "We have . . . no visits, no communications we've picked up . . . the evidence says, no one's out there."[128]

Philosopher David Lamb argues that:

> Generous estimates of the number of planets with intelligent communicative life suffered a serious setback in 1992 following the completion of a radio search conducted by D.G. Blair . . . The search covered the neighbourhoods of 176 stars . . . within forty light years of the Earth. No signal was detected. The negative results weaken [the] assumption that technological intelligence will inevitably emerge through enough time on an Earth-sized planet near a Sun-like star.[129]

Theoretical physicist Jim Al-Khalili reports that: "Between 1995 and 2004, Project Pheonix used radio telescopes to look at hundreds of Sun-like stars within a couple of hundred light years of Earth' without detecting any sign of alien civilization."[130] As detailed in a 2013 *Astrophysical Journal* paper, a targeted search of "86 Kepler Objects of Interest . . . hosting [164] planet candidates judged to be most amenable to the presence of Earth-like life"[131] looked for narrow band radio emissions but found "No signals of extraterrestrial origin . . . no evidence of advanced technology indicative of intelligent life,"[132] thus "placing limits on the presence of intelligent life in the galaxy . . ."[133] In 2017, the Berkeley SETI Research Center "Breakthrough Listen" project published its first results, explaining in a press release that they'd "examined data on 692 stars from the primary target list . . . Eleven events rose above the pipeline threshold

---

124. Webb, *Where Is Everybody?*, 101.
125. Webb, *Where Is Everybody?*, 88–105.
126. Bassala, *Civilized Life In The Universe*, 167.
127. Webb, *Where Is Everybody?*, 25.
128. Borucki quoted in Westcott, ""No one's out there"."
129. Lamb, *The Search for Extraterrestrial Intelligence: a Philosophical Inquiry*, 55.
130. Al-Khalili, *Aliens*, 3.
131. Siemion et al., "A 1.1 to 1.9 GHz SETI Survey of the Kepler Field," 3.
132. Siemion et al., "A 1.1 to 1.9 GHz SETI Survey of the Kepler Field," 13.
133. Siemion et al., "A 1.1 to 1.9 GHz SETI Survey of the Kepler Field," 14.

for significance, but further detailed analysis indicates that it is unlikely that any of these signals originate from artificial extraterrestrial sources."[134]

As well as investigating individual stars, astronomers have searched at the galactic level for the energetic signatures of any civilizations using much of a galaxy's starlight to satisfy their power requirements.[135] In 1999, the *Journal of the British Interplanetary Society* reported the results of one such search, noting: "For a sample of 137 galaxies, no such outliers are found."[136] A Swedish study of 1359 spiral galaxies, published in 2015, failed to detect signs of any galactic civilizations.[137] Also in 2015, another research group published the results of their extensive search for "the thermodynamic consequences of galactic-scale colonization."[138] As reported in *Scientific American*: "After examining some 100,000 nearby large galaxies a team of researchers led by The Pennsylvania State University astronomer Jason Wright has concluded that none of them contain any obvious signs of highly advanced technological civilizations."[139]

This ever-growing absence of evidence isn't a conclusive evidence for the absence of alien life per se, but it does disconfirm the idea that technologically advanced civilizations abound in or around our neck of the cosmos.

The absence of alien civilizations is the simplest answer to "the Fermi paradox—the contradiction between the apparent absence of aliens, and the common expectation that we should see evidence of their existence."[140] Observing that "we've seen no convincing evidence of other civilizations among the stars in our skies," astrobiologist Lewis Dartnell concludes that technologically sophisticated intelligent life "may well be vanishingly rare in the Galaxy."[141] Andrew Norton, Professor of Astrophysics at the Open University agrees that "intelligent, communicating life may well be extremely rare..."[142]

It's one thing for intelligent aliens to exist, but another for them to develop sophisticated technology (not to mention technology outstripping our own). As botanist William C. Burger observes: "Whether here on planet Earth or elsewhere in the universe, the assumption that since science happened once, science ought to happen often is wishful thinking."[143]

---

134. See: "Breakthrough Listen Initiative Publishes Initial Results."

135. See: "Kardashev scale."

136. Annis, "Placing a Limit on Star-fed Kardashev Type III Civilisations."

137. See: Zackrisson et al., "Extragalactic SETI."

138. Billings, "Alien Supercivilizations Absent from 100,000 Nearby Galaxies." See also: Griffith et al., "The Ĝ Infrared Search For Extraterrestrial Civilizations."

139. Billings, "Alien Supercivilizations Absent from 100,000 Nearby Galaxies." See also: "The Fermi Paradox and Our Search for Alien Life."

140. Webb, *Where Is Everybody?*, ix.

141. Dartnell, "(Un)welcome Visitors," 25. See also: O'Connell, "Alien Megastructure "Discovery;"" Ross, "Our Only Hope?"

142. Norton, "Ross 128 Mystery Signals Aren't From Aliens."

143. Berger, *How Unique Are We?*, 270.

First, "the march of technological advance from the Stone Age . . . was only possible because of what would appear to be an outrageously fortuitous set of environmental conditions, without which, despite our genius . . . no advance beyond the most primitive stone tools would have been possible."[144] As biologist Michael Denton explains:

> There is . . . every justification for viewing our planetary home with its oxygen-containing atmosphere, large land masses covered in trees, with its readily available and well scattered metal-bearing rocks as an ideal and perhaps unique environment for the use of fire and the development of metallurgy and ultimately the emergence of a technologically advanced complex society . . .[145]

Second, consider the fact that, as Indian philosopher Vishal Mangalwadi remarks: "The scientific perspective flowered in Europe as an outworking of medieval biblical theology."[146] As agnostic theoretical physicist Paul Davies explains:

> It was from the intellectual ferment brought about by the merging of Greek philosophy and Judeo-Islamic-Christian thought that modern science emerged, with its unidirectional linear time, its insistence on nature's rationality, and its emphasis on mathematical principles . . . [Today] even the most atheistic scientist accepts as an act of faith that the universe is not absurd, that there is a rational basis to physical existence manifested as a lawlike order in nature that is at least in part comprehensible to us. So science can proceed only if the scientist adopts an essentially theological worldview.[147]

In contrast to pagan and pantheistic worldviews, Christian belief in the incarnation elevated "the dignity of matter and of manual work . . . Modern science was possible only when investigators became willing to dirty their hands in workshops and laboratories, and only when they began to see all material things, which have been created by God, as good in themselves."[148]

In short:

> The origin of modern science and technology depend on a precise configuration of economic, cultural, philosophical, and theological precursors, and an unusually long-lasting and stable warm climate. Technology requires dexterity and a level of capacity to communicate that, of millions of known species of

---

144. Denton, *Fire Maker*, 614. See also: Parker et al., "The Pyrophilic Primate Hypothesis," 54–63; Berger, *How Unique Are We?*, 241–44.

145. Denton, *Nature's Destiny*, 394.

146. Mangalwadi, *The Book That Made Your World*, 223. See also: "The Theological Roots of Science;" Hannam, "How Christianity Led to the Rise of Modern Science;" Berger, *How Unique Are We?*, 251–70; Chapman, *Stargazers*; Chapman, *Slaying The Dragons*; Grant, *A History of Natural Philosophy*; Hannam, *God's Philosophers*; Harrison, *The Bible, Protestantism, and the Rise of Natural Science*.

147. Davies, "Physics and the Mind of God."

148. Koons, "Science and Theism," 83.

life, only humans possess. It also requires access to an oxygen-rich atmosphere, dry land, and concentrated ores. The laws of physics did not uniquely determine any of these. Until these factors came together, no civilization developed technology advanced enough to harness radio communication. And even on Earth, this has happened only once. What justification do we have for assuming that it's an inevitable result of life, even intelligent life, everywhere?[149]

Hence, as astrophysicist John Gribbin argues, "the kind of intelligent, technological civilization that has emerged on Earth may be unique, at least in our Milky Way Galaxy."[150]

Even if technologically sophisticated aliens exist, they might lack the means of visiting us (whether in person or via some sort of technological proxy). After all, our *closest* extrasolar star (a red dwarf called Proxima Centauri[151]) is 4.22 light years away (one light year, or the distance light travels in one year, being "roughly 9.5 billion km or 5.9 billion miles"[152]). According to Dartnell: "The laws of physics . . . strongly constrain movement across the vast gulfs between stars."[153] Atheist and science writer Michael White concludes: "All forms of sub-light travel restrict meaningful interstellar travel and the options for circumventing the light-speed barrier present huge technical difficulties."[154] While Krauss finds it "hard to believe that we are alone,"[155] he calculates that "Energy expenditures beyond our current wildest dreams would be needed"[156] to facilitate interstellar travel and concludes that "we probably don't have to worry too much about being abducted by aliens."[157] Likewise, Christopher Hitchens notes that "travel from Alpha Centauri . . . would involve some bending of the laws of physics . . ."[158]

Dawkins reckons that intelligent life "is probably extremely rare and isolated on far-flung islands of life, like a celestial Polynesia" and consequently concludes that

---

149. Gonzalez and Richards, *The Privileged Planet*, 287–88. See also: Berger, *How Unique Are We?*; Denton, *Fire Maker*; Dartnell, *Life in the Universe*, chapter eight; Denton, *Nature's Destiny*; Gribbin, *Alone in the Universe*, 204; Webb, *Where Is Everybody?*, 211–32.

150. Gribbin, *Alone in the Universe*, xiv.

151. Although Proxima Centauri has planets, it probably doesn't have any habitable planets. See: Tran, "An Earth-like Atmosphere May Not Survive Proxima b's Orbit;" Mack, ""Goldilocks" planets might not be so nice;" Davis, "Proxima b: could we live on this newly found planet—or could something else?"

152. Gribbin, *Alone in the Universe*, 1.

153. Dartnell, "(Un)welcome Visitors," 31.

154. White, *The Science of The X Files*, 19.

155. Krauss, *The Physics of Star Trek*, 127.

156. Krauss, *The Physics of Star Trek*, 128.

157. Krauss, *The Physics of Star Trek*, See also: Krauss, *Beyond Star Trek*.

158. Hitchens, *God Is Not Great*, 144.

"Visitations to one island by another are hugely more likely to be in the form of radio waves than visitations by corporeal beings."[159]

Even if technologically sophisticated aliens existed and had the ability to visit Earth, why would they visit in the first century? As Dartnell notes: "if the Galaxy does contain other intelligent life forms, they would likely be oblivious to our recent appearance . . . humanity has only been detectably civilised [that is, broadcasting radio waves] for about a century . . ."[160]

The alien conspiracy hypothesis is not only convoluted and highly *ad hoc*, but several facets of the theory are strongly *disconfirmed* by the available evidence.

Watch: "Is the Resurrection Hypothesis Really As Absurd as the Alien Hypothesis?" by William Lane Craig: https://youtu.be/QW97epVeN7Y

"Aliens & UFOs" Youtube playlist: www.youtube.com/playlist?list=PLQhh3qcwVEWii xwhvDhbqSoO3qcIK7zu5

"The Origin of Life" Youtube playlist: www.youtube.com/playlist?list=PLQhh3qcwVE WggFeEP9H7k1LyccfxzvoSr

"The Rare Earth Hypothesis" Youtube playlist: www.youtube.com/playlist?list=PLQhh 3qcwVEWiLU4H5kBr2JzSAzfIlTRst

"Physical Preconditions of Science & Technology" Youtube playlist: www.youtube. com/playlist?list=PLQhh3qcwVEWiEbtcuD5f8bK0DHH31Lg6Y

"The Theological Roots of Science" Youtube playlist: www.youtube.com/playlist?list=P LQhh3qcwVEWh3jDVYqFFzWSnTbtIUeCg3

Listen: "Scientific Rebuttals to Ancient Alien Conspiracy Theories as Alternatives to Biblical History" by Peter S. Williams: http://podcast.peterswilliams.com/e/scientific-rebuttals-to-ancient-alien-conspiracy-theories-as-popular-alternatives-to-biblical-history/

Read: "7 times that science explained aliens" by Nsikan Akpan and Joshua Barajas: www.pbs.org/newshour/updates/7-times-aliens-explained-science/

"Abduction by Aliens or Sleep Paralysis?" by Susan Blackmore: www.csicop.org/si/show/abduction_by_aliens_or_sleep_paralysis

"Ezekiel's Vision: An Alien UFO?" by Kyle Butt: www.apologeticspress.org/apcontent.aspx?category=11&article=1061

"Close encounters of the psychological kind" by Christopher C. French: https://thepsychologist.bps.org.uk/volume-28/october-2015/close-encounters-psychological-kind

"What About Alien Abductions?" by Erich Goode: www.psychologytoday.com/blog/the-paranormal/201205/what-about-alien-abductions

"Would Extraterrestrial Intelligent Life Spell Doom for Christianity?" by Guillermo Gonzalez: www.equip.org/article/would-extraterrestrial-intelligent-life-spell-doom-for-christianity/

"How Christianity Led to the Rise Of Modern Science" by James Hannam: www.equip.org/PDF/JAF3384.pdf

"Abductions and Hoaxes" by Joe Nickell: www.csicop.org/si/show/abductions_and_hoaxes

---

159. Dawkins, *Science In The Soul*, 210.
160. Dartnell, "(Un)welcome Visitors," 33.

"Von Däniken's Chariots: A Primer in the Art of Cooked Science" by John T. Omohundro: www.csicop.org/si/show/von_daumlnikenrsquos_chariots_a_primer_in_the_art_of_cooked_science

"Alien Abductions: The Real Deal?" by Kaja Perina: www.psychologytoday.com/articles/200303/alien-abductions-the-real-deal

"Toronto Aetherius Society: Jesus, Venusians, and some bad astronomy (Part 1)" by Karl Mamer: www.skepticnorth.com/2012/01/toronto-aetherius-society-jesus-venusians-and-some-bad-astronomy-part-1/

"Toronto Aetherius Society: His Master's Voice, stuff that goes boom, and a lack of proof (Part 2)" by Karl Mamer: www.skepticnorth.com/2012/01/toronto-aetherius-society-his-masters-voice-stuff-that-goes-boom-and-a-lack-of-proof-part-2/

Civilized Life In The Universe: Scientists On Intelligent Extraterrestrials by George Bassala

How Unique Are We? Perfect Planet, Clever Species by William C. Berger

Abducted: How People Come To Believe They Were Kidnapped By Aliens by Susan A. Clancy

The Cult Of Alien Gods: H.P. Lovecraft and Extraterrestrial Pop Culture by James Colavito

The Design of Life by William A. Dembski and Jonathan Wells

Fire Maker: How Humans Were Designed to Harness Fire and Transform Our Planet by Michael Denton

God, Life; Intelligence & the Universe edited by Terence J. Kelly SJ and Hilary D Regan

The Privileged Planet: How Our Place In The Cosmos Is Designed For Discovery by Guillermo Gonzalez and Jay W. Richards

Alone In The Universe: Why Our Planet Is Unique by John Gribbin

Lucky Planet: Why Earth is Exceptional—and What that Means for Life in the Universe by David Waltham

Rare Earth: Why Complex Life is Uncommon in the Universe by Peter C. Ward and Donald Brownlee

Where Is Everybody? Fifty Solutions To The Fermi Paradox And The Problem Of Extraterrestrial Life by Stephen Webb

The Past Is Human by Peter White

3c) Conspiracy involving time travel, etc.

We can generate a hypothesis with good explanatory scope if we posit that a human from the future went back in time and gave Jesus access to a time machine, along with other advanced technology. Having been born in Bethlehem and growing up to meet our hypothetical time traveller, Jesus could travel forward in time to Easter Sunday, appearing alive to the witnesses (with fake wounds?), having teleported his own corpse out of the tomb (he could also use the teleporter to come and/or go during his appearances). At or after his "ascension" (perhaps using "anti-gravity" or a "tractor beam"), Jesus could vanish by going back in time to be crucified on Good Friday.

Alternatively, technology from the future could be used to make it *look like* Jesus was crucified (one can imagine a scenario involving a stand-in and plastic surgery, or a clone). In any case, Jesus *was* seen alive after his death/apparent death, and the tomb *was* emptied, but the explanation is "technological" rather than "supernatural": no miracle needed.

The first question faced by this *ad hoc* "science" of the gaps hypothesis is: *would* Jesus participate in such a conspiracy? Such behavior seems to be disconfirmed by our evidence about his character. Attempts to explain away such disconfirmed behavior would only increase the already *ad hoc* nature of this hypothesis.

The second question faced by this hypothesis is: *could* Jesus participate in such a conspiracy? As noted above, teleportation doesn't appear to be technologically practicable, and it's doubtful that traveling back and forth in time is any more practicable.

While scientists have described some exotic theoretical scenarios under which Einstein's theory of general relativity is consistent with time-travel, they've yet to show that any of these scenarios are physically possible. In his book on *The Physics of Star Trek*, Lawrence Krauss reports:

> Kurt Gödel's time-machine solution in general relativity involves a universe with constant uniform energy density and zero pressure which spins but does not expand. More recently, a proposed time machine involving "cosmic strings" was ... shown to be unphysical. While wormhole time travel has yet to be definitively ruled out, preliminary investigations suggest that the quantum gravitational fluctuations themselves may cause wormholes to self-destruct before they could lead to time travel.[161]

In 2016, Ping Gao and Daniel Jafferis of Harvard University and Aron Wall of Stanford University published a paper describing how "a new species of traversable wormhole"[162] could theoretically result from the quantum coupling of two black holes linked by Hawking radiation, such that "something tossed into one will shimmy along the wormhole and, following certain events in the outside universe, exit the second [as Hawking radiation]."[163] Whilst quantum coupling "allows information to be recovered from black holes," it also "precludes using these traversable wormholes as time machines ... the wormhole doesn't offer any superluminal boost that could be exploited for time travel."[164] As Professor Robert Matthews comments:

> According to Jaefferis, calculations based on the wormhole types studied so far suggest that using them would actually be slower than simply travelling directly through space ... The laws of nature seem to insist that wormholes

---

161. Krauss, *The Physics of Star Trek*, 50–51.

162. Wolchover, "Newfound Wormhole Allows Information to Escape Black Holes." See also: Eck, "New Wormhole Could Resolve the Black Hole Information Paradox."

163. Wolchover, "Newfound Wormhole Allows Information to Escape Black Holes."

164. Wolchover, "Newfound Wormhole Allows Information to Escape Black Holes."

can either perform amazing feats but collapse in an instant, or be traversable but useless.[165]

In recent years, several scientists have proposed the theoretical possibility that dark matter (the existence of which "is still a hypothesis, albeit a rather well supported one"[166]) could facilitate the existence of large, stable wormholes, either in the center of our galaxy, or else in the galactic halo.[167] If one could travel at the speed of light, it would take about 25,000 years to reach the centre of the galaxy from Earth.[168] Earth may be closer to the galactic halo, at a distance of around 12,500 light-years.[169]

To claim that dark matter *could* facilitate wormholes in these locations isn't the same as showing that there *are* wormholes in these locations. Dr. Luke Barnes, a post-doctoral researcher at the Sydney Institute for Astronomy, says there's no reason to think there's a wormhole in the center of our galaxy:

> the hypothesis that there is a black hole at the centre of our galaxy explains the data [in particular, studies by Andrea Ghez of UCLA and her collaborators on the orbits of stars near the centre of our galaxy[170]] just fine. Furthermore, we know how to make a black hole—just collapse some matter and then keep feeding it to make it grow. We don't have any realistic astrophysical scenario to make a wormhole.[171]

Barnes points out that the halo wormhole hypothesis is disconfirmed by observational evidence, since "Wormholes are areas of extremely strong gravitational field, but all our observations of the halo are in very weak field regimes."[172] Indeed, Barnes reports that "all our observations are in the weak field, even those around the black hole at the centre of the galaxy ... the surrounds of the black hole at the centre of the galaxy have only been observed in the weak field limit. Newtonian gravity still works fine at the orbits of the stars we see around the black hole."[173]

Barnes additionally notes that we can see plenty of stars inside the enormous wormhole radii postulated by some of these scientists, and "it is hard to see how

---

165. Matthews, "Through The Wormhole," 44.
166. Lincoln, "Is Dark Matter Real?"
167. See: Dimopoulos, "Active galaxies may harbour wormholes if dark matter is axionic;" Li and Bambi, "Distinguishing black holes and wormholes with orbiting hot spots;" Rahaman et al., "Possible existence of wormholes in the galactic halo region;" Rahaman et al., "Could wormholes form in dark matter galactic halos?"
168. See: Williams, "Where is Earth in the Milky Way?"
169. See: Murmson, "How Did Astronomers Determine Where the Earth Is Located."
170. See: Sokol, "The Black-Hole Hunter Peering Into the Heart of Our Galaxy."
171. Personal correspondence.
172. Personal correspondence.
173. Personal correspondence.

there could be such an extreme warping of spacetime without any of the stars being affected."[174]

In any case, even if some such wormhole did exist, could be reached, and were traversable, there's no reason to think it would take you anywhere near any specific place and/or time you wanted to visit.

Krauss cautions: "My understanding of wormholes is that we have no idea how to make them stable and traversable without exotic unknown forms of energy, so any discussion of traversable wormholes as realistic travel devices is highly speculative at best."[175] Nobel-Prize-winning theoretical physicist Kip Thorne muses that "If a wormhole can be held open, the precise details of *how* remain a mystery,"[176] and states: "I doubt the laws of physics permit traversable wormholes . . . If they *can* exist, I doubt very much that they can form naturally in the astrophysical universe."[177] Thorne concludes: "there are very strong indications that wormholes that a human could travel through are forbidden by the laws of physics . . ."[178]

It's worth remembering that wormholes remain "hypothetical constructs."[179] According to Dr. Eric Christian and Dr. Louis Barbier of NASA: "Wormholes are allowed to exist in the math of 'General Relativity' . . . [So, if] general relativity is correct, there may be wormholes. But no one has any idea how they would be created, and there is no evidence for anything like a wormhole in the observed Universe."[180]

Moreover, there are serious *philosophical* questions about whether one can travel back in time, however one proposes to do it. As Krauss observes: "There are . . . perplexing questions that crop up the moment you think about time travel."[181]

In short, the "time travel, etc." hypothesis is *ad hoc*, has low *plausibility,* and is *disconfirmed* by the available evidence. As Krauss concludes: "While the possibility of time travel continues to tantalize physicists and laypeople alike, the odds are against it."[182]

Watch: "Thinking About Time Travel" Youtube playlist: www.youtube.com/playlist?list=PLQhh3qcwVEWi1ih_D_hJINA5ozXguom_c

"The hunt for a supermassive black hole" by Andrea Ghez: https://youtu.be/c8re1U9rCo4

Read: "God and Time" by William Lane Craig: www.reasonablefaith.org/god-and-time

---

174. Personal correspondence.
175. Krauss quoted in Wall, "Interstellar Reality Check."
176. Thorne, *The Science of* Interstellar, 132.
177. Thorne, *The Science of* Interstellar, 136.
178. Thorne quoted in Redd, "What is a Wormhole?"
179. Al-Khalili, *Paradox*, 203.
180. Christian, "Space Physics."
181. Krauss, *The Physics of Star Trek*, 14.
182. Krauss, "What Einstein and Bill Gates Teach Us About Time Travel."

"The Quantum Physics of Time Travel" by David Deutch and Michael Lockwood: http://ieas.unideb.hu/admin/file_7226.pdf

"The Metaphysics of D-CTCs: On the Underlying Assumptions of Deutsch's Quantum Solution to the Paradoxes of Time Travel" by Lucas Dunlap: http://philsci-archive.pitt.edu/11374/1/SMS_DCTC_AEDU_Version.pdf

"Why wormholes (probably) don't exist" by Matthew Francis: https://galileospendulum.org/2015/01/26/why-wormholes-probably-dont-exist/

"No Time Travel For Presentists" by Steven D. Hales: http://logos-and-episteme.acadiasi.ro/wp-content/uploads/2015/02/NO-TIME-TRAVEL-FOR-PRESENTISTS.pdf

"Would Astronauts Survive an Interstellar Trip Through a Wormhole?" by Victoria Jaggard: www.smithsonianmag.com/science-nature/would-astronauts-survive-interstellar-trip-through-wormhole-180953269/

"What Einstein and Bill Gates Teach Us About Time Travel" by Lawrence M. Krauss: www.nbcnews.com/storyline/the-big-questions/what-einstein-bill-gates-teach-us-about-time-travel-n757291

"Interstellar Reality Check: Could Our Galaxy Host a Wormhole?" www.nbcnews.com/science/weird-science/interstellar-reality-check-could-our-galaxy-host-wormhole-n290861

"Wormhole Time Travel "Possible" (If You're a Photon)" by Ian O'Neill: www.livescience.com/45812-wormhole-time-travel-possible-for-photons.html

"Do Not Book Your Trip Through Our Huge Galactic Wormhole Yet!" by Bob Novella: www.theskepticsguide.org/do-not-book-your-trip-through-our-huge-galactic-wormhole-yet

"Is Time Travel Possible For The Presentist?": www.tutorhunt.com/resource/4715/

"What is a Wormhole?" by Nola Taylor Redd: www.space.com/20881-wormholes.html

"Are Wormholes a Dead End for Faster-Than-Light Travel?" by Paul Sutter: www.scientificamerican.com/article/are-wormholes-a-dead-end-for-faster-than-light-travel/

The Only Wise God: The Compatibility of Divine Foreknowledge and Human Freedom by William Lane Craig

Time and Eternity: Exploring God's Relationship To Time by William Lane Craig

The Physics of Star Trek by Lawrence K. Krauss

Metaphysics: An Introduction by Alyssa Ney

3d) Conspiracy involving the virtual reality hypothesis.

A final conspiracy theory, which philosopher Richard Hanley suggests as a response to any miracle claim, would be to adopt the "virtual reality hypothesis" and to explain away the resurrection as a deliberate "glitch" within the world-simulation we inhabit. We've already discussed the problems with such a hypothesis (see: chapter one).

Alternative 4: Delusion theories

Delusion theories have the merit of recognizing the obvious sincerity of the disciples' testimony (as do conspiracy theories that include third parties who intentionally mislead the disciples). Delusion theories may be categorized into theories of "mundane" delusion (from observational mistakes to hallucinations) and theories of "paranormal" delusion. We will begin with the former, but the search to avoid the resurrection hypothesis will drive us to contemplate the latter.

Tomb delusion theories

Most delusion theories relate to the resurrection appearances, but some focus on trying to explain the empty tomb.

4a) THE WRONG TOMB

In 1907 theologian Kirsopp Lake suggested that the women disciples went to the wrong tomb on the Sunday morning, resulting in the delusional belief that Jesus' tomb was empty. Lake's *ad hoc* hypothesis ignores the evidence that the women knew where Jesus had been entombed: "The women who had come with Jesus from Galilee followed Joseph and saw the tomb and how his body was laid in it." (Luke 23:55)

Jesus was buried in a new family tomb with no other occupants (see: Matthew 27:60, Luke 23:53, John 19:41–42), and such a tomb is hard to confuse with another. As Robert Stein comments:

> this was no Forest Lawn Cemetary—Jerusalem Branch, where one could mistake tomb 10,358 with look-alike tomb 18,494! This was a private burial tomb. We have no reason for concluding that there were similar tombs in the immediate area that could have been confused with this one.[183]

Even if the women did get it wrong, Joseph (and Nicodemus) knew where Jesus was entombed (see: Mark 15:46; Luke 23:55; Matthew 27:59–60; John 19:38–39). Likewise, are we to believe the Jewish authorities posted a guard on the wrong tomb?

Moreover, when "Peter and the other disciple" (John 20:3) checked up on the women's reports about the empty tomb, they found Jesus' grave clothes inside (see: Luke 24:12; John 20:1–9).

4b) EARTHQUAKE

In 1913, the Austrian spiritualist Rudolf Steiner opined that one of the earthquakes reported by Matthew:

---

183. Stein, *Jesus the Messiah*, 267.

shook the tomb in which Jesus' body lay—and the stone which had been placed before the tomb was ripped away and a crevice opened in the ground and the body fell onto the crevice. Further vibrations caused the ground to close over the crevice. And when the people came in the morning the tomb was empty, for the earth had received Jesus' body; the stone, however, remained apart from the tomb.[184]

On this theory, the shared belief that the tomb was empty because Jesus' body had been deliberately removed (whether the agency involved was human or divine) was a delusion facilitated by the non-intelligent action of geological forces.

Modern science suggests that a fissure caused by an earthquake a) wouldn't form in the rock out of which the tombs around Jerusalem are hewn, b) probably wouldn't be wide enough for a body to fall into (fissures are typically only a few inches wide), c) probably wouldn't be deep enough to make a body disappear from view, and d) wouldn't close up after its formation.[185] As Ross Pomeroy explains:

> most fissures that result from earthquakes . . . form due to associated landslides or slumps tied to the rapid withdrawal of groundwater. "Most such cracks are on unconsolidated ground (as opposed to bedrock)," University of Utah seismologist James Pechmann told RCScience . . . These common fissures take time to form and are often no more than a few feet deep . . . The fissure type perpetuated by Hollywood—where the ground rapidly ruptures and swallows unsuspecting bystanders—is almost certainly a myth. When a normal fault slips, the soil near the surface can potentially rip apart, creating jagged cracks in the ground up to a meter in width. However, fissures of this variety aren't very deep or long—you could probably safely stand in them—and they definitely don't . . . seal themselves back up.[186]

In other words, even in the highly unlikely eventuality of the earth opening up under Jesus' corpse (and if it did, it wouldn't have left his grave-clothes behind!), it would have been obvious to one and all where the body had gone (in other words, this hypothesis lacks *explanatory power*).

Moreover, on the plausible assumption that the Church of the Holy Sepulcher marks the site of Jesus' burial, we can say that archaeology *disconfirms* Steiner's theory, since the rock shelf on which Jesus' corpse was laid is intact.

Finally, a general problem with the theories advanced by Lake and Steiner is that *they lack explanatory scope*, because they don't address either the resurrection appearance reports or the origin of belief in Jesus' resurrection.

---

184. Steiner, "The Fifth Gospel, Lecture 2."
185. See: Achenbach, "Gaping Earthquake Fissures Exist Only in People's Fears and Hollywood Movies."
186. Pomeroy, "Do People Ever Fall Down Earthquake Chasms?"

4c) Mistaken identity

Turning to delusion theories that attempt to deal with the reported resurrection appearances (but which fail to account for the empty tomb), Carl Stecher suggests the possibility of delusion by mistaken identity:

> After Jesus' execution, a disciple in great excitement tells the other disciples "I was in the market this morning, and I saw Jesus! I called to him, but the Roman legionnaires marched between us, and when they were gone he was no longer there." Remember, eyeglasses, like hearing aids, were not invented until centuries later. Near-sighted people had no help. And in several of the appearances reported in the gospels, notably that on the road to Emmaus and Mary Magdalene's encounter with Jesus, there were problems recognizing him. Such misidentifications of the dead are common to this day. Following Elvis' death and burial many people believed that he was still alive; they had seen him . . . driving in a convertible.[187]

One can understand how grieving disciples might well have "seen Jesus" in the crowd, although it seems unlikely that *all* the disciples had such experiences, and the disciples were apparently more concerned with hiding from the authorities than wandering around misidentifying strangers (see: John 20:19).

Indeed, the disciples no doubt understood both that such episodes of misidentification are possible and that they wouldn't be good grounds upon which to conclude that Jesus was alive, let alone resurrected. As Wright observes: "If the disciples had simply seen, or thought they had seen, someone they took to be Jesus, that would not by itself have generated the stories we have."[188] Moreover, what can this theory say about Saul?

The misidentification theory doesn't square with the intimate and prolonged nature of several of Jesus' resurrection appearances as reported by the four gospels. The misidentification of a distant figure briefly seen in a crowd, whether as a friend whom you believe to be dead or a stranger whom you believe to be alive (even someone, like Elvis, that you believe to be alive despite their reported death), just isn't the same as mistaking a person with whom you are in sustained close proximity as a friend whom you believe to be dead but now take to have been resurrected.

Moreover, the insufficiency of the misidentification theory is highlighted by the fact that on several occasions, those who met the resurrected Jesus *didn't recognize him* until later on in an extended meeting. For example, in a report that passes the criteria of embarrassment and the criteria of Semitisms (among others), Mary Magdalene initially mistook the resurrected Jesus for the cemetery's gardener (see: John 20:11–15). However, she recognized Jesus when he spoke to her by name (see: John 20:16). Moreover, he told her not to hold onto him (see: John 20:17), which indicates

---

187. Stecher, personal correspondence, September 14 2016.
188. Wright, *Surprised by Hope*, 69.

that she touched him. Again, in the case of the two disciples on the road to Emmaus, while they didn't recognize Jesus while he walked with them on the road (see: Luke 24:16), they recognized him at table when he blessed the bread for their evening meal (see: Luke 24:30–31).

Even if the mistaken identity theory were a good description of the reported resurrection appearances (which it isn't), and even if such experiences offered a plausible explanation for anyone to change their mind about Jesus' fate (which they don't), it would at best explain people coming to believe that Jesus hadn't died after all, or that he'd been miraculously resuscitated (like Lazarus), not that he'd been *resurrected* after being dead.

4d) Misleading "memories"

Stecher suggests that another source of appearance stories might be the phenomenon of co-opted false memories:

> We are . . . prone to completely co-opt memories of events as if they had happened to us when in fact someone else experienced the events and told us about them. Research is beginning to give us an understanding of how false memories of complete, emotional and self-participatory experiences are created in adults. False memories are constructed by combining actual memories with the content of suggestions received from others.[189]

Stecher provides an example:

> Some years ago I read an anecdote in the *Reader's Digest* about a woman from the Midwest shopping for jewelry in a Boston department store. This woman was confused when a clerk asked her "Do you have P-S-D-S?" She eventually worked out that this was the Boston way of asking, "Do you have pierced ears?" I related this story to my wife, who was very amused. Several years later, I heard my wife tell the story to friends. But in my wife's version, this had happened while she was shopping in Boston with her mother—my wife and her mother both having been born in Wisconsin. I told her that the story had actually originated in the *Reader's Digest*, but my wife still believes that it happened as she remembers.[190]

Although someone may misremember an event they heard about having happened to someone else as having happened to them, in such a case the event in question still *happened to someone* (indeed, perhaps both women simply had similar shopping experiences)!

---

189. McCormick, *Atheism and the Case Against Christ*, 88.
190. Stecher, personal correspondence, September 14 2016.

Moreover, this supposed appropriation of an experience happened in a context far removed from one in which the originating experience is being repeatedly discussed, perhaps even by the person who had that original experience. Would Mrs. Stecher have mistakenly co-opted the *Reader's Digest* story (if that's what happened) if Mr. Stecher had read that story out to her not just the once, but on a regular basis? Such a situation would surely be closer to someone hearing about a resurrection appearance in the early Christian community. Moreover, in the case Stecher relates we have conflicting accounts of who had the experience in question. When it comes to the resurrection we find no disputes over who had which experiences.

While experiments conducted by cognitive psychologist Elizabeth Loftus found that about 25 percent of subjects (5 out of 24 subjects) could be induced to develop a false memory of an event they had not experienced (e.g. being lost in a shopping mall as a small child[191]), about 75 percent of test subjects were not induced to develop a false memory.[192] Other researchers have found that "at least some kind of false memory could be implanted in between 20 percent and 40 percent of participants."[193] Of course, that leaves the majority (60–80 perecent) of people whose memories were *not* co-opted: "Overwhelmingly, most participants in these studies disbelieve the childhood event ever happened, and they doubt any apparently new memories that arise, despite the pressure to think otherwise."[194] As Pomeroy warns: "implanting a false memory in a person, and having them fully believe it, takes some doing. Even in the lab, researchers succeed less than half of the time . . ."[195]

In their paper "Creating Memories for False Autobiographical Events in Childhood: A Systematic Review," Chris R. Brewin and Bernice Andrews conclude:

> susceptibility to false memories of childhood events appears more limited than has been suggested. The data emphasise the complex judgements involved in distinguishing real from imaginary recollections and caution against accepting investigator-based ratings as necessarily corresponding to participants' self-reports.[196]

According to Brewin and Andrews:

> memory implantation studies . . . demonstrate that substantial numbers of college students can be encouraged to have false recollective experiences when they are misled by authoritative sources into believing that certain events

---

191. To make the suggestions plausible, relatives of the subjects provided researchers with details of shopping malls that they could have been, but were not, lost in as children. See: "Implanting False Memories: Lost in the Mall & Paul Ingram."

192. Wilson, "War & Remembrance."

193. Hyman and Pentland quoted in O'Leary, "Unravelling "Recovered Memory.""

194. Fradera, "It's easy to implant false childhood memories, right?"

195. Pomeroy, "Do People Ever Fall Down Earthquake Chasms?"

196. Brewin and Andrews, "Creating Memories for False Autobiographical Events in Childhood," 1.

happened to them in childhood. It is clear, however, that the results of these studies are highly variable and that a high proportion of these "memories" are speculative, partial or only in the form of images. Many participants harbour doubts about their authenticity, and they are not on average rated as being comparable with memories of true events. Attempts to adopt more stringent definitions of what constitutes a memory reduce the mean percentage of participants who respond to the suggestions from 47% to 15%.[197]

Even when "some recollective experience for the suggested events is induced" in memory implantation studies, "only in 15% [of study subjects] are these experiences likely to be rated as full memories."[198] For example, Loftus reports an experiment by researchers:

> who asked 27 highly hypnotizable individuals during hypnosis to choose a night from the previous week and to describe their activities during the half hour before going to sleep. The subjects were then instructed to relive that night, and a suggestion was implanted that they had heard some loud noises and had awakened. Almost one half (13) of the 27 subjects accepted the suggestion and stated *after* hypnosis that the suggested event had actually taken place. Of the 13, 6 were unequivocal in their certainty.[199]

Hence, even with a group of "highly hypnotizable individuals," most of the experimental subjects rejected the hypnotist's suggestion, and below a quarter of subjects were subjectively certain about the false memory. Indeed, Brewin and Andrews report that:

> average scores on measures of recollective experience and confidence in memory for false events all fell at or below the midpoint of the scales used. Even when clear memories were identified by the investigators, participants' confidence in them was below the scale midpoint.[200]

This experimental data disconfirms the hypothesis that the disciple's belief in Jesus' resurrection—a belief in which they placed so much confidence that they were prepared to suffer persecution and even death—was grounded in false and/or co-opted memories.

Again, Brewin and Andrews note that, under a stringent definition of memory (one that excludes images not experienced as memories), the percentage of participants in memory implantation studies who falsely came to believe they could recall

---

197. Brewin and Andrews, "Creating Memories for False Autobiographical Events in Childhood," 16.
198. Brewin and Andrews, "Creating Memories for False Autobiographical Events in Childhood," 1.
199. Loftus, "The Reality of Repressed Memories."
200. Brewin and Andrews, "Creating Memories for False Autobiographical Events in Childhood," 16.

an event from childhood: "ranged from 0% for events selected for being implausible (Pezdek et al., 1997, Study 2, receiving an enema) to 65% (Lindsay et al., 2004, put Slime in teacher's desk)."[201] That is, it's hard to implant false memories of events people judge to be unlikely:

> Pre-existing beliefs play a causal role in the acceptance of potential false memories as authentic... plausibility is an important factor in making such decisions. Whereas a fleeting memory of an ostensibly anomalous experience might be dismissed as probably being the memory of a dream by a sceptic, a believer is more likely to accept that it may reflect something that actually happened.[202]

If it's hard to get people to falsely believe they put slime in their teacher's desk or had an enema as a child, it must be harder to convince first-century Jews that they recently met a crucified man who had been *resurrected* from the dead.

While Robyn Fivush, Professor of Psychology at Emory University, acknowledges that it's possible to "introduce error into memory," he cautions that this can be done "only under certain conditions with certain people in certain ways."[203] Writing for *Scientific American*, Steven Ross Pomeroy lists eight conditions that maximize one's chances of generating a false memory in a subject:

1) "select one of your mates who, in your estimation, is 'prone to suggestion.'"

2) "you should be acquainted with this friend for at least five years, and have shared experiences with him or her. This will enhance your believability, and thus your odds of success."

3) "The false memory should have 'taken place' at least a year in the past... Choosing a childhood memory will give you the best odds of success. You'll have an easier time implanting something that supposedly occurred far in the past."

4) The proposed false memory should "not be unduly intricate... Studies have shown that it's easy to make people falsely recall small details about events, but as the fake memories grow in complexity and specificity, implantation grows progressively harder"

5) The proposed false memory should "not be something that might engender strong feelings of emotion... your target might not be as apt to accept a false memory if you told him or her that they experienced something highly emotional."

6) "If you're skilled at editing images, you could also try doctoring a photo [as one memory implantation study using a fake photograph had a 50% success rate]."

---

201. Brewin and Andrews, "Creating Memories for False Autobiographical Events in Childhood," 13.

202. French, "Fantastic Memories," 169.

203. Wilson, "War & Remembrance."

7) "You'll also need corroborators; the more the better."

8) "The memory may not stick right away; you'll probably have to bring it up multiple times over a span of days or even weeks."[204]

To this list we can add a ninth condition:

9) Your odds of success are better if you select a false memory your subject doesn't consider to be intrinsically improbable

Note that in the case of Jesus' purported resurrection:

1) It is unlikely that all of the witnesses would have been prone to suggestion.

2) Even in those cases where one or more disciple's memories could have influenced one or more other disciple's memories, many of the resurrection witnesses would have known each other for less than three years (the length of Jesus' public ministry).

3) The resurrection was an event the witnesses believed happened in the very recent past.

4) Several of the resurrection reports are quite intricate. For example, some of the resurrection appearances involve long conversations, or specific details about location, time of day, who was or wasn't there, the specific food that was eaten, etc. Belief in a resurrection appearance wasn't belief in a small detail about some event, but in a highly complex and specific event.

5) The resurrection appearances naturally engendered very strong emotions.

6) No one had a doctored photo of a resurrected Jesus, because no one had invented photography.

7) Although some appearance memories were formed in a context containing (sincere) "corroborators," they were clearly unable to exert much peer pressure upon those who reportedly disbelieved them (e.g. the male disciples disbelieved the women, Thomas disbelieved the other male disciples, Saul disbelieved all Christians). Moreover, no one was (even sincerely) playing the role of Pomeroy's coordinating memory prankster in these scenarios (unless one counts some of Jesus' own predictions about his fate, predictions that no one seems to have understood until after the fact). Note that, even if the story of an angelic appearance to the women at the empty tomb is accepted as historical (see: Matthew 28:6, Mark 16:6; Luke 24:6), the angels describe what had happened to Jesus' body using the *general* term for "raised up" (i.e. ēgerthē[205]), and neither the women nor the disciples from Emmaus knew what to make of their *non-specific* report that Jesus was "alive" (see: Luke 24:5; 24:22–24). Perhaps they wondered if they should

---

204. Pomeroy, "How to Install False Memories."
205. See: Bible Hub Commentaries, "ēgerthē."

take this statement in the spiritual sense used by Jesus when he told Martha: "Whoever believes in me, though he die, yet shall he live, and everyone who lives and believes in me shall never die." (John 11:25–26, ESV). Meanwhile, Mary Magdalene clearly thought Jesus' corpse was in need of being located until she believed she had met Jesus, having first mistaken him for the gardener (see: John 20:1–16).

8) It's clear that in many instances the witnesses' memories of a resurrected Jesus weren't formed over a span of days, but on the very day they made their appearance claims.

9) All of the resurrection witnesses would have considered a historical resurrection something they were very unlikely to experience.

Hence, in the first three purported appearances highlighted in Fig. 22 (see: chapter four), the evidence is against seven or eight out of our nine conditions for success. Furthermore, in the other cases highlighted in Fig. 22, the witnesses' memories were formed in the presence of, *at best*, only four of our nine conditions.

It's worth noting that these are conditions for maximizing success in inculcating a false memory *when someone armed with a modern knowledge of cognitive science is deliberately coordinating an attempt to achieve this goal* and that this pre-condition of conditions 1–9 remains unfulfilled in the case of the resurrection.

Indeed, positing the *deliberate* inculcation of false memories in the resurrection witnesses takes us back to a *conspiracy* theory, and does so in the absence of anyone to play the role of psychological experimenter. As Alex Fradera comments:

> It's clear that false memory paradigms can shift how we evaluate past events, and can for a minority of participants provoke memory-like experiences. But the rates are very low and the effects variable, and the one that produces the strongest effect—memory implantation—is also the most invasive, and least likely to match the experiences of people in normal life . . .[206]

Memory implantation experiments involve "authority figures conniving over multiple sessions to persuade a participant that an event really happened in their childhood"[207] and are thus fundamentally disanalogous to the experience of the resurrection witnesses.

Watch: "Memory Implantation" Youtube playlist: www.youtube.com/playlist?list=PLQhh3qcwVEWjoBnrBC8UZrQuIoMR5Hsq7

Read: "Creating Memories for False Autobiographical Events in Childhood: A Systematic Review" by Chris R. Brewin and Bernice Andrews: http://onlinelibrary.wiley.com/doi/10.1002/acp.3220/full

206. Fradera, "It's easy to implant false childhood memories, right?"
207. Fradera, "It's easy to implant false childhood memories, right?"

"Fantastic Memories: The Relevance of Research into eyewitness Testimony and False Memories for Reports of Anomalous Experiences" by Christopher C. French in *PSI Wars: Getting To Grips With The Paranormal* edited by James Alcock et al.

4e) Dream on

Stecher suggests "still another possibility"[208] that offers a source for the resurrection concept that's neither another person's reported experience nor the deceptive suggestion of some manipulative "experimenter":

> It's been widely noted that there was rivalry between Jesus' disciples . . . This too could have been a source of appearance stories. Andrew reports a vivid dream in which he was sure Jesus was speaking to him. Not to be outdone, Peter claims that Jesus appeared to him too . . . Years later, because of memory distortion, Peter fully believes that Jesus appeared to him. And that it wasn't a dream.[209]

It's not clear if Stecher imagines that Andrew's dream concerned a *resurrected* Jesus, or if Peter is supposed to have added this innovation. Either way, the proposed explanation lacks explanatory power.

Note that Stecher gives his delusion theories time to work that the NT evidence doesn't permit, saying that talk of dreams and/or misidentified strangers, "passed from one person to another before finally being recorded in the gospels . . ."[210] The faster the naturalistic mechanisms Stecher suggests are required to produce belief in Jesus' resurrection, the less plausible they become. However, all the evidence we have says that the disciple's resurrection experiences turned their world upside-down from the Sunday morning after the evening of Good Friday, and that they were successfully preaching a resurrected Jesus around 40 days thereafter in Jerusalem (Acts 1:3)! Peter didn't come to believe in the resurrection "years later"[211] as Stecher suggests, but was proclaiming the resurrection of Christ in Jerusalem *within weeks* of the crucifixion (see: Acts 2:14–40). Then again, multiple individual and group appearances were codified in creedal form by the Jerusalem church *within a few years or even months* of the crucifixion (see: 1 Corinthians 15).

Besides, if Andrew related what he knew to be a dream, how did he come to believe in the resurrection (it's historically plausible that Andrew was martyred by crucifixion[212])? Waking up from a dream about the dead usually only serves to re-

---

208. Stecher, personal correspondence, September 14 2016.
209. Stecher, personal correspondence, September 14 2016.
210. Stecher, personal correspondence, September 14 2016.
211. Stecher, personal correspondence, September 14 2016.
212. See: McDowell, "Did the Apostles die as Martyrs?"

mind one *that they are dead*. Why didn't Andrew point out to Peter and/or the other disciples that Peter had co-opted his dream as if it were something that had happened to him? And why did all the other disciples believe in the resurrection?

Again, what about Saul's resurrection experience? Saul wasn't part of the rivalry between disciples (nor, as far as we know, were Mary Magdalene or the other women). While Saul had no doubt heard about the disciples' belief in Jesus' resurrection a) he obviously didn't believe it until his road to Damascus experience, and b) he'd probably have heard about Jesus' purported ascension as well, which would have likely seemed to one and all to preclude Jesus appearing to anyone before the end of the world (see: Acts 1:11).

4f) Hallucinations

"there is nothing like the resurrection appearances in the psychological casebooks."
—WILLIAM LANE CRAIG[213]

A hallucination is an apparent perception via the physical senses lacking a corresponding external physical stimulus. The hypothesis that the disciples suffered hallucinations that convinced them Jesus had been resurrected traces back to Celsus in the second century, who said the resurrection was the "cock and bull story" of a "hysterical female" who "through wishful thinking had a hallucination due to some mistaken notion."[214]

Having sensibly dismissed what he calls "silly pop-history explanations never worthy of serious consideration: that Jesus only swooned on the cross and was revived; that his disciples stole the body; that Jesus had a twin brother," Carl Stecher likewise suggests what he calls the "more substantial possibility of grief hallucinations."[215] However, as Dale Allison writes:

> when assessed by standard criteria used for testing historical descriptions, [the] Hallucination Hypothesis is seen to have narrow explanatory scope, to have weak explanatory power, to be implausible, to be unacceptably ad hoc, to contradict quite a large number of accepted beliefs [i.e. to be disconfirmed by evidence], and not to outstrip its rivals in meeting these tests.[216]

Hallucinations are rare occurrences. Carl E. Olson observes that "group hallucinations are, at best, incredibly rare."[217] Indeed, many psychologists deny that group hallucinations happen, or are even possible. Joseph W. Bergeron and Gary R. Haber-

---

213. Craig, "Dale Allison on the Resurrection of Jesus."
214. Chadwick, *Origen*, 109.
215. Stecher, personal correspondence, September 14 2016.
216. Allison, "Resurrecting Jesus."
217. Olson, *Did Jesus Really Rise From the Dead?*, 108.

mas note that: "While some may consider the disciple's post-crucifixion encounters with the resurrected Jesus as collective simultaneous hallucinations, such an explanation is far outside mainstream clinical thought..."[218] They report:

> the concept of collective-hallucination is not found in peer reviewed medical and psychological literature ... and there is no mention of such phenomena in the Diagnostic and Statistical Manuel of Mental Disorders. As such, the concept of collective hallucinations is not part of current psychiatric understanding or accepted pathology. Collective hallucinations as an explanation for the disciple's post-crucifixion group experiences of Jesus is indefensible.[219]

Clinical psychologist Gary Collins argues:

> Hallucinations are individual occurrences. By their very nature only one person can see a given hallucination at a time. They certainly are not something which can be seen by a group of people ... Since a hallucination exists only in the subjective, personal sense, it is obvious that others cannot witness it.[220]

Clinical psychologist Gary A. Sibey writes:

> I have surveyed the professional literature (peer reviewed journal articles and books) written by psychologists, psychiatrists, and other relevant healthcare professionals during the past two decades and have yet to find a single documented case of a group hallucination...[221]

Bergeron and Habermas comment:

> Individuals within a group simply do not "collectively" experience identical simultaneous hallucinations. Rather ... when collective visionary experiences occur, some individuals in the group may experience similar but not identical personal hallucinations.[222]

They add that "the earliest list of resurrection appearances in 1 Cor. 15:3ff. alone presents an amazing array of visits to both individuals and especially groups, which is simply unparalleled in the bereavement literature."[223]

A 1971 survey of widows experiencing grief hallucinations showed that the duration of marriage "had a positive linear correlation to the percentage of persons describing bereavement experiences. Thus, the longer the marriage, the more likely it was for the living spouse to have bereavement experiences."[224] Even assuming that

---

218. Bergeron and Habermas, "The Resurrection of Jesus."
219. Bergeron and Habermas, "The Resurrection of Jesus."
220. Collins quoted in McDowell and Sterrett, *Did the Resurrection Happen...Really?*, 125.
221. Sibey quoted in Licona, *The Resurrection Of Jesus*, 484.
222. Bergeron and Habermas, "The Resurrection of Jesus."
223. Bergeron and Habermas, "The Resurrection of Jesus."
224. Bergeron and Habermas, "The Resurrection of Jesus."

experiences on the part of unmarried friends would be just as strong, most of the disciples would have known Jesus for only three years or less. Moreover, 46 percent of widows merely reported "feeling the presence" of the deceased. Visual experiences (more common in those over 40 years old) made up just 14 percent of such experiences, speaking with the spouse (more common in those over 60) 11.6 percent and tactile experiences only 2.7 percent.[225] The disciples reportedly touched Jesus on multiple occasions (see: John 20:17-28; Matthew 28:9; Luke 24:39).

A 2011 survey of recently bereaved individuals found that visual experiences of the deceased had a prevalence of just 4 percent.[226] A 2016 study by Gothenburg University found that 80 percent of elderly people (in their 70s) experienced a hallucination shortly after the death of a spouse. Half of the fifty participants in this study said they "felt a presence," while one in three said they either saw or heard their departed spouse. None of these bereavement experiences were taken by those having them to indicate that the deceased was alive, let alone resurrected!

According to the 1971 study: "If the spouse attempted to speak with the apparition, the vision would dissipate."[227] The resurrected Jesus held extended conversations in the presence of multiple individuals and groups (see: Luke 24:13-32 and 24:36-49; John 20:11-18; 20:19-23; 21:1-25; Acts 1:3 and 9:1-19). Hallucinations usually last seconds, or minutes at most. Jesus hung around for long stretches of time. Hallucinations usually happen only once. Jesus returned to the disciples many times (see: John 20:19; Acts 1:3). Bereavement hallucinations usually persist over years, not the limited time period reported by the NT. Hallucinations don't consume food. According to multiple reports, including two eyewitnesses, Jesus ate, and on at least two separate occasions (see: Luke 24:42-43, John 21:1-14, and Peter's testimony in Acts 10:41). Hallucinations come from within and draw upon what we already believe, so are unlikely to do surprising or unexpected things. The resurrected Jesus constantly surprised people: "the resurrection of Jesus involved ideas utterly foreign to the disciple's minds."[228] Finally: "hallucinations rarely produce longstanding convictions or radical lifestyle changes. But belief in the resurrection of Jesus did both."[229]

Hence, even in the unlikely case that the disciples suffered from multiple grief-induced hallucinations, it remains unlikely that they would all *see and hear* Jesus, let alone *an unexpectedly resurrected Jesus*, let alone *talk with* him, let alone *touch* him, let alone *see and hear and talk with and touch* him, let alone *in multiple individual and group settings*, and clearly not *over an extended length of time*! As Kreeft and Tacelli observe: "it is unlikely that so many various people under so many varied

---

225. See: Bergeron and Habermas, "The Resurrection of Jesus."
226. Simon et al., "Informing the Symptoms Profile of Complicated Grief," 118–26.
227. Bergeron and Habermas, "The Resurrection of Jesus."
228. Craig, "Dale Allison on the Resurrection of Jesus," 114.
229. Davis, *Rational Faith*, 76.

circumstances could experience [the requisite] hallucinations."[230] Indeed, as Winfried Corduan observes: "in the case of the Resurrection appearances, everything we know about hallucinations is violated."[231] In other words, because the hallucination hypothesis lacks *explanatory power* and is very strongly *disconfirmed* by the known nature of hallucinations, the theory implicitly amounts to the postulation of a *miraculous* hallucinatory sequence of delusional experiences, an *ad hoc* and *implausible* supernatural explanation that lacks the *explanatory scope* to address the empty tomb.

In purported cases of group hallucinations "expectation is a necessary prerequisite,"[232] but the evidence demonstrates that the disciples weren't expecting the resurrection appearances. Neither Mary Magdalene, nor the other women, nor the disciples from Emmaus, nor the ten disciples, nor Thomas, nor Saul believed Jesus was alive, let alone resurrected, until they had personal experiences of meeting him (during which experiences neither Mary nor the Emmaus disciples even recognized Jesus at first). As Vermes writes:

> The cross and the resurrection were unexpected, perplexing, indeed incomprehensible for the apostles . . . As for the resurrection, no one was awaiting it, nor were the apostles willing to believe the good news brought to them by the women who had visited the tomb of Jesus.[233]

It is *doubly embarrassing* that the disciples a) *failed to believe* the good news brought to them b) by the initial *female* witnesses. Hence the fact that male disciples dismissed the women's reports—as noted by Luke and John (see: Luke 24:11; John 20:25)—disconfirms the hallucination hypothesis by showing that they weren't in the receptive frame of mind the hypothesis requires. Besides, if the disciples were susceptible to hallucinations given circumstance of grief, guilt, etc., why didn't they hallucinate that Jesus had been vindicated in terms of the culturally well-established concept of having ascended to heaven to be with Abraham in paradise?

Consider again the road to Damascus incident. Although only Saul got the religiously significant detail of the experience, his companions saw a light and heard a noise (it's possible that they didn't see Jesus because they didn't look directly into the light that caused Saul's temporary blindness, and that they heard Jesus' voice without understanding what it said because they didn't speak the right language). Either Saul and his non-grief-stricken companions spontaneously suffered a coordinated set of hallucinations, or something objective happened. We've already considered and rejected an attempt at providing a naturalistic account of what that something might have been (the meteor thesis).

---

230. Kreeft and Tacelli, *Handbook of Christian Apologetics*, 120.
231. Corduan, *No Doubt About It*.
232. Kreeft and Tacelli, *Handbook of Christian Apologetics*, 84.
233. Vermes, *Jesus the Jew*, 86.

We might suppose, for the sake of argument, that Saul and his companions all witnessed a natural phenomenon of some kind or other and that Saul just happened to be in a state of mind such that this phenomenon triggered a hallucination. Even so, we must ask, why did he hallucinate *about Jesus*? More than that, why a *visual* hallucination that also *conversed* with him at some length (and gave him instructions that meshed with instructions Ananias thought he received from God in a vision)? More than that, why hallucinate a *resurrected* Jesus? To follow this road the skeptic has to swallow one unproven and unlikely *ad hoc* supposition on top of another:

> even if Paul felt sorrow for his mistreatment of his fellow Jews who had become Christians, it seems implausible to posit that as the basis of a hallucination vindicating Jesus in Paul's mind. It's one thing to experience remorse for having a hand in the death of someone you regard as peddling a false messiah; it's another thing for one's guilt to lead you to embrace the false messiah as true and to hallucinate a vision of him.[234]

Of course, "We have no indication that prior to his encounter with the risen Jesus Paul felt guilt for persecuting Christians."[235] But even if Paul felt some guilt, sorrow, or uncertainty about his mission, and even if his subconscious conjured up a hallucination to deal with the situation, why didn't it concoct a vision of God reassuring him that he was following the divine will? Such a hallucination would have cohered with Saul's cultural expectations and would have allowed him to retain his position of power and prestige. Instead, Saul had an experience on the Damascus road that cut against his cultural expectations and which led him to move from the position of the persecutor to that of the persecuted. The pile of *ad hoc* assumptions needed to explain away just the road to Damascus event puts one in mind of a stack of building blocks in proximity to a toddler.

Jake O'Connell makes another significant point about hallucinations and expectations when he points out that *even if a first-century Jew were predisposed to hallucinate a resurrected person*:

> many of those at the resurrection appearances would have expected Jesus to make a glorious appearance [see: Daniel 12:2; Mark 12:25; 2 Baruch; 1 Enoch; Testament of Job 40:3] . . . but the Gospels present us with purely non-glorious appearances . . . the evidence indicates that if stories of glorious appearances ever existed they would have been preserved by the tradition, and the absence of glorious appearances from the Gospel narratives is therefore indicative of the absence of any stories of glorious appearances at any point between AD 30 and 70. Since stories of glorious appearances should have been preserved if

---

234. Olson, *Did Jesus Really Rise From The Dead?*, 109.

235. Olson, *Did Jesus Really Rise From The Dead?*, 109. Of course, Paul needn't have felt sorrow or guilt about his persecution of Christians in order to ask or permit God to step in if he was on the wrong track. *Perhaps* he prayed that God would aid him in his mission against the Christians "if it was his will"?

the resurrection appearances were hallucinatory, their absence from the Gospel narratives serves as a strong argument against the hallucinatory nature of the appearances.[236]

Again, O'Connell points out that in the rare claimed cases of simultaneous hallucinations "not all present see the vision,"[237] whereas the evidence suggests that everyone present saw the resurrected Jesus. In purported cases of collective hallucination "Those who do see the vision see it differently,"[238] whereas in the case of the resurrection appearances, the experiences were coordinated (e.g. *neither* disciple on the road to Emmaus recognized Jesus until he broke bread with them, whereupon they *both* recognized him; *all* the disciples saw Jesus *cooking fish* for breakfast, etc.).

Perhaps most damningly, O'Connell points out that:

> a group conversation would be impossible if the vision was a hallucination . . . while expectation seems theoretically capable of accounting for collective visual hallucinations, it would not be able to give rise to a collective hallucinatory conversation. This is because, while a group of people could go expecting to see Jesus, or even go expecting to hear a short statement from Jesus . . . they could not possibly go with an entire conversation planned out in their mind.[239]

But the resurrection narratives present us with multiple conversations between Jesus and the disciples (e.g. Luke 24:13–35; John 20:10–18 and 24–29; John 21:15–24; Acts 1:3–9 and Acts 9:1–9). Hence O'Connell argues:

> if the hallucination hypothesis is correct [the] group appearances . . . 1) would have been expected; 2) would probably have involved some external signs of extreme stress (e.g. fainting); 3) would have involved Jesus being seen only by some members of the group; 4) would have involved Jesus being seen differently by those who did see him; 5) would not have involved Jesus conducting group conversations.[240]

Since the evidence contradicts each and every one of these predictions, O'Connell concludes that "the [resurrection] narratives are inconsistent with collective hallucinations . . ."[241]

C.S. Lewis highlighted the difficulty that "Any theory of hallucination breaks down on the fact . . . that on three separate occasions this hallucination was not

---

236. O'Connell, "Jesus' Resurrection and Collective Hallucinations," 105.
237. O'Connell, "Jesus' Resurrection and Collective Hallucinations," 85.
238. O'Connell, "Jesus' Resurrection and Collective Hallucinations," 85. While Paul and his traveling companions didn't share exactly the same experience, they all saw the bright light and heard a voice talking to Paul, absent any apparent expectation of such experiences (see: Acts 9:7 and 22:9).
239. O'Connell, "Jesus' Resurrection and Collective Hallucinations," 86.
240. O'Connell, "Jesus' Resurrection and Collective Hallucinations," 87–88.
241. O'Connell, "Jesus' Resurrection and Collective Hallucinations," 88.

immediately recognized as Jesus [Luke 24:13–31; John 20:15; 21:4]."[242] Why would the grieving disciples hallucinate *a Jesus that they didn't recognize*?

The need for multiple, sustained, collective, and coordinated multisensory episodes, without a context of expectation and involving unexpected content, puts an intolerable strain on any hallucination hypothesis:

> The resurrection of Jesus looks like an unlikely candidate for hallucination. The considerations here are several: Jesus' followers were not expecting a resurrection; many people saw the risen Jesus; the encounters were located in various places and times; some . . . only recognized him with difficulty (so they were certainly not *all* hallucinating); there were no drugs, high fever, or lack of food or water mentioned; and longstanding convictions and permanent lifestyle changes were produced. Taken together, these points constitute a powerful cumulative case against hallucination.[243]

Robert H. Gundry emphasizes the point that the hallucination theory simply fails to provide an adequate explanation for the disciples' belief in Jesus' *resurrection*:

> Normally, visions of deceased people have not been thought to imply physical resurrections resulting in empty tombs; rather, they have been thought to consist of ghostly apparitions. So it is hard to accept [the] thesis that reports concerning the emptiness of Jesus' tomb were made up because subjective visions of the post-mortem Jesus were thought to imply his physical resurrection.[244]

Christopher Bryan makes a broader point along the same lines as Gundry, about delusion theories in general:

> Everyone in the ancient world took it for granted that people had strange experiences of encountering dead people. They knew at least as much as we do about visions, ghosts, dreams, and the fact that when somebody is grieving over a person who has just died, they sometimes see, briefly, a figure that seems to be like that person appearing to them. This is not a modern invention or discovery; ancient literature is full of it. They had language for that sort of phenomena, and that language was not "resurrection."[245]

As Wright argues, any hypothesis proposed to explain the relevant historical data must grapple with the fact that:

> If the disciples had simply seen, or thought they had seen, someone they took to be Jesus, that would not by itself have generated the stories we have. Everyone in the ancient world took it for granted that people sometimes had strange experiences involving encounters with the dead, particularly the recently

---

242. Lewis, *Miracles*, chapter 16.
243. Davis, *Disputed Issues*, 72.
244. Gundry, *Jesus' Resurrection*, 109.
245. Bryan, "The Resurrection of the Messiah."

dead. They knew at least as much as we do about such visions, about ghosts and dreams—and the fact that such things often occurred within the context of bereavement or grief. They had language for this, and it wasn't "resurrection." However many such visions they had had, they wouldn't have said Jesus was raised from the dead; they weren't expecting such a resurrection.[246]

Dunn likewise stresses the need to convincingly account for:

> the first disciple's interpretation of their experience. For them to have understood that they were seeing the crucified Jesus *as risen from the dead* rather than as (simply!) translated or glorified was quite extraordinary. That it led them to the conclusion that God had raised Jesus from the dead, that Jesus had been raised as the beginning of the end-time general resurrection of the dead, was exceptional and unprecedented. That is why I am [confident] that this first Christian interpretation deserves a very high respect, and that Christians, on its basis, need have no qualms about affirming their faith in Jesus as risen.[247]

Watch: "Can hallucinations explain the resurrection?" Youtube playlist: www.youtube.com/playlist?list=PLQhh3qcwVEWgVNLsZOUCB5i64lC51Zsji

Read: "The Resurrection of Jesus: a Clinical Review of Psychiatric Hypotheses for the Biblical Story of Easter" by Joseph W. Bergeron and Gary R. Habermas: www.garyhabermas.com/articles/irish-theological-quarterly/Habermas_Resurrection%20of%20Jesus.pdf

"Jesus' Resurrection and Collective Hallucinations" by Jake O'Connell: www.tyndalehouse.com/Bulletin/60=2009/5%20O%27Connell.pdf

"Visions of Jesus: A Critical Assessment of Gerd Lüdemann's Hallucination Hypothesis" by William Lane Craig: www.reasonablefaith.org/visions-of-jesus-a-critical-assessment-of-gerd-ludemanns

---

4g) *Delusional pick and mix*

Suppose just one person had a grief-induced hallucination or a dream, which they mistook for an experience of a resurrected Jesus. Once that person has a deluded belief in the resurrection of Jesus, mightn't their delusion be co-opted as false memories by the other disciples? Perhaps this process might be helped along by the odd misidentification of distant men in the market?

Such a combination of delusion theories still requires *someone* to hit upon the concept of a *resurrected* Jesus in the absence of a plausible horizon of expectation, but it does have the merit of only requiring this to happen once. Moreover, such a scenario gains plausibility by avoiding appeals to group hallucinations. The problem is that

---

246. Wright, *Surprised by Hope*, 69.
247. Dunn, "In Grateful Dialogue," 321–22.

this mixed delusion theory buys a measure of internal plausibility at the cost of riding roughshod over the relevant external evidence.

The hypothesis of a chain of delusion transmitted via false memories has difficulty accounting for the fact that the resurrection appearances reported by the NT writers vary significantly from one another. They vary as to *when* they happened (e.g. morning or evening?), *where* they happened (e.g. inside or outside? Jerusalem or Galilee?) and *who* was there (e.g. women or men? Was Thomas there or not?), as well as the specifics of *what* happened (e.g. what did Jesus say and/or do? Did anyone touch Jesus?).

Indeed, the resurrection appearances cannot be arranged in a sequence of common descent through which one person's delusion could be co-opted by all the others. Mary Magdalene clearly didn't expect her encounter with the resurrected Jesus. The other women (another group experience) hadn't heard about Mary Magdalene's solo encounter.

Cleopas and his wife Mary (see: John 19:25) on the Emmaus road later that day apparently hadn't heard about the appearances to Mary Magdalene or the other women, and were simply bemused by the reported angelic affirmation that Jesus was alive (see: Luke 24:13–35). While the male disciples in the upper room (a third group experience) had heard the female disciples' report of encountering Jesus, "they did not believe the women, because their words seemed to them like nonsense" (Luke 24:11). Their rejection of the women's testimony (which is embarrassing in light of their later claims) makes it implausible that they co-opted the women's experience as their own.

Not that we can speak so easily of one group of people co-opting another group of people's group experience. For example, it makes no sense to think that the male disciples could have co-opted the women's experience of going to tend to Jesus' corpse, or of being told by Jesus to go and give a message *to the male disciples*, as their own experience! Even if they did co-opt the women's memory as their own, you'd think someone would point out that the women claimed to have exactly the same experience, only without the male disciples having been involved!

Likewise, although Thomas had heard the testimony of the other disciples, he didn't believe in the resurrection until he saw for himself. When he did, his (embarrassing) experience was unique, not a copy of anyone else's experience. Moreover, the group experience of the other disciples when Thomas met the resurrected Jesus for the first time was clearly distinguished from their previous group meeting with Jesus when Thomas wasn't with them.

Although Saul had no doubt heard claims about the resurrection of Jesus from Christians, he clearly didn't believe them. Moreover, Saul had likely heard from Christians about Jesus' purported ascension, which would have probably seemed to one and all to exclude Jesus appearing to anyone before his predicted second coming, even if Jesus was who Christians believed him to be (see: Acts 1:11; 1 Corinthians 15:8). It's clear that neither Saul nor his companions were co-opting anyone's memory of a resurrection appearance since a) Saul's experience was unique and b) Saul's companions didn't experience the resurrected Jesus (although they did experience a light and a voice that would require a further group hallucination to explain away). In sum, an appeal to false memory syndrome can't replace the appeal to *multiple* hallucinations, including *multiple group hallucinations*.

General problems with delusion theories

One general problem with theories positing mundane delusions to explain away the resurrection experiences is that in many of the documented cases, those experiences weren't *generic* experiences that could easily be "transmitted" from one person to another (like a false memory of being lost in a shopping mall). Instead, the resurrection experiences have various features that make them specific to the individual or individuals that had them.

Mundane delusion theories make *ad hoc* assumptions and rely upon ignoring disconfirming evidence. For example, to suggest that Mary Magdalene's belief in the resurrection resulted from mistaken identity or a hallucination means ignoring the evidence that:

- Mary thought Jesus' tomb was empty because his *corpse* had been moved.
- Far from mistaking the gardener for Jesus, Mary mistook Jesus for the gardener!
- Mary recognized Jesus at close quarters during the course of a conversation wherein she probably touched him.

As Kreeft and Tacelli observe: "The apostles could not have believed in the 'hallucination' if Jesus' corpse had still been in the tomb . . . for if it was a hallucination, where was the corpse? They would have checked for it [indeed, they did, see: Luke 24:12 and John 20:3–9]; if it was there, they could not have believed."[248]

Indeed, delusion theories that address the empty tomb fail to address the putative resurrection appearances, whilst delusion theories that address the putative resurrection appearances fail to address the empty tomb. To rectify this lack of explanatory scope, any delusion theory must be conjoined with an independent hypothesis that seeks to address the other relevant data. Of course, expanding the explanatory scope of one's theory in this way (e.g. combining grief-hallucinations with an earthquake) inevitably increases the *ad hoc* nature and complexity of one's theory.

In short, as agnostic philosopher Antony O'Hear concludes: "the standard rationalistic explanations in terms of auto-suggestion seem altogether too glib . . ."[249] Hence we need to turn our attention to less standard explanations.

---

248. Kreeft and Tacelli, *Handbook of Christian Apologetics*, 187–88.
249. O'Hear, *Jesus for Beginners*, 97.

Paranormal delusions

Let us draw a distinction between theories involving standard "mundane" psychological delusions and theories involving non-standard "paranormal" delusions. "Paranormal" is a term that designates phenomena "beyond the scope of normal scientific understanding."[250] This label leaves open the issue of whether the purported phenomenon at issue has a supernatural explanation or an as-yet-undiscovered or generally unrecognized, naturalistic explanation. Rational investigation of the paranormal should of course prioritize evidence over worldview presuppositions: "in a fair and critical hearing matters of evidence and logic must be paramount."[251]

4h) Psychic delusions

One might expand on a delusion theory by entertaining the possibility that one person's dream or hallucination of meeting a resurrected Jesus might be communicated to other people via some sort of psychic phenomenon, thereby positing a paranormal solution to the lack of "common descent" among the resurrection witnesses. However, there are many problems with the "psychic delusion" hypothesis:

1) The psychic delusion hypothesis doesn't address the *origin* of belief in the resurrection.

2) Caroline Watt, Senior Lecturer in Psychology and a founder member of the Koestler Parapsychology Unit at the University of Edinburgh, reports that "despite many advances in experimentation and analysis, the evidence for psychic abilities continues to be controversial."[252] Victor Stenger rejected what he called "the dead horse of psychic claims."[253] Sam Harris states: "While I remain open to evidence of psi phenomena—clairvoyance, telepathy, and so forth—the fact that they haven't been conclusively demonstrated in the lab is a very strong indication that they do not exist."[254]

3) Lest we are landed back with a conspiracy theory (subject to the inherent problems thereof), the paranormal powers posited by the psychic delusion theory need to operate *unintentionally* before being subsequently mistaken for an experience involving normal sensory faculties. However, parapsychological experiments almost inevitably focus upon the *intentional* use of psychic powers. Even research on spontaneous telepathic dreams involves a researcher deliberately

---

250. See: "Paranormal."
251. Roberts, "Science and experience," 18.
252. Watt, *Parapsychology*, 185.
253. Stenger, "Victor J. Stenger," 211.
254. Harris, "Response to Controversy."

trying to "send" information to the dreamer.[255] While there are anecdotal reports of spontaneous ESP during dreams, "foremost among these accounts are themes of death or danger,"[256] which is the opposite of the resurrection experiences!

4) Even granting the reality of the requisite psychic powers, it's unlikely that all the right disciples would just so happen to be psychically gifted/sensitive in a way that could bridge the "belief gaps" in the "common descent" between resurrection witnesses.

5) While it doesn't seem likely that people would confuse psychic experiences with everyday sensory experience (at least not within a matter of days), the resurrected Jesus was reportedly experienced via normal sensory faculties (sight, sound, touch) within days of his crucifixion.

6) Even according to paranormal researchers who believe in the reality of ESP, "ESP impressions can be vague and fleeting. It is rare for the receiver to give an exact and unambiguous description of the ESP target . . . ESP impression resemble weak sensory impressions, where one obtains only incomplete information which may be distorted or only partially represented in conscious awareness."[257] Brian Clegg describes remote viewing experiments as "at best" producing "remote impression gathering . . ."[258] However, we have multiple reports of protracted individual and group encounters with a resurrected Jesus featuring various different details that nevertheless cohere together.

7) The psychic delusion hypothesis posits a *transmission* of resurrection appearances and so fails to explain the witnesses reporting such *varied* experiences of the resurrected Jesus. Suggesting that the psychic influence of one deluded disciple might cause other people to hallucinate the widely *different* resurrection encounters reported in the NT is *ad hoc*.

8) Finally, even if they are real, such psychic phenomena lack the explanatory scope to explain the empty tomb.

Watch: "Telepathy" Youtube playlist: www.youtube.com/playlist?list=PLQhh3qcwVEWg YUp52F1huI_yr38G6QDxB

Read: "Further Possible Psychological Connectedness Between Identical Twins: The London Study" by Adrian Parker and Christian Jensen: www.deanradin.com/evidence/Parker2013.pdf

"Replicable Functional Magnetic Resonance Imaging Evidence of Correlated Brain Signals Between Physically and Sensory Isolated Subjects" by Todd R. Richards et al.: www.deanradin.com/evidence/RichardsKozak2005.pdf

255. See: Henry, *Parapsychology*, 103.
256. Mueller and Roberts, "Dreams," 98.
257. Watt, "Paranormal cognition," 136.
258. Clegg, *Extra Sensory*, 128.

"A Bayes Factor Meta-Analysis of Recent Extrasensory Perception Experiments: Comment on Storm, Tressoldi, and Di Risio (2010)" by Jeffrey N. Rouder et al.: www.deanradin.com/evidence/Rouder2013Bayes.pdf

"Testing the Storm et al. (2010) Meta-Analysis Using Bayesian and Frequentist Approaches: Reply to Rouder et al. (2013)" by Lance Storm et al.: www.deanradin.com/evidence/Storm2013reply.pdf

"Revisiting the Ganzfeld ESP Debate: A Basic Review And Assessment" by Brian J. Williams: www.deanradin.com/evidence/Williams2011Ganz.pdf

PSI Wars: Getting To Grips With The Paranormal edited by James Alcock et al.

Extra Sensory: The Science And Pseudoscience Of Telepathy And Other Powers Of The Mind by Brian Clegg

Parapsychology: The Science of Unusual Experience edited by David Groome and Ron Roberts

Beginners Guides: Parapsychology by Caroline Watt

4i) Ghostly goings-on

Many people believe in ghosts.[259] Michael White collates reports of ghosts into two phenomenological categories:

> apparitions and poltergeists . . . apparitions are largely *passive*, whereas poltergeists are *active*. Apparitions are usually witnessed as images, which impart information or respond to living beings only rarely, whereas poltergeists are frequently reported to interact with the living and are often said to be malevolent, even murderous.[260]

White observes that "The most common time to see a ghost is late at night and usually at the point of going to sleep," a fact that suggests the plausibility of explaining most such encounters in terms of sleep-related hallucinations. Indeed, it seems plausible to chalk up most ghost reports to the misidentification of mundane phenomena or to hallucinations of various kinds (while some reports are hoaxes).[261] Nevertheless, it might be conjectured that appearances by Jesus' ghost sparked belief in his resurrection. Moreover, paranormal investigators have proposed some explanations for "ghosts" that naturalists might try to apply to Jesus' purported resurrection appearances.

One naturalistic hypothesis advanced to explain one class of "ghost" reports is that "there may be some natural mechanism by which the energy of an event or person

---

259. David Groome and Ron Roberts report: "a survey carried out in the UK (Theos, 2009) of 2,060 British adults found that 39 percent believe in ghosts . . . Similarly, a survey carried out in the USA (Harris Poll, 2013) of 2,250 American adults found that 42 percent believe in ghosts . . ."–*Parapsychology*, 2.

260. White, *The Science of* The X-Files, 115.

261. See: Watt, *Parapsychology*, 120–22.

could be recorded in the environment."²⁶² Maurice Townsend, former chairman of the *Association for the Scientific Study of Anomalous Phenomena*, explains: "We all know cases where the same kind of phenomena recur at the same places time after time. Some people have hypothesised that the phenomenon is, in fact, a real recording of a past event, somehow imprinted onto the local surroundings."²⁶³

White reports:

> The majority of ghosts appear to individuals, invariably at night or in darkness and have little or no interaction with the environment . . . [These] apparitions usually perform a basic set of movements (and occasionally sounds) within a limited frame of reference. They appear to be tied in some way to a particular building or even a specific room, and to follow through repeated, identical movements—for example a walk along a corridor or across a room—and many appear only at certain times or under special conditions.²⁶⁴

There's a *prima facie* plausibility about treating repetitive, non-interacting "ghosts" as some sort of environmental "recording." On this "place memory" hypothesis,²⁶⁵ what the resurrection witnesses experienced wasn't a resurrected Jesus, but the playback of historical recordings somehow encoded into and projected out of the physical environment.

Although White reckons that mundane explanations (hallucinations, etc.) are adequate to account for most ghost reports, he remains open to the "place memory" hypothesis as an explanation for some "ghost" experiences. By contrast, Townsend records his "severe doubts about the 'recording' theory of ghosts," arguing that "Cases of apparent 'recording' can generally be explained just as well by other causes, such as environmentally stimulated hallucinations."²⁶⁶

Since some poltergeist cases are known to have mundane explanations (for example, some are known to have been hoaxes), one might conclude that all poltergeist cases have mundane explanations. Nevertheless, parapsychologists William Roll and Craig Hamilton-Parker suggest that some poltergeists might be instances of "recurrent spontaneous psychokinesis" that "result from psychokinetic energy projected from" a person whose "inner problems" express themselves by making objects move.²⁶⁷ Alternatively, Italian scientists Pierro Brovetto and Vera Maxia hypothesize that:

> changes in the brain that occur at puberty involve fluctuations in electron activity that, in rare cases, can create disturbances up to a few metres around

---

262. White, *The Science of* The X-Files, 116.
263. Townsend, "Recording Ghosts?"
264. White, *The Science of* The X-Files, 115–16.
265. See: Heath, "A New Theory of Place Memory;" Persinger and Dotta, "Temporal Patterns of Photon Emissions Can Be Stored."
266. Townsend, "Recording Ghosts?" See also: Townsend, "Magnetic Fields Causing Ghosts?"
267. See: "Poltergeist."

the outside of the brain. These disturbances . . . would substantially enhance the presence of the virtual particles surrounding the person. This could slowly increase the pressure of air around them, moving objects and even sending them hurtling across the room.[268]

It bears noting that the statistical evidence for even micro-psychokinetic effects (e.g. on random number generators), let alone macro-psychokinetic effects as required by human-centric poltergeist theories, is highly controversial.[269] As Watt reports: "the majority of academic parapsychologists do not find the evidence compelling in favour of macro-PK."[270] Nobel laureate physicist Brian Josephson calls the Brovetto-Maxia hypothesis "distinctly flaky."[271]

There's no evidence Jesus visited the Jerusalem tombs or Emmaus before his death. This makes the hypothesis of place-memory apparitions in these locations *ad hoc*. Again, while place-memory apparitions are supposed to be recurrent phenomena, in no resurrection appearance is Jesus reported as reenacting a previous appearance. Instead, the resurrected Jesus is reported as doing new things.

While the *active* Jesus of the resurrection reports is in this respect a better fit with the *active* poltergeist category than the *passive* apparition category, the resurrection reports depict *the wrong sort of activity* to fit the poltergeist category. The resurrection reports simply don't square with the unseen, object-flinging force typical of poltergeist activity. However, neither do the resurrection reports square with White's description of apparitions as phenomena that appear mainly to individuals rather than groups, rarely make sounds, are limited to a single location, repeatedly follow identical movements, and only appear at certain times or under special conditions. The Jesus of the resurrection reports spoke, conversed, and otherwise interacted with his environment (being touched and eating food) for sustained periods of time in a variety of different locations and at different times of day. The resurrected Jesus wasn't experienced as an apparition repeatedly replaying scenes from a life like a recording but as a living personality interacting with the world around him.

Moreover, while a place memory apparition is reportedly a long-term phenomenon, the disciples didn't experience the resurrected Jesus after his ascension.

Finally, since the disciples' folk ontology accepted the reality of ghosts (see: Mark 6:49 and Matthew 14:26), if the resurrection appearances could be contained within this category, why would they proclaim that Jesus had been *resurrected*?

In sum, paranormal place-memory and psychokinetic theories fail to explain the disciples' belief in Jesus' resurrection. The hypothesis of environmentally triggered hallucinations is also inadequate, especially given the variety of reported resurrection

---

268. Merali, "They're Here."
269. See: Bösch et al., "Examining Psychokinesis;" Henry, "Psychokinesis;" Alcock et al., *PSI Wars*.
270. Watt, *Parapsychology*, 37.
271. Josephson quoted in Merali, "They're Here."

encounters in different locations. Neither would any such experiences explain the empty tomb.

Watch: "Ghosts and Science" Youtube playlist: www.youtube.com/playlist?list=PLQhh3q cwVEWhIqjrqHG_X5vIbzlUSZz_t

Read: "Examining Psychokinesis: The Interaction of Human Intention with Random Number Generators. A Meta-Analysis" by Holger Bösch et al.: www.ebo.de/publikationen/pk_ma.pdf

"Temporal Patterns of Photon Emissions Can Be Stored and Retrieved Several Days Later From the "Same Space": Experimental and Quantitative Evidence" by M.A. Persinger and B.T. Dotta: www.neuroquantology.com/index.php/journal/article/download/467/443

"Testing the Storm et al. (2010) Meta-Analysis Using Baysean and Frequentist Approaches: Reply to Rorder et al. (2013)" by Lance Storm et al.: www.deanradin.com/evidence/Storm2013reply.pdf

"An investigation into alleged "hauntings"" by Richard Wiseman et al.: www.richardwiseman.com/resources/BJP-hauntings.pdf

Extra Sensory: The Science And Pseudoscience Of Telepathy And Other Powers Of The Mind by Brian Clegg

Beginners Guides: Parapsychology by Caroline Watt

4j) Apparitions and/or supernatural visions

Given the problems with naturalistic paranormal theories, one might wonder if the resurrected Jesus was some sort of a ghostly "apparition" or supernatural "objective vision" (especially if one is not dogmatically wedded to a naturalistic worldview).

Parapsychologists Andrew MacKenzie and Jane Henry write:

> The "churchyard" ghost of fiction is usually described as a white, wispy, semi-transparent figure, seen at night. In real life, in experiences reported by reliable witnesses, an apparition is often mistaken for a living person, being three-dimensional, often showing some awareness of the living, and sometimes able to speak a few words . . . appearances are often for a minute or less. Although the figure is seemingly solid we would not be able to grasp it . . . Apparitional . . . experiences have been reported for centuries and include collective cases, where more than one person sees the same apparition, and crisis apparitions, where, on some occasions, people appear to gain correct information about the death of a relative they would not otherwise have known.[272]

In this context, an "apparition" can be defined as a dead person revealing themselves to the living in a physically perceptible manner, an occurrence that's attributed to an *intrinsic* ability of the human mind or spirit. Around 10 percent of the population

---

272. MacKenzie and Henry, "Apparitions and encounters," 176, 185.

claims to have seen an apparition. Of course, one must consider how many of these claims are best explained naturalistically.[273]

Jake H. O'Connell notes that "to argue that the resurrection appearances are the same phenomenon as typical apparitions is to argue that . . . we should expect that whatever laws typical apparitions follow . . . were followed in the resurrection appearances."[274]

The "objective vision" hypothesis posits postmortem visions of Jesus *with an extrinsic supernatural cause* (i.e. God). O'Connell notes that on this hypothesis, "since the cause is entirely supernatural, we should not expect the resurrection appearances to be bound by the laws of apparitions."[275]

A third hypothesis combines the apparition and vision hypotheses. This is a hypothesis "according to which the resurrection appearances generally followed the laws of apparitions, but which proposes that God in some instances intervened so that the appearances did not always follow these laws."[276]

Finally, "physical mediums" claim that certain physical phenomena are produced by or with help from the agency of the dead during séances, including the "materialization" (in whole or in part) of "ectoplasmic" bodies, the "direct voice" (wherein a deceased person allegedly speaks from mid-air), and the *Star Trek* transporter-like "apport." Might a combination of these phenomena have produced belief in the resurrection?

These hypotheses are delusion hypotheses in the sense that they posit that the disciples came to believe in Jesus' resurrection on the basis of experiences that didn't involve a resurrected Jesus. Nevertheless, it should be noted that in all the hypothetical cases described above: "Jesus is still thought to have been literally revealed in some real sense . . ."[277]

A GHOST OF A CHANCE

The more one pays attention to the historically established details of the resurrection reports, the further one is forced to stretch the apparition hypothesis to accommodate those details and the less plausible the hypothesis becomes. Habermas emphasizes that "[A] number of Jesus' appearances, even to groups of observers, including the specific messages and other details that require a patchwork comparison of apparitions, along with the glorified appearance to Paul, are each at least fairly well evidenced."[278] In other words, the apparitional hypothesis *lacks explanatory power* compared to the

---

273. See: O'Connell, *Jesus' Resurrection and Apparitions*, 2.
274. O'Connell, *Jesus' Resurrection and Apparitions*, 12.
275. O'Connell, *Jesus' Resurrection and Apparitions*, 13.
276. O'Connell, *Jesus' Resurrection and Apparitions*, 13.
277. Habermas, "The Resurrection Appearances of Jesus," 272–73.
278. O'Connell, *Jesus' Resurrection and Apparitions*, 311.

resurrection hypothesis when we take into account the number and nature of the appearance reports supported by multiple criteria of authenticity. As Licona observes:

> Apparitions are not usually observed by groups . . . are not usually touched . . . and are not usually accompanied by belief that the person has been raised bodily from the dead . . . In fact, there are no cases in the literature of such an apparition.[279]

While apparitions reportedly appear to groups in about ten percent of cases, Andrew MacKenzie and Jane Henry note that "all present may not share the experience."[280] There's no resurrection report wherein it seems that anyone present failed to share the experience. In sum, it would take multiple unprecedented apparitional episodes to account for Jesus' postmortem appearances.

Having studied the paranormal literature on apparitions, O'Connell highlights numerous points where the apparitional hypothesis has low explanatory power, especially as compared to the resurrection hypothesis. For example, he reports:

> I have reviewed a large number of cases of collective apparitions, and . . . I have not found a single well-evidenced case of an apparition which appeared to more than four people. Thus the appearance to . . . the eleven . . . the 500, and all the apostles would be exceedingly improbable given the apparition hypothesis. However, these appearances are not exceedingly improbable given the resurrection hypothesis.[281]

Moreover, "An apparition which appears both recurrently and collectively is a quite uncommon find in the apparition literature . . ."[282] While many of Jesus' appearances lasted a long time, "Long appearances are exceedingly improbable given the apparition hypothesis, for apparitions rarely, if ever, last very long."[283] Caroline Watt also notes the "often fleeting nature of apparitional experiences."[284] Jesus' appearances were reportedly sustained over the course of conversations, long walks, and meals. Furthermore, "apparitions which appear to persecutors, or which make an appearance which is in any way analogous to an appearance to a persecutor, are very uncommon."[285] Yet Jesus reportedly appeared to Saul (as well as to his skeptical brother James).

O'Connell concludes that the resurrection appearances fail "to be bound by the laws of apparitions."[286] Dale Allison concludes that, with reference to understanding

---

279. Licona, *The Resurrection of Jesus*, 635.
280. See: MacKenzie and Henry, "Apparitions and encounters," 177.
281. O'Connell, *Jesus' Resurrection and Apparitions*, 224–25.
282. O'Connell, *Jesus' Resurrection and Apparitions*, 226.
283. O'Connell, *Jesus' Resurrection and Apparitions*,, 233.
284. Watt, *Parapsychology*, 111.
285. O'Connell, *Jesus' Resurrection and Apparitions*, 228.
286. O'Connell, *Jesus' Resurrection and Apparitions*, 13.

what happened to Jesus, the literature on apparitions "should be understood as heuristic, not as supplying a reductionist explanation."[287]

Turning from apparitions to visions, O'Connell argues that:

> First, the early Christians clearly believed the appearances were physical . . . and second, the Gospels present us with much data indicating that the appearances were indeed physical (e.g. Jesus eating and saying he is resurrected).[288]

Indeed, O'Connell emphasizes:

> The most pressing problem for [the apparition and/or objective vision] hypothesis is the fact that Jesus tells the disciples he is raised. Jesus tells the disciples he has risen from the dead, and in fact, even tells them he is not an apparition.[289]

According to Luke (writing in the middle of the first century) the resurrected Jesus was at pains to counter the male disciples' *culturally plausible* but nevertheless *embarrassing* initial assumption *that they were seeing a ghost*:

> While they were all talking about this, Jesus himself stood among them and told them, "Peace be with you." They were startled and terrified, thinking they were seeing a ghost. But Jesus told them, "What's frightening you? And why are you doubting? Look at my hands and my feet, because it's really me. Touch me and look at me, because a ghost doesn't have flesh and bones as you see that I have." After he had said this, he showed them his hands and his feet. Even though they were still skeptical due to their joy and astonishment, Jesus asked them, "Do you have anything here to eat?" They gave him a piece of broiled fish, and he took it and ate it in their presence. (Luke 24:36–43, ISV)

This incident is mentioned c. AD 108 by Ignatius in an apparently independent form:

> Some unbelievers say [Jesus] suffered in appearance only. Not so . . . when he came to Peter and his companions he said, "Take hold and feel me, and see that I am not a bodiless phantom." And immediately they touched him and believed, when they had contact with his flesh and blood.[290]

It's worth remembering that Ignatius knew Peter and John the apostle, as well as people (e.g. Polycarp and Papias) who knew John (either the apostle or the elder) and the four daughters of Phillip the evangelist.

To accept the objective vision hypothesis is to accept a supernatural hypothesis that implies a divine stamp of approval upon the elevated personal claims made by

---

287. Allison, "Resurrecting Jesus," 333.
288. O'Connell, *Jesus' Resurrection and Apparitions*, 255.
289. O'Connell, *Jesus' Resurrection and Apparitions*, 235.
290. Bettenson, *The Early Christian Fathers*, 48–49.

Jesus *prior* to his death. However, Jesus' claims also included prophecies (see: Mark 8:31, 9:9, and 10:34; Luke 18:33, 24:7, and 24:46; John 2:19–21, Mark 14:57–58; Matthew 26:61 and 16:4, Luke 11:29–30; Jonah 1:17[291]) of Jesus' resurrection (or at least his return to embodied life) soon after his death. Again, Jesus claimed to fulfill OT prophecies about the messiah, and these plausibly include prophecy of his resurrection (e.g. Isaiah 53[292]). Moreover, Jesus claimed that the Holy Spirit would guide his apostles into the truth about him (see: John 16:13), and this surely applies to the central Christian belief in his resurrection.[293]

O'Connell concludes:

> the resurrection appearances do not merely differ from typical apparitions, but they differ in just the manner we would expect them to differ if the resurrection appearances were appearances of a physical being—for . . . there is a large amount of data which is more probable given that Jesus was resurrected than given that he was an apparition. Hence if the combination apparition/vision theory is true . . . the disciples [are presented] with data designed to mislead them into thinking he is physically raised. Therefore, this theory carries all of the same problems as the objective vision theory in its simpler form . . . If we think the probability God would actually raise Jesus from the dead is higher than the probability God would mislead the disciples into thinking Jesus was raised from the dead, then the resurrection hypothesis is the most probable . . .[294]

As Habermas observes, although apparitions "were well-known in the ancient world [they] were not expressed as resurrections . . . To the contrary, although these apparitions may have comforted the mourners, we must not lose sight of the fact that these persons were definitely known to have remained dead!"[295] Likewise, visionary experiences were recognized but were not expressed in terms of resurrection. Hence neither hypothesis explains why experiencing such culturally-expected phenomena would lead the disciples to the culturally-unprecedented belief that Jesus had been *resurrected*:

> the New Testament writers consistently distinguished between the resurrection appearances of Jesus and later visions. Something set these appearances apart . . . the resurrection appearances seem to have been of a different quality . . . while there is clearly some overlap between Jesus's appearances and

---

291. See: McLatchie, "The fallacy of the sign of Jonah objection;" Craig, "Problems with the Old Testament."
292. See: Piper, "The Risen Christ."
293. See: Bible Hub Commentaries, "John 16:13."
294. O'Connell, *Jesus' Resurrection and Apparitions*, 260–61.
295. Habermas, "Dale Allison's Resurrection Skepticism," 309.

apparitions . . . Jesus's appearances do what the New Testament writers attest—they break all the categories. They were indeed unique.[296]

Moreover, the hypothesis of supernatural apparitions and/or visions *lacks explanatory scope* because it fails to account for the empty tomb.

Read: "Dale Allison on Jesus' Empty Tomb, his Postmortem Appearances, and the Origin of the Disciples' Belief in his Resurrection" by William Lane Craig: www.reasonablefaith.org/writings/scholarly-writings/historical-jesus/dale-allison-on-jesus-empty-tomb-his-post-mortem-appearances-and-the-origin/

"Dale Allison on the Resurrection of Jesus" by William Lane Craig: www.reasonablefaith.org/question-answer/P20/dale-allison-on-the-resurrection-of-jesus

"Dale Alison's Resurrection Skepticism: A Critique" by Gary R. Habermas: www.garyhabermas.com/articles/phil_christi/habermas_phil_christi_dale_allisons_res_skept.htm

"An investigation into alleged "hauntings"" by Richard Wiseman et al.: www.richardwiseman.com/resources/BJP-hauntings.pdf

Jesus' Resurrection and Apparitions: A Bayesian Analysis by Jake H. O'Connell

---

The physical mediumship hypothesis

Finally, what about a hypothesis that appeals to physical mediumship? Former president of the Society for Psychical Research and paranormal investigator G.N.M. Tyrrell comments that the society "investigated a number of physical mediums, and in all, or nearly all, has discovered fraud," adding: "I am not aware that any case of complete 'materialization,' investigated by critical observers, has resulted in a favourable verdict. 'Materializations' consisting of regurgitated cheese-cloth are well-known."[297] Watt reports that early work investigating materializations "often revealed evidence of fraud, trickery, and self-deception."[298] Thus, the mediumship hypothesis leads us back to a form of the conspiracy theory, with all the attendant problems thereof.

Nevertheless, one might attempt to explain (or to explain away) the resurrection appearances by appealing to the hypothesis of "ectoplasmic materializations" during séances. However, the resurrection reports are at odds with the expectant atmosphere of a darkened séance. There is no medium. There is no atmosphere of expectation. The appearances take place in a wide variety of locations, including outside in daylight. (These criticisms also apply to any hypothesis involving non-physical mediumship.)

Not that "ectoplasmic materializations" would have been mistaken for a *resurrected* Jesus, especially not a resurrected Jesus *who wasn't at first recognized as such* on several occasions (but was mistaken for ordinary human beings)!

296. Habermas, "Dale Allison's Resurrection Skepticism," 309, 311.
297. Tyrrell, "Physical Mediumship."
298. Watt, *Parapsychology*, 77.

Not that the Jewish resurrection witnesses would engage in what they would have regarded as a "detestable" practice outlawed by God (see: Deuteronomy 18:9–13).

Again, one might try explaining the empty tomb as resulting from an unusually large "apport" wherein "spirit-guides" supposedly magically materialize a physical object magically "dematerialised" from elsewhere into a "psychic circle."[299] However, appealing to a psychic circle turns the physical mediumship hypothesis into a conspiracy theory. After all, the appearance of Jesus' corpse in a psychic circle would only serve to confirm his deceased status to those present. Moreover, the lack of evidence for a psychic circle makes such a suggestion *ad hoc*, even if one thinks psychic teleportation a plausible hypothesis in the first place.

One should note that combining the hypothesis of psychic materialization with so-called "direct voice" phenomena and psychic teleportation purchases greater (but still inadequate) explanatory scope only at the cost of being more *ad hoc* and *complex* than the resurrection hypothesis, which explains both the empty tomb *and* the multi-sensory resurrection appearances with economy.

Watch: "Spiritualism" Youtube playlist: www.youtube.com/playlist?list=PLQhh3qcwVEWjNSfstQpdhOU9_YyURPaB2

Read: *Extra Sensory: The Science And Pseudoscience Of Telepathy And Other Powers Of The Mind* by Brian Clegg

Parapsychology: The Science of Unusual Experience by David Groome and Ron Roberts

---

Pick and mix remix

Finally, as with combining psychic hypotheses, so with combining any of the above hypotheses. This or that particular combination of hypotheses may purchase *explanatory scope* (e.g. aliens teleport Jesus' body out of the tomb whilst the disciples coincidentally experience hallucinations and/or place-memory apparitions of Jesus), but this gain would inevitably come at the cost of an exponential increase in explanatory *ad hoc*-ness and *complexity*. Moreover, the component parts of such expanded hypotheses would still suffer from other problems, such as *low explanatory power* (e.g. neither hallucinations nor place-memory apparitions would be likely to produce belief in Jesus' *resurrection*) and being subject to *evidential disconfirmation* (e.g. transporter using aliens probably haven't visited Earth).

---

299. Fuller, "What is Physical Mediumship?"

WHERE DO WE GO FROM HERE?

"'Even the most skeptical historian [must] postulate some other event that is not the disciples' faith, but the reason for their faith, in order to account for their experiences. Of course, both natural and supernatural options have been proposed."

—Reginald Fuller[300]

"there is a patch of first-century history that makes perfect sense from a Christian perspective but from no other."

—Stephen T. Davis[301]

As Stephen T. Davis writes: "no one who denies that Jesus was raised from the dead or who offers reductive theories of the resurrection has yet been able to account adequately for [the] widely accepted facts."[302] For example, having decided to reject all miracle-claims, philosopher Charles Hartshorne acknowledged: "it is remarkable that a crucified man should have been the source of so vast a company of believers. I cannot explain this convincingly."[303] Likewise, the late Antony Flew admitted: "I don't think it's possible to offer any satisfactory naturalistic account of what happened."[304]

Many alternative explanations that have been proposed, from dismissing the resurrection as a myth to the suggestion that Jesus swooned on the cross, are falsified by firmly established historical facts (such as Jesus' death by crucifixion or the evident sincerity of the disciples' belief in his resurrection), while other theories are strongly disconfirmed by other data (e.g. the implausibility of time travel or the nature of grief-hallucinations). Even "paranormal" and frankly supernatural hypotheses that deny Jesus rose from the dead (e.g. theories that posit psychic phenomena, miraculous hallucinations, apparitions, or objective visions) fall short of explaining the relevant historical facts with the combination of explanatory economy, plausibility, power, and scope exhibited by the resurrection hypothesis.

The failure of rival theories is reflected in the fact that "Modern scholarship recognizes no plausible explanatory alternative to the resurrection of Jesus. Those who refuse to accept the resurrection as a fact of history are simply self-confessedly left without an explanation."[305] Indeed, as Paul Barnett observes, "it is striking that those who reject the resurrection of Jesus have not settled on one major objection to its

---

300. Fuller, "The Formation of the Resurrection Narratives," 142.
301. Davis, *Rational Faith*, 80.
302. Davis, *Risen Indeed*, 180–81.
303. Hartshorne, "Charles Hartshorne," 137.
304. Flew and Ankerberg, *Resurrected?*, 29.
305. Craig, "Contemporary Scholarship and the Historical Resurrection of Jesus Christ."

historicity."[306] With Robert J. Hutchinson, I think this lack of agreement is obviously because "none of the alternative explanations for what happened with the resurrection adequately explain all the historical evidence..."[307]

It is from this point of widely-acknowledged perplexity that we leave behind any hope of scholarly agreement across worldviews, because the question of how to explain historical data inevitably intersects with philosophical issues. As Pannenberg concludes: "The negative judgement on the bodily resurrection of Jesus as having occurred in historical fact is not a result of the historical critical examination of the Biblical Easter tradition, but a postulate that precedes any such examination."[308]

Bart Ehrman comments that: "The reason [the resurrection is] rational and makes sense to Bill [Craig] is because he's a believer in God, and so, of course, God can act in the world. Why not? . . . Well, that presupposes a belief in God."[309] On the one hand, note Ehrman's admission that *belief in Jesus' resurrection makes sense if you already believe in God*. On the other hand, note that this admission doesn't go far enough, because agnostics and even non-dogmatic atheists can admit at least the possibility that God might exist and act miraculously in the world. As Habermas argues:

> it is undeniable that everyone generally operates within his or her own concept of reality . . . Having said this, however, the factual data are still equally crucial . . . We do need to be informed by the data we receive. And sometimes this is precisely what happens—the evidence on a subject convinces us against our indecisiveness or even contrary to our former position.[310]

Standing up for the resurrection hypothesis

"That he arose is the only plausible explanation for what happened after his death and what still exists today as a consequence."

—Dallas Willard[311]

In the words of F.F. Bruce: "the one interpretation which best accounts for all the data . . . is that Jesus' bodily resurrection from the dead was a real objective event."[312] As N.T. Wright contends:

---

306. Barnett, "Is The New Testament Historically Reliable?," 250.
307. Hutchinson, *Searching for Jesus*, 250.
308. Pannenberg, "History and the Reality of the Resurrection," 64.
309. Ehrman, "Is There Historical Evidence for the Resurrection of Jesus? Ehrman's Second Rebuttal."
310. Habermas, "Did Jesus Perform Miracles?," 126.
311. Willard, *Knowing Christ Today*, 134.
312. Bruce, *The New Testament Documents*, 64.

the historian may and must say that all other explanations for why Christianity arose and took the shape it did are far less convincing as historical explanations than the one the early Christians themselves offer: that Jesus really did rise from the dead . . . the sort of reasoning historians characteristically employ—inference to the best explanations, tested rigorously in terms of the explanatory power of the hypothesis thus generated—points strongly toward the bodily resurrection of Jesus.[313]

The "problem" with the resurrection hypothesis is that it requires us to accept that a miracle happened; but the failure of arguments against the occurrence and rational believability of miracles leaves the resurrection hypothesis standing tall as *the best explanation of the relevant historical data.*

The evidence for the proposition that "God raised Jesus from the dead," in the sense that "after his death Jesus was physically alive again," is naturally stronger than it is for the proposition that Jesus' renewed physical form had the *resurrected* nature of what Paul called the "spiritual body." Of course, the first proposition still constitutes a miracle that validates Jesus' ministry: "one is justified in inferring a supernatural act of God on behalf of Jesus. Whether this event also involved Jesus' risen body being invested with properties of invulnerability, indestructability, etc., can be left as an open question . . ."[314]

That said, the proposition that Jesus was *resurrected* in the full New Testament sense of the term *is* evidentially supported. Indeed, it provides the most convincing explanation of why Jesus' disciples came to believe in his *resurrection* and not merely in his *revivification*. It also provides a single unifying explanation for the *multiply attested* facts that a) several people who knew Jesus well failed to recognize him for a while when they met him after his death (see: Luke 24:13–35; John 20:14 and 21:12), and that b) Jesus suddenly appeared to witnesses inside a locked room (see: Luke 24:36–43; John 20:19 and 26), and that c) Jesus disappeared in front of witnesses (see: Luke 24:30–31 and 50–53; Acts 1:9).

A particular case in point: the "ascension" of Jesus is not only narrated twice by Luke (Luke 24:50–53; Acts 1:9–10) but it is also prefigured by John (see: John 20:17; see also: Ephesians 4:8, 1 Timothy 3:16 and Hebrews 4:14), thereby passing the criterion of *multiple independent attestation*. With Stephen T. Davis:

> I see the [ascension] primarily as a symbolic act performed for the sake of the disciples. By means of it, God showed them that Jesus was henceforth to be apart from them in space and time. . . The ascension of Jesus. . . was visibly symbolized for the disciples by a change of location.[315]

Finally, William Lane Craig argues that:

---

313. Wright, "Jesus' Resurrection and Christian Origins," 136–7.
314. Craig, *A Reasonable Response*, 306.
315. Davis, "The Question of Miracles, Ascension & Anti-Semitism," 79–80.

in inferring that Jesus was risen from the dead in the full, Jewish sense of that term, one is inferring to the best explanation of the data . . . This conclusion is especially manifest if Jesus predicted His death and resurrection by Israel's God, for He was speaking of resurrection in the full Jewish sense.[316]

Listen: "Jesus: Risen, Ascended, Glorified" by Peter S. Williams: www.podbean.com/media/share/pb-cmr3y-6451e3

COYNE'S COMPLAINTS

What do the New Atheists make of the argument for the resurrection? Very little, inasmuch as few of them consider the question of Jesus' resurrection from an evidential standpoint at all. Jerry A. Coyne's *Faith vs. Fact* offers the most extended neo-atheist engagement with the historical evidence for the resurrection in print, but that's not saying much. As David H. Glass comments:

> Coyne adopts the standard New Atheist approach of being able to reject [the resurrection] without having to consider the arguments in favour of it seriously . . . We are told that there are "many alternative and non-miraculous explanations" . . . and he then appeals to the Jesus Seminar to assure us that there is no credible evidence for the empty tomb or Jesus's post-mortem appearances. It's interesting that Coyne draws on such an extreme group, whose views have been widely criticized in the academic literature, in order to deny two facts that are widely accepted by historical scholars, whether religious or not, on evidential grounds. Coyne accuses religious believers of confirmation bias, but his approach to the historical Jesus looks like a perfect example.[317]

Instead of interacting with the cumulative case (built upon multiple standard criteria of authenticity) for each of the relevant historical facts, Coyne focuses upon the supposed failure of the data to pass a couple of rather *naive* measures of historicity.

Coyne asserts (without argumentation) that "the biblical account of the Crucifixion and Resurrection fails" the "elementary tests" for historicity "because the sources are not independent . . ."[318] However, all five historical facts bearing on the resurrection are supported by "independent" evidence from multiple sources, sometimes including non-Christian sources. Then again, multiple testimonial sources (sometimes embarrassingly) only believed Jesus was alive because they experienced meeting him alive. Their testimony is "independent" in the robust sense (discussed in chapter four) that it isn't dependent upon anyone else's testimony and even includes multiple

---

316. Craig, *A Reasonable Response*, 306.
317. Glass, "Jerry Coyne on the Incompatibility of Science and Religion."
318. Coyne, *Faith vs. Fact*, 121.

reports from people who didn't stand in any relationship of common descent with anyone who already believed in the resurrection.

In any case, one can hardly make having independent sources, in whatever sense, a prerequisite for historical knowledge. That would generate an insatiable infinite regress. It would also mean ignoring all the other criteria of authenticity. For example, all five historical facts pass Coyne's (also overly stringent) demand for "accounts that are contemporaneous with the event,"[319] assuming we take this to mean accounts written *within living memory* of an event.

Coyne also attempts to cast doubt on the biblical sources for Jesus' crucifixion and resurrection by stating that "none are by eyewitnesses . . ."[320] All other things being equal, eyewitness sources are preferable to non-eyewitness sources. Nevertheless, eyewitness sources are hardly the be-all-and-end-all of historical research. That said, eyewitness testimony *does* support at least four out of five of our historical facts pertaining to the resurrection, including the resurrection appearances.

Why not Mormonism?

> "if we are to take the Jesus story as truth why not the stories of the Mormons?"
> —Michael Ruse[321]

Having demanded eyewitness testimony for the resurrection, Coyne has an objection to eyewitness testimony:

> consider the "testimonies" that begin the book of Mormon. Opening the book, you'll find two statements, signed by eleven named witnesses, all swearing they actually saw the golden plates given to Joseph Smith by the angel Moroni. Three of the witnesses—Oliver Cowdery, David Whitmer, and Martin Harris—add that an angel personally laid the plates before them.[322]

As with Sam Harris's uninformed assumption of evidential parity between Christianity and Islam, Coyne asks how Christians can justify rejecting this testimony to the truth of Mormonism whilst accepting "the tales about Jesus in the New Testament"?[323] The answer is that the testimonies that begin the Book of Mormon are disanalogous to those contained in the NT. The original "eyewitnesses" to the purportedly Golden Plates that Joseph Smith claimed contained the Book of Mormon went on to retract their support for Mormonism (something Coyne neglects to mention):

---

319. Coyne, *Faith vs. Fact*, 121.
320. Coyne, *Faith vs. Fact*, 121.
321. Ruse, "Not Reasonable But Not Unreasonable," 118.
322. Ruse, "Not Reasonable But Not Unreasonable," 118.
323. Ruse, "Not Reasonable But Not Unreasonable," 118.

Oliver Cowdery

Cowdery exposed Joseph Smith's affair with Fanny Alger and, as a result, was excommunicated from the Mormon Church. Smith described Cowdery as a thief, liar, perjurer, counterfeiter, adulterer and leader of "scoundrels of the deepest degree." Cowdery eventually became a Methodist and denied the Book of Mormon, publicly stating that he had "sorrow and shame" over his connection with Mormonism.

Martin Harris

Harris was a member of five different religious groups prior to becoming a Mormon and eight different religious groups after leaving Mormonism. Like Cowdery, Harris was also excommunicated from the Mormon Church. He recanted his "eyewitness" testimony related to the Golden Plates and reported that he did not see them as Joseph Smith maintained. Harris instead said that he saw the plates spiritually in a "state of entrancement" after praying for three days.

David Whitmer

Whitmer, like Cowdery and Harris, was eventually excommunicated from the Mormon Church . . . Whitmer later admitted that he saw the Golden Plates "by the eye of faith" rather than with his physical eyes.[324]

It was only these original three men who testified to anything beyond the mere existence of "plates" which Smith (1805–1844) kept under wraps (i.e. in a box or under a table-cloth[325]).

Smith added eight additional "eyewitnesses" to his list of authenticators in 1829, limiting his choices to close friends and family members.[326] Two of the eight died in 1835 and 1836 respectively; the rest abandoned Mormonism after Joseph Smith's death in 1844. Indeed: "By 1847 not a single one of the surviving eleven witnesses were part of the Mormon church."[327] By contrast, the apostles testified to the resurrection without wavering, and many of them died a martyr's death for what they claimed:

> None of the apostles recanted their stories. None of the apostles later said their observations of the Risen Christ were simply spiritual sightings or visions. None of the apostles left Christianity to become active in other religious

---

324. Wallace, "The Witnesses of the Resurrection."
325. Vogel, "Book of Mormon Witnesses Revisited."
326. See: Wallace, "The Witnesses of the Resurrection."
327. "Can I get a witness to the Book of Mormon translated?"

groups. None of the apostles were condemned or publicly scorned by the leaders of Christianity.[328]

Besides, we know that in 1842 several men and women followed Smith's lead by lying under oath in the pages of the official periodical of the Mormon Church, *Times and Seasons*, to fend off the true accusation that Smith was a polygamist (which he had been since the 1830s).[329] The point here isn't about Smith's polygamy, but that "Smith suborned perjury, a criminal act."[330]

The negative evidential situation of Mormonism

Just as the testimonies of men like Paul and Peter and women like Mary Magdeline are only one element in the overall evidential situation of Christianity, so the testimonies that open the Book of Mormon are only one element in the overall evidential situation of Mormonism. Whilst the NT testimonies are consistent with the positive evidential situation of Christianity, the testimonies of Cowdery et al. are at odds with the negative evidential situation of Mormonism.

Trouble with theology

According to traditional Mormon doctrine, stemming from the later teachings of Joseph Smith, "God" was actually once a man on another planet (we've already seen some of the problems with such a hypothesis) who became divine by following the laws of the god he served (a process called "exaltation").[331] That god in turn was exalted by *his* god, who was exalted by *his* god, *ad infinitum*. Hence Mormonism teaches an infinite temporal regress of causes. However, there are strong conceptual arguments against the existence of an infinite causal regress.[332] For example, if climbing out of an infinitely deep well one ladder rung at a time is impossible, then so too is arriving at the present time if the past is infinite. And yet we *have* arrived at the present time one event at a time. In which case, it is plausible to conclude that the past isn't infinite:

> Wittgenstein thought it ridiculous that one might come across a person saying, '-5, -4, -3, -2, -1, 0!' and who, when asked what he was doing, claimed that he had just finished reciting the series of negative numbers backwards

---

328. Wallace, "The Witnesses of the Resurrection."

329. See: "False Witnesses and Lost Credibility;" Burningham, *An American Fraud*, 218.

330. Beverley, *Mormon Crisis*, 46.

331. See: Bowman, "From Monotheism to Eternal Progression;" Critchley, "Why I Love Mormonism;" "Teachings of Presidents of the Church."

332. See: Beckwith, "Philosophical Problems with the Mormon Concept of God;" Craig, "Philosophical and Scientific Pointers;" Guthrie, "Russell, Infinity, and the Tristram Shandy Paradox;" Holt, "Maths and the finitude of the past;" Moreland, *Scaling the Secular City*; Reichenbach, *The Cosmological Argument*; Williams, *A Faithful Guide to Philosophy*.

from infinity . . . if the reciter claimed to have finished his job on April 9, 2006, surely we would be entitled to ask why he had finished *then* rather than, say . . . November 30, 1363 or January 12, 5041. The very date of completion requires an explanation, yet if the scenario were real, an explanation would be in principle impossible.[333]

Logical problems aside, the hypothesis of an infinite past is disconfirmed by contemporary cosmology. As atheist cosmologist Alexander Vilenkin says: "there are no [cosmological] models at this time that provide a satisfactory model for a universe without a beginning."[334]

Trouble with history

Turning to historical matters, the Book of Abraham (part of *The Pearl of Great Price*) was "translated" by Joseph Smith from Egyptian papyri purchased in 1835, supposedly using his paranormal powers as a "seer":

> With the rediscovery of [at least some of] the papyri at the Metropolitan Museum in New York in 1967, analysis by John Wilson, Richard Parker and Klaus Baer (all 1968), and even the LDS apologist Hugh Nibley (in 1975) disproved any possibility that the Book of Abraham could be an acceptable translation of the surviving Egyptian papyri [which were] misunderstood and mistranslated by Joseph Smith.[335]

The art of reading Egyptian hieroglyphics vanished in the fourth century and was only recovered by the French scholar Jean-François Champollion in the 1820s. News of this academic breakthrough didn't reach America until the 1840s. Mormon apologists openly admit that "Joseph couldn't translate Egyptian. At that time, nobody could translate Egyptian"[336] whilst affirming that "Joseph was able to receive the text of the Book of Abraham . . . by revelation."[337] However, as Matt Slick comments:

> When Joseph first gave his translation, hieroglyphics were undecipherable. Today they are. He was safe in saying anything he wanted to, and there would be no way of proving him wrong. But with the resurfacing of [at least some of] the same papyri he used to do his Book of Abraham translation and the fact

---

333. Oderberg, "The Cosmological Argument," 348.

334. Vilenkin, "Did the Universe Have a Beginning?" See also: Craig, "'Honesty, Transparency, Full Disclosure;'" Grossman, "Death of the eternal cosmos;" Mithani and Vilenkin, "Did the Universe Have a Beginning?"

335. Ritner, "'Translation and Historicity of the Book of Abraham'—A Response."

336. "The method by which Joseph Smith produced the Book of Abraham."

337. "The method by which Joseph Smith produced the Book of Abraham."

that he did not in any way do it correctly should be proof enough that Joseph Smith lied about his abilities from God.[338]

As Thomas Stuart Ferguson, founder of the *New World Archaeological Foundation*, concluded: "the Egyptian papyri showed that Joseph Smith could not read Egyptian and simply faked it when he was presented with a MS."[339]

Joseph Smith's anachronism-filled former "translation" of the supposedly ancient "plates" allegedly containing The Book of Mormon (which he dictated, without using the "plates," with his head in a hat containing a seer stone[340]) borrows from the King James Bible:

> Jewish and Christian Scripture was originally written in Hebrew, Aramaic and Greek without chapter or verse divisions. But Joseph's translation of the *Book of Mormon* includes verbatim quotes from the KJV with the verse and chapter divisions intact . . . To make matters worse, we now know the KJV contained a number of translation errors . . . The *Book of Mormon* lifts passages from the KJV without correcting these errors.[341]

Professor Thomas J. Finley concludes: "There is no solid evidence that the Book of Mormon was written by Semites in ancient times. Contrary evidence makes it more likely that the book is a product of Joseph Smith's time, with the KJV strongly influencing it."[342]

Mormon Richard Lyman Bushman correctly observes that, like the gospels: "The Book of Mormon [is] susceptible to historical analysis . . . a history of a migrant band of Israelites to America is open to investigation."[343] However, such analysis has consistently disconfirmed Mormon truth-claims. For example: "The only Book of Mormon geographies which avoid insurmountable difficulties are those which merely show relationships between lands and make no attempt to locate places on a map of the real world."[344]

According to Michael Coe, Professor Emeritus of Anthropology at Yale University: "nothing, absolutely nothing, has ever shown up in any New World excavation which would suggest to a dispassionate observer that the Book of Mormon, as claimed by Joseph Smith, is a historical document relating to the history of early migrants to our

---

338. Slick, "The Book of Abraham Papyri and Joseph Smith."
339. Ferguson quoted in Larson, *Quest For The Gold Plates*, 118.
340. See: Burningham, *An American Fraud*, 262–65.
341. Wallace, "Investigating the Evidence for Mormonism in Six Steps."
342. Finley, "Does the Book of Mormon Reflect an Ancient Near Eastern Background?," 366.
343. Bushman, *Mormonism*, 32.
344. Larson, *Quest for the Gold Plates*, 9.

hemisphere."[345] According to Dr. David Johnson (Professor of Anthropology, Brigham Young University): "there is no archaeological proof of the Book of Mormon."[346]

For example, Mormon 6:10–15 claims that hundreds of thousands of people were killed on or near the hill Cumorah during a battle:

> It says that "*their flesh, and bones, and blood lay upon the face of the earth, being left by the hands of those who slew them to molder upon the land, and to crumble and to return to their mother earth*" (Mormon 6:15). In other words, their bodies were left there, unburied . . . If 6,000 men died on the battlefield at Gettysburg, what would a battlefield look like with hundreds of thousands dead? Since they were left unburied at hill Cumorah, wouldn't there be some artifacts made of metal and stone? Bullets by the thousands are found at Gettysburg. Nothing however has been found at hill Cumorah.[347]

This is the sort of absence of evidence that constitutes evidence of absence. Indeed, as James A. Beverley explains, *contrary* to the material culture depicted in the Book of Mormon:

> no archaeological or anthropological evidence exists for the Book of Mormon's version of events in the Americas from 2200 BC through AD 400 . . . American Indians had no wheat, barley, oats, millet, rice, cattle, pigs, chickens, horses, donkeys, or camels before 1492 . . . steel, glass, and silk were not used in the New World before 1492 . . .[348]

Coyne himself points out that:

> a critical claim of Mormonism is that Native Americans . . . descended from a group of people who migrated to North America from the Middle East around 600 BCE. Genetics, evolutionary biology, and archaeology show . . . these claims are dead wrong . . . all native peoples in the New World, descended from East Asians—Siberians—who migrated over the Bering Strait roughly fifteen thousand (not twenty-six hundred) years ago.[349]

Hence, while Coyne's critique of the resurrection depends upon a close analogy between Mormon and Christian revelation claims, the two claims are *not* analogous. Indeed, in a public discussion with Richard Dawkins, Lawrence Krauss passed the following comment (with which Dawkins agreed):

---

345. Coe quoted in Beverley, *Mormon Crisis*, 72.
346. Johnson quoted in Licona, "Archaeology & 'The Book of Mormon.'"
347. Licona, "Archaeology & 'The Book of Mormon.'" See also: Burningham, *An American Fraud*, 266–67.
348. Beverley, *Mormon Crisis*, 71.
349. Coyne, *Faith vs. Fact,* 125, 131. See also: Bolnick et al., "Civilizations Lost and Found;" Southerton, *Losing a Lost Tribe*.

More importantly, unlike some of the, I mean, we also read that the biblical stories are equally ridiculous, but the difference is, we don't know they were written by known con-men; but in fact he [Joseph Smith] was a known felon.[350]

In other words, even some of Coyne's fellow New Atheists concede that the writings of Joseph Smith are in a worse evidentiary position than the writings of the NT. As William Lane Craig comments: "unlike the stories of Joseph Smith and the golden tablets, the Gospel narratives cannot be plausibly written off as due to fraud."[351]

Watch: "Mormonism" Youtube playlist: www.youtube.com/playlist?list=PLQhh3qcwVEWjOn4gyNXipluUzVuNsJjjI

Listen: "The Mormon View of Creation" by William Lane Craig: www.rfmedia.org/RF_audio_video/RF_podcast/The_Mormon_View_of_Creation.mp3

"Mormonism—an introductory critique" by Peter S. Williams: www.podbean.com/media/share/pb-49qub-5d19e9

Read: "Museum Walls Proclaim Fraud of Mormon Prophet": https://timesmachine.nytimes.com/timesmachine/1912/12/29/100076264.pdf

"Philosophical Problems with the Mormon Concept of God" by Francis J. Beckwith: www.equip.org/article/philosophical-problems-with-the-mormon-concept-of-god/

"Civilizations Lost and Found: Fabricating History—Part One: An Alternate Reality" by Kenneth Feder et al.: www.csicop.org/si/show/civilizations_lost_and_found_fabricating_history_-_part_one_an_alternate_re

"Civilizations Lost and Found: Fabricating History—Part Two: False Messages in Stone" by Kenneth Feder et al.: www.csicop.org/si/show/civilizations_lost_and_found_fabricating_history_-_part_two_false_messages

"Civilizations Lost and Found: Fabricating History—Part Three: Real Messages in DNA" by Kenneth Feder et al.: www.csicop.org/si/show/civilizations_lost_and_found_fabricating_history_-_part_three_real_messages

"What to say to Mormons" by Michael R. Licona: www.bethinking.org/mormons/what-to-say-to-mormons

""Translation and Historicity of the Book of Abraham"—A Response" by Robert K. Ritner: https://oi.uchicago.edu/sites/oi.uchicago.edu/files/uploads/shared/docs/Research_Archives/Translation%20and%20Historicity%20of%20the%20Book%20of%20Abraham%20final-2.pdf

"The Book of Abraham Papyri and Joseph Smith" by Matt Slick: https://carm.org/book-abraham-papyri-and-joseph-smith

"Book of Mormon Witnesses Revisited" by Dan Vogel: www.mormonthink.com/vogelwitnesses.htm

"Mormonism" by J. Warner Wallace: http://coldcasechristianity.com/tag/mormonism/

The New Mormon Challenge: Responding to the Latest Defences of a Fast Growing Movement edited by Francis J. Beckwith et al.

---

350. Krauss in "Dawkins and Krauss on Mormonism." See also: Burningham, *An American Fraud*, 278–79.

351. Craig, "Reply to Our Respondents," 160.

Mormon Crisis: Anatomy of A Failing Religion by James A. Beverley

Quest for the Gold Plates: Thomas Stuart Ferguson's Archaeological Search for The Book of Mormon by Stan Larson

Leaving Mormonism: Why Four Scholars Changed Their Minds edited by Corey Miller

The Mormon Mirage: A Former Member Looks at the Mormon Church Today by Latayne C. Scott

Losing a Lost Tribe: Native Americans, DNA, and the Mormon Church by Simon G. Southerton

---

Coyne vs. the Christ event

Coyne complains that "all contemporary writers outside of Scripture fail to mention the event . . ."[352] If by "the event" Coyne means the crucifixion of Jesus, his statement is incorrect.[353] If by "the event" he means the resurrection of Jesus, the failure of extant works of contemporary writers outside of Scripture to directly reference the resurrection is hardly a surprising evidence of absence (as opposed to a mere absence of evidence). Moreover, one can't simply pit the positive evidence of sources X against an absence of evidence in sources Y. That's like dismissing some event reported in several newspapers (e.g. *The Times, The Telegraph,* and *The Washington Post*) simply because *The Sun* and *The Star* didn't mention it. Just like journalists, ancient writers had different interests that influenced what they wrote about. Then again, any first-century writer who believed in the resurrection was likely on that count to become a Christian, and any report they wrote and that survives is likely to be found in the NT.

Perhaps various "sources outside of Scripture" *did* directly reference the resurrection, or at least belief in the resurrection, without believing in it themselves; but even if they did, it's unlikely that their report would have survived to the present day and have been discovered by us. However, there is arguably an *indirect* reference to Jesus' resurrection in *The Annals* of Tacitus, who reports:

> The originator of the name, Christ, was executed as a criminal by the procurator Pontius Pilate during the reign of Tiberius; and though repressed, this destructive superstition erupted again, not only through Judea, which was the origin of this evil, but also through the city of Rome, to which all that is horrible and shameful floods together and is celebrated.[354]

---

352. Coyne, *Faith vs. Fact,* 121.

353. See: Gleghorne, "Ancient Evidence for Jesus from Non-Christian Sources;" Habermas, *The Verdict of History,* 178.

354. Tacitus, *Annals,* 44.3.

Historian N.D. Anderson suggests that Tacitus is here "bearing indirect . . . testimony to the conviction of the early church that the Christ who had been crucified had risen from the grave."[355]

Again, it's possible that Josephus touched upon the resurrection in *Antiquities* 18:63, which in its extant form states that Jesus "appeared to [his disciples] on the third day restored to life."[356] The Arabic version of the so-called *Testimonium Flavianum*, which is likely closer to the unvarnished autograph, states with greater circumspection that: "his disciples . . . reported that he had appeared to them three days after his crucifixion and that he was alive."[357] (A Christian interpolation would likely have been clearer about Jesus having been *resurrected*.)

Coyne complains that "the details of the Resurrection and empty tomb—even among the Gospels and the letters of Paul—show serious discrepancies."[358] We've already dealt with this allegation. However, it's worth reiterating the fact that the historical method we are using here—i.e. sifting sources using criteria of authenticity—is designed to sidestep worries about discrepancies and the general reliability or unreliability of our historical sources. As Habermas and Miethe emphasize:

> Our arguments [for the resurrection are] based on a *limited number* of knowable historical facts and *verified by critical procedures*. Therefore, contemporary scholars should not spurn such evidence by referring to 'discrepancies' in the New Testament texts or to its general 'unreliability' . . . Jesus' resurrection appearances can be historically demonstrated *based only on a limited amount of critically recognized historical facts*.[359]

Surpassing Coyne's standards

Coyne asserts that "no religious miracle even comes close" to meeting the evidential standard of "massive, well-documented, and . . . independently corroborated evidence from multiple and reliable sources."[360] However, the resurrection of Jesus is supported by data that meets the evidential standard of well-documented evidence that's independently corroborated in the sense that it comes from multiple reliable sources (and much of this testimony is "independent" in the robust sense that it clearly isn't dependent upon anyone else's testimony). Indeed, when we consider the cumulative case for our five historical facts pertaining to the resurrection, we see that the evidence *surpasses* Coyne's naïve standards.

355. Anderson quoted in Habermas, *The Historical Jesus*, 189–90.
356. Maier, "Josephus and Jesus."
357. Maier, "Josephus and Jesus."
358. Coyne, *Faith vs. Fact*, 121.
359. Miethe and Habermas, *Why Believe?*, 273–74.
360. Coyne, *Faith vs. Fact*, 124.

Whether or not the evidence for the resurrection qualifies as "massive" rather depends on what Coyne means by the term. If what he means is in the tradition of the "extraordinary claims require extraordinary evidence" slogan (see: chapter one), erecting an unreachable target that effectively begs the question against miracles, then we should reject this attempt to stack the deck against the resurrection. If he means something sensible by the term, then I submit that the evidence for the resurrection plausibly qualifies as "massive" (the case for all five historical facts is strong), whilst noting that the evidence need only qualify as *adequate* for the argument about how best to explain it to proceed.

CONCLUSION

"The purpose of the historian is not to construct a history from preconceived notions and to adjust it to his own likings, but rather to reproduce it from the best evidence and to let it speak for itself."

—Philip Schaff[361]

It follows from the falsity of the myth hypothesis (see above) that "the disciples must have been either deceivers, deceived, or telling the truth about the resurrection,"[362] but as Lydia McGrew argues:

> The details and context of the disciple's claims preclude the first two options . . . It is these [historically established] details [e.g. Jesus' death by crucifixion, burial and empty tomb, the pattern of multi-sensory resurrection appearances to multiple groups and individuals, the disciple's firm belief in Jesus' resurrection in its first century socio-religious context] that give such tremendous force to the apostle's testimony and to their willingness to die for it, for it is from these details that we can conclude with confidence that they were not hallucinating, experiencing some sort of non-physical, paranormal event, having visions, or merely mistaken.[363]

If one grants that miracles are both possible and knowable—and especially if one takes into account the context of Jesus' claims and character, and the evidence pertaining to his reputation as a miracle worker and his fulfillment of prophecy—the best explanation of the relevant historical facts is apparently the one given by the eyewitnesses: God raised Jesus from the dead.

---

361. Schaff, *History of the Christian Church*, 175.
362. McGrew, *Hidden In Plain View*, 221.
363. McGrew, *Hidden In Plain View*, 221, 223.

What follows from this? Well, as Craig A. Evans observes: "if Jesus was raised, then what he said prior to his crucifixion and what he said to his followers ... probably should be accepted as true."[364] The resurrection is pregnant with significance:

> Jesus made extravagant claims about himself as to his authority, mission, and origin, and the resurrection was a divine affirmation that those claims were good. Viewed this way, the resurrection *magnified* rather than *manufactured* Jesus' claims to a divine status. Viewed this way, the resurrection *intensified* rather than *initiated* belief in Jesus' unique relationship with God.[365]

In pursuit of a cause opposed to this recognition, the New Atheists have a tendency to issue ill-considered demands for historical evidence that they avoid examining on the basis of discredited philosophical arguments. What little examination of the evidence there is within the movement is decidedly lackluster. As Professor Painter observes: "The irony at the core of New Atheist historiography lies precisely in their failure to carry out their abstract appeals to reason in the specifics of the history they invoke ... The problem with New Atheist historiography is its ignorance of history."[366]

It seems to me that if one follows the relevant philosophical and historical evidence where it leads, it leads to the conclusion that while the New Atheism is the bearer of fake news, the New Testament is the bearer of good news.

Watch: "The Resurrection of Jesus" Youtube playlist: www.youtube.com/playlist?list=PLQhh3qcwVEWjFoVbpQ9sPUUivlyF5n0wB

"Debating the Resurrection" Youtube playlist: www.youtube.com/playlist?list=PLQhh3qcwVEWhAPCkcpFsSwEXrYKuBhoaq

Websites: *William Lane Craig: Reasonable Faith* www.reasonablefaith.org

Gary R. Habermas: www.garyhabermas.com/

Michael Licona: http://risenjesus.com/

Read: "Jesus' Resurrection" by William Lane Craig: www.reasonablefaith.org/writings/scholarly-writings/historical-jesus/jesus-resurrection/

"The Argument from Miracles: A Cumulative Case for the Resurrection of Jesus of Nazareth" by Timothy and Lydia McGrew: www.lydiamcgrew.com/Resurrectionarticlesinglefile.pdf

Did The Resurrection Happen? edited by David Baggett

Resurrection: Faith or Fact? A Scholars' Debate Between a Skeptic and a Christian by Craig Blomberg and Carl Stecher with contributions by Richard Carrier and Peter S. Williams

The Resurrection Fact: Responding to Modern Critics edited by John J. Bombaro and Adam S. Francisco

Will The Real Jesus Please Stand Up? A Debate between William Lane Craig and John Dominic Crossan edited by Paul Copan

---

364. Evans, "The Christ of Faith is the Jesus of History," 465.
365. Bird, "Did Jesus Think He Was God?," 67.
366. Painter, *The New Atheist Denial of History*, 4, 167.

Getting at the Best Explanation

Jesus' Resurrection: Fact or Figment? A Debate between William Lane Craig and Gerd Lüdemann edited by Paul Copan and Ronald K. Tacelli

The Son Rises by William Lane Craig

Risen Indeed: Making Sense of the Resurrection by Stephen T. Davis

Did Jesus Rise From the Dead? The Resurrection Debate by Gary R. Habermas, Antony Flew, and Terry L. Miethe

The Resurrection of Jesus: A New Historiographical Approach by Michael R. Licona

Paul Meets Muhammad: A Christian-Muslim Debate On The Resurrection by Michael R. Licona

Jesus' Resurrection and Apparitions: A Bayesian Analysis by Jake H. O'Connell

No God But One: A Former Muslim Investigates The Evidence For Islam & Christianity by Nabeel Qureshi

The Case for Christ by Lee Strobel

The Case for the Real Jesus by Lee Strobel

The Resurrection of God Incarnate by Richard Swinburne

The Resurrection of the Son of God by N.T. Wright

Conclusion

Getting at Jesus with Neo-Atheist Concessions to Historical Reality

> "There is objective truth out there and it is our business to find it."
> —Richard Dawkins[1]

As documented in the foregoing chapters, the New Atheism purveys a lot of nonsense about "the historical Jesus." Nevertheless, individual neo-atheists occasionally make concessions to reality. If we take these concessions together, we discover a series of significant methodological and historical truths consonant with Richard Bauckham's conclusion that the real Jesus was (and therefore is) "the much-more-than-historical, but not less-than-historical Jesus."[2]

1) A genuine search for truth must be open to the facts

Christopher Hitchens affirms:

- "Objectivity means the search for truth no matter what."[3]

Sam Harris writes:

- "Nothing is more sacred than the facts. No one, therefore, should win any points in our discourse for deluding himself. The litmus test for reasonableness should be obvious: anyone who wants to know how the world is, whether in physical or spiritual terms, will be open to new evidence."[4]

---

1. Dawkins, *Science in the Soul*, 7.
2. Bauckham, "A Life with the Bible," 24.
3. Hitchens quoted in Mann, *The Quotable Hitchens*, 207.
4. Harris, *The End of Faith*, 225.

2) Miracles are possible (and knowable)

Neo-atheists frequently evince the following double standard: On the one hand, they claim that scientific, empirical methods are the only way to know anything and that the problem with the Christian revelation claim is a lack of *a posteriori* evidence. On the other hand, they justify their failure to seriously engage with the relevant *a posteriori* evidence by appealing to Hume's *a priori* philosophical argument against belief in miracles. However, some neo-atheists take issue with the procrustean foundations of this question-begging hypocrisy. For example, Lawrence M. Krauss admits that miracles can't be ruled out *a priori* unless one first rules out the possibility that God exists:

- "A god who can create the laws of nature can presumably also circumvent them at will."[5]

And while neo-atheists tend to genuflect to Hume's discredited arguments about miracles, Jerry A. Coyne admits:

- "Hume took it too far. No amount of evidence, it seems, could ever override his conviction that miracles were really the result of fraud, ignorance, or misrepresentation. Yet perhaps there are some events . . . when a [miracle] is more likely than human error or deception."[6]

Coyne recommends approaching the question of miracles with an open mind, stating:

- "It would be a closed minded scientist who would say that miracles are impossible in principle."[7]

3) Christianity makes truth-claims that are open to historical investigation

Richard Dawkins writes:

- "Did Jesus raise Lazarus from the dead? Did he himself come alive again, three days after being crucified? There is an answer to every such question, whether or not we can discover it in practice, and it is a strictly scientific answer."[8]

Victor J. Stenger asserts:

- "Physical and historical evidence might have been found for the miraculous events . . . of the scriptures."[9]

Coyne comments:

---

5. Krauss, *A Universe from Nothing*, 142.
6. Coyne, *Faith vs. Fact*, 124.
7. Coyne, *Faith vs. Fact*, 124.
8. Dawkins, *The God Delusion*, 59.
9. Stenger, "Victor J. Stenger," 211.

- "nothing in science prohibits us from considering supernatural explanations . . . If something is supposed to exist in a way that has tangible effects on the universe, it falls within the ambit of science. And supernatural beings and phenomena can have real-world effects."[10]

Of course, to accept that claims about the tangible effects of supernatural beings fall "within the ambit of science," or history, does not mean denying the relevance of philosophical and theological perspectives on said events or beings.[11]

4) There was a historical Jesus

Dawkins acknowledges:

- "Jesus existed."[12]

Harris writes of:

- "Jesus, the Buddha, Lao Tzu, and the other saints and sages of history . . ."[13]

Krauss admits that Jesus:

- "was a real, historical person."[14]

Again, Krauss says:

- "If you asked me, is the weight of historical evidence such that Jesus was a real historical figure, I would say, the weight of historical evidence is that Jesus was a historical figure . . . I do not dispute that the weight of historical evidence suggests that he was a real person."[15]

5) The historical Jesus hasn't been obscured by pagan mythology

Krauss concedes:

- "One may argue that these connections [between Jesus and pagan myths] are spurious, and I'm willing to accept that."[16]

---

10. Coyne, *Faith vs. Fact*, 93, 94.
11. After all, "science" is best understood as "natural philosophy"—see Peter S. Williams, *A Faithful Guide to Philosophy*, chapter sixteen.
12. Dawkins, "Richard Dawkins Admits Jesus Existed."
13. Harris, *Waking Up*, 5.
14. Krauss and Craig, "Life, the Universe, and Nothing."
15. Krauss and Craig, "Life, the Universe, and Nothing."
16. Krauss and Craig, "Life, the Universe, and Nothing."

6) New Testament writers wrote what they honestly believed to be the truth about Jesus

According to Michel Onfray:

- "Mark, Matthew, Luke and John did not knowingly deceive. Neither did Paul . . . they said what they believed was true and believed that what they said was true . . . Clearly they believed what they wrote."[17]

7) Jesus did think that he was divine

Hitchens acknowledged that Jesus:

- "reportedly believed himself, at least some of the time, to be god or the son of god."[18]

Krauss states that Jesus:

- "had delusions of being God."[19]

8) Jesus wasn't a lunatic or a liar

Harris records realizing:

- "Jesus, the Buddha, Lao Tzu, and the other saints and sages of history had not all been epileptics, schizophrenics, or frauds."[20]

Harris bears witness to Jesus' goodness and wisdom by grouping him together with "the other saints and sages of history . . ."[21] Moreover, Harris repudiates any dismissal of those "saints and sages," including Jesus, as "epileptics, schizophrenics, or frauds."[22]

On the one hand, as Dawkins admits:

- "There's no evidence Jesus himself was barking mad."[23]

On the other hand, Dawkins says we know enough about Jesus to conclude that he:

- "was a great moral teacher."[24]

---

17. Onfray, *In Defence of Atheism*, 125.
18. Hitchens, *God is Not Great*, 118, emphasis added.
19. Krauss and Craig, "Life, the Universe, and Nothing."
20. Harris, *Waking Up*, 5.
21. Harris, *Waking Up*, 5.
22. Harris, *Waking Up*, 5.
23. Dawkins, "Interview in *Playboy*."
24. Dawkins, "Atheists for Jesus."

Conclusion

Dawkins's risible attempt to suggest that Jesus was just "honestly mistaken"[25] about his divinity constitutes a backhanded compliment to the "trilemma" argument for the truth of his exulted claims.

9) Jesus was executed by crucifixion

Coyne states:

- "Jesus was crucified, ending everyone's hope of glory."[26]

10) Some people believed they met Jesus alive after his death

Krauss allows that:

- "In fact, the fact that people may have seen Jesus walking [after his death], if they did, if they report that, I'm willing to accept their belief that they did."[27]

A CLOSING, OPENING THOUGHT

"Truth obeys no one. That is why it is free, and freeing."
—ANDRE COMPT-SPONVILLE[28]

Despite the dogmatic skepticism about the historical Jesus that characterizes the New Atheism, individual neo-atheists admit one or more significant points of historical method and/or historical fact that, when taken together, jointly constitute the core elements in the case for thinking that the historical Jesus is the figure Christianity takes him to be.

At the very least, contrary to the generic message of the New Atheism, these neo-atheist concessions to reality (and the reasons for making them) should encourage us to agree with I. Howard Marshall that: "The historian must be open to . . . the significance of Jesus which is suggested to him by the evidence. And that significance may be expressed in terms of the supernatural without the historian feeling that he has sacrificed his intellect . . ."[29]

---

25. Dawkins, *The God Delusion*, 117.
26. Coyne, *Faith vs. Fact*, 123.
27. Krauss, *A Universe from Nothing*, 142.
28. Compte-Sponville, *The Book of Atheist Spirituality*, 185.
29. Marshall, *I Believe in the Historical Jesus*, 244.

Selected Resources

PETER S. WILLIAMS

Website: www.peterswilliams.com
Podcast: http://peterswilliams.podbean.com/?source=pb
YouTube playlists: www.youtube.com/user/peterswilliamsvid/playlists?view=1&flow=grid

WEBSITES

BeThinking: www.bethinking.org
William Lane Craig: *Reasonable Faith:* www.reasonablefaith.org
Gary R. Habermas: www.garyhabermas.com/
Michael Licona: http://risenjesus.com/

BOOKS

Bauckham, Richard. *Jesus and the Eyewitnesses*: *The Gospels as Eyewitness Testimony* (Eerdmans, 2017)
Barnett, Paul. *Messiah: Jesus—the evidence of history* (IVP, 2009)
———. *Finding the Historical Christ* (Eerdmans, 2009)
———. *Paul: Missionary of Jesus* (Eerdmans, 2008)
———. *The Birth of Christianity*: *The First Twenty Years* (Eerdmans, 2005)
Beckwith, Francis J., ed. *To Everyone an Answer*: *A Case for the Christian Worldview* (IVP, 2004)
Bird, Michael F., et al. *How God Became Jesus*: *The Real Origins of Belief in Jesus' Divine Nature—A Response to Bart D. Ehrman* (Zondervan, 2014)
Blomberg, Craig and Carl Stecher with contributions by Richard Carrier and Peter S. Williams. *Resurrection: Faith or Fact? A Scholars' Debate Between a Skeptic and a Christian* (Pitchstone, 2019)
Blomberg, Craig L. *The Historical Reliability of the Gospels* (IVP, 2008)
Bock, Darrell L. and Robert L. Webb, eds. *Key Events In The Life of the Historical Jesus*: *A Collaborative Exploration of Context and Coherence* (Eerdmans, 2010)

Selected Resources

Bock, Darrell L. and Daniel B. Wallace. *Dethroning Jesus: Exposing Popular Culture's Quest to Unseat the Biblical Christ* (Thomas Nelson, 2007)

Bowman, Robert and Ed Komoszewski. *Putting Jesus in His Place: The Case for the Deity of Christ* (Kregel, 2007)

Burridge, Richard A. *What Are the Gospels? A Comparison with Graeco-Roman Biography* (Cambridge University Press, 2004)

Charlesworth, James H., ed. *Jesus Research: New Methodologies and Perceptions* (Eerdmans, 2014)

Copan, Paul, ed. *Will The Real Jesus Please Stand Up? A Debate between William Lane Craig and John Dominic Crossan* (Baker, 1998)

Copan, Paul, and Paul K. Moser, eds. *The Rationality of Theism* (Routledge, 2003)

Craig, William Lane. *On Guard For Students: Defending Your Faith with Reason and Precision* (David C. Cook, 2015)

Craig, William Lane, and J.P. Moreland, eds. *The Blackwell Companion To Natural Theology* (Wiley-Blackwell, 2009)

———. *Naturalism: A Critical Analysis* (Routledge, 2001)

Davis, Stephen T. *Christian Philosophical Theology* (Oxford University Press, 2016)

———. *Risen Indeed: Making Sense of the Resurrection* (SPCK, 1993)

Eddy, Paul Rhodes, and Gregory A. Boyd. *The Jesus Legend: A Case For The Reliability of the Synoptic Jesus Tradition* (Baker Academic, 2007)

Evans, Craig A. *Fabricating Jesus: How Modern Scholars Distort the Gospels* (IVP, 2007)

———. *Jesus And His World: The archaeological evidence* (SPCK, 2012)

Evans, C. Stephen. *The Historical Christ & The Jesus of Faith: The Incarnational Narrative as History* (Clarendon Press, 2004)

Geivett, R. Douglas, and Gary R. Habermas, eds. *In Defence of Miracles: A Comprehensive Case for God's Action in History* (Apollos, 1997)

Gilson, Tom, and Carson Weitnauer, eds. *True Reason: Confronting the Irrationality of the New Atheism* (Kregel, 2013)

Glass, David H. *Atheism's New Clothes: Exploring and Exposing the Claims of the New Atheists* (Apollos, 2012)

Howard, Jeremy Royal, ed. *The Holman Apologetics Commentary On The Bible: The Gospels and Acts* (Holman, 2013)

Hutchinson, Robert J. *Searching For Jesus: New Discoveries In The Quest For Jesus Of Nazareth—And How They Confirm The Gospel Accounts* (Nelson, 2015)

Jones, Timothy Paul. *Misquoting Truth: A Guide to the Fallacies of Bart Ehrman's Misquoting Jesus* (IVP, 2007)

Keener, Craig S. and Edward T. Wright, eds. *Biographies and Jesus: What Does It Mean for the Gospels to be Biographies?* (Emeth Press, 2016)

Kreeft, Peter. *Between Heaven & Hell: A Dialog Somewhere Beyond Death with John F. Kennedy, C.S. Lewis & Aldous Huxley* (IVP, 2008)

Kostenberger, Andreas J., and Justin Taylor. *The Final Days of Jesus* (Crossway, 2014)

Larmer, Robert A. *The Legitimacy of Miracle* (Lexington, 2014)

Lennox, John C. *God's Undertaker: Has Science Buried God?* (Lion, 2009)

Lewis, C.S. *Miracles*. (Fount, 1998)

Licona, Michael R. *The Resurrection of Jesus: A New Historiographical Approach* (IVP/Apollos, 2010)

May, Peter. *The Search for God And The Path To Persuasion* (Malcolm Down, 2016)

McGrew, Lydia. *Hidden In Plain View: Undesigned Coincidences in the Gospels and Acts* (DeWard, 2017)

Meister, Chad, and James K. Drew Jr., eds. *God And Evil: The Case for God In A World Filled With Pain* (IVP, 2013)

Miller, Corey, and Paul Gould, eds. *Is Faith in God Reasonable?* (Routledge, 2014)

Miller, Troy A., ed. *Jesus: The Final Days* (SPCK, 2008)

Moreland, J.P. *Scaling the Secular City: A Defence of Christianity* (Baker, 1987)

Moreland, J.P., and Kai Nielsen. *Does God Exist? The Debate Between Theists & Atheists* (Prometheus, 1993)

Moreland, J.P., and William Lane Craig. *Philosophical Foundations for a Christian Worldview* (IVP, 2017)

Morrow, Jonathan. *Questioning the Bible: 11 Major Challenges to the Bible's Authority* (Moody Press, 2014)

Murray, Michael J., ed. *Reason For The Hope Within* (Eerdmans, 1999)

Pitre, Brant. *The Case For Jesus: The Biblical And Historical Evidence For Christ* (Image, 2016)

Qureshi, Nabeel. *No God But One: Allah or Jesus?* (Zondervan 2016)

Roberts, Mark D. *Can We Trust the Gospels?* (Crossway, 2007)

Sennett, James F., and Douglas Groothuis, eds. *In Defence of Natural Theology: A Post-Humean Assessment* (IVP, 2005)

Smart, J.J.C., and J.J. Haldane. *Atheism & Theism* (Blackwell, 2003)

Strobel, Lee. *The Case For Christ* (Zondervan, 2018)

———. *The Case for Miracles* (Zondervan, 2016)

———. *In Defence of Jesus* (Zondervan, 2016)

Swinburne, Richard. *The Resurrection of God Incarnate* (Clarendon Press, 2003)

———. *Was Jesus God?* (Oxford University Press, 2008)

Wallace, J. Warner. *Cold Case Christianity: A Homicide Detective Investigates The Claims Of The Gospels* (David C, Cook, 2013)

Walls, Jerry L. and Trent Dougherty, eds. *Two Dozen (Or So) Arguments For God: The Plantinga Project* (Oxford University Press, 2018)

Wilkins, Michael J., and J.P. Moreland, eds. *Jesus Under Fire: Modern Scholarship Reinvents the Historical Jesus* (Zondervan, 1995)

Williams, Peter S. *C. S. Lewis vs. the New Atheists* (Paternoster, 2013)

———. *A Faithful Guide to Philosophy: A Christian Introduction to the Love of Wisdom* (Wipf & Stock, forthcoming)

———. *I Wish I Could Believe In Meaning : A Response To Nihilism* (Damaris, 2004)

———. *Understanding Jesus: Five Ways to Spiritual Enlightenment* (Paternoster, 2011)

———. *A Sceptic's Guide to Atheism* (Paternoster, 2009)

Wright, N.T. *The Resurrection of the Son of God* (SPCK, 2003)

Zacharias, Ravi. *Can Man Live Without God* (Word, 1994)

References

Abel, David L., ed. *The First Gene*. New York: LongView, 2011.

———. *Primordial Prescription*: *The Most Plaguing Problem of Life Origin Science*. New York: Long View, 2015.

"Abila—Tomb Q-4." http://users.stlcc.edu/mfuller/abila/AbilaTombQ4.html.

"A.C. Grayling vs. Peter S. Williams on *The God Argument*." www.bethinking.org/does-god-exist/unbelievable-ac-graylings-the-god-argument.

Achenbach, Joe. "Gaping Earthquake Fissures Exist Only in People's Fears and Hollywood Movies." www.deseretnews.com/article/192109/GAPING-EARTHQUAKE-FISSURES-EXIST-ONLY-IN-PEOPLES-FEARS-AND—HOLLYWOOD.html.

Adamson, James B. *The Epistle of James*. Grand Rapids: Eerdmans, 1977.

Akpan, Nsikan and Joshua Barajas. "7 times that science explained aliens." www.pbs.org/newshour/updates/7-times-aliens-explained-science/.

Al-Khalili, Jim. "Introduction." In *Aliens: Science Asks: Is Anyone Out There?*, edited by Jim Al-Khalili. London: Profile, 2016.

———. *Paradox*. London: Black Swan, 2012.

Alcock, James, et al., eds. *PSI Wars: Getting To Grips With The Paranormal*. Exeter, UK: Imprint Academic, 2003.

Alexander, Denis. *Rebuilding the Matrix*. Oxford: Lion, 2001.

Alexander, Loveday. "What is a Gospel?" In *The Cambridge Companion To the Gospels*, edited by Stephen C. Barton, 13–33. Cambridge, UK: Cambridge University Press, 2006.

Ali, Abdullah Yusuf. *The Meaning of the Holy Qur'an*. Beltsville, MD: Amana, 1999.

"Aliens & UFOs." www.youtube.com/playlist?list=PLQhh3qcwVEWiixwhvDhbqSoO3qcIK7zu5.

Allen, Charlotte. *The Human Christ: The Search for the Historical Jesus*. Oxford: Lion, 1998.

Allison, C. Fitz Simons. "Modernity or Christianity? John Spong's Culture of Disbelief." In *Can A Bishop Be Wrong? Ten Scholars Challenge John Shelby Spong*, edited by Peter C. Moore, 40–54. Harrisburg: Morehouse, 1998.

Allison, Dale C., Jr. "Matthew." In *The Oxford Bible Commentary: The Gospels*, edited by John Muddiman and John Baron, 844–86. Oxford: Oxford University Press, 2013.

———. "Resurrecting Jesus: The Earliest Christian Tradition and Its Interpreters." https://jamesbishopblog.wordpress.com/2015/06/29/jesus-really-did-appear-to-the-disciples-and-skeptics-after-his-death-40-quotes-by-scholars/.

———. *Resurrecting Jesus: The Earliest Christian Tradition and its Interpreters*. New York: T & T Clark, 2005.

References

Alston, William P. "Historical Criticism of the Synoptic Gospels." In *Behind The Text: Historical and Biblical Interpretation*, edited by Craig Bartholomew, C. Stephen Evans, Mary Healy, and Murray Rea, 151–80. Grand Rapids: Zondervan, 2003.

Amarasingam, Amarnath. "A Review of Michel Onfray's *In Defense of Atheism: The Case Against Christianity, Judaism, and Islam*." www.theotherjournal.com/article.php?id=320.

Ambrosino, Brandon. "From Nietzsche to Richard Dawkins: a Conversation on Modern Atheism." www.vox.com/2014/7/20/5912283/from-nietzsche-to-richard-dawkins-a-brief-history-of-modern-atheism.

Anderson, J.N.D. "The Resurrection of Christ." *Christianity Today* (March 1968) 4-9.

Annis, J. "Placing a Limit on Star-fed Kardashev Type III Civilisations." *Journal of the British Interplanetary Society* 52 (1999) 33–36. www.jbis.org.uk/paper.php?p=1999.52.33.

"Apologia: A Sermon Series in Defense of the Faith—Part IIb: 'Can We Trust the Bible?'" www.walkingtogetherministries.com/2015/07/05/apologia-a-sermon-series-in-defense-of-the-faith-part-iib-can-we-trust-the-bible/.

Arav, Rami and John Rousseau. *Jesus and His World: An Archaeological and Cultural Dictionary*. Minneapolis: Fortress, 1995.

Archaeological Study Bible: An Illustrated Walk Through Biblical History and Culture. Grand Rapids: Zondervan, 2005.

"Archaeology and the New Testament." http://youtu.be/rloyZgQyjuw.

Argubright, John. "Historical Evidence for Pontius Pilate." www.biblehistory.net/newsletter/pontius_pilate.htm.

"The Argument from Desire." www.youtube.com/playlist?list=PLQhh3qcwVEWj3nK3TBydEVAFRtdqfrpW2.

Arnold, Clinton E., ed. *Zondervan Illustrated Bible Backgrounds Commentary: Acts*. Grand Rapids: Zondervan, 2002.

———, ed. *Zondervan Illustrated Bible Background Commentary: Volume 1, Matthew, Mark, Luke*. Grand Rapids: Zondervan, 2002.

Aron, Jacob. "Falling Meteor May Have Changed the Course of Christianity." *New Scientist* 3018 (April 2015). www.newscientist.com/article/mg22630183-700-falling-meteor-may-have-changed-the-course-of-christianity.

Aslan, Reza. *Zealot: The Life and Times of Jesus of Nazareth*. New York: Westbourne, 2014.

Atkins, Peter. *On Being*. Oxford: Oxford University Press, 2011.

Aune, David E. "Greco-Roman Biography." In *Greco-Roman Literature and the New Testament: Selected Forms and Genres*, 107–26. Atlanta: Scholars Press, 1988.

Avis, Paul. "The Resurrection of Jesus." In *The Resurrection of Jesus Christ*, edited by Paul Avis, 1–22. London: DLT, 1993.

Axe, Douglas. *Undeniable: How Biology Confirms Our Intuition That Life Is Designed*. San Francisco: HarperOne, 2016.

Baggett, David, ed. *Did the Resurrection Happen? A Conversation with Gary Habermas and Antony Flew*. Downers Grove, IL: IVP, 2009.

Baggini, Julian. "A flawed attempt to shed light on genius." *The New Review, The Observer* (October 4, 2016) 38.

Bahat, D. "Does the Holy Sepulchre Church Mark the Burial of Jesus?" *Biblical Archaeological Review* 12 (1986) 26-45.

Bannister, Andy. *The Atheist Who Didn't Exist*. Oxford: Monarch, 2015.

Barclay, John M.G. "The Resurrection In Contemporary New Testament Scholarship." In *Resurrection Reconsidered*, edited by Gavin D'Costa, 13–30. Oxford: OneWorld, 1996.

Bargiel, Joe. "Phlegon of Tralles Scientifically Established as a Credible Source on Jesus." https://joebargiel.wordpress.com/2016/03/22/phlegon-of-tralles-scientifically-established-as-a-credible-source/.

Barkman, Adam. *C.S. Lewis & Philosophy As A Way Of Life*. Allentown, PA: Zossima, 2009.

Barnett, Paul W. *The Birth of Christianity: The First Twenty Years*. Grand Rapids: Eerdmans, 2005.

———. *Finding the Historical Christ*. Grand Rapids: Eerdmans, 2009.

———. *Gospel Truth: Answering New Atheist attacks on the Gospels*. Nottingham: IVP, 2012.

———. "Is The New Testament Historically Reliable?" In *In Defence of The Bible*, edited by Steven B. Cowen and Terry L. Wilder, 223–65. Nashville: B&H, 2013.

———. *Is The New Testament Reliable?* Downers Grove, IL: IVP, 2003.

———. *Messiah: Jesus—The Evidence of History*. Nottingham: IVP, 2009.

———. *Paul: Missionary of Jesus*. Grand Rapids: Eerdmans, 2008.

———. "The Quest for the Historical Pilate." http://paulbarnett.info/2011/04/the-quest-for-the-historical-pontius-pilate/.

———. *The Truth about Jesus: The Challenge of Evidence*. Sydney: Aquila, 2004.

Bartlett, Jonathan. "Philosophical Shortcomings of Methodological Naturalism and the Path Forward." In *Naturalism And Its Alternatives In Scientific Methodologies*, edited by Jonathan Bartlett and Eric Holloway, 13–37. Broken Arrow, OK: Blyth Institute, 2016.

Bassala, George. *Civilized Life In The Universe: Scientists On Intelligent Extraterrestrials*. Oxford: Oxford University Press, 2006.

Bassham, Gregory ed. *C.S. Lewis' Apologetics: Pro and Con*. Leiden, NL-ZH: Rodopi-Brill, 2015.

Bauckham, Richard. *Jesus and the Eyewitnesses*. Grand Rapids: Eerdmans, 2006.

———. "A Life with the Bible." In *I Still Believe: Leading Bible Scholars Share Their Stories Of Faith And Scholarship*, edited by Joel N. Lohr and John Byron, 17–28. Grand Rapids: Zondervan, 2015.

———. *Jesus: A Very Short Introduction*. Oxford: Oxford University Press, 2011.

"Baylor ISR "Two Dozen (or so) Theistic Arguments" Alvin Plantinga Conference (2014)." www.youtube.com/playlist?list=PLoJmtbsEea3gcN5eNq-oJXq2qTwDg7L_Q.

Beckwith, Francis J. *David Hume's Argument Against Miracles: A Critical Analysis*. Lanham: University Press of America, 1989.

———. *God Crucified: Monotheism and Christology in the New Testament*. Grand Rapids: Eerdmans, 1999.

———. *Jesus and the Eyewitnesses: The Gospels as Eyewitness Testimony*. Grand Rapids: Eerdmans, 2017.

———. *Jesus and the Eyewitnesses: The Gospels as Eyewitness Testimony*. Grand Rapids: Eerdmans, 2006.

———. "The Irrationality of Richard Dawkins." www.firstthings.com/onthesquare/?p=776.

———. "Philosophical Problems with the Mormon Concept of God." www.equip.org/article/philosophical-problems-with-the-mormon-concept-of-god/.

———. "Theism, Miracles, And the Modern Mind." In *The Rationality of Theism*, edited by Paul Copan and Paul K. Moser, 221–36. London: Routledge, 2003.

Beckwith, Francis J., and Gregory Koukl. *Relativism: Feet Firmly Planted in Mid-Air*. Grand Rapids: Baker, 1998.

Behe, Michael J. *Darwin's Black Box: The Biochemical Challenge to Evolution*. New York: Free Press, 2006.

References

———. *The Edge of Evolution: The Search for the Limits of Darwinism*. New York: Free Press, 2007.

Behm, J. *TDNT*. 4:752.

"Bentham, Jeremy." *Internet Encyclopedia of Philosophy*. www.iep.utm.edu/bentham/.

Berger, William C. *How Unique Are We? Perfect Planet, Clever Species*. New York: Prometheus, 2003.

Bergeron, Joseph W. and Gary R. Habermas. "The Resurrection of Jesus: a Clinical Review of Psychiatric Hypotheses for the Biblical Story of Easter." www.garyhabermas.com/articles/irish-theological-quarterly/Habermas_Resurrection%20of%20Jesus.pdf.

Bermejo-Rubio, Fernando. "Was the Hypothetical Vorlage of the Testimonium Flavianum a "Neutral" Text? Challenging the Common Wisdom on Antiquitates Judaicae 18.63–64." *Journal for the Study of Judaism* 45 (2014), 326–365.

Bethune, Brian. "Did Jesus Really Exist?" www.macleans.ca/society/life/did-jesus-really-exist-2/.

Bettenson, Henry, ed. and trans. *The Early Christian Fathers*. Oxford: Oxford University Press, 1969.

Beverley, James A. *Mormon Crisis: Anatomy of A Failing Religion*. Lagoon City, ON: Castle Quay, 2013.

Beverley, James A., and Craig A. Evans. *Getting Jesus Right: How Muslims Get Jesus And Islam Wrong*. Lagoon City, ON: Castle Quay, 2015.

Bible Hub Commentaries. "1 Corinthians 15:42." http://biblehub.com/commentaries/1_corinthians/15-42.htm.

———. "2 Corinthians 8:18." http://biblehub.com/text/2_corinthians/8-18.htm.

———. "asphaleia." http://biblehub.com/greek/803.htm.

———. "blasphémó." http://biblehub.com/greek/987.htm.

———. "de." http://biblehub.com/greek/1161.htm.

———. "egeiró." http://biblehub.com/greek/1453.htm.

———. "isos." http://biblehub.com/greek/2470.htm.

———. "James 2:7 Commentaries." http://biblehub.com/commentaries/james/2-7.htm.

———. "James 2:7." http://biblehub.com/text/james/2-7.htm.

———. "John 11:24." http://biblehub.com/text/john/11-24.htm.

———. "John 16:13 Commentaries." http://biblehub.com/commentaries/john/16-13.htm.

———. "katapiptó." http://biblehub.com/greek/2667.htm.

———. "Mark 12:25." http://biblehub.com/text/mark/12-25.htm.

———. "phóné." http://biblehub.com/greek/5456.htm.

"Bible Query—Early Manuscripts of 1 Corinthians." www.biblequery.org/1cormss.htm.

"Biblical Archaeology 40: The Pilate Stone." https://theosophical.wordpress.com/2011/09/20/biblical-archaeology-40-the-pilate-stone/.

Biblical Archaeological Society Staff. "A Tomb in Jerusalem Reveals the History of Crucifixion and Roman Crucifixion Methods." www.biblicalarchaeology.org/daily/biblical-topics/crucifixion/a-tomb-in-jerusalem-reveals-the-history-of-crucifixion-and-roman-crucifixion-methods/.

Biddle, Martin. *The Tomb Of Christ*. Stroud: Sutton Publishing, 1999.

Billings, Lee. "Alien Supercivilizations Absent from 100,000 Nearby Galaxies." *Scientific American*. https://www.scientificamerican.com/article/alien-supercivilizations-absent-from-100-000-nearby-galaxies/.

References

Bird, Michael F. "Did Jesus Think He Was God?" In *How God Became Jesus: The Real Origins of Belief in Jesus' Divine Nature*, 45–70. Grand Rapids: Zondervan, 2014.

———. "The Story of Jesus and the Story of God." In *How God Became Jesus: The Real Origins of Belief in Jesus' Divine Nature*, 11-21. Grand Rapids: Zondervan, 2014.

Bird, Michael F., and James Crossley. *How Did Christianity Begin? A Believer and Non-believer Examine the Evidence.* London: SPCK, 2008.

Bishop, James. "30 Common New Testament Challenges by Skeptics Answered." https://jamesbishopblog.wordpress.com/2015/02/01/30-common-new-testament-challenges-by-sceptics-answered/.

"Bitter Water." www.studylight.org/dictionaries/hbd/view.cgi?number=T971.

Bivin, David N. "Farewell to the Emmaus Road." www.jerusalemperspective.com/16208/.

Blackford, Russell. "Philosophy in an age of propaganda." *The Philosophers' Magazine* 72 (2016) 27–28.

Blackford, Russell, and Udo Schuklenk. *50 Great Myths About Atheism*. Oxford: Wiley Blackwell, 2013.

Blackmore, Susan. "Abduction by Aliens or Sleep Paralysis?" www.csicop.org/si/show/abduction_by_aliens_or_sleep_paralysis.

Blackmore, Susan, and Marcus Cox. "Alien Abductions, Sleep Paralysis and the Temporal Lobe." www.susanblackmore.co.uk/articles/alien-abductions-sleep-paralysis-and-the-temporal-lobe/.

Blaiklock, E.M. *Jesus Christ: Man or Myth*. Homebush West: Anzea, 1983.

"Blasphemy." www.biblestudytools.com/dictionaries/bakers-evangelical-dictionary/blasphemy.html.

Blomberg, Craig L. *The Historical Reliability of the Gospels*. Nottingham: Apollos/IVP, 2007.

———. *The Historical Reliability of John's Gospel: Issues & Commentary*. Leicester: Apollos, 2001.

———. *Jesus and the Gospels*. Leicester: Apollos, 1997.

———. *Jesus and the Gospels: An Introduction and Survey*. Nashville: B&H, 2009.

———. *Making Sense of the New Testament: Three Crucial Questions*. Leicester: IVP, 2003.

———. *The New American Commentary: Matthew*. Nashville: B&H, 1992.

———. "Where Do We Start Studying Jesus?" In *Jesus Under Fire*, edited by Michael J. Wilkins and J.P. Moreland, 17–50. Carlisle: Paternoster, 1995.

Blomberg, Craig L., and Carl Stecher. *Resurrection: Faith or Fact? A Scholars' Debate Between a Skeptic and a Christian*. Durham, NC: Pitchstone, forthcoming.

Bock, Darrell L. *Acts*. Grand Rapids: Baker Academic, 2007.

———. *Studying the Historical Jesus: A Guide to Sources and Methods*. Leicester: Apollos, 2007.

Bock, Darrell L. and Daniel B. Wallace. *Dethroning Jesus: Exposing Popular Culture's Quest To Unseat The Biblical Christ*. Nashville: Thomas Nelson, 2007.

———. "Precision and Accuracy: Making Distinctions in the Cultural Context." In *Do Historical Matters Matter To Faith? A Critical Appraisal of Modern and Postmodern Approaches to Scripture*, edited by James K. Hoffmeier and Denis R. Magary, 367–81. Wheaton, IL: Crossway, 2012.

———. "The Words of Jesus in the Gospels: Live, Jive, or Memorex?" *Jesus Under Fire: Modern Scholarship Reinvents the Historical Jesus*, edited by Michael J. Wilkins, 73–99. Grand Rapids: Zondervan, 1995.

"Bodmer Papyri." http://en.wikipedia.org/wiki/Bodmer_Papyri.

References

Bolnick, Deborah A., et al. "Civilizations Lost and Found: Fabricating History—Part Three: Real Messages in DNA." www.csicop.org/si/show/civilizations_lost_and_found_fabricating_history_-_part_three_real_messages.

Bombaro, John J. "Introduction." In *The Resurrection Fact: Responding to Modern Critics*, edited by John J. Bombaro and Adam S. Francisco, 1–15. Irvine, CA: NRP, 2016.

Bond, Helen K. *The Historical Jesus: A Guide for the Perplexed*. London: Bloomsbury T. & T. Clark, 2013.

———. *Jesus: A Very Brief History*. London: SPCK, 2017.

Bonevac, Daniel. "The Argument from Miracles." http://bonevac.info/papers/Miracles Oxford.pdf.

Borg, Marcus. "Jesus, A New Vision: Spirit, Culture, and The Life of Discipleship." https://jamesbishopblog.com/2015/04/23/what-do-scholars-make-of-jesus-miracles-58-quotes-by-scholars/.

———. "The Meaning of Jesus: Two Visions." https://jamesbishopblog.wordpress.com/2015/02/01/30-common-new-testament-challenges-by-sceptics-answered/.

Borg, Marcus, and N.T. Wright. *The Meaning of Jesus*. San Francisco: HarperSanFrancisco, 1999.

Bösch, Holger, et al. "Examining Psychokinesis: The Interaction of Human Intention with Random Number Generators. A Meta-Analysis." *Psychological Bulletin* 132 (2006) 74-157. www.ebo.de/publikationen/pk_ma.pdf.

Bowman, Robert, Jr. "From Monotheism to Eternal Progression: The Evolution of the Mormon Doctrine of Exaltation." http://mit.irr.org/monotheism-eternal-progression-evolution-of-mormon-doctrine-of-exaltation.

———. "Did they hear what Paul heard? Acts 9:7 and 22:9 Revisited." www.academia.edu/19770469/Did_They_Hear_What_Paul_Heard_Acts_9_7_and_22_9_Revisited.

Bowman, Robert, Jr., and J. Ed Komoszewski. *Putting Jesus In His Place: The Case for the Deity of Christ*. Grand Rapids: Kregel, 2007.

Boyd, Gregory A. *Letters From a Skeptic*. Downers Grove, IL: IVP, 2000.

Boyd, Gregory A., and Paul R. Eddy. *Lord or Legend? Wrestling with the Jesus Dilemma*. Grand Rapids: Baker, 2007.

Braaten, Carl. *History and Hermeneutics*. New Directions in Theology Today 2. Philadelphia: Westminster, 1966.

Brandon, S.G.F. *Jesus and the Zealots*. New York: Charles Scribner's, 1976.

Braun, Michael A. "James' Use of Amos at the Jerusalem Council: Steps Toward a Possible Solution of the Textual and Theological Problems." www.etsjets.org/files/JETS-PDFs/20/20-2/20-2-pp113-121_JETS.pdf.

"Breakthrough Listen Initiative Publishes Initial Results." https://breakthroughinitiatives.org/News/10.

Brewer, David Instone. "Jesus of Nazareth's Trial in Sanhedrin 43a." www.tyndale.cam.ac.uk/Tyndale/staff/Instone-Brewer/prepub/Sanhedrin%2043a%20censored.pdf.

Brewin, Chris R. and Bernice Andrews. "Creating Memories for False Autobiographical Events in Childhood: A Systematic Review." *Applied Cognitive Studies* 31 (April 2016) 2-23. http://onlinelibrary.wiley.com/doi/10.1002/acp.3220/full.

Brierley, Justin. *Unbelievable?* London: SPCK, 2017.

Brindle, Wayne. "The Census And Quirinius: Luke 2:2." www.etsjets.org/files/JETS-PDFs/27/27-1/27-1-pp043-052_JETS.pdf.

References

Bromwich, Jonah. "Bright Lights, Strange Shapes and Talk of U.F.O.s." *New York Times* (November 2015). www.nytimes.com/2015/11/13/us/bright-lights-strange-shapes-and-talk-of-ufos.html?_r=0.

Broocks, Rice. *God's Not Dead: Evidence For God In An Age Of Uncertainty*. Nashville: Thomas Nelson, 2013.

Brown, Andrew. "Dawkins the Dogmatist." *Prospect Magazine* 127 (October 2006). https://prospectmagazine.co.uk/magazine/dawkinsthedogmatist.

Brown, Dan. *The Da Vinci Code*. New York: Doubleday, 2003.

Brown, Raymond. *The Death of the Messiah: from Gethsemane to the grave : a commentary on the Passion narratives in the four Gospels* 2. New York: Doubleday, 1994.

Bruce, F.F. "Christianity Under Claudius." *Bulletin of the John Rylands Library* 44 (March 1962) 309-326. http://biblicalstudies.org.uk/pdf/bjrl/claudius_bruce.pdf.

———. *The Epistle to the Hebrews*. Grand Rapids: Eerdmans, 2012.

———. *The Gospel of John: Introduction, Exposition and Notes*. Grand Rapids: Eerdmans, 1983.

———. *The New Testament Documents: Are They Reliable?* Downers Grove, IL: IVP, 2006.

———. *The New Testament Documents: Are They Reliable?* Leicester: IVP, 1981.

———, ed. *Zondervan Bible Commentary*. Grand Rapids: Zondervan, 2008.

Bryan, Christopher. "The Resurrection of the Messiah." https://jamesbishopblog.wordpress.com/2015/06/29/jesus-really-did-appear-to-the-disciples-and-skeptics-after-his-death-40-quotes-by-scholars/.

———. *The Resurrection of the Messiah*. Oxford University Press, 2011.

Bullivant, Stephen. "The New Atheism And Sociology." In *Religion And The New Atheism: A Critical Appraisal*, edited by Amarnath Amarasingam, 109–24. Chicago: Haymarket, 2012.

Bultmann, Rudolf. *Kerygma and Myth*. New York: Harper & Row, 1961.

———. *Kerygma and Myth: A Theological Debate*. edited by Hans Werner Bartsch and translated by Reginald H. Fuller. London: Billing and Sons, 1954.

———. *The History of the Synoptic Tradition*. Translated by John Marsh. Oxford: Blackwell, 1972.

Burningham, Kay. *An American Fraud: One Lawyer's Case Against Mormonism*. Amica Veritatis, 2011.

Burridge, Richard A. *What Are the Gospels? A Comparison with Graeco-Roman Biography*. Grand Rapids: Eerdmans, 2004.

Bushman, Richard Lyman. *Mormonism: A Very Short Introduction*. Oxford: Oxford University Press, 2008.

Bylica, Piotr and Dariusz Sagan. "God, Design, and Naturalism: Implications of Methodological Naturalism in Science for Science-Religion Relation." *Pensamiento* 64 (2008) 621–38. https://docs7.chomikuj.pl/2540786018,PL,0,0,146.pdf.

Cabal, Ted, ed. *The Apologetics Study Bible*. Nashville: Holman, 2007.

Came, Daniel. "Richard Dawkins's Refusal to Debate is Cynical and Anti-intellectualist." www.theguardian.com/commentisfree/belief/2011/oct/22/richard-dawkins-refusal-debate-william-lane-craig.

Campbell, Charlie H. *Archaeological Evidence for The Bible*. Carlsbad, CA: AlwaysBeReady, 2012.

Campbell, John Angus and Stephen C. Meyer, eds. *Darwinism, Design, and Public Education*. East Lansing, MI: Michigan State University Press, 2003.

References

"Can I get a witness to the Book of Mormon translated?" www.letusreason.org/LDS14.htm

Carson, Donald A. *The Gospel According to John*. Grand Rapids: Eerdmans, 1991.

Casey, Maurice. *Jesus: Evidence And Argument Or Mythicist Myths?* London: Bloomsbury, 2014.

———. *Jesus of Nazareth: An Independent Historian's Account of His Life and Teaching*. London: T. & T. Clark, 2010.

Chadwick, Henry. *Origen: Contra Celsus*. Cambridge, UK: Cambridge University Press, 2003.

Chaffey, Tim. *In Defence of Easter*. Midwest Apologetics, 2014.

Chapman, Allan. *Slaying The Dragons: Destroying Myths In The History Of Science And Faith*. Oxford: Lion, 2013.

———. *Stargazers: Copernicus, Galileo, the Telescope and the Church—The Astronomical Renaissance 1500–1700*. Oxford: Lion, 2014.

Charlesworth, James H. *The Historical Jesus: An Essential Guide*. Nashville: Abingdon, 2008.

"Chester Beatty Papyri." http://en.wikipedia.org/wiki/Chester_Beatty_Papyri.

Chesterton, G.K. *The Everlasting Man*. London: Hodder & Stoughton, 1927.

Chilton, B.D. and C.A. Evans, eds. *Authenticating the Activities of Jesus*. New Testament Tools and Studies 28.2. Leiden: Brill, 1998.

Christian, Eric. "Space Physics: Wormholes, Time Travel, and Faster-Than-Speed-of-Light Theories." *NASA*. https://helios.gsfc.nasa.gov/qa_sp_sl.htm.

"Christianity Not A Source of Violence: A Statement from the EPS." www.epsociety.org/library/articles.asp?pid=96&mode=detail

Churchill, Leigh. *The Blood of Martyrs: The History of the Christian Church from Pentecost to the age of Theodosius*. Milton Keynes: Paternoster, 2005.

Clancy, Susan A. *Abducted: How People Come To Believe They Were Kidnapped By Aliens*. Cambridge, MA: Harvard University Press, 2005.

Clegg, Brian. *Extra Sensory: The Science And Pseudoscience Of Telepathy And Other Powers Of The Mind*. New York: St. Martin's Press, 2013.

Cline, Austin. "Dating and Origins of Mark's Gospel." http://atheism.about.com/od/biblegospelofmark/a/dating.htm.

Clowney, Edmund. *The Message of 1 Peter*. Nottingham: IVP, 2010.

Colavito, James. *The Cult of Alien Gods: H.P. Lovecraft and Extraterrestrial Pop Culture*. New York: Prometheus, 2005.

Cole, R. Alan. *Mark*. Tyndale New Testament Commentaries 2. Downers Grove: IVP, 2008.

Collins, Francis S. "The Language of God." In *A Place for Truth*, edited by Dallas Willard, 72–98. Downers Grove: IVP, 2010.

———. *The Language of God: A Scientist Presents Evidence For Belief*. New York: Free Press, 2006.

Collins, Steven. *The Defendable Faith: Lessons in Christian Apologetics*. Albuquerque: Trinity Southwest University Press, 2012.

Comfort, Philip W. and Jason Driesbach. *The Many Gospels of Jesus: Sorting Out the Story of the Life of Jesus*. Carol Stream, IL: Tyndale House Publishers, 2008.

Compte-Sponville, Andre. *The Book Of Atheist Spirituality*. London: Bantam, 2007.

Consolmagno, Guy. "Was St. Paul Converted by a Meteor Fall?" www.vofoundation.org/blog/was-st-paul-converted-by-a-meteorite-fall/.

Cook, Steven R. "Introduction to the Letter of James." https://youtu.be/hYc9cdUgQfQ.

Cooper, John W. *Body, Soul, and Life Everlasting: Biblical Anthropology and the Monism-Dualism Debate*. Grand Rapids, MI: Eerdmans, 1989.

Copan, Paul. "Interview with Paul Copan: Is Yahweh a Moral Monster?" www.epsociety.org/blog/2008/04/interview-with-paul-copan-is-yahweh.asp.

———. *True For You But Not For Me: Overcoming Objections to Christian Faith*. Minneapolis: Bethany House, 2009.

Copan, Paul, and Ronald K. Tacelli, eds. *Jesus' Resurrection: Fact or Figment? A Debate between William Lane Craig and Gerd Lüdemann*. Downers Grove, IL: IVP, 2000.

Copan, Paul, and William Lane Craig, eds. *Contending with Christianity's Critics: Answering New Atheists and Other Objectors*. Nashville: B&H, 2009.

Corduan, Winfried. *In The Beginning God: A Fresh Look At The Case For Original Monotheism*. Nashville: B&H, 2013.

———. *No Doubt About It: The Case for Christianity*. Nashville: B&H, 1997.

"Cornelius Tacitus." www.earlychristianwritings.com/tacitus.html

Cottingham, John. *Why Believe?* London: Continuum, 2009.

Cover, J.A. "Miracles and Christian Theism." In *Reason for the Hope Within*, edited by Michael J. Murray, 345–74. Grand Rapids: Eerdmans, 1999.

Cowan, Steven B. "Discerning the Voice of God: The Apologetic Function of Miracles." *Areopagus Journal* 8 (March/April 2008) 10–13.

Coyne, Jerry A. *Faith vs. Fact: Why Science And Religion Are Incompatible*. New York: Viking, 2015.

———. "It's Time to Ponder Whether Jesus Really Existed." https://whyevolutionistrue.wordpress.com/2016/04/03/its-time-to-think-about-whether-jesus-really-existed/.

———. "Once Again: Was There a Historical Jesus?" https://whyevolutionistrue.wordpress.com/2014/10/03/once-again-was-there-a-historical-jesus/.

———. "What is a "true" religion?" http://whyevolutionistrue.wordpress.com/2014/09/12/what-is-a-true-religion/.

Craig, Olga. "DNA Test Pinpoints St Luke the Apostle's Remains to Padua." *The Telegraph* (October 2001). www.telegraph.co.uk/news/worldnews/europe/italy/1360095/DNA-test-pinpoints-St-Luke-the-apostles-remains-to-Padua.html.

Craig, William Lane. "Atheists Gone Wild?" www.reasonablefaith.org/atheists-gone-wild#ixzz4t1TpNp8G.

———. "The Bodily Resurrection of Jesus." https://www.reasonablefaith.org/writings/scholarly-writings/historical-jesus/the-bodily-resurrection-of-jesus/.

———. "A Classical Apologist's Response." In *Five Views on Apologetics*, edited by Steven B. Cowen, 122–28. Grand Rapids: Zondervan, 2000.

———. "Contemporary Scholarship and the Historical Resurrection of Jesus Christ." www.leaderu.com/truth/1truth22.html.

———. "Creation and Divine Action." In *The Routledge Companion to Philosophy of Religion*, edited by Chad Meister and Paul Copan, 318–328. London: Routledge, 2010.

———. "Dale Allison on Jesus's Empty Tomb." *Philosophia Christi* 10 (2008) 293–301.

———. "Dale Allison on the Resurrection of Jesus." www.reasonablefaith.org/dale-allison-on-the-resurrection-of-jesus#ixzz4bUNI8Gng.

———. "The Definition That Will Not Die." www.reasonablefaith.org/the-definition-that-will-not-die.

———. "The Doctrine of Christ (Part 18)." www.reasonablefaith.org/defenders-1-podcast/transcript/s13–18.

———. "The Empty Tomb of Jesus." In *Gospel Perspectives: Studies of History and Tradition in the Gospels, Volume II*, edited by R.T. France and David Wenham, 173–200. Sheffield: JSOT Press, 1981.

———. "The Evidence for Jesus." www.reasonablefaith.org/the-evidence-for-jesus.

———. "Excavating the Tomb of Jesus." www.reasonablefaith.org/excavating-the-tomb-of-jesus#ixzz4Q3vk6rxS.

———. "The Guard on the Tomb." www.reasonablefaith.org/site/News2?page=NewsArticle&id=5211.

———. "'Honesty, Transparency, Full Disclosure'" and the Borde-Guth-Vilenkin Theorem." www.reasonablefaith.org/honesty-transparency-full-disclosure-and-bgv-theorem.

———. "Is Mormonism a Cult?" www.reasonablefaith.org/is-mormonism-a-cult.

———. "Jesus and pagan mythology." www.reasonablefaith.org/jesus-and-pagan-mythology.

———. "Jesus the Son of God." www.reasonablefaith.org/site/News2?page=NewsArticle&id=6247.

———. "Naturalism and Intelligent Design." In *Intelligent Design*, edited by Robert B. Stewart, 58–71. Minneapolis: Fortress, 2007.

———. *On Guard*. Colorado Springs: David C. Cook, 2009.

———. "Philosophical and Scientific Pointers to Creation Ex Nihilo." www.asa3.org/ASA/PSCF/1980/JASA3-80Craig.html.

———. "Problems with the Old Testament." www.reasonablefaith.org/problems-with-the-old-testament.

———. "Qualms about the resurrection of Jesus." www.reasonablefaith.org/site/News2?page=NewsArticle&id=6503.

———. *Reasonable Faith: Christian Truth and Apologetics*. Wheaton, IL: Crossway, 2008.

———. *A Reasonable Response*. Chicago: Moody, 2013.

———. "Rediscovering the Historical Jesus: Presuppositions and Pretensions of the Jesus Seminar." www.leaderu.com/offices/billcraig/docs/rediscover1.html.

———. "Reply to Our Respondents." In *Is Faith In God Reasonable?*, edited by Corey Miller and Paul Gould, 153–165. London: Routledge, 2014.

———. "The Resurrection of Jesus." www.reasonablefaith.org/the-resurrection-of-jesus.

———. "Richard Dawkins' Argument for Atheism in The God Delusion." www.reasonablefaith.org/site/News2?page=NewsArticle&id=5493.

———. "Richard Dawkins on Argument for God." In *God Is Great, God Is Good: Why Believing in God Is Reasonable and Responsible*, edited by William Lane Craig and Chad Meister, 13–31. Downers Grove, IL: IVP, 2009.

———. *The Son Rises: The Historical Evidence For The Resurrection Of Jesus*. Eugene, OR: Wipf & Stock, 2000.'

———. "The Soul Provides Continuity Between the Physical and Resurrection Body." https://youtu.be/4I9otrxUoN4.

———. "Visions of Jesus: A Critical Assessment of Gerd Lüdemann's Hallucination Hypothesis." www.reasonablefaith.org/visions-of-jesus-a-critical-assessment-of-gerd-ludemanns.

———. "What About Pre-Christ Resurrection Myths?" https://youtu.be/qrCYVk6xrXg.

———. "What was Herod thinking?" www.reasonablefaith.org/what-was-herod-thinking#ixzz4VLykpVnY.

References

Craig, William Lane. "Who Was Jesus? A Christian Perspective." In *Who Was Jesus? A Jewish–Christian Dialogue*, edited by Paul Copan and Craig A. Evans, 21–28. Louisville, KY: Westminster John Knox, 2001.

———. "William Lane Craig at the Bible and Beer Consortium in Dallas, Texas (2015)." https://youtu.be/VKudgsPT6No.

———. "The Work of Bart Ehrman." www.reasonablefaith.org/videos/lectures/the-work-of-bart-ehrman-gracepoint-church/.

Craig, William Lane, and Walter Sinnott-Armstrong. *God? A Debate between a Christian and an Atheist*. Oxford: Oxford University Press, 2004.

Critchley, Simon. "Why I Love Mormonism." *The New York Times* (September 2012). https://opinionator.blogs.nytimes.com/2012/09/16/why-i-love-mormonism/?mcubz=0.

Crossan, John D. *The Historical Jesus: The Life of a Mediterranean Jewish Peasant*. Edinburgh: T. & T. Clark, 1992.

———. *Jesus: A Revolutionary Biography*. San Francisco: HarperOne, 1994.

Crossley, James G. "Against the Historical Plausibility of the Empty Tomb Story and the Bodily Resurrection of Jesus: A Response to N.T. Wright. *Journal for the Study of the Historical Jesus* 3 (2005) 171–86.

———. *The Date of Mark's Gospel: Insight from the Law in Earliest Christianity*. London: T. & T. Clark, 2004.

———. "The Resurrection Probably Did Not Happen." In *Debating Christian Theism*, edited by J.P. Moreland, 484–94. Oxford: Oxford University Press, 2013.

Crowe, Brandon D. *Was Jesus Really Born Of A Virgin?* Philadelphia: Westminster Seminary, 2013.

Cullmann, Oscar. *The New Testament*. London: SCM, 1968.

Dartnell, Lewis. *Life in the Universe—Beginner's Guides*. London: OneWorld, 2012.

———. "(Un)welcome Visitors: Why Aliens Might Visit Us." In *Aliens: Science Asks: Is There Anyone Out There?*, edited by Jim Al-Khalili. Profile, 2016.

Das-Bhaumik, Raj. "Falling meteor may have changed the course of Christianity." *New Scientist* (April 2015). www.newscientist.com/article/mg22630183-700-falling-meteor-may-have-changed-the-course-of-christianity.

Davids, Peter H. "James." In *The New Bible Commentary*, edited by D.A. Carson et al., 1354–68. Leicester: IVP, 1994.

Davies, Paul. "Physics and the Mind of God." www.firstthings.com/article/1995/08/003-physics-and-the-mind-of-god-the-templeton-prize-address-24.

Davis, C. Truman. "The Crucifixion of Jesus. The Passion of Christ from a Medical Point of View." *Arizona Medicine* 22 (March 1965) 183–7.

Davis, Nicola. "Proxima b: Could we Live on This Newly Found Planet—or Could Something Else?" *The Guardian* (August 2016). www.theguardian.com/science/2016/aug/27/proxima-b-could-we-live-on-this-newly-found-planet-or-could-something-else.

Davis, Stephen T. "The Question Of Miracles, Ascension & Anti-Semitism." In *Jesus's Resurrection: Fact or Figment?: A Debate Between William Lane Craig & Gerd Ludemann*, edited by Paul Copan, 72–85. Leicester: IVP, 2000.

———. *Christian Philosophical Theology*. Oxford: Oxford University Press, 2016.

———. *Disputed Issues*. Waco, TX: Baylor University Press, 2009.

———. "James D.G. Dunn on the resurrection of Jesus." In *Memories of Jesus: A Critical Appraisal of James D.G. Dunn's Jesus Remembered*, edited by Robert B. Stewart and Gary R. Habermas, 255–66. Nashville: B&H, 2010.

———. "The Mad/Bad/God Trilemma: A Reply to Daniel Howard Snyder." www.lastseminary.com/trilemma.

———. *Rational Faith: A Philosopher's Defence of Christianity*. Oxford: Lion, 2017.

———. *Risen Indeed: Making Sense of the Resurrection*. London: SPCK, 1993.

———. "Was Jesus Raised Bodily." In *Christian Philosophical Theology*, 111–28. Oxford: Oxford University Press, 2006.

"Dawkins and Krauss on Mormonism." https://youtu.be/KN4M8PvpmW4.

Dawkins, Richard. "Afterword." In *What Is Your Dangerous Idea?*, edited by John Brockman, 305–9. London: Pocket, 2006.

———. "Atheists for Jesus." www.richarddawkins.net/articles/20.

———. *A Devil's Chaplain*. London: Weidenfeld & Nicolson, 2003.

———. *The God Delusion*. London: Bantam, 2006.

———. *The God Delusion*. London: Black Swan, 2007.

———. "Hugh interviews atheist Richard Dawkins." *Townhall Review*. www.hughhewitt.com/hugh-interviews-atheist-richard-dawkins/.

———. Interview in *Playboy* (August, 2012). https://scrapsfromtheloft.com/2018/01/02/richard-dawkins-playboy-interview-chip-rowe/.

———. "Is Science a Religion?" In *What's So Great About Christianity?* by Dinesh D'Souza, 180. Washington: Regnery, 2007.

———. "Lecture at the Edinburgh International Science Festival." April 15, 1992.

———. "Let's all stop beating Basil's car." http://edge.org/response-detail/11416.

———. *The Magic of Reality: How we know what's really true*. London: Bantam, 2011.

———. *Reddit* (2016) www.reddit.com/r/IAmA/comments/4lbjwa/i_am_richard_dawkins_evolutionary_biologist_and/.

———. "Richard Dawkins Admits Jesus Existed." https://youtu.be/m5EjA-JNiVk.

———. "Richard Dawkins on Studio 4 in Vancouver—Part 3 of 5." www.youtube.com/watch?v=XwWQamTzjA0&feature=related.

———. *Science In The Soul: Selected Writings Of A Passionate Rationalist*. London: Bantam, 2017.

———. *The Selfish Gene*. Oxford: Oxford Paperbacks, 1989.

Dawnes, Gregory. *Theism and Explanation*. London: Routledge, 2009.

Deem, Rich. "Book Review: *Cold-Case Christianity*." www.godandscience.org/apologetics/cold-case_christianity.html.

Dembski, William A. "The Incompleteness of Scientific Naturalism." www.leaderu.com/orgs/fte/darwinism/chapter7.html.

———. *No Free Lunch: Why Specified Complexity Cannot Be Purchased Without Intelligence*. Oxford: Rowman & Littlefield, 2002.

———, ed. *Uncommon Dissent: Intellectuals Who Find Darwinism Unconvincing*. Wilmington, Delaware: ISI, 2004.

Dembski, William A., and Jonathan Wells, *The Design of Life*. Dallas: The Foundation for Thought and Ethics, 2008.

Dennett, Daniel. "Afterword." In *The God Delusion* by Richard Dawkins, 421–26. London: Black Swan, 2016.

———. *Breaking the Spell: Religion as a Natural Phenomenon*. London: Penguin, 2006.

———. "Is Religion a Threat to Rationality and Science." www.theguardian.com/education/2008/apr/22/highereducation.uk5.

———. Quoted in "Mounting Disbelief" by Nick Spencer. *Thirdway Magazine* (Jul/Aug, 2013). https://thirdway.hymnsam.co.uk/editions/julyaugust-2013/high-profile/mounting-disbelief.aspx.

———. "The Q&A." *New Humanist* (Summer 2017).

———. "Review of Richard Dawkins' *The God Delusion*." *Free Inquiry* (October 2006). www.philvaz.com/apologetics/DawkinsGodDelusionReviewFreeInquiry.pdf.

———. "What is a "true" religion?" http://whyevolutionistrue.wordpress.com/2014/09/12/what-is-a-true-religion/.

Denton, Michael J. *Fire Maker: How Humans Were Designed to Harness Fire and Transform Our Planet*. Seattle: Discovery Institute, 2016.

———. *Nature's Destiny: How the Laws of Biology Reveal Purpose in the Universe*. New York: Free Press, 1998.

DePoe, John M. "How to Confirm a Miracle." http://apollos.ws/miracles/How%20to%20Confirm%20a%20Miracle.pdf.

DeWeese Garrett J., and J.P. Moreland. *Philosophy Made Slightly Less Difficult*. Downers Grove, IL: IVP, 2005.

Dickson, John, and Greg Clarke. *Life of Jesus*. Sydney: CPX, 2009.

Dickson, John. "I'll Eat a Page from my Bible if Jesus Didn't Exist." www.abc.net.au/,news/2014-10-17/dickson-ill-eat-a-page-from-my-bible-if-jesus-didnt-exist/5820620.

———. *Investigating Jesus: An Historian's Quest*. Oxford: Lion, 2010.

———. "The New Atheist's Questionable History: Part 1." http://youtu.be/c3pwNDUgwfM.

———. "The New Atheist's Questionable History: Part 2." http://youtu.be/6lzza11g3LA.

———. "The Nouveau Atheists on the Historical Jesus." http://ho-logos.blogspot.co.uk/2009/02/nouveau-atheists-on-historical-jesus.html.

"Did Prophet Muhammad Split the Moon?" www.quran-islam.org/faq/did_muhammad_split_the_moon_(P1414).html.

Dimopoulos, Konstantinos. "Active galaxies may harbour wormholes if dark matter is axionic." https://arxiv.org/pdf/1603.04671v2.pdf.

"Divine Hiddenness." www.youtube.com/playlist?list=PLQhh3qcwVEWjdEpbDWJYgLlQjJQC8hCgo.

Dobson, Kent. "James: Introduction." In *NIV First Century Study Bible*, p. 1579. Grand Rapids: Zondervan, 2014.

Dodd, C.H. *The Founder of Christianity*. London: Collins Fontana, 1973.

———. *The Founder of Christianity*. London: Collins, Fontana Religious, 1974.

Douglas, J.D., and Merrill C. Tenny. *Zondervan Illustrated Bible Dictionary*. Grand Rapids: Zondervan, 2011.

Drane, John. *Introducing the New Testament*. Oxford: Lion, 1999.

Drange, Theodore M. "Some Philosophical Aspects of the Craig-Rosenberg Debate." In *Is Faith in God Reasonable?*, ed. Corey Miller and Paul Gould, 84–96. London: Routledge, 2014.

Duncan, John. Quoted in *C.S. Lewis: The Work of Christ Revealed* by P. H. Brazier. Eugene, OR: Pickwick, 2012.

Dunn, James D.G. *The Evidence for Jesus*. London: SCM, 1985.

———. *Jesus Remembered*. Christianity in the Making 1. Grand Rapids: Eerdmans, 2003.

———. "In Grateful Dialogue." In *Memories of Jesus: a Critical Appraisal of James D.G. Dunn's Jesus Remembered*, edited by Robert B. Stewart and Gary R. Habermas, 287–323. Nashville: B&H Academic, 2010.

———. "Myth." In *Dictionary of Jesus and the Gospels*. Downers Grove, IL: IVP, 1993.

———. "The New Testament As History." In *Different Gospels: Modern Orthodoxy and Modern Theologies*, edited by Andrew Walker, 43–53. London: SPCK, 1993.

———. "Remembering Jesus: How the Quest for the Historical Jesus Lost Its Way." In *The Historical Jesus: Five Views*, edited by James K. Beilby and Paul R. Eddy, 199–225. London: SPCK, 2010.

———. "Social Memory and the Oral Jesus Tradition." In *Memory in the Bible and Antiquity*, 179–194. Mohr Siebeck, 2007.

———. *Why Believe in Jesus' Resurrection?* London: SPCK, 2016.

Eagleton, Terry. *Culture and the Death of God*. New Haven: Yale University Press, 2015.

———. "Lunging, Flailing, Mispunching." *London Review of Books* 28 (October 2006) 32–34. www.lrb.co.uk/v28/n20/eaglo1_.html.

———. *Reason, Faith, and Revolution: Reflections on the God Debate*. New Haven: Yale University Press, 2009.

Dyke, Daniel J., and Hugh Henry. "A Hypernatural Miracle: Elijah and the Fire from Heaven." www.reasons.org/articles/a-hypernatural-miracle-elijah-and-the-fire-from-heaven.

"Earliest Known Picture of Jesus Goes on Display." www.rejesus.co.uk/blog/post/earliest_known_picture_of_jesus_goes_on_display/

Earman, John. *Hume's Abject Failure*. Oxford: Oxford University Press, 2000.

Easley, Kendell H. *Holman Quick Source Guide To Understanding The Bible*. Nashville Tennessee: Holman, 2002.

Eck, Allison. "New Wormhole Could Resolve the Black Hole Information Paradox." *Nova Next* (October 2007). www.pbs.org/wgbh/nova/next/physics/new-wormhole-could-resolve-the-black-hole-information-paradox/.

Eddy, Paul Rhodes and Gregory A. Boyd. *The Jesus Legend: A Case for the Historical Reliability of the Synoptic Jesus Tradition*. Grand Rapids: Baker Academic, 2007.

Edwards, Chuck. "Dawkins' Delusional Arguments Against God." www.summit.org/resource/tc/archive/0407/.

Edwards, Douglas. *The Virgin Birth In History And Faith*. London: Faber & Faber, 1943.

Edwards, James R. "Archaeology Gives New Reality To Paul's Ephesus Riot." *Biblical Archaeology Review* 42 (July/August 2016) 24–32.

Ehrenkranz, N.J., and D.A. Sampson. "Origin of the Old Testament Plagues: Explications and Implications." *Yale Journal of Biology and Medicine* 81 (March 2008) 31–42. www.ncbi.nlm.nih.gov/pmc/articles/PMC2442724/.

Ehrman, Bart D. "Bart D. Ehrman Interview." www.thebestschools.org/special/ehrman-licona-dialogue-reliability-new-testament/bart-ehrman-interview/.

———. *Did Jesus Exist? The Historical Argument for Jesus of Nazareth*. San Francisco: HarperOne, 2012.

———. "Is There Historical Evidence for the Resurrection of Jesus? Ehrman's Opening Statement." www.reasonablefaith.org/site/DocServer/resurrection-debate-transcript.pdf?docID=621.

———. "Is There Historical Evidence for the Resurrection of Jesus? Ehrman's Second Rebuttal." www.reasonablefaith.org/site/DocServer/resurrection-debate-transcript.pdf?docID=621.

———. "Jesus as God in the Synoptics." https://ehrmanblog.org/jesus-as-god-in-the-synoptics-for-members/.

———. *Jesus Interrupted*: *Revealing the Hidden Contradictions in the Bible (and Why We Don't Know About Them)*. San Francisco: HarperOne, 2009.

———. "On the Existence of Jesus." http://1peter315.wordpress.com/2011/07/23/bart-ehrman-on-the-existence-of-jesus/.

———. "Opening Statement." www.holycross.edu/departments/crec/website/resurrection-debate-manuscript.pdf.

———. *The New Testament*: *A Historical Introduction to the Early Christian Writings*. Oxford: Oxford University Press, 2004.

———. "The Significance of an Astounding New Discovery." http://ehrmanblog.org/the-significance-of-an-astounding-new-discovery/.

———. "What was the Council of Nicea?" www.beliefnet.com/Faiths/Christianity/2005/06/What-Was-The-Council-Of-Nicea.aspx.

———. "Who Cares? Do the Varients in the Manuscripts Matter For Anything?" http://ehrmanblog.org/who-cares-do-the-variants-in-the-manuscripts-matter-for-anything/.

Elwell, Walter A., and Robert W. Yarborough. *Encountering the New Testament*: *A Historical and Theological Survey*. Grand Rapids: Baker, 2013.

———. *Encountering the New Testament*. Grand Rapids: Baker Books, 1998.

Emery, Emery. "A Child Was Born on Christmas Day." In *There's Probably No God*: *The Atheist's Guide to Christmas*, edited by Ariane Sherine, 15–19. London: Friday, 2009.

Engwer, Jason. "Early External Evidence for an Early Date for Luke-Acts." http://triablogue.blogspot.co.uk/2014/07/early-external-evidence-for-early-date.html.

"Evaluating Information: The cornerstone of civic online reasoning." https://sheg.stanford.edu/upload/V3LessonPlans/Executive%20Summary%2011.21.16.pdf

Evans, Craig A. "The Burial and Empty Tomb Traditions." www.youtube.com/watch?v=ZKvy9e5UMKE.

———. "The Christ of Faith is the Jesus of History." In *Debating Christian Theism*, edited by J.P. Moreland, Chad Meister and Khaldoun A. Sweis, 458–467. Oxford: Oxford University Press, 2013.

———. *Fabricating Jesus*: *How Modern Scholars Distort the Gospels*. Downers Grove, IL: IVP, 2006.

———. "Foreword." *Why Are There Difference In The Gospels? What We Can Learn From Ancient Biography*, by Michael R. Licona. Oxford: Oxford University Press, 2017.

———. "The Historical Jesus and the Deified Christ: How Did the One Lead to the Other?" In *The Nature of Religious Language*: *A Colloquium*, edited by Stanley E. Porter, 47–67. Sheffield: Sheffield Academic Press, 1996.

———. *Jesus And His World*: *The Archaeological Evidence*. London: SPCK, 2012.

———. "The Jesus of History and the Christ of Faith: Toward Jewish-Christian Dialogue." In *Who Was Jesus? A Jewish-Christian Dialogue*, edited by Paul Copan and Craig A. Evans, 59–72. Louisville, KY: WJK, 2001.

———. *Jesus and the Remains of His Day*: *Studies in Jesus and the Evidence of Material Culture*. Peabody, MA: Hendrickson, 2015.

———. "Jewish Burial Traditions and the Resurrection of Jesus." http://craigaevans.com/Burial_Traditions.pdf.

———. "Resurrection." In *The Routledge Companion to Philosophy of Religion*, edited by Chad Meister and Paul Copan, 566–75. London: Routledge, 2010.

References

———. "Textual Criticism And Textual Confidence: How Reliable Is Scripture?" In *The Reliability of The New Testament: Bart D. Ehrman and Daniel B. Wallace In Dialogue*, edited by Robert B. Stewart, 161–72. Minneapolis: Fortress 2011.

Evans, Ernie. "Jewish Burial Customs and the Resurrection of Jesus." http://craigaevans.com/Burial_Traditions.pdf.

Evans, C. Stephen. *The Historical Christ & the Jesus of Faith*. Oxford: Clarendon, 2004.

———. *Philosophy of Religion: Thinking about Faith*. Downers Grove, IL: IVP, 1982.

———. *Why Christian Faith Still Makes Sense*. Grand Rapids: Baker Academic, 2015.

Evans, C. Stephen, and R. Zachary Manis. *Philosophy of Religion: Thinking About Faith*. Downers Grove, IL: IVP Academic, 2009.

"Everyday Mysteries: Is it true that no two snow crystals are alike?" www.loc.gov/rr/scitech/mysteries/snowcrystals.html.

"The Exodus." www.youtube.com/playlist?list=PLQhh3qcwVEWjbiCIsVBzoXW4bFq72c3EJ.

"Extrabiblical Evidence for King David." http://theophilogue.com/2009/04/24/extrabiblical-evidence-for-king-david/.

Fabricatore, Dan. *Form of God, Form of a Servant*. Lanham, MD: University Press of America, 2009.

"False Witnesses and Lost Credibility." http://thoughtsonthingsandstuff.com/false-witnesses-and-lost-credibility/.

Feder, Kenneth L. "Help! I'm Being Followed by Ancient Aliens!" www.csicop.org/si/show/help_im_being_followed_by_ancient_aliens.

Feldmeier, Peter. *The God Conflict*. Ligouri, MO: Liguori, 2014.

Ferguson, Everett. *Baptism in the Early Church: History, Theology and Liturgy in the First Five Centuries*. Grand Rapids: Eerdmans, 2009.

Fergusson, David. *Faith and Its Critics: A Conversation*. Oxford: Oxford University Press, 2011.

"The Fermi Paradox and Our Search for Alien Life." https://youtu.be/5tjnuVheDoY.

Fernandes, Phil, et al. *Hijacking the Historical Jesus: Answering Recent Attacks on the Jesus of the Bible*. CreateSpace, 2012.

Fingas, Jon. "Study: Most Students Can't Spot Fake News." www.engadget.com/2016/11/21/students-have-trouble-spotting-fake-news/.

Finley, Thomas J. "Does the Book of Mormon Reflect an Ancient Near Eastern Background?" In *The New Mormon Challenge*, edited by Francis Beckwith and Carl Mosser, 337–66. Grand Rapids: Zondervan, 2002.

Flew, Antony. "Book Review: The God Delusion." *Philosophia Christi* 10(2008). www.bethinking.org/atheism/professor-antony-flew-reviews-the-god-delusion.

———. Quoted in *Did Jesus Rise From the Dead? The Resurrection Debate*, edited by Terry L. Miethe. Eugene, OR: Wipf & Stock, 2003.

———. "My Pilgrimage from Atheism to Theism: An Exclusive Interview with Former British Atheist Professor Antony Flew." https://digitalcommons.liberty.edu/cgi/viewcontent.cgi?article=1336&context=lts_fac_pubs.

———. "Professor Antony Flew Reviews *The God Delusion*." www.bethinking.org/atheism/professor-antony-flew-reviews-the-god-delusion.

Flew, Antony, and John F. Ankerberg, eds. *Resurrected? An Atheist and Theist Dialogue*. New York: Rowman & Littlefield, 2005.

Flusser, David. *The Sage from Galilee*. Grand Rapids: Eerdmans, 2007.

References

Foster, Charles. *The Christmas Mystery: What On Earth Happened At Bethlehem?* Milton Keynes: Authentic, 2007.

Foster, John. *The Jesus Inquest*. Oxford: Monarch, 2006.

Fradera, Alex. "It's easy to implant false childhood memories, right? Wrong, says a new review." *Research Digest* (May 2016). https://digest.bps.org.uk/2016/05/26/its-easy-to-implant-false-childhood-memories-right-wrong-says-a-new-review/

France, R.T. *The Evidence for Jesus*. London: Hodder & Stoughton, 1986.

———. *Matthew*. Nottingham: IVP, 2008.

Francisco, Adam S. "Can a Historian Explain the Empty Tomb with the Resurrection of Jesus?" In *The Resurrection Fact: Responding to Modern Critics*, edited by John J. Bombaro and Adam S. Francisco, 43–58. Irvine, CA: NRP, 2016.

Frazer, James G. *The Golden Bough: a Study in Magic and Religion*. London: Macmillan, 1913.

Fredriksen, Paula. *Jesus of Nazareth, King of the Jews*. New York: Vintage, 2002.

———. *Jesus of Nazareth: King of the Jews*. New York: Vintage, 1999.

———. Quoted in *The Search for Jesus* with Peter Jennings (2000).

French, Christopher C. "Close Encounters of the Psychological Kind." https://thepsychologist.bps.org.uk/volume-28/october-2015/close-encounters-psychological-kind

———. "Fantastic Memories: The Relevance of Research into Eyewitness Testimony and False Memories for Reports of Anomalous Experience." In *PSI Wars: Getting To Grips With The Paranormal*, edited by James Alcock et al., 153–74. Exeter: Imprint, 2003.

French, Christopher C., et al. "Psychological Aspects of the Alien Contact Experience." https://research.gold.ac.uk/4223/2/French%252Bet%252Bal%252BAliens%252Bwith%252BEffect%252BSizes%252Baccept. . ..pdf.

Friedrichsen, T.A. "Critical Observations on a Team Effort: *Beyond the Q Impasse—Luke's Use of Matthew*." www.markgoodacre.org/synoptic-l/friedrichsen.pdf.

Fudge, Edward William. *Hebrews: Ancient Encouragement For Believers Today*. Abilene, Texas: Leafwood, 2009.

Fulks, Robie. "God isn't Real." In *There's Probably No God: The Atheist's Guide to Christmas*, edited by Artiane Sherine, 261–69. London: Friday Books, 2009.

Fuller, Reginald. *The Formation of the Resurrection Narratives*. New York: Macmillan, 1980.

———. *The Foundations of New Testament Christology*. New York: Scribner, 1965.

Fuller, Steve. "Science & Religion: Exploring the Spectrum Podcast—Part 1." https://youtu.be/FyAWr7VtQoA.

———. *Science vs. Religion? Intelligent Design and the Problem of Evolution*. Cambridge, UK: Polity, 2007.

Fuller, Vincent. "What is Physical Mediumship?" www.vincentfuller.co.uk/physical_mediumship.html.

Funk, Robert W. *Honest to Jesus*. New York: HarperSanFrancisco, 1996.

Funk, Robert W., and The Jesus Seminar. *The Acts of Jesus: The Search for the Authentic Deeds of Jesus*. San Francisco: Harper San Francisco, 1999.

G.M. Barclay, John. "The Resurrection in Contemporary New Testament Scholarship." In *Resurrection Reconsidered*, edited by Gavin D'Costa, 13–30. Oxford: OneWorld, 1996.

Gaskin, J.C.A. *Hume's Philosophy of Religion*. London: Macmillan, 1978.

Gathercole, Simon J. "Did Jesus Think He Was God?" In *How God Became Jesus* by Michael F. Bird et al., 94–116. Grand Rapids: Zondervan, 2014.

Gatt, Elaine Gerada. "The mystery of St. Paul's shipwreck." www.um.edu.mt/think/the-mystery-of-st-pauls-shipwreck/.

References

Gauch, Hugh G., Jr. "The Methodology of Ramified Natural Theology." *Philosophia Christi* 15 (2013) 283–98.

Geisler, Norman L. *Baker Encyclopedia of Christian Apologetics*. Grand Rapids: Baker, 1999.

———. *Christian Apologetics*. Grand Rapids: Baker, 1996.

———. *Christian Apologetics*. Grand Rapids: Baker, 2013.

———. "Has the Bible Been Accurately Copied Down Through the Centuries?" In *If God Made the Universe, Who Made God? 130 Arguments For Christian Faith*, 44–45. Nashville: Holman Bible Publishers, 2012.

———. "Miracles & the Modern Mind." In *In Defence of Miracles*, edited by R. Douglas Geivett and Gary R. Habermas, 73–85. Leicester: Apollos, 1997.

———. *A Popular Survey of the New Testament*. Grand Rapids, Michigan: Baker, 2007.

———. *A Popular Survey of the New Testament*. Grand Rapids, Michigan: Baker, 2014.

———. "Updating the Manuscript Evidence for the New Testament." www.normgeisler.com/articles/Bible/Reliability/Norman%20Geisler%20-%20Updating%20the%20Manuscript%20Evidence%20for%20the%20New%20Testament.pdf.

Geisler, Norman L., and Abdul Saleeb. *Answering Islam: The Crescent in Light of the Cross*. Grand Rapids: Baker, 2002.

Geisler, Norman L., and Frank Turek. *I Don't Have Enough Faith to be an Atheist*. Wheaton, IL: Crossway, 2005.

Geisler, Norman L., and Peter Bocchino. *Unshakeable Foundations*. Minneapolis: Bethany House, 2001.

Geisler, Norman L., and William D. Watkins. *Worlds Apart: A Handbook On World Views*. Grand Rapids: Baker, 1989.

Geivett, R. Douglas. "Is Jesus The Only Way?" In *Jesus Under Fire: Modern Scholarship Reinvents the Historical Jesus*, edited by Michael J. Wilkins and J.P. Moreland, 177–205. Grand Rapids: Zondervan, 1995.

Gibson, Shimon. *The Final Days of Jesus*. San Francisco: Harper Collins, 2009.

"Gill's Exposition of the Entire Bible." www.biblehub.com/commentaries/luke/24-33.htm.

Gilson, Tom. "Gabriel Revelation (Stone Tablet)." www.thinkingchristian.net/posts/2008/07/gabriel-revelation-the-stone-tablet/.

———. "The Party of Reason?" In *True Reason: Confronting the Irrationality of the New Atheism*, 15–24. Grand Rapids: Kregel, 2013.

Glass, David H. *Atheism's New Clothes: Exploring and Exposing the Claims of the New Atheists*. Nottingham: Apollos, 2012.

———. "Four Poor Reasons to Reject the Resurrection." www.saintsandsceptics.org/four-poor-reasons-for-rejecting-the-resurrection/.

———. "Jerry Coyne on the Incompatibility of Science and Religion." www.saintsandsceptics.org/jerry-coyne-on-the-incompatibility-of-science-and-religion/.

———. "Jerry Coyne on the Incompatibility of Science and Religion: Part 3." www.saintsandsceptics.org/jerry-coyne-on-the-incompatibility-of-science-and-religion-part-3/?utm_content=bufferc74a0&utm_medium=social&utm_source=twitter.com&utm_campaign=buffer.

Gleghorne, Michael. "Ancient Evidence for Jesus from Non-Christian Sources." www.bethinking.org/jesus/ancient-evidence-for-jesus-from-non-christian-sources.

Godfrey, Neil. "What do Biblical scholars make of the Resurrection?" http://vridar.org/2011/03/13/what-do-biblical-scholars-make-of-the-resurrection/.

Goetz, Stewart. "Is Sam Harris Right About Free Will?" http://cct.biola.edu/blog/2014/may/26/sam-harris-free-will-book-review/.

Goldberg, G.J. "The Coincidences of the Emmaus Narrative of Luke and the Testimonium of Josephus." *The Journal for the Study of the Pseudepigrapha* 13 (1995) 59–77. www.josephus.org/GoldbergJosephusLuke1995.pdf.

Gonzalez, Guillermo and Jay W. Richards. *The Privileged Planet: How Our Place in The Cosmos is Designed for Discovery*. Washington: Regnery, 2004.

Goodacre, Mark. "Beyond the Q Impasse or Down a Blind Alley?" www.academia.edu/2429504/Beyond_the_Q_Impasse_or_Down_a_Blind_Alley

Goode, Erich. "What About Alien Abductions?" www.psychologytoday.com/blog/the-paranormal/201205/what-about-alien-abductions.

Gould, Paul M. "The Imperialistic, Elitist and Foolish Scientism of Neo-Atheism." www.paulgould.com/2015/03/09/the-imperialistic-elitist-and-foolish-scientism-of-neo-atheism/.

Gordon, Bruce L. and William A. Dembski, eds. *The Nature of Nature: Examining the Role of Naturalism in Science*. Wilmington, DE: ISI, 2011.

Grant, Edward. *A History of Natural Philosophy: From the Ancient World to the Nineteenth Century*. Cambridge, UK: Cambridge University Press, 2007.

Grant, Michael. *Jesus: An Historian's Review Of The Gospels*. New York: Charles Scribner's, 1977.

Gray, John. "The Closed Mind of Richard Dawkins." *New Republic* (October 2014). https://newrepublic.com/article/119596/appetite-wonder-review-closed-mind-richard-dawkins.

———. "The ghost at the atheist feast." *New Statesman* (March 2014). https://www.newstatesman.com/culture/2014/03/ghost-atheist-feast-was-nietzsche-right-about-religion.

———. *Seven Types of Atheism*. New York: Farrar, Straus and Giroux, 2018.

———. "Sex, Atheism and Piano Legs." In *Heresies: Against Progress and Other Illusions*, 41–48. London: Granta, 2004.

Grayling, A.C. "A.C. Grayling." In *Conversations on Religion*, edited by Mark Gordon and Chris Wilkinson, 1–15. London: Continuum, 2008.

———. *The God Argument*. London: Bloomsbury, 2013.

———. "A Happy Christmas." In *There's Probably No God: The Atheist's Guide to Christmas*, edited by Ariane Sherine, 195–99. London: Friday, 2009.

Green, Michael. *The Books The Church Suppressed: What The Da Vinci Code Doesn't Tell You*. Oxford: Monarch, 2005.

———. "Jesus in the New Testament." In *The Truth of God Incarnate*, edited by Michael Green, 17–57. London: Hodder & Stoughton, 1977.

———. *Lies, Lies, Lies! Exposing Myths About The Real Jesus*. Nottingham: IVP, 2009.

Green, Samuel. "The Gospel of Barnabas." www.answering-islam.org/Green/barnabas.htm.

Greenleaf, Simon. *The Testimony of the Evangelists: The Gospels Examined by the Rules of Evidence*. Grand Rapids: Kregel Classics, 1995.

Gribbin, John. *Alone in the Universe: Why Our Planet is Unique*. Hoboken, NJ: Wiley, 2011.

Griffith, Roger L., et al. "The Ĝ Infrared Search FOR Extraterrestrial Civilizations With Large Energy Supplies III. The Reddest Extended Sources in Wise." *The Astrophysical Journal Supplement Series* 217 (April 2015). http://iopscience.iop.org/article/10.1088/0067-0049/217/2/25/pdf.

References

Groome, David and Ron Roberts. *Parapsychology: The Science of Unusual Experience*. New York: Routledge, 2017.

Groothuis, Douglas. *Christian Apologetics: A Comprehensive Case for Biblical Faith*. Nottingham: IVP, 2011.

Grossman, Lisa. "Death of the eternal cosmos." *New Scientist* 213 (January 2012) 6–7.

Grudem, Wayne A. *Tyndale New Testament Commentaries: 1 Peter*. Nottingham: IVP, 2009.

Gundry, Robert H. "Trimming The Debate" In *Jesus' Resurrection—Fact or Figment?* edited by Paul Copan and Ronald K. Tacelli, 104-23. Downers Grove, IL: IVP, 2004.

Gumbel, Nicky. *Is God a Delusion?* London: Alpha, 2008.

Guthrie, Donald. *New Testament Introduction*. Downers Grove, IL: IVP, 1990.

Guthrie, Shandon L. "Russell, Infinity, and the Tristram Shandy Paradox." http://sguthrie.net/infinity.htm.

Habermas, Gary R. "The Case for Christ's Resurrection." In *To Everyone An Answer*, edited by Francis J. Beckwith et al., 180–98. Downers Grove, IL: IVP, 2004.

———. "Dale Allison's Resurrection Skepticism: A Critique." *Philosophia Christi* 10 (2008) 303-313.

———. "Did Jesus Perform Miracles?" In *Jesus Under Fire*, edited by Michael J. Wilkins and J.P. Moreland, 117–40. Carlisle: Paternoster, 1996.

———. "Evidential Apologetics." In *Five Views on Apologetics*, edited by Steven B. Cowan, 91-121. Grand Rapids, MI: Zondervan, 2000.

———. "Filling the Naturalistic Void." https://youtu.be/ycWkKRzx65k.

———. *The Investigator: Finding The Truth Is All That Matters—Solve The Most Famous Cold Case In History*. Gabriel's Messenger Films, 2017.

———. "The Plight of the New Atheism: A Critique." www.garyhabermas.com/articles/J_Evangelical_Theological_Soc/h.

———. "The Resurrection Appearances of Jesus." In *In Defence of Miracles*, edited by R. Douglas Geivett and Gary R. Habermas, 262–75. Leicester: Apollos, 1997.

———. *The Risen Jesus & The Future Hope*. Rowman & Littlefield, 2003.

———. "Tracing Jesus' Resurrection to Its Earliest Eyewitness Accounts." In *God Is Good, God Is Great*, edited by William Lane Craig and Chad Meister, 202–16. Downers Grove: IVP, 2009.

———. *The Verdict of History: Conclusive Evidence From Beyond the Bible for the Life of Jesus*. Eastbourne: Monarch, 1990.

———. "Why I Believe the New Testament is Historically Reliable." www.apologetics.com/index.php?option=com_content&view=article&id=165:why-i-believe-the-new-testament-is-historically-reliable&catid=39:historical-apologetics&Itemid=54.

Habermas, Gary R., et al eds. *Did Jesus Rise from the Dead?* Eugene, OR: Wipf & Stock, 2003.

Hanley, Richard. "Miracles and Wonders: Science Fiction as Epistemology." In *Science Fiction And Philosophy: From Time Travel To Superintelligence*, edited by Susan Schneider, 385–92. Oxford: Wiley Blackwell, 2016.

Hann, Scott, and Curtis Mitch. *Ignatius Catholic Study Bible, The Letter of St. James, the First and Second Letters of St. Peter and the Letter of St. Jude: Commentary, Notes & Study Questions*. San Francisco: Ignatius, 2008.

Hannam, James. "An Evening With G.A. Wells." http://www.bede.org.uk/gawells.htm.

———. *The Genesis of Science: How The Christian Middle Ages Launched The Scientific Revolution*. Washington, DC: Regnery, 2011.

———. "*The God Delusion* by Richard Dawkins." www.bede.org.uk/goddelusion.htm.

———. *God's Philosophers: How The Medieval World Laid The Foundations Of Modern Science*. London: Icon, 2009.

———. "A Historical Introduction to the Myth that Jesus Never Existed." In *Shattering the Christ Myth: Did Jesus Not Exist?*, edited by James Patrick Holding, xi–xvii. Maitland, FL: Xulon, 2008.

———. "How Christianity Led to the Rise of Modern Science." www.equip.org/PDF/JAF3384.pdf.

Hardman, Randall. "Historical Evidences For the Gospels." In *True Reason: Confronting the Irrationality of the New Atheism*, edited by Tom Gilson and Carson Weitnauer, 225–54. Grand Rapids: Kregel, 2013.

Harris, Murray J. *From Grave to Glory*. Grand Rapids: Zondervan, 1990.

———. *Raised Immortal: Resurrection and Immortality in the New Testament*. Grand Rapids: Eerdmans, 1985.

Harris, Sam. *The End of Faith: Religion, Terror, And The Future Of Reason*. London: Free Press, 2006.

———. *Free Will*. New York: Free Press, 2012.

———. *Letter to a Christian Nation*. London: Bantam, 2007.

———. *The Moral Landscape*. London: Bantam, 2010.

———. "Response to Controversy." https://samharris.org/response-to-controversy/#paranormal.

———. *Waking Up: Searching for Spirituality Without Religion*. London: Black Swan, 2014.

Harris, Sam, and Maajid Nawaz. *Islam And The Future Of Tolerance*. Cambridge, MA: Harvard University Press, 2015.

Harrison, Peter. *The Bible, Protestantism, and the Rise of Natural Science*. Cambridge, UK: Cambridge University Press, 2008.

Hart, David Bentley. *Atheist Delusions: The Christian Revolution and Its Fashionable Enemies*. New Haven: Yale University Press, 2009.

———. "Daniel Dennett Hunts the Snark." www.orthodoxytoday.org/articles7/HartDennet.php.

Hartley, L.P. *The Go-Between*. London: Hamish Hamilton, 1953.

Hartshorne, Charles. "Charles Hartshorne." In *Did Jesus Rise from the Dead? The Resurrection Debate*, edited by Gary R. Habermas, Antony Flew, and Terry L., 137–42. Miethe. Eugene, OR: Wipf & Stock, 2003.

Harvey, A.E. "Christology and the Evidence of the New Testament." In *God Incarnate: Story and Belief*. London: SPCK, 1981.

Hashim, Hasrol. "The Gospel of Barnabas." www.slideshare.net/hasrulkhat/the-gospel-of-barnabas.

Hazen, Craig A. "Ever Hearing but Never Understanding: A Response to Mark Hutchins's Critique of John Warwick Montgomery's Historical Apologetics." In *Tough-Minded Christianity: Honoring the Legacy of John Warwick Montgomery*, edited by William Dembski and Thomas Schirrmacher, 20–32. Nashville: B&H, 2008.

———. "What's in a Name?" *Biola Magazine* (Spring 2012). http://magazine.biola.edu/article/12-spring/whats-in-a-name/.

Head, Peter M. and Peter J. Williams. "Q Review." www.tyndale.cam.ac.uk/Tyndale/staff/Williams/HeadandWilliamsQReview.pdf.

Heath, Pamela Rae. "A New Theory of Place Memory." *Australian Journal of Parapsychology* 5 (2005) 40-58. http://nonfiction.pamelaheath.com/PDF/PlaceMemory2.pdf.

Hebblethwaite, Brian. *In Defence of Christianity*. Oxford: Oxford University Press, 2006.

"Hegesippus." www.earlychristianwritings.com/text/hegesippus.html.

Hengel, Martin. *Studies in the Gospel of Mark*. London: SCM, 1985.

Henry, Jane, ed. *Parapsychology: Research on Exceptional Experiences*. London: Routledge, 2005.

———. "Psychokinesis." In *Parapsychology: Research on Exceptional Experiences*, edited by Jane Henry, 125–36. London: Routledge, 2005.

Herman, Ben. "Jewish Witnesses: Who Qualifies?" https://rabbibenherman.com/2015/08/23/jewish-witnesses-who-qualifies/.

Hicks, John Mark. "James Interprets Amos 9:11–12." http://johnmarkhicks.com/2013/05/10/james-interprets-amos-911-12-acts-1513-18/

"High-context and low-context cultures." https://en.wikipedia.org/wiki/High-_and_low-context_cultures

Hill, C.E. *Who Chose the Gospels?* Oxford: Oxford University Press, 2010.

Hitchens, Christopher. *God is Not Great*. London: Atlantic Books, 2007.

———. *Hitch-22*. New York: Twelve, 2010.

———. "In the Name of the father, the Sons . . .," *New York Times* (July 2010).

———. Quoted in "Q&A: Christopher Hitchens" by Dave Morris. *The Walrus* (July 2009).

———. Quoted in *Red Eye*. Fox News. May 12 2017.

———. Quoted in "The World According to Hitch" by Mindy Belz. *World Magazine* (June 3, 2006). https://world.wng.org/2006/06/the_world_according_to_hitch.

———. "Zombies? LOL—Christopher Hitchens debunks the resurrection of Jesus Christ" https://youtu.be/R2GM_g7VCJI.

Hixson, Elijah. "Despite Disappointing Some, New Mark Manuscript Is Earliest Yet." *Christianity Today* (May 2018). www.christianitytoday.com/ct/2018/may-web-only/mark-manuscript-earliest-not-first-century-fcm.html.

Hoffmann, R. Joseph. "Mythic Pizza and Cold-Cocked Scholars." https://rjosephhoffmann.wordpress.com/2012/04/23/mythic-pizza-and-cold-cocked-scholars/.

Hoffmier, James K. *Ancient Israel in Sinai: The Evidence for the Authenticity of the Wilderness Tradition*. Oxford: Oxford University Press, 2005.

———. *Israel in Egypt: The Evidence for the Authenticity of the Exodus Tradition*. Oxford: Oxford University Press, 1996.

Hoffmier, James K., et al, eds. *"Did I Not Israel Out Bring of Egypt?": Biblical, Archaeological, and Egyptological Perspectives on the Exodus Narratives*. Warsaw, IN: Eisenbrauns, 2016.

Holden, Joseph, and Norman L. Geisler. *The Popular Handbook of Archaeology and the Bible*. Harvest House, 2013.

Holding, James Patrick, ed. "Appendix: Hallucinations and Expectations." In *Defending the Resurrection*, 369–375. Maitland, FL: Xulon, 2010.

———. "The Authorship of James." In *Trusting the New Testament*, 221–24. Maitland, FL: Xulon, 2009.

———. *Defending the Resurrection*. Maitland, FL: Xulon, 2010.

———. "Pagan Christs, Persian Front: Mithra and Zoroaster." In *Shattering the Christ Myth: Did Jesus Not Exist?* 203–16. Maitland, FL: Xulon, 2008.

———. "Sam Harris' "Letter to a Christian Nation" Refuted." www.tektonics.org/gk/harrisletter.php.

———. "Secular references to Jesus: Josephus." www.tektonics.org/jesusexist/josephus.html.

———. *Trusting the New Testament: Is the Bible Reliable?* Maitland, FL: Xulon, 2009.

———. "Was Joseph of Arimathea a Myth?" In *Defending the Resurrection*, 285–89. Maitland, FL: Xulon, 2010.
Holt, Jim. "Beyond Belief." *The New York Times* (October 2006). www.nytimes.com/2006/10/22/books/review/Holt.t.html?_r=2&ei=5070&en=4269d64c4939d0f6&ex=1189828800&pagewanted=a&oref=slogin&oref=slogin.
———. "Maths and the finitude of the past." www.philosophyofreligion.info/mathsfinitepast.html.
Horgan, John. "Book by Biologist Jerry Coyne Goes Too Far in Denouncing Religion, Defending Science." *Scientific American* (June 2015). http://blogs.scientificamerican.com/cross-check/book-by-biologist-jerry-coyne-goes-too-far-in-denouncing-religion-defending-science/.
Horn, Trent. *Hard Sayings: A Catholic Approach to Answering Bible Difficulties*. El Cajon, CA: Catholic Answers, 2016.
Howard-Snyder, Daniel. "The Argument from Divine Hiddenness." http://apollos.ws/divine-hiddenness/The%20Argument%20from%20Divine%20Hiddenness.pdf.
Howe, Timothy. "The Letter of James." https://youtu.be/nT3FNt4i7w4.
http://ancienthistory.about.com/library/bl/bl_text_plinyltrstrajan.htm.
Hughes, Austin L. "Faith, Fact, and False Dichotomies." *The New Atlantis* 45 (2015) 111–17. https://www.thenewatlantis.com/publications/faith-fact-and-false-dichotomies.
Hume, David. *An Enquiry Concerning Human Understanding*. Oxford: Clarendon, 1975.
———. "Of Miracles." In *The Portable Atheist*, edited by Christopher Hitchens, 32–45. London: Da Capo, 2007.
Humphreys, Colin. *The Miracles of Exodus*. London: Continuum, 2003.
———. *The Mystery of The Last Supper: Reconstructing the Final Days of Jesus*. Cambridge, UK: Cambridge University Press, 2011.
Hunt, Julia. "'Fake news' Named Collins Dictionary's Official Word of the Year for 2017." www.independent.co.uk/news/uk/home-news/fake-news-word-of-the-year-2017-collins-dictionary-donald-trump-kellyanne-conway-antifa-corbynmania-a8032751.htm.
Hurtado, Larry W. *Lord Jesus Christ—Devotion to Jesus in Earliest Christianity*. Grand Rapids: Eerdmans, 2003.
Huston, J. *Reported Miracles*. Cambridge, UK: Cambridge University Press, 2007.
Hutchinson, Robert J. *Searching For Jesus: New Discoveries In The Quest For Jesus Of Nazareth—And How They Confirm The Gospel Accounts*. Nashville: Nelson, 2015.
Hunter, Cornelius G. *Science's Blind Spot: The Unseen Religion of Scientific Naturalism*. Grand Rapids: Brazos, 2007.
Ibrahim, Ayman S. "Did Muhammad Perform Miracles?" www.firstthings.com/web-exclusives/2015/09/did-muhammad-perform-miracles.
"Implanting False Memories: Lost in the Mall and Paul Ingram." www.spring.org.uk/2008/02/implanting-false-memories-lost-in-mall.php.
"Intelligent Design." www.youtube.com/playlist?list=PLQhh3qcwVEWjckJboK1rfuBKPcHiMFTSO.
"Interview with Steve Fuller." www.alrasub.com/interview-with-steve-fuller/.
Ignatius Catholic Study Bible New Testament. San Francisco: Ignatius, 2010.
Isbouts, Jean-Pierre. *Jesus and the Origins of Christianity*. New York: National Geographic, 2016.

References

———. *National Geographic: The Story of Jesus*. Washington, DC: National Geographic, 2016.

Jackson, Wayne. "Does the Expression "the Eleven" (Luke 24:33) Constitute an Error?" www.christiancourier.com/articles/732-does-the-expression-the-eleven-luke-24-33-constitute-an-error.

Jacobs, Louis. "The Death Penalty in Jewish Tradition." www.myjewishlearning.com/article/the-death-penalty-in-jewish-tradition/#.

"James 2:7." www.biblestudytools.com/james/2-7-compare.html.

"James 2:7 Commentary: Meyer's NT Commentary." https://biblehub.com/commentaries/james/2-7.htm.

Jarus, Owen. "World's Earliest Christian Engraving Shows Surprising Pagan Elements." www.livescience.com/16319-earliest-christian-inscription-pagan-artifacts.htm.

Jeremias, Joachim. "Die alteste Schicht der Osterberlieferung." In *Resurrexit*, edited by Edouard Dhanis, 185–206. Rome: Editrice Libreria Vaticana, 1974.

"Jesus of Testimony." https://youtu.be/mpwQFYnhqEs

Johnson, David. *Hume*. Ithaca, NY: Cornell University Press.

Johnson, Donald E. *Programming of Life*. Sylacauga, AL: Big Mac, 2010.

Johnson, Luke Timothy. *Brother Of Jesus, Friend Of God: Studies In The Letter Of James*. Grand Rapids: Eerdmans, 2004.

———. *The Real Jesus*. San Francisco: HarperOne, 1997.

Johnson, Philip E. *Darwin on Trial*. Downers Grove, IL: IVP, 2010.

———. *The Wedge of Truth*. Downers Grove, IL: IVP, 2000.

Johnson, Samuel. Quoted in *The Faith of Christopher Hitchens*, by Larry Alex Taunton. Nashville: Nelson, 2016.

Jones, Timothy Paul. *Misquoting Truth: A Guide to the Fallacies of Bart Ehrman's Misquoting Jesus*. Downers Grove, IL: IVP, 2007

———. *Why Trust the Bible?* Torrance, CA: Rose, 2008. .

Judge, E.A. "Foreword." In *The Truth About Jesus: The Challenge of Evidence*, by Paul Barnet, v–vi. Sydney: Aquila, 2004.

"Kardashev scale." https://en.wikipedia.org/wiki/Kardashev_scale.

Keener, Craig S. *The Historical Jesus of the Gospels*. Grand Rapids: Eerdmans, 2009.

———. "Introduction." In *Biographies and Jesus: What Does It Mean for the Gospels to be Biographies?* by Craig S. Keener and Edward T. Wright, 1–45. Lexington: Emeth, 2016.

———. *The IVP Bible Background Commentary: New Testament*. Downers Grove, IL: IVP, 2014.

———. "Jesus Existed." *Huffington Post* (May 2014). www.huffingtonpost.com/craig-s-keener/jesus-existed_b_1652435.htm.

———. *Miracles: The Credibility Of The New Testament Accounts*. Grand Rapids: Baker, 2011.

Keim, Karl Theodor. *The History of Jesus of Nazareth* 6. Translated by Arthur Ransom. London: Williams and Norgate, 1873-82.

Keller, Timothy. *The Reason for God*. London: Hodder & Stoughton, 2008.

Kelly, Joseph F. *An Introduction to the New Testament for Catholics*. Collegeville, MN: Liturgical, 2006.

Kendall, Jonathan. "Hallucinations and the Risen Jesus." In *Defending the Resurrection: Did Jesus Rise from the Dead?* edited by James Patrick Holding, 307–71. Maitland, FL: Xulon, 2010.

Kessler, Ed. *Jesus: Pocket Giants*. Stroud: The History, 2016.

King, Mike. *The God Delusion Revisited*. Lulu, 2007.
Kirby, Peter. "Testimonium Flavianum: Josephus' Reference to Jesus." www.earlychristianwritings.com/testimonium.htm.
Kirsch, Adam. "If Men Are From Mars, What's God." www.nysun.com/article/27182.
Kitchen, Kenneth A. *On the Reliability of the Old Testament*. Grand Rapids: Eerdmans, 2003.
Kitcher, Philip. *Abusing Science*. Cambridge, MA: MIT Press, 1983.
Klinghoffer, David A. *Debating Darwin's Doubt*. Seattle: Discovery Institute, 2015.
———, ed. *Signature Of Controversy: Responses to Critics of Signature In The Cell*. Seattle: Discovery Institute, 2010.
Kneale, Matthew. *An Atheist's History of Belief*. London: Vintage, 2014.
Kolarik, Ruth E. "Mosaics of the Early Church at Stobi." Dumbarton Oaks Papers 41 (1987) 295–306.
Komoszewski, J. Ed, et al. *Reinventing Jesus: How Contemporary Skeptics Miss The Real Jesus And Mislead Popular Culture*. Grand Rapids: Kregel, 2006.
Koons, Robert C. "Science and Theism: Concord, not Conflict." In *The Rationality of Theism*, edited by Paul Copan and Paul Moser, 72–90. London: Routledge, 2003. http://robkoons.net/media/69b0dd04a9d2fc6dffff80b3ffffd524.pdf.
Koperski, Jeffrey. "Two Bad Ways to Attack Intelligent Design and Two Good Ones." *Zygon* 43 (June 2008) 433–49.
Kostenberger, Andreas J., et al. *Truth Matters: Confident Faith in a Confusing World*. Nashville: B&H, 2014.
Kostenberger, Andreas J. and Justin Taylor. *The Final Days of Jesus*. Wheaton, IL: Crossway, 2014.
Koukl, Gregory. *Faith Is Not Wishing*. STR, 2011.
Krauss, Lawrence M. *Beyond Star Trek: Physics from Alien Invasions to the End of Time*. New York: Basic, 1997.
———. "Dealing with William Lane Craig." http://old.richarddawkins.net/articles/612104-dealing-with-william-lane-craig.
———. "Krauss, Meyer, Lamoureux: What's Behind it all? God, Science and the Universe." www.youtube.com/watch?v=mMuy58DaqOk.
———. *The Physics of Star Trek*. London: Flamingo, 1997.
———. *A Universe from Nothing*. New York: Free Press, 2012.
———. "What Einstein and Bill Gates Teach Us About Time Travel." www.nbcnews.com/storyline/the-big-questions/what-einstein-bill-gates-teach-us-about-time-travel-n757291.
Krauss, Lawrence M., and William Lane Craig. "Life, The Universe, and Nothing: Is It Reasonable To Believe in a God?" http://youtu.be/7xcgjtps5ks.
Kraut, Richard. "Socrates." www.britannica.com/EBchecked/topic/551948/Socrates.
Kreeft, Peter. *Between Heaven & Hell: A Dialog Somewhere Beyond Death with John F. Kennedy, C.S. Lewis & Aldous Huxley*. Downers Grove, IL: IVP, 1982.
———. "Why I Believe Jesus is the Son of God." In *Why I Am A Christian*, edited by Norman L. Geisler and Paul K. Hoffman, 239–52. Grand Rapids: Baker, 2006.
Kreeft, Peter, and Ronald Tacelli. *Handbook of Christian Apologetics*. Downers Grove, IL: IVP, 1994.
Kruger, Michael J. *The Question of Canon: Challenging the Status Quo in the New Testament Debate*. Nottingham: Apollos, 2013.

———. "The NT Canon Was Not Decided at Nicea." http://michaeljkruger.com/ten-basic-facts-about-the-nt-canon-that-every-christian-should-memorize-8-the-nt-canon-was-not-decided-at-nicea-nor-any-other-church-council.

———. "Some NT Writers Quote Other NT Writers as Scripture." http://michaeljkruger.com/ten-basic-facts-about-the-nt-canon-that-every-christian-should-memorize-4-some-nt-writers-quote-other-nt-writers-as-scripture/.

Kumar, Steve. *Christianity for Skeptics*. John Hunt, 2000.

Lamb, David. *The Search for Extraterrestrial Intelligence: a Philosophical Inquiry*. London: Routledge, 2001.

Lapide, Pinchas. *The Resurrection of Jesus*. London: SPCK, 1984.

———. *The Resurrection of Jesus: A Jewish Perspective*. Minneapolis: Ausberg, 1983.

Larmer, Robert A. "Is Methodological Naturalism Question-Begging?" http://epsociety.org/userfiles/art-Larmer%20(MethodologicalNaturalismQuestion-Begging).pdf.

———. *The Legitimacy of Miracle*. Lanham: Lexington, 2014.

———. "Miracles as Inconsistent with the Perfection of God." *EPS* (2015). http://epsociety.org/library/articles.asp?pid=257.

———. "Miracles and the Principle of the Conservation of Energy." *EPS* (2015). http://epsociety.org/library/articles.asp?pid=248.

Larson, Stan. *Quest for the Gold Plates: Thomas Stuart Ferguson's Archaeological Search for The Book of Mormon*. Herriman, UT: Freethinker, 2004.

Lennox, John C. *Against the Flow: The Inspiration Of Daniel In An Age Of Relativism*. Oxford: Monarch, 2015.

———. *God's Undertaker: Has Science Buried God?* Oxford: Lion, 2009.

———. *Gunning for God: Why the New Atheists Are Missing the Target*. Oxford: Lion, 2011.

———. "Has Science Buried God?" https://youtu.be/f7kjNu9CUwo.

Lewis, C.S. *Christian Reflections*. London: Geoffrey Bles, 1967.

———. "Fern-seed and Elephants." In *Fern-seed and Elephants: And Other Essays on Christianity*, edited by Walter Hooper, 104–25. Glasgow: Fount, 1975.

———. "Letter to Owen Barfield, April 1932." *Letters*. London: Fount, 1991.

———. "Letter to Arthur Greeves, December 1916." *Letters*. London: Fount, 1991.

———. *Mere Christianity*. London: Collins, 1952.

———. *Miracles*. London: Fount, 1998.

———. "Modern Theology and Biblical Criticism." In *The Essential C.S. Lewis*. New York: Touchstone, 1996.

———. *Studies in Words*. Cambridge, UK: Cambridge University Press, 1967.

———. "What are we to make of Jesus Christ?" In *God in the Dock*, 79–84. London: Fount, 1979.

Li, Zilong and Cosimo Bambi. "Distinguishing black holes and wormholes with orbiting hot spots." https://arxiv.org/pdf/ Zilong 1405.1883.pdf.

Libbrecht, Kenneth G. "Is it really true that no two snowflakes are alike?" www.its.caltech.edu/~atomic/snowcrystals/alike/alike.htm.

Licona, Michael R. "Archaeology & "The Book of Mormon."" www.bethinking.org/mormons/what-to-say-to-mormons/4-mormon-archaeology.

———. "Bart D. Ehrman, *Forged: Writing in the Name of God* . . . a Review by Michael R. Licona." http://risenjesus.com/articles/52-review-of-forged.

———. "Can We Be Certain that Jesus Died on a Cross?" In *Evidence for God*, edited by William A. Dembski and Michael R. Licona, 164–67. Grand Rapids: Baker 2010.

References

———. "The Evidence For Jesus' Resurrection." In *The Big Argument: Does God Exist?*, edited by John Ashton and Michael Westacott, 359–74. Green Forest, AR: Master Books, 2006.

———. "Fish Tales." In *Come Let Us Reason: New Essays in Christian Apologetics*, edited by Paul Copan and William Lane Craig, 137–50. Nashville: B&H, 2012.

———. "Historians and Miracle Claims." *Journal For The Study Of The Historical Jesus* 12 (2014) 106–129.

———. "Jesus—the Son of Man?" www.bethinking.org/jesus/jesus-the-son-of-man.

———. "Michael Licona Interview." www.thebestschools.org/special/ehrman-licona-dialogue-reliability-new-testament/michael-licona-interview/.

———. "Michael Licona vs. Elaine Pagels: The Gospel of Thomas." https://youtu.be/N7HOBt5yrz0.

———. "Paul and the Nature of the Resurrection Body." In *Buried Hope or Risen Savior? The Search For The Jesus Tomb*, edited by Charles L. Quarles, 177–98. Nashville: Holman, 2008.

———. *Paul Meets Muhammad: A Christian-Muslim Debate On The Resurrection*. Grand Rapids: Baker, 2006.

———. *The Resurrection of Jesus*. Nottingham: Apollos, 2010.

———. "Were the Resurrection Appearances of Jesus Hallucinations?" In *Evidence for God*, edited by William A. Dembski and Michael R. Licona, 176–78. Grand Rapids: Baker, 2010.

———. *Why Are There Difference In The Gospels? What We Can Learn From Ancient Biography*. Oxford: Oxford University Press, 2017.

Lincoln, Don. "Is Dark Matter Real?" www.livescience.com/59814-is-dark-matter-real.htm.

Lindars, Barnabas. *The New Century Bible Commentary: The Gospel of John*. London: Eerdmans, 1995.

———. "The Resurrection and the Empty Tomb." In *The Resurrection of Jesus Christ*, edited by Paul Avis, 116–35. London: DLT, 1993.

Lodge, Carey. "New book claiming Jesus did not exist dismissed by historians." https://www.christiantoday.com/article/new-book-claiming-jesus-did-not-exist-dismissed-by-historians/41234.htm

Loftus, Elizabeth. "The Reality of Repressed Memories." https://faculty.washington.edu/eloftus/Articles/lof93.htm.

Loftus, John W. *Why I Became An Atheist: A Former Preacher Rejects Christianity*. New York: Prometheus Books, 2008.

Lüdemann, Gerd. Quoted in *Jesus' Resurrection*, edited by Paul Copan and Ronald K. Tacelli. Downers Grove: IVP, 2009.

———. *The Resurrection of Christ: A Historical Inquiry*. New York: Prometheus, 2004.

———. *What Really Happened to Jesus: A Historical Approach to the Resurrection*. Louisville, KY: Westminster John Knox, 1996.

"Luke, Gospel of." *Holman Bible Dictionary*. https://www.studylight.org/dictionaries/hbd/l/luke-gospel-of.html.

Lyons, Eric. "Did Jesus Rise "On" or "After" the Third Day?" www.apologeticspress.org/apcontent.aspx?category=6&article=756.

———. "Jesus' Sermon on . . . the Mount or the Plain?" www.apologeticspress.org/apcontent.aspx?category=6&article=800.

References

Macdonald, Fiona. "Bad news: 80% of students can't tell the difference between real and fake news." www.sciencealert.com/bad-news-study-finds-80-of-students-can-t-tell-the-difference-between-real-and-fake-news.

Machen, J. Gresham. *The Virgin Birth of Christ*. London: James Clark, 1958.

Mack, Katie. "'Goldilocks' Planets Might Not Be So Nice." *Cosmos* (January 2017). https://cosmosmagazine.com/space/goldilocks-planets-might-not-be-so-nice.

MacKenzie, Andrew, and Jane Henry. "Apparitions and encounters." In *Parapsychology: Research on Exceptional Experience*, edited by Jane Henry, 175–87. New York: Routledge, 2005.

Magee, Greg. "The Origins of the Church at Rome." https://bible.org/article/origins-church-rome

Maier, Paul L. "Biblical History." www.equip.org/article/biblical-history-the-faulty-criticism-of-biblical-historicity/.

———. "Did Jesus Really Exist?" In *Evidence for God*, edited by William A. Dembski and Michael R. Licona, 143–46. Grand Rapids: Baker, 2010.

———. "The James Ossuary." www.mtio.com/articles/bissar95.htm.

———. "Josephus and Jesus." www.4truth.net/fourtruthpbjesus.aspx?pageid=8589952897.

Mangalwadi, Vishal. *The Book That Made Your World: How the Bible Created the Soul of Western Civilization*. Nashville: Thomas Nelson, 2011.

Mann, Windsor, ed. *The Quotable Hitchens*. Cambridge, MA: Da Capo, 2011.

Manson, T.W. *Studies in the Gospels and Epistles*. Manchester: Manchester University Press, 1962.

Markos, Louis. *Apologetics for the 21st Century*. Wheaton, IL: Crossway, 2010.

Marks, Robert J. II, et al, *Introduction To Evolutionary Informatics*. London: World Scientific, 2017.

Marshall, David. "The Resurrection of Jesus in the Qur'an." In *Resurrection Reconsidered*, edited by Gavin D'Costa, 168–83. Oxford: OneWorld, 1996.

Marshall, I. Howard. *Acts*. Nottingham: IVP, 2008.

———. *I Believe in the Historical Jesus*. London: Hodder & Stoughton, 1977.

Marshall, I. Howard, et al. *Exploring the New Testament: A Guide to the Letters & Revelation*. Downers Grove, IL: IVP, 2011.

Martin, Robert. "The New Atheists and the New Testament." In *Disbelieving Disbelief*, edited by Philip Brown, 54–73. Northcote Vic: Morning Star, 2012.

"The Martyrdom of Ignatius." www.mb-soft.com/believe/txv/ignatiuc.htm.

Matthews, Cate. "It's True That No Two Snowflakes Are Alike, But Not For The Reason You Think." *Huffington Post* (2014). www.huffingtonpost.com/2014/01/10/no-two-snowflakes-alike-video_n_4569491.htm.

Matthews, Robert. "Through The Wormhole." *Focus* 322 (June 2018). www.sciencefocus.com/space/through-the-wormhole-2/.

Mawson, T.J. *Belief In God: An Introduction to the Philosophy of Religion*. Oxford: Clarendon, 2009.

May, Peter. *The Search for God and the Path to Persuasion*. Malcolm Down, 2016.

McCallum, Dennis. "A Chronological Study of Paul's Ministry." www.xenos.org/classes/chronop.htm.

McCormick, Matthew S. *Atheism and the Case Against Christ*. Amherst, NY: Prometheus, 2012.

References

McCullagh, C. Behan. *Justifying Historical Descriptions*. Cambridge, UK: Cambridge University Press, 1984.

McDonald, Glenn. "We Are Not Living In A Simulation. Probably." *Fast Company* (March 2018). www.fastcompany.com/40537955/we-are-not-living-in-a-simulation-probably.

McDowell, Josh. *The New Evidence That Demands a Verdict*. Nashville: Thomas Nelson, 1999.

McDowell, Josh, and Bill Wilson. *He Walked Among Us: Evidence for the Historical Jesus*. Carlisle: Alpha, 2000.

McDowell, Josh, and Dave Sterrett. *Did the Resurrection Happen . . . Really?* Chicago: Moody Publishers, 2011.

McDowell, Josh, and Sean McDowell. *Evidence That Demands a Verdict*. Nashville, TN: Thomas Nelson, 2017.

McDowell, Sean. "Did the Apostles Die as Martyrs?" https://youtu.be/elXMJoJA3cQ.

McGinn, Colin. *The Making of a Philosopher*. London: Scribner, 2002.

McGuire, A. "List of the Parables of Jesus." http://ww3.haverford.edu/religion/courses/301F09/List%20of%20Parables.htm.

McGrath, Alister. *Jesus: Who He Is and Why He Matters*. Leicester: IVP, 1994.

———. *NIV Bible Handbook*. London: Hodder & Stoughton, 2014.

———. "Resurrection and Incarnation." In *Different Gospels: Christian Orthodoxy and Modern Theologies*, edited by Andrew Walker, 79–96. London: SPCK, 1988.

———. "The Spell of the Meme." www.st-edmunds.cam.ac.uk/faraday/issues/McGrath%20RSA%20Lecture%2013-03-06.pdf.

———. *The Twilight of Atheism: The Rise And Fall Of Disbelief In The Modern World*. London: Rider, 2004.

McGrath, James. "Maurice Casey, Jesus: Evidence and Argument or Mythicist Myths?" *Review of Biblical Literature* (June 2015). www.bookreviews.org/pdf/9729_10748.pdf.

McGrew, Lydia. "Bart Ehrman and the Authorship of the Gospels." http://lydiaswebpage.blogspot.co.uk/2015/07/on-bart-ehrman-and-authorship-of-gospels.htm.

———. *Hidden In Plain View: Undesigned Coincidences in the Gospels and Acts*. Chillicothe, OH: DeWard, 2017.

———. "Licona gospel examples IV: More over-reading." http://projectthreesixty.org/index.php/2018/01/06/licona-gospel-examples-iv-reading/.

———. "Probabilistic Issues Concerning Jesus of Nazareth and Messianic Death Prophecies." *Philosophia Christi* 15 (2013) 311–28.

McGrew, Timothy. "Do Miracles Really Violate the Laws of Science?" *Slate*. www.slate.com/bigideas/are-miracles-possible/essays-and-opinions/timothy-mcgrew-opinion.

———. "Extraordinary claims require extraordinary evidence." https://youtu.be/H7Gv8Fw_fFE.

———. "Internal Evidence for the Truth of the Gospels and Acts." https://slideplayer.com/slide/274333/.

———. "Science, Doubt and Miracles." http://enrichmentjournal.ag.org/201204/201204_122_science_doubt_miracles.cfm.

———. "There Are Serious Reasons for Belief in the Existence of God." In *Is Faith in God Reasonable?*, edited by Corey Miller and Paul Gould, 97–111. London: Routledge, 2014.

McKnight, Scott. "Who Is Jesus? An Introduction to Jesus Studies." In *Jesus Under Fire: Modern Scholarship Reinvents the Historical Jesus*, edited by Michael J. Wilkins and J.P. Moreland, 51–72. Grand Rapids: Zondervan, 1995.

References

McLatchie, Jonathan. "The fallacy of the sign of Jonah objection." http://apologeticsuk.blogspot.co.uk/2012/01/fallacy-of-sign-of-jonah-objection.htm.

———. "The Nativity Defended." http://crossexamined.org/the-nativity-defended/.

McRay, John. *Archaeology & the New Testament*. Grand Rapids: Baker, 2008.

Meades, Jonathan. "Ben Building: Mussolini, Monuments and Modernism." *BBC Four* (January 3 2017).

Meadors, Gary T. "The 'Poor' in the Beatitudes of Matthew and Luke." http://faculty.gordon.edu/hu/bi/ted_hildebrandt/ntesources/ntarticles/gtj-nt/meadors-lukepoor-gtj-85.pdf.

Meier, John P. *A Marginal Jew: Rethinking the Historical Jesus: The Roots of the Problem and the Person, Vol 1*. New York: Doubleday, 1991.

Meister, Chad. *Building Belief: Constructing Faith from the Ground Up*. Eugene, OR: Wipf & Stock, 2009.

———. "Evil and the Hiddenness of God." In *God And Evil: The Case For God In A World Filled With Pain*, edited by Chad Meister and James K. Drew, Jr., 138–51. Downers Grove, IL: IVP, 2013.

———. *Philosophy of Religion*. London: Palgrave, 2014.

Meister, Chad, and James K. Drew, Jr., eds. *God And Evil: The Case For God In A World Filled With Pain*. Downers Grove, Illinois: IVP, 2013.

Menuge, Angus. *Agents Under Fire: Materialism And The Rationality Of Science*. Lanham, MD: Rowman & Littlefield, 2004.

Merali, Zeeya. "They're Here: The Mechanism of Poltergeist Activity." *New Scientist* (April 2008). www.newscientist.com/article/dn13563-theyre-here-the-mechanism-of-poltergeist-activity/

Metaxas, Eric. "Hello, Hezekiah!" www.breakpoint.org/bpcommentaries/entry/13/28557.

———. *Miracles*. London: Hodder & Stoughton, 2014.

"The method by which Joseph Smith produced the Book of Abraham." www.fairmormon.org/answers/Book_of_Abraham/How_was_it_produced.

Mettinger, T.N.D. *The Riddle of Resurrection: 'Dying and Rising Gods' in the Ancient Near East*. Stockholm: Almqvist & Wiksell, 2001.

Meyer, Stephen C. *Darwin's Doubt: The Explosive Origin of Animal Life and the Case for Intelligent Design*. New York: HarperOne, 2013.

———. "DNA and the Origin of Life: Information, Specification, and Explanation." *Discovery* (May 2004). www.discovery.org/a/2184.

———. "The Methodological Equivalence of Design and Descent." In *The Creation Hypothesis*, edited by J.P. Moreland, 67–112. Downers Grove, IL: IVP, 1994.

———. "The Return of the God Hypothesis." http://037f521.netsolhost.com/docs/meyer/sm_returnofgod.pdf.

———. *Signature in the Cell: DNA and the Evidence for Intelligent Design*. San Francisco: HarperOne, 2009.

Micklethwaite, John, and Adrian Wooldridge. *God Is Back: How The Global Rise Of Faith Is Changing The World*. London: Allen Lane, 2009.

Midgley, Mary. *Are You an Illusion?* Stocksfield, UK: Acumen, 2014.

Miethe, Terry L., and Gary R. Habermas. *Why Believe? God Exists!* Joplin, MO: College Press, 1998.

Millar, Glenn. "Question: Was Jesus of Alien Parentage?" http://christianthinktank.com/alien2.html.

References

———. "Was the Burial of Jesus a Temporary One Because of Time Constraints?" http://christianthinktank.com/shellgame.htm.

Miller, Thomas A. *Did Jesus Really Rise From The Dead? A Surgeon-Scientist Examines the Evidence*. Wheaton, IL: Crossway, 2013.

Millican, Peter. The Craig-Millican debate at Birmingham University, 2011. https://youtu.be/fEw8VzzXcjE.

Milne, Bruce. *The Message of John*. Leicester: IVP, 1993.

Milstei, Mati. ""Oldest Church" Discovery "Ridiculous," Critics Say." *National Geographic News* (June 2008). http://news.nationalgeographic.com/news/2008/06/080613-old-church.htm.

Mishkin, David. *Jewish Scholarship on the Resurrection of Jesus*. Eugene, OR: Pickwick, 2017.

Mithani, Audrey, and Alexander Vilenkin. "Did the Universe Have a Beginning?" https://arxiv.org/pdf/1204.4658.pdf.

Mittleberg, Mark. *The Questions Christians Hope No One Will Ask (With Answers)*. Carol Stream, IL: Tyndale, 2010.

"Modern Myth: All but 11 Verses of the NT Could be Constructed from the Writings of the Early Church Fathers." http://theosophical.wordpress.com/2012/01/17/modern-myth-all-but-11-verses-of-the-nt-could-be-constructed-from-the-writings-of-the-early-church-fathers/.

Mohler, Albert R. "When The Bible Speaks, God Speaks: The Classic Doctrine Of Biblical Inerrancy." *Five Views on Biblical Inerrancy*, edited by J. Merrick et al., 29–58. Grand Rapids: Zondervan, 2013.

Montefiore, Hugh. *A Commentary on the Epistle to the Hebrews*. London: A & C Black, 1977.

———. *The Miracles of Jesus*. London: SPCK, 2005.

———. *The Womb And The Tomb*. London: Fount, 1992.

Montefiore, Simon Seabag. *Jerusalem: The Biography*. London: Weidenfeld & Nicolson, 2011.

Montgomery, John Warwick. *Faith Founded On Fact: Essays in Evidential Apologetics*. Irvine: NRP, 2015.

———. "Faith, History and the Resurrection." In *History and Christianity* 81–110. Minneapolis: Bethany House, 1986.

———. *History And Christianity*. Minneapolis: Bethany House, 1971.

———. *History, Law and Christianity*. Corona, CA: NRP Books, 2014.

———. *How Do We Know There is a God? and other questions inappropriate in polite society*. Minneapolis: Dimension, 1973.

———. "Miracle Evidence: How Philosophers Go Wrong." In *Philosophia Christi* 17 (2015) 199–204.

Montgomery, John Warwick, ed. *Evidence for Faith*. Dallas: Probe, 1991.

Monton, Bradley. "Is Intelligent Design Science? Dissecting the Dover Decision." http://philsci-archive.pitt.edu/archive/00002592/01/Methodological_Naturalism_Dover_3.doc.

———. *Seeking God in Science: An Atheist Defends Intelligent Design*. Toronto: Broadview, 2009.

Moo, Douglas J. *Tyndale New Testament Commentaries: James*. Nottingham: IVP, 2009.

Moore, Peter C. *Can A Bishop Be Wrong? Ten Scholars Challenge John Shelby Spong*. New York: Morehouse Publishing, 1998.

Moreland, J.P. *The God Question: An Invitation to a Life of Meaning*. Eugene, OR: Harvest House, 2009.

References

———. "Intelligent Design and the Nature of Science." In *Intelligent Design 101*, edited by H. Wayne House, 41–65. Grand Rapids: Kregel, 2008.

———. *The Recalcitrant Imago Dei: Human Persons and the Failure of Naturalism*. London: SCM, 2009.

———. *Scaling the Secular City*. Grand Rapids: Baker, 1987.

Moreland, J.P., and William Lane Craig. *Philosophical Foundations for a Christian Worldview*. Downers Grove: IVP, 2017.

Morison, Frank. *Who Moved the Stone?* London: Faber & Faber, 1981.

Morris, Leon. *Tyndale New Testament Commentaries: Luke*. Nottingham: IVP, 2008.

Morris, Thomas V. *Our Idea of God: An Introduction to Philosophical Theology*. Notre Dame, IN: University of Notre Dame Press, 1991.

Morrow, Jeffrey L. *Jesus' Resurrection: A Jewish Convert Examines the Evidence*. Toledo, OH: Principium Institute, 2017.

Morrow, Jonathan. *Questioning the Bible*. Chicago: Moody, 2014.

Motyer, Alec. *The Message of James*. Leicester: IVP, 2003.

Moxnes, Halvor. *A Short History Of The New Testament*. London: I.B. Tauris, 2014.

Moyes, Angus. "The Reliability of John's Gospel." www.theologynetwork.org/christian-beliefs/the-bible/starting-out/the-reliability-of-johns-gospel-.htm.

Mueller, Antje, and Ron Roberts. "Dreams." In *Parapsychology*, edited by Ron Roberts and David Groome, 86–101. New York: Arnold, 2001.

"Muhammad and Miracles." www.answering-islam.org/Responses/Azmy/mhd_miracles.html.

Murmson, Serm. "How Did Astronomers Determine Where the Earth Is Located Within the Milky Way?" https://sciencing.com/did-astronomers-determine-earth-located-within-milky-way-19463.htm.

Myers, P.Z. "Bad Religion." http://richarddawkins.net/article,211,Bad-Religion,PZ-Myers—Seed-Magazine.

Nagel, Thomas. "Dawkins and Atheism." In *Secular Philosophy and the Religious Temperament*, 19–26. Oxford: Oxford University Press, 2010.

———. "Fear of Religion." *The New Republic* (October 2006). www.tnr.com/article/the-fear-religion

———. *Mind and Cosmos: Why The Materialist Neo-Darwinian Conception Of Nature Is Almost Certainly False*. Oxford: Oxford University Press, 2012.

———. "Public Education and Intelligent Design." In *Secular Philosophy and the Religious Temperament*, 41-57. Oxford: Oxford University Press, 2010.

Nash, Ronald H. *Faith & Reason: Searching for a Rational Faith*. Grand Rapids: Zondervan, 1988.

———. *The Gospel and the Greeks: Did the New Testament Borrow from Pagan Thought?* Phillipsburg, NJ: P&R, 2003.

"The Nativity." www.youtube.com/playlist?list=PLQhh3qcwVEWjXCwcSr2FYzpj5-uQrLKIR.

Nelson, Mary. "Paul Survives a Shipwreck." https://missionbibleclass.org/1b0-new-testament/new-testament-part-2/acts-paul-the-prisoner-spreads-the-gospel-from-jerusalem-to-rome/pauls-shipwreck/.

Neufeld, Thomas R. Yoder. *Recovering Jesus: The Witness of the New Testament*. Grand Rapids: SPCK, 2007.

References

Nicholl, Colin R. *The Great Christ Comet: Revealing The True Star Of Bethlehem*. Wheaton, IL: Crossway, 2015.

Nickell, Joe. "Abductions and Hoaxes: The Man Who Attracts Aliens." www.csicop.org/si/show/abductions_and_hoaxes.

Nielsen, Kai. "An Atheist's Rebuttal." In *Does God Exist? The Debate between Theists and Atheists,* by J.P. Moreland and Kai Nielsen, 64–68. Amherst, NY: Prometheus, 1993.

NIV Thompson Student Bible. Indianapolis, IN: Kirkbride Bible Company, 1999.

Norton, Andrew. "Ross 128 Mystery Signals Aren't From Aliens. But What Would Happen If They Were?" *Newsweek* (July 2017). www.newsweek.com/ross-128-mystery-signals-aliens-what-happens-638172.

Novakovic, Lidija. "Jesus' Resurrection and Historiography." In *Jesus Research: New Methodologies and Perceptions,* edited by James H. Charlesworth, 910–33. Grand Rapids: Eerdmans, 2014.

O'Brien, Peter T. *The Epistle to the Philippians (The New International Greek Commentary)*. Grand Rapids: Eerdmans, 1991.

O'Collins, Gerald. *The Resurrection of Jesus Christ*. Pennsylvania: Judson, 1973.

———. "The Resurrection: The State of the Question." In *The Resurrection*, edited by Stephen T. Davis, 5–28. Oxford: Oxford University Press, 1998.

O'Connell, Cathal. "Alien Megastructure "Discovery": a Review of the Facts." *Cosmos* (August 2016). https://cosmosmagazine.com/space/alien-megastructure-discovery-a-review-of-the-facts.

O'Connell, Jake H. *Jesus' Resurrection and Apparitions: A Baysian Analysis*. Eugene, OR: Resource, 2016.

———. "Jesus' Resurrection and Collective Hallucinations." *Tyndale Bulletin* 60 (2009) 69-105.

O'Hear, Anthony. *Beyond Evolution*. Oxford: Clarendon Press, 1997.

———. *Jesus for Beginners*. London: Icon, 1993.

O'Leary, Denyse. "Unravelling 'Recovered Memory.'" www.mercatornet.com/conjugality/view/unravelling-recovered-memories/18887.

Oakes, John. "A Response to Recent False Claims by Muslims About the Gospel of Barnabas." http://evidenceforchristianity.org/a-response-to-recent-false-claims-by-muslims-about-the-gospel-of-barnabas/.

———. "What is the Significance of the Gabriel Stone? What will be its Effect on Christianity?" http://evidenceforchristianity.org/what-is-the-significance-of-the-gabriel-stone-what-will-be-its-affect-on-christianity/.

Oderberg, David S. "The Cosmological Argument." In *The Routledge Companion to Philosophy of Religion*, edited by Chad Meister and Paul Copan, 341–50. London: Routledge, 2010.

"Of Course Jesus Existed! Have a Bit of Sense!" www.saintsandsceptics.org/of-course-jesus-really-existed-have-a-bit-of-sense/.

Olson, Carl E. *Did Jesus Really Rise From the Dead*? San Francisco: Ignatius, 2016.

Omohundro, John T. "Von Däniken's Chariots: A Primer in the Art of Cooked Science." www.csicop.org/si/show/von_daumlnikenrsquos_chariots_a_primer_in_the_art_of_cooked_science.

Onfray, Michael. *In Defence of Atheism: The Case Against Christianity, Judaism and Islam*. Translated by Jeremy Leggatt. London: Serpent's Tail, 2007.

———. *Atheist Manifesto*. New York: Arcade, 2011.

References

"The Origin of Life." www.youtube.com/playlist?list=PLQhh3qcwVEWggFeEP9H7k1Lyccfxzvosr.

Orr, H. Allan. "The God Delusion." www.nybooks.com/articles/2007/03/01/the-god-delusion/.

Osborne, Grant R. "Jesus' Empty Tomb and His Appearances in Jerusalem." In *Key Events In The Life of the Historical Jesus*, edited by Darrell L. Bock and Robert L. Webb, 775–823. Grand Rapids: Eerdmans, 2009.

Overman, Dean L. *A Case for the Divinity of Jesus: Examining the Earliest Evidence*. Plymouth, UK: Rowman & Littlefield, 2009.

Owen, H.P. *Christian Theism: A Study in its Basic Principles*. Edinburgh: T&T Clark, 1984.

Painter, Borden W., Jr. *The New Atheist Denial of History*. New York: Palgrave Macmillan, 2014.

Paley, William. *A View of the Evidences of Christianity*. Westmead, England: Gregg, 1970.

Pannenberg, Wolfhart. "History and the Reality of the Resurrection." In *Resurrection Reconsidered*, edited by Gavin D'Costa, 62–72. Oxford: OneWorld, 1996.

———. *Jesus—God and Man*. Translated by L.L. Wilkins and D.A. Preibe. Philadelphia: Westminster, 1974.

Papias. "Fragments of Papias." www.newadvent.org/fathers/0125.htm.

"Papyrus 52." http://en.wikipedia.org/wiki/Papyrus_52.

"Paranormal." https://en.oxforddictionaries.com/definition/paranormal.

Parker, Christopher H., et al. "The Pyrophilic Primate Hypothesis." *Evolutionary Anthropology* 25 (March/April 2016) 54–63. www.researchgate.net/publication/301252297_The_pyrophilic_primate_hypothesis.

Parsons, Keith M. "Old Atheism." http://dangerousidea.blogspot.co.uk/2016/04/parsons-and-feser-on-coyne.htm.

———. "Review of Michael Ruse, *Can a Darwinian be a Christian*? (2001)." www.infidels.org/library/modern/keith_parsons/darwinian.html.

"Parting the waters: Computer modeling applies physics to Red Sea escape route." www.sciencedaily.com/releases/2010/09/100921143930.htm.

Pascal, Blasé. *Pensees*. New York: E.P. Dutton, 1958.

Pate, C. Marvin. *40 Questions About the Historical Jesus*. Grand Rapids: Kregel, 2015.

Patterson, Paige. "James, the Letter." *Holman Bible Dictionary*. www.studylight.org/dictionaries/hbd/j/james-the-letter.html.

Pearcey, Nancy R. and Charles B. Thaxton. *The Soul of Science: Christian Faith and Natural Philosophy*. Wheaton, IL: Crossway, 1994.

Perina, Kaja. "Alien Abductions: The Real Deal?" www.psychologytoday.com/articles/200303/alien-abductions-the-real-deal.

Persinger, M.A. and B.T. Dotta. "Temporal Patterns of Photon Emissions Can Be Stored and Retrieved Several Days Later From the "Same Space": Experimental and Quantitative Evidence." *NeuroQuantology* 9 (2011) 605–13. www.neuroquantology.com/index.php/journal/article/download/467/443.

Peterson, Michael, et al. *Reason & Religious Belief*. Oxford: Oxford University Press, 2009.

Pew Research Center. "The Changing Global Religious Landscape." www.pewforum.org/2017/04/05/the-changing-global-religious-landscape/?utm_content=buffer49cb2&utm_medium=social&utm_source=twitter.com&utm_campaign=buffer.

Pigliucci, Massimo. "New Atheism and the Scientistic Turn in the Atheism Movement." *Midwest Studies In Philosophy* 37 (2013) 142-53. http://philpapers.org/archive/PIGNAA.pdf.

Piper, John. "The Risen Christ: Satisfied with his Suffering." www.desiringgod.org/messages/the-risen-christ-satisfied-with-his-suffering.

Pitre, Brant. *The Case For Jesus: The Biblical And Historical Evidence For Christ*. New York: Image, 2016.

Plantinga, Alvin. "The Dawkins Confusion." www.philvaz.com/apologetics/DawkinsGodDelusionPlantingaReview.pdf.

———. "Two Dozen or so Theistic Arguments." http://appearedtoblogly.files.wordpress.com/2011/05/plantinga-alvin-22two-dozen-or-so-theistic-arguments221.pdf & www.calvin.edu/academic/philosophy/virtual_library/articles/plantinga_alvin/two_dozen_or_so_theistic_arguments.pdf.

———. *Warranted Christian Belief*. Oxford: Oxford University Press, 2000.

———. *Where the Conflict Really Lies: Science, Religion, & Naturalism*. Oxford: Oxford University Press, 2011.

———. "Whether ID Is Science Isn't Semantics." www.discovery.org/scripts/viewDB/index.php?command=view&id=3331.

Plotinsky, Benjamin A. "The Fanatical Philosopher: Michel Onfray's Weak Case Against Monotheism." www.city-journal.org/html/rev2007-02-01bp.htm.

Polhill, John B. *The New American Commentary: Acts*. Nashville: B&H, 1992.

Polkinghorne, John. *Encountering Scripture: A Scientist Explores the Bible*. London: SPCK, 2010.

"Poltergeist." http://skepdic.com/poltergeist.html.

"Polycarp." *Catholic Encyclopedia*. www.newadvent.org/cathen/12219b.htm.

Pomeroy, Stephen Ross. "Do People Ever Fall Down Earthquake Chasms? Yeah, When the Earth Swallows Cows." www.realclearscience.com/blog/2013/01/do-people-ever-fall-down-earthquake-chasms-yeah-when-the-earth-swallows-cows.htm.

———. "How to Install False Memories." *Scientific American* (February 2013). https://blogs.scientificamerican.com/guest-blog/how-to-instill-false-memories/#.

Poole, Michael. *Miracles: Science, The Bible & Experience*. London: Scripture Union, 1992.

Porter, Daniel. "What is Photokeratitis—Including Snow Blindness?" www.aao.org/eye-health/diseases/photokeratitis-snow-blindness.

Porter, Stanley E. "How Do We Know What We Think We Know?" In *Jesus Research: New Methodologies and Perceptions*, edited by Charles H. Charlesworth, 82–99. Grand Rapids: Eerdmans, 2014.

———. *How We Got the New Testament: Text, Transmission, Translation*. Grand Rapids: Baker, 2013.

"Post Truth & Fake News." https://youtu.be/sCRI-K4VWGc.

Powell, Doug. *Holman Quick Source Guide to Christian Apologetics*. Nashville: Holman, 2006.

———. *Resurrection iWitness*. Nashville: B&H, 2012.

Powell, Mark Allan. *Introducing the New Testament: A Historical, Literary, and Theological Survey*. Grand Rapids: Baker, 2009.

———. *The Jesus Debate: Modern Historians Investigate the Life of Jesus*. Oxford: Lion, 1998.

Powers, Daniel G. *New Beacon Commentary: 1 & 2 Peter, Jude: A Commentary in the Wesleyan Tradition*. Kansas City: Beacon Hill, 2010.

References

Powers, Tom. "Treasures in the Storeroom: Family Tomb of Simon of Cyrene." In *Biblical Archaeology Review* 29 (July/August 2003) 46–59.

Prachett, Terry. "I create gods all the time—now I think one might exist, says fantasy author Terry Pratchett." *Daily Mail Online* (June 2008). www.dailymail.co.uk/femail/article-1028222/I-create-gods-time—I-think-exist.htm.

Price, Christopher. "The Miracles of Jesus: A Historical Inquiry." www.christianorigins.com/miracles.htm

"Prison Makes Way for the Holy Land's Oldest Church." www.biblicalarchaeology.org/daily/biblical-sites-places/biblical-archaeology-places/prison-makes-way-for-the-holy-lands-oldest-church/.

Pritchard, John. *Why Go to Church?* London: SPCK, 2015.

Provan, Iain, et al. *A Biblical History of Israel*. Louisville, KY: WJK, 2015.

Pullen, Stuart. *Intelligent Design or Evolution? Why the Origin of Life and the Evolution of Molecular Knowledge Imply Design*. Raleigh, NC: Intelligent Design, 2005.

Purtill, Richard. "Defining Miracles." In *In Defence of Miracles*, edited by R. Douglas Geivett and Gary R. Habermas, 61–72. Leicester: Apollos, 1997.

———. "Miracles: What If They Happen?" In *Miracles*, edited by Richard Swinburne, 189–205. New York: Macmillan, 1989.

———. *Reason to Believe: Why Faith Makes Sense*. San Francisco: Ignatius, 2009.

Quarles, Charles L. "Higher Criticism: What Has It Shown?" In *In Defence of the Bible*, edited by Steven B. Cowan and Terry L. Wilder, 63–88. Nashville: B&H, 2013.

———. *Midrash Criticism: Introduction and Appraisal*. Lanham, MD: University Press of America, 1998.

Quine, W.V. "Naturalism; or, Living within One's Means." *Dialectica* 49 (1995) 251-61.

Qureshi, Nabeel. *No God But One: Allah or Jesus? A Former Muslim Investigates The Evidence For Islam & Christianity*. Grand Rapids: Zondervan 2016.

Rahaman, Farook, et al. "Could wormholes form in dark matter galactic halos?" https://arxiv.org/pdf/1609.00155.pdf.

———. "Possible existence of wormholes in the galactic halo region." https://arxiv.org/pdf/1307.1237.pdf.

Rayner, Claire. "How to Have a Peaceful Pagan Christmas." In *There's Probably No God: The Atheist's Guide to Christmas*, edited by Ariane Sherine, 107–114. London: Friday, 2009.

Rea, Ernie, et al. "Virgin Birth." www.bbc.co.uk/programmes/b08578tm.

Redd, Nola Taylor. "What is a Wormhole?" www.space.com/20881-wormholes.htm.

Redford, John. *Born Of A Virgin: Proving the Miracle from the Gospels*. London: St. Pauls, 2007.

Reichenbach, Bruce R. *The Cosmological Argument: A Reassessment*. Springfield, IL: Charles C. Thomas, 1972.

Reiher, Jim. "Violent Language—a Clue to the Historical Occasion of James." *Evangelical Quarterly* 85 (July 2013). www.paternosterperiodicals.co.uk/back-issues/evangelical-quarterly/evangelical-quarterly-volume-85-issue-3-july-2013.

Reinhartz, Adele. "John." In *The Gospels and Acts: Fortress Commentary on the Bible—Study Edition*, edited by Margaret Aymer, et al., 265–307. Minneapolis: Fortress, 2016.

"Religious Experience." www.youtube.com/playlist?list=PLQhh3qcwVEWjccogWzetsujJ_3BtcyLJT.

"Removal of fill from inside of the Christian House Church at Dura Europos showing the Good Shepherd wall painting." http://users.stlcc.edu/mfuller/DuraChurch.html.

References

Reppert, Victor. "Miracles and the Case for Theism." *Philosophy of Religion* 25 (1989) 33–51.

"Reza Aslan vs Lauren Green." https://youtu.be/H7UU6FQoU_g.

Reymond, Robert L. *Faith's Reasons for Believing*. Fearns, Ross-Shire: Mentor, 2008.

Richards, Jay Wesley. "Divine Simplicity: The Good, the Bad, and the Ugly." In *For Faith And Clarity: Philosophical Contributions to Christian Theology*, edited by James K. Beilby, 157–77. Grand Rapids: Baker, 2006.

———. "How Phil Johnson Changed My Mind." In *Darwin's Nemesis: Phillip Johnson and the Intelligent Design Movement*, edited by William A. Dembski, 48–61. Leicester: IVP, 2006.

Richardson, Alan. *Christian Apologetics*. London: SCM, 1948.

Richardson, Kurt A. *The New American Commentary: James*. Nashville: B&H, 1997.

Ritner, Robert K. ""Translation and Historicity of the Book of Abraham"—A Response." http://mit.irr.org/files/files/ritner_translation_and_historicity_of_the_book_of_abraham_-_response.pdf.

Roberts, Alexander, et al. *The Ante-Nicene Fathers Vol. III: Translations of the Writings of the Fathers Down to A.D. 325*. Oak Harbor, WA: Logos Research Systems, 1997.

Roberts, Alexander, and James Donaldson, trans. 1 Clement. www.earlychristianwritings.com/text/1clement-roberts.html.

Roberts, Mark D. *Can We Trust the Gospels?: Investigating the Reliability of Matthew, Mark, Luke and John*. Wheaton, IL: Crossway, 2007.

———. "*God is Not Great* by Christopher Hitchens: A Response." www.markdroberts.com/htmfiles/resources/godisnotgreat.htm.

Roberts, Michael Symonds. *The Miracles of Jesus*. Oxford: Lion, 2006.

Roberts, Ron. "Science and Experience." In *Parapsychology: The Science of Unusual Experience*, edited by Ron Roberts and David Groome, 7–18. London: Arnold, 2001.

Robertson, David. *Magnificent Obsession: Why Jesus Is Great*. Fearns, Ross-Shire: Christian Focus, 2013.

Robinson, J.A.T. *Can We Trust The New Testament?* London: Mowbrays, 1977.

———. *The Human Face of God*. Philadelphia: Westminster, 1973.

———. *Redating the New Testament*. London: SCM, 1976.

Romer, John. *Testament: The Bible and History*. London: Michael O'Mara, 1988.

Romey, Kristen. "The Real Jesus." *National Geographic* (December 2017). http://press.nationalgeographic.com/2017/11/13/national-geographic-magazine-december-2017/.

———. "Unsealing of Christ's Reputed Tomb Turns Up New Revelations." *National Geographic* (October 2016). http://news.nationalgeographic.com/2016/10/jesus-christ-tomb-burial-church-holy-sepulchre/.

Rosenberg, Alex. *The Atheist's Guide to Reality: Enjoying Life Without Illusions*. London: W.W. Norton, 2011.

Rosenblatt, Helena. "The Christian Enlightenment." In *Enlightenment, Reawakening and Revolution 1660–1815*, edited by Stewart J. Brown and Timothy Tackett, 283–301. Cambridge, UK: Cambridge University Press, 2006. http://histories.cambridge.org/extract?id=chol9780521816052_CHOL9780521816052A017.

Rosenfeld, A., et al. "The Authenticity of the James Ossuary." *Open Journal of Geology* 4 (2014) 69-78.

Ross, Hugh. "Our Only Hope? A New Search for Extraterrestrial Intelligent Life." www.reasons.org/articles/our-only-hope-a-new-search-for-extraterrestrial-intelligent-life.

Rountree, Clarke. "Faith, Not Reason, Underwrites the Belief in God." In *Is Faith in God Reasonable?*, edited by Corey Miller and Paul Gould, 136–50. London: Routledge, 2014.

Ruse, Michael. *Atheism: What Everyone Needs To Know*. Oxford: Oxford University Press, 2015.

———. "The God Delusion." *Isis* 98 (December 2007) 814-16.

———. "Not Reasonable But Not Unreasonable." In *Is Faith in God Reasonable?*, edited by Corey Miller and Paul Gould, 112–121. London: Routledge, 2014.

Saaduev, Muhammadrasul. "What Is the Meaning of Prophet Muhammad's (PBUH) Suffering?" http://islam.ru/en/content/story/what-meaning-prophet-muhammad-s-pbuh-suffering.

Sacks, Jonathan. Quoted in *The Global Public Square*, by Os Guinness. Downers Grove, IL: IVP, 2013.

Safrai, Shemuel. *The Jewish People in the First Century*. Philadelphia: Van Gorcum/Fortress, 1976.

"Saint Luke." www.britannica.com/EBchecked/topic/351086/Saint-Luke.

Sanders, E.P. *The Historical Figure of Jesus*. New York: Penguin, 1993.

Sandmel, Samuel. "Parallelomania." *JBL* 81 (1962) 1–13.

Schaff, Philip. *History of the Christian Church, Volume I*.

Schmit, Tom. "The Contribution of 1 Thessalonians 3:11–13 to a Pauline Christology." http://ttschmidt.com/wp-content/uploads/2012/11/1-Thess-3-and-Pauline-Christology.pdf.

Schweitzer, Albert. *The Quest of the Historical Jesus*. Translated by W. Montgomery. London: A. & C. Black, 1954.

Scott, J.C. "Matthew's Intention to Write History." https://faculty.gordon.edu/hu/bi/ted_hildebrandt/ntesources/ntarticles/wtj-nt/scott-matthewhistory-wtj.pdf.

Senor, Thomas D. "The Incarnation and the Trinity." In *Reason For The Hope Within*, edited by Michael J. Murray, 238–60. Grand Rapids: Eerdmans, 1999.

Serapion, Mara bar. "Testimony on Jesus." www.tektonics.org/jesusexist/serapion.php.

Serrao, C. Jeanne Orjala. *James: A Commentary in the Wesleyan Tradition*. Kansas City: Beacon Hill, 2010.

Shamoun, Sam. "A Series of Answers to Common Questions." www.answering-islam.org/Shamoun/q_mt28_19.htm.

Shanks, Hershel. *The Brother of Jesus: The Dramatic Story & Meaning of the First Archaeological Link to Jesus & His Family*. London: Continuum, 2003.

———. "The James Ossuary is Authentic." *Biblical Archaeological Review* 38 (July/August 2012) 26–28. http://members.bib-arch.org/publication.asp?PubID=BSBA&Volume=38&Issue=4&ArticleID=2.

Sheaffer, Robert. "An Examination of the Claims that Extraterrestrial Visitors to Earth are Being Observed." In *Extraterrestrials: Where Are They?*, edited by B Zucherman and M.H. Hart, 20–28. New York: Pergamon, 1982.

Shenvi, Neil. "A Long Response to Sam Harris' *The End Of Faith*." www.shenvi.org/Essays/HarrisResponse.htm.

Sherer, Michael. "Trump Truth: The President With False Claims Faces Reality." *Time Magazine* (April 2017). http://time.com/4710614/donald-trump-fbi-surveillance-house-intelligence-committee/.

Sherwood, Harriet. "People of no Religion Outnumber Christians in England and Wales—Study." *The Guardian* (May 2016). www.theguardian.com/world/2016/may/23/no-religion-outnumber-christians-england-wales-study.

References

Short, A. Rendle. *Why Believe?* London: Inter-Varsity Fellowship, 1962.

Siemion, Andrew P.V., et al. "A 1.1 to 1.9 GHz SETI Survey of the Kepler Field: I. A Search for Narrow-band Emission from Select Targets." http://iopscience.iop.org/article/10.1088/0004-637X/767/1/94/pdf.

Siemon-Netto, Uwe. "God Not So Dead: Atheism in Decline Worldwide." *World Tribune* (March 2005). www.worldtribune.com/worldtribune/05/breaking2453432.91875.htm.

Simon, Naomi M., et al. "Informing the Symptoms Profile of Complicated Grief." *Depression and Anxiety* 28 (2011) 118–26.

Slick, Matt. "The Book of Abraham Papyri and Joseph Smith." https://carm.org/book-abraham-papyri-and-joseph-smith.

———. "Regarding the quotes from the historian Josephus about Jesus." http://carm.org/regarding-quotes-historian-josephus-about-jesus.

Small, Keith E. *Textual Criticism and the Qur'an Manuscripts*. Lanham, MD: Lexington, 2011.

Smith, Barry D. "James." www.mycrandall.ca/courses/NTIntro/Jas.htm.

Smith, Jonathan Z. "Dying and Rising Gods." In *Encyclopedia of Religion,* Vol 5, 2535–40. New York: Macmillan, 2005.

Smith, Mark D. *The Final Days of Jesus*: *The Thrill of Defeat, The Agony of Victory. A Classical Historian Explores Jesus's Arrest, Trial, and Execution*. Cambridge, UK: Lutterworth, 2018.

Smith, Wilbur M. *Therefore Stand*: *Christian Apologetics*. Grand Rapids: Baker, 1976.

Sokol, Joshua. "The Black-Hole Hunter Peering Into the Heart of Our Galaxy." www.theatlantic.com/science/archive/2017/07/andrea-ghez-black-hole-hunter/535296/.

Sosa, Ernest. "Knowledge: Instrumental and Testimonial." In *The Epistemology of Testimony*, edited by Jennifer lackey and Ernest Sosa, 116–23. Oxford: Clarendon, 2006.

Southerton, Simon G. *Losing a Lost Tribe*: *Native Americans, DNA, and the Mormon Church*. Salt Lake City: Signature, 2004.

Spencer, Robert. *A Religion of Peace? Why Christianity Is and Islam Isn't*. Washington, DC: Regnery, 2007.

Stannard, Russell. *Science and Wonders*. London: Faber & Faber, 1996.

Stanton, Graham. *A Gospel for a New People*: *Studies in Matthew*. Edinburgh: T & T Clark, 1992.

———. *The Gospels and Jesus*. Oxford: Oxford University Press, 1993.

———. *The Gospels and Jesus*. Oxford: Oxford University Press, 2002.

Stark, Rodney. *The Triumph of Christianity*. New York: HarperOne, 2011.

Stein, Robert H. "The "Criteria" for Authenticity." https://biblicalstudies.org.uk/pdf/gp/gp1_authenticity_stein.pdf?

———. "Criteria for the Gospel's Authenticity." In *Contending With Christianity's Critics*: *Answering New Atheists & Other Objectors*, edited by Paul Copan and William Lane Craig, 88–103. Nashville: B&H, 2009.

———. *Jesus the Messiah*. IVP, 1996.

Steiner, Rudolf. "The Fifth Gospel: Lecture 2." http://wn.rsarchive.org/Lectures/GA/GA0148/19131002p01.html.

Stenger, Victor J. "Victor J. Stenger." In *Science & Religion*: *5 Questions*, edited by Gregg D. Caruso, 209–18. New York: Automatic, 2014.

———. *The New Atheism: Taking a Stand for Science and Reason*. New York: Prometheus, 2009.

———. "What's New About The New Atheism?" www.colorado.edu/philosophy/vstenger/MagArticles/NewAthPhilNow.pdf.

Stephens, Bret. "The Dying Art of Disagreement." *The New York Times* (September 2017). www.nytimes.com/2017/09/24/opinion/dying-art-of-disagreement.html?smid=tw-share.

Stewart, Robert B., ed. *The Future of Atheism: Alister McGrath & Daniel Dennett in Dialogue*. London: SPCK, 2008.

———. *The Reliability of The New Testament: Bart D. Ehrman and Daniel B. Wallace In Dialogue*. Minneapolis: Fortress 2011.

Stewart, Roy A. "Judicial Procedure in New Testament Times." *The Evangelical Quarterly* 47 (1975) 94–109. https://biblicalstudies.org.uk/pdf/eq/1975-2_094.pdf.

Stoeger, William. "Describing God's Action in the World in Light of Scientific Knowledge of Reality." In *Chaos and Complexity: Scientific Perspectives on Divine Action*, edited by Robert John Russell 239–61. The Vatican Observatory, 1995.

Stott, John R.W. *Basic Introduction to the New Testament*. Grand Rapids: Eerdmans, 1964.

———. *Basic Christianity*. Edinburgh: IVP, 1958.

Strauss, David. *A New Life of Jesus, Volume 1*. Edinburgh: Williams & Norgate, 1879.

Strauss, Mark. *Four Portraits, One Jesus: An Introduction to Jesus and the Gospels*. Grand Rapids: Zondervan, 2007.

———. *Introducing Jesus: A short guide to the gospel's history and message*. Grand Rapids: Zondervan, 2018.

Strauss, Michael G. "Extraordinary Claims Require Extraordinary Evidence." www.michaelgstrauss.com/2017/05/extraordinary-claims-and-extraordinary.html.

Strobel, Lee. *The Case for a Creator*. Grand Rapids: Zondervan, 2004.

———. *The Case for Christ*. Grand Rapids: Zondervan, 1998.

———. *The Case for Miracles: A Journalist Investigates Evidence for the Supernatural*. Grand Rapids: Zondervan, 2018.

———. *The Case for the Real Jesus*. Grand Rapids: Zondervan, 2007.

Stroll, Avrum. "Did Jesus Really Exist?" In *History, Law and Christianity* by John Warwick Montgomery, 79–94. Corona, CA: NRP Books, 2014.

Sullivan, Thomas D. and Sandrra Menssen. "Revelation and Miracles." In *Christian Philosophical Theology*, edited by Charles Taliaferro and Chad Meister, 201–15. Cambridge, UK: Cambridge University Press, 2010.

Swaine, Jon. "Donald Trump's team defends "alternative facts" after widespread protests." www.theguardian.com/us-news/2017/jan/22/donald-trump-kellyanne-conway-inauguration-alternative-facts.

Sweetman, Brendan. *Religion: Key Concepts in Philosophy*. London: Continuum, 2007.

Swift, David. *Evolution Under the Microscope: a Scientific Critique of the Theory of Evolution*. Stirling: Leighton, 2002.

Swinburne, Richard. *The Christian God*. Oxford: Clarendon, 1994.

———. "Divine Action In The World And Human History." In *Great Thinkers On Great Questions*, edited by Roy Abraham Varghese, 212–13. Oxford: OneWorld, 2009.

———. *Mind, Brain, and Free Will*. Oxford: Oxford University Press, 2013.

———. "Response to Richard Dawkins' Comments on my Writings in his Book *The God Delusion*." http://users.ox.ac.uk/~orie0087/framesetpdfs.shtml.

———. *The Resurrection of God Incarnate*. Oxford: Clarendon, 2003.

———. *Revelation: From metaphor to analogy*. Oxford: Oxford University Press, 2008.

———. *Was Jesus God?* Oxford: Oxford University Press, 2008.
"Talking Jesus." www.talkingjesus.org.
Tappy, Connie Gundry. "The Gospels and Acts: John." In *The Eerdmans Companion to the Bible,* edited by Gordon D. Fee and Robert L. Hubbard, Jr, 582–97. Grand Rapids: Eerdmans, 2011.
Taunton, Larry Alex. *The Faith of Christopher Hitchens.* Nashville: Nelson, 2016.
Taylor, Charles. *A Secular Age.* Cambridge, MA: Harvard University Press, 2007.
Taylor, James E. *Introducing Apologetics: Cultivating Christian Commitment.* Grand Rapids: Baker, 2006.
———. "The New Atheists." www.iep.utm.edu/n-atheis/.
"Teachings of Presidents of the Church: Lorenzo Snow. Chapter 5: The Grand Destiny of the Faithful." www.lds.org/manual/teachings-of-presidents-of-the-church-lorenzo-snow/chapter-5-the-grand-destiny-of-the-faithful?lang=eng.
Tepper, Yotam. *A Christian Prayer Hall of the Third Century CE at Kefar 'othnay (legio): Excavations at the Megiddo Prison 2005.* Jerusalem: Israel Antiquities Authority, 2006.
Tertullian. *The Apology of Tertullian.* Translated by William Reeve. www.tertullian.org/articles/reeve_apology.htm.
Thatcher, Tom. "Philo on Pilate: Rhetoric or Reality?" *Restoration Quarterly* 37 (1995) 215–18. www.acu.edu/sponsored/restoration_quarterly/documents/thatcher-37-4.pdf.
Thayer, Joseph. *Thayer's Greek-English Lexicon of the New Testament.* Peabody, MA: Hendrickson, 2012.
"The Theological Roots of Science." www.youtube.com/playlist?list=PLQhh3qcwVEWh3jDVYqFFzWSnTbtlUeCg3.
Thiede, *The Emmaus Mystery.* London: Continuum, 2005.
———. *Jesus: Life or Legend?* Oxford: Lion, 1990.
Thorne, Kip. *The Science of Interstellar.* New York: W.W. Norton, 2014.
Tidmarsh, Marcus. "Saint Luke." www.catholic-saints.info/patron-saints/saint-luke.htm.
Tilby, Angela. *Son of God.* London: Hodder & Stoughton, 2001.
"Timeline of the Apostle Paul." www.blueletterbible.org/study/paul/timeline.cfm.
Tobin, Paul. "The Death of James." www.rejectionofpascalswager.net/jamesdeath.html.
Tomes, Nigel. "Is This Simon of Cyrene's Tomb?" http://churchintoronto.blogspot.co.uk/2012/03/is-this-simon-of-cyrenes-tomb.html.
Tour, James. "An Open Letter to My Colleagues." *Interface: International Review of Science* 3 (August, 2017). http://inference-review.com/article/an-open-letter-to-my-colleagues.
———. "The Origin of Life: An Inside Story—2016 Lectures." https://youtu.be/_zQXgJ-dXM4.
Townsend, Maurice. "Magnetic Fields Causing Ghosts?" www.assap.ac.uk/newsite/articles/Magnetic%20ghosts.html.
———. "Recording Ghosts?" www.assap.ac.uk/newsite/articles/Recording%20ghosts.html.
Townsend, Michael J. *The Epistle of James.* London: Epworth, 1994.
Townsend, Peter. *Questioning Islam.* CreateSpace, 2014.
Tran, Lina. "An Earth-like Atmosphere May Not Survive Proxima b's Orbit." www.nasa.gov/feature/goddard/2017/an-earth-like-atmosphere-may-not-survive-proxima-b-s-orbit.
Tuckett, Christopher. "Sources and Methods." In *The Cambridge Companion to Jesus*, edited by Markus Bockmuehl, 121–37. Cambridge, UK: Cambridge University Press, 2001.

References

Twelftree, Graham H. "What About 'Gospels' Not In Our New Testament?" In *If God Made the Universe, Who Made God? 130 Arguments For Christian Faith*, 57–58. Nashville: Holman Bible Publishers, 2012.

Tyrrell, G.N.M. "Physical Mediumship: Is there Anything Besides Fraud in the Physical Séance Room?" www.survivalafterdeath.info/articles/tyrrell/fraud.htm.

Tzaferis, V. "Inscribed to 'God Jesus Christ': Early Christian Prayer Hall Found in Megiddo Prison." *Biblical Archaeology Review* 33 (2007) 38-49.

Upton, John. "Ancient Sea Rise Tale Told Accurately for 10,000 Years." *Scientific American* (January 2015). www.scientificamerican.com/article/ancient-sea-rise-tale-told-accurately-for-10-000-years/.

Van der Breggen, Hendrik. "Hume's Scale: How Hume Counts a Miracle's Improbability Twice." *Philosophia Christi* Volume 4, Number 2 (2002) 443–53.

———. "Reasonable Skepticism about Radical Skepticism." www.equip.org/article/reasonable-skepticism-about-radical-skepticism/.

Van Inwagen, Peter. "Of 'Of Miracles.'" In *Philosophy Of Religion: An Anthology*, edited by Michael Rea and Louis Pojman, 447–87. Boston: Cengage Learning, 2015.

Van Voorst, Robert E. *Jesus Outside the New Testament: An Introduction to the Ancient Evidence*. Grand Rapids: Eerdmans, 2000.

Vaughn, Richard. "Teach students how to spot fake news stories, say academics." *i* 12 (January 2017). https://inews.co.uk/news/education/teach-students-spot-fake-news-say-academics/.

Veale, Graham. *New Atheism: A Survival Guide*. Fearn, Ross-shire: Christian Focus, 2013.

Vermes, Geza. "Jesus in the Eyes of Josephus." http://standpointmag.co.uk/node/2507/full.

———. *Jesus the Jew. A Historian's Reading of the Gospels*. London: Collins, 1973.

———. *The Passion: The True Story of an Event That Changed Human History*. New York: Penguin: 2006.

———. *The Resurrection*. London: Penguin, 2008.

———. "Was Crucifixion a Jewish Penalty?" http://standpointmag.co.uk/node/4936/full.

Viegas, Jennifer. "Day of Jesus' Crucifixion Believed Determined." *Discovery News* (May 2012). www.nbcnews.com/id/47555983/ns/technology_and_science-science/t/quake-reveals-day-jesus-crucifixion-researchers-believe/#.WxWeoiOZPmI.

Vilenkin, Alexander. "Did the Universe Have a Beginning?" https://youtu.be/NXCQelhKJ7A.

Vogel, Dan. "Book of Mormon Witnesses Revisited." www.mormonthink.com/vogelwitnesses.htm.

Voorst, Van. *Jesus Outside the New Testament*. Grand Rapids: Eerdmans, 2000.

Wade, Nicholas. "Body of St. Luke Gains Credibility." *New York Times* (October 2001). www.nytimes.com/2001/10/16/world/body-of-st-luke-gains-credibility.html.

Wagner, Paul D., et al. "Do We Have the Right Canon?" In *In Defence Of The Bible*, edited by Steven B. Cowan and Terry L. Wilder, 393–428. Nashville: B&H, 2013.

Wainwright, William J. *Philosophy of Religion*. Toronto: Wadsworth, 1999.

Walker, Peter. *In The Steps of Jesus: An Illustrated Guide To The Places Of The Holy Land*. Oxford: Lion, 2006.

Wall, Mike. "Interstellar Reality Check: Could Our Galaxy Host a Wormhole?" *NBC News* (January 2015). www.nbcnews.com/science/weird-science/interstellar-reality-check-could-our-galaxy-host-wormhole-n290861.

Wallace, Daniel B. "Daniel B. Wallace Interview Transcript." www.apologetics315.com/2013/06/daniel-b-wallace-interview-transcript.html.

———. "Earliest Manuscript of the New Testament Discovered?" www.dts.edu/read/wallace-new-testament-manscript-first-century/.

———. "James: Introduction, Outline, and Argument." https://bible.org/seriespage/20-james-introduction-outline-and-argument#_ftn12.

———. "The Post Resurrection Behavior of Jesus Eliminates the Possibility of an Imposter." http://coldcasechristianity.com/2016/the-post-resurrection-behavior-of-jesus-eliminates-the-possibility-of-an-imposter/?utm_content=bufferc6adf&utm_medium=social&utm_source=twitter.com&utm_campaign=buffer.

———. "Predictable Christmas fare: Newsweek's Tirade against the Bible." https://jamesbishopblog.wordpress.com/2015/02/01/30-common-new-testament-challenges-by-sceptics-answered/.

———. "Symposia Christi." www.symposiachristi.com.

———. "Why the pre-Jesus mythologies fail to prove Jesus was a myth." http://coldcasechristianity.com/2013/why-the-pre-jesus-mythologies-fail-to-prove-jesus-is-a-myth/.

———. "The Witnesses of the Resurrection Compared to the Witnesses of the Golden Plates." http://coldcasechristianity.com/2013/the-witnesses-of-the-resurrection-compared-to-the-witnesses-of-the-golden-plates/.

Wallace, J. Warner. *Cold-Case Christianity: A Homicide Detective Investigates The Claims Of The Gospels*. Colorado Springs: David C. Cook, 2013.

———. "Investigating the Evidence for Mormonism in Six Steps." http://coldcasechristianity.com/2014/investigating-the-evidence-for-mormonism-in-six-steps/.

———. "Is there any evidence for Jesus outside the Bible?" http://coldcasechristianity.com/2017/is-there-any-evidence-for-jesus-outside-the-bible/.

Wanamaker, Charles A. "Philippians." In *Eerdmans Commentary on the Bible*, edited by James D. G. Dunn and John W. Rogerson, 1394–1403. Grand Rapids: Eerdmans, 2003.

Warburton, Nigel. *Thinking: From A to Z*. London: Routledge, 1998.

Ward, Keith. *The Big Questions in Science and Religion*. West Conshohocken, Pennsylvania: Templeton, 2008.

———. "*The God Argument* by A.C. Grayling." www.bethinking.org/does-god-exist/book-review-ac-graylings-the-god-argument.

———. *Is Religion Dangerous?* Oxford: Lion, 2006.

"Was Jesus an Alien?" https://youtu.be/Ey4eAodAAN8.

"Was the stone sealing Jesus's tomb square-shaped?" https://beliefmap.org/jesus-resurrected/tomb-square-stone/.

Watson, Francis. "The Quest for the Real Jesus." In *The Cambridge Companion to Jesus*, edited by Markus Bockmuehel, 156–69. Cambridge, UK: Cambridge University Press.

Watson, R. Gregg. "James." In *Holman Illustrated Bible Commentary*, edited by R. Ray Clendenen and Jeremy Royal Howard, 1347–54. Nashville: Holman, 2015.

Watt, Caroline. *Beginners Guides: Parapsychology*. London: OneWorld, 2016.

———. "Paranormal Cognition." In *Parapsychology*, edited by Ron Roberts and David Groome, 130–40. London: Arnold, 2001.

Watts, Geoff. "Is There Life on Other Planets?" In *Big Questions In Science*, edited by Harriet Swain, 200–203. London: Jonathan Cape, 2002.

Webb, Robert L. "The Historical Enterprise and Historical Jesus Research." In *Key Events in The Life of the Historical Jesus*, edited by Darrell L. Bock and Robert L. Webb, 9–93. Grand Rapids: Eerdmans, 2009.

———. "The Roman Examination and Crucifixion of Jesus." In *Key Events In The Life of the Historical Jesus*, edited by Darrell L. Bock and Robert L. Webb, 669–773. Grand Rapids: Eerdmans, 2009.

Webb, Stephen. *Where Is Everybody? Fifty Solutions To The Fermi Paradox And The Problem Of Extraterrestrial Life*. New York: Copernicus, 2010.

Wedderburn, A.J.M. *Beyond Resurrection*. Peabody, MA: Henderickson, 1999.

Wells, G.A. "Earliest Christianity." www.infidels.org/library/modern/g_a_wells/earliest.html.

Wells, H.G. "H.G. Wells on the Historicity of Jesus." www.apologetics315.com/2013/06/hg-wells-on-historicity-of-jesus.html.

Wenham, David. "Did Peter Go to Rome in AD 42?" *Tyndale Bulletin* 23 (1972), 94–102.

———. *Did St Paul Get Jesus Right?* Oxford: Lion, 2010.

Wenham, David, and Steve Walton. *Exploring the New Testament: A Guide to the Gospels & Acts*. Downers Grove, IL: IVP, 2001.

———. *New Testament: Volume One—Exploring the New Testament: A Guide to the Gospels & Acts*. Downers Grove, IL: IVP, 2001.

Werther, David. "Freedom, Temptation, and Incarnation." In *Philosophy And The Christian Worldview: Analysis, Assessment and Development*, edited by David Werther and Mark D. Linville, 252–64. London: Continuum, 2012.

Westcott, Ben. ""No One's Out There": We're Likely Alone in the Milky Way, says Shaw Prize Astronomy Winner as he Visits Hong Kong for Award Ceremony." *South China Morning Post* (September 2015). www.scmp.com/news/hong-kong/health-environment/article/1860781/no-ones-out-there-shaw-prize-astronomy-winner-says.

White, Michael. *The Science of the X Files: the truth . . .* London: Legend, 1996.

White, Peter. *The Past Is Human*. London: Angus & Robertson, 1976.

Wielenberg, Erik. "Dawkins's Gambit, Hume's Aroma, and God's Simplicity." *Philosophia Christi* 11 (2009) 113–27. www.academia.edu/19893604/Dawkinss_Gambit_Humes_Aroma_and_Gods_Simplicity.

Wierenga, Edward. *The Philosophy of Religion*. Oxford: Wiley Blackwell, 2016.

Wieseltier, Leon. "The God Genome." www.nytimes.com/2006/02/19/books/review/19wieseltier.htm.

Wilkins, Michael J. "Matthew." In *Zondervan Illustrated Bible Background Commentary: Volume 1, Matthew, Mark, Luke*, edited by Clinton E. Arnold, 2–203. Grand Rapids: Zondervan, 2002.

———. *The Holman Apologetics Commentary on the Bible: The Gospel and Acts*. Nashville: Holman, 2013.

Wilkins, Ulrich. "Auferstehung." *Themen der Theologie* 4 (1970) 114–44.

Willard, Dallas. *Knowing Christ Today*. New York: HarperOne, 2009.

Williams, Jefferson B., et al. "An early first-century earthquake in the Dead Sea." *International Geology Review* 54 (2012) 1219–28. www.academia.edu/6108262/Quake_Article.

Williams, Matt. "Where is Earth in the Milky Way?" www.universetoday.com/65601/where-is-earth-in-the-milky-way/.

Williams, Peter S. "The Big Bad Wolf, Theism and the Foundations of Intelligent Design Theory." http://epsociety.org/library/articles.asp?pid=53.

———. *The Case for Angels*. Carlisle: Paternoster, 2002.

———. *The Case for God*. Oxford: Monarch, 1999.

———. "Contra Grayling: A Critique of *Against All Gods*." www.peterswilliams.com/2016/02/09/contra-grayling-a-critique-of-against-all-gods/.

———. *C.S. Lewis vs. the New Atheists*. Carlisle: Paternoster, 2013.

———. "Dawkins and the Public Understanding of Scientism." www.bethinking.org/atheism/dawkins-and-the-public-understanding-of-scientism.

———. *Digging for Evidence*. London: Christian Evidence Society, 2016. http://christianevidence.org/docs/booklets/digging_for_evidence.pdf.

———. "Dissecting Dawkins' Defence of *The God Delusion*." http://peterswilliams.podbean.com/mf/feed/rr7cd9/SUCU_Dawkins_Delusion_2016.mp3,

———. "The Emperor's Incoherent New Clothes—Pointing the Finger at Dawkins' Atheism." *Think* 9 (2010) 29–33.

———. *A Faithful Guide to Philosophy*. Carlisle: Paternoster, 2013.

———. "Hebrews 11 and faith in the new atheists." http://peterswilliams.podbean.com/mf/feed/dizgnf/Heb_11.mp3.

———. "In Defence of Arguments from Desire." www.peterswilliams.com/2016/11/02/in-defence-of-arguments-from-desire/.

———. "Is Christianity Unscientific?" https://youtu.be/mWiU2p_PIE8.

———. "The Nativity." http://peterswilliams.podbean.com/mf/feed/rh7ek3/rf_nativity.mp3.

———. "Old Testament Archaeology." http://peterswilliams.podbean.com/mf/feed/hgncuq/otarchaeologyathomegroup.mp3.

———. "Old Testament Miracles." http://peterswilliams.podbean.com/mf/feed/vip63m/otmiracles.mp3.

———. *A Sceptic's Guide to Atheism: God Is Not Dead*. Carlisle: Paternoster, 2009.

———. "Understanding the Trinity" www.bethinking.org/god/understanding-the-trinity.

———. *Understanding Jesus: Five Ways to Spiritual Enlightenment*. Carlisle: Paternoster, 2013.

———. "A Universe From Someone: Against Lawrence Krauss." www.bethinking.org/is-there-a-creator/a-universe-from-someone-against-lawrence-krauss.

———. "Who's Afraid of the Big Bad Wolf? Richard Dawkins' Failed Rebuttal of Natural Theology." www.arn.org/docs/williams/pw_goddelusionreview2.htm.

Williams, Rowan. *Meeting God in Mark*. London: SPCK, 2014.

Williams, Roy. *God, Actually*. Oxford: Monarch, 2009.

Wilson, Amy. "War & Remembrance: Controversy is a Constant for Memory Researcher Elizabeth Loftus, Newly Installed at UCI." *The Orange County Register* (November 2002). http://williamcalvin.com/2002/OrangeCtyRegister.htm.

Wilson, A.N. *Paul: The Mind Of The Apostle*. London: Sinclair-Stevenson, 1997.

Winter, David. *The Search for the Real Jesus*. London: Hodder & Stoughton, 1982.

Witherington, Ben, III. *The Acts Of The Apostles: A Socio-Rhetorical Commentary*. Grand Rapids: Eerdmans, 1998.

———. "Christianity in the Making." In *Memories of Jesus: A Critical Appraisal of James D.G. Dunn's Jesus Remembered*, edited by Robert B. Stewart and Gary R. Habermas, 197–226. Nashville: B&H, 2010.

———. "The Death and Resurrection of Messiah—written in stone." http://benwitherington.blogspot.co.uk/2008/07/death-and-resurrection-of-messiah.html.

———. *Invitation to the New Testament: First Things*. Oxford: Oxford University Press, 2017.

Wolchover, Natalie. "Newfound Wormhole Allows Information to Escape Black Holes." *Quanta* (October 2017). www.quantamagazine.org/newfound-wormhole-allows-information-to-escape-black-holes-20171023/.

References

Wolf, Gary. "The Church of the Non-Believers." *Wired* 14 (November 2006). www.wired.com/wired/archive/14.11/atheism.html.

Woolmer, John. *Healing and Deliverance*. Tunbridge Wells: Monarch, 1999.

"Word of the Year 2016 is. . ." https://en.oxforddictionaries.com/word-of-the-year/word-of-the-year-2016.

Wright, N.T. "Can a Scientist Believe in the Resurrection." In *Surprised by Scripture*, 41–64. London: SPCK, 2014.

———. *The Challenge of Jesus*. London: SPCK, 2001.

———. "Foreword." In *The New Testament Documents: Are They Reliable?* by F. F. Bruce, vii–xi. Grand Rapids: Eerdmans, 2000.

———. *Jesus and the Victory of God*. Minneapolis: Fortress, 1996.

———. "Jesus' Resurrection and Christian Origins." In *Passionate Conviction: Contemporary Discourses on Christian Apologetics*, edited by Paul Copan and William Lane Craig, 123–37. Nashville: B&H, 2007.

———. *Judas and the Gospel of Jesus*. London: SPCK, 2006.

———. *The Resurrection of the Son of God*. London: SPCK, 2003.

Wright, Tom. *Simply Christian*. London: SPCK, 2006.

———. *Surprised by Hope*. London: SPCK, 2007.

———. *Why Read the Bible?*. London: SPCK, 2015.

Yarborough, Robert W. "The Date of Papias: A Reassessment" *Journal of the Evangelical Theological Society* 26 (June 1983) 181–91. www.etsjets.org/files/JETS-PDFs/26/26-2/26-2-pp181-191_JETS.pdf.

Zaas, Peter. "Questions and Answers." In *Who Was Jesus? A Jewish-Christian Dialogue*, edited by Paul Copan and Craig A. Evans, 36 42. London: WJK, 2001.

Zackrisson, Erik, et al. "Extragalactic SETI: The Tully-Fisher Relation as a Probe of Dysonian Astroengineering In Disk Galaxies." *The Astrophysical Journal* 810 (September 2015) 23–35. http://iopscience.iop.org/article/10.1088/0004-637X/810/1/23/pdf.

Zaimov, Stoyan. "Atheist Author Phillip Pullman: Jesus Is Important for Child Education." www.christianpost.com/news/atheist-author-phillip-pullman-jesus-is-important-for-child-education-92108/.

Zalonski, Paul A. "Saint Luke the Evangelist." http://communio.stblogs.org/index.php/2011/10/saint-luke-the-evangelist/.

Zwartz, Barney. "*The God Delusion*." www.theage.com.au/entertainment/books/the-god-delusion-20061125-ge3ndu.html.

Lightning Source UK Ltd.
Milton Keynes UK
UKHW030603260219
338002UK00004B/247/P